Insatiable Appetite

Insatiable Appetite

The United States and the
Ecological Degradation
of the Tropical World

Richard P. Tucker

UNIVERSITY OF CALIFORNIA PRESS
Berkeley · Los Angeles · London

University of California Press
Berkeley and Los Angeles, California

University of California Press, Ltd.
London, England

© 2000 by the Regents of the University of California

Library of Congress Cataloging-in-Publication Data
Tucker, Richard P., 1938–
    Insatiable appetite : the United States and the ecological degradation of the
tropical world / Richard P. Tucker.
        p. cm.
    Includes bibliographical references and index.
    ISBN 0-520-22087-0 (cloth : alk. paper)
        1. Tropical crops—Economic aspects—History—20th century. 2. Tropical
crops—Environmental aspects—History—20th century. 3. Investments,
American—Tropics—History—20th century. 4. Environmental degradation—
Tropics—History—20th century. I. Title.

HD1417.T83 2000
333.7'0913—dc21   00-037774

Manufactured in the United States of America

09   08   07   06   05   04   03   02   01   00
10   9   8   7   6   5   4   3   2   1

The paper used in this publication meets the minimum requirements of ANSI/NISO Z39.48-1992
(R 1997) (*Permanence of Paper*).

For Lia
and Sarah and Rachel
and Olivia

Contents

Acknowledgments

At professional gatherings of environmental historians, one participant is likely to ask another how on earth she or he ever became enmeshed in such an impossibly complex field. The response is often idiosyncratic: the practitioner traces the meandering path that led to a fusion of work and play, profession and citizenship, and the painstaking effort to marry social and biological understanding.

I had been immersed for some years in research on the interplay between British imperial administrators and the Anglicized elite of Victorian India, when I began to see that some of their key controversies centered on the distribution of access to natural resources, such as forest and grazing resources. In the summer of 1979 I began to explore the colonial forestry archives in England, and I soon faced the difficulty of explaining to colleagues why I had become interested in trees and goats, species that leave no archival documents and in that sense have no history. But foresters understood; indeed, shepherds understood. Later that season I attended an international forest history conference at the Ecole Nationale des Eaux et Forêts in Nancy, France, hoping to find historians or foresters working on the impact of European forestry traditions in their tropical and subtropical empires. There was none, but I was encouraged by the fact that my colleagues instantly saw the significance of the question.

By 1981, when some of us met again in Kyoto at a global gathering of the International Union of Forest Research Organizations, we were ready to organize an international network on the history of tropical forest use and depletion. Many useful works on that subject have emerged since then; some of them are building blocks in chapter 7 of this book. European colonial regimes maintained massive records of their work, including those kept for their technical agencies such as forestry. In contrast, the global reach of the United States, which came to dominate large parts of Latin America and the Pacific Basin about a century ago, was not a formal empire, apart from its short period of governing the Philippine Islands. American corporate investors and speculators in tropical resources did not have to answer to their countrymen in colonized countries, and Yankee officialdom did not organize and maintain the governmental agencies of tropical countries. I was a citizen of the country whose economy had become the most voracious consumer of global resources in the twentieth century world, but the evolution of that epochal story was virtually impossible to discern. By the early 1980s many writers had given glimpses of how the global environmental impact of the United States had been shaped, but no historian had addressed the subject as the central issue. During five months in 1983 on a research appointment at the University of California in Berkeley, I began to define the scope of the subject within its global and comparative context, with the help of geographers Robert Reed, James Parsons, Hilgard O'Reilly Sternberg, and other colleagues and students of the two great geographers Clarence Glacken and Carl Sauer. Anthropologists James Anderson and Gerald Berreman and historians Barbara and Thomas Metcalf were equally stimulating in discussions of the shape of global environmental history.

In the same years, as a member of the International Programs Committee of the Sierra Club, I joined the discussion of the specific links between the American economy and the degradation of tropical natural resources. Over the years since then I have particularly valued Bill Mankin's insights and his skill in designing programs to challenge these forms of overconsumption.

When the World Resources Institute invited me in 1985 to attempt an overview of this dimension of tropical environmental history, the task was daunting but irresistible. My greatest of many debts is to WRI for financial and logistical support for my first two years' work, and sustained critical support since then. I am grateful especially to Andrew Maguire, Robert Repetto, Walter Reid, and above all, Janet Welsh Brown. WRI also organized an advisory committee for the work; I have benefited in countless ways from the wisdom of Raymond Dasmann, Robert Reed, Raymond Vernon, and above all the historians John Richards and Donald Worster. During those two years at Clark University, my work was enriched by support and commentary from Richard Ford, Barbara Thomas Slater, Billie Lee Turner II, and various others. During my frequent trips to Yale University I benefited from the insight of Joseph Miller, Timothy Weiskel, Harold Conklin, and others.

In the years since then, as my discoveries of American entrepreneurs and expatriates took me to regions of the world that were newer to me, I learned much from historians Peter Boomgaard, Albert Crosby, Warren Dean, Richard Grove, Clayton Koppes, John McNeill, Elinor Melville, and Ravi Rajan. At the University of Hawaii James and Sonia Juvik, Mark Merlin, and Fritz Rehbock oriented me to the history and biogeography of the Pacific Basin. At the East-West Center, Jeff Fox and Larry Hamilton enriched my sense of the legacy of American entanglements in the Pacific.

Since my work had begun with analyses of tropical forest history, I accumulated major debts to tropical foresters and forest historians, especially James Burchfield, Harold Steen, and Frank Wadsworth among the Americans, as well as Jeff Burley and others at the Oxford Forestry Institute, John Dargavel at Australian National University, and Joanny Guillard of the French Forestry Institute.

Material relevant to such a multifaceted subject is virtually endless. The long process of letting the seeds ripen into the full discussion would not have been possible without the seasoning of teaching my course on global environmental change in the modern world, which I first launched at Oakland University. I remember many students there fondly, for insisting on clarity and a sense of the subject's drama and relevance to their lives. I think with delight of the contributions I have received from virtually every member of the History Department, most abundantly from Mary Karash, and from Oakland colleagues Peter Bertocci, Vincent Khapoya, and Don Mayer.

When the School of Natural Resources and Environment at the University of Michigan invited me to add global environmental history to its offerings, I began a uniquely enriching cluster of collaborations. This book in its mature form would be unimaginable without the input of colleagues, friends, and students in Ann Arbor. Faculty collaborators and advisors there have included Steve Brechin, Jim Crowfoot, Lisa Curran, Maria Montoya, Gayl Ness, Ivette Perfecto, Tom Princen, Michael

Ross, Rebecca Scott, Ann Stoler, John Vandermeer, and Patrick West. A range of students too long to list, especially a decade of splendid teaching assistants, have added their probing analyses to the work.

Behind this web of concerned scholars lies the influence of environmental historians and scientists in India, especially Neeladri Bhattacharya, Ramachandra Guha, Mahesh Rangarajan, Vasant Saberwal, and Chetan Singh, whose work has contributed to my understanding of the determining force of global power relations in the control over the natural wealth of lands under Western economic and political hegemony.

My quest for information on the course of the American ecological empire led me to numerous libraries and archives: the National Archives in Washington, the Forest History Society in Durham N.C., the U.S. Forest Service's tropical research center in Río Piedras, Puerto Rico, the U.S. Army Corps of Engineers in Virginia, the Bureau of Reclamation in Denver, and the Bishop Museum in Honolulu, as well as universities mentioned above. I also consulted the India Office Library in London, the Centre Technique Forestier Tropical in Paris, the Indian Forest Research Institute in Dehra Dun, and the Malaysian Forest Research Institute in Kepong. I am grateful to the staffs of all these archives for their thoughtfulness and efficiency.

Numerous people have read chapters of various drafts of the resulting manuscript and given invaluable suggestions and corrections, including Raymond Dasmann, Crystal Fortwangler, Michael Hathaway, David McCreery, Michael Ross, Richard Slatta, Harold Steen, John Vandermeer, and Peter Wilshusen. The full manuscript, in one draft or another, was read with exceeding patience and insight by Janet Brown, Lia Frede, Donald Worster, and three careful readers for the University of California Press. For editorial assistance in tightening and clarifying the manuscript, I have nothing but praise for the University of California Press. Howard Boyer, Danielle Jatlow, and Dore Brown were unfailingly supportive; my copy editor, Rebecca Frazier, did wonders with the manuscript, polishing and clarifying it at many points; Bill Nelson produced maps that are both informative and beautiful. Roberta Engleman prepared the index. Whatever deficiencies remain in the manuscript surely represent what I have missed from the advice of all these collaborators.

In addition to the core funding from World Resources Institute for this project, I am grateful for smaller grants from Oakland University, which enabled me to visit several archival collections, a travel grant from the Forest History Society, and more recently the MacArthur Fund, which assisted me in pursuing the evolution of American consumerism in its connections to tropical products. This work has also benefited indirectly from grants from the National Endowment for the Humanities, the Social Science Research Council, and the Smithsonian Institution for related research projects.

Every completed project is built on its own unique bedrock. Mine has been provided by my wife, Lia Frede. To sustain me in the work, she selflessly loaned me her study on a Himalayan mountain ridge, then built another writer's retreat in the Hawaiian ohia forest. More than that, she was willing to postpone or curtail other adventures of the spirit as part of her contribution to our understanding of the consequences of our collective appetites. I am forever grateful to her.

A Consuming Passion

The United States as Exploiter of Tropical Nature

It is a splendid victory over Nature, the stern but fair giant-
ess who enforces the decree that the soil of this earth shall
yield its treasures only to those who battle with her, but
who smilingly submits to the ardent and intelligent tres-
passer on her domains.

Frederick Upham Adams, 1914

Since the late 1960s a groundswell of changing consciousness has been
shaping us as we assess the political and environmental dimensions of
America's global power. In earlier years the idea of the exploitation of
Nature had strongly positive connotations, expressing our success in
harnessing Nature's abundance to fulfill human needs and desires. In
contrast, to speak of the exploitation of certain social groups by others
was more often a denunciation. In recent years we have begun to be
collectively more self-critical of our interaction with our environment,
as evidence mounts that social exploitation has been closely linked with
a damaging exploitation of natural resources. Humans have always
shaped their environments to sustain themselves—one of our earliest
tools, fire, is still one of our most powerful—and modern capital and
modern industry can be seen as essential tools for the accelerating human drive for survival, security, and domination over Nature. Modern
man has increasingly unified the international flow of resources. Tamed
and domesticated Nature, a network of landscapes shaped by human
priorities, is now the inescapable character of the biosphere.

The task of a historian is to describe the institutions and cultures that
have brought about that domestication and the exquisite complexity of

that process. The task of an ecologist and a global citizen is to evaluate that change, to determine which forms of domestication are damaging, and to define the criteria for that judgment. An environmental historian can hardly avoid bringing the concerns of both ecologist and citizen into the viewpoint of his work, since the narrative that a historian produces must be concerned with where we are heading and how that will affect the web of life that is our planetary home. As an environmental historian who is also a United States citizen, I became concerned with a specific challenge: to understand how American history came to be inseparably linked to the worldwide degradation of the biosphere in our fateful century.[1]

Americans' involvement with the natural wealth of the tropics began in the 1700s, but a turning point came in 1898, when victory in the war with Spain, a political and military event, opened the door to the creation of an American empire in Latin America and the islands of the Pacific. From that time onward Americans moved with extraordinary speed and bravado to supplant earlier European empires, even that of the British, in commanding the natural resources of the tropical world to contribute to U.S. domestic affluence.

In the half century after victory in World War I, the United States dominated the global consumption of tropical natural resources, both mineral and biological. The nation of new consumers supported a network of investors and marketers who profited from satisfying their demands. Few consumers knew anything about what was happening at the tropical sources of their satisfaction. Indeed, few of the corporate planners who provided the financing, technology, and managerial skills to create those products and place them in consumers' hands knew much more. In the industrial era the distance between producer and consumer increased immeasurably over that of the almost-mythical past, only a generation or two earlier, when consumers grew and harvested their own food and fiber or else traded them face to face in far more restricted local economies.

This study, then, is an overview of the links between producing regions in many parts of the tropical and subtropical world and the multifaceted power of a boisterous young industrial and economic giant, the United States. Although America's power to command global resources, and the ecological consequences of that power, reached its greatest height in the years after World War II, the fuller story reaches not only back to the seventeenth century, when the first New England sea captains sailed into warm Caribbean waters, but also forward into the last decades of the twentieth century.

The decades from the 1890s to the 1960s constituted the era of American hegemony. American influence was paramount in a great geographical arc of the planet that stretched from Latin America across the Pacific into Southeast Asia. The strength of America's empire was vested not only in strategic domination and economic penetration, it was equally based on ecological exploitation. Americans played major roles in transforming a wide spectrum of tropical ecosystems and their natural resources into commodities for their own and others' consumption.[2] Corporate America and the consumers of its products became co-workers with Washington in creating that empire.

Although this study centers on the American role in the 1890s through the 1960s, it places that saga in the broader context of five hundred years of European commercial and industrial influence around the world.[3] For well over half of that time, North America was itself a frontier for the extraction of resources by European powers. By the mid-1800s the natural abundance of the continent was transformed, and in many instances degraded, by the financial and technological powers of Europe—primarily Great Britain, which led the world into the industrial era and dominated global development processes through most of the nineteenth century.

In the late 1800s the United States began to surpass its mentors in its extractive reach into the tropics. Advance agents of American power were the commercial companies that had penetrated colonial Europe's profit networks in the American tropics from the mid-eighteenth century on. From ports along the entire East Coast, from Portland to Savannah, the colonial entrepreneurs opened niches in Havana, Vera Cruz, and beyond, trading cod, timber, and wheat for sugar and products that refused to grow in Yankee back yards. Virtually the instant the colonies gained independence, they began extending the long lines of speculation until they reached around Tierra del Fuego to Honolulu, Manila, and Canton.

Speculators in the Mississippi Valley, from New Orleans up to Chicago, joined the imperial venture after 1800, providing capital, processing, and markets for the Caribbean Basin and beyond. Mexico ceded California to the United States in 1848, and the acquisition of Texas and the New Mexico Territory from Mexico by 1853 extended the hungry giant's reach. Holdings in the Pacific Northwest completed the consolidation of the colossus, enabling Yankee agents to penetrate Central America and the west coast of South America and, beyond that, across the Pacific to Hawaii and on to the South China Sea.

This geographic reach over half the planet was inseparable from the extension of American strategic hegemony, which was essential to the larger process of gathering profits and fruits of affluence for the nation's consumers. Unlike Europe's direct colonial occupation of tropical regions, America's access to tropical resources did not entail actual political annexation except in the Philippines. The collapse of the Spanish empire in the 1820s created a power vacuum in Latin America and the west coast of North America, which allowed Americans to trade and invest in the land on better than equal terms with their competitors. Even where European colonies remained—Spanish Cuba, the Dutch East Indies, and British Malaya—the power of Yankee capital was gradually established. American money was sometimes distrusted, but often it was welcomed by the older European powers.

In the last decades of the nineteenth century the United States took what it had learned in the tropics from its century-long apprenticeship in the European colonies and formed its own ecological empire. Once the United States displaced the last remnant of Spain's formal empire in Cuba, Puerto Rico, and the Philippines in 1898, the path was clear to draw the wealth of tropical Nature north. This transmission of resources was largely unimpeded by older European rivals. Americans competed with the British in many places until the global reach of Great Britain was severely weakened by World War I. The United States took the initiative, and by 1900 Americans matched the British in industrial technology and corporate organization, investment capital and consumer appetites for tropical products.

In addition, the depth of U.S. penetration into tropical lands and societies rested on the work of tropical science, in particular agronomy, livestock and pasture management, and forestry. Later, in the 1930s, soil scientists and wildlife biologists joined the coalition.

Together these Americans undertook what they liked to call the "Conquest of the Tropics." They saw themselves as bringing civilization to benighted peoples and cultivation to unruly tropical Nature. Traders, agronomists and engineers, ranchers and loggers all migrated south and southwest from nearly every region of the United States. American investments in the Western Hemisphere were backed by the diplomatic and military protection provided by the Monroe Doctrine. In Puerto Rico, Hawaii, and the Philippines Americans could work under direct colonial administration, with greater security but also with a few more restraints. In Indonesia and Malaya they prospered or foundered under the skeptical but tolerant eye of Dutch and British colonial regimes and European corporate competitors.

Beyond U.S. borders Americans had to adapt to existing power structures and extraction systems to gain access to cane sugar, coffee, tropical fruit, hardwood timber, and even pasturelands. In the southern Pacific and the South China Sea, international trade networks that long antedated the European presence were in Chinese, Malay, and other hands. As newcomers to those lands, languages, and cultures, Americans forged links or rivalries with local agrarian, commercial, and political elites. Like their European counterparts, Americans usually succeeded in subordinating local elites through a mutually profitable transformation of landholding patterns and agricultural labor. In the process they destroyed or subordinated indigenous cultures and displaced their collective subsistence use of field and forest with private property regimes linked to cash economies. These social transformations were inseparable from ecological change.

The process was far more complex and dynamic than one of merely domesticating tropical Nature into plantations and ranches. As Great Britain's global investments in the nineteenth century showed, the extraction of tropical resources depended on construction of a new worldwide system of transport infrastructure. The railroads, port facilities, and roads that were carved into the forests to support northern investments had secondary impacts that range far beyond the immediate area of farms or logging sites. The secondary effects of the global industrial web are virtually impossible to measure with any precision since the boundaries of systemic change are partly a matter of definition. These ripple effects on the tropical frontiers of settlement must not be discounted, however; they are suggested at many points in this account. In sum, virtually every aspect of the transformation of tropical societies is relevant to our understanding of the domestication and reduction of tropical Nature in the twentieth century.

The term *tropical forest* covers a range of ecosystems that are far more varied than the temperate forest ecosystems of Japan, Europe, and North America, where the first professional forestry traditions emerged. Indeed, one of the worst problems for northerners who intended to extract or manage tropical timber resources was their total lack of experience with the dazzling variety of tree species in the rainforest. That variety makes any generalization about tropical forest ecosystems risky, but for present purposes we can sketch four types and focus on the two that the Americans confronted.

The true rainforest, in which a significant amount of rain falls every month of the year, has the world's greatest variety of terrestrial species of plants and animals. Occurring at low elevations, generally below 1,000 meters, the rainforest's dominant tree species are an entirely different group on each of the three equatorial continents. Dominant species are slow-growing hardwoods: mahogany in the Caribbean Basin, the *Dipterocarps* such as the lauan in the Philippines and northern Borneo, and a number of dominant species in equatorial Africa and South America. Each species of tropical hardwood, such as Honduran mahogany, teak, meranti, lauan, or ebony, grows naturally in only one zone, which comprises climate, soils, and elevation. Each hardwood species is mixed with as many as several hundred other species in each hectare of forest, so a hectare may have as few as two or three mature trees of each marketable timber species—a dramatic contrast to hardwood forests of temperate zones.

A somewhat different pattern occurs in the monsoon forests of tropical Asia, where species are adapted to long hot dry seasons each year, alternating with heavy rains from June into December. In some of these seasonally dry regions one hardwood species such as teak can thrive in a single-species forest and under the right conditions be sustainably managed as a modern timber plantation. Teak, more than any other species, can grow successfully in parts of the world where it never evolved naturally, such as the Pacific coastal lowlands of Central America, where the climate approximates its homeland on the southwest coast of India and the central hill zone of Southeast Asia. North American foresters, who had little involvement in the forests of mainland tropical Asia before the 1960s, nonetheless successfully used teak for their reforestation plantations in Central America.

A third broad type of tropical forest is the open dry savanna woodlands of large parts of Africa, which are dominated by drought-resistant species such as acacias. These forests have never been linked to significant American political and economic interests and thus have never attracted American foresters or forest biologists outside research circles.

The fourth type of tropical forest, the conifer forests, did draw the attention of American corporations, and its commercial potential presented attractive challenges to Yankee foresters. Conifer zones are found in drier hill regions with poor soils (either nutrient-poor or porous) in Mexico, Central America, some Caribbean islands, and some inland areas of the Philippines. These woodlands approach the character of single-species forests, and most have been shaped by centuries of human settlement.

The linkages between American initiatives and ecological change in that broad equatorial region of the planet were widely varied in character—direct and indirect, specific and systemic. The American middle-level manager running a sugar plantation and the Yankee engineer supervising its refining factory were directly and daily responsible for the domestication of tropical soil and vegetation systems. A coffee roaster in New York, a fruit wholesaler in New Orleans, and a mahogany furniture craftsman in Grand Rapids worked at greater distances from their sources of supply, but they were equally crucial links in the American consumption of tropical Nature. So too were the Americans who purchased retail products like Jamaican rum, Philippine sugar, or Sumatran rubber.

Even when Americans were not the consumers, Yankee technicians and traders provided the means for selling primary products of the tropics to eager consumers elsewhere in the temperate world: a Massachusetts sea captain might carry Hawaiian sandalwood to Canton, a Chicago meat packer might run a slaughterhouse in Buenos Aires for beef eaters in England, a livestock breeder in northern Mexico might improve beef production for the Mexico City market, a forester from the Great Lakes might increase a timber company's efficiency so that it could cut Philippine mahogany for markets around the Pacific.

Just as this was an era of Yankee money, machines, and appetites, it was equally an era of Yankee enthusiasm, optimism, and moralism. To be sure, many of the Yankees were small-scale operators who risked their health and solvency in the tropics just to make ends meet, to reconstitute lives disrupted back home, or to escape the boredom and mediocrity of life in the small towns and farm communities of their birth. But the few who wrote about their work portrayed themselves as making major contributions to progress and prosperity, not only for the American economy but for tropical societies as well. In their initial ignorance of tropical cultures and biology, they were precursors of the Ugly American, who had no idea that he might be contributing to a gathering storm of troubles—to the decline rather than the rise of life in the tropics.

The chapters of this book follow the course of major American investment and consumer demand in the tropics, broadly defined. The earliest investments were in sugar production in the moist lowlands of the Caribbean Basin, where New England shippers were trading with

European colonial slave plantations by the 1700s. The shippers' power expanded into direct control in Cuba, which they turned into a semi-colony in the late 1800s, a situation that continued until 1959. There Americans dominated engineering, processing, banking, distribution, and management of the estates. They supplanted both natural and domesticated landscapes; they destroyed both mahogany forests and pastureland.

The predominant market demand in the United States in the 1800s was in the eastern states, where most of the population lived. As white settlement spread westward to California, markets in the western states produced new consumer demand that increased pressure on the Pacific tropics for products such as cane sugar. This led to the establishment of the American-held territory of Hawaii. A concentrated monocrop that usually demands large-scale irrigation, cane sugar displaced varying biotas in Hawaii, where the plantations were directly owned and managed by U.S. corporations. After 1900 sugar corporations extended their reach even farther, into the Philippines, where local landlords owned and usually managed the estates. Americans provided technology, capital, and export systems, but took no responsibility for brutal labor conditions or severe watershed damage.

Consequences were very different for coffee production in the cooler hill zones of South and Central America. Coffee trees thrive in more temperate climates, but in some settings their cultivation has caused severe soil erosion on hill slopes. American investment had a great impact on the social organization of coffee production as well. Smallholders in many countries could grow the brown gold as competitively as could large estate owners. Beginning in the early 1800s in southern Brazil, Americans purchased coffee from local exporters on the coast (Santos in southern Brazil, then Barranquilla in Colombia) and controlled international marketing. Coffee prices were determined on the New York and London markets. American and British coffee traders, who did not undertake direct management of coffee plantations, probably had less direct knowledge of or responsibility for the social and environmental effects of production than did their counterparts in the cane sugar business.

From the 1890s on, the corporate production of bananas in the lowland rainforests of Central America and then northern South America saw a direct, massive American investment in forest clearance, fruit cultivation, and transportation. This investment embraced the entire process, from leveling the forest to growing the delicate yellow fruit to delivering it to distant markets. In this tropical business as in no other, the growth of production resulted in the vertical integration of corporate interests. Moreover, bananas were produced under a notoriously unstable cropping system until the 1950s. At that point production was stabilized with new biological varieties, but this accomplishment was accompanied by intensive pesticide use.

After 1910 rubber became the target of major American investment first in tropical Southeast Asia, and later in Amazonia and West Africa. Rubber was the industrial era's paramount demand on tropical Nature. U.S. (and French) companies followed Dutch and British firms into Southeast Asia. The Americans shared technology with the Europeans, but competed with them for capital investment and price management. They cleared large sections of the rainforest for a monocrop that proved to be quite stable, although it caused some soil erosion. The American companies, The Goodyear Tire and Rubber Company and its competitors, which were the major rubber corporations of the eastern industrial belt, sent their managers directly into the rainforests, to supervise their clearing and replacement by a single species of tree crop. It was only when the Japanese military cut off American access to Southeast Asian rubber that petroleum-based rubber appeared and claimed roughly half the world's rubber market. The acreage of tropical land under rubber then stabilized, rather than expanding as rapidly as the mass market otherwise would have demanded.

Beef, the crop on hooves, had a long history of Yankee investment in Mexico. Beef production was far more varied and widespread than that of any plant crop, but it began to have an impact on the moist tropics only in the 1950s, when beef became a large-scale commercial export to the United States. Beginning in the mid-1800s, cattle production fostered a complex interaction between Hispanic and Anglo ranching systems in the grasslands. The beef packing industry of Chicago joined its British competitors to transform Argentina's savannas and economy, for European markets. Then Texan capital and veterinary and breeding science led the beef industry into the rainforest. From the 1950s American fast-food consumers added Central American beef to their diets. So the clearing of rainforest for cattle production reflected American consumer demand only in Central America, not farther south.

This survey concludes with the production of tropical timber. Tropical logging did not replace the forest with an agricultural monocrop, but with trees that were harvested as a commodity in their own right. Historically this story began around 1700 when the import of mahogany to East Coast furniture makers began. Yankee importers roamed the entire Caribbean Basin with European mahogany loggers, using primitive technology and small-scale investment to harvest the trees. Mahogany soon faced depletion, forcing a gradual diversification of species that were exploited by the timber industry. The search for new species took Americans into the Philippines after 1900, where they concentrated on harvesting Philippine mahogany as a substitute for true Caribbean Basin mahogany. Research and management under the colonial Philippine government introduced advanced sawmill technology and developed Pacific Rim markets as well as American markets. The result in the Philippines was rapid forest depletion. In tropical America the logging industry and the forestry profession ushered in a similar trend, but there it developed much more slowly.

None of these transformations of tropical ecosystems can be properly understood without an awareness of the markets that purchased their products, especially in the metropolitan economies of the northern world. Its first phase was the era of commercial capitalism in sixteenth century Iberia, then seventeenth century Netherlands. A second and vastly more powerful phase was the consumerism associated with industrial urbanization in England from the mid-eighteenth century on.[4]

The American economy's rise toward first place in tropical consumption accelerated after the Civil War, as an expression of rapid industrialization and the creation of an urban consuming class.[5] Like its European predecessors, this was a broad-spectrum consumerism. Within that trend individual tropical crops represent specific ecological changes, which directly resulted from the clearing of forests.

The years after World War I saw a rapid expansion of the consumerist ethos.[6] Access to bananas and rubber tires helped fulfill the dream of abundance for the expanding middle class. The Depression and another world war slowed consumption, but they created huge pent-up demand for security and affluence. In the quarter-century after 1945, mass consumption accelerated beyond anything ever seen before. It was epitomized in the new fast-food industry, which featured instant coffee, to the delight of Brazilian and Colombian producers. Another feature was lean beef for billions of American hamburgers; for the first time, American beef producers reached into the tropical rainforest.[7] In an era of accelerated consumer affluence, the Colossus of the North had the technological and strategic power to penetrate most tropical sources for the commodities that Americans desired.

Inexorably it became more important to consider whether tropical agriculture and forestry could learn to create sustainable product systems. Tropical agronomists working for corporations like the United Fruit Company or Goodyear were grafted onto a long European colonial tradition of studying tropical soils, botany, and diseases.[8] Dutch, French, and British economic botanists and later agronomists had worked in the employ of the colonial regimes for three centuries and more before they were joined by Americans after 1900. The European agronomists were constrained by the developmental priorities of those regimes, but they also enjoyed a continuity of work and influence on colonial administration that Americans working in the tropics rarely had.

Tropical forestry science, and its application in administrative systems, took long steps forward under American aegis in the Philippines and later in Puerto Rico. Americans worked closely with their British counterparts in Southeast Asia and India, and marginally also with Dutch and French colonial foresters. They were at the service of the loggers, however, just as the tropical crop and soil scientists were at the service of the plantation companies. In both cases extraction moved much faster and farther than systematic knowledge did. The process of learning from their mistakes, as well as their successes, always lagged behind.

That race to stabilize production systems in the tropics is still being lost, just as the effort to preserve a remnant of tropical nature in something like its pristine forms is still being lost. Capital investments, technological skills, and mass consumer appetites have spread to dozens of additional countries in the final four decades of the century. Understanding of the processes and planning for their control are also accelerating. If this book contributes to an understanding of our interconnections with our living planet, it will have been well worth the effort.

Croplands

CHAPTER I

America's Sweet Tooth

The Sugar Trust and
the Caribbean Lowlands

Sucrose is, in both its production and its consumption,
at the contact points of capitalist intent.
                                                Sidney Mintz, 1985

MERCANTILE CAPITALISM
TRANSFORMS TROPICAL LOWLANDS

Sugar cane was the first tropical plantation crop grown in the Americas for European consumption, linking tropical land and vegetation systems directly with the global economic web of the mercantilist empires. Of all Latin America's export crops, sugar cane has had the most influential role in the region's history, transforming its economic, political, and societal structures. It was the first crop to arrive with the Europeans; it was associated with one of the most ruthless of all labor systems, African slavery; and it has been the most widespread in replacing tropical rainforests. Only bananas can rival sugar as a dominant monocrop, and that has been only in the twentieth century. In the long perspective of global cane sugar production, the United States was a latecomer, not becoming involved until the 1650s.

From early colonial times onward, buyers of molasses and rum on the wharves of Boston, New York, Baltimore, and other ports helped strengthen the slave sugar system. The ultimate consumers of cane sugar had no direct responsibility for the social costs of its production and virtually no awareness of its ecological costs, but they were players nonetheless. By the end of the slave era, in the last years of the 1800s, Yankee investors and engineers had become the largest-scale players in the game. Protected by the U.S. flag, they achieved an unprecedented scale of industrialized agriculture in the cane fields of Cuba. This was the first flowering of American ecological imperialism. By the end of the nineteenth century U.S. producers were also growing cane in Florida, Louisiana, California, and Hawaii, and their competitors who produced sugar beets were growing that cool climate crop in more than thirty states. Cuba was the world's largest producer of cane sugar, however, and the American estates there were inheritors of a four-century European tradition that had intensely involved every imperial power. Sugar cane has been the crop most entangled with American economic and political interests in Cuba since the nineteenth century. This has resulted in fateful political consequences for U.S. relations with the entire region.

The international environmental impacts of sugar monocropping have been massive. In many locations primary forest was cleared expressly to plant cane. In other instances the record suggests that cane displaced field crops and pastures. Where cane grew, the cornucopia of flora and fauna was eliminated, replaced by wide acreage of only one species. In many locations the higher slopes above the cane were gradually stripped of timber to provide fuel for boiling the raw cane juice and cooking the workers' food. Moreover, the field workers' need for food and fiber led plantation owners to import those materials from great distances. More than any other crop, cane drew to itself the social and ecological resources of temperate as well as tropical lands, in the form of food (wheat and codfish), clothing (cotton), shelter (timber) and labor. Beyond this, the transport systems built to take cane to the refineries and from there to worldwide markets opened to domestication whole regions that had previously been inaccessible to international capital.[1]

On the other hand, sugar cane proved less susceptible to epidemic disease than most other major tropical export crops, and the impact of sustained sugar production on soils over long periods has been less severely depleting than that of some crops such as cotton or tobacco. Once the initial transformation from natural to domesticated ecology was completed, and as experience in working cane soils accumulated, it became possible to sustain the growth of sugar cane, something that was not possible with some other monocrops. Once planted in cane, these lands have mostly remained productive over extended periods of time.[2]

Sugar cane originated in the island biotas of Oceania, where several related species of tall grasses produced sucrose in their moisture-laden stems.[3] Throughout the human history of the Pacific, local people have enjoyed the moderate sweetness of natural cane varieties. Hybridization to produce a plant with higher amounts of sucrose began centuries ago. Raw sugar was enjoyed in northern India by at least 500 B.C. Migrating slowly westward, it was used for medicinal purposes in Persia and Byzantium.[4] It reached the eastern Mediterranean by the early eighth century. Arab traders took it westward from the Levant to Sicily and Valencia. French crusaders discovered it in Syria in the late 1200s and planted it in Cyprus. They conveyed the new craving back to regions north of the Mediterranean littoral, an unintended gift of the crusades to northern Europe.

By the late 1500s northern Europeans, led by the Dutch and English, began aggressively looking for a way to circumvent their Catholic and Muslim suppliers of Oriental goods. In the early 1600s sugar became a major item in imports from Asia. The Dutch East India Company exported sugar from southern China and Taiwan to Europe.[5]

The driving force behind these investments was an expanding market in Europe, where sugar became one of the luxuries of the aristocracy in the sixteenth century. The affluent began to satisfy their desire for sweeteners with something other than honey collected from farms and wood lands.[6] Common people could only dream of tasting sugar regularly because it remained available in such limited quantities throughout the eighteenth century. The first true mass market for sugar was created in the industrial era of the nineteenth century.[7] By 1800 England consumed 150,000 tons of sugar annually, much of it added to the new British addiction, tea. Sugar consumption on this scale would not have been possible without massive supply zones in tropical America. Nor would it have been possible without one of history's most brutal systems of human exploitation, the use of African slaves to clear lands in the New World for plantations.[8]

SLAVE SUGAR EMPIRES IN TROPICAL AMERICA

Portuguese entrepreneurs were the first Europeans to compete with Arab traders by producing sugar themselves. Sugar cane would not grow on mainland Portugal, so the Portuguese reached out into the Atlantic, to three island groups that became Iberia's steppingstones to the world. Their first sugar plantations were on Madeira, where they built the first water-driven sugar mill in 1452. In 1456 the first Madeiran sugar shipment arrived in England, and the sweetener also went to France, Flanders, and Italy before the decade was over. The hills of Madeira were stripped of their forest cover in the process. The "wooded isle," as it was known by the first Europeans to arrive there, was wooded no longer.

From Madeira it was relatively easy for the Iberians to reach the other Atlantic islands, the Canaries and Azores. The Spanish seized the Canaries, which are south of Madeira, off the Moroccan coast, and quickly drove to extinction the Guanchos, a Berber group that had immigrated from northwest Africa centuries before.[9] The first sugar mill there began operations in 1484. The cultivation of sugar cane and other export crops quickly reduced the forest cover of the mountains to a fragment of its former extent. Soil erosion and depletion followed, leaving the islands severely degraded. The Canaries were the first island ecosystem to be a casualty of European imperialism. Only an ambitious reforestation program organized by the government of Spain in the 1920s began to reverse the damage in some locations in the Canaries.[10]

It was only one more long reach across the Atlantic to the Caribbean islands and the east coast of South America. In the sixteenth century the Portuguese were the primary European sugar producers; they grew sugar cane along the coast of Brazil. Markets throughout western Europe were so lucrative that the Spanish—and soon the Dutch, the English, and the French—set up competing plantations in the Caribbean to assure themselves of a steady supply of the great sweetener and to fill their treasuries with the wealth that Portugal might otherwise siphon away. In the mercantile rivalry that resulted, the forest ecosystems of coastal Brazil and the Caribbean islands were ecologically transformed and degraded.

The Portuguese took sugar to Brazil's northeast coast in the early sixteenth century from their plantations on Madeira. In the 1520s they began planting cane on the narrow lowlands of Bahia and Pernambuco below the high escarpments that defended the interior plateau from penetration. In the following few decades they cleared more and more of the unique rainforest biome of the coastal zone. Throughout the 1500s Brazil was the largest sugar supplier in the Atlantic world.[11]

Clearing virgin tropical forest, and then growing and harvesting sugar cane, was back-breaking labor that required a concentrated, controlled labor force. People of the indigenous coastal cultures either died from European diseases or refused to work as slaves. They knew how to vanish into the higher hinterland, where they established small exile communities that lasted for generations. So the Portuguese turned to slaves imported from West Africa. Africans cleared extensive areas of coastal and riverside forests for the sugar plantations, using ax and hoe and then burning the severed vegetation. Growers preferred the rich clay soil of the lowlands, but found that the better-drained sandy soils of adjacent areas also produced well, although they were more quickly exhausted of nutrients.

The cane they planted, which became known as Creole sugar, was Puri stock from India. It had high juice and fiber content but poor yields of processed sugar. Yet it was the only variety used in the Americas for 250 years, until more productive varieties arrived from the South Pacific via French plantations in Mauritius in the late eighteenth century.[12]

To process the cane into semirefined *muscovado* sugar, investors built *trapiches,* simple mills along the banks of the coastal rivers, which used power supplied by oxen (cattle were an integral element of sugar plantations) or water to grind the cane and extensive amounts of fuelwood to boil the juice into marketable sugar. On the Bahia and Pernambuco coasts no irrigation was needed; hence the Portuguese growers did not need to reconstruct the natural water systems of the sugar region, unlike some later sugar-producing regions in dry settings. More intrusive was the effort needed to process the cane: each cartload of sugar cane used nearly half a cartload of firewood. The first plantations had adequate forest reserves for their needs, but by the early seventeenth century the forest frontier gradually receded into the hills and the rising cost of hauling wood greater distances became one of the growers' major troubles. Sugar from northeastern Brazil began to lose out to competition from the Caribbean islands.[13]

The need to import food supplies resulted in a vast extension of the resource base required to produce cane sugar. Nutrition for Africans and Europeans alike did not come from the foods of the wet New World tropics, but from foods bought from other areas. Slave owners imported wheat from the Spanish-controlled highlands of Mexico; by the 1570s over 150,000 bushels left Veracruz for Brazil each year. The Spaniards also shipped smaller amounts of wheat from Lima's high hinterland in the Peruvian Andes, transporting it by ship around nearly the entire coast of South America.

Animal protein for the plantation population was supplied by beef from Criollo cattle, which had first stepped onto Brazilian shores in the 1530s. Cattle grazing led the expansion of the plantation economy over the escarpments to the *sertão,* the drier, more open woodlands in the vast interior, where plantation crops would not grow. By the 1550s beef and leather were being exported from the inlands to the coastal plantations.[14]

In 1580 the Spanish empire swallowed Portugal, and this dynastic event on the Iberian peninsula reverberated into the history and bio-history of the tropical New World. For sixty years, until 1640, Madrid controlled Lisbon, permanently weakening the Portuguese empire in Brazil. By the time Portugal was independent again, its financial structure was largely controlled by English capital and its trade with Brazil had been largely captured by Dutch sea captains.

Farther north, sugar cane was one of the most important plant species that accompanied the Spanish when they established colonies in Mexico and the Caribbean islands. Cane was introduced in the Caribbean as early as 1493, when Columbus took it to Española, or Hispaniola, the "Spanish island" that he had discovered a year before. Sugar and cattle became the mainstay and the curse of the island.[15] Many early attempts to grow sugar cane profitably failed. Growers gained Hapsburg imperial patronage when Charles V ordered sugar masters and technicians to migrate from the Canaries to Hispaniola. There were thirty-four mills on the island by the late 1530s. From Hispaniola sugar production spread quickly along the Spanish conquest route. It migrated to Mexico in the 1520s with Cortez's invaders, where the cane thrived on the coastal lowlands north and south of the beachhead at Veracruz. Shortly thereafter sugar cane began to set roots in the volcanic soils of Central America's Pacific lowlands, especially in Guatemala. It accompanied Pizarro to the coastal lowlands of Peru, and then reappeared far beyond the Andes in the Rio de la Plata lowlands of colonial Uruguay and Argentina.[16] In the long run, the Spanish empire's most important home was the Caribbean island of Cuba, where Spain presided over slave-based plantations for nearly four centuries, until its island holdings collapsed in 1898. The rise of Cuban sugar to preeminence among the islands did not occur until the late 1700s, after a long period of Dutch, English, and French dominance.

Sugar's most dramatic transformations of societies and landscapes were in the biotically fragile settings of the Caribbean islands. Island ecosystems support limited biodiversity because of their small overall extent and relative isolation from other landmasses. Species composition varies greatly from one island to another; hence islands sustain many endemic species of flora and fauna, each of which exists nowhere else in the natural world. Each species occupies limited territorial extent and links intricately to many other species.[17]

Branching off from the mountain system of the Central American isthmus, two great mountain chains run eastward into the Caribbean Sea. Their lower slopes are submerged; their higher slopes form the islands of the Antilles. (See appendix, maps 1 and 2.) The northernmost chain forms Cuba and Hispaniola and its highest peak, rising 10,400 feet, is in the Dominican Republic. Except for the richly fertile central plain of Cuba, nearly all land in the islands is ruggedly mountainous. The islands' soils range from limestone and sandstone to barren granite; apart from the bottomlands, these soils are only marginal for agriculture of any sort. Since colonial times their forests have been subject to deforestation, especially in the service of agriculture.

Land use in the Caribbean basin before the Spanish conquest was determined by the migration of Arawak and Carib populations, which together amounted to around one million people in 1490. The Arawaks practiced a complex pattern of multicrop farming, along with hunting, gathering, and fishing. European ideas of private property would have been incomprehensible to them. The Caribs, more aggressive even to the point of cannibalizing their captives in war, developed less in the way of agriculture.[18]

Within a few years after 1492 the Spaniards and their allied cultures virtually wiped out the indigenous populations of the Caribbean islands and weakened the island ecosystems, leaving a demographic vacuum that was filled from the Old World. Sugar and slaves, both biological exotics, further damaged the natural systems of the islands. From the 1590s onward Dutch sea captains and slave traders, financed by the merchant aristocracy of Amsterdam, transferred the plantation system from Brazil to the Caribbean.[19] By the 1630s Dutch shippers and technicians had wrested control of Brazilian sugar exports from the Portuguese. They learned production processes in Pernambuco and Bahia and quickly established new plantations on Curaçao and several other small Caribbean islands, displacing Brazil as the major source for world markets. Thus the geographical focus and ecological consequences of sugar production shifted to the fragile islands.

For the sugar lords everything depended on markets in Europe. Whoever could control sugar shipments to the great emerging entrepôts of Holland and England in the early 1600s could shape sugar production and tropical land use in the Americas. The British led the large-scale development of sugar production in the islands, after they defeated the Dutch in a series of naval wars in the western Atlantic in the mid-1600s. The British prevailed, but the Dutch were ready in any case to experiment with sugar production in their Southeast Asian colony of Java.

English buccaneers had been probing Caribbean trade possibilities for sugar, and Belize mahogany as well, from the late 1500s onward.

Then, between 1600 and 1620, sugar consumption escalated rapidly in England. From the 1640s onward the British-controlled island of Barbados was the main source of cane sugar. Taken by Britain in the early 1600s, the island was soon dominated by sugar plantations. England gained a windfall from the internal ethnic struggles of their southern rivals when Portuguese Jews skilled in sugar production and refinement, who had been banished from Brazil by the Spanish crown, settled on islands governed by the more tolerant, pragmatic English.[20]

British planters and their slaves cleared the lowland forests of Barbados to make way for cane in the rich soils. The forested hills of the watersheds above, unsuitable for sugar cultivation, were more gradually cleared of trees for fuel to boil the cane juice. Dense slave populations for clearing the forest and growing and harvesting the cane were concentrated in the plantation lowlands. Their need for cooking fuel further increased the demand for wood. Soil erosion and depletion began to be evident by 1650 because the planters grew cane in trenches regardless of their angle to slopes.[21]

Dramatic environmental damage resulted within a few decades. By 1665 only one small hill forest remained on the entire island of Barbados. The island had suffered almost total loss of its ecologically complex forest.[22] Some species extinctions ensued, since the island had many endemic species: one species of palmito, mastick (a timber tree), and shrub and ground plants were quickly depleted, and several monkey and bird species of the forest canopy were decimated. In their stead appeared invader species from Europe and other islands, including rats, weeds, and tree species including logwood, guava, and coconut.[23] Such a complete transformation led to the first conservationist countermeasures: fragmentary efforts to replant trees on the higher watersheds.[24] Unfortunately, political conditions did not allow effective forest laws to be established or reclamation work to begin for another two centuries, until shortly after 1900.[25]

In the early eighteenth century, British sugar planters, who were constantly searching for new soils, arrived on Jamaica. Over twenty times the size of Barbados, Jamaica is the third largest island in the Caribbean. It lies directly south of eastern Cuba. Slightly smaller than Connecticut, it is mostly high, rolling hills that loom over coastal plains and alluvial river basins. Well-drained limestone soils cover three quarters of the island. It is moderately rainy most of the year, served by trade winds from the northeast. Several sheltered harbors lie on the leeward south coast, the finest of which host Port Royal and Kingston. The smaller harbor of Morant Bay lies farther along the southeast coast.[26]

British planters chose the most fertile, best watered lowland soils on which to plant the precious cane. They could concentrate labor just as they wished for clearing the forest, preparing, tilling, and weeding the cane fields, digging irrigation systems, and the myriad other tasks of plantation life. For growing much of their food, slaves were allotted small plots of land that were unsuitable for cane; this was called the "provision ground" system. It enabled the slaves to maintain their skills at growing subsistence crops, skills upon which they relied for survival when the plantation system collapsed after emancipation.[27] The major portion of estate land was maintained as pasture or left in woodlands.

In early colonial times upland forests were declared the property of the Crown in an attempt to insure that the high watersheds would be conserved from the deforestation that was causing severe problems in Barbados.[28] Despite this precaution it was not easy to prevent squatters from entering the mountain forests and slashing small patches to grow subsistence crops.

Plantation slavery was necessary for maintaining a labor force when there was much empty land in the hills above, land into which field laborers could vanish. Escaped slaves, called "maroons," were responsible for clearing many tiny patches of hill forest throughout tropical America's slave region. Owners made frequent efforts to recapture them, sometimes succeeding. Afro-Jamaicans who left plantations for "the mountain" grew subsistence crops in these small clearings in the forest, but they soon began producing cash crops too. Their crops included fruit, yams, plantains, breadfruit, sugar, ginger, and coffee. Some of these were introductions from the Old World, but they provided a far wider biological spectrum than the monocrop system of commercial plantations.

Out of this contrast arose a controversy that has echoed through the centuries to today. The Africans' attitude toward the land was that it was to be used, not locked up in forest reserves. They treated it as a private holding if it was farmed; otherwise it was considered available for others' subsistence. The Europeans, in contrast, believed that commercial monocropping was the most civilized form of land use. Philip Curtin writes of the "mystique" of one-crop planting—that is, the European belief that there was nobility in crops like sugar and, later, coffee.[29] Most British were contemptuous of the African system of multicrop plantings in the forest commons, seeing it as economically backward and damaging to the forest cover. Ultimately others saw its greater complexity and ambiguity. Well after 1900 a former governor, Sydney Haldane Olivier, looked back in retrospect and concluded:

> The trees of high woodland are felled and burnt or where they resist are lopped of their branches, the trunks left standing sometimes like blackened obelisks. Roots are levered out and the soil turned up with sharpened stakes or hoes. . . . No doubt it appears chaotic. But it is planted for a rotation. The knowledgeable cultivator studies the ground and sets each plant or seed where the soil will suit it and the growth fit in most conveniently with the general purpose. The selections and combinations are very varied. . . . This art of food cultivation is, for its purposes, highly efficient. On a well-chosen and well-handled plot the quantity of food produced is astonishing and the yield is continuous.[30]

Lord Olivier was too knowledgeable to romanticize Afro-Jamaican multicropping uncritically, however, and he knew how intense the conflict between the two cultures' systems of agronomy was.

> But the [African] method exhausts the land and the plot has presently to be abandoned. A nomad habit is fostered. Dwellings are shifted. Spent land must be abandoned to rest. . . . When the yield no longer repays the labour the plot is allowed to grow up in bush. After a period of years the new jungle is again cut down and fired. . . . What the African husbandman likes best is virgin woodland. The accumulated fertility repays the heavy labour of clearing. The forest is ruined, to the grief of the lover of timber. After the land has been cleared once or more, it frequently happens that, by the time the cultivators have finished with it, exposure to weather has caused a good deal of the soil to be washed away. . . . To Europeans, who have long had no land to waste, who have long ceased their migrations and have had to devise a system of static husbandry and renew their soil by manuring, native African agriculture is an abomination.[31]

By the end of the eighteenth century, the English sugar islands were in long-term decline brought on by the combined systems of forest clearance and soil depletion. When the United States became independent, the former colonies were excluded from West Indian trade under the British Navigation Laws, depriving the sugar islands of supplies and markets. In addition, Britain began moving toward the abolition of slavery, which made the plantation economy even more unstable. In London Parliament abolished the British Caribbean slave trade in 1807; all slavery was formally ended in Jamaica in 1834. In that year Jamaica had 650 sugar estates, holding a total of 650,000 acres, but only 100,000 acres were planted to cane. Under slavery the planter could concentrate labor on the acreage he chose; after emancipation, the freedmen were tempted to migrate to hill land owned by the British Crown and to begin a new life of forest clearing for subsistence farming, as their counterparts had done *en masse* in Haiti a generation before.[32]

In consequence of boom prices in the early nineteenth century, some parcels of marginal hill land had been cleared of forest and planted to sugar. When sugar prices fell during the Napoleonic Wars and after, these estates were forced to close. In acts that were both economically foolhardy and ecologically damaging, land speculators replaced forests with estates that were financially viable only as long as international prices were high. By the time the slave system was abolished on Jamaica in 1834, large areas of land had lost their natural forest to sugar and all of its systemic demands. The British worried that desolation of the economy and the land was the only alternative to the plantation system. This was not necessarily so: it represented European assumptions about a properly managed landscape. After emancipation, hill and forest land was open to purchase, rent, or squat, and many former slaves settled there and raised survival and cash crops. Despite this availability of fertile land, the depression created a large surplus of mobile labor. Many Afro-Jamaican men were willing to go anywhere in the Caribbean basin to find paying work. They were to provide much of the free labor that cleared forests for the American sugar and banana plantations that were established around the region in the decades after 1890.

Meanwhile, in Saint Domingue, later Haiti, the western third of Hispaniola, the French experiment with tropical cane production had played itself out into a social and ecological disaster. In the course of the 1600s Saint Domingue became France's primary source of sugar from the tropical Americas. The first plantations, established in the 1640s, were on the moist and fertile northern lowland plains. From there cane spread southward to drier areas, but only after complex irrigation canals were put in place. As French planters imported African slaves to clear lowland forests, the population of Saint Domingue became one of the densest in the Antilles. In 1789 there were twenty Africans for every Frenchman, the highest ratio in the Caribbean.

In such a labor-intensive economy as slave sugar, the provision of a nutritional base to keep the slaves working presented a dilemma for the French planters. Wheat, a staple in the slaves' diet, would compete for the same soils as sugar, and they were unwilling to devote acreage to the less lucrative crop. Instead they imported wheat from New Orleans. This market was one significant factor in the spread of wheat farming into the lower Mississippi Valley. Thus slave sugar entangled yet another region of continental North America in its web.

Conditions for slaves on the French plantations of Haiti were as brutal as any in the entire Caribbean. When the Ancien Régime in France fell in 1789, the chaos that followed the storming of the Bastille became another European export to the Caribbean. It was not long before the slave populations of Haiti learned of the events in Paris. In 1791 they rose against their masters, either killing them or forcing them to flee from the island. Within the first few weeks, 2,000 Europeans died and 180 sugar plantations were burned. Those planters and their families who could escape fled to Havana, home of the Spanish sugar aristocracy, where they added their skills to the expansion of Cuban sugar production. In Haiti, spasms of fighting continued until 1804, when the ex-slave republic was officially established. By then the sugar industry had collapsed, and Haiti reverted from a supplier of France's sweetener to a subsistence economy that depended on degraded lands, which grew steadily more degraded as the largely African population changed over to subsistence farming.[33] As they spread into the hills, they increasingly practiced a form of multicrop farming that had been better adapted to their African homelands. The forest and soil cover were steadily depleted, until Haiti became modern tropical America's most desperately poor and degraded country.[34]

By 1800 soil exhaustion was rampant in the lowlands of all the older sugar islands. The mountainous hinterland felt the impact of sugar production too, as ex-slaves moved into the hills and returned to subsistence farming, disrupting forests and watersheds throughout the nineteenth century. Many ultimately became members of a landless work force that supplied labor for plantations elsewhere around the Caribbean. In sum, sugar plantation capitalism resulted in three concentric circles of ecological disruption: the plantation lands themselves, the hill hinterlands that supported plantation workers before and after emancipation, and the far-flung lands and oceans from which the plantation system drew its supplies.

CUBA: KING SUGAR AND THE AMERICAN EMPIRE

THE SPANISH PLANTATIONS

The Spanish-held islands, especially Cuba, began their move to dominate world sugar production when French and British markets were

disrupted during the Napoleonic Wars. By the time Spanish power collapsed in Cuba in 1898, the island was the world's greatest exporter of
sugar and the target of massive investment from the United States.

It is difficult to assess the full environmental costs of sugar production
in Cuba, since detailed data on forest cover and soil erosion are not
readily available. But a broad picture can be traced. Estimates of the
history of Cuba's forest cover suggest that some 60 percent of the country was forested when the Spanish conquistadors first attacked and decimated the indigenous population; the other 40 percent was in lowland
savannas or local clearings, particularly in the east, for the subsistence
agriculture of perhaps 1 million people. After four hundred years of
Spanish rule, the 1899 census indicated that about 50 percent of the
island was still forested, in spite of massive clearings for sugar. The
population, which had dropped calamitously after 1500, leaving most
of the pre-Hispanic clearings to revert to forest, had recovered to about
1.5 million.[35]

The colonial transformation of Cuba's vegetation systems reflected
the island's topography and climate.[36] The largest island in the Caribbean, Cuba is 800 miles long and varies from 25 to 120 miles wide.
Cuba is the least mountainous of the Antillean islands and thus is the
best endowed for large-scale agriculture. In the west, a range of low hills
is the home of some of the world's finest tobacco.[37] East of those hills
lie the rich plains of Matanzas, where sugar has dominated the landscape
in modern times, making Cuba the world's greatest sugar producer. The
gentle slopes and ecologically stable lowlands of these central plains hold
the fertile red Matanzas clay, composed of residues from dissolved lime
stone, fine-grained and permeable, which guarantees good drainage.
Sometimes over twenty-five feet deep, this soil still provides one-third
of the nation's sugar acreage.[38] The open, rolling lands and rich soils
are perfectly suited for the maximum production and easy transport of
sugar. Most sugar is grown below 300 feet; no cane grows above 1,000
feet. The region also has an ideal climate: an evenly spaced annual rainfall of 40 to 60 inches alternates with a reliable dry season for the *zafra,*
or harvest. Moreover, the long thin profile of the island meant that for
colonial growers the best sugar areas were only short distances from
numerous pocket harbors along the coast, although portions of the
south coast were blocked by long mangrove swamps and high hills in
Trinidad and the Sierra Maestra.[39]

Cattle were closely associated with sugar production from the moment the Spaniards arrived on Hispaniola. Forty percent of Cuba's land

became pasture of one sort or another. Over the years most cattle have grazed on poorer lands in the provinces of Camagüey and Oriente, where large ranches flourished until 1959 under colonial rancheros and their descendants. Much land was rotated between pasture and sugar.[40]

Until major U.S. investments vastly expanded sugar acreage after 1900, production was far less intensive in the eastern provinces of the island. East of the central plain, in Camagüey province, the topography is more hilly, with varied and fragile soils. That region was long lightly populated and isolated from important ports. It produced little in the way of cash crops before the post-1900 extension of American-built railroads eastward across the island. In the hills of Camagüey and Oriente, forest clearance for sugar production was more risky. Cropland was less productive, and fields were more prone to soil erosion.

Cuba's highest mountains, the Sierra Maestra, rise ruggedly beyond Camagüey in the east; they are Cuba's greatest source of forest wealth, but their mountain soils are generally thin and easily eroded except for a few alluvial bottomlands. There in Oriente, remote and poor, many rebellions of the peasantry against central authority have been nurtured, including the most fateful, Fidel Castro's revolution in the 1950s.

The story of political turmoil and variable environmental change in Cuba must be traced against the background of Cuba's colonial economy. Eighteenth-century Cuban society was dominated by a handful of Andalusian families, mostly living in Havana, who had cattle haciendas on nearby savanna lands. Eighteenth-century Havana was an impressive city. The 1778 census counted 40,737 inhabitants of the city plus 41,000 more in its immediate hinterland, out of the island's total population of 179,484.[41] Havana was the largest port in Spanish America, its population exceeded only by those of Mexico City and Lima. In its hinterland, tobacco farms coexisted with large cattle ranches, which raised beef for local consumption and hides for export. Neither tobacco nor beef was likely to expand much: Madrid had imposed a royal monopoly on tobacco in 1717, and the Cuban towns fixed beef prices low.

Havana's shipyards were a key to the power of the entire Spanish empire. Between 1714 and 1762 sixty-six warships were built in Havana for the Bourbon fleet, two-fifths of total Spanish shipbuilding. The ships were constructed from timber harvested in the magnificent mahogany forests that lay east and southeast of Havana. Several fortunes were built from the mahogany ships, such as that of the Justi family, landowners in Matanzas, near Havana, whose interests included sugar and to-bacco.[42]

The Spanish Crown controlled the harvest of timber species that were used in shipbuilding, and it forbade private sales. This inhibited the expansion of acreage under sugar cane, since trees were in the way. Timber was needed by the planters as well, for fuel and packing crates; as early as 1770 Havana began importing wood from Louisiana.

By the time of the Seven Years' War in the 1750s, some fifty patrician families controlled Havana's political offices and Cuba's economy from their sugar and cattle estates in the Matanzas plains. In the relative prosperity that followed that war, those families steadily expanded their sugar harvests, an expansion that was financed by the import of Mexican silver. The trend toward international free trade in the Caribbean furthered their interests. In 1765 the Crown opened Havana's shipping to many European ports. Sugar acreage expanded rapidly: between 1760 and 1791 production tripled, sending Cuba from eleventh to fourth place in world production. After the slave revolt in Haiti in 1791, Spain's policies in Cuba became even more liberal. With Haiti's sugar industry in collapse, Cuban sugar production doubled again in the 1790s. Sugar thus expanded at the expense of cattle pasturage, small tobacco farms, and especially forests.[43]

In that decade the landlords of Havana were joined by those Haitian sugar planters who were able to escape with their lives when their slaves rose and destroyed Haiti's plantation economy. When most of Latin America joined the revolution against Spanish and Portuguese control after 1810, many *hacendados* from revolutionary areas of Latin America also moved to Cuba. They added their wealth and skills to Havana society and joined a surge of new investment in Matanzas, on what one historian has called "virgin land of remarkable fertility."[44]

As the nineteenth century wore on, sugar refining demanded increasingly complex machinery, which required more concentrated capital resources. In the early nineteenth century, an *ingenio*—the larger steam-powered mill that was replacing the smaller, animal-powered *trapiche*—cost thirty to forty thousand dollars. In 1827 Cuba had some 1,000 *ingenios,* producing 90,000 tons of sugar annually. The rapid increase in the scale of the island's sugar production is reflected in the fact that by the early 1850s production grew remarkably without significant technical changes: 1,500 *ingenios* were producing 300,000 tons annually. The extraction process was crude and wasteful, and the sugar quality was low: the process extracted less than half of the sugar in the cane. Improvements in engineering, most of them designed by Americans, were about to revolutionize the refining process, making it far more efficient but further centralizing ownership and profits.

YANKEE MERCHANTS AND THE CARIBBEAN

The role of U.S. capital, entrepreneurship, and engineering in transforming tropical lands was nowhere more influential than in the Cuban sugar industry, and nowhere did it have earlier beginnings. Ship owners from Boston and other New England coastal towns competed with their European rivals from the mid-1600s onward, first in trade, then through capital investment in production processes. These men were the forerunners of speculative entrepreneurs who brought industrial capitalism to the islands, transforming sugar production into an industrial process.

By 1700 North Atlantic maritime trade produced complex exchanges between the temperate and tropical Atlantic bioregions. The triangular trade, fatefully linked to the African slave trade, provided New England, New York, Philadelphia, and Baltimore with sugar's major by-products: molasses and the rum that was distilled from molasses. According to a survey made in 1769, Boston imported 1,190,754 gallons of molasses and only 71,937 gallons of rum, while Philadelphia took 352,855 gallons of molasses and 734,342 gallons of rum. There was only a small market for refined sugar, for that was an expensive luxury. Poor people used molasses as their sweetener. Aside from sugar products, the English-speaking colonies imported little else from the West Indies—they developed only a small demand for ginger, indigo, and pimento. In other words, they generated little demand for other tropical products, a demand that would have had a direct environmental impact.

Hard cash was scarce in the colonies, a result of the narrowly limited market, and sugar was a highly versatile article of trade. In the West Indies most planters insisted on paying for goods with goods: they accepted sugar and tobacco as currency throughout the 1600s. Throughout the 1700s rum and molasses were commonly bartered for bread, tobacco, spermaceti candles, clothes, and even houses, land, ships, and construction labor.[45]

During the eighteenth century both continental North America and the Caribbean islands were still frontiers of European capitalist and industrial expansion. The two regions were linked in a two-way trade that consisted largely of primary products of land and sea. Yet the trade between the temperate and tropical climate zones of the New World had momentous ecological consequences in itself.

The West Indian economy demanded timber from northern New England and the maritime provinces of Canada. Colonial ports and sugar plantations needed pine for construction. Havana and lesser ports needed naval stores, such as pine pitch and resin for shipbuilding, and some hardwoods.[46] Equally important for the trade between ecological zones, the West Indies desired codfish from the teeming spawning grounds of the Grand Banks off Newfoundland. Caribbean slave owners looking for protein to keep their chattel working found it in salt cod, which they purchased in massive amounts from northern shippers. These shippers bought the cod from an international fishing fleet that competed in an endless free-for-all, in unregulated international waters, for a seemingly bottomless source of profit.[47]

In the years immediately following independence, American commercial and political relations with the European powers in the western Atlantic were so unsettled that the fortunes of Yankee traders in the Caribbean were never secure. Their links with Havana became steadily stronger, however, from all the major ports on the Atlantic coast. American hinterlands provided a wide range of natural and agricultural resources, which paid for the constantly accelerating purchase of sugar products, linking the clearing of forestlands in eastern North America with the decline of mahogany forests in the Caribbean. One example of this linkage was the mercantile relationship between Philadelphia and Havana. From about 1770 onward Cuban farms made little attempt to provide adequate wheat for Havana's urban population. Havana's bakers in any case preferred Philadelphia's flour, made from wheat grown on the farms of eastern Pennsylvania, which they used to provision the imperial fleet and the region's populace. In the early 1790s Havana was able to shift its rural acreage into sugar production largely because of Pennsylvania's wheat farmers.

American investment in Cuba grew steadily. As a recent analysis puts it, "The rapidly expanding white and black populations, the annual influx of thousands of silver pesos from New Spain, as well as the de facto loosening of Bourbon commercial restrictions during wartime, made Cuba ever more attractive to merchants on the American mainland."[48] These investments were highly speculative and risky: by the definitions of Spanish colonial law, the North Americans were smugglers and pirates. Financiers usually chose to make limited annual investments or, at most, short-term business partnerships. Usually they stopped only briefly in port to unload and load cargo. Mercantilist Bourbon Spain attempted to maintain a monopoly of trade with its Caribbean possessions, but its weakening power in the 1700s gradually led Madrid toward tolerating other traders, including the North Americans.

For a century Havana was the most important port for Yankee traders in the tropical Caribbean, in a network that stretched around the Caribbean's shores to Veracruz and Cartagena, and even as far along South America's Atlantic seaboard as Buenos Aires. By the early 1740s

> the colonial merchants had obtained almost a monopoly of the West Indian business: they owned and operated the ships, and marketed in the French and Spanish as well as in the British islands the large surplus of products which the mainland colonies had for export. In exchange they brought back sugar and molasses to supply the innumerable distilleries scattered along the thousand-mile coast from Maine to Georgia. Every mainland port and nearly every mainland merchant had ties in the West Indies—family ties and property holdings, such as the Livingstons of New York and the Dickensons of Philadelphia; speculators like the Beekmans of New York; general exporters and ship-owners like the Browns of Providence; agencies like that of Peter Faneuil of Boston and Richard Derby of Salem who dealt in enemy sugar during the Seven Years War, handling the affairs of Frenchmen as well as their own. In short, the West Indian trade permeated all parts of the mainland economy and contributed substantially to the wealth of the seaboard merchants.[49]

The strategic rivalries of the North Atlantic did not end when the United States became independent. A vaster vision of American imperial leadership in the future of the Americas was emerging, as Jefferson noted in 1786: "Our confederacy must be viewed as the nest, from which all America, North and South, is to be peopled. We should take care too, not to think it for the interest of that great continent to press too soon on the Spaniards. Those countries cannot be in better hands."[50]

Intense maritime competition between the British and Yankee merchant marines continued just short of overt conflict. The British succeeded in increasingly disrupting Yankee trade with the West Indies, and in 1812 the two countries again resorted to open hostilities. It took three years of inconclusive naval skirmishes before a peace treaty in 1815 permanently ended open violence between the two. The rivalry continued, however, dominating the imperialists' struggle for hegemony over the rich natural resources of the New World's tropics for another century.

After war ended in Europe and the North Atlantic in 1815, an increasing stream of Yankee adventurers turned up in Havana and its hinterland. American investment in the Cuban sugar industry began to expand after 1820. At that time New York surpassed Philadelphia in foreign trade because of its aggressive development of trade connections with Europe, which enabled Manhattan's merchants and bankers to offer Cubans an entire range of trade and financial services.[51] By the 1830s numerous U.S. citizens were investing in Cuban sugar. Drake Brothers and Company, based in New York, imported Cuban sugar and owned one of the best Cuban plantations in collaboration with the United States Mail Steamship Company. Another New Yorker playing the Cuban hand was George Law, politician and partner in the New York Mail Steamship Company. As in Boston and other old colonial ports, trade and shipping provided the basis for investment in Cuban sugar.

Nor was the eastern seaboard the only major player. New Orleans could draw on the resources of the entire Mississippi Valley for its trade with the West Indies. By the mid-nineteenth century its cotton, grain, and cattle exports made it second only to New York in its foreign trade. As a relative newcomer to the city, J. D. B. DeBow wrote in *DeBow's Monthly* in 1850, "We have a destiny to perform, a 'manifest destiny' over all Mexico, over South America, over the West Indies and Canada."[52] By mid-century the Illinois Central Railroad, the great valley's new railroad system, efficiently linked New Orleans with the economic magnet, Chicago. The railroad's owners planned to trade wheat and pork for Cuban sugar.

New Orleans was particularly notorious for its political shenanigans toward Cuba. Filibuster Narciso Lopez organized three personal invasions of Cuba from New Orleans between 1849 and 1851, with help from John L. O'Sullivan, Jefferson Davis, and others. Like other U.S. adventurers in later years, Lopez misjudged his importance to the Cubans. No popular uprising greeted his appearance, and Spanish soldiers shot him on his third landing.[53]

Cuba has a strategic location, as Spain had always known. Whoever held Havana could neutralize other nations throughout the western Caribbean, including the aggressive new empire to the north, which might turn the Caribbean into an American lake. By the early 1850s the United States was importing more from Cuba than was Spain, its nominal colonial overlord, as the taste for sugar in the American market rapidly rose. Between 1840 and 1860, U.S. imports expanded fourfold. Businessmen in New York and New Orleans with sugar connections in Havana joined southern slaveholders to accelerate the long-standing campaign to annex Cuba and its slave economy. The Irish-born New Yorker John L. O'Sullivan, who had family ties to Cuban sugar, argued that in return for guaranteed protection of the slave system, the Cuban sugar barons would surely buy the island from Spain and present it to Washington. In 1848 August Belmont, a New York banker who had been the Rothschilds' agent in Naples and Havana, tried to persuade the Rothschilds to force Spain to sell Cuba to the United States, since the family's fortune provided wherewithal for the bankers of financially strapped Spain. Nothing came of this grandiose scheme either.[54]

The annexation movement failed; the northern states' antislavery opposition to the annexation effectively postponed a U.S. invasion until 1898. Nonetheless, a pattern was being set: the penetration of Yankee capital was followed by political and military support from Washington to guarantee American access to land and resources. U.S. dominance of Cuba's lands would evolve gradually over the next half century, and its character would be deeply conditioned by global sugar production and marketing.

By the mid-1800s an additional complication entered the picture, when sugar beets grown in the northern United States became an important market factor. Sugar is the only major commodity on world markets that can be produced not only in tropical zones but also far northward into the zone of cold winters, because it can be economically derived from two very different plant sources: cane and beets.

Beet sugar was known by 1575 in Germany, but it was only in 1747 that a German chemist efficiently extracted refined sugar from beets.[55] Sugar beets were first cultivated on a large scale in northern Europe during the Napoleonic wars, when the British naval blockade of France forced the French to provide home-grown substitutes for many of their habitual imports. In the years after Napoleon's defeat, first northern German and then Austrian, Polish, and Russian farmers moved into large-scale sugar beet production.

The United States was not far behind. In several northern states beet farmers began major production to supply domestic U.S. markets. Beet sugar refining was introduced into Northampton, Massachusetts, in the 1830s by men who learned the technique in Paris. Soon Philadelphia joined the industry, and from there it spread rapidly westward as more states were settled by white farmers. In the 1860s German immigrants in Ohio, Illinois, Michigan, and Wisconsin began to grow sugar beets. From there the cultivation moved across the plains states to Colorado, Utah, and finally California.[56]

The result was a revolution in world sugar production. In 1853 only 14 percent of the world's sugar was produced from beets, but by 1884 the percentage had risen to 53 percent. Consequently international prices fell rapidly, and the Cuban sugar-producing elite began to experience the unpredictable price variations that have haunted developing world commodity production ever since. After the 1870s Europe no longer imported significant amounts of Cuban sugar. Thereafter the United States was free to dominate the Cuban export market and thus dictate the biotic fate of the island. Internal events in Cuba prepared the way.

The production of beet sugar plus the import of cane sugar (and some cane sugar production in Louisiana) kept pace with the growth of the domestic market demand. An international pattern of supply had been established by the last years of the 1800s. It was shaped through an intensive political process in which continental beet producers competed with cane sugar interests centered in New York (and later San Francisco) over import tariffs and quotas. In that struggle the Cuban sugar lobby in New York was able to hold its own.

In the 1870s the Cuban economy was weakened by the internal upheavals known as the Ten Years' War. In 1868 a patriotic revolution broke out, led by discontented stockmen and coffee growers of Camagüey and Bayamo in eastern Cuba, who had been losing status against the prospering sugarmen.[57] Counterattacking government forces destroyed their ranches and crippled coffee production in the rebellious region. As a result eastern Cuba was in decline for decades; land clearance nearly halted in the resulting depression, and control of the economy resided with the sugar interests farther west.

In the prevailing economic doldrums after the Ten Years' War, inexpensive land was available throughout Cuba. Many small U.S. investors moved in, buying coffee, sugar, cocoa, tobacco, and cattle properties. U.S. ship owners, traders, and small bankers arrived with them, building a growing role in the export trade. One American had already built the first Cuban railroad in 1837, penetrating inland from Havana; another had designed steam engine machinery that made sugar processing more efficient. Yankee engineers were contributing to Yankee control of the island.

Regardless of nationality, Cuban sugar exporters faced steadily falling prices in the U.S. market after the 1870s. The average price for duty-paid raw sugar on the New York market fell from 11 cents per pound in 1877 to 8.6 cents in 1884 to a low of 3.2 cents ten years later.

Consequently, after the 1870s, heavy competition developed for efficient, low-cost production. Moreover, consumer tastes in the industrialized countries were shifting decisively to refined white sugar. In order to survive in this international market, sugar refiners were forced to adopt the fundamental changes that were appearing in sugar refining technology, and this transformed the scale and quality of operations.

In the late nineteenth century new refining technology accelerated the infusion of investment capital and the purchase of new machinery. By raising the degree of purity in refined sugar and increasing the scale of production, the new technology drove sugar produced by older methods out of international markets. In the process a group of large-scale investors consolidated control over large areas of land and determined how the nominally free peasantry was to work the soil. Most of the new machinery—hydraulic pressure regulators, vacuum pan and centrifugal apparatus to purge and crystallize sugar from juice, steam power generators to replace open fires—was designed by Americans. In 1885 there were some two hundred engineers and machinists in Cuban refineries from the Boston area alone. As a result, by the 1890s the scale of competitive sugar refining increased exponentially, and large investors centered in New York increasingly dominated the process. The new sugar refineries, or centrals, were major industrial operations. Because harvested cane rapidly loses its sugar content, it has to be squeezed within hours of cutting, and early refineries had to be located close to the fields. New railroads financed by the centrals owners greatly extended the distance that freshly cut cane could be moved before it lost its sugar content. In the process over 1,000 Cuban mills closed. Only 400 were left in 1894; after 1898 there were fewer than 200.

The work force in the cane fields was also transformed in this period. In 1886 Spain belatedly abolished slavery in Cuba, and the work force became, nominally, free labor.[58] But the *colonos*, the workers in the sugar fields, were hardly better off than before: they contracted with a nearby central to plant an agreed acreage; advances from the central covered their cultivation costs. This forced workers to take on most of the risk of poor harvests or low export prices, and it placed them in permanent debt to the centrals. Furthermore, the owners of the centrals made little effort to intensify production; their interest was restricted to the technology of refining. Workers thus escaped slavery but not hunger, and in the years after 1884 many fled to the hills of Oriente, where they became squatters in forest refuges, joining the ranks of the dispossessed who ultimately allied themselves with Fidel Castro in the late 1950s.[59] Although the extent cannot be measured closely, marginal hill forests were degraded by frontier colonizers as a direct result of the workings of capitalist export agriculture.

THE AMERICAN CONQUEST OF THE CUBAN LANDSCAPE

Many American investors were partners of Cuban and Spanish interests. The most prosperous Spanish and Cuban planters were already loosely formed into the "Club de la Habana," a landed elite whose culture and ostentation matched that of the most elegant society anywhere in Latin America. They were almost as much at home in New York as in Havana. By now their U.S. partners had no difficulty in crossing language and cultural boundaries to work in the same business. Thus the elite that controlled the island until 1959 was a binational and closely intertwined network.

A primary example of a cooperative venture, one of the earliest and best run, was owned by the Atkins family of Boston, whose long-established trading connections with Havana took them deeply into the sugar lands and sustained a long romance with rural Cuba. The Atkins story, as told in Edwin Atkins' autobiography, shows how Yankee interests worked with changing conditions in Cuba through the 1800s, being drawn more and more deeply into the fortunes of an agrarian economy that was transformed by the end of slavery and Spanish rule.

The Atkins family had long been in Boston's maritime trade, frequenting India Wharf and Central Wharf, "the headquarters of the West Indian trade." By the mid-1800s they were in banking as well as commission business with Cuba, advancing money on sugar crops, usually 5 percent on the selling price. That was the setting in which Edwin Atkins did his early apprenticeship, settling in as manager of his father's Havana office. In his memoirs he describes the process of taking over ownership of a great estate in the turbulent 1880s: "1882 might be said to mark the beginning of our sugar-producing business in Cuba. Two years earlier foreclosure proceedings had been begun against the Sarria Estates. Soledad, the most important of these estates, was developed by old Juan Sarria before 1850. Some years later he built up Rosario, an adjacent estate, from the resources of Soledad."[60] But he managed Soledad badly, and in the rebellion that began in 1868, bad business conditions thrust him deeply into debt. In 1883 Atkins and Company and their local correspondents, the Torriente brothers, decided to take a joint mortgage on both estates as well as two others whose product they were marketing.

The reasons for the move were revealed in the Atkins family papers. The Ten Years' War, which ended in 1878, badly disrupted the region's economy. During the early 1880s many sugar estates were in a financial tailspin. In a letter to his father, dated 13 February 1884, young Atkins asked rhetorically, "Had we better nurse them along hoping for something to be done by Spain, or allow the properties to be abandoned for want of funds?" Six days later, in his next letter, he answered his own question. "Under the present financial condition of the Island it would be prudent for us to take the property in our name," allowing the Torrientes to continue managing it. The family bought Soledad Estate, which they had been financing for years, and entered the life of the planter class. In retrospect, many years later, Atkins added, "In Cuba then it was worth any effort to make private settlement rather than take even a clear case into court where interminable delay and crooked practice of the law were sure to bring you to a worse result than you could negotiate yourself."[61]

Soledad was somewhat inland, upriver from the small port of Cienfuegos, which lay on the central south coast of Cuba.[62] It was a bucolic tropical paradise. After an early visit from Boston, Mrs. Atkins wrote enthusiastically, "The sail [upriver from Cienfuegos] is delightful, the river is so still and the banks very pretty. Crabs and long-legged birds seem to be abundant on the shores."[63]

Atkins, cultured and philanthropic, established Harvard Garden on his estate, which became one of the outstanding botanical gardens and research centers in Latin America. In 1908 the Harvard biologist Thomas Barbour visited the Soledad plantation, beginning a long working connection there. Barbour described the Atkins home at Soledad in effusive terms. "The great thick walls, the thirty-foot ceilings, the high barred windows and prodigious doors, produce the sensation of being cool, even when the temperature outside is pretty high."[64] The graciousness and antique charm of the successful plantation owner's surroundings complemented his managerial acumen.

Underlying Atkins's love for the neocolonial life and his enthusiasm for natural history lay his firm belief in the virtue of free trade and modern industrial methods, freed from the plethora of Spanish bureaucratic regulations and its inevitable consequence, official corruption. His correspondence criticizes the high Spanish and U.S. tariffs for choking off Cuba's economic development. England, he argued, had established factories in Spain in order to get inside the Spanish empire's tariff walls, shipping its manufactures to Cuba and elsewhere.

Atkins, now a prominent merchant and banker, was in a position to do something about American policy, for his family had influence in the highest circles in Washington. His father was one of several Bostonian bankers who had financed the Union Pacific Railroad; the senior Atkins ran its finances as vice president of the railroad. He and the secretary of state, James G. Blaine, had joint railroad interests. The younger Atkins could catch Blaine's ear and argue the strategic value of lowering American sugar duties by casting reciprocal agreements with Spain.[65]

By 1890 Atkins was one of the two most powerful American investors in Cuba, along with Horace Havemeyer of New York. Between them they held the key to the Cuban sugar economy. Atkins alone controlled 12,000 acres, including 5,000 in cane, and twenty-three miles of narrow-gauge railway. These lands were already in sugar when he arrived, but other investors had to clear forest or grassland to plant the new cane. Havemeyer, the most aggressive Yankee investor of all, combined nineteen refineries into one operation in 1888, including Atkins's interests, when the two merged. In 1890 Havemeyer's budding empire became the American Sugar Refining Company, or more simply and ominously, the Sugar Trust.

Sugar refining in the United States had begun in the late eighteenth century in New York, then spread to Philadelphia and Baltimore and other port cities in Rhode Island and Massachusetts. Monopoly efforts, or the "trust movement"—the effort to unify control of the refineries and the marketing system and thereby control prices—began in 1881, when Havemeyer and the Brooklyn Sugar Refining Company reached an agreement to reduce production so as to drive up prices. Under Havemeyer's lead in 1887, eight companies combined into the Sugar Refineries Company to coordinate their marketing strategies. When they closed ten of their twenty plants, efficiency and production rose.

There were some governmental efforts to control the Sugar Trust, but they were far too feeble to have much effect. In 1889 the state Supreme Court dissolved the Trust, but it quickly reorganized under the more permissive law of New Jersey, which was just across the Hudson from Manhattan. The five major East Coast independents, plus the San Francisco magnate Claus Spreckels (who bought a competing refinery in Philadelphia), organized a rate war, challenging the Sugar Trust. The Trust won by buying out the independents. Havemeyer and his dependents soon controlled 90 percent of sugar cane production in the United States—all except the cane grown in the Louisiana fields.[66] The Sugar Trust was now in a position to attempt domination of sugar production in the Caribbean as well.

The extent and pace of Cuba's land clearance for sugar now depended on sugar wars in the halls of Congress. Havemeyer's success in the United States was built on the support of the U.S. government, which provided an open door to imports from Cuba, in direct competition with domestic sugar beet interests, through the manipulation of import tariffs. If the beet sugar lobby could persuade Congress to defend domestic production by setting an import tax on imported cane sugar, not only would the cane sugar importers suffer, but a major impetus to cut down tropical forests in Cuba and elsewhere would be inhibited.

In the years around 1890 the U.S. government was basking in a period of budget surpluses. Hence, when it passed a new tariff law that year, the Cuban-American sugar lobby had little trouble in gaining a clause that totally exempted its product from any duty. Cuban sugar production immediately boomed: in 1893 it passed one million tons for the first time. But the victory was brief-lived. The U.S. beet sugar lobby retaliated quickly and successfully. The 1894 Wilson-Gorman Tariff Act set a new duty on raw cane sugar. Until then the Sugar Trust had been refining its raw sugar within the United States, guaranteeing a more uniform and highly refined quality than sugar refined in the Cuban *ingenios*—and forcing Cuban exporters to market their sugar through Havemeyer. Seventy to ninety percent of the refined cane sugar consumed in the United States was controlled by the Sugar Trust. Washington's tariff powers enabled American business to dominate marketing, and therefore production, of the crop, which in turn dominated Cuba's lands.

As yet few American investors actually owned and managed Cuban sugar estates. That step followed quickly when the United States replaced Spain in 1898 as Cuba's overlord. In 1895 Cubans had reopened their war of independence against Spain, frustrated by Spain's increasingly restrictive tariff policies. In 1898 the United States declared war on Spain and quickly swept the old regime off the island. The Treaty of Paris, signed by Spain in the same year, granted Cuba independence, but the island was under American military occupation for the following four years. It was during this period that Congress, fearing European intervention or further disorder in the Cuban countryside, passed the Platt Amendment. The amendment was part of an appropriations bill

for the U.S. Army, but its provisions were inserted into the Cuban constitution, which was adopted in 1901, at the insistence of the United
States. The provisions arrogated for the U.S. "the right to intervene for
the preservation of Cuban independence, [and] the maintenance of a
government adequate for the protection of life, property, and individual
liberty."[67] Thus, unilaterally, Congress assured American investors that
their government was prepared to send its army back onto the island in
order to guarantee the safety of their investments. Although political in
form, the proviso was to have profound consequences for Cuba's landscape, for it placed the full potential force of the American military
behind the investors who came to dominate Cuba's economy in the
following years.

Almost immediately, competitors to Havemeyer's Sugar Trust, including the United Fruit Company, moved into Cuba under the Platt
guarantee. United Fruit, which was on its way to dominating the rainforest region of coastal Central America, had bought the Boston Fruit
Company in 1899, and with it the Banes Fruit Company in Cuba.
United's great capital resources enabled it in 1900 to spend one million
dollars to install the most advanced sugar mill in Cuba at the time.[68] No
Cuban producer could match this scale of operation. Technological escalation and corporate centralization under American control were creating a new empire over Nature in Cuba virtually overnight.

No sugar central could function without efficient facilities for transportation, and American engineers moved rapidly into the Cuban hinterland after 1902. The U.S. role in building the infrastructure for economic development had at least as important long-range environmental
consequences as did investment in the land itself. The key to opening
eastern Cuba to world sugar markets was a west-to-east railroad across
the country. Sir William Van Horne, who in his earlier years had built
the Canadian Pacific Railroad and then speculated in Guatemalan railroad construction, assigned himself the task. Born in Illinois of Dutch
parents, he became a naturalized British citizen; he was fully familiar
with both U.S. and British capital markets. Impatient with slow-moving
governments, he waited for no franchise, right of way, government sub-
sidy, or declaration of eminent domain, but in 1900 began purchasing
private properties and building his line. He completed it several years
later in Oriente. His tracks made possible a vast expansion of large
American-owned estates into the lowlands and hills of Camagüey and
Oriente. The way was now paved for American-financed clearing of the
remaining rich lowland soils of central and eastern Cuba.[69] As long as

virgin soil remained available, and transport systems penetrated far enough, high price levels for primary commodities on world markets immediately resulted in deforestation unrestrained by any government regulation. Over the years this expansion proved to be both economically and environmentally unstable.

Van Horne's railroad also led to the transformation of a poverty-stricken but free subsistence peasantry into proletarian plantation laborers.

> Ironically, Van Horne saw himself as a champion of the small farmer, intending that his line would give free campesinos access to wider markets for their produce, and result in a conservative and prosperous small capitalist class. As he remarked at the time, "The country can only reach its highest prosperity and greatest stability of government through the widest possible ownership of the lands by the people who cultivate them. In countries where the percentage of individuals holding real estate is greatest, conservatism prevails and insurrections are unknown."[70]

Sugar production had already become a highly centralized and capital-intensive process, and even Van Horne's strategy of lowering freight rates by as much as 90 percent could not preserve the campesinos. Only the revolutionary victory of the campesino more than a half-century later under Fidel Castro could achieve that, and the environmental significance of that more recent upheaval is still unclear.

Washington, prodded by the Havana–New York coalition, continued to maintain favorable tariff levels for Cuban sugar imports, paving the way for its greatest boom during and after World War I. The war brought devastation to Europe's sugar beet production. European sugar production dropped from 8 million tons just before the war to 2.6 million by 1919. War on the sea also disrupted shipment of New World sugar to Europe. In the wartime emergency Allied governments were willing to abandon the free trade principles that had governed their approach to the global commodities market for decades. Thus began an era of coordinated intergovernmental planning of international markets, which directly and massively triggered forest clearance.

Great Britain led in establishing the International Sugar Board during the fighting, and the United States joined. Complementing that action in 1917, as the United States entered the war, Congress passed the Lever Act, giving the president power to control the production and marketing of foods for the duration of the war. Faced with intense competition between American beet sugar and Cuban cane sugar growers, Washington set up the Sugar Equalization Board the following year, which guaranteed Cuban and Yankee growers high profit levels. Growers continued leveling the forests to the east, along the route of Van Horne's tracks, at a rapid pace. This was also a major opportunity for American banks and importers to achieve their long-imagined goal of displacing European capital in the Caribbean economies. Yankee protection during the war was a bonanza for the Cubans. Cuba's production spiraled upward; by 1919 it surpassed four million tons for the first time. In 1909 Cuba had produced 10 percent of the world's sugar; ten years later it produced 25 percent. Sugar was also now overwhelming the rest of Cuba's economy. In 1908 it had provided 54 percent of Cuba's exports; by 1919 it provided 89 percent.[71]

By the end of 1918 an unprecedented speculative race was on, popularly dubbed the "Dance of the Millions." New York banks lent millions to Cuban growers, and even Havana's bankers committed all the capital they could command. As historian Leland Jenks noted acidly, "there developed in Cuba between 1917 and 1920 most of the phenomena of speculation, industrial combination, price-fixing, bank manipulation, pyramiding of credits, and over capitalization, which we are accustomed to regard as the peculiar gift of the highly civilized Anglo-Saxons."[72]

In order to achieve this production boom, growers brought great new areas of land under sugar production; they still did not attempt to increase the efficiency of growing and harvesting the cane. Engineers preferred innovating with machines to improving the working conditions of the campesinos. The result, for lack of a technological and social alternative, was a further attack on the natural landscape. Acreage statistics are unavailable, but narrative accounts indicate that this was the final great period of clearing Cuba's natural forest. Small amounts of previously unclaimed land in the central plains were appropriated, but little of this uncleared lowland remained. The ominous result was that by 1920 many areas of marginal hill forest in Camagüey and Oriente were put into sugar by eager speculators, areas whose soils could not grow sugar competitively except in times of inflated international prices. When price levels collapsed shortly after 1920, some of these areas reverted to degraded scrub forest or were taken over by squatters.[73]

In 1921, as European beet sugar production recovered, inflated global sugar prices crashed in a classic disaster of an extreme price-supply cycle. Many Cuban sugar barons defaulted on their loans from New York banks, and control of the industry shifted decisively to the United States. In New York the National City Bank alone took control of fifty mills in the summer of 1921.[74] The Cuban government, under its weak new president Alfredo Zayas, drifted toward bankruptcy. That year its fiscal affairs were turned over to the American president's personal envoy, Enoch Crowder, who saved the government from collapse only by arranging a massive new loan from J. P. Morgan.[75] This further consolidated American control of the Cuban economy.

International sugar prices recovered after two years and were strong again through the mid-1920s. But the short sharp depression had done its transformative work. By 1927 Cuba produced six million tons, 62 percent of which was now directly under U.S. control. Atkins and Havemeyer raised new capital in New England and Pennsylvania, combined into a new corporation named Lowry & Company, and prospered.

To make the most of the international boom in sugar prices, the estate owners in Camagüey and northern Oriente scrambled to clear additional forestland or plow old cattle pasture, even though slopes were progressively steeper and soils increasingly marginal. Large tracts of forest were simply cut and burned. Harry Franck, an American businessman and traveler, wandered through Oriente in 1920. He recorded the virtual frenzy of land clearing and its impact on the natural ecosystem.

> Here vast stretches of virgin forest, often three to five thousand acres in extent, are turned into cane fields in a few months' time. The usual method is to let contracts for the entire process, and to pay fixed sums for completely replacing the forests by growing cane. . . . The woodsmen [are] more often Jamaican or Haitian negroes than Cubans. . . . With machetes and axes which to the Northerner would seem extremely crude—though nearly all of them come from our own State of Connecticut—they attack the immense and seemingly impenetrable wilderness. The underbrush and saplings fall first under the slashing machetes. Next the big trees—and some of these are indeed giants of the forest—succumb before the heavy axes and, denuded of their larger branches, are left where they lie.[76]

At a time when international prices gave a premium to the production of sugar, it made little economic sense to attempt to market the mahogany and Spanish cedar that had been felled. It was simply not worth the investment and labor to haul the trees to a river or coastline for shipment to distant markets. Instead, the hardwoods were burned along with all the other chopped vegetation when it had dried. Many species of trees went up in smoke, and any chance that a timber industry might be developed by giving market value to the Cuban hardwoods was destroyed as well.[77] This large-scale slash-and-burn method was essentially identical to the technique being used around the tropics to make way for coffee, bananas, rubber, cotton, and other market crops. Franck's account continues, "The burning usually takes place during the first fortnight of March, at the end of the longest dry season. . . . When at last the fires are set and sweep across the immense region with all the fury of the element, fuel sufficient to keep an entire Northern city warm during the whole winter is swept away in a single day."[78]

At least this one traveler caught the fuller significance of what was happening to the land. He concluded by warning, "The time is near . . . when the Cubans must regulate this wholesale destruction of their forests or see the island suffer from one of those changes of climate which has been the partial ruination of their motherland, Spain."[79] In a significant oversight, he made no mention of the Yankee capital that was largely responsible for the Cuban workers' efforts.

The Dance of the Millions was responsible for that particular firestorm in the forest. But the brief, giddy postwar boom was part of a quarter-century of massive land clearances. Between 1905 and 1921 sixteen new processing factories were built in central and western Camagüey to encourage growers to plant cane in forests and grazing lands. Six more went up in eastern Camagüey and twenty-four in Oriente.[80]

The impact on the land of these transformations was illustrated by the new Manatí central and its adjacent lands on Manatí Bay, on the north coast of Oriente.[81] Some natural forest still stood in that area, a mixture of partially logged mahogany and coastal palms. Interspersed with the forests were savannas of guinea and parana grass, which grew on well drained but sandy soil and had formerly been used to run cattle. The forest soils were richer in organic matter than adjacent savannas, and were therefore more interesting to sugar planters. The local coastal town, Victoria de las Tunas, had exported cattle and timber since colonial times.

In 1911 Manuel Rionda y Polledo, a Cuban living in New York, joined with Yankee investment partners to purchase a huge tract of 150 square miles of land near Victoria for $1.5 million. They built a new central, capable of producing 250,000 bags or 40,000 tons of sugar per year, and began burning the forest. Within two years they cleared 15,000 acres with a work force of 3,000, and had 10,000 acres in sugar production. During the wartime boom they expanded production to 43,000 acres, 25,000 of which the company owned directly. By 1923 the Manatí Sugar Company produced almost 90,000 tons of semirefined sugar.

But trouble was in store for Cuba's sugar industry. The onset of global depression in October 1929 affected it dramatically: by early 1930 consumer demand in the United States and all other industrial economies began to fall precipitously, leaving one-crop export economies like Cuba's desperate. Faced with a catastrophic collapse of consumer demand, the International Sugar Board was powerless to stabilize prices. The world sugar price, which had stood at 2.78 cents per pound in 1927, plunged to .78 in 1932, took until 1937 to reach 1.00 again, and would finally return to the 1927 level only as World War II ended in 1945. Compounding the fall in prices, sugar production in Cuba fell by nearly one-half in the early 1930s. Cuban estate owners' income, which had risen from $100 million in 1920 to $200 million in 1929, collapsed to $40 million in 1932.[82]

The effects on Cuban land use would have been even greater but for the political power of the American importers to manipulate import tariffs. To protect American producers, Congress in 1930 passed its most restrictive tariff law, the Smoot-Hawley Tariff Act, building in a high sugar tariff for Cuba and its Caribbean neighbors. By 1934, as the worst effects of the market collapse began to pass in the United States, the rate was lowered and, in a more significant change, Congress established the first guaranteed minimum quota for Cuban sugar imports. This resulted from such intensive pressure from the importers that Secretary of Agriculture Henry Wallace called their lobbying "one of the most astounding exhibitions I have ever seen."[83] A new system for the American import of tropical crops was emerging from the Depression, one in which governments, and therefore lobbyists, would have a more dominant role. After 1945 the terms of production and trade for tropical agriculture would be very different.

In primary producing countries of the tropics, economic collapse during the Depression made it clearer than ever before that land use patterns and their environmental consequences depend heavily on political circumstances, particularly on the relations among a country's elite, its rural work force, and those who control its exports. The financial disaster of the Depression brought intense political and social pressures to Cuba, which had been ruled by Gerardo Machado since 1925, when he became the elected president of the republic. American control of the sugar economy rested directly on his regime. Machado eventually became one of Cuba's most repressive dictators. His style of governing has been characterized as "brutal but businesslike. . . . Machado's methods were those of a small-scale Mussolini. They included imprisonment without trial, torture of prisoners, political assassinations, and all the highly developed modern apparatus for preventing the expression of opinion."[84] For a time he succeeded in controlling the plantation labor force under Depression conditions, and his American friends continued to visit Havana comfortably. But social and political upheaval, the nemesis of the investors, was inevitable in the battered one-crop economy. In 1933 a coup eliminated Machado and brought to power a young army officer, Fulgencio Batista. From then until his overthrow in 1959, Batista was the kingpin of Cuban politics and economics, maintaining his predecessor's repressive ways.

Washington, as always in that era, gave its pliant junior partner full support. Under the strategic net of the Monroe Doctrine, the 1901 Platt Amendment, and President Theodore Roosevelt's corollary to the Monroe Doctrine (added to the 1823 policy in 1904), the United States officially reserved the right to intervene militarily throughout the region, to prevent European powers from gaining strategic leverage, and to protect American investments. After World War I European imperial ambitions, even those of the British, had battered each other so severely that the United States no longer had to worry about major strategic challenges from across the Atlantic in its own Latin American back yard. From 1933 onward President Franklin Roosevelt pursued his Good Neighbor style of diplomacy, working to maintain Yankee hegemony through local regimes whose controlling elites were closely and profitably tied to the American economy. The U.S. government's support of Batista and his friends was a classic example of that strategy.[85]

No study has looked systematically at the Depression in terms of its effect on Cuba's lands, just as few studies have probed the specific ecological impacts of the Depression anywhere in the primary producing countries. Some tentative conclusions are possible, however. Export markets in the 1930s were so reduced that no one opened new land to produce export crops. Indeed, the trend was toward deserting sugar production in eastern Cuba, where marginal hill lands had recently come under sugar cultivation. Frequently, *colonos* who had grown sugar independently and sold it to centrals reverted to planting maize and beans to avoid starvation. In a perverse way, agricultural production in Cuba moved back toward a balance between subsistence and export cropping. Some cultivated lands rested briefly in the absence of consumer pressure from the United States, reverting to secondary woodland or scrub cattle pasture and usually suffering soil erosion and depletion. When World

War II demanded increased sugar production from Cuba, it was at last achieved through greater efficiency of production, not additional acreage under cane.[86]

By the late 1940s some American owners began divesting their direct holdings in Cuban estates by selling their lands to their Cuban counterparts and partners, although they maintained their massive marketing investments. They saw the dangers of political instability and the headaches of direct management of land and labor. By the mid-1950s all but seven of the fifty mills in central Cuba were owned by Cuban companies, and only four were owned by Americans.[87] Most were absentee owners, living in palatial homes in Havana and New York, close to the power intrigues of Batista and his gringo supporters. The effect was a drift back toward the pattern of the late 1800s, when the original Sugar Trust in New York had controlled production in Cuba by controlling its international markets but had exercised no responsibility for social or environmental conditions on the land.

In other regions more American corporate owners remained in Cuba. Hershey Chocolate had held lands and centrals in northeastern La Habana province since early in the century. Between 1948 and 1952 Central Hershey, the twelfth largest mill in Cuba, produced nearly 600,000 sacks of sugar. In Camagüey, the major region of Yankee investment in the 1920s, the Americans held on, controlling sixteen centrals in 1956, in contrast with nine owned by Cubans. Farthest east, in the more precarious sugar region of the Oriente mountains, twenty-five were American-owned and thirteen had Cuban owners by 1956.[88]

After 1948, in the early years of the Cold War, both the Truman and Eisenhower governments staunchly supported Batista's regime, so as to protect still massive American investments. This eliminated any possibility of economic reform in the industry, reform that might have averted the revolutionary upheaval that transformed Cuba's land politics in 1959.

POSTSCRIPT: CASTRO'S REVOLUTION AND CUBAN LAND USE

In 1956 Fidel Castro and his supporters launched a revolt in the hills of Oriente, using the same guerrilla base that their predecessors had used since the late 1860s. Soon they gained support from rising numbers of sugar workers around the country. By the time they entered Havana victorious in 1959, the sugar aristocracy was already in exile in Miami and New York. The Eisenhower government's response in 1960 was to cut Cuba's sugar quota by 95 percent and then, a few months later, to declare an embargo on trade with Cuba. The next chapter of Cuba's environmental history was shaped by the sudden extinction of the American market and the Soviet movement into the resulting vacuum. Once again, ecological and political history were fatefully linked.

The Caribbean historian Eric Williams has written,

> The Castro revolution was a belated attempt to catch up with the nationalist movement in the rest of the Caribbean. [In 1959] Cuba presented the following picture: 75 percent of rural dwellings were huts made from the palm tree. . . . Only 4 percent of the Cuban peasantry ate meat as a regular part of their diet; while 1 percent ate fish, less than 2 percent eggs, 3 percent bread, 11 percent milk; none ate green vegetables. . . . 82 percent of Cuba's total land area was farm land, but only 22 percent of that was cultivated. . . . American sugar companies controlled about 75 percent of Cuba's arable land.[89]

It proved extremely difficult to move out of the old pattern of one-crop exploitation. Fundamentally the new regime was still oriented to the conquest of Nature. Castro's planners wanted to reverse the patterns of imperialism and, specifically, to put idle land and labor back to work. In 1961 they adopted a policy of diversifying production on the sugar lands, devoting some acreage to soybeans, peanuts, and cattle, in addition to growing additional food for local consumption.[90] A revival of cattle ranching in particular seemed worthwhile, to provide more meat and leather for Cuban consumption as well as expanded exports. Large private farmers cultivated previously idle land to avoid expropriation, while government planners and estate managers made a major effort in the early 1960s to drain marshy lands, especially along the coasts. By 1962 up to 440,000 acres of "new land"—forestlands that were cleared or fallow lands that were replanted—had been cultivated.[91]

Cuban agricultural planners took some land out of sugar entirely, and production fell severely on other sugar soils as workers reduced their hours of labor and repairs of refinery machinery began to run behind. Weeding and irrigation were neglected, the replantings needed in 1959 and 1960 were ignored, and in 1962 and 1963 droughts hit the island. The United States, which had been Cuba's source of farm machinery and parts, fertilizer, pesticides, and even seeds, cut off all equipment shipments to Cuba in 1960.[92] Once again Cuba's economy was haunted by food deficits, a perennial problem. Food imports, now coming from Europe and the Soviet Union, were running at $125 million to $150 million annually, requiring massive export sales to finance them. In 1962 a crisis in the balance of payments descended on Cuba, a country now cut off from its near-monopoly sugar buyer: by the end of the year it faced a $170 million deficit. There was no choice but to reemphasize sugar production and to sell on the new market provided by the Soviet alliance.

Through the 1960s Cuban sugar production rose again, this time with the stress on intensifying cultivation and expanding sugar acreage. Fortunately for the effort, no major disease epidemic threatened the cane, unlike in the fruit agroindustry of Central America. Sugar export earnings rose from 80 percent of total export income in 1957 to 83 percent by 1982. In a major irony, by 1982 cane covered 75 percent of all cultivated land, in comparison to 60 percent in 1958.[93]

In sum, Cuba's century-long experience as the world's greatest producer of the oldest colonial monocrop left it with continued reliance on that crop. This kept the country tied politically to its major buyer, although the buyer had changed. Cuba was linked with the Soviet Union in a variant of the dependency that characterized so many of the colonial systems over the years. The pattern of land use changed only marginally until the collapse of the Soviet market after 1990. That jolt, combined with the continuing U.S. embargo, forced Cuban agriculture to shift from chemical-intensive export sugar to organic multicropping. In short order Cuba became the hemisphere's leader in genuinely sustainable agriculture.[94]

Evidence on environmental trends in the 1960s and 1970s is inconclusive, but some inferences may be drawn. Soil conditions on the Matanzas plains remained stable. Farther east, after the intense speculative expansion of sugar cultivation in the 1920s, problems of deforestation and soil loss in Camagüey and the Sierra Maestra were severe. By the late 1960s the Cuban forestry agency was able to begin reforestation measures with the assistance of Czech foresters.[95] In contrast, an unfortunate environmental legacy of U.S.–Cuba relations continued to haunt the rest of the Caribbean region. As long as American political alliances remained tied to landlord regimes, U.S. policy could not consistently support environmentally sound resource management, for those regimes perpetuated a range of damaging land-use practices. Moreover, as long as American policy refused to deal with any inter-American organization that recognized the new Cuban government, it was crippled in contributing to environmentally sound planning for the Caribbean Basin as a whole.[96]

REGIONAL SHIFTS IN AMERICAN DEMAND AFTER 1960

No other commodity was as dramatically involved as sugar was in the international ecological impact of the political shifts triggered by the Cold War. What transpired in the Americas immediately after 1960 was the most sudden and massive example in history of the power of political policy to determine tropical land use. The cancellation of sugar imports from Cuba necessitated that the U.S. government expand imports rapidly from other countries if the Kennedy administration was to avoid facing the politically damaging prospect of skyrocketing prices for sugar on supermarket shelves.

Domestic beet sugar producers, although delighted at the elimination of their biggest competitor, could not meet more than a small fraction of the import gap by themselves. Markets in the western United States had drawn sugar from the Pacific islands, including the American territory of Hawaii and the colony of the Philippines. The San Francisco and Honolulu interests ensured that their source areas in the Pacific would benefit from the U.S. government's posture toward Castro's regime. Their rivals, the Sugar Trust of New York, were more interested in their clients in the Caribbean and new sources of supply for purchase in Mexico and Brazil.

In the Caribbean the major economic beneficiaries of the suddenly expanded U.S. import quotas were the other islands of the Greater Antilles east of Cuba: the Dominican Republic and the U.S. territory of Puerto Rico. On the Latin American mainland, the Atlantic coastal lowlands of Mexico and Brazil felt the shift most sharply. In each of these four regions the sudden expansion of American imports produced rapid, dramatic increases of acreage diverted to sugar cane from other crops, cattle pasture, or natural vegetation.

THE DOMINICAN REPUBLIC

The first Caribbean country to feel the sudden bite of the Yankee sweet tooth in the early 1960s was the Dominican Republic, the eastern two-thirds of Hispaniola. This second largest Caribbean island is separated from the eastern tip of Cuba only by the ten-mile-wide Windward Passage. As on adjacent islands, the Spaniards had cultivated cane there for local consumption since Columbus introduced it in 1493. Cane was grown primarily on the southeast coastal lowlands, where fairly gently sloping mountains allow passage of the trade winds from the northeast and fertile soils had accumulated through geological time.[97]

Santo Domingo, as the country was known in colonial times, felt the tremors of the wars of independence from Spain in the early 1800s. Spain's departure left a vacuum that was quickly filled by forces from heavily populated Haiti. The French-speaking Afro-Haitians occupied Santo Domingo's main towns until 1844, when the Spanish-speaking local people finally achieved full independence and renamed their new country the Dominican Republic.

Sugar's impact on the Dominican Republic was somewhat similar in character and timing to the Cuban situation. For most of the four centuries of Spanish rule the colony had remained an economic backwater. Agricultural production on its slave plantations was geared more toward mixed cropping and cattle grazing for local consumption than any intensive single cropping for export to Europe. By the mid-1800s most of the mountain region was still heavily forested and had not been domesticated for economic production.

Industrialized sugar production for export emerged in the last third of the nineteenth century in response to the steady rise in both European and American import demand and the end of slavery.[98] The establishment of capital-intensive plantations linked to steam-driven refining machinery was a direct consequence of events in Cuba. The disruptions of Cuban sugar society in the Ten Years' War led planters from Cienfuegos and Oriente to leave the country. Some of them took their skills to Santo Domingo, where forested land with humus-rich soils was still available at very low prices. There they set up several *ingenios* and began to compete in North American and German markets.

The strategic interests of American politicians conjoined with Dominican sugar in the early 1870s. Determined to pursue the expansion of Yankee power throughout the Caribbean, President Ulysses S. Grant spoke of the new republic in 1876 in his last message to Congress: "Santo Domingo is fertile, and upon its soil may be grown just those tropical fruits of which the United States use so much, and which are produced or prepared for market now by slave-labor almost exclusively; namely sugar, coffee, dye-woods, mahogany, tropical fruits, and tobacco."[99]

Grant asserted that free trade with the United States would be beneficial for both countries. Indeed, direct American annexation of the country might be even more attractive, for Spain was still intransigently maintaining both slavery and tariff barriers against American imports.

Moreover, cultivating Santo Domingo could help undermine Spanish power in Cuba as well, and it could also provide a haven for freed slaves from the southern United States.

> The island is but sparsely settled, while it has an area sufficiently [large] for the profitable employment of several millions of people. The soil would soon have fallen into the hands of United States capitalists. The products are so valuable in commerce that emigration there would have been encouraged, the emancipated race of the South would have found there a congenial home.[100]

The president was not merely philosophizing. In 1873 Grant's business associates founded a new company in New York, the Samana Bay Company, named for the largest bay on the north side of the island. The New Yorkers purchased from the government of the Dominican Republic "the sovereignty of the Bay of Samana and islands therein and of the Peninsula of Samana and water adjacent"[101] and immediately set about clearing 10,000 acres of forest for the plantation, the largest on that island.

A collapse of international sugar prices in 1883 precipitated an emergency for Dominican landholders. The country's dictator, Ulises Heureaux, courted American investors, signing a trade agreement with the United States in 1891 that opened the country to accelerated Yankee investment. It reduced U.S. tariffs on Dominican sugar, in return for reduced or cancelled tariffs on imports of American industrial goods. The Dominican Republic thereby sold its autonomy to the high bidder from the north. Dominican landlords were now in a position to modernize their sugar production, with the enthusiastic cooperation of American investors. Capital, managers, and machinery flowed into the country. In 1911 a new law allowed state land to be sold to sugar planters; it made possible still further clearing of forestlands. By 1920 sugar acreage had increased 30 percent from its 1910 figure, reaching 400,000 acres.[102]

The fledgling republic had little experience in managing its own internal security or fiscal affairs. Its treasury fell rapidly into debt, and until World War I the British were always at hand to assist with financial bailouts. When Woodrow Wilson assumed the American presidency, he and Secretary of State Robert Lansing watched the British closely as Dominican financial management became more corrupt and ineffectual. In 1916, as war in Europe ate at the heart of British resources, Wilson sent the Marines into the Dominican Republic to guarantee political stability and the security of American investments. The American military

occupation lasted until 1924, long after the threat of European intervention had totally vanished.

Under the strategic umbrella of the Roosevelt Corollary, the Washington–New York nexus gradually turned the little country into an economic as well as a political protectorate. The steady expansion of Dominican sugar estates and refineries was largely funded by American
investors led by the National City Bank of New York.[103] Some small-
scale Yankee operators also settled on Dominican land, but corporate
investment was far more powerful. By the early 1900s American interests dominated almost all Dominican sugar land; they also built and
owned the new processing plants and railroad network. Just as on the
other islands, forests were cleared and some hill areas suffered soil erosion. Sugar cane came to command the best lowland soils, and in a
familiar pattern of social and environmental disruption sugar production drove food-growing farmers either onto marginal hill lands or into
tenancy on the new corporate holdings. Some managed to survive as
colonos, growing sugar on their own lands to provide to the new mills.
The plantations' own labor force became a mixture of local campesinos
and Haitian and Jamaican ex-slaves who were willing to go great distances to find work and food.[104]

Major cane estates were centered in the southeastern coastal plain
and the adjacent interior hills, where large-scale production had begun
when Cuban refugees arrived in the 1870s. Sugar production, which
had been less than 5,000 tons in 1870, surpassed 350,000 tons in the
late 1920s. After the turbulent years of Depression and war, production
tripled again by 1960, when the figure rose to 1,112,000 tons.[105]

Until 1960 most Dominican sugar was sold to buyers from Great
Britain and continental Europe. But immediately after 1960 the expanded production went to the United States. American imports shifted
from a mere 15,000 tons in 1950 to a late-1950s average of 92,000
tons, and then by a quantum leap upward to 582,000 tons in 1962, a
figure that roughly stabilized over the following decade. These exports
to the United States undermined those to Europe, which fell from
451,000 tons in 1960 to only 42,000 tons five years later.

By the mid-1960s sugar constituted over half of the Dominican Republic's exports. The dictator Rafael Trujillo, in power from 1930 until
he was assassinated in 1960, had consolidated most of the sugar land
under his personal control, using modernized refining equipment and
cheap Haitian labor.[106] When the government failed to stabilize after
Trujillo's death, President Lyndon Johnson ordered 20,000 troops into

the Dominican Republic in 1965 to protect the country from "disorder"; this was a replay of the Marines' appearance there in 1916. The United States was mollified by the election of the more moderate, pro-American Joaquin Balaguer in 1966. He guaranteed the continuing control of land and commercial agriculture by a political cadre loyal to U.S. directives. Plantation sugar, which reduced the biological diversity of wide reaches of land to little more than one species, continued as a major arm of American control of the Caribbean basin during the later years of the Cold War.

PUERTO RICO

U.S. hegemony began to penetrate Puerto Rico, the easternmost and smallest of the three islands of the Greater Antilles, in the 1870s, as it had in Cuba and Hispaniola. Policies of the U.S. government became direct and dominant following its annexation of Puerto Rico in 1898. The island is shaped by a west-east volcanic spine that rises to jagged, forested peaks. On its northern, windward shores lies a narrow, moist coastal plain, which supported rainforest through the precolonial millennia. During Spanish colonial times, when Madrid's navy dominated coastal waters from its capital at San Juan, the only port on the north coast, that lowland was gradually cleared as the region became densely populated and intensively farmed.

The rich forest biome of the higher hills, well watered across the entire island, became the home of subsistence squatter peasants. After 1800 experimental coffee plantations began to appear in those cooler elevations. On the south side of the island the mountains subside more gradually to the leeward, drier coast. A series of streams flow southward from the heavily forested watershed into the semiarid lowlands where xerophytic tropical woodlands confronted early European colonists. Soils there are excellent for agriculture, but intensive cropping on a large scale necessitated ambitious irrigation schemes to divert water from the streams. Short of that, these lands most easily supported cattle ranching; Criollo cattle of hardy Spanish stock subsisted on the hot, dry lands, while ranchers built city homes in Ponce on the south coast.

As Spanish rule declined to its nadir in the 1890s, Puerto Rico's destiny shifted toward the northern giant. In 1898 the smaller island moved under the American umbrella along with Cuba, but unlike Cuba, Puerto Rico remained under direct American rule throughout the twentieth century. It was designated a commonwealth, and granted many tax and tariff preferences. This gave it a unique status among the Caribbean islands, tying it more directly to the American economy than any other island.[107]

In an ironic contrast with Cuba, Puerto Rican sugar estates did not fall under direct American management, but the results were similar. Under American administration, the old Puerto Rican landed gentry, many of them with close links to New York, developed a series of sugar plantations along the southern reaches of the island. The sugar barons channeled American capital into new centrals for processing the cane and ambitious new irrigation systems that took water from other uses and turned the patchwork of semiarid pasturelands, subsistence food-crop plots, and open woodlands of the southern slopes into fewer, larger expanses of uniform green.

Estate owners turned many subsistence farmers into hired laborers or tenants. Other poor farmers were forced upward into hill lands, clearing forest for small food plots. By 1940 only 16 percent of the cultivated land in Puerto Rico was in farms under twenty acres, and most of that was on marginal hill land. Some fifty corporations, many of them closely linked to New York, controlled 250,000 acres of Puerto Rico's best land.[108]

Sugar was supreme, as long as its northern market was guaranteed within the U.S. quota system. By the mid-1960s sugar cane was Puerto Rico's most important export crop; it was grown on the better half of all the arable land on the island. Formerly it had been grown only on gently sloping lowland soils. In the boom years of the 1960s its cultivation expanded onto fragile hillsides and marginal soils, just as it had in Cuba in the 1920s. Yields were lower on the poorer soils of steeper slopes, and soil erosion was greater as the slopes increased. In those years Puerto Rico, under Governor Luis Muñoz Marin, was industrializing rapidly. Displaced peasants, who in most Latin American countries were migrating into fragile hill forests as subsistence squatters, had the option of looking for work in the industrial economies of San Juan or Manhattan. Consequently the forested watersheds of the island were put under relatively less pressure from intensified market cropping in the lowlands than were their counterparts in most of tropical Latin America.

Still, the Dominican Republic and Puerto Rico taken together could not make up for the flood of Cuban sucrose that had been diverted from North America to Europe and the Soviet Union. To fill demand, New York buyers turned to two major South American producers, Mexico and Brazil, whose sugar exports had gone largely to Europe until 1960.

MEXICO

Mexico's participation in the sudden shift in tropical sugar production after 1960 was concentrated in the perpetually hot, humid lowlands of Veracruz, below the eastern slopes of the Sierra Madre. Sugar had been grown in the moist alluvial soils of the region between the cities of Veracruz and Tampico since the early 1500s, in counterpoint to low-intensity cattle ranching on the wide semiarid reaches. During colonial times many small *trapiches,* powered either by water or by cattle, dotted the region, as the coastal forests and wetlands were gradually cleared by mahogany loggers and mixed-crop farmers.

In the early 1800s Mexico's long War of Independence, a wrenching war of attrition, left the country independent but the rural economy and towns in shambles. For decades thereafter the lowlands underwent a somnolent economic depression. The export economy did not flourish, monocropping did not expand significantly either for export or for the Mexico City market, and technical innovation in sugar refining was out of the question.

American mercantile houses had been operating branch offices in the city of Veracruz since the eighteenth century.[109] These merchants, along with the U.S. consuls stationed there, monitored commercial possibilities—they were the permanent Yankee presence that foretold the major sugar purchases of the 1960s. At no time in these past two centuries, however, were these Americans interested in purchasing land rights in the hinterland and becoming estate owners or managers themselves. Their link to changes in land use in the region remained indirect.

When Porfirio Díaz seized the presidency of Mexico in 1876, he and his associates were determined to modernize the country's economy by attracting foreign investment in mining, industry, and large-scale export agriculture. Sugar producers in the eastern lowlands responded in the same way as had their Cuban counterparts. By 1900 the small local sugar producers were flanked by some thirty large plantations and steam-operated *ingenios,* which were spread as far south as the lower Papaloapan river basin.

During the revolution that ravaged Mexico from 1911 to the early 1920s, the estates were expropriated and broken up into small private holdings or collective *ejidos.* Crops were cultivated as they always had been, with simple hand tools.[110] These years were not the time for corporate transformation of agricultural systems, nor were the Depression years which followed.

In the more stable and prosperous years after World War II the sugar economy expanded and modernized steadily. Mexico's total sugar production tripled from an annual average of 192,000 tons in the late 1920s to 589,000 tons in the late 1950s.[111] The market for this production was almost entirely domestic until the 1950s. Domestic consumption rose from an average of 278,000 tons annually in the late 1930s to 710,000 tons in the early 1950s.

A significant export market emerged in the 1950s, growing from almost nothing at the beginning of the decade to 150,000 tons in 1959. This increasing flow headed to Europe and the United States. U.S. imports rose from a trivial 2,000 tons in 1950 to 61,000 tons in 1959, as American buyers began to diversify their sources, shying away from total dependence on politically shaky Cuba.

These growing and changing market patterns had profound consequences for land use in Mexico's lowlands. As markets increased, more and more land was diverted from other uses into sugar. The total acreage under cane, still primarily in the eastern lowlands, quadrupled from 150,000 acres in the late 1930s to 625,000 acres in the late 1950s. In the early 1960s a sudden quantum jump in production levels and acreage resulted directly from the dramatic shift in American demand that followed Castro's victory in Cuba. Mexico's sugar production rose from 1,518,000 tons in 1960 to 2,107,000 in 1965. Its exports to the United States rose by fully 800 percent from the late 1950s to an average of over 468,000 tons in the mid-1960s.

In response to the expansion of domestic and North American demand, the national acreage under sugar expanded sharply, from slightly over 625,000 acres in the late 1950s to nearly one million by the mid-1960s. In the major production area, the Veracruz coastal lowlands, the acreage devoted to sugar more than doubled, and sugar production tripled. This large an expansion, accomplished virtually overnight, meant widespread and disruptive changes in land use. Cane fields displaced a combination of other cropland, pasture, scrub forest, and coastal wetlands.

BRAZIL

The other immediate beneficiary of the changes in American sugar import quotas was Brazil, where sugar production was still located primarily along the Pernambuco coast, as it had been for well over four hundred years. American sugar purchases in Recife and Salvador had previously been far fewer than Brazil's perennial exports to Europe. As late as 1959 exports to Europe totaled 237,000 tons, whereas only 11,000 tons went north to the United States.[112] The almost total destruction of the coastal rainforest biome in Brazil was not an American achievement.

By 1960 the Brazilian government was turning its attention to development efforts in the Amazonian basin, the planet's greatest reserve of rainforest and biodiversity. Sugar became one tool of conquest in Amazonia, just at the time when the export flow changed sharply toward American markets. The Castro-era changes in American policy played at least a minor role in the penetration of lower Amazonia.

Brazil's total sugar production in 1960 was 3,319,000 tons; by 1965 it had risen to 4,614,000 tons. The national acreage harvested exploded from 2 million acres in 1960 to 4,050,000 in 1967, doubling in seven years. As with other major crops, Brazil's domestic demand was so great that the increased American demand was responsible for less than one-tenth of the total pressure on the land. In the early 1960s South America's giant consumed an annual average of 2,732,000 tons of sugar. By 1965 Brazil exported 818,000 tons; of this only 117,000 tons crossed to Europe, and 332,000 tons, a tripling in five years, went north to the United States.

American expansion into the Brazilian sugar economy cannot be listed as a major determinant of environmental change in the sugar-producing areas of that great country, in contrast to the island countries of the Caribbean, where the American role in environmental history after 1898 was overwhelming. As we shall see in chapter 4, however, even massive Brazil was not large enough to be independent of American purchasing power when it came to its premier export crop, coffee. The alliance between the world's largest grower of coffee and the largest consumer of coffee produced an intense ecological shock in southern Brazil.

REGIONAL POSTSCRIPT

For the international sugar economy as a whole, cane sugar production continued to be plagued through the 1960s with unstable prices and heavy competition among cane growers.[113] The entire Caribbean sugar industry faced severe stress by the early 1970s. In all the sugar islands the costs of production and processing had been growing inexorably since the late 1940s, and cane workers had slowly been organizing into unions. For many years they had expressed their discontent with harsh working conditions, low wages, and the threat of mechanization. Burning standing cane in the fields made it easier to harvest the cane, but it had the environmental effect of depriving the fields of the mulch that could counteract soil erosion and rebuild nutrients for further crops.

The sugar industry was beset by the troubles of foreign corporations and workers' growing resentment of the continuing domination of the industry by foreigners. Island governments responded by buying out major foreign sugar holdings, including the British sugar giant Tate and Lyle in Trinidad, Jamaica, and Belize. The Dominican industry, which faced a perennial labor shortage, had been importing 20,000 Haitian workers each year for harvesting and planting. The instability of that system was pushing planters there to attempt to use new American harvesting machinery, but the harvesters worked poorly on sloping terrain, and breakdowns were a constant threat.[114]

The global era of governmentally managed markets came to an end in 1973 with an international agreement to end national quotas on sugar imports. Artificially protected markets in many consumer countries had encouraged overproduction of sugar that had become increasingly expensive to maintain. The consequence of ending national import quotas was the instability and stubborn depression in the global market that is still evident today.

CONCLUSION: SUGAR EMPIRES AND ECOLOGICAL CHANGE IN TROPICAL AMERICA

Commercial cane sugar production had produced an inexorable downward trend in the ecological health of tropical American lowlands for almost four centuries before the United States became dominant in the Caribbean sugar economy. Plantation sugar has been the most severe exploiter and transformer of both social and ecological systems over the past half millennium throughout the region as a whole.

The most decisive ecological impact of sugar plantations was the clearing of native forests to gain access to rich soils for monocropping. Untold numbers of forest species of flora and fauna were lost when trees were cleared for plantation acreage. Hill forests above the plantations came under secondary pressure, gradually being cleared or degraded.

Moreover, as always happened with plantation agriculture, the resources drawn into one-crop production systems entailed far wider ecological reverberations than simply what happened on the estate lands and their peripheries. The sugar economy was responsible for major developments in transport infrastructures such as port facilities, railroads, and paved motor roads, which linked the cane lands to the world economy and acted as funnels for wider expansion of commercial economies. Migrations of large numbers of people, especially enslaved Africans, to the Americas' moist lowlands and beyond was one of history's most dramatic demographic shifts, paralleling the expansion of the European population to the temperate zones of the world.

The exchange of food was another facet of the systemic changes and exchanges between climate zones brought about by the production of cane sugar. In the slave era on the Caribbean islands, planters drew on food sources from great distances, such as cod from the North Atlantic fishing banks. Purchases of wheat for slaves were a major factor in the spread of wheat farming in the middle Atlantic colonies and the Mississippi valley in the 1700s. Managing the sugar plantations thereby involved domesticating bioregions far removed from the actual sites of sugar production.

The American era of sugar production in the Caribbean basin was largely in the postslavery period, a result of the U.S. government's political displacement of Spain from Cuba, the Dominican Republic, and Puerto Rico in 1898. American capital, corporate organization, and machinery produced a quantum escalation of scale—a pattern approximated in other capitalist crops as well—which marginalized small-scale producers. Even then, large-scale, heavily capitalized sugar production remained unstable in its socioeconomic and political impacts. Because sugar production was labor intensive in the fields, coercion of a semi-proletarian labor force was the norm in most locations of large-scale export production. It repeatedly led to some of the deepest class conflicts ever seen in the tropical world.

These manipulations and upheavals rested ultimately on consumer demand. For half a millennium the collective sweet tooth of European and American retail sugar purchasers played a major role in determining the patterns of imperial exploitation of African labor and lowland forests across tropical America. By the late 1930s Americans consumed 6 million tons of cane and domestic beet sugar per year, nearly as much as all of western Europe, which consumed 6.8 million tons annually. In the early 1960s the ratio was similar: Americans ingested 9 million tons in comparison with western Europe's 11 million.[115]

In sum, sugar demonstrated powerfully that tropical America's economic dependency upon the imperial and industrial North had profound ecological costs. The sugar industry reduced integrated natural ecosystems to a series of isolated commodities, and it did not value or even recognize any species that did not have immediate market value. It caused a radical species simplification wherever it spread.

Within that overall picture, was sugar cane production moving toward becoming a stable agroecological system? Cane sugar is less susceptible to epidemic disease than crops such as bananas and less punishing to soil nutrients than tobacco and cotton. But sustainability depends on far more than the biological potential of a single crop. To what extent sugar monocropping was integrated into a balanced agroecological system varied from one country and location to another; it depended on a perpetually slippery equation of international prices, national political economies, and local ecological realities. In other parts of the tropical world, such as the cane producing areas of the Pacific, the variations were startling.

CHAPTER 2

Lords of the Pacific

*Sugar Barons in the Hawaiian
and Philippine Islands*

If on some ultimate judgment day the sugar industry should
ever have need for justification, it could rest its case upon
its irrigation work and submit no further evidence. There is
scarcely an acre of the tens of thousands that the ditches
serve that was not worthless before money and the wise use
of it brought water.

John W. Vandercook, 1939

YANKEE MERCHANTS AND THE CHINA TRADE

The American pursuit of the natural wealth of the Pacific began in the
1790s, almost as early as America's penetration of the Caribbean, and
it was a direct extension of the Caribbean trade. American commercial
interests were closely linked with the country's strategic expansion into
those seas, and European rivals provided competition for commercial
and strategic ambitions alike. Among the many natural products that
contributed to American wealth and power, sugar cane was preeminent. King Cane led Americans into political, sociological, and ecological transformations of an oceanic world that some of sugar's managers began to envision as an American lake.

In contrast to the Caribbean, in the Pacific westerners confronted
highly developed, centuries-old trade networks for spices, timber, cloth,
and many other products both natural and processed. Chinese maritime
traders had been key throughout the region for centuries, vying with
many other ethnic groups to control the commercial and maritime
knowledge that ensured survival in a complex and competitive arena.
In sharp contrast to their experiences in the Atlantic and Caribbean

regions, the Europeans and their North American progeny found that
to compete successfully they had to learn the rules of a preexisting, monetized regional economy.[1] That task took fully three centuries to master.

The first direct European contacts with Southeast Asia and the
South China Sea were driven by romantic tales of the unbounded riches
and resources to be seized in Asia and the distant oceans.[2] The first
to reach Asian shores were the Portuguese, beginning with Afonso
d'Albuquerque's conquest of Malacca in 1511 from a base in India. For
the Spanish king, Ferdinand Magellan matched Albuquerque with a
westward crossing of the Pacific in 1519, reaching the Philippines in
1521. The Spaniards consolidated that route when Miguel López de
Legazpi sailed in 1564 from Acapulco on Mexico's west coast, reaching
the Philippines the next year. The Dutch East India Company, founded
in 1602, soon displaced Portugal from the Indies and the South China
Sea. Another 180 years elapsed before the British captain James Cook
and the French captain Louis-Antoine de Bougainville completed the
first sketchy exploration of the entire Pacific in the late 1760s through
the 1770s.[3] Their discoveries led directly to the rampant commercialization of the North Pacific's shores, exploitation of its riches, and the
depletion of the resources of previously isolated archipelagos.

At the end of that extraordinary route across the Pacific was Canton,
the key to the riches of China. The Ch'ing, or Manchu, dynasty maintained relative peace but severely limited all foreign access to China in
the eighteenth century, restricting all foreign trade to Canton. The first
resources harvested from the Pacific for Chinese markets were the primary products of the ocean and its coasts. Hardly had the American
colonies become independent from Britain in 1784 than New England
merchants began extending their maritime rivalry with the English beyond the Caribbean, around Cape Horn and across the Pacific, past the
farthest limits of the Spanish empire, as far as Canton.[4] New England
merchants were not to be left out of England's new openings on the
western shores of the Pacific. Imbued with rivalry against British merchant ships, they followed the East India Company closely. In subsequent years the diplomatic weight of the U.S. government worked in
tandem with its private capitalists. The first American consul in Canton,
Major Samuel Shaw, launched the firm of Shaw and Randall in 1786,
the first American company resident in Asia, which he designed to aid
nonspecialist firms in trade negotiations with Chinese authorities.

Massachusetts coastal firms soon began reaching across the Pacific to meet their customers' new rage for chinoiserie: lacquered chinaware, tea, elegant silks, and less expensive nankeen cotton cloth.[5] New England family firms expanded their investments rapidly. By 1830 U.S. investments in Canton were valued at about three million dollars.

The long-term ecological price of that competition with the British East India Company and others began with the decimation of the sea otters of the northern coasts of the Pacific.[6] Profits from the sale of otter furs in Canton gave New Englanders the capital and experience necessary to penetrate more competitively into the southern Pacific. Then, as the Americans and their European rivals turned to the land resources of the island groups of the Pacific and Southeast Asia, they transformed some of those regions' best agricultural lands into export monocrop plantations for northern consumers, weakening a variety of precapitalist cultures and damaging the ecosystems that they had inhabited.

From the northwest, Russian imperial expansion was driven by the same limitless appetite for commercially valuable natural resources. In the 1700s Russian fur traders struggled across Siberia in an effort to profit from the great eastward expansion of Europe's luxury economy. They searched for sables and other furbearing mammals, moving onward as local populations of these animals were decimated. The Russian traders reached Kamchatka, on Siberia's eastern seaboard, in the early 1700s.[7] From there they moved into the Pacific coastal zone and the home of the sea otter, the largest member of the weasel family but the smallest marine mammal. The Russian traders quickly made the sea otter's fur the most valuable fur on the world market.

Otter fur is exquisitely lustrous and warm. Mandarin taste recognized the elegance of otter, and it commanded the highest price of any fur worn in Peking, which is located in the cold winter climate of north China.[8] The furbearing animals of the north Pacific coasts thus became the first link between the consumers of China and the capitalist traders of the North Atlantic. Together they began to devour the natural resources of the Pacific.[9]

On his third and final voyage in 1776–1779, Cook had explored the northwest coast of what is now the United States. He had contacted Russian fur hunters and their Aleut subordinate allies on the coasts of Alaska and the Aleutian Islands, and there he learned of their lucrative harvests of sea otter pelts. John Ledyard, who sailed with Cook on his last voyage, returned home to Boston with reports of the great sea otter populations along the entire North Pacific littoral. Sea otters flourished from northern Japan to lower California, for the southward-drifting California Current allowed this animal, which loves cool waters, to breed as far south as Baja California.[10]

New England traders would have to be aggressive if they were to exploit this beckoning wealth, since ocean resources were open property, not under the effective control or protection of any individual or nation. Robert Gray was the first American to sail around the globe, leaving Boston in 1787 and completing the voyage in 1790, and the first to stop on the northwest coast along the way. After this, most northwest voyages were launched from Boston. The triangular trade—from Boston to the Pacific Northwest, from there to Canton, and finally homeward—became New England's most prestigious trade route. Historian Samuel Eliot Morison called it "Boston's high-school of commerce for forty years."[11] In the classic contemporary account, *Two Years Before the Mast,* William Henry Dana explained,

> The style and gentility of a ship and her crew depend upon the length and character of the voyage. An India or China voyage always is *the thing,* and a voyage to the Northwest coast . . . for furs is romantic and mysterious, and if it takes the ship round the world, by way of the [Hawaiian] Islands and China, it out-ranks them all.[12]

The first U.S. ship in the triangular trade was named the *Otter;* it was captained by Ebenezer Dorr of Boston, who bought 1,000 pelts from northwest coast Indians in 1796 and, after a stop in Hawaii, sold them in Canton. The Spaniards protested against the operations of the *contrabandistas,* as they labeled the New Englanders, but Spain had no ships capable of adequately patrolling the California coast—and the Yankees had no respect for faded Iberian imperial pretensions. Other Boston traders followed Dorr. The most important proved to be Charles Winship, whose first ship arrived in San Diego in 1800, via a long reach to Honolulu; Winship soon became one of the most powerful American trading houses in Hawaii.

Soon the Bostonians began to dream of displacing the Russians. The Russians were based on Kodiak Island, and they built fortified outposts as far south as northern California. They protested the activities of the Yankee interlopers, but they could not consistently control the coast south of the Straits of Juan de Fuca, today's border between Canada and the United States. In 1803 Joseph O'Cain, a merchant captain from Boston, proposed to Aleksandr Baranov, the Russian viceroy for North

America, that O'Cain be licensed to operate along the coast for a season, providing the clippers while Baranov contributed Aleut hunters and their kayaks. The two men would split the fur profits. Baranov agreed to this alliance, not being able to supply the larger ships himself.

Adele Ogden, the sea otters' historian, estimated that the California otter population began to decline around 1815.[13] The largest year's catch was in 1811, when four boats manned by 300 men and 150 canoes took 9,356 pelts—according to written records. Others were surely taken but not recorded, and the Indians who lived in California's Spanish missions perennially harvested small numbers. As one commentator put it, "Too many ships [were] chasing too few skins."[14] Available skins were becoming scarcer, lower in quality, and more expensive to catch, and the Chinese market was beginning to show signs of leveling off. By 1817 the pelts averaged less than one-quarter of their former value.

After 1822 the California provincial arm of the newly independent Mexican government allowed foreign trade, but by that time the sea otter population was already severely reduced. Each year for two decades dozens of ships, mostly from New England, had taken as many as 1,000 to 2,000 pelts each to Canton. No species of marine mammal could reproduce fast enough to withstand that level of pressure.[15]

Two thousand miles to the southwest, the kingdom of Hawaii had been reaping the profits of the trans-Pacific otter trade. The Winships and others had established bases along the California coast and in Honolulu, even though by 1828 American ships began arriving in Honolulu with few pelts, and thus little to trade. The seas provided a substitute product that more than compensated for the loss of the otter in Pacific maritime trade: whales.

Just as the otter hunt was ebbing, an even more romantic, bloody, and highly publicized struggle was launched on the open Pacific, an utterly unrestrained international hunt to "harvest" the great whales. Applying the skills and capital that the slaughter of the otters had provided, New Englanders moved on to the cetaceans. Once again consumer demand in the urban western world imposed unprecedented, very specific, and virtually unlimited pressure on a limited natural resource.[16]

International demand for whale oil to light the lamps of Europe and North America burgeoned in the late eighteenth century, and it lasted until about 1870, when whale oil was largely replaced by kerosene. New England whalers were necessarily latecomers in the North Atlantic ad-

venture, learning their trade from the European fishermen who had
added whale oil to fish products nearly a millennium before.[17] Ships
from the newly founded colony of Massachusetts were the first to join
the race, followed by others from Connecticut and New York.

The whalers learned that the oil of each species varied somewhat from
the others, and they gradually came to recognize that the most desirable
oil for lighting came from the majestic seventy-foot sperm whales of
both the Atlantic and Pacific oceans. The male migrates into Arctic waters in spring and summer, then returns to its mating grounds around
the Grand Banks, the Carolinas, and the Bahamas in the Atlantic, and
the Hawaiian and Galapagos Islands in the Pacific. Sperm whales were
most abundant in the Pacific. Moreover, because they often concentrate
in large pods, they were the most easily hunted, and therefore the most
reliable in terms of returns to investors.

The sperm whale led the parade of Yankee clippers around Cape
Horn. The first New England whaler to reach the Pacific was the *Amelia,*
which was owned in London but sailed from 1787 to 1790 with an
American crew, including a harpooner from Nantucket. The *Amelia*'s
mixed sponsorship epitomized international whaling for decades to follow. Nantucket led the way, and New England's ships gradually displaced most competition, even the British, from the Pacific. New England's maritime economy was temporarily disrupted during the War
of 1812, but the moment the war was over, the whalers again raced for
the Pacific. The profits from these voyages were usually so great that
whaling remained the largest single shipping investment in New England
for half a century despite the dangers facing every ship that rounded
Tierra del Fuego.

Whalers first found and harried the whales in the coastal waters off
Chile, then their kin north of the equator. In 1818 they discovered pods
of whales migrating much farther offshore, in the deep waters of the
central Pacific leading toward Hawaii. The first U.S. whaler reached
Hawaii in 1819. In 1821 the ships began cruising the Japanese coast;
every ship on that run used the port of Lahaina on the Hawaiian island
of Maui to reprovision.

In 1824 there were more than 100 ships; in 1829 that number rose
to 170. By 1830 Nantucket whalers no longer paid attention to the
whales in the Atlantic. Off the shores of the Hawaiian Islands more and
more ships chased the humpback whales, which migrated annually to
wintering grounds in shallow waters such as the Maui Straits. U.S. whalers reached the height of adventure, and profit, after the discovery in

1838 of the bowhead whale populations of the North Pacific. In 1846, the peak year, 736 ships were registered in the New England whaling fleet, and almost 600 of these stopped in the Hawaiian Islands. In the most chaotic and rapacious competition the Pacific ever witnessed, whalers extended ever farther northward in their search for oil and bone, expanding their prey from sperm and humpback whales to the gray whales of the northeastern Pacific.

In Lahaina and Honolulu, where brothels and the sale of liquor were legal, sailors brawled and caroused after a catch, while captains and ship owners spent so lavishly that by the 1840s the islands' commercial economy rested precariously on the giants of the sea.[18] Outfitting firms, many of them offshoots of Boston trading houses, expanded frantically in Honolulu. "The mere thought that the whaling industry might collapse some day was enough to give nightmares to the calmest businessman at the islands."[19] The catch and the resulting spending sprees were very unpredictable; at least one year in five produced disastrously low whale "harvests," and each time the Hawaiian commercial economy went into a downward spiral.

Diseases accompanied the sailors, adding microbial attacks on indigenous people to the multidimensional onslaught produced by whaling. Syphilis and smallpox, and probably also cholera, soon ravaged the islanders, who had never been exposed to European diseases before. Captain Cook tried to control the spread of venereal disease but failed. In Hawaii, as in all the Pacific Islands, the indigenous population began a precipitous decline. This, combined with King Kamehameha I's conquest of the islands in the same years, reduced the population by perhaps as much as one-third by 1800.[20]

Provisioning the sailing ships had an additional impact on the Hawaiian biota, especially in the hinterland of Honolulu, for Oahu had good soils on which crops suiting western tastes could be grown. New commercial crops, including pumpkins, melons, oranges, tobacco, cotton, beans, cabbages, cucumbers, and onions, soon displaced traditional food crops. The simultaneous introduction of cattle, horses, sheep, and goats compounded the deleterious effect. Both native vegetation communities and the Hawaiian people who subsisted on them suffered in consequence.[21]

The rise of San Francisco as a major market after the gold rush of 1848 guaranteed a decade of prosperity for the whalers and disaster for the Pacific whales. In 1860 the industry began a permanent decline, which was caused by events on the mainland in addition to the growing scarcity of whales.[22] The world's first oil well was drilled in Pennsylvania in 1859, and the resulting availability of crude oil greatly increased the manufacture of kerosene, providing an alternative oil for lamps. Then, during the Civil War, many New England whaling ships were either converted to merchantmen or taken by the Union navy. Others were scuttled in the Pacific by the Confederate captain James Waddell and his raider, the *Shenandoah*. In the aftermath of the war, kerosene, which was inexpensive, abundant, and reliably obtained, replaced whale oil in most North American homes. During the last third of the century, market prices for whale oil steadily declined throughout the United States. From the whalers' perspective, the law of supply and demand no longer worked in their favor: as the supply shrank toward the vanishing point, the bottom also dropped out of the market.

Those who invested in whaling became more painfully aware of their perennial, and increasing, problem: the uncertainty of a catch. The great risks associated with the trade, which had been the heart of its romance and adventure for decades, contributed to its demise. In 1871 and again in 1876 entire fleets of whaling ships, pushed northward in their pursuit of smaller and smaller numbers of whales, were crushed in Arctic ice-packs before they could escape southward for the winter.

For U.S. interests in the Pacific in the nineteenth century, though, the economic and technical gains from the whaling era provided another opening. The skills and profits acquired from the unrestrained gathering of the ocean's resources could be applied to extracting the more stable land-based products of the Pacific Islands. These entrepreneurs had gathered storehouses of information on the central Pacific, a region totally unknown to the western world before 1770. Half a century later, the geographical information that would provide supremacy over the sea and its islands was recorded in American maritime logbooks. As Congressman J. N. Reynolds of New York put it in 1828, "Too much credit cannot be given to our whalers, sealers, and traffickers for the information they have acquired. . . . [A]fter all their exertions, justice to ourselves, as a great people, requires that this mass of information should be reviewed, analyzed, classified, and preserved" for the purpose of exploiting the riches of the Pacific Basin.[23] Trade in sea otters and whales provided the shipping and trading knowledge that made plantation agriculture in the Pacific region possible. Coastal and marine mammals were ultimately superceded by products of the land in a new era of venture capitalism.

THE PLUNDER OF SANDALWOOD

As Darwin discovered during his journey across the Pacific aboard the *Beagle,* island ecosystems are uniquely fragile. Their flora and fauna, as well as their cultures, have evolved in semi-isolation for many millennia. Many species are endemic to individual islands or island groups, natural to those locations and nowhere else on the planet. They are precisely adapted to narrow ecological niches and have limited geographic range. Few predators evolved to threaten localized island species. Consequently, endemic species were easily disrupted and even pushed to extinction by alien species imported by humans.[24]

Europeans were not the first to introduce exotic species experimentally onto newly discovered islands. Long before Captain Cook explored the North Pacific in the 1770s, and even before the first Portuguese mariners passed the Strait of Malacca in the early 1500s, other cultures had taken their domesticated plants and animals to islands previously isolated from human experiments. Some indigenous species thus became extinct, and some island ecosystems were greatly remodeled by human effort. But no pre-European transformations prepared the islands of the Pacific for the overwhelming speed or scope of change that Europeans and Americans introduced.

The Hawaiian Islands, the northernmost archipelago in the Pacific, are broadly representative of these processes. Hawaii was the American staging point for the penetration of the southern and western Pacific, and it became the only island group to be absorbed fully into the United States. The islands of Hawaii rise in lonely grandeur in the mid-Pacific at a latitude similar to that of Mexico City, farther from a major landmass than any other archipelago on the planet. The eight major islands are formed from a series of volcanic peaks, most of them long inactive, from one to seventy million years old. (See appendix, map 3.) The highest peaks, Mauna Kea and Mauna Loa on the Big Island, Hawaii, rise over 13,000 feet above sea level and are snow-covered most winters. Most of the year the islands are watered by the rains produced by the North Pacific trade winds, which drift in from the northeast, bringing as much as 300 inches of rain to the windward coasts, but as little as 10 inches and less on the driest leeward coasts. This extreme variation in elevation and moisture has resulted in the evolution of many locally unique plant and animal communities.[25]

Polynesian explorers, probably from Tahiti, first reached the uninhabited Hawaiian Islands as early as 1,800 years ago. They discovered many species of plants and birds that had evolved only there.[26] Koa, ohia, mamane, and naio trees, all endemic, blanketed the mid-elevation forests; at lower elevations grew a variety of medicinal plants that the immigrants from the South Seas used to help maintain their health. They also discovered major gaps in the Hawaiian flora and fauna; for example, no land mammals had evolved there. Over long periods of time, the Polynesian immigrants supplemented the islands' limited range of species by importing plants and animals that even today are the basis of subsistence. Taro, sweet potato, and breadfruit provided the carbohydrate core of the Hawaiian diet; sugar cane sweetened it; coconut had many food and fiber uses. Animal protein was provided primarily by fish from the coastal waters, mostly pan-Pacific species familiar to them from Polynesia. They supplemented their offshore catch with species raised in delicately balanced brackish ponds at numerous points along the coasts.

The immigrant Polynesians also brought the mammals that were familiar to them farther south but which made dramatic changes in the islands' ecological balance.[27] They brought dogs and chickens, which roamed around their villages, and pigs, which went wild, ranging over large vegetated areas of the islands, putting pressure on indigenous plant species in both moist and arid forests. In addition they inadvertently introduced roof rats, hitchhikers that crossed the central Pacific with them and devoured ground-nesting birds and their eggs, pointing a few species toward extinction.[28]

In the traditional Hawaiian land tenure system only the chiefs of each island or district controlled land, in great wedges called *ahupua'a,* which stretched from the volcanic mountain heights down to the broad watery reaches beyond the reefs. The chiefs gave major land grants to the *ali'i,* the heads of aristocratic clans, to manage the commoners and their farming systems. Commoners had a traditional right to work the land, but they could not own it. Each wedge included all elevation zones, ensuring that all crop zones were included in each community's shared lands and that wood and water from the mountain forests were available for their needs. Taro needed irrigation in the arid lowlands, so the Hawaiians developed complex irrigation systems in a communal effort of construction and maintenance directed by the landholding aristocrats. On mountainsides that had weathered into gorges with permanent streams, especially on the windward slopes, the elaborate systems provided reliable water.[29] Irrigation systems also tapped underground watercourses.

Cropping and gathering cleared an indeterminable acreage of dry low-elevation woodland, probably with some desiccation from a resulting decline of rainfall on arid leeward lands. In higher elevations the Hawaiians cut koa and other hardwoods for canoes, housing, and utensils, but it is unlikely that this caused any serious depletion or species-shift in the extensive moist upland forests.[30]

Thus the landscapes and seashores of Hawaii were no longer unaltered, but were cultivated and civilized when European eyes first saw them in the 1770s. Yet the consequences of Polynesian occupation were nothing like the explosive impact of the species introduced by the Europeans, beginning with James Cook and his ragged crew. After Cook's death in 1779 and the opening of Canton to western trade not long thereafter, Europeans and Americans established a string of stations throughout the Pacific Islands for replenishing naval stores, water, food, and fuel. They left goats, cattle, and other European livestock deliberately, and new diseases inadvertently, on all the islands they touched. The familiar result was the decimation of indigenous populations, both human and biotic. For example, more than a third of all endemic Hawaiian bird species and subspecies have been exterminated since the first Europeans arrived—more species than have been lost in the entire continental United States.

The most ruthless exploitation of any indigenous Pacific Island species for the new international markets, and the one that led white men most directly toward domination of the land itself, was the plunder of sandalwood. The luxury market for furs was not the only Chinese contribution to the decimation of animals and plants in the Pacific basin during the early nineteenth century. For centuries specialty timbers from throughout tropical Asia had been in demand for luxury construction and Mandarin household goods.[31] Sandalwood was prized for furniture and household items, but even more as a sacred incense, especially in Buddhist temples throughout much of Asia. Significant international trade began as early as eighteen hundred years ago, when Buddhist travelers using sandalwood for ritual purposes took it from their homeland in India to China, where it did not grow. Chinese and Arab traders imported it into southern China from about the sixth century on.

Some sixteen species of sandalwood grow in a great arc from India through the Pacific Islands as far north as Hawaii.[32] For centuries the most famed sandalwood was the highly aromatic wood that grows in the monsoon forests of southern India.[33] Closely related species are endemic to islands in Melanesia and Polynesia, including the Hawaiian

Islands. Each species of sandalwood is a small tree, growing to a maximum height of about twenty-five feet. It thrives on poor hilly soils on the leeward side of islands. It is valued only for its aromatic heartwood; even its root cortex is fragrant.

Before 1800 the extraction of sandalwood from groves on numerous islands was small in scale, and this harvest apparently caused no extinction of the species in significant areas. Likewise, its harvest and sale to outside traders caused no serious disruption to local social and cultural systems.

Beginning in the 1780s westerners (the Hawaiians called them *haoles*, or men without souls) transformed the trade by escalating the scale and speed of extraction. In a pattern that closely resembled the trade in otter pelts, British and then American and Australian ships precipitated violent confrontations with local cultures, trading firearms, alcohol, and tobacco for sandalwood to ship to Canton. Sandalwood was one of the few foreign products that interested Cantonese merchants. It could thus be sold in Canton to pay for the revolution in tea drinking that was sweeping England and the United States. The result was, in the leading authority's description, "rushes . . . that were not unlike gold rushes in some respects: in the secrecy surrounding the find, in the gambling spirit of the whole venture and in the magnitude of their effects on tiny areas."[34]

As each island's groves were located, a near total depletion of its sandalwood ensued within two to five years. In the Marquesas, sandalwood was decimated by the British and Americans in three years, between 1814 and 1816; in Fiji it was nearly gone at about the same time. By then the British and a growing fleet from Salem, Massachusetts, dominated exports from southern and central Melanesia.[35] Violence and chicanery were the rule of the day: one trader held a chieftain hostage until his people filled his ships with wood, then murdered the chief and his family and burned their village to suppress the spread of information about the supply and the rapine.[36]

The first Hawaiian sandalwood was shipped to Canton in 1804; it soon became a standard complement to fur in the clippers' holds. Kamehameha I, on his way to consolidating the first kingdom over all the islands of Hawaii, declared sandalwood a royal monopoly. He intended to sell it for Spanish silver dollars, which he would use to modernize his army and navy so that he could complete his conquests.[37] Using the aristocratic clans as his intermediaries, he required all commoners to harvest sandalwood. Sandal is a heavy, dense wood, difficult to carry long distances. Moreover, since only the heartwood was used, commercial cutting wasted a large percentage of each log, leaving marketable pieces from two to eight feet long by one to eighteen inches in diameter. Work gangs as large as five thousand people went into the high hills and carried logs as far as eighteen miles down to the harbors.

In 1810 Jonathan and Nathan Winship negotiated with Kamehameha I for a ten-year trading monopoly of the islands' sandalwood, in return for one-fourth of the profits.[38] The king gained little net profit, though, because another Yankee war with England broke out two years later, decreasing American international shipping. In 1814 Kamehameha broke the contract, allowing other New England shippers into the sandalwood scramble as well.

Kamehameha the Great died in 1819. His son Liholiho (Kamehameha II) was much less fully in control than his father had been, and he allowed the Hawaiian aristocrats to enter the trade. They had followed the royal house in their eagerness to collect western luxury goods, and by then their debts to the white men were huge; many had been contracted by the use of promissory notes payable in sandalwood. By 1821 they owed the foreigners at least 18,000 piculs of wood (a common standard of measurement in that era, a picul is 133 and one-third pounds). The immediate result was a sandalwood harvesting boom in the early 1820s, which was a disaster to the Hawaiian commoners, as well as to the trees.

The commoners were required to find, saw, and transport the trees from wherever they could be found on the higher slopes. The harvest went on around the year and involved one-quarter to one-third of the total population, workers who were forced to neglect their lowland crops. "The dank highlands were stripped of sandalwood in defiance of the traditional ethic of *aloha aina,* the feeling of affection and respect for nature, and especially the reverence for *mana,* the vital and sacred essence shared by all living things."[39] As wood became scarcer, longer labor was necessary to find and transport it. Near famine and exposure to cold mountain rains debilitated many commoners.

The escalation continued. In 1826, to pay his royal debts, Kamehameha II placed a tax on every native islander, payable in money or sandalwood. In 1827 30,000 piculs of the fragrant wood were harvested and shipped. This degree of avarice finally tested Nature's limit: within another year most sandalwood was eliminated from Hawaii. In 1828 the harvest was only 5,000 piculs, and prices were driven down by a glut of the wood in the Canton market. In 1829 an agent of Bryant and

Sturgis, one of the largest Boston-Honolulu-Canton firms, reported from Hawaii that "Sandal Wood is an article which has become so scarce here, that we get little other [than] Chips, the gleanings of the mountains, the refuse of better days."[40]

The politics of ecological imperialism were clearly visible in this frenetic maneuvering. American traders, in order to ensure that their debts were collected, demanded that U.S. gunships enforce their actions. Four navy ships appeared in Hawaiian waters between 1826 and 1836 to remind the islanders of the sanctity of contracts. As the sandalwood supply ran out, it could no longer bail out the Hawaiian aristocrats from their decade-long experiment in massive consumerism. When too many chiefs defaulted, the royal government was forced to take over a collective $200,000 debt, Hawaii's first public debt. Ecological and financial insolvency went hand in hand.

Hawaii was by no means unique in those decades. In Melanesia, to the south, sandalwood was harvested island by island from 1828 into the 1860s. The Australians were the largest presence here, especially after 1834, when the British East India Company's monopoly of the British Empire's trade in the Pacific ended. On Negros island in the central Philippines, sandalwood was taken from forests that were later converted to sugar estates, some of which were financed out of Honolulu.[41]

In most locations a few sandalwood trees survived the onslaught, and in the twentieth century most subspecies made a very slow recovery. The trade in the aromatic wood provided important capital as well as commercial and maritime information for the increasingly diverse trans-Pacific trade, but it nearly eliminated the tree from the islands where it grew. More ominous were the violence and the intensity of the extraction, which were key elements in wounding the cultures of those islands. Prior to the arrival of modern technology and the transformation of sandalwood into a high-value commodity, those cultures had been stable. Fragrant wood was one of the few commercially valuable commodities that islanders could trade for western goods, however, and their desire for trade accelerated the decline of their culture as well as the depletion of the resource.

The demographic fate of native Hawaiians was more or less typical of the West's deadly impact on the indigenous populations of the Pacific Islands. In 1778, the year before James Cook died at Kealakekua Bay, estimates of Hawaii's population range up to 400,000; the most recent study estimates between 200,000 and 250,000.[42] By 1831, in the wake of the sandalwood disruptions, it had fallen to approximately 130,000. The 1890 census counted 34,436 pure Hawaiians; by 1970 they numbered only 7,697. Had a wildlife biologist seen these numbers, the Hawaiians would have been put on the endangered species list.

Hawaiian demography is a bit more ambiguous than that, however. Even those sobering figures do not represent the horrific population collapse of 90 percent and more that some islands experienced within a generation or two, a die-off similar in severity to what had happened to the indigenous populations on the mainland of the Americas. Moreover, the Hawaiians had little cultural resistance to intermarriage with outsiders—Europeans, Americans, or Asians. As a result, the part-Hawaiian population rose as the pure Hawaiian population fell. An early count estimated in 1853 that there were 983 part-Hawaiians on the islands, including members of some royal and aristocratic families. By 1900 part-Hawaiians numbered 9,857; by 1970 the census counted 125,224. They had become an important segment of the new multiracial, multicultural population of Hawaii, and many part-Hawaiians saw themselves as culturally Hawaiian.[43] Such a complex mixture could only have resulted from a massive movement of other peoples into the islands. Sandalwood extraction and other maritime trade alone could not have produced that transformation. More than anything else, sugar transformed Hawaii. The islands' great plantation economy had its beginnings in the 1830s, just after the demise of the sandalwood forests and during the height of the whaling race.

THE YANKEE SUGAR BARONS OF HAWAII

Even during the height of whaling in the Pacific, entrepreneurs in Hawaii worried about the instability of their prosperity. Each year business was brisk only as long as the ships were in port, and the whalers' fast-dispersed profits depended on an unpredictable harvest of a precarious and elusive resource. By the 1840s investors were actively searching for sustainable commodities that could be produced on the islands for mainland markets. California's booming markets in the 1850s provided the key: a sweet tooth, which could be satisfied with sugar from the cane that grew wild in the forests of the Hawaiian slopes.

Americans grew sugar cane in other locations, but growing cane on these islands was a very different matter. The islands' soils are mostly weathered lava, rich in nutrients but often very thin or coarse. In a few places deeper humus had developed from centuries of vegetation, but

these areas were not extensive. To grow cane commercially on lava soil
was a new challenge.

Water sources presented as great a challenge as soil. Not that there
is a lack of fresh water on the islands: on many higher mountain slopes
the trade winds bring over one hundred inches of rain each year, and
fog lingers for weeks at a time. The lush wet forestlands of the upper
elevations retain that moisture, guaranteeing a permanent source of
fresh water for the dry lands closer to sea level, at least on the windward
side of the islands. Some of the best cane soils, however, are on the
leeward side of several islands, where perennial aridity had allowed only
the scrub vegetation of drought-resistant species to grow. A foreign eye
whose reference was the North American landscape would, at first
glance, have seen only cattle ranching as a possible productive use of
the islands' arid lands. Yankee experimentation found other strategies,
however, in a process of trial and error, setbacks and innovation.

Several new settlers from New England, plus children of the first generation of missionaries who arrived in the 1830s, experimented with
growing sugar from that decade onward. In 1835 the first Hawaiian
plantation was established on Kauai by Ladd & Company, a mercantile
firm in Honolulu. Its founders, New England businessmen, were reck-
lessly speculative, and they scrambled to raise capital for their plantation
as far away as Belgium. The original experiment collapsed in 1844, and
it had to be reorganized more than once in its long subsequent history.[44]
All other efforts before 1850 also failed. Growers soon found that native
cane had very low sugar content, and machinery was not available on
the islands to refine it to the commercial standards of the mainland. As
Cuban growers were learning at the same time, greater efficiency and
competitiveness necessitated a larger scale of investment in all aspects
of sugar production. The prerequisite for that sort of progress was the
establishment of a private property system in Hawaii, as a guarantee of
haole investments against unpredictable royalty and *ali'i*. Under pressure
from the white settlers, King Kauikeauoli declared the Great Mahele in
1848, reserving for himself a set of crown lands, allowing the chiefs to
take full ownership of their existing holdings, and making it legal for
commoners to buy parcels from them. This was not quite enough to
satisfy the whites, most of whom were still citizens not of Hawaii but
of the United States and European countries. In 1850 they were fully
satisfied when a supplementary decree made it legal for foreigners to
purchase property outright. The islands of the mid-Pacific could now
pass fully into the capitalist orbit of the white world. Sugar planters

could begin making deserts bloom under a new regime of what they saw as civilization and progress. Ultimately about one-third of the total territory of the islands was cultivated for sugar cane.[45] Many of the lands consolidated into plantations seem to have been carved out of mountaintop-to-ocean wedges purchased from their traditional managers, the native aristocrats.

The California sugar market boomed from 1848 to 1851, and rampant speculation drew in risk-takers from great distances. The islands' sugar mills produced poor quality, semirefined sugar, which captured only about 85 percent of the sucrose from the cane and failed to extract all the molasses. Other producers by then were able to produce a uniform white sugar, which was coming to dominate the North American and European markets. Hawaiian producers would have to follow suit, intensifying the process of sugar refining, if they were to command any significant portion of the export market.

That feat of finance and engineering was not long in coming. In 1853 David Watson, founder of Honolulu Iron Works, built the first centrifuge on the islands, which separated sugar from molasses in minutes, instead of the weeks needed by older methods. In 1861 the vacuum pan was first used at Kaupakuea Plantation on Hawaii. Cane juice could be boiled at a much lower temperature in a partial vacuum, which avoided the danger of scorching and increased the quality and quantity of sugar produced.[46]

With a system of property law and expanding markets in place, white planters began to transform the volcanic lowlands of several islands into a virtual sugar colony of the U.S. Pacific coast. As soon as the 1850 law was in place, many Honolulu merchant houses entered a speculative rush to buy arable land, betting that sugar could siphon gold from California. One of the most powerful, Castle and Cooke, founded by two former missionaries, led the way; the great C & C sugar and fruit empire is still an international concern. The gold boom in California was short-lived, but it established Hawaii as a major sugar producer for the West Coast.

A decade later the Civil War crippled northern access to southern sugar, and Hawaiian planters prospered. In 1860 they had exported less than 1.5 million pounds of semirefined sugar; in 1866 the figure approached 18 million pounds. Sugar became Hawaii's largest export, and the islands' balance of trade began showing a steady surplus for the first time. Markets were notoriously unpredictable, fluctuating in a series of booms and collapses. In an abrupt shift shortly after the Civil War, the mainland sugar market crashed again, and several Hawaiian plantations collapsed. By the end of the decade another rapid recovery ensued, and by the 1870s this single crop began to dominate the life of the mid-Pacific islands. Expanding markets dictated that additional acreage be shifted from food crops or natural vegetation to the monocrop. With extraordinary speed the acreage under sugar multiplied ten times between 1876 and 1898, reaching 125,000 acres by the end of the century. By 1890 exports had grown from 12 million pounds to 250 million, and by 1897 the figure had spiraled up to 500 million pounds, 10 percent of total mainland U.S. consumption.[47]

Two key elements were necessary to achieve this great expansion: a reliable, massive supply of water, and a stable mainland market. The first was a technical and managerial challenge; the second was political. The search for water became the single greatest engineering impact on the natural systems of the islands, for the high volcanic islands in mid-ocean presented peculiar problems of water supply. Windward slopes receive heavy annual precipitation, but the leeward slopes are perennially arid. The northeast coasts, the windward coasts, all had plantations by 1900, but the weather there was too cloudy for maximum growth. Fine soils and optimal sunshine were available on the dry leeward slopes, if water could reach them. Planters had three sources of water: mountain streams, groundwater held in "dikes," impervious basalt catchments on the mountainsides, and the basal water table under each island. The engineers' challenge was to move water to the leeward areas.

Hydroengineering transformed the arid rain-shadow lowlands of several islands, where only scrub grazing lands and sleepy ranches had been before, into highly profitable sugar cane plantations. The first irrigation complex was built at Lihue Plantation on Maui in 1856. In 1876 Samuel T. Alexander and Henry P. Baldwin, both Hawaiian-born sons of New England missionaries, completed construction of the Hamakua Ditch on Maui. They were determined to find ways of moving water from the rain-soaked windward slopes of the 10,000-foot Haleakala volcano to the desiccated plains of central Maui. Building the canal was a highly speculative operation—it ultimately cost $80,000, an enormous sum for the day—but the speculators produced an engineering breakthrough that became legendary for its daring and sheer power of will.[48] When the canal was completed, it ran seventeen miles, cutting across gorges and through cliffs, tapping many roiling streams, and using a system of inverted siphons to lift the water where necessary. It provided forty million gallons of water per day. The Alexander and Baldwin venture

proved to be an immense financial success; the water supplied by the
canal allowed the partners to produce the sugar that they exported from
the early whaling ports of Lahaina and Kahului.

This effort demonstrated that the ecological and technical difficulties
of opening the islands' dry lands to sugar cultivation could be overcome.
Hawaii's irrigation systems became the most elaborate of any cane irrigation systems in the world. A much larger scale of financing and
technical skill would be necessary to put Hawaiian sugar production
into the world picture, however. The islands' plantation economy, competing with many other sources of sugar for a place in American kitchens, would not be financially viable without guaranteed mainland markets.

In the mid-1870s Hawaii's most powerful *haoles* centered their attention on Washington, generating a campaign of political maneuvering
that rivaled even that of the New York–Havana cartel. Inevitably their
effort was linked to the broader issue of the Hawaiian economy's ties
to the United States. They achieved total success in the Reciprocity
Treaty of 1875, which allowed an unlimited amount of every grade of
Hawaiian sugar to enter the United States duty free. This single act of a
reluctant Senate in Washington was the key to transforming the political
system of Hawaii and also the patterns of land use and employment on
the islands. The global consequences of the treaty showed that U.S. tariff
regulations could have a major influence on land use and ecological
change in any area of the planet that supplied mainland markets.

In exploiting the profit possibilities of the Reciprocity Treaty, no one
could keep pace with Claus Spreckels. Born in Germany, he had immigrated as a young man to New York.[49] The boom created by California's
gold rush drew him farther westward: in the 1850s Spreckels sold his
New York businesses and moved to San Francisco. Spreckels's ambitions were boundless. He set his sights on controlling the entire process
of sugar production and sale on the Pacific coast. When the Reciprocity
Treaty was about to be signed in Washington, he hurried to Hawaii for
the first time and quickly cornered half of the island's entire crop for the
year. By the next year he was in a position to outflank the missionary
sons with his own grandiose scheme for an irrigation canal. He and a
partner bought 16,000 acres of dry pasturage in central Maui; he then
leased a nearby 24,000 acres from the government, "a dreary expanse
of sand and shifting sandhills, with a dismal growth in some places of
thornless thistles and indigo," according to one observer.[50] This assessment ignored the indigenous dryland plant and animal species that were

being displaced, for they had no identifiable commercial value in the
new system of things.

For such a vast estate, large amounts of absolutely reliable water were
necessary, for it takes two thousand pounds of water to produce one
pound of sugar. Spreckels needed to lease water rights from members of
King Kalakaua's cabinet, some of whom were tied to local sugar interests.
When they dragged their heels, Spreckels—who by then was financing
the king's debts—had only to entertain the king for a champagne-ridden
evening. By the next morning, 1 July 1878, Kalakaua had a new set of
cabinet ministers and within a week the requisite permission was granted to His Royal Saccharinity, as Spreckels was beginning to be called.

By the terms of the water rights decree, Spreckels' Ditch had to be
fully functioning within six years. Spreckels turned to California, bringing hydraulic engineers from his San Francisco home area to confront
the challenge. The job was completed in two years: water coursed down
the canal and the first cane was growing on Spreckelsville Plantation in
1880. Surpassing even the Hamakua Ditch, the great canal was thirty
miles long, crossing thirty ravines as deep as four hundred feet by massive flumes and trestles constructed with wood from the nearby forests.
Chinese laborers blasted twenty-eight tunnels as long as five hundred
feet through the lava. The project cost half a million dollars, but it delivered fifty to sixty million gallons a day, almost as much as San Francisco's entire use. To western eyes in Hawaii this was the ultimate engineering marvel. When it was completed one admirer wrote,

> On the sandy isthmus connecting East and West Maui, and on a plain which
> was formerly an arid desert, where neither a tree and scarcely a blade of grass
> could formerly be found, can now be seen green pastures, beautiful flower
> gardens, avenues of trees and twelve thousand acres of growing sugar cane,
> and a sugar mill capable of manufacturing 100 to 110 tons of sugar per day.
> . . . This is by far the grandest piece of engineering that these islands can
> boast.[51]

A Honolulu newspaper added, "Without the treaty, the bringing down
of this water would be a bonanza to East Maui, but with the treaty—it
simply assures a magnificent near future for the planters of that region."[52] In terms of management and technology, Spreckelsville Plantation became the pacesetter for the sugar industry in Hawaii. In 1881
it introduced a five-roller mill, squeezing bagasse so dry that it was immediately ready to be used as fuel, thus avoiding the lengthy process of
drying it in trash houses, which often burned.

These were also the years when steam was replacing sail for oceanic transport. In 1883 Oceanic Steamship Line, Spreckels's line of ships, changed to steam engines; thereafter it provided regular semimonthly service between San Francisco and Honolulu. Thus was born a fully integrated system of production, refining, and marketing of sugar in the islands. Like others, Spreckels at first worked through a marketing agent in Honolulu, W. G. Irwin & Co. Spreckels, however, bought a half share in the firm, and by 1882 Spreckels and William Irwin controlled the marketing of most Hawaiian sugar.

The boom and bust cycle was decisive for island politics as well as the international price of sugar. In 1886 the king tired of Spreckels's imperious dealings with cabinet and legislature alike, and closed his door to him. The man who had been Sugar King for a decade returned, fuming, to his empire in California, leaving the islands' sugar to a group of the established planter families. His vision of enormous scale and driving efficiency had transformed the islands' economy; the long-term environmental consequences were still uncertain.

The 1880s ushered in the era of sugar baron paternalism, which lasted through the 1950s. Through those years the sugar companies known as the Big Five dominated the land, the economy, and the politics of Hawaii. Owners and managers of the great estates merged with the financial and export houses of Honolulu into a new and tightly knit aristocracy. In addition to Castle and Cooke was Theo. H. Davies & Company, which later became the most powerful sugar exporter in the Philippines. Alexander and Baldwin, the two original families on Maui, remained dominant there. On Oahu the German immigrant H. Hackfeld expanded from his beginnings in a dry goods store in downtown Honolulu to major financial and transport dealings, and, ultimately, control of important plantations. C. Brewer and Company, on Hawaii, completed the group of five.

These five controlled 75 percent of Hawaiian sugar by 1910, and 96 percent by 1933. They expanded to control shipping among the islands and to California, banking, insurance, railroads, and even a large share of public utilities and merchandising on the islands. Between 1896 and 1932 the number of plantations dropped from fifty-six to forty-two, but acreage increased and the labor force doubled from 25,000 to 50,000. Production rose from 250,000 tons to over 1 million tons.[53]

Not content with merely centralizing economic power, the Big Five had seen in the 1880s that they could also control political power, shaping the political destiny—and eventually the demise—of the kingdom. Gavan Daws, today's leading historian of the islands, has called this group one of the most centralized and streamlined power elites on the planet.[54] Alarmed by Spreckels's blatant manipulation of the king's court, they concluded after his departure that the old royal system was both archaic and too independent. A convoluted series of maneuvers in Honolulu and Washington culminated in the *haole* elite precipitating a coup in 1893, overthrowing the monarchy and establishing a new republic with timely help from U.S. Navy gunboats, which appeared off Honolulu to remind doubters of who held real power in the mid-Pacific.

The Republic of Hawaii chose Sanford Dole, head of one of the leading planter families and one of the most progressive of the paternalists, as its president. He was its only president, for the republic lived only five years. In fact, it was a transitional form of government that led to direct American control. In 1898, when the United States was busy taking Cuba and the Philippines from Spain, Washington also annexed the Hawaiian Islands, turning them into a territory functioning under U.S. law in 1900. Hawaii remained a territory until 1959, when it became the fiftieth state

With the political system stabilized to their satisfaction after 1898, the Big Five could turn to further centralization of operations and cooperation among themselves, which was their strategy against their mainland sugar competitors—the producers of cane sugar in California and Louisiana, and the producers of beet sugar in other states.[55] Spreckels was still a threat. In 1898 Castle and Cooke combined with Alexander and Baldwin in a successful stock battle for control of the Spreckelsville operations on Maui. Spreckels's mainland refineries still processed the Hawaiian sugar shipped to the United States for North American markets, so in 1905 the Hawaiian cartel bought a refinery at Crockett, California, which became the single largest in the world. Once again, oligopolistic competition produced gigantism. In 1915, shortly before the United States entered World War I, sugar comprised 90 percent of Hawaii's agricultural production, employing 20 percent of its population. The oligarchy's members owned forty-four of the forty-seven plantations on the islands. A dozen men effectively controlled Hawaii's sugar industry; they often lunched together at Honolulu's elite Pacific Club and Oahu Country Club.[56]

The final major move in the corporate consolidation of the sugar industry was initiated in Washington during World War I. Since Hackfeld was still a German citizen, his assets were confiscated by the U.S. government in 1918. The attorney general, Mitchell Palmer, a notorious nativist who was equally hostile to Germans and Russians, invited the other four companies to buy Hackfeld's operations at bargain basement prices. They quickly organized a new corporate entity, which they patriotically named American Factors, purchasing Hackfeld's assets for seven million dollars, perhaps half the market value. Although the war ended shortly thereafter, his subsequent lawsuits to recover his assets came to nothing, and the Hawaiian sugar industry was more tightly centralized than ever.[57]

A similar story was true for the shipping industry between the islands and the American mainland. In 1909 Spreckels's former partner Irwin merged with the C. Brewer Company, giving Brewer control of the Oceanic Steamship Line. In the early 1930s Matson Lines, which was controlled by an interlocking directorate representing the Big Five, absorbed the Los Angeles Steamship Company and the Oceanic Steamship Line, creating a shipping monopoly. By 1935 Matson, with fifty oceangoing ships, was owned outright by Castle and Cooke.[58]

THE PLANTATION SYSTEM

In the years after 1893 Hawaiian sugar lands achieved the highest yields in the world. Lying on the Tropic of Capricorn, they are in a somewhat milder climate than are most cane growing regions. Winter storms bring rain, and summers are drier, in contrast to the equatorial Pacific Islands, where monsoon rains fall during summer heat, making the cane grow much faster, ready for harvesting in nine to twelve months. Hawaii's cane takes anywhere from twenty-one to thirty months to mature, but the two-year crop produces a thicker, taller plant with proportionately more juice and sugar. In 1940 the average Hawaiian yield was 65.5 tons of cane per acre, producing 14,500 pounds of refined sugar. In the same year, Florida produced 29 tons of cane per acre and 6,000 pounds of sugar, and Louisiana produced 13.8 tons per acre, resulting in 2,200 pounds of sugar. Moreover, raising two crops in two years is more expensive than raising a single crop in two years, especially for labor. In Hawaii a fully resident labor force could plant, care for, and harvest growing canes in a year-round rotation.[59]

Such results were indebted partly to Nature's bounty and partly to a highly efficient, paternalistic plantation regime. Isolated from the rural towns that dotted the islands, the plantations provided and controlled all services for their workers, including housing, fire and police departments, infirmaries, churches and schools, general stores, and cultural and recreational facilities. On the plantation the manager's word was law, rather like the old Hawaiian society in which commoners were bound to particular segments of land under aristocratic control. As one financial historian put it (reflecting *haole,* not Hawaiian, values), "The major difference was that on the plantation, in contrast to the ahupuaa [traditional Hawaiian land unit], everyone worked hard, including the manager."[60]

Commercially competitive processing of the sugar demanded the most modern centrifugal refineries. The Hawaiian planters introduced a series, each capable of processing up to 80,000 tons of cane per year. The first Hawaiian centrifugal factory was built in 1851, immediately after the land law made large-scale production possible.[61]

The planters' greatest challenge was the need for a rapid expansion of the labor force. Without that, the transformation of natural Hawaii would be impossible. Assembling the labor force led to more than just replacing Nature with sugar cane on a particular acreage; it ultimately led to a concentrated population and the expansion of towns and cities. Until World War II sugar was the most important element in the Americanization of the entire life system of the islands.

Most Hawaiians resisted the long hours and strict discipline of the cane fields, preferring to maintain their traditional rural subsistence, however degraded and poverty-stricken their cultural and agricultural landscape was under the *haole* system. Desperate for workers during the early years, the plantation owners dabbled in blackbirding, the notorious practice of impressing unwilling laborers into service, which the captains of British and American sailing ships had employed throughout the Pacific, using alcohol, drugs, false promises, or force to drag them aboard.[62] In the last half of the century the planters recruited aggressively throughout Europe, Asia, and the Pacific, creating the basis for Hawaii's multiethnic population.[63] The planters usually imported labor on three-year indenture contracts. Almost all the recruits were illiterate; most intended to return home at the end of their indenture contracts, although few did. In the early years these workers were docile and apolitical, precisely the proletariat that these rural factories required.

In 1852 the planters imported the first boatload of Chinese contract laborers—293 landless peasants from Canton's hinterland. Soon thousands were arriving each year. A flood of Chinese workers was also arriving on the mainland, and some European Americans began to fear racial pollution. In 1882 Congress passed the Chinese Exclusion Act, banning the further import of Chinese labor. The annexation of Hawaii in 1898 meant that the mainland's laws went into force, cutting off the islands' supply of landless peasants from south China. By then 400,000 Chinese laborers had arrived to stay in Hawaii.

When the flow of Chinese was stopped, the planters turned primarily to Japan. Between 1896 and 1900 the number of Japanese in the islands rose from under 25,000 to over 60,000; by 1907, 100,000 Japanese had arrived, mostly poor peasants from the crowded countryside of southwest Japan. Once again, just as a quarter century before, racism on the mainland complicated life for the Big Five planters. In 1907 the Gentlemen's Agreement between the American and Japanese governments stopped the import of Japanese laborers.

The planters attempted to recruit more Europeans, but they proved too expensive. Then they turned to the Philippines, which had been under American rule for a decade and which also had a large pool of landless or destitute labor. The governments of Hawaii and the Philippines could cooperate closely in organizing the mass movement of workers. By 1932 over 100,000 Filipino men were brought northeast to Hawaii.

The squeeze on workers' budgets intensified after 1909. Despite the inflationary pressures of World War I and its immediate aftermath, Japanese plantation workers' wages remained at seventy-seven cents per day. Japanese workers on Oahu went on strike in 1920, staying out for weeks. It was an ugly time. The planters' agents brought in non-Japanese strikebreakers and evicted the strikers from their homes on the plantations. The strike collapsed, but the Japanese workers' struggles began to have a ripple effect. In 1924 Pablo Manlapit organized the Filipino Higher Wages Movement, and led three thousand Filipinos in a plantation strike on Kauai. This time the strike was repressed by the National Guard, which forced Manlapit to leave Hawaii. With their control of the state's police force the planters were not accustomed to this sort of labor bargaining. After Manlapit's failure there were no more strikes until the Depression in the 1930s.

Changes were in motion, though. After World War II the labor movement became increasingly powerful. By 1959, when Hawaii became the fiftieth state of the United States, its sugar workers were receiving the highest plantation wages in the world.[64] New opportunities for the children of immigrant laborers were not just in the form of better wages for their fathers. As early as 1899, only 362 of 791 overseers on the sugar plantations were *haole;* the rest were Hawaiian, Portuguese, Japanese, and Chinese, in that order. The system was paternalistic but ethnically permeable.[65] Moreover, the Chinese and Japanese in particular found new opportunities in urban Hawaii. When their three-year labor contracts were completed, many of them entered the middle class: they moved into towns, especially Honolulu, opened shops, and educated their children.

The cost of producing sugar in Hawaii and shipping it to distant markets had begun to rise faster than the costs experienced by competing producers elsewhere. Beginning shortly after 1900 the planters used every possible technique of controlling costs and modernizing the technology of their operations. The long-term environmental consequences were to be as complex, distinctive, and sometimes paradoxical as the socioeconomic results.

The plantation owners first mechanized water supplies and irrigation systems on a grand scale. In addition to tapping upland streams, they installed great pumps to lift the groundwater that had drained through lava strata on volcanic mountainsides to roughly sea level. One pump on Maui was the world's largest, delivering up to fifty million gallons daily.[66] Ultimately, by the late 1930s, 240,000 miles of irrigation ditching was at work on the thirty-six great plantations owned and operated by the Big Five. The romance of large irrigation systems seemed irresistible. In the rhapsodic prose that decorated the descriptions of many Yankee projects in the tropical world, John Vandercook, the historian of Hawaiian sugar, wrote in 1939,

> The Hawaiian irrigation projects, though they are so far away and function so smoothly that few ever think of them, are the most remarkable and permanent change that man has wrought in the islands. If on some ultimate judgment day the sugar industry should ever have need for justification, it could rest its case upon its irrigation work and submit no further evidence. There is scarcely an acre of the tens of thousands that the ditches serve that was not worthless before money and the wise use of it brought water.[67]

According to the industry's boosters, the Big Five were harnessing Nature's abundance, integrating her resources and putting them to more productive use than Nature herself was able to do. In fact, the muscular work of the hydroengineers was not the only pride of the planters. They were just as strongly committed to research in agronomy, soil science, and forestry. They used profits, political control, and social stability to construct agricultural research facilities that were more advanced than what the New York–Cuban cartel ever managed. In many ways the sugar lands in Hawaii became the best managed on the planet.

AGRICULTURAL RESEARCH: THE HAWAIIAN
SUGAR PLANTERS' ASSOCIATION

In 1850, 127 farmers and ranchers organized the Royal Hawaiian Agricultural Society, modeling their organization after similar civic and
agricultural improvement societies that were springing up around the
United States. Its purpose was broadly stated: to foster "the interests of
agriculture in all its various branches, and the mechanical arts; and to
increase the amount of industrial production in this group of islands."[68]
It was short-lived, collapsing in 1857 after a serious drought and the
post–Gold Rush depression in the California market. Forty years later
a similar organization became the spearhead of the sugar industry.

The Hawaiian Sugar Planters' Association was born in 1895, its
members the thirty-six consolidated plantations that totally dominated
Hawaiian sugar production. Its charter pointed to the "advancement,
improvement and protection of the sugar industry of Hawaii, the support of an Experiment Station, the maintenance of a sufficient supply of
labor for the sugar plantations of Hawaii and the development of agriculture in general."[69]

The HSPA quickly and aggressively established world standards in
technical research, setting up an experiment station in a Honolulu suburb, which became the world's most sophisticated sugar research facility. Within a few years it fostered substations on other Hawaiian islands
and American Samoa as well. By 1949 its network coordinated over
500 technologists in the experiment station's network and on the plantations. The station itself soon had twelve departments: agricultural
engineering, agronomy, biochemistry, botany, chemistry, climatology,
entomology, genetics, geology, pathology, physiology, and sugar technology. Its library, set up in 1907, attracted sugar researchers from
around the world.

The HSPA's scientists concentrated their early efforts on the search
for exotic sugar varieties that would prosper on the islands and defenses
against the diseases that ravaged the monocrop. In a monocrop agriculture such as this, the geneticists and entomologists were urgently
needed. As early as 1854 planters had begun using the Tahitian Lahaina
variety on Maui, with bountiful results. Propagation had been by cuttings, and a deadly root rot appeared shortly after 1900. In response,
HSPA succeeded in 1905 in developing its own hybrid, H-109, from the
plant's microscopic seeds, bypassing the root disease. H-109 was hit

hard by another disease, eyespot, on higher, damper fields. Gradually it was phased out by hybrid descendants derived from wild earlier stock from New Guinea, which were immune to eyespot but had low sugar content.

The experiment station's department of entomology had its hands full in the struggle against insects.[70] One of the most destructive, the sugar cane leafhopper from Australia, was discovered in 1900. One plantation showed what the leafhopper could accomplish: the Pahala Plantation on the Big Island harvested 18,888 tons of sugar in 1903 but only 1,620 tons in 1905 and 826 in 1906.[71] The fledgling entomology department went into action and soon found a leafhopper parasite in Queensland. Similarly, when the dreaded cane borer arrived from New Guinea, Frederick Muir of the experiment station searched the southern Pacific until he found a parasite that controlled it. The annals of the HSPA are full of such stories. The results were not always benign: the mongoose and the cane toad, which became major pests throughout the islands, were given similar entry visas.[72]

The genetic search for a perfectly adapted sugar cane variety continued. By the 1930s HSPA had developed 25 major varieties that were suited to specific sites around the islands, with 250 other varieties available in nurseries. In 1932 they introduced the 32–8560 cross between Indian and Javanese stock, which proved a winner; by 1947, 45 percent of Hawaiian sugar acreage was planted with this variety.

The remodeling of Nature in the Pacific, which had been accelerating ever since Captain Cook's first visit, was now drawing on the genetic resources of the entire tropical world and gaining the prestige of high scientific legitimacy. Vandercook once again expressed the industry's euphoria most vividly:

> Plants from the far quarters of earth, by men's intention, are here brought together in combinations that could not have occurred in ten million years of drifting time without human agency. . . . Tomorrow there will be new life, life that never before had existence. It is somehow a stirring anticipation. Genius can occur among plants as well as among men. And it is genius that transforms the world.[73]

Through intensive efforts to apply biological controls to pests, HSPA was able to resist using pesticides on the fields for many years. No commercial pesticide was applied until the 1960s. Fertilizers were a separate problem on the varied, often rich but often chemically unbalanced volcanic soils. In the 1800s the planters had imported guano, rich in nitrogen, from seabird rookeries of other Pacific Islands to maintain soil fertility. Along with Australia, the continental United States, and England, they drew on the pelagic nitrogenous capital of centuries to compensate for the overuse of soil nutrients.

Naturally concentrated nitrogen could not satisfy the islands' agricultural needs for long. With the dawn of the agrochemical era around 1900, new industrial possibilities began to emerge. The experiment station's first head was a soil chemist, Walter Maxwell, who was brought in from the Louisiana cane industry. Under his direction, soil studies were pursued intently from the beginning, including research on irrigation techniques, the application of manure, the use of green fertilizers, and fallowing to maintain soil quality.[74] The pressure to increase sugar production meant that as soon as the petrochemical industry on the mainland produced the right inorganic fertilizers in bulk, in the 1930s, the Hawaiians bought them. The oldest of the plantations, Koloa on Kauai, had spent $50,000 on inorganic fertilizer by 1939. One specialist reported in 1947 that "more chemical fertilizer is used on Hawaiian sugar cane than on any other staple crop in the world."[75] This fertilizer was mostly imported from the mainland, already at the high cost of $4 million to $7 million per year, and eventually chemical buildup in runoff water began to threaten coastal ecosystems, including the superb coral beds of several of the islands.

Fresh water is the ultimate limited resource on islands surrounded by salt water. Without water, none of Hawaii's impressive sugar production would have been possible. The sugar industry gained the power to control this resource in its early years, and this control posed the threat that the industry might deplete the virtually unrenewable underground water resources in one location or another, depriving others of access to the life-sustaining resource. The first such case was on heavily populated and tilled Oahu, where James Campbell tapped into the basal reservoir on the dry Ewa plain outside Honolulu for his sugar plantation from 1879 onward. Campbell brought in a San Francisco driller, who was the first to sink a major artesian well successfully in the islands. The results were impressive: by 1896 those fields' average yield was 12.5 tons per acre, and some irrigated fields were yielding up to 20 tons.[76]

A major dike was tapped—and gradually depleted—for the Waiahole irrigation system which fed the Oahu Sugar Company's fields on arid central leeward plains above Pearl Harbor. That massive system, constructed between 1913 and 1916, was twenty-two miles long, and used forty-five tunnels drilled into the Koolau Range's windward side to carry an average of 40 million gallons per day, and up to 125 million per day in the rainy winter season. In the long run, Oahu's increasingly dense population eventually asserted competing demands for that limited water supply, calling the plantation's use extravagant.

Even mountain streams, which capture each year's rainfall, could be disrupted if continuing damage to the montane forests was tolerated. Long before 1900 some people saw the need to control and manage the upper watersheds, which assured the investors of a permanent supply of precious water. That factor more than any other led to the conservation of mountain forests in Hawaii. In 1903 the Hawaiian Sugar Planters' Association introduced a bill into the legislature to set up a department of agriculture and forestry "for protecting and developing the springs, streams, and sources of water supply."[77] The bill was quickly passed and signed that April by Sanford Dole, governor of the islands and one of the leading plantation voices.

The law established a board of commissioners, which consulted with Gifford Pinchot, head of the U.S. Bureau of Forestry in Washington. That same year Pinchot began to recruit fresh graduates from his alma mater, Yale College, to organize forestry operations in the newly conquered Philippine Islands. At Pinchot's recommendation, Hawaii appointed Ralph Hosmer as first superintendent of forestry. Hosmer's successor in 1915, Charles Judd, was the grandson of one of the first medical missionaries, G. P. Judd, who had arrived in Hawaii in 1827. Over the years Hosmer, Judd, and their staff worked closely with sugar plantation managers and HSPA soil and plant scientists. In 1918 the HSPA took its own complementary step when it formed a department of botany and forestry, whose chief function was to protect watersheds. The department's head in its first years, H. L. Lyon, was a forester who specialized in watershed management.[78]

Years later Hosmer succinctly summarized the priority of Hawaiian forestry, writing, "in Hawaii the most valuable product of the forest is water, rather than wood."[79] What valuable timber had originally grown in the upland forests—sandalwood and a few other hardwood species such as the endemic koa tree—had long since been depleted. Cattle ranching had sprawled over many upland forest areas, and the nonnative rats, goats, and pigs had done considerable damage to native vegetation and fauna. Native Hawaiians in some cases had lost their pre-Mahele access to upland streams. By the 1920s the sugar planters and foresters had assured that the mountain watersheds of islands with extreme variations between their arid and wet slopes were stabilized. This much cannot be said of many tropical mountain zones in the areas of Latin America and Southeast Asia where Americans were becoming involved.

THE SUGAR ECONOMY AND CHANGING LAND USE

As production rose and acreage expanded, the entire plantation system—both the acreage of cane itself and the complex mobilization of resources necessary to produce the sugar—radiated outward from the cane fields across the islands. Aside from annual ups and downs, the trend of production was strongly upward for the first third of the new century. In 1912 the industry produced 600,000 tons of refined sugar; in 1932 it reached its first million-ton year.[80]

During the early Depression years Hawaiian sugar actually prospered. Acreage under cane rose from 240,000 acres in 1929 to 255,000 acres four years later, and the labor force remained constant, at 52,000 workers.[81] The International Sugar Agreement of 1937 established domestic production controls and foreign import quotas. The various sugar lobbies had maneuvered adroitly to preserve their local interests, and Hawaii fared well in the outcome. The Hawaiian production quota was reduced by only 10 percent, and the law guaranteed "reasonable" profits to mainland and Hawaiian sugar.

Japan's bombing of Pearl Harbor on 7 December 1941 plunged the islands into the vortex of all-out war and launched a new era of Hawaiian agriculture. Huge military installations were thrown up, and this new industry quickly surpassed the sugar industry as the dominant economic, demographic, and ecological force of those years. Most of those installations, and most of the military population that lived and worked on them, remained after the post-1945 demobilization. The future of Hawaii's military economy was assured when the Cold War commenced in 1948 and the Korean War two years later.

Wartime sugar production was curtailed somewhat as the military's need for manpower drained workers off the plantations and the corporations had to cut back operations. By 1945 the acreage in cane was reduced to 211,000 acres, worked by only 21,000 laborers.[82] In the 1950s Oahu in particular prospered from major military investment. Land values on that relatively small island skyrocketed, spurred also by accelerating urban sprawl in Honolulu. Oahu's economic boom drew in large numbers of people from the other islands, which fell into relative depression and even experienced a net decline in population in the 1950s.[83]

The years after the end of the war in the Pacific brought profound changes to Hawaii's sugar industry. It remained the technically most efficient sugar production system in the world, and increasing harvests were being brought in from gradually decreasing acreage. During the war laborsaving machinery had been introduced to do the work of laborers who had left the fields. Producers further mechanized their operations in response to a cost squeeze that resulted primarily from rapidly rising labor costs.[84] Between 1944 and 1947 a new union, the International Longshoremen's and Warehousemen's Union, began organizing the sugar workers on the islands for collective bargaining. The ILWU's membership grew to 37,000 within a short time.[85] By the 1950s Hawaiian sugar workers were the highest paid in the world.

Profit margins were very tight for the planter aristocracy: in 1957 they earned only 4.2 percent on net assets, a very low figure for capital investment in those years.[86] For that reason if no other the planters continued rapid mechanization. In 1946 in Hawaii it took 3.77 man-hours of labor to produce one ton of sugar; by 1969 that figure had dropped to 1.17 man-hours. In contrast, in 1969 in Louisiana cane fields, one ton of sugar required 2.33 man-hours; in Florida it took 1.80 man-hours; and on the inefficient Puerto Rican estates, where workers were paid far lower wages, 3.05 hours were required for the same production.[87] The results were complex for the Hawaiian industry. In 1946 the plantations marketed 6,002,000 tons of sugar; the amount rose steadily until 1959, the year of statehood, when production reached 9,416,000 tons. In 1968 the figure hit 11,280,000 tons, the highest ever. In terms of value, however, Hawaii's total sugar sales fell from $81 million in 1955 to $69,800,000 in 1959, then rose gradually again through the 1960s.[88] Moreover, mainland U.S. beet growers and Asian cane producers were highly competitive. When Hawaii entered the Union in 1959, there were sixty-nine sugar beet factories in the fifteen states where most Hawaiian sugar was sold, and eleven western states had twice as much sugar in storage as that year's market demand.[89]

In order to avoid or at least postpone the closure of entire estates, the planters took one of their most environmentally significant steps: introducing commercial pesticides on a large scale for the first time in the early 1960s. Although the crop itself was effectively defended from predators, damaging effects began to accumulate downhill from the plantations, especially in the coastal zones, where shoreline fisheries and coral reef ecosystems began to decline. Controversy still rages over how severe the ecological damage has been, how much responsibility belongs to the plantations, and how much damage has been caused by the broader impact of growing coastal towns and tourist resorts. The existence of a new kind of ecological stress, however, has not been seriously disputed.

By the end of the 1940s the Big Five began to respond to rising land and labor prices and widening investment possibilities by diversifying their funds and bringing in mainland executives with new approaches to corporate management. The era of the classic plantation economy was in decline. Some of the long-established plantations closed down, and their workers were pensioned off. The Puna Sugar Company, located on the rainy side of the Big Island, closed in the early 1960s. Theo. H. Davies and Company had managed twenty-two plantations at one time, but by 1959 only three plantations were still under its control.

In other instances the sugar barons diversified their lands into new crops, beginning with tropical fruits. The rise of the tropical fruit industry ultimately linked Hawaiian sugar investments with Central American banana companies and, after 1960, agricultural concerns in the Philippines. The first fruit mass-produced in Hawaii was pineapple, which became the second most important export crop in the islands. In 1922 the Dole family's Hawaiian Pineapple Company bought the island of Lanai for something over one million dollars and turned the entire island into a single family-run pineapple plantation. By 1931 Lanai contributed 38 percent of the islands' total pineapple production, and the Hawaiian Pineapple Company was one of largest single producers of pineapples in the world.[90]

In 1940, 78,000 acres of the islands were planted in pineapples and the industry employed 35,000 workers. After the Japanese attack on Pearl Harbor, which was near the cannery, the U.S. military declared that pineapples as well as sugar were a wartime necessity. The military supported production and marketing of the golden fruit until peace returned in 1945. At the end of the war, the islands had cornered 75 percent of total world production.[91]

By 1958 that figure had fallen to 57 percent, a reflection of several factors (factors that were pressing in on the sugar industry as well): rising labor costs, new taxes, rising land values, and a burgeoning pineapple industry in other tropical locations, especially Puerto Rico, Malaysia, South Africa, the Philippines, Taiwan, and the Ivory Coast.[92] Hawaiian pineapple faced two major mainland competitors in the 1950s: California Packing Corporation and Libby McNeill and Libby. In 1960 the Hawaiian Pineapple Company was renamed the Dole Corporation, a subsidiary of Castle and Cooke.[93] In a controversial move, they relocated to the Philippines in the 1960s, to the southern island of Mindanao, where they forcefully displaced many small highland farmers as they consolidated pineapple plantations.

Dole's major island competitor, Del Monte, also faced severe pressures. Its Hawaiian pineapple production went into a long decline from the early 1960s onward, facing competition from pineapples grown by cheaper labor elsewhere. In 1973 Hawaiian workers received $2.79 per hour, in contrast to Taiwan, where they earned $.17. The Hawaiian share of world pineapple production fell from 72 percent in 1950 to 33 percent in 1973.[94] Yet even in the late 1960s the industry maintained some 75,000 acres in production, using 10,000 workers year-round and another 11,000 during the harvest season from June to September. Pineapples remained the second largest export crop in the islands, in terms of both market value and acreage under cultivation.

Far more complex forces than sugar prices continued to accelerate the diversification of the sugar corporations and the decline of the old plantations. Simply put, other opportunities for capital resided elsewhere. Corporate managers were moving their headquarters to San Francisco and beyond and gradually phasing out their Hawaiian plantations.[95] The result was a gradual reduction of sugar acreage on Hawaii's volcanic slopes and in her valleys. From an all-time high of 145,000 acres in 1933, the acreage under cane fell one-third to roughly 100,000 acres in cultivation by 1970.[96] The rest reverted to long-term fallow: rolling slopes of weedy grasses punctuated by random stalks of persistent cane, waiting for some future transformation into another profitable agroeconomic system.

CONCLUSION: THE ECOLOGICAL IMPACT OF SUGAR IN HAWAII

What can be concluded, then, about the long-term role played by King Sugar in the ecological transformation of the Hawaiian Islands? In contrast with the sugar economy of Cuba and the other Caribbean islands, Hawaii's industry was better managed, and in the long run it was more socially responsible. In part this reflected the fact that the islands were directly under the American umbrella, where agrotechnology developed freely and the labor movement ultimately succeeded in representing its workers' needs. The Hawaiian cane industry was also the world's most productive, but by the 1960s it had entered the agrochemical era. Its

viability was thus no longer organic but artificial, although the environmental costs of the accumulating residues from commercial fertilizers
and pesticides were mostly felt not on the cane fields but by the species
that lived below them.

Much biological value was lost in payment for the Hawaiian sugar
plantations. Obvious and fundamental changes occurred on the sugar
lands themselves, and secondary impacts of sugar farming were felt on
adjacent croplands and settlements. Irrigation systems enabled thirsty
sugar cane to thrive where a variety of natural forests, woodlands, and
scrub vegetation had grown before. Each of these habitats had a distinctive population, for many unique species had evolved in the strikingly varied microclimates of these islands.[97] Many endemic species
(found nowhere else on the planet in a natural state) were threatened
with extinction by the monocrop and its supporting production system.
It is impossible to know how many species vanished as part of sugar's
legacy in Hawaii, but surely the number was far greater than it was in
the more widespread and less locally varied sugar lands of tropical
America.

In the higher mountains above the cane fields, oligopolistic control
of upland water sources restricted the Hawaiians' traditional access to
the flora and fauna of the cool moist forests. It did, however, help preserve watersheds, in contrast to the Philippines. There the sugar plantation system resulted in massive damage to forested watersheds.

The coastal zones, where croplands and fishing waters meet and coral
reefs maintain an additional richly varied biota, also felt the impact of
the sugar economy. Along the coast the mainlanders added commercial
settlements, which were first established for exporting sugar and cattle,
and *haole* resorts; inland they built railroads and then motor roads. This
basket of changes disrupted the Hawaiians' old ways, leading to a gradual collapse of the coastal fishing villages, which had been an essential
element of Polynesian culture. From the 1960s on pesticides began polluting coastal waters to an extent that is still in dispute.

The precapitalist Hawaiian system of mixed cropping and harvesting
for subsistence was displaced by the sugar industry and Polynesian culture was replaced by the broader European-American culture that sugar
represented, including industrial technology and global commerce. In
Hawaii those systems took specific forms, such as raids on sandalwood
and the introduction of exotic livestock like goats and cattle. Despite
the unequal distribution of resources that resulted from its class hierarchy, native Hawaiian culture was far better adapted to the resources

of land, sea, and climate than the culture that overwhelmed it and the fragile islands.

The most systemic impact was the intensification of land use throughout the islands and the burgeoning of urban settlements and populations, to which the Asian immigrant labor on the plantations contributed. Here the environmental changes spearheaded by sugar merge into the broader environmental changes wrought in the islands since World War II.

Finally, through the era of sugar's prosperity, the Hawaiian land and people provided corporate profits to the Big Five and their offshoot companies that enabled them to spread beyond Hawaii. By 1900, American capital, including that of the Hawaiian sugar interests, was aggressively surveying the lands of the entire South Pacific and Southeast Asia for more opportunities to domesticate the tropics. In the Philippine Islands, the American colony thousands of miles to the southwest across the open ocean, another system of American-supported sugar plantations had far different and more damaging results, both ecological and social.

SUGAR ESTATES AND ENVIRONMENTAL DEGRADATION IN THE PHILIPPINES

By the early 1800s sugar plantations had become a feature on Dutch colonial Java and other European-controlled islands. For many centuries sugar cane juice had been part of local subsistence in this, its original homeland. Early colonial rulers experimented with small-scale plantations of sugar, producing semirefined brown sugars of several grades. Then, as global production and trade expanded after 1815, international markets in Europe and East Asia grew rapidly. Chinese traders who had been spreading throughout the southern Pacific and Southeast Asia stimulated much expansion of sugar cane acreage for Chinese markets.[98] The westerners were not the only economic and ecological imperialists.

American control of the Hawaiian Islands was a step toward its stewardship of the Philippines, where American entrepreneurs became junior players in a preexisting system of social and ecological exploitation run by a landlord-commercial class rooted in Spanish colonial and even pre-European times. The American impact there was based less on direct exploitation of the land than on the power of U.S. capital and markets to capture and manipulate the Philippine political economy, reinforcing the extraction system that was already in place. From the start Americans therefore had little sense of direct responsibility for their impact on the land. Furthermore, in the Philippines Yankee interests confronted the Asian tropics for the first time, as American investors moved into unfamiliar ecological and socioeconomic systems. Their efforts to study the soil and climate conditions associated with sugar production were limited by the economics of the plantation system within which they worked. In this there was a certain similarity with the research pursued by American fruit companies in Central America.

In 1898 the U.S. Navy seized control of the Philippines from Spain, along with Cuba and Puerto Rico; all these territories later became major sugar producers for American markets. But for a century before that, Yankee trading firms had been gaining a foothold in Manila, the colonial capital established in the 1560s by Legazpi during his voyage across the Pacific. American commercial interests began doing business in Manila in the 1790s, primarily as a link in the Canton trade. There they coexisted with Spaniards, Englishmen, and other Europeans, as well as the long-established Chinese trading community that controlled small-scale local trade and exports to China. The British, as they did in many other colonial ports around the globe, dominated Manila's trade and banking as late as 1900.

In order to prosper in that intense competition, the New England firms had to establish close ties with Filipino counterparts. U.S.–Filipino commercial ties developed into a variety of joint ventures in the 1800s under the Spanish umbrella. Those ties set a pattern of American partnership with the Filipino landed and commercial elite which was never seriously challenged under American rule of the islands from 1898 to 1946 and, indeed, has shaped land and resource use to the landlords' interests until today.[99] In the nineteenth century those partnerships focused on four major export crops: coconut products, tobacco, abaca fiber for ropes and matting, and sugar.[100] Americans, in competition with Europeans once again, provided capital, technology, and marketing networks, but rarely managed the land directly. Thus they remained one step removed from the environmental consequences that their economic interests engendered. Although the prominence of sugar in the Philippines was supported by American interests, it had been an essential element of the islands' economy for centuries.

PLANTATION SUGAR AND ECOLOGICAL CHANGE

Long before the first Spanish galleons appeared in Manila Bay, the Filipino people chewed the ripe indigenous sugar cane for its sweet juice;

they did not refine it into the brown, molasses-laced *muscovado* sugar that fed the nineteenth-century world. In the last third of the sixteenth century Spanish adventurers began the gradual conquest of the islands, centering their attention on Luzon, the northernmost island. (See appendix, map 4.) Establishing their colonial capital at Manila, they penetrated north into the central lowlands, encountering a great variety of indigenous peoples and languages as they headed toward the northern mountains. The Spaniards were looking for easy riches, just as they had in Latin America. The agricultural potential of the rich alluvial river valleys was of no interest to them.

The partial exception to this lack of foresight was demonstrated by the Catholic Church. Whereas secular Spanish conquerors preferred the urban life of Manila, missionary friars representing several monastic orders began developing rural estates in central Luzon in the early 1600s as their base for the conversion of the islanders to what they fervently believed was the true faith and true civilization.

Colonial exploitation of land and labor in the lowlands of central Luzon was unusual by the global standards of the sugar industry because it relied on a tenancy system that was already well developed. Dating far back into pre-colonial times, the society of central Luzon was characterized by clustered rural communities of subsistence rice farmers controlled by large landowners, or *caciques,* whose power the Spanish conquerors never seriously attempted to undermine. The Spanish added to each rural town a church, a municipal administration, a public plaza, and fine homes for the most influential and affluent members of the administration, including the plantation owners.

Sugar was among the important crops on the early plantations in Pampanga province, in central Luzon.[101] The plantations emerged organically from the older social strata, the peasants acting as tenant farmers on their lords' estates. Until about 1850 sugar production remained localized and was only a minor item in the export trade. Then markets began to grow, and sugar production expanded rapidly on Spanish and Filipino estates on the Pampanga plain. Here fortunes made in the galleon trade with Mexico were put into the safer investment of rich farmland. Pampanga is located on the alluvial plain of the Pampanga River, and its soil is a sandy, friable loam; it had long supported prosperous rice farming for a relatively dense population.[102] These lands did not need to be cleared from the primary forest that blanketed many parts of the islands.[103] In a foreshadowing of troubles to come, access to the world sugar market encouraged landlords to transform croplands, cultivating sugar instead of food crops, especially rice. Until the 1870s there was usually a rice surplus for export. After more land on the large estates was converted to sugar production, chronic rice shortages necessitated its import from Cochin China, Burma, and Thailand.[104]

American whalers sailing to Java and Canton first purchased sugar in Manila around 1815.[105] Sugar moved onto global markets in quantity in the 1850s; by 1870 it was the islands' largest export item in dollar value and export earnings, and it remained the largest, in most years, until the 1960s. Exports were financed primarily by British and American investors. Important markets included Spain, China, and Japan, but even before 1898 the U.S. market was claiming an expanding share.

The rising international demand encouraged sugar estates to expand beyond their sleepy beginnings in central Luzon to other islands that had much smaller populations. Market demand initiated large-scale deforestation of the tropical forest frontier on the island of Negros in the central Visayas, some 300 miles south of Manila. In contrast to the old farmlands and colonial towns of central Luzon, Negros was a mountainous, lushly forested but lightly populated island lying between the much more densely populated rice-producing islands of Panay and Cebu. The mountain spine of Negros, which runs north and south for 150 miles, is dominated by volcanic Mount Canlaon. Alluvial lowlands favorable for paddy rice or sugar cane are found only along the west coast, in a narrow strip that extends around to the northeast.

Before the mid-nineteenth century, patches in the forest had been cleared by the island's small population of rice-growing peasants, who were closely related to the nearby rice peasants and urban weavers of Panay, across the Guimaras Strait. The northwest coast of Negros lies thirty miles across the strait from Iloilo City on Panay, the only well-protected port in the region.[106] Iloilo had been a colonial administrative center from the late sixteenth century and a major center of the island's cotton weaving industry. In the nineteenth century the availability of British factory-made cloth undermined Iloilo's weaving industry, causing severe unemployment—this was one of the most remote disruptions of the early industrial revolution. Some of the unemployed cotton workers were among the first to become seasonal laborers on the sugar frontier of Negros. In the higher mountains of Negros survived a small indigenous tribal population who shifted their subsistence agriculture when soils became depleted. They had been on the defensive against lowland peoples for several centuries.[107]

In the 1860s the British entrepreneur-diplomat Nicholas Loney, who was already involved in the cotton market, began organizing the sugar trade from his headquarters in Iloilo, controlling the early growth of several Negros estates by providing capital and machinery to local landlords.[108] Americans also arrived on the scene quickly. Russell and Sturgis, by then the largest Yankee firm in Manila, opened the first American warehouse in Iloilo in 1863. They were soon followed by the second largest Yankee firm in the Philippines, Peele, Hubbell and Company. Thus a pattern of dual ownership of Negros sugar lands developed, in which power was shared between foreign investor-exporters and Filipino landlords. On the haciendas of Negros foreigners had little or no direct responsibility for management of the land or its social and environmental outcomes. Although foreigners had less control here than they did in Hawaii or Cuba, they were vital to the transformation of sugar production into rural industrial capitalism.

In the years that followed, sugar growers transformed Negros's moist lowland forest to a belt of monocrop agriculture that was approximately eighty miles long by thirty miles wide. Under the rugged cordillera, the rich volcanic soils and typhoon-free climate provided conditions for sugar production that were even more favorable than those on Luzon.

The little plantation communities that sprang into being on Negros were the advance guard of the attack on the forest ecosystem. As late as 1900 a visiting American military officer wrote:

> Each hacienda was a community in itself—a feudal community of which the *hacendero* was the overlord. The hacendero's house, like a baron's fortress of the Middle Ages, stood in the centre of the buildings and dependants' huts. Many miles of almost uninhabited country might separate one hacienda from the next.[109]

On the early plantations milling was done in the traditional *trapiches*, producing low-profit, semirefined *muscovado*, still laced with molasses.[110] The boiling process was fueled primarily by wood until the late 1800s, when severe forest depletion in the vicinity of the sugar cane fields forced a gradual shift to using bagasse as fuel.[111] The same years saw a shift to iron milling, using machinery imported from England. In 1919 Claus Spreckels reached out from San Francisco and founded the Pampanga Sugar Mills. His operation introduced the twentieth-century technology of centrifugal refining to the Philippines, illustrating the transformative power of large-scale industrial capital and technology.

Under the direction of landlords from nearby Panay, sugar exports from Negros had begun to expand in the 1860s. In 1880, 200,000 tons left the island, and the population of the sugar-producing region had grown from 35,000 in 1845 to roughly 150,000 in 1880.[112] The land-lords' future seemed rosy well into the 1880s. Then a serious downturn in the market combined with the rise of violent resistance among the displaced lowland rice farmers and upland tribal swidden communities threatened to make the sugar era short-lived on Negros. These two forces coincided with the turbulent last years of the Spanish colonial era; by the time it collapsed in 1898 the planters seemed to have no protector left.

Even by the 1880s the outlines of a major ecological transformation in northern Negros were clear. As international demand for sugar pen-etrated to one of the farthest points of the plantation frontier, cane fields displaced both acreage for food production and natural forest in the lowlands, then gradually extended up steeper hillsides. On newly cleared soils early yields were as much as 40 percent higher than those on the more depleted soils of the older plantations on Luzon. As clearance for cane fields and fuelwood accelerated, watersheds began to be stripped, posing a threat to water supplies originating on high forested slopes.

From the start, the indigenous tribes in Negros's mountains resisted the incursions of settlers and land speculators. In response the Spanish governor launched pacification campaigns, slaughtering many tribal people in the hills in a bloody example of what was happening in many mountainous locations in the tropics.[113] By the mid-1890s scattered re-sistance against Spanish rule was escalating into guerrilla warfare on all the major islands of the Philippines. On Negros the class and ethnic violence took the form of a revolt on the western slopes of Mount Can-laon in 1896, led by Papa Isio, an immigrant from Iloilo who had lost his farm to a powerful planter. Isio had worked on a plantation until he tried to kill its owner. When the attempt failed, he fled to the moun-tains, where he was joined by other sugar laborers. The guerrillas fought a series of indecisive battles against Spanish military units until the col-lapse of the Spanish regime in 1898. From then on the fate of the sugar aristocracy, their tenant and tribal opponents, and the land itself would rest in American hands.

SUGAR OLIGARCHS AND AMERICAN BUYERS

In 1896 the Filipino War of Independence took an organized form when its leader, Emilio Aguinaldo, proclaimed the Philippine Republic. Not a landed aristocrat himself, but from a more modest middle-class background, Aguinaldo was educated in Spain. On Luzon his movement centered its challenge on the sugar estates run by Catholic friars. By 1898 the ecclesiastical landlords were on their way back to Spain, and the future of the rich lands that they had turned from food production to sugar for export was entirely uncertain.

From Washington that year, President William McKinley sent an American fleet under Admiral George Dewey across the Pacific to take Manila. Dewey summarily annihilated the ancient Spanish gunboats, an action that was timed to coincide with American military operations in Cuba. The American business community had little enthusiasm for a colony on the far side of the Pacific. The striking exception was the cane sugar cartel centered in New York. Horace Havemeyer, Edwin Atkins and the rest of the Sugar Trust were struggling against the sugar beet interests of the midwest and western states. They were members of the circle of Republican expansionists around McKinley and were closely associated with Theodore Roosevelt, then governor of New York. From early 1898 this group pressed for annexation of the Philippines, for they had their eyes on the sugar lands of Luzon and Negros.[114]

The sugar magnates expected little opposition to the liberation from the Filipinos themselves. They were grossly mistaken. Neither Aguinaldo's forces nor most other Filipinos wanted another foreign power to replace Spain. The American takeover of the rural Philippines was a protracted and bloody process, involving as many as 250,000 American troops. Wide-ranging nationalist guerrilla forces resisted the American army for six long years—the United States offered a far more tenacious opposition than had Spain.

From the start those who favored the annexation of the Philippines faced heavy opposition in Congress and around the country. They had to convince their opponents that the American presence in the Philippines was humanitarian, bringing civilized modern values to a primitive population, and not merely the self-interested action of a financial cabal.

McKinley declared martial law in 1900 and moved quickly to instate a civilian government. He convinced William Howard Taft, a federal lawyer in Ohio with ambitions for a Supreme Court appointment, to head the protocolonial administration, although Taft knew nothing about the islands. Taft needed Filipino allies whom he could appoint to new civilian administrative posts, and he looked to the sugar gentry. On Luzon the Catholic friars had already been sent packing back to Spain, but on Negros the landlord class was intact, if badly shaken by the depressed sugar market and the guerrilla campaign.

Taft had little respect for the Negros landlords, writing bluntly in private to Secretary of State Elihu Root that they

> are generally lacking in moral character; are with some notable exceptions prone to yield to any pecuniary considerations, and are difficult persons out of whom to make an honest government. We shall have to do the best we can with them. They are born politicians; are as ambitious as Satan and as jealous as possible of each other's preferment.[115]

But Taft saw little alternative, since no other social class on any of the islands had any common interest with the Americans.

It was not difficult to convince the planter class of the advantages of the American alliance. The first and foremost was military protection. In 1899 Papa Isio's insurgents looted and burned fifty-six plantations. Then the U.S. Army replaced the Spaniards, organizing pacification campaigns and finally defeating Papa Isio's scattered force in 1907 [116] The planters' dominance was once again assured by a sympathetic regime. With American political support, their capacity to transform land and society in Negros was now assured, and they became a major force in the Philippine government throughout the twentieth century.

The decade of military campaigns had resulted in a severe disruption of sugar production on the estates.[117] Iloilo landlords held on through years of near-collapse, cultivating first Spanish and then American rulers. With a return of calm to the countryside, both Filipino and American sugar interests revived, forming a new coalition that was much more dynamic than it had been under Spanish rule.

In Washington widespread opposition to formal colonialism could not prevent annexation of the Philippines, but it did prevent American investors from taking over the friar estates on Luzon. The colonial constitution of 1902 was a compromise, reflecting the Democratic Party's hostility to direct economic control of Philippine estates. The constitution placed a 2,500-acre limit on the purchase of government lands, specifically the former friar estates, by American companies. Thus from the start Washington's political control was able to support American corporate control of land in the colony only to a strictly limited degree.[118] This arrangement was a forerunner of the international system that developed after 1945, in which foreign firms controlled the transport and marketing of crops produced by local owners, rather than directly managing the estates themselves.

In one way the acreage limitation accomplished just what it intended. Under its restrictions American investors were very reluctant to take

direct control of land, since they were barred from the direct purchase
of estate-size parcels. By 1938 Americans owned only 423,185 acres of
agricultural land for all crops throughout the islands, which represented
only 2 percent of all land in private hands.[119]

The American political takeover of the Negros sugar lands was quite
different from America's intervention in Hawaii, where there was no
preexisting colonial landlord class and sugar estates had to be constructed from scratch. The takeover in Negros did not give Yankee sugar
barons the leeway or need to buy and directly manage the old estates,
as they were doing at the same time in Cuba. American investors in
Negros sugar had another, more tempting alternative. Wary of the entanglements of direct land ownership, they forged associations with local
landlords, somewhat similar to the way that Honolulu business interests
had provided capital, technology, and management to the rural planters
of Hawaii. Thus a system emerged in which Filipino sugar barons and
their Yankee backers were able to evade the acreage limitation by reg-
istering maximum parcels under the names of several family members
or associates, or even by deeding small properties to workers and then
leasing them back on terms dictated by the landlords. Official American
colonial policy was essentially passive in response, since its underlying
strategic purpose was to support social stability and economic expansion, which meant supporting the agricultural gentry and their closely
linked commercial interests in Manila. American policy thus perpetuated and even promoted the social and economic polarization that had
long existed in the Philippines.[120]

At first U.S. sugar investors moved cautiously, for they did not have
the political support from the colonial government necessary to guarantee big investments in highly mechanized sugar centrals.[121] They soon
gained powerful backing by institutions of the colonial state, despite
opposition from the U.S. sugar beet lobby. The Payne-Aldrich Tariff of
1909 provided for an annual American import of 300,000 tons of Philippine sugar duty-free. Additional production could enter the United
States at very low duty rates, the only Filipino product so favored. The
1913 Underwood Tariff Act went even further, removing all limitations
on the amount of sugar imported. This tightly tied Philippine sugar to
the American economy, and it remained there until the entire global
system of import quotas was dismantled in 1974.

The colonial administration went further, establishing a national
sugar board in 1915, with legal authority to aid new centrals. A year
later the Philippine National Bank was incorporated to provide finance

capital for new centrals for a few Filipino owners as well as crop loans to the sugar planters.[122] The power of the colonial capitalist state, backed by Washington, was firmly behind the local sugar landlords.

There was room for them all during the production and export boom. The opening of the Panama Canal in 1914 made it feasible for Philippine sugar to compete in East Coast markets. Rapid expansion continued during World War I, when European beet sugar was cut off from the international market by the disruption of Atlantic shipping. By 1920 there were twenty modern centrals in the islands, nearly all owned by U.S. interests, including fifteen on Negros and four on Luzon. Expansion was the theme throughout the 1920s, even though world prices were volatile. The greatest harvest ever was in 1934, at the height of the international depression.

In 1908 the U.S. Department of Interior's Bureau of Science designated its top soil chemist, Herbert Walker, to do a systematic study of Negros. His report gave potential investors a close-up assessment. In retrospect, it reveals an authoritative American technocrat's view of how to modernize sugar technology and transform primary forest into a marketable commodity. It also documents the engineer's attitudes toward the social and ecological systems that enabled that transformation.

Walker described the existing Negros sugar belt as rich in fine volcanic soils, but added the caveat that a good portion of that land was "by no means suitable for growing cane. Much of it along the coast is covered by [mangrove] swamps, and the soil inland toward the mountains is often rocky and nearly barren."[123] In contrast, south of the existing plantation belt "there is a large extent of forest land, mostly hilly, but containing several level plains where . . . sugar cane may be as profitably grown as in any other portion of the island. However, this region is as yet undeveloped and it is impossible to give exact data as to its resources."[124]

Walker's census counted 484 planters, who controlled 162,000 acres of land suitable for sugar cane, of which only 67,000 acres were actually cultivated. Production in 1908 was 73,462 metric tons. The type of cane in use was almost entirely *cana morada*, or purple cane, very different from Luzon yellow or white cane and well suited to the soil and climate conditions of lowland Negros. Purple cane had few parasites and produced excellent yields.

Turning to the social organization of the haciendas, Walker reported that the hacenderos—the planters—were either Spanish mestizos or native Visayans; there were also a few Swiss and Chinese mestizos. All spoke Spanish; a few spoke broken English when absolutely necessary. Walker was cautiously impressed with some of them, but noted that "the average yield for the island is greatly reduced by the comparatively large number of small growers who lack either the resources or the ability properly to care for their cane."[125] Efficiency and modernization and, ultimately, the capacity to compete on volatile international markets were possible only on large haciendas. Walker described the industry as widespread but decentralized, using primitive and wasteful technology that produced only about half the yield (an average of 6.7 tons of sugar per acre, far less than Hawaiian or Cuban yields) that better management could achieve.

Walker accepted the hacenderos' view that local people refused to be drawn into the capitalist plantation system. He quoted a Spanish study of 1894 that asserted that locals "will not work, preferring to enjoy the abundance of plains and mountains plentiful with fruit, of rivers and of seas, which for slight effort yield to man his daily sustenance."[126] The larger haciendas were beginning to swallow up the small rice farmers of the lowlands. Since Negros cane matured within twelve months, cane could be immediately replanted after harvest. During the few months of harvest and planting more than twice as many workers were needed as were needed during the off-season. For that intensive but seasonal labor, planters had to go to the poverty-stricken, over-populated nearby islands of Panay and Cebu. The flow of seasonal workers was difficult to organize. Planters gave labor contractors advances with prepaid bonuses of around $10 and the first month's wage, but many laborers, they complained, took the money and disappeared. Worse yet, under the American system imprisonment for debt was not allowed.

The sugar refining process struck Walker as quaintly archaic. Bagasse was used for fuel in the steam mills, and sugar juice was boiled in "a train of open, hemispherical, iron kettles set over a direct fire [of bagasse]."[127] In the fifth kettle, the *massecuite,* no effort was made to separate molasses from sugar. The semirefined solid was simply taken to Iloilo in small boats and sold.

To Walker it was self-evident that modernization and mechanization were vitally necessary. If a planter sold fresh cane to a central, this would raise the quality of sugar to internationally competitive levels, raise the profit level per acre, and allow the planter to concentrate on better management of the land. As an important consequence, planters could then put much more land under cultivation. This process would improve labor conditions, since it would raise workers' wages and benefits and allow nearly all of them to work the fields. Walker noted that there was "still considerable virgin forest land as yet undeveloped" toward the south and that much lowland used only for rice could also support sugar if proper drainage were constructed. Much sugar was planted every year with no soil enrichment, and under that system it inexorably declined. Commercial fertilizers were probably not feasible; but workers could greatly improve yields "by a more common utilization of the materials available on every estate, such as bagasse ash, sugar-house refuse, animal manure, and green manuring by planting occasional leguminous crops."[128]

Walker's report epitomized the technocratic attitude of the American administration in the Philippines. It revealed a belief in the efficient use of social as well as natural resources coupled with an acceleration of the industry to a capitalist scale under American tutelage. It reflected the best agronomic research of its day, and its proposals were rooted in an emphatic concern for maintaining soil quality against erosion and nutrient depletion. Walker's report also firmly recommended the expansion of commercial agriculture by clearing the natural forest. The report was flawed, however, in its complacent acceptance of the local gentry as the link between foreign interests and the land. The social consequences of the Negros system would be uglier than Walker sanguinely envisioned, and severe ecological disruptions would be closely linked with the social dislocations.

When the American sugar barons arrived, they did so in a powerful way, led by the New York, California, and Hawaii interests—men who brought capital and technology to the refining process on an unprecedented scale. Within a few years they established a new generation of sugar centrals in the Philippines, built to international standards.

The first of the Americans to arrive was Horace Havemeyer of the American Sugar Refining Company in 1909. Havemeyer, a New Yorker, working with Dean Worcester, the commissioner of the territory, reached out beyond his already massive Cuban holdings and purchased the 58,000-acre San Jose estate on Mindoro island, using the help of Filipino politicians to circumvent the acreage limitation.[129] Claus Spreckels and the other San Francisco interests were not far behind. In 1912 Spreckels's associates organized the San Carlos central on the northeast coast of Negros. By 1934 production at that one refinery drew cane from 13,000 acres of prime soil, and achieved the highest yield per acre in the Philippines. The San Carlos central milled nearly all the sugar produced in one district for thirty years, paying the hacendero suppliers 60 percent of the manufactured sugar. By contrast, during the wartime market boom, many long-term contracts paid only 50 percent to plantation owners.[130]

In 1918 the San Carlos combine opened its second Negros central, through the Hawaiian-Philippine Company, which was run by Theo. H. Davies & Company, one of Hawaii's Big Five companies.[131] The Hawaiian-Philippine Company was organized in 1918 by Davies and other members of the Hawaiian Sugar Planters' Association. The company wanted to use Filipino laborers locally rather than incur the costs of sending them to the Hawaiian Islands. The association could not reach an agreement with planters in Pampanga, so it built a new central at Silay on Negros. Silay was very successful financially, paying its shareholders handsome dividends even in the early years of the Depression. The efficiency of its sucrose extraction process matched that of mills in Hawaii, Java, Louisiana, and Cuba. The Hawaiian-Philippine Company organized an association of its nearby grower-suppliers and maintained experimental facilities for hybrid types of sugar, technical advice, and access to fertilizers.[132]

The technological improvements introduced by Americans were mostly in manufacturing and marketing, which transformed sugar plantation management step by step. Technicians on both American and Filipino plantations in the 1920s were mostly Americans. One of the most prominent was John Switzer. A veteran of the Philippine-American War, Switzer joined the Pacific Commercial Company (the Castle Brothers affiliate in California) in 1899. The company, which sold produce to the U.S. Army in the Philippines, grew into the largest American import-export firm in the islands. When the Pacific Commercial Company was reorganized in 1911, Switzer became its general manager. In 1912 he went into sugar milling, first in Pampanga, where, with financial help from Spreckels, he founded the Pasumil central on old friar lands. In 1917 the company was absorbed into the Pacific Development Corporation, a conglomerate with major holdings in New York and San Francisco and close connections with top American officials in the Philippines. In 1919 Switzer moved to New York, where he headed the Manhattan office of the PDC until the mid-1920s and became a member of the politically powerful Philippine-American Chamber of Commerce.[133]

The culminating organizational step in the American system was the founding of the Philippine Sugar Association in 1922 as a technical forum for the entire industry. The Philippine Sugar Association was somewhat more decentralized than the Hawaiian Sugar Planters' Association, in that individuals, rather than the association, developed new cane varieties, studied production systems, and improved milling procedures. The sugar association was the islands' clearinghouse for technical information. More important, it orchestrated legislative lobbying in Manila and New York, coordinating many major Filipino, Spanish, and Yankee hacenderos in their efforts against the anti-Philippine sugar lobbies, which included National City Bank, United Fruit Company, Hershey in Cuba, and others in Puerto Rico and Hawaii.

The Philippine lobby was highly successful, maintaining privileged access to American markets through tariff preferences, even into the mid-1930s. The American sweet tooth assured steadily rising sugar production in the southwestern Pacific. In 1922 twenty-six American-owned refineries produced 233,770 tons of centrifugal sugar. By 1934, at the depth of the Depression, they produced a remarkable 998,123 tons. These centrals improved the extraction of sugar by 20 percent and produced a highly refined uniform product, plus large amounts of alcohol. The western Negros plantations expanded their acreage by 44 percent in the 1920s and production per acre also rose, although unevenly.

The capacity of the centrifugal refineries was so great that U.S. owners had to draw cane from large tracts of land under consolidated ownership. Land clearing continued rapidly, in some cases onto increasingly marginal hill soils in a process very similar to the eastward extension of cane fields in Cuba during the 1920s. By 1938, 49 percent of Negros's arable land was in sugar, producing over half the total national sugar yield. On Negros even the hardwood timber from some new clearings was marketed. Insular Lumber Company, owned in Seattle and the largest and most modern timber company in the Philippines, built its fortune on large timber-harvesting concessions in the Negros lowlands.

The modernization of the refining process, which was under American control, inexorably replaced the old sugar haciendas with industrially administered plantations. Between 1914 and 1927 some 820 haciendas were consolidated as the suppliers for 17 centrals. By 1930 most sugar refining on Negros and Luzon had switched to centrifugal technology since this was necessary to insure that the sugar was of export quality for U.S. markets. Aspects of sugar production that were technically competitive, including machinery, hybrid cane, and fertilizer, were managed by the Big Five companies of Honolulu. The Hawaiian Sugar Planters' Association sent technicians from the Philippines to

Honolulu for training at its experiment station. The primitive transport system of Negros was improved with the construction of several rail grids, with branches often over one hundred miles in length, and new port facilities at several refinery towns ultimately outflanked Iloilo's port facilities entirely.

Thomas McHale, an American and a former sugar executive at Victorias, reminisced later about their inflexible managerial demands.

> The new central mills clearly represented a quantum jump in technical and economic efficiency. Drawing cane from many sources and with no direct vested interest in the specific problems or prosperity of individual cane planters, however, the mills tended to be highly impersonal in their dealings with planters. As a result, planters began to complain that the contracts were onerous in that they required them to plant cane irrespective of weather cycles, disease infestations, price movements or other problems and that the mills had the right to take over management of their land if they didn't comply with their contract regardless of the reason.[134]

Small-scale hacenderos were often undercapitalized and less able to compete with the big estates. Their owners lacked the skills or the funds to improve irrigation, seed selection, fertilization, or mechanization. Many small owners fell into debt and some even lost their properties, victims of the centralization process. Corporate industrial growth was rapidly transforming the land tenure system.

An extreme polarization developed between wealthy owners and poorly paid laborers. Hacienda owners were mostly Spanish-Filipino or Chinese-Filipino mestizos who had emigrated from Iloilo after the decline of the cloth industry there. These men were powerful figures on the land, and they reveled in "almost unimaginable wealth": "Mansions, servants, luxury cars, and round-the-world trips were commonplace for the owners of the large haciendas and the sugar mills."[135] Within a short time, in alliance with the Luzon sugar planters, they became the most powerful politicians in Manila, shaping the legislative process from 1912 onward, when the American rulers passed power on to their Filipino subjects.

On the land itself, aside from a few plantations linked to American interests, production was never mechanized. Expanded production meant additional removal of forest rather than more efficient production; in Negros forest clearance exceeded even that in Cuba. The Negros landlords' power was so great that they could assure that the initial labor cost of opening new land was minimal. Few land titles were clear, and the planters' clearance strategies typically included fraudulently taking peasant farms by falsifying title deeds. Alternatively they made loans to small farmers at high interest, with land as collateral, then foreclosed when it suited them. The dispossessed peasants, both original locals and first-generation immigrants, had to retreat into the hills, where they began removing the forest cover from steep slopes in order to grow survival crops.[136] Thus the plantations, like lowland monocrop systems throughout the tropics, were responsible for damage to watersheds that were located far beyond the sugar acreage itself, in part through the social dislocations that they caused.

Negros was still a frontier society: many peasants homesteaded or squatted in the hills, landlords grabbed land with armed force if necessary, and cattle rustlers and robber bands roamed the land. As on most of the Philippine Islands, guns were omnipresent in towns and on plantations, and discipline was harsh. Life for workers in the fields was an utter contrast to the luxury enjoyed by their masters. Plantation managers had to import labor twice each year, first to clear forestland or rice paddies and establish the cane fields, then, from October to March, to harvest the cane. The spreading plantations took both land and labor from rice production and led to perennial shortages of this staple on Negros plantations.

In the early 1900s, poor peasants flocked in from alluvial lowlands and the depressed weaving towns of Panay. From the 1920s on, *sacada* workers, men on short-term contracts of up to five months per year, were shipped in by the thousands from the overpopulated lowlands of nearby Cebu and other central Visayan islands. Many were caught in perennial debt bondage. The system encouraged a high level of fraud and coercion; corporal punishment was commonplace. The government in Manila, increasingly under the control of the landlords of the islands, could be counted on to look the other way.

Under these social conditions the Negros plantations boomed in the 1920s, well able to compete with Hawaii for international markets, especially in the western United States. From 290,000 tons in 1921, half of which went to the United States, exports rose in eight years to over 670,000 tons, 94 percent of which was funneled into American kitchens.[137]

When the Depression descended on the islands after 1929, the Philippine sugar industry might have been expected to suffer as much as other producing areas, but ironically the outcome was quite different. It rested on a new fight over tariff revisions in Washington, which would be the controlling factor in Negros sugar production, and thus in its environmental impacts. Despite the best efforts of an American-Filipino joint sugar lobby, in 1934 U.S. beet producers and Caribbean cane growers, under the Depression's sagging consumer demand, won a major victory in Congress. The 1934 Tydings-McDuffie Act set a quota of 1,015,185 tons for the Philippines and stated that the tonnage should be allocated to producers on the basis of recent performance. In response, every planter pushed to increase production. In a grim sequence, more forests fell while markets were frozen, although the ultimate effect of the law was to create a ceiling for the expansion of cultivated acreage.[138]

The turmoil of the 1930s was followed immediately by the disasters of World War II. Philippine plantations were badly damaged during the three years of Japanese occupation, and many centrals were destroyed. By 1945 only twenty-six of the former forty-two centrals remained in operation on the islands, including seven of sixteen on Luzon and eleven of eighteen on Negros. During the war a large but indeterminate acreage reverted temporarily to food production, as tenant farmers struggled for survival, or reverted to tenaciously rooted, low-value cogon grass. In 1945 hardly any cane at all was harvested.[139]

LANDLORDS AND AMERICANS AFTER INDEPENDENCE

The Philippines became fully independent on 4 July 1946, a year after the war ended. The United States fulfilled the promise it had made a decade before despite the massive disruptions of the Japanese occupation. Independence was tied to the continuing subordination of the Philippine economy to American markets. That same year the Bell Trade Act, which regulated the new commercial relationship between the two sovereign states, established a figure of 980,000 tons as the Philippines' duty-free sugar quota for the American market, a system that lasted until 1974, when the era of international sugar quotas was ended. This guaranteed the sugar lords continued prosperity and power. At first the Philippine sugar industry, in its severely damaged condition, was unable to come near to filling its quota: in 1947 the Philippines exported only 18,850 tons of sugar to the United States. Philippine shipments did not approach recovery until 1955, when they reached 927,000 tons.

Independence in 1946 also caused a realignment of American involvement in the Philippine sugar economy. In the pervasive corruption that developed, outsiders had to maneuver for whatever political influence they could command amidst frequent scandals. It became increasingly difficult for foreigners to function, especially in rural areas far from Manila. In 1950 U.S. direct private investment in Philippine agriculture was only $15 million. In 1957 it dropped to $14 million. By 1960 it probably amounted to no more than 3 percent of total U.S. direct private investment in the Philippines.[140]

American owners of sugar interests gradually sold their stakes in the centrals to Filipinos. In 1957 the Bishop Trust of Hawaii sold the last of them, the San Carlos Milling Company, to a newly established corporation in Manila. Control of the sugar industry in the Philippines had passed to the old Filipino elite. The flow of technical assistance from Hawaii stopped, guaranteeing that the estates would continue to be managed along increasingly outdated lines. The Philippine estates were moving in precisely the opposite direction from those in Hawaii.

More and more acreage was required to maintain the same output. The Philippine lobby struggled to maintain its free access to the crucial U.S. market. The 1956 Laurel-Langley tariff raised the quota slightly to 1,050,000 tons, but, as a concession to rival interests, the act also established a gradually rising duty for Philippine sugar. By 1974, when the law lapsed, sugar from the Philippines carried the same duty as that produced in other countries.

Another vital test of the Philippine sugar lobby's political influence in Washington came in 1961, when the United States cancelled Cuban imports and turned to other sources. Congress, while sharply raising the quotas of Mexico, Brazil, and several Caribbean island countries, kept the Philippine quota at one million tons, a political defeat for Manila's lobby. To compensate, sugar producers in the Philippines expanded the acreage in cane once again, just as the sugar barons had in the 1930s in response to falling profits. From approximately 500,000 acres in sugar cane in 1960, the national figure expanded to slightly over 1,250,000 acres in 1975, just after the quotas were lifted. Within four years, the effect of the long depression in the sugar market was beginning to show on the land: in 1979 the acreage fell to 1,075,000 acres.[141]

Sugar production in the Philippines had become highly politicized. Political feuding among landlord factions in Manila, not the business of producing and marketing sugar, was dictating production and use of the land. The United States government continued to play a major role in the political structure of the Philippine state throughout the Cold War, in contrast to the steady withdrawal of American investors from the sugar industry. U.S. diplomacy supported the oligarchy against protest movements from below, which turned bloody in the Hukbalahap rebellion of 1946–1954. In the mid-1950s the more moderate President Ramon Magsaysay had elaborate American support, from the money that was funneled into his election campaign to the plans for his counterinsurgency strategy. When his plane crashed in the mountains of Luzon, the moderate era ended for a quarter-century. American policy returned to support of the political and landlord oligarchy, whose firm stance against Communism well suited U.S. Cold War strategies in that part of the world.

The worst abuse of plantation politics occurred after Ferdinand Marcos became president in 1965. Marcos, who hailed from central Luzon, was determined to break up the old sugar elite in favor of his friends. He lavishly rewarded his supporters, men like Roberto Benedicto, the new sugar king of Negros.[142] Marcos added twelve new refineries on several other islands. Politics thus extended sugar acreage at the expense of food production and forest preservation in many areas. The expansion onto marginal land meant that production per acre dropped by about one-third.[143] Moreover, the industry increased mechanization to make the prices of Philippine crops on world markets more competitive.[144] Nationwide the use of fertilizers on the country's croplands rose from 101,200 metric tons in 1956 to 563,000 in 1972. The application of pesticides, especially fungicides and agricultural insecticides, increased similarly. Until 1966 all fertilizers and pesticides were imported, primarily from the United States.[145]

World prices remained high until the mid-1970s. In 1974 the U.S. Sugar Act lapsed, and the resulting global price collapse hit the Philippines hard. By then 65 percent of Negros's arable land was planted in sugar cane, which accounted for 55 percent of the Philippines' total sugar production, employing 440,000 workers. The international price of sugar in 1974 was sixty-five cents per pound; within a year the market price plummeted by 90 percent, and sugar sales met only half the cost of producing the sugar. The sugar industry was in general bankruptcy by 1985. Two hundred thousand workers were laid off with no severance benefits. Many haciendas closed or became only marginally productive. The acreage in sugar steadily fell. On some of it poverty-stricken squatters began to raise food; much of it began to revert to secondary woodlands or cogon grass.

The depression and mass unemployment that occurred after 1974 produced intense social and environmental stress. On Negros, where Benedicto had taken over the family estates of old-guard politicians, severe malnutrition emerged, partly because workers had become utterly dependent on the haciendas and possessed no skills that allowed them to raise alternative crops or find industrial jobs. In 1978 food riots broke out among the desperate urban poor in the festering port of Bacolod. The National Federation of Sugarcane Workers organized communes on leased lands, but the owners suppressed them ruthlessly. Gary Hawes, a leading observer of the Philippine economy under Marcos, observed, "The industry today is in crisis—sugar planters are deeply in debt, many of the sugar mills are on the verge of being closed, workers are without work, without land to plant food on, almost without hope."[146] The hinterland of Bacolod became a center of the New People's Army in the mid-1980s, which recruited several hundred thousand unemployed sugar workers, threatening to create the very socioeconomic revolution that the United States had always feared.[147]

Social chaos was closely linked to escalating environmental devastation in the region around the plantations. Both the lowland sugar estates and the upland forestlands reeled under the conflict. No rational land management was possible, watershed forests suffered endless blows, and erosion accelerated throughout the islands' natural systems. In the long run, Negros suffered some of the most severe ecological disruption in the islands. For many years the watersheds above the cane fields had been stripped of their forests, and streams had run ever lower in the dry season. Sugar planters had been forced to construct large water storage tanks to capture what water they could.[148] Today much land on the periphery of the estates is virtual wasteland, so badly eroded that even tiny food plots are almost impossible to maintain.[149] Politically outspoken priests report a region of denuded hills and stony ridges pocked by squatters' huts above the plantations' good lowland soils: "treeless hills covered with brown *cogon* grass, eroded gullies, and isolated, bamboo-stilt houses clinging to the slopes."[150] Many migrants moved up from the lowlands, forced off their plots by the sugar barons, and are left stranded on land that is incapable of sustaining them or even sustaining itself under the pressure of their desperation.

CONCLUSION: PLANTATION SUGAR AND ECOLOGICAL DETERIORATION

In Hawaii the planters imported hundreds of thousands of laborers over a century-long period. Many of them and their descendants (especially the Chinese and Japanese) ultimately prospered, moving into the middle class and into towns and cities. As urban consumers they put pressure on the limited food resources of the islands. The large number of immigrants who entered Hawaii from Luzon did less well, remaining mostly tied to the plantations and recently facing massive layoffs. They, however, fared better than their counterparts back home in the Philippines.

The plantations of Negros faced a similar labor shortage, but workers were found among the surplus populations on nearby islands. Planters, who comprised an ostentatiously wealthy aristocracy, were able to import thousands of seasonal laborers. These *sacadas* shared the misery of local year-round labor only in the hinterland of Bacolod. On Negros, as in other areas of the tropics where social polarization created a landless labor class, the marginalization of sugar workers put increasing pressure on delicate forest ecosystems where some workers attempted to create an extra-legal squatter society. On Negros, as in some areas of tropical America, U.S. financial interests and consumer markets provided key elements of that marginalization.

Americans' consumption of Pacific sugar replaced indigenous cultures with proletarian concentrations of ethnically uprooted laborers. These were not slave systems, like those on the earlier Caribbean and Brazilian sugar lands, since Pacific sugar plantations arose after the end of the global era of African slave labor. Sugar laborers in the Pacific were hired on short-term indenture contracts and lived in conditions that varied from appalling and politically explosive in Negros to more tolerable and temporary in Hawaii.

The natural ecosystems replaced by sugar cane were widely diverse. On the Hawaiian Islands, the indigenous vegetation systems varied from dryland scrub on slopes facing away from the northeast trade winds to the lush grasslands and forests of the windward slopes. On Negros, cane plantations replaced some subsistence rice paddy lands, but mostly virgin rainforest.

Sugar corporations centralized control of vast acreages of land. In Hawaii this entailed the detailed management of estates under intense market competition. The planters invested heavily in agronomic research, which for many years emphasized the search for biological controls of sugar pests. In sharp contrast, on Negros the Americans remained offshore. They tolerated—and were indirectly responsible for—the severe social and ecological damage that the local sugar barons perpetrated.

Were cane plantations, as artificial ecosystems, biologically sustainable? Sugar cane did not suffer devastating disease attacks—as did Gros

Michel bananas or Brazilian rubber—although there were parasites and diseases that attacked some varieties when they were grown as a monocrop. Research centers overcame those challenges, but ultimately only by increasing applications of commercial fertilizers and pesticides. The impact of that intensification on soil and water depended largely on local production systems, since sugar cane itself does not deplete soil nutrients as severely as several other tropical monocrops.

In the broader picture of the impact of European-American culture on the Pacific region, the ecological devastation caused by the cane plantations was the corporate agriculture equivalent of the depletion of the great ocean's peripheral lands and pelagic depths. To be sure, this was not like the "mining" of the aquatic mammals or sandalwood trees, none of which could be artificially propagated in plantation densities. None of these species is yet extinct, although some whale species are endangered. They were harvested until they were so scarce that they could no longer be found in commercially adequate quantities. Later, either beyond the reach of the market or protected by law, their numbers began to rise slowly. In contrast, plantation monocrops like sugar (and rubber, the other commodity that led Americans into the South Pacific) could be produced in virtually limitless amounts. Consuming more sugar resulted in the reduction of the biologically diverse natural ecosystems that sugar cane displaced.

CHAPTER 3

Banana Republics

*Yankee Fruit Companies and the
Tropical American Lowlands*

Banana cultivation does not enhance the beauty of landscape. Its foliage is of a sober, apologetic green, not har-
monising well with the native verdure; and the texture of
its surfaces decidedly tedious.

Sydney Haldane Olivier, 1935

INTRODUCTION: FOREST CLEARANCE
IN THE BANANA BELT

The steadily increasing appetite of North Americans and Europeans for
tropical fruit, especially bananas, produced impacts in the tropics that
were very similar to those that resulted from the consumer demand for
cane sugar. Bananas and cane thrive in the same setting, so, in the first
half of the twentieth century, American fruit companies joined the sugar
producers in their frontal attack on the rainforest lowlands of the Caribbean Basin and northern South America.

In the mid-twentieth century, most of the bananas grown in the tropical world were destined for local consumption, not international trade.
In the 1950s about 20 million tons of bananas were produced annually
worldwide, 17 million of which were consumed within the producing
countries. Africa represented more than half of this production. Because
of the banana's importance in African diets, most bananas—of numerous varieties—were consumed at home, although several African countries produced increasing amounts for export to Europe. A similar pattern of small-scale local production and sale typified tropical Asia from
India east through Indonesia and the Philippines.

The picture was dramatically different in Latin America. There the balance of domestic versus foreign consumption was tipped toward massive exports. Several countries' economies—and patterns of ecological change—were radically shaped by North American corporations and markets. In 1970 Latin America exported 3 million tons of bananas, worth about $200 million, mostly from small countries in Central America and northern South America. A generation earlier, even in the Depression years of the mid-1930s, 2.4 million tons were exported annually from Central America alone. In those days Americans consumed over half of that. By the mid-1950s 3 million tons were exported; the expansion was due mostly to additional European consumption. By then bananas were the world's fourth largest fruit crop—40 percent of all fruit in international trade. In the United States they were 10 percent of fresh produce sales.[1]

The history of northern consumption of this fragile tropical fruit is the most controversial story in the annals of export monocropping and expatriate corporate power in Latin America. For North Americans the story began on the wharves of Port Morant, Jamaica, and led to Boston harbor, where the United Fruit Company was born. The company prospered, ultimately becoming a major force in the economies and politics of countries throughout Central and South America. Its plantations, and the transport networks that served them, cut deeply into previously intact forests and displaced small frontier and Indian settlements in each country.

POST-SLAVERY JAMAICA AND THE BOSTON FRUIT COMPANY

United Fruit made a major contribution to the transformation of the Jamaican landscape. Its influence extended from the depression that followed the postslavery collapse of the sugar economy to the new export-based dynamic built on the banana trade. The agroecology that resulted was a complex patchwork of changing vegetation on both crop and forestlands.

Jamaica and Barbados were the great sugar producers of the British colonies. That era came to an end in Jamaica when the slaves were emancipated in 1834, transforming the social basis of the island's economy. In the following decade sugar prices dropped by half, the island went into a deep depression, and many cane fields went out of production. The impoverished Creole planters—the British landowners who had been born on the island—watched with distress as former cane fields reverted to rank second-growth vegetation. They viewed the landscape with a culturally determined perception of Nature's processes. For them, orderly, groomed fields were the ecological aspect of civilized existence. They believed that natural as well as socioeconomic desolation would inevitably be the consequence of abandoning the plantations. In about 1840 the planters' association defined their view of civilized society:

> Without the produce of the large properties we should have scarcely any export trade, and consequently no contact with the outside world sufficient to keep us in the march of civilization and improvement: and without the existence of an upper class giving tone to society by its manners and example, [the workers] would soon revert to a state of barbarism.[2]

In their eyes the collapse of the ordered hierarchy of plantation society foretold the end of civilized tropical society. Its natural counterpoint, the reversion of cultivated fields to Nature's own processes, was no different from primeval chaos. A decade later one planter expressed the link between economic and biological landscapes in the imagination of his class:

> [W]herever the eye is turned, wide-spread ruin meets the view. The bustle of business is no longer perceived in our towns; shipping has almost deserted our harbours; the busy industry of the sugar-estate has given place to the stillness of desolation, and the cultivated field is lapsing fast into its primeval state of weeds and jungle.[3]

The Creole planters had not seen the final chapter of the colonial venture. Lowland areas that had once produced sugar cane were switched to coffee groves or cattle ranches; some reverted to almost continuous forest. Bananas could be grown just as well on small, multicrop farms as on large, monocrop plantations; wealth could be based on a system other than the slave hierarchy of sugar. Many uncultivated estates had been settled by ex-slave squatters; other estates were sold in relatively small lots to new arrivals from Europe. Freedmen who settled on plots where soil and climate were suitable for African subsistence crops such as yams and other root crops and who also grew coffee or bananas for cash became fairly prosperous.[4] Within forty years of emancipation, bananas began to replace sugar as Jamaica's lowland cash crop.

The Gros Michel banana had been introduced from the nearby French island of Martinique in the 1830s.[5] At first it was grown largely for subsistence, or as shade for cacao, citrus, and coffee. Daniel Morris, the director of public gardens and plantations on Jamaica, reported that

[a]s the bananas are utilized in many cases as nurse-plants for cacao, nut-megs, oranges, Liberian coffee, cinnamon, coconuts, cardamoms and rubber-yielding plants, the banana culture is leading to numerous permanent culti-vations, which will remain after the bananas have died out. In this respect, it is the means of permanently reclaiming extensive areas that hitherto had been utterly neglected.[6]

A major shift toward more intensive, large-scale planting of bananas began in the 1870s, when shipping companies discovered that the fruit could be sent successfully to distant northern markets. In the moist northeast region of the island estate owners and smallholder freedmen began growing bananas for export to England and the United States. They gravitated toward forming marketing cooperatives that combined the production of many small- and medium-scale farms. In the long run this produced a patchwork quilt of vegetation on the undulating land-scape, a striking contrast to the vast single-species agroindustrial pattern introduced elsewhere by their American competitors.

The year 1870 initiated a major transition in the island's environ-mental history, as Yankees began to move toward more direct involve-ment in the island's agricultural economy. They had previously played only a peripheral role on Jamaica, as buyers of sugar and rum in the coastal ports. Discovering that bananas were available for speculative sales in the United States, they first pursued purchase and marketing and then production and land management. The resulting transformation of Jamaica's agricultural economy made the island the world's largest ex-porter of bananas until the 1920s and launched another monocrop rev-olution in the tropics. By the 1920s some 80,000 acres were in banana production.

The first American entrepreneur in the island's banana economy was Lorenzo Dow Baker of Boston, who put into Port Morant with his sloop *Telegraph* for caulking and repairs in 1870. He discovered large num-bers of bananas and coconuts for sale on the wharves. In a modest speculative move that launched an international industry, he bought 160 stems of bananas, selling them profitably fourteen days later at Jersey City for the New York area market. Returning to Port Morant a year later, he bought 400 stems and sold them in Boston for the New England market. Increasingly confident, in 1876 Baker launched the Standard Steam Navigation Company and the Boston Fruit Company, the fore-runner of the United Fruit Company. In 1877 he diversified his markets further, beginning regular shipments to New Orleans for the lower Mis-sissippi regional market. Baker switched to steamships when they made

sailing ships obsolete in the 1880s, which reduced the shipping time to
Boston to ten and then to eight days, a major advantage for the fragile
cargo.

Success brought competition. By the 1880s several other U.S. shippers
were competing with Baker, transporting bananas to New Orleans, Baltimore, Philadelphia, New York, and Boston. In those early days it was
a commercial free-for-all: seventeen shippers bought bananas in Jamaica, including old British firms such as Cunard, Atlas, Royal Mail,
and the Glasgow Line, which had found successful banana markets in
the British Isles.

British-owned estates formerly dedicated to sugar cane began growing and shipping bananas to England in the early 1870s, guaranteeing
that the Yankees would have severe difficulty entering the trans-Atlantic
market. John Pringle, who owned one of the largest idle estates, found
that bananas gave it a new viability. Pringle began buying additional
land, and by 1912 he was able to accumulate a total of nearly 5,000
acres. He then sold the lot to the Standard Fruit Company of New Orleans, one of two emerging American banana giants; Standard maintained this acreage as its Jamaican holdings. The Boston Fruit Company
also began to buy Jamaican banana lands. In 1899, when it reincorporated as the United Fruit Company, it had a value of $20 million. By
1913 United Fruit managed 7,500 acres, its maximum holding, which
it maintained until 1929.[7]

Until 1920 United Fruit ran an innovative, even socially and environmentally progressive system of banana production in Jamaica. Lord
Olivier reflected in the mid-1930s, three decades after his time as Governor of Jamaica, that United Fruit

> led the way in the arable field culture of bananas, and although they had
> many Creole rivals in the intelligent study of planting, cultivation, pruning,
> manuring and other agricultural arts for improving the yield of the crop, they
> have continuously devoted liberal expenditure, and the intelligence of qual-
> ified scientific and practical agriculturists to this object. They have always
> preferred to employ, whenever they could, native Jamaicans in every grade
> of their business, and have found themselves well served by them.[8]

United was ruthless in its competition for markets, using every possible technique to gain a monopoly of Jamaican banana exports. It temporarily raised the price it paid to small growers to outflank its competitors, and it cut retail prices in the United States to defeat competitors
in Boston, New York, Philadelphia, Baltimore, and New Orleans. Jamaican planters tried to circumvent that campaign by negotiating long-

term contracts with Italian-American fruit wholesalers and distributors. In 1903 they amalgamated with Italian companies in New York and Philadelphia, forming the Atlantic Fruit Company so that they could trade directly with Jamaican exporters. This precipitated a trade war with United Fruit, which United won by buying Atlantic, assuring itself a monopoly of Jamaican banana exports to the eastern United States thereafter.

The Jamaican producers were not finished. In 1927 they formed the Jamaica Banana Producers' Cooperative Association, unique in the world, to compete with United Fruit. By 1933 the cooperative had 15,000 members, representing 66,000 acres in bananas. It was a union of small producers: 99 percent of its members owned under 50 acres. In that year they marketed 27 percent of the island's bananas across the Atlantic. By the late 1960s the United Kingdom was still responsible for 90 percent of Jamaica's banana exports, at a level of 400,000 tons per year.[9]

In 1929 the United Fruit Company, which had just extended its range into Honduras by buying the Cuyamel Fruit Company on the north coast, reviewed its corporate strategy and began selling its Jamaican lands; by the early 1940s it no longer cultivated any soil in Jamaica. United Fruit had shifted its major emphasis to the Central American mainland, where there was no competition from British planters and traders, where there was no highly developed land tenure system, and where governments gave it carte blanche to clear forests for massive banana plantations.

THE CONQUEST OF THE CENTRAL AMERICAN RAINFOREST

A second and larger wedge of the industry developed on the Central American mainland, this time in largely untouched lowland rainforest— a setting very different from Jamaica's old plantation lands. On the mainland were great stretches of forest for the taking, with few existing land rights that could be defended by local communities. Land was far less expensive here than in Jamaica, and development contracts were readily granted to ambitious foreign capitalists by pliant, inexperienced regimes eager to consume the crumbs from the corporate tables. From the 1870s on banana growers opened a vast new biotic region to forest clearance and settlement by growing and exporting tropical fruits, first in the Caribbean lowlands, then later in the Pacific coastal lowlands on the opposite slopes of the cordillera.

Seventy percent of Central America, from Belize through Honduras, Nicaragua, Costa Rica, and Panama, drains into the Caribbean. Its five most extensive river systems all flow east, carrying abundant year-round water supplies. The largest segment of lowland rainforest is along the north coast of Honduras. At Cape Gracias a Dios the rainforest turns south, running down the Miskito Coast of eastern Nicaragua and traversing the San Juan River, which marks the border of Costa Rica. The forest continues southeast to Panama, where the group of islands called Bocas del Toro guard Chiriquí Lagoon, a semi-enclosed bay, from the open Caribbean. (See appendix, map 5.)

This is the *tierra caliente,* the hot land, a broad plain broken by occasional low hills and cut by a series of short rivers that plunge from the interior mountains to the flat lowlands, where they slow to a meander and release rich alluvium on wide natural terraces. Except for these terraces, the lowland soils are mostly heavy clays, acidic and nutrient-deficient, and they are quickly leached by the year-round rains brought by the Caribbean trade winds. When clearing the forest eliminates its thin humus content, the plain can support little but degraded pasture on which only cattle can be raised profitably. Near the coast the rainforest is broken by extensive swamps that support a wide range of flora and fauna, including a spectacular variety of migratory birds that spend summers ranging throughout North America.

To capitalist adventurers in the late 1800s the Caribbean coastal lowlands presented all the difficulties found in wet tropical frontiers anywhere. In contrast to the hill region above, the lowland zone was hostile to human health. Diseases of the rainforest, especially malaria, yellow fever, and hookworm, were daunting. The work force for any industrial-scale agricultural venture faced a defensive war against an invisible foe: parasites were the legions of Nature in primeval form. The economic cost of that warfare to investors was very high until modern medicine began to win victories.

The transformation of the natural vegetation of the lowland rainforest—an area with some of the planet's richest species diversity—to one-species banana plantations was predominantly the work of Americans. Two powerful corporations, first the United Fruit Company and shortly thereafter the Standard Fruit Company, penetrated the rainforest on invitation from local governments. Together they opened for exploitation regions that were remote from the national capitals in the hilly agricultural zone.

No all-weather roads ran from the hills to the Caribbean coastal plain. Virtually the only transportation available was along a series of meandering rivers that drained the northeastern slopes of the cordillera, and only a few tiny ports dotted the coastal marshes and beaches, usually near river mouths. The fertile flood plains were ideal for growing the demanding banana. Temperatures were high year-round, and the annual rainfall was between 80 and 120 inches. The dry season was so brief, usually only a month, that bananas could be harvested year-round.[10]

Spanish colonial control had never effectively penetrated the Caribbean forest zone. Throughout the three centuries of rule from distant Madrid, the Ladinos, Spanish-speaking settlers, stayed in the hills, avoiding the wet lowlands. The Iberians detested the rainforest and its pre-Columbian inhabitants. An occasional traveler might float down a river to safety on the shore, but only a few eccentrics or misfits remained in the forest.

The Central American countries won independence from Spain in the early 1820s, as an afterthought to Mexico's struggle for liberation. The region's oligarchs were monarchists; they wanted nothing of Mexican republicanism or the threatened Mexican imperialism. Francisco Morazan, a Honduran, organized the United Provinces of Central America in 1823, but the government was never strongly united, and the old landed elites, proud of their Spanish lineage, broke up the federation in 1838. Today's independent countries of Guatemala, El Salvador, Honduras, Nicaragua, and Costa Rica took its place.

From then on the hill estate owners, their power rooted in bands of followers loyal to them as individuals alone, ruled what they could of their territories. They had no administrative or technological capacity to reach to the Caribbean lowlands or past them to the coast. The coastal towns became the staging ground for faction leaders challenging upland regimes: throughout the early decades of independence, Ladino governments were harassed by rebellions based on this remote coast. Ladino leaders dreamed of luring railroad builders and their financial resources from England and the United States to Central America to help them consolidate their power.

The unstable regimes also had a financial motive, backed by an ideology of progress, in their efforts to settle the lowlands and clear the rainforest. From the early years of independence onward, Central American governments attempted to attract agricultural colonists, either individuals or corporations, to their large holdings of financially unproductive forestland. Each regime designed laws to turn its forest domain into private property in such a way that it would be cleared and cultivated. Searching for new capital by offering their chief form of wealth, they attempted to attract European and American settlers or investors.[11]

American strategic interests in the Caribbean lowlands were triggered suddenly when gold was discovered in California in 1848. In the two decades before the transcontinental railroad was completed, many Easterners, frantic to join the race for instant riches, tried to reach California quickly by crossing the Central American isthmus. Ships, controlled by transport magnate Cornelius Vanderbilt, took adventurers across the Caribbean, but there the trip became complicated. The gold seekers had to transfer first to river boats, which struggled up the San Juan River to its headwaters in Lake Nicaragua, then to pack trains, which carried the gold seekers the short distance remaining to the Pacific shore. Once they reached the Pacific, Vanderbilt's ships took them up the coast.

Morazan had dreamed of an interocean canal; Vanderbilt revived plans for an isthmian canal across Nicaragua. If Americans could build and control it, using the Monroe Doctrine as a justification to keep European interests out, the United States' strategic and economic domination of the entire Caribbean Basin would be assured. As yet, though, Great Britain's financial, industrial, and naval resources were far too great, precluding an American challenge. In 1850 the two countries temporarily resolved the issue by signing the Clayton-Bulwer Treaty, agreeing to work jointly if any canal were built. For the next half-century and more, the effort to finance and build the canal was the linchpin of the region's geopolitics.

Through the rest of the 1800s this mix of political instability, intrigue, and northerners' dreams of empire and fortune attracted a particular sort of reckless, highly individualistic gringo to Central America. Several of them, labeled "filibusters" by the press, attempted to organize private militias among the motley cosmopolitan underclass of American ports and then to conquer territories south of the Rio Grande. They were like the Yankees who had infiltrated Texas and wrenched it away from Mexico in the 1840s: collectively they were responsible to no one but themselves; they were contemptuous of the *caudillos* who controlled the Central American regimes; and they saw the region's lands and resources purely in terms of the power and wealth that could be extracted.[12]

The most notorious of the gringo filibusters in Central America was

William Walker, who organized a private army in New Orleans in the early 1850s with financial support from eastern speculators. Walker led his men to Nicaragua, where he occupied the capital, Managua, in 1855. Washington actually recognized his government—the U.S. State Department could see little difference between Walker and the *caudillos* whom he had defeated. Vanderbilt saw it differently, for Walker had challenged his political influence and economic bonanza on the route that spanned the isthmus. Within two years of gaining glory, Walker was crushed by Vanderbilt's Nicaraguan friends in 1857.[13] Walker was chased down the coast to Costa Rica, where he was cornered by his enemies and shot at a ranch house in the dry cattle country. The house still stands today, a minor tourist attraction in Guanacaste National Park.

Most of the early Yankee adventurers in the Central American tropics did not organize private armies; they were restless individuals who traveled beyond the westward-drifting frontier of European-American culture and politics, using the same techniques that they would have employed in Kansas or Arizona. One of the first hucksters on the Caribbean coast was Henry L. Kinney, originally from Pennsylvania, who had already speculated on land in Texas. He arrived on Nicaragua's Miskito Coast in the 1850s, where he negotiated with the distant Managuan regime a questionable title to a vaguely defined area of some hundreds of thousand acres of rainforest. No one inquired whether anyone, either Miskito or Ladino, might already be in possession of the land. He put the land title in the name of a new corporation, the Central America Company, the first of numerous gringo companies organized for the purpose of land speculation in Central America. Like many of his contemporaries on the frontier of commercial land in the western United States, Kinney sold stock carrying "title" to land at twenty-five cents an acre to unwary investors back east.[14] Kinney's company failed before long, as did most early land speculation companies, and he faded back into obscurity. Indeed, for every Yankee entrepreneur or adventurer who succeeded over the long haul in Central America, there were probably a dozen who quickly vanished. Land development corporations, and the employment and income that they offered, did not appear until after 1900. The American presence was tenuous and dispersed until the high risks and formidable development problems of the rainforest frontier were bested by the superior resources and long-term staying power of large-scale corporations.

THE UNITED FRUIT COMPANY IN PANAMA AND COSTA RICA

At first the United Fruit Company exports were diversified, including oranges, cattle, coconut, rubber, cacao, and sugar as well as bananas. Bananas proved so profitable that they soon dominated the company's other crops. In the early years United purchased most of its bananas from small producers. As late as 1911 it bought 65 percent of its bananas on the open market or through contracts, but the economies and discipline of centralized large-scale production produced an efficiency that was too attractive to ignore. The company soon decided to control 80 percent of production by growing bananas on its own plantations.

By the late nineteenth century, local governments were determined to establish effective control over their Caribbean lowlands, and they saw that railroads were the key. Never before had they dared to hope that the impenetrable jungle beyond the mountains could be vanquished. They were willing to lease government-claimed lands to foreigners for long terms—a strategy modeled on the sale of railroad land in the western United States. Governments were so eager to attract foreign capital that they granted American companies almost total independence in their operations until the 1930s. This was the era of the banana barons, and directly and indirectly they were responsible for clearing entire regions of lowland forest.

Many local Ladinos attempted to grow bananas for export as early as the 1860s, but big plantations did not appear until the 1890s. When they did emerge, the result was a classic case of enclave economies. In corporate banana operations the entire work force was controlled and managed like a great factory. The companies built housing for managers and workers in a strictly hierarchical system. The companies also provided schools, hospitals, recreation facilities, and stores that carried only company-controlled goods. These outlets were virtually the only source of food for many plantation workers, since the companies reserved the fertile alluvial terraces for the commercial crop or cattle pasture.

These facilities radically reshaped the natural environment. In the jungle the companies clear-cut forests, filled in low and swampy areas, and installed sewage, drainage, and water systems. They transformed natural or roughly settled ecosystems into rational, orderly biofactories.[15] The companies changed the economic base of the forest region from low-density farming and ranching, which supported small market towns on the riverbanks, to an ordered industrial hierarchy with a semi-proletarian work force. There was little resident population in the rainforest. The main rivers and coastlines were lightly populated by forest Indians, notably the Miskitos on the Honduran and Nicaraguan coastal lowlands.[16] Entrepreneurs had to import labor for large plantations, for the highland Indians and Ladinos both resisted migrating into the steaming, malarial lowlands.

During colonial times Costa Rica had been a remote, untraveled land that lay between the route that crossed the Panamanian isthmus and the Spanish regional center in Guatemala. Costa Rica was always more lightly populated and less developed than many parts of Central America. To travel to the Caribbean coast from San José, Costa Rica's capital in the central valley, was a difficult challenge. The trip began with the climb up to any of several passes through the volcanic cordillera. The struggle to cross the mountains was minor compared to the transit of the tropical lowlands, where there were no all-weather roads. Before the railroad era the only possible lowland routes were the rivers that drained the slopes east of the volcanic spine. Small boats taxied the occasional traveler down these streams.

After the 1820s the newly independent nation's government encouraged the growth of coffee plantations as the route to profit and progress, but that crop's only route to Europe from the central valley was by mule to Puntarenas on the Pacific, and from there by boat around Cape Horn. By 1870 the government was dreaming of building a rail line to Puerto Limón on the Caribbean coast. The elite of San José embraced the international romance of the iron horse: railroads were opening frontiers across the globe to settlement and prosperous agriculture.[17]

In 1871, just as Lorenzo Baker was beginning his operations in Jamaica, the Costa Rican government began courting Henry Meiggs, the American who was building Peru's first railroad. Meiggs was preoccupied in the Andes, so he sent his nephew Minor Keith to San José. The United Fruit Company's operations in Costa Rica rose out of the railroad-building contract that Keith signed with the government. In return for building a railroad from San José through the hills to Turrialba and then down through the lowland forest to Puerto Limón, the Costa Rican government gave Keith a ninety-nine-year lease on the land for the proposed line, plus 800,000 acres of government land along its route or anywhere else he chose within the country.[18]

Until the stipulated length of railroad was complete, the Costa Rican government would grant only a provisional title to the land to Keith. This led to endless wrangling, but Keith moved ahead with construction. Coffee, a seasonal crop, could not bring business and profits to a railroad by itself, so Keith began to search for other goods, especially new export crops, which could be hauled on the same tracks throughout the year. Most of the rainforest lands of Sarapiquí, the hinterland of Puerto Limón, were very thinly populated. The alluvial riverine terraces had supported cacao plantations in colonial times, but many of these had been deserted by the local Indians, who were harassed by Miskito raiders based along the Nicaraguan coast.[19] A tiny peasant population lived scattered throughout the forest by Keith's time, almost totally isolated from commercial markets. One of the products of their mixed subsistence cropping was bananas. Later, under pressure from the railroad and fruit company, they increased their banana production for export at prices dictated by the monopoly. In his railroad's first years, Keith bought and shipped bananas from many sources, both small-holdings and private plantations run by Costa Ricans with Jamaican workers.[20]

Baker and other Yankee commercial banana shippers had also been surveying the entire arc of Caribbean coastal lowlands from Mexico to Colombia, searching for supply areas that could replace hurricane-prone Jamaica. Baker's interest focused on the north coast of Panama, which had attracted American strategic notice as early as 1846, when President James Polk signed a treaty with Colombia that gave the United States the right to build a canal across Panama (then still a region of Colombia). The effort by the French engineer Ferdinand de Lesseps to build an isthmian canal across Panama in the 1880s emphasized the strategic importance of that land bridge. France's attempt hardened the resolve of both Great Britain and the United States in their confrontation over Colombia and Panama. When yellow fever destroyed the French effort in 1888, unemployed European and Jamaican laborers remained behind.[21]

In 1903, under President Roosevelt's encouragement, Panama broke free from Colombia and the United States began its successful effort to build a canal. In 1904 the president announced the Roosevelt Corollary to the Monroe Doctrine, officially extending America's power in Central America: henceforth the United States would act as policeman for the region. After 1904 the Panamanian government and economy were effectively dominated by the United States.[22]

United Fruit was attracted to an unpenetrated belt of rainforest along the Caribbean coast, in the Bocas del Toro area of northwest Panama across the border from the Sarapiquí lowlands of Costa Rica. Chiriquí Lagoon, which is partially protected by Bocas del Toro, is some fifty by twenty miles in extent. Strategically located, it lies 150 miles west of where the Panama Canal would ultimately be built. Frederick Adams, the early chronicler of the United Fruit Company, sailed around the bay and its islands in 1914. His lyrical account of Chiriquí Lagoon expresses the delight of northern adventurers in the overwhelming beauty of tropical Nature at its most pristine. In Adams's mind there was no contradiction between delight in wilderness and eagerness to domesticate it.

> The Chiriqui Lagoon is a mass of islands . . . several thousands of them—a perfect labyrinth of tropical islands in a setting which mocks description. Some of these islands rise in cliffs hundreds of feet sheer above the crystal waters that lave their bases. The crests of these heights are fringed with palms and with other tropical trees laden with huge flowers of flaunting colors. Ferns and clinging vines soften the lines of the cliffs. In places the passage between these precipitous islands is so narrow that there is barely room to float a canoe. Only the Indian guides can safely find a way in and out of this tropical wonderland.

On that part of the Panama coast, where rain falls every month of the year, the climate is excellent for growing bananas. Nearly a decade before Adams described this picturesque area, Minor Keith had already organized the Snyder Banana Company in Panama and the Colombia Land Company in the Santa Marta lowlands in a consortium with British investors. Keith preferred American partners, however, and in 1899 he merged his interests with Baker's Boston Fruit Company, creating the United Fruit Company.[23] No one could foresee at the time that this one company would transform the politics and ecology of an entire region and that it would earn the ominous name of "El Pulpo," the octopus. More often it was simply referred to as "the Company."

The new company built its Caribbean headquarters in the little town of Bocas del Toro, on the inland side of Colón Island, looking twenty miles across Almirante Bay to the mainland mountains on the evening horizon. In 1900 the town was a swampy village, with a squatter population of English-speaking Jamaicans living in squalor and disease, probably the descendants of slaves who had escaped the sugar plantations generations before. On higher grounds the company built permanent houses, shops, and a hospital that served its entire operation in western Panama and adjacent Costa Rica.

The first plantations were on Colón Island and along the mainland shore. By 1914 United Fruit controlled 109,000 acres, of which 40,000 acres were already in banana production, and employed nearly 7,000 workers. The company grew Changuinola bananas, the biggest and most expensive on international markets. These bananas averaged sixty-four pounds per bunch, ten pounds heavier than any others. The infrastructure for the operation was impressive: the company built 250 miles of railway spurs, all lined with plantations, through the former wilderness. Although the company's interests were highly specialized, its infrastructure began to open the entire region for general settlement and forest clearance.[24]

United Fruit constructed an integrated operation that ranged from soil management to overland and oversea shipping to wholesale markets in American ports. Keith lost money on most of his railroad contracts, since he had trouble finding enough freight to pay his costs in the first years, but his empire grew in related areas. The Costa Rican government relied on Keith to build the infrastructure of an entire modern economy; in the long run this work probably had as great an impact on the country as the banana operations themselves. Within another few years Keith landed a $600,000 contract to build a municipal tram service for San José and another for the old colonial capital of Cartago. He built a bank in San José, central markets for Cartago and Heredia, and an ice plant in Limón. No one else in the country could remotely compete with him.

Keith and his men were also determined to conquer the lowland diseases. In 1892 the government awarded him a $489,000 contract to build a sanitation and public health system for Limón. San José's *El Heraldo* described the work in grand rhetorical flourishes.

> The work of sanitation is the most urgent. The swamp and the reefs there are stocked with the germs of fever and anemia. No force is too great if it be directed to the destruction of this enemy. But the undertaking is large; it is an enormous undertaking to bring to conclusion this giant task. The necessary man is in Costa Rica. There is Mr. Keith. . . . He is the strength of a long-haired lion mistakenly placed in the body of a man. Nothing is more merited than his . . . fame; he is constant and tireless.[25]

Adams agreed. He offered a condescending assessment of how the region had been before the introduction of Anglo civilization.

> The peoples of Central America were highlanders in the true sense of the word. Nothing but absolute necessity could induce them to venture into the disease-stricken wildernesses which bounded them on the Pacific Ocean and the Caribbean Sea. These desolate regions had for them an absolute terror, and that dread of the lowlands still exists in all classes. . . . No words can describe the horrors and dangers of the few squalid villages which once lay on the water edge of these jungles. Nature had infested these wastes with most of the enemies of mankind, but the ignorance and indifference of those who clustered there added new and more deadly menaces.[26]

The conquest of tropical Nature, bringing the rainforest under the domesticating hand of technology and corporate organization, necessitated the conquest of malaria and yellow fever through municipal drainage and public health projects.

> By filling, draining, oiling and otherwise destroying the breeding places of the poisoning mosquito, and by thoroughly screening all human habitations, yellow fever could be stopped at its source. The epidemics that had ravaged Cuba and the tropics, that had periodically swept over the South and occasionally reached even the ports of New York, Philadelphia and Boston, might, if the work were done effectively, be ended forever.[27]

In retrospect, the eradication of tropical disease was probably the most humanitarian effort that the company made. But even this crusade had an ecological cost in the draining and oiling of coastal wetlands.

Profit from the banana trade continued to be United Fruit's primary interest, and in its pursuit the company extended itself far beyond the borders of Central America. From the start it moved into international transport and marketing, building a totally integrated operation that stretched from plantation to consumer. By 1902 United's own fleet of banana boats, the famous "Great White Fleet," controlled most banana shipping to Europe as well as the United States. By 1912 it also controlled International Railways of Central America; a year later it created the Tropical Radio Telegraph Company, Central America's first, to communicate with its jungle stations. United Fruit had become a managerial and technological empire, indispensable to the republics in which it operated.

Through their operations, the United Fruit Company and its chief competitor, the Standard Fruit Company in Honduras, made the first third of this century the first great era of the banana republics and the first period of extensive clearing of the rainforest. By 1930 United alone exported 65 million bunches of bananas to the United States; it owned 3,482,042 acres of lowland forest, equal to Connecticut and Rhode Island combined. Eighty-five percent of that land was unused, maintained for future exploitation and kept out of the hands of potential competitors.[28]

For its labor force—those anonymous men whose daily struggle was the actual point of confrontation between society and Nature—United relied upon the impoverished rural descendants of Jamaican ex-slaves. The legacy of sugar slavery on that island provided a large pool of laborers. In the decades after emancipation, they were willing to go wherever the wages were good. When the French were making their abortive attempt to build the Panama Canal, 25,000 Jamaicans hired on. When the project failed, the unemployed workers looked for other wage labor in Central America. When the United States revived work on the canal, nearly 50,000 Jamaicans joined the massive crew, earning at least twice what they could have at home. By 1910 Jamaicans had also spread to the banana plantations in Costa Rica, Colombia, Nicaragua, and Honduras and to the sugar plantations in Cuba.

Lorenzo Baker once commented to Olivier that although Jamaican workers did not work well at home, they did in Costa Rica, where they labored on estates for good pay and could be disciplined, if they refused to work, by being arrested and deported. In Costa Rica they had no land on which they could grow food; rather, they bought provisions from company stores at what Baker called reasonable rates. Moreover, he added, company housing was superior to their hovels at home.[29] Indeed, the company had a high degree of control over all aspects of its operations, but although it rewarded disciplined labor, the system could not guarantee that workers would be content or docile forever.

In Costa Rica, United Fruit hired migrant Jamaicans as the primary labor force on its 50,000 acres in Sarapiquí, for the company preferred English speakers. In 1911, 40,000 Jamaicans were working for United in Central America, not only as laborers, but also as foremen, engineers, clerks, managers, and teachers. Although many of these workers were on temporary contracts and moved on when their contracts expired, others remained as squatters, living on the fringes of the plantations.[30] The uprooted men, bound only to industrial and cash structures, had no organic connection to the land.

When it chose a new site for a plantation, the company preferred virgin soil, especially alluvium on riverine terraces. Company laborers removed undergrowth, girdled high trees, and planted banana suckers immediately. Then they felled and burned the tall trees, leaving only native rubber trees standing. Bananas grew fast, smothering the weeds and natural second growth. Long, rational ranks of a single species replaced the infinite, complex variety of the natural forest.

Insatiably expanding, and not constrained by any political boundaries, United Fruit searched for additional potential banana lands along the entire rainforest arc of Central America, including the major Caribbean islands. The company negotiated long leases with governments, or it bought lands outright, often through local middlemen. It was easy to ignore the occupancy rights of indigenous populations in the forest, for they were invisible to both politicians and corporate managers. By 1913

United owned or leased 852,560 acres of rainforest land, including 221,837 acres under cultivation, in Jamaica, Santo Domingo, Cuba, Nicaragua, Honduras, Costa Rica, Panama, and Colombia.

THE FRUIT COMPANIES IN HONDURAS

The biggest prize of all was the windward lowlands of Honduras, which were the largest segment of the Caribbean rainforest belt. The government in Tegucigalpa was eager to have it conquered, for the wide Caribbean coastal plains of Honduras were even more effectively cut off from the centers of settlement in the hills than they were in Costa Rica. In colonial times, the sparse Indian population had been nearly wiped out. The river basins became the major Ladino settlement areas, but even these people were widely dispersed. Through the nineteenth century Honduras had no major export crop and thus achieved little economic growth. By the 1890s the Honduran government had fallen deeply into debt. With an annual income of around $1.6 million, it had contracted $124 million in loans from private banks in London, a staggering debt ratio. Great Britain's fiscal control of Central American regimes was at its peak.

The Caribbean coastal rainforests could provide the wealth needed to lift the country out of lethargy and foreign debt, but massive new investments were necessary to develop them. This is a lowland region, but the terrain is broken by a series of low hill ranges, reaching up to 2,000 feet or so, their soils mostly thin and nutrient-poor. The region is dissected by streams and rivers, the largest being the Ulua and Aguán. Each year brought fresh alluvial sediments down from the hills, slowly building terraces that were ideal for growing bananas. Mangrove swamps alternated with sandy beaches along the coast and farther inland were many marshy areas and shallow lakes.

The American writer O. Henry, describing a fictional town on the adjacent Miskito Coast of Nicaragua in 1912, caught the note of dread and hostility in Yankee perceptions of the rainforest:

> Between the sea and the foothills stretched the five miles' breadth of alluvial coast. Here was the flora of the tropics in its rankest and most prodigal growth. Spaces here and there had been wrested from the jungle and planted with bananas and cane and orange groves. The rest was a riot of wild vegetation, the home of monkeys, tapirs, jaguars, alligators and prodigious reptiles and insects. Where no road was cut a serpent could scarcely make its way through the tangle of vines and creepers. Across the treacherous mangrove swamps few things without wings could safely pass.[31]

The few small riverine and coastal settlements were almost entirely cut off from the interior: indeed, there was no all-weather motor road or railroad to the inland capital of Tegucigalpa until after 1950. This thwarted the Honduran government's efforts to control its tropical frontier when the region began to develop autonomously from the interior hills. By the mid-twentieth century, the northern coast zone had over 20 percent of the national population, and produced half of the national export revenue, its entire railroad system, and most of its industry.[32] This massive and independent development was largely the work of the gringo banana barons, but they in turn built upon a previous generation of local entrepreneurship, ultimately overwhelming it.

When the first foreign banana purchasers dropped anchor off the north coast of Honduras in the late 1870s, they found a series of towns spread along the coast and for some thirty miles up the main rivers. The largest town, with a population of 1,200, was San Pedro Sula, located near the mouth of the Ulua River, just east of the Guatemala border. The local gentry were growing several crops on a small scale, including coconuts, cacao, rubber, bananas, and citrus, for sale to the steamship captains who occasionally stopped along the coast.[33] On acreage that had been cleared for crops and then degraded, they ran scrub Criollo cattle on the meager grass cover, in the traditional Hispanic hacendero style.

Most of the banana growers were *poquiteros,* or small-scale private landowners. One 1899 survey of the north coast counted 1,032 farmers, most of whom had a small acreage of bananas: two-thirds of them cultivated fewer than 10 acres of bananas along with other crops. Yet a total banana acreage of 15,000 acres produced over one million stems for export that year, not a trivial amount for the local economy.

The *poquiteros* cultivated bananas by ancient methods of forest clearing. They cut down the brush and small trees, then burned the slash when it was dry enough. Using wooden dibble sticks in the ashes, they planted bananas and related species of plantains. Weeding was done only once a year and was rough, just enough to inhibit fast-growing weed species from competing with the bananas until the bananas were tall enough to shade the weeds. This system minimized soil and nutrient loss, and it was a sharp contrast to the European practice of clean weeding, which eliminated competition for soil nutrients and was neat and esthetically satisfying to northern eyes. The northern system was labor intensive, and it produced much more soil erosion than tropical techniques.

Local banana growers struggled against cattle ranchers for control of the land. Local growers converted some existing grazing land to export crops, and the municipal governments that they controlled turned over additional public land, most of it still wooded, to local commercial growers. The problem of transporting their crops to northern markets was severe, and they struggled to find reliable steamship purchasers. Looking for economic growth, they began to form growers' associations in 1887 to negotiate with purchasers; they even attempted to set up a steamship service to New Orleans. In the long run, all these local co-operatives failed, either because of internal dissension or because they were overwhelmed by the gringos' corporate scale and market knowledge.

In the 1890s the commercial gentry, impatient for market growth and increased profits, turned their hopes to railroads as a replacement for river transport, which was risky and unpredictable. They lobbied the national government for land concessions to foreign railroad builders. They found an attentive ear in the governing elite, who were moving in the same direction by encouraging industrial technology and corporate investment, influenced by the doctrines of European liberalism. One of its tenets was "scientific agriculture," which assumed that agricultural expansion was the basis of a strong economy and that monoculture, efficiency, and a standard quality of product were the hallmarks of progress. By 1890 this ideology exercised a strong influence on government policies.

This all meant opportunities for Yankee immigrants. A miscellaneous lot of Americans had already begun filtering into the region. As early as the 1870s there were three hundred of them in San Pedro Sula, one-fourth of the town's population, looking for land grants and commercial contracts. U.S. consulates had been involved in commercial probes since the 1830s. Working with the International Office of the U.S. Department of Commerce, they monitored commercial possibilities and sent reports back to Washington.

By the 1870s American steamships were stopping at all the coastal towns. In 1877 the Oteri and Brothers steamship line began service from New Orleans. Soon it had several competitors, most of them from New Orleans but some from New York; all were irregular and unpredictable. In 1894 the Honduran government exempted two U.S. companies, Macheca Brothers of New Orleans and Williams and Renkin of New York, from port duties. Even with this advantage, the two companies could not withstand the challenge of the ultimate winners.

By the late 1890s small-scale farmers on the Mississippi delta had become a major source of fruits and vegetables for urban markets around the southern states. Many Italian and Sicilian immigrants were attracted by the region's intensive agriculture and marketing, including Joseph, Luca, and Felix Vaccaro. The brothers became successful brokers of locally grown oranges. Louisiana citrus farming was wiped out in February 1899 by a cold wave that plunged temperatures to minus seven degrees Fahrenheit, the coldest temperature ever recorded that far south. Having nothing to lose, the Vaccaro brothers decided to turn their entrepreneurial talents to Honduras, where crops would never be touched by frost and where they could diversify by purchasing coconuts and bananas as well as oranges. The brothers founded the Standard Fruit Company, which proved so successful that it became United Fruit's primary competitor in the international banana business and more than its equal in southern U.S. markets.

A competitor of the Vaccaros, Samuel Zemurray, arrived in Honduras from New Orleans in 1905. By 1910 he had leased 5,000 acres on the Cuyamel River, and founded the Cuyamel Fruit Company. Shortly thereafter Zemurray gambled with the future by buying an additional 15,000 acres, so as to outflank the Vaccaros. This triggered a corporate race to control Central America's largest rainforest, and soon the north coast was largely controlled by the rivalry of the two companies. Great banana plantations arose around San Pedro Sula, in the Ulúa-Chamelecón basin near the Guatemalan border; San Pedro Sula became the second largest city of Honduras in the process.[34]

The economic success of the foreign fruit companies depended on the efficiencies of large-scale production, processing, and transportation, which would be viable only if the companies could be sure of major land leases and infrastructure concessions for long periods of time. They insisted on full legal support from the government, which was far less stable than its Costa Rican counterpart. This led to intricate political maneuvering in which the fruit companies had the full backing of the United States government.

The Honduran government wanted a share of the profits. In 1893 it passed the first national law related to the banana industry, establishing a 2 percent duty on the value of exported bananas. This tax was collected quixotically, for the government had barely begun to develop a presence on the coast. More important was its power to grant land concessions. The government was desperately eager to establish fast, reliable transport from the capital to the coastal region. Following the international strategy of the time, it granted foreign firms extensive land rights in return for a commitment to build railroad lines not only from the coast into the areas that the companies wanted to open for banana production, but all the way through the hills to Tegucigalpa. In the early years most concessions were either fifty-year leases of government land or outright land sales. The government, eager to convert forest to taxable agriculture, commonly stipulated to private purchasers that the alienated lands had to be cleared for agriculture within a certain period, often five years. This provision was rarely enforced against the banana corporations.

The Honduran government was inconsistent regarding sales to foreigners. An 1895 law guaranteed homesteaders alternate lots along railroads, so as to prevent the companies from completely dominating vast regions of rainforest. Moreover, an 1898 agrarian law prohibited public land sales within eight miles of the coast. In 1906, in a rising tide of anti-American feeling, this was extended to thirty miles from the coast. But the major companies could usually either evade the restrictions or force their repeal. In many instances the companies bought the proscribed lots through intermediaries or from the individuals that owned them.[35]

These manipulations went too far for the nationalist element in the Honduran Congress, where anti-American feeling was running strong. A new law promulgated in 1909 required the government to grant only temporary use of government lands to foreigners—they were not to be given full title. Facing severe factionalism and political instability in Tegucigalpa, the companies fought fire with fire, financing rival contestants for power. Honduras's two political parties, locked in a protracted struggle, encouraged the meddling of the banana barons. The companies insisted on favors in return.

In a particularly notorious instance, Zemurray cultivated close relations with Honduran president Manuel Bonilla. When forces supporting Bonilla's anti-American rival, Miguel Dávila, overthrew him in 1907 and the British demanded repayment of their loans, the U.S. State Department saw a strategic opportunity. Secretary of State Philander Knox, working with J. P. Morgan and other American private bankers, was attempting to replace British banking interests throughout the Caribbean Basin. Not to be displaced, Zemurray financed a little army led by a New Orleans soldier of fortune named Lee Christmas, which invaded Honduras by a north coast landing in 1911 in support of Bonilla. The United States withdrew its support from Dávila and reinstated Bonilla.

As a reward for his efforts, Christmas was appointed U.S. consul for Honduras. In gratitude to Zemurray, President Bonilla had the land law revoked by his congress, paving the way for large sales of land to northern speculators. As historian Walter LaFeber acidly concludes, "If Honduras was dependent on the fruit companies before 1912, it was virtually indistinguishable from them after 1912."[36]

This suited U.S. strategic interests. In 1911 President William Howard Taft proclaimed, "It should be the policy of this Government, especially with respect to countries in geographical proximity to the Canal Zone, to give to them when requested all proper assistance . . . in the promotion of peace, in the development of their resources, and in a sound reorganization of their fiscal systems."[37] The strategic ambitions of the American imperium were forging an alliance with the corporate powers that were leading the conquest of the rainforest.

No more than a year later two concessions were sold to Zemurray, who proceeded to make one of them, Tela, the center of his operations. Through their influence, the Vaccaro brothers had gained only the use of alternating plots; Zemurray gained ownership of 766 acres per mile, including the land under his branch lines.

The fruit companies did not uphold their side of the bargain in the railroad contracts. Between them in the years that followed they built 1,000 miles of railroad to serve the region's fruit economy, but they did not complete the connection through the hills to Tegucigalpa that they had agreed to build. The link would bring them no profits, only greater government influence over their operations.

In the tropical lowlands land laws might be in place, but little land was actually surveyed in detail, and local ownership or usufruct rights were rarely clear. Entrepreneurs eager to get on with their work did not bother to wait for the surveyors to arrive. Instead, they used what was called a denouncement procedure, similar to the one used by homesteaders in the United States. Anyone interested in a specific parcel of land could "denounce" it in public, then request an auction. This procedure was abused—as it was in the western United States—by agents of local and foreign speculators.[38] The fruit companies were free to accelerate the process of forest clearance.

On the north coast the fruit companies proceeded to transform land—mostly marshland and forests—into plantations. From the start they had to build a transport infrastructure, where little or none existed. They built railroads and port facilities. They straightened riverbeds, applying technology that the U.S. Army Corps of Engineers had been developing in the eastern United States since the early 1800s. Streambed by streambed the corps had domesticated eastern North America's rivers by 1900.

Standard Fruit set about transforming the hinterland of La Ceiba on the central north coast.[39] Between 1904 and 1910 the Vaccaros gained three railroad concessions to link plantations with La Ceiba, and by 1915 they had built 96 miles of rail lines. At the port they built a long pier so that bananas could be loaded directly from boxcars onto waiting steamers. In 1913 they exported over 2.8 million stems; by 1919 the figure had risen to a spectacular 5.5 million stems.

In 1919 Standard Fruit began extending its railroad east into previously untouched forestlands in the Aguán River valley. The company planted not just bananas; in addition it put some acreage into sugar cane and some into oranges. Degraded lands that came into its hands were turned into largely unmanaged cattle pasture. By the late 1920s the hinterland of La Ceiba was a patchwork of forest and banana plantations, interspersed with smaller amounts of other crops, pasture, and an occasional abandoned field in which random stalks of sugar cane were being choked out by weedy secondary woodland species. Company-built railroads were opening up the region to general settlement; old towns grew and new ones were established.[40]

Standard's major competitor was Sam Zemurray's Cuyamel Fruit Company. Zemurray founded his railroad, the Tela Railroad Company, in 1912 on the basis of the land concession that he extracted from the Honduran government.[41] His crews immediately attacked the forests growing on the rich soils of the Ulúa River lowlands. Zemurray imported construction materials duty-free and assembled a crew of 500 workers. By 1921 they had built 200 miles of track, including both mainline and narrow-gauge feeder lines. Banana exports from Tela rose exponentially. In 1915 the tiny port shipped 1,203,500 stems; five years later, in 1920, that figure leaped to 4,576,500. Most of the farms that produced those millions of stems were created on valley and bottomland that was newly cleared of species ranging from mangrove to palm to mixed hardwood and bamboo.

The poorly drained, marshy lands impeded the extension of the rail lines, so Zemurray began draining wide areas of wetlands.[42] Paul Standley, the leading Mesoamerica biologist of those years, surveyed the area in 1927–1928 and wrote an incisive description of the transformation.

Practically all the land within this area that is fit for the purpose is covered
with banana plants, which, however beautiful when standing alone or in
moderate quantities, become exceedingly monotonous when massed in plantations many miles in extent. Between banana plantations however are large
areas unsuited for their cultivation. These consist, near the coast, of wide
marshes and of densely wooded swamps which cannot, or at least have not,
been drained. . . . Much swamp land has been ditched and planted. The most
spectacular of these unused areas is the great Toloa Swamp that is crossed
by the railroad as it approaches the Ulúa River from Tela. It is like many
other swamps or marshes in Central America, a shallow lake with an abundance of aquatic plants, and such a profusion of water birds as one sees only
in the tropics.[43]

Draining the marshlands reduced avian habitat, including that of migratory birds. By the 1920s Cuyamel, steadily expanding its engineering
works, also diverted silt-laden annual floodwaters into lagoons to build
them up for banana production. By 1930 its system of drainage canals
and dikes included 90,000 feet of canals and 44,000 feet of dikes. The
company's enormous extent of domesticated land enabled it to export
over ten million stems of bananas that year. By then, although the upland forests on its concessions remained largely in their natural condition, the species composition in the valleys and river bottoms had
changed to the monotony of acre after acre of bananas.

In these years Zemurray held two major territorial concessions in
addition to his holdings in Tela. One provided the base for his Truxillo
Railroad Company, which he built farther east in Colón province, where
there had been little farming and settlement before 1900 and no banana
exports.[44] When Zemurray began construction in Colón he found the
usual mix of coconut and rubber groves and many small cattle haciendas, as well as some small timber operations that were busy extracting
mahogany. After 1915 the Truxillo Railroad opened rail lines and established its own plantations, but it also continued to buy bananas from
local small producers.

In the beginning Zemurray optimistically projected a potential of 20
million stems from that area, but that turned out to be far too optimistic.
This region had poor soils and it suffered periodic drought, plagues of
grasshoppers, and powerful storm winds, which made the investment
less securely profitable than Zemurray had originally imagined. A less
grandiose or better informed plan might have resulted in the clearance
of less natural land, but the dream of limitless profits dictated otherwise.
Zemurray continued opening new plantations as his crews built more
feeder lines and leveled more forest. In 1919 the Truxillo Company had

32,250 acres in bananas, producing 7.6 million stems. By the early 1930s new plantations covered both banks of the lower Aguán valley.

Between 1910 and 1930 Zemurray's largest operation was the Cuyamel Fruit Company, his original holding, which exploited a region farther west, the hinterland of Puerto Cortes, almost to the Guatemalan border.[45] Here the Hondurans themselves had built the national railroad in the 1890s, penetrating inland from Puerto Cortes for sixty miles and opening the Ulúa and Chamelecón river valleys.

In 1910 three major growers shipped 1.5 million stems of bananas from Cortes, produced on over 17,500 acres of plantation land. Cuyamel and Standard were two of these growers; the third was an American, William Streich, who had extracted a land concession from the Honduran government in 1902. This was a vast area of forests, banana groves, marshes, and coastal mangrove swamps. Its thickest vegetation grew on alluvial terraces close to riverbanks, precisely the land on which a sea of banana plants would grow. This great tract was so extensive that many independent growers, who owned a few to a few thousand acres, could continue to produce bananas for export from Puerto Cortes. This area did not become a monolithic unit of ownership and management.

In the 1920s the Cuyamel Fruit Company opened a large area of the adjacent Ulúa and Chamelecón river basins. There the company grew bananas on lands cleared from virgin forest and on acreage that had been under other crops. On part of that concession Zemurray set up the Sula Sugar Company, with a modern processing plant ten miles east of San Pedro Sula.

Banana exports from Puerto Cortes reached 5.1 million stems in 1925. The figure declined to 4.0 million in 1926, reflecting a series of troubles: fires in the cane fields, blowdowns from windstorms, and grasshoppers. In 1927 the Sula Sugar Company exported 20,000 tons of semirefined sugar from the basin.

In 1927 Zemurray negotiated a new contract with the Honduran government that allowed him to construct major irrigation works along the Ulúa and Chamelecón rivers. The contract stipulated that he could tap groundwater but must not disrupt river navigation. His crews proceeded to drain swamps and divert nutrient-rich silt into other lowlands. By 1930 the Cuyamel Company was irrigating 15,561 acres for banana plantations, had an additional 54,120 acres in bananas, sugar, and coconuts, and owned an additional 56,810 acres of forest and swamp.

The north coast as a whole reached its maximum banana production between 1929 and 1931, when 30 million bunches were exported from Honduras annually, a remarkable one-third of total world exports. Most of them were shipped directly to ports on the East and Gulf Coasts of the United States. For an operation on that scale, Zemurray and the Vaccaro brothers brought in a very large population of workers and their dependants. This had a regionwide ecological impact that added to the accumulating damage that a disrupted peasantry both reflected and accelerated.

Traditional economic wisdom has maintained that the corporate enclaves were almost entirely self-contained and contributed little to national economies. Recent research has begun to show that this somewhat misses the point. As in any plantation system (including the colonial slave sugar estates), workers were drawn from a wide area, which affected their home locations, and food had to be grown to feed them. The environmental consequences of plantation enclaves, therefore, were complex and wide reaching, becoming more difficult to distinguish from other factors as they spread farther from the plantation lands.[46]

United's operations from Guatemala to Colombia were inextricably entwined with American strategic and economic interests throughout the region. The company was closely linked with Washington from President Woodrow Wilson's administration onward, as part of an overall American strategy to displace British economic hegemony throughout Central America.[47] This was as clear in Guatemala as in Honduras.

Across the border from United's plantations on the north coast of Honduras lay Guatemala, which was becoming another U.S. protectorate. Until the 1930s banana production in Guatemala was centered in the lower Motagua River valley in the Caribbean lowlands, where the Cuyamel Fruit Company had expanded from Honduras under Zemurray's direction. Between 1913 and 1929 Guatemala's banana exports to the United States rose by over 150 percent. In 1929, the country's exports totaled $25 million—$17 million were coffee and $3 million were bananas; all the bananas were grown in the lower Motagua valley. Then the bonanza burst: subsequent production declined because of the low international prices for bananas during the Depression.

In Honduras and Guatemala, as well as in Costa Rica and Panama, the economic difficulties of the Depression intersected with an ecological crisis that hit the banana companies in the form of soil depletion and plant disease. Both United, which had bought Zemurray's empire in 1929, and Standard were forced into the major task of shifting their production bases from the Caribbean to the Pacific coast. The damage they had done in the Caribbean lowlands was about to be repeated—with the concurrence of all four national governments—on the other coast.

MONOCROP DISEASES AND CORPORATE RESPONSES

The heady early days of the corporate plantations were more precarious than any banana grower had dreamed at the dawn of the banana era. Monocrop agriculture destabilized tropical nature, inviting disaster. Subsistence producers had always grown several varieties of bananas and plantains for their own and local consumption, but a large concentration of any single-species product virtually assured massive attack by some species of micropredator. Disaster struck in the form of a root mold, *Fusarium,* which attacked the Gros Michel banana, the only banana variety then in mass production. Discovered first in 1903 on a plantation in Panama, it was soon known as Panama disease.

Panama disease was carried in the soil. Commercial propagation of the banana, thousands of plants at a time, could be done only by dividing the rootstock of existing plants, a process that transmitted the root mold. The planters could not interrupt the disease cycle, as they might have if propagation had been done by seed. After Panama disease struck, plantations usually lived only for eight to ten years before they shriveled. The first local production declines were in 1913, and by the 1920s the epidemic was advancing rapidly through the entire Caribbean coastal region, threatening to destroy the entire industry. In Honduras Panama disease was a serious problem on the oldest plantations by 1918. Production on Standard Fruit's first plantations began falling severely in the early 1920s. Production dropped from 4,337,000 bunches in 1922 to 1,920,000 bunches in 1927. The Cuyamel Fruit Company began steadily abandoning farms from the mid-1920s onward. On the great Truxillo concession, old farms were gradually closed. In the early 1920s an annual average of 30,000 to 37,500 acres were in bananas, but by 1928 25,000 acres had been abandoned. In the early 1930s the Truxillo Railroad Company's concession gave its new owner, United Fruit, management of 132,500 acres of national lands, and legal rights to 217,500 acres more, but in 1933 the company "magnanimously" renounced these additional lands. Primarily because of Panama disease, United had abandoned this great tract by the early 1930s.[48]

Operations as far-flung as these, in which many millions of dollars were invested, had to be supported by agronomic research on a scale that no small producer could finance. Zemurray had the financial resources to hire the best available tropical botanists. The Cuyamel Fruit Company set up a research laboratory and experimental farm at Lancetilla, a short distance inland from Tela, which quickly became the finest tropical crop research center in all of Central America. In 1925 Zemurray hired Wilson Popenoe, the leading American tropical botanist of his time, to head the laboratory and experimental farm; after Cuyamel was sold to the United Fruit Company in 1929, Popenoe became head agronomist of the company's research operations. The son of a mining engineer who had spent many years in Central and South America, Popenoe was a pomologist (more specifically a world authority on avocados) and soil expert. He had compiled years of experience as an agricultural explorer for the U.S. Department of Agriculture's Division of Foreign Seed and Plant Introduction and was the author of a standard book on tropical agronomy.[49] Popenoe was responsible (as his biographer later put it) for "overseeing production on more than one hundred thousand acres of banana plantation in seven or eight Middle American countries and directing the fight against the various diseases attacking the banana plant; and the creator of a tropical experimental garden in the jungles of Lancetilla Valley."[50]

Popenoe and the plant pathologists at United Fruit's chemical laboratory worked feverishly to eradicate or at least control Panama disease, but had no success, even after years of effort. Exacerbating the growers' difficulties, in the 1920s a second disease appeared on the monocrop plantations, Sigatoka. First detected in the Fiji Islands, Sigatoka was an airborne fungus, attacking the leaves of the banana plants, withering them as their fruit neared ripening. Sigatoka hit Central America hard, compounding the damage caused by Panama disease. By the mid-1930s Sigatoka had infected 80 percent of Honduras's crop, and its effects were almost as bad elsewhere.

By the mid-1920s—rather quickly—United's pathologists had learned that Sigatoka could be controlled by spraying the plants with Bordeaux mixture, a copper sulfate or arsenic solution. The treatment was expensive. Many small growers, who could not afford the additional expense, were ruined, which helped to increase the corporations' monopoly of commercial production. No remedy for Panama disease had been found, however, and the viability of the commercial growers was at grave risk as well. It was ironic: the monocrop system established by the banana barons had increased their profits, but it also spread the devastating diseases that increased the chance that their empires might literally wither away.

Two strategies could possibly save the industry from total collapse. Growers could move their plantations to new soil every decade, clearing new forest each time. This course would be extremely expensive—and ecologically disastrous. The alternative was to develop disease-resistant varieties of banana that would be commercially acceptable in the United States and Europe. Researchers strove to perfect these bananas, working on variants of the Giant Cavendish banana, but they did not achieve real success until the late 1950s. Until then the only available strategy was to continue moving every ten years or so, abandoning the banana plantations to other crops.

In Costa Rica large-scale abandonment of Caribbean coast plantations began in 1926, when United Fruit closed operations on the large Santa Clara tract near Limón.[51] After removing everything with any monetary value, the company turned over some of its banana lands to the government. It left other lands to its Jamaican workers, whom it had to lay off because the government refused to allow Afro-Caribbeans to work in United's new plantations on the Pacific coast. Workers' towns crumbled. A vivid example was Limón, United's chief port in Costa Rica, which was left to decay when its Santa Clara division was abandoned. In Talamanca, near the Panama border, where banana production also collapsed in the late 1920s, the company removed everything, including rails, bridges, and telephones. Only a mixed population of Jamaicans, Ladinos, and Indians were left on and around the abandoned plantations. They cultivated a variety of food crops on small plots while secondary woodlands grew up around them and weeds reclaimed the streets of formerly bustling towns.[52]

THE SHIFT TO THE PACIFIC COAST

Even before the Depression settled in along the Caribbean coast, bringing economic dislocation, Panama disease had caused such devastation on the older banana plantations that the two major companies had begun to shift their operations across the peninsula to the previously undeveloped Pacific lowlands. The Pacific coastal plain, which lies against the steep slopes of the cordillera, is far narrower at most points than are the Caribbean lowlands. On the Central American peninsula the rain is brought from the northeast by Caribbean trade winds; along the north-western coast of South America it is brought off the Pacific by the Humboldt Current. Where the central mountains are high enough to block the moisture-laden trade winds—from Mexico and Guatemala as far south as Guanacaste and the Nicoya Peninsula in western Costa Rica—the Pacific lowlands are dry during the cool months. Beyond that, along the rest of Costa Rica and Panama, and south along the Pacific through Colombia and Ecuador, lies a rainforest belt that is wet nearly all year. The moisture and the rich volcanic soils that had collected in alluvial fans along the area's many short rivers supported a rainforest that in the 1920s was as biotically varied as the Caribbean forest.

Writings of the times give glimpses of the anonymous individual gringos, many of them rootless, who assisted with the conquest of tropical Nature throughout the region. In 1929 Samuel Crowther described the still tenuous connection between Tegucigalpa and the coast. One rough dirt road snaked up through the mountains; "over it go all the goods from the Pacific on mule back, or ox cart, or in American motor trucks manned by daredevil, cheerful looking American drivers who have drifted into this section of the world. They manage to stand ten hours a day of steady bumping."[53] Any expatriate Yankee who could work the powerful new machinery made his contribution, but no individual could match the systemic power of the great companies.

In 1920, United Fruit obtained approximately 175,000 acres on the Pacific coast of Costa Rica. In order to buy land cheaply at auction, United frequently used local intermediaries, who disguised the fact that they were in the giant's pocket. This practice put it at odds with the Costa Rican government, which by then was attempting to curb the company's power.

> Although sub-rosa the company and the government endeavored to seek some satisfactory solution, on the surface neither appeared to be doing anything. The company maintained its exploring and investigating parties in different parts of the country and even after the withdrawal of its proposals it acquired large tracts of land which had been bought by individuals who undoubtedly were using company money.[54]

By 1938 United had shifted all its Costa Rican operations to the Pacific coast.

In Panama the company's strategy was the same. United bought 17,000 acres of forest through its intermediary, C. W. Mueller of Panama City, and took thirty-year leases from the Panamanian government on two large parcels in the Puerto Armuelles district on the Pacific coast,

just east of the Costa Rica border. A year later the company abandoned
its Bocas del Toro operations and, operating through its subsidiary, the
Chiriquí Land Company, moved to the new little port of Puerto Armuelles, located at the head of the Burica Peninsula. Panama's government paid for a thirty-four-mile extension of its national railroad
through the company's new region to the coast. United paid for the new
wharf facilities that made Puerto Armuelles a viable deep-water port.
The company and a compliant government thus opened a previously
"neglected" section of Panama's rainforest region to general development.

In Guatemala, Panama disease and Sigatoka hit the Motagua valley
plantations in the late 1920s, so United shifted this operation to the
Tiquisate area of the Pacific lowlands. The company had begun to explore that coast in the early 1920s in response to European and Cali-
fornian competitors' efforts to develop a source for West Coast markets.[55] The company faced serious disadvantages on the Pacific coast of
Guatemala: Tiquisate did not have a good harbor, the construction of
communication and transportation systems to the interior had hardly
begun, and the area was prone to drought. Yet by the late 1930s the
region's annual production averaged 167,000 tons.[56]

Throughout Central America the banana frontier was shifting from
one coast to the other, clearing additional rainforest in large blocks.
Whenever the companies moved on, they left behind a degraded landscape and unemployed workers who had to improvise to survive on the
land.

BANANA POLITICS AND THE CONTROL
OF NATURAL RESOURCES

In the same years political conditions were beginning to shift in ways
that would ultimately change the pattern of land management in Central
America, ending the total domination of foreign corporations that were
largely committed to one crop, the Gros Michel banana. The Depression
years witnessed increasing controversy between United Fruit and an assertive Costa Rican government.[57]

In the 1930s the foreign corporations' power was seriously challenged, both by governments determined to claim a larger share of the
wealth and by workers determined to improve their pay and working
conditions. By the late 1930s the companies could no longer operate
with a totally free hand. By the 1950s this shift in power led the com-

panies to sell most of their direct interests in Central American land. Instead they worked through local subsidiaries or semi-independent producers, which for the most part eliminated any direct American corporate connection to the labor force or to working conditions on the land. This arrangement presented a more elusive target for nationalist attacks: it became more difficult to determine where responsibility lay for sustainable land management.

Neither governments nor organized labor were yet consciously concerned about resource sustainability, for the rainforest was still just beginning to be penetrated on a large scale. Forest cover was still abundant on the frontier of every Central American country except El Salvador. National governments tried to maintain the delicate balance between enticing the companies and giving away sovereignty. Once the companies were deeply committed, governments could begin harder bargaining.

The government of Costa Rica led the way throughout this long period in devising ways of holding the companies accountable to the terms of their contracts and assuring the division of their profits.[58] From as early as 1892 the Costa Rican congress made efforts to establish an export tax on bananas. For a long period it mostly failed, outmaneuvered by the foreign monopoly's great economic and political power. The classic contract between United Fruit and a Central American government was signed in 1900, allowing United to export all of its bananas without a tariff for ten years, even though local exporters had to pay the banana tax. In 1910 the Costa Rican congress established an export tax of one cent per bunch, but United forced it to lock that trivial figure in place for twenty years.

In 1929, shortly before the Depression's onset, the Costa Rican government negotiated a new contract with United Fruit for the next twenty years. The government's first proposal projected a tax of five cents per bunch for the first six million bunches per year, four cents for the next eight million, and three cents beyond that. In response, United threatened to move its operations entirely out of Costa Rica to rival countries. This was not an idle threat. After the onset of the banana diseases, the company had hired some of the world's highest paid soil scientists to look for new sites.

A compromise contract adopted in 1930 showed how little even a strong local government could yet do against a corporate giant and the benefits that it alone could promise. The contract established a tax of two cents on each bunch of bananas until 1950. It also allowed the company to expand its railroads wherever necessary for its crops and to remove or change rail lines even on public lands. Further, United gained the right to build a new port, Golfito, on the Golfo Dulce on the Pacific. In return the company agreed to give the government a trivial 5,300 acres of abandoned plantation land outside Limón, on which the government would establish new agricultural colonies for local workers who had been left unemployed by the company's move to the Pacific coast.[59] This agreement blatantly favored the interests of United Fruit: the company could now legally expand its operations to an entirely new sector of the region.

United Fruit found that such favorable treatment no longer could be acquired without a political price. The forces of Latin nationalism had strengthened against Yankee imperialism. When the agreement was ratified in the legislature, twelve deputies walked out. They protested that "[t]he United Fruit Company has imposed upon our Atlantic coast an economic system with a notorious trend. . . . [I]t has exhausted the lands while accumulating its wealth."[60] The first priority of the Costa Rican Congress was to institute higher export taxes and strengthen regulatory control over the company. This goal could not be achieved during the Depression decade, for Costa Rica's economy, like those of its neighbors, was in disarray from the steep decline in primary exports brought on by the international economic crisis. Any new agricultural development had to be welcomed, on whatever terms could be negotiated.

Anti-American sentiment was nothing new. It arose in each country of Latin America almost as early as U.S. capital penetrated its frontiers. The Latin American labor movement, greatly influenced by rising Bolshevism in Russia, combined resistance to oligarchic government with hostility toward gringo corporate imperialism. The movement emerged first in Mexico; the constitution of 1917 included provisions for labor reform and curbs on the foreign ownership of land. By 1919 Communist parties had been established in many Latin American countries.

Naturally enough, nationalist fervor tended to focus on major corporations like the United Fruit Company. In the first years of the century confident Yankee executives and their defenders were accustomed to treating that sentiment as another routinely annoying hindrance to their work. As early as 1914, Crowther, who was an apologist for United Fruit, wrote,

> There is a considerable amount of anti-American propaganda throughout
> the Caribbean countries. It is in part communistic and in part commercial
> and also it is mixed up with Pan-Latinism. . . . It is something for the intel-
> ligentsia to write about and it is a safe subject for orators. The communistic
> movement is not important and has no real following. It becomes important
> only when it is used for some ulterior purpose such as stirring up strikes on
> American property or covering revolutionary movements or for some other
> political necessity.[61]

The labor movement meant far more than that. Peasants who had
been transformed by American interests into a concentrated wage labor
force were in a position to organize. The first major labor protest in
Central America focused on the United Fruit Company in Honduras. In
the early 1920s its headquarters in Tela was the target of a series of
strikes. The actions of the fruit corporations were supported by the expanding strategic interests of the American government, which was determined to maintain its hegemony over the Panama Canal and the surrounding region. That policy led the United States to prop up any local
regime that supported U.S. economic investment and, thus, furthered
American domination of Central America and the Caribbean. Frank
Polk, the U.S. undersecretary of state, said of U.S. policy in World War
I, "It is sure that the State Department . . . tried to keep alive the fruit
trade with Central America, not because we wanted to send anything
there, but because the export of fruit was the sole means of support of
several of these republics."[62]

In the 1920s, in the isolationist days of Warren Harding's administration, Washington moved gradually away from direct intervention in
the region toward more indirect control by backing, often implicitly, the
financial and corporate domination of the region by private banks and
corporations.[63] Dana Munro, a top Central America specialist in the U.S.
Department of State throughout the 1920s, argued in retrospect many
years later that the department

> was interested in promoting trade and finding profitable opportunities for
> the investment of American capital abroad. Helping Americans who found
> themselves in difficulties in foreign countries was an important part of its
> work. . . . [Indeed,] the fruit companies in Central America often took care
> of their own interests in ways that the department strongly disapproved of.[64]

The policy of the U.S. government by the mid-1920s was to protect
American hegemony in the western hemisphere without going so far as
to maintain its protectorates. In 1923 Secretary of State Charles Evans
Hughes put it clearly, stating that the United States should withdraw

from Caribbean protectorates, but he insisted on orderly governments that could effectively protect free international trade, which clearly meant the work of American firms.

> No arrangement should be entered into, or resolution concurred in, which could possibly be interpreted as curtailing in any way the full scope of the rights today asserted by the U.S. under the Monroe Doctrine. Thus there should be no opening for curtailment of those rights through acquiescence in any arrangement whereby an American State could at will accept even the slightest non-American control of its territory or independence.

Hughes's principles included promoting stability and resisting confiscation of property. "In promoting stability we do not threaten independence, but seek to conserve it. We are not aiming at control, but endeavoring to establish self-control. We are not seeking to add to our territory or to impose our rule upon other peoples."[65] But he insisted on countries' responsibility to guard foreign property.

Throughout Central America Yankee political hegemony was reinforced as antigringo nationalism and Marxist workers' movements heated up. The government in Washington and corporate investors in New York and elsewhere cooperated closely, for imports of several primary products from Central America were increasing rapidly. By 1929 the United States was the dominant importer of bananas from all Central American countries except El Salvador, where Germany remained dominant, and Costa Rica, where Britain was primary.[66]

The closest ongoing link between the fruit companies and the U.S. government was the group of American consuls at their posts, who were the key sources of commercial intelligence for the companies. Their reports to the U.S. Department of Commerce gave detailed on-the-spot analyses of market conditions and investment opportunities and sometimes in the process offered insights into environmental conditions on the land.[67]

Central American governments set about repressing labor resistance with the full backing of American power. In the late 1920s international markets for tropical commodities were increasingly unstable, sending tremors through the neocolonial agricultural economies and drawing governments and the fruit companies closer together as unemployment rose and workers became more distressed.

In Nicaragua César Augusto Sandino raised a rebellion against the oligarchy in 1926 by organizing a guerrilla movement in the hills east of Managua. He also turned his attention to the United Fruit Company, pushing for better working conditions and higher wages for the plantation workers. The liberals demanded dismantling of the great estates, or *latifundia,* so that good soils would be available to peasants to grow their own subsistence crops. This policy gradually began to change management of the banana lands and surrounding forest areas.

The Depression accelerated the trend toward political unrest, as Americans and Europeans cut back on their consumption of such optional items in their market baskets as bananas. Markets and production shrank drastically; unemployment was widespread, and worker desperation was rising against companies and governments alike. Economic losses were so massive that governments saw themselves squeezed between the demands of the labor movements and the demands of the fruit companies.

The most intense Depression-triggered conflict occurred, once again, in Honduras, where a protest against United Fruit broke out in 1931, most specifically over water rights. United's 1929 purchase of the Cuyamel Fruit Company had included a sophisticated irrigation system that watered thousands of acres in the Aguán valley. In 1931 United wanted to add 24,000 acres more to the system, and it petitioned the Honduran congress for the water rights, using the usual array of pressure tactics to gain its goal. However, a 1927 law stipulated that irrigation water was to be delivered free to holdings under 50 acres; for any larger acreage a fee of $2.50 per acre per year would be charged for using national waters. United's request was met by public demonstrations that demanded that the company be charged $25 per acre. Soon an insurrection broke out. Intended to end the alliance between the company and the government, it was yet another of the armed conflicts that had wracked Honduras for decades. The fighting began with a small uprising at Progreso, located in the banana zone. It was led by General Gregorio Ferrera, a full-blooded Indian who had attempted a revolution against the Honduran government in 1924 and again in 1925. Government forces retaliated, and Ferrera was killed in June. As the death toll rose, the insurrection faded away, and no further threat to the company's operations arose during the Depression years.[68]

In Costa Rica a more sustained labor protest movement developed. There the Communist Party was founded in 1931. Under its leadership a massive strike of banana workers began in 1934. The Costa Rican government, less repressive than other Central American regimes, finally forced United Fruit to instate better working conditions.[69] The days of totally unregulated company control of its concessions were ending. The challenges that United and Standard faced in the coming years were even more desperate.

THE CAVENDISH ERA AND INTERNATIONAL DIVERSIFICATION

By the early postwar years the virtually autonomous power that the monolithic corporations asserted over entire rainforest regions was beginning to fade. Major shifts in both export purchases and production locations occurred in the postwar years. During World War II, crop shipments to Europe had been badly disrupted. Total exports from Central America fell by over one-half and did not begin to rise again until 1945. The United States maintained production and import figures that were closer to prewar levels, despite the difficulties with banana diseases and the diversion of much of United Fruit's Great White Fleet into wartime work.[70] In 1945 the American fruit corporations dominated international markets even more than they had before the war. In the immediate postwar years U.S. consumption remained almost steady. Although the American population grew rapidly during the baby boom, per capita consumption had fallen by about 20 percent by the mid-1960s. The nation's annual imports, which averaged 1,301,000 stems in 1938, rose only to 1,675,000 in 1964.[71]

Western Europe's consumption of bananas, in contrast, rose rapidly in its recovery period, but several countries of the new Common Market preferred the product of specialized sources in Africa. Italy imported its bananas mostly from Somalia, while France imported them from its colonies in West Africa. West Germany and the Low Countries drew from Latin America. The United Kingdom still imported 90 percent of its bananas from the Commonwealth soils of Jamaica and the Windward Islands.[72] Western Europe's average annual imports of 741,000 stems in the mid-1930s rose to 1,989,000 by 1964.[73]

The banana companies made a major genetic and commercial breakthrough in the 1950s, when they finally established that a different species of banana, the Giant Cavendish, did not carry Panama disease. They began a long and complex process of changing production in Central America from the Gros Michel to varieties of Cavendish, which they developed on their experimental farms. They also continued to search for new locations and to diversify the range of fruits and other export crops that they produced.

THE GEOGRAPHICAL MOBILITY OF THE
MULTINATIONALS: COLOMBIA AND ECUADOR

In Colombia and Ecuador the political economy of fruit production was
rather different from that in Central America: the banana corporations
never dominated the national governments, as they did in the smaller
countries to the north. In the early 1900s United Fruit organized some
plantations in Colombia, but in both countries after World War II the
companies worked largely through smallholder producers, returning to
a system reminiscent of the earliest operations in Central America. Yet
in each variation of the political and agronomic system forests were
cleared and new regions were opened to colonization. United Fruit had
set roots in Colombia almost as early as it had established its first Central
American operations. The banana region was carved from the complex
and varied hinterland of Santa Marta, a small port that dated from
colonial times.[74] East of Santa Marta half a dozen small rivers flow out
of the Sierra Nevada de Santa Marta, through broad floodplains, and
into the Caribbean. West, toward Barranquilla, in the wide valley where
the Cauca and Magdalena rivers merge, lies the great coastal Salt
Swamp. Away from the coast behind the swamp lies a third area, the
Magdalena savanna.

In pre-Columbian times the floodplains had been farmed by Indians
who irrigated their land during the long dry summers and grew two
crops annually. Under the Spanish onslaught in the 1500s the region
was largely depopulated; most Spaniards preferred to move through the
disease-ridden lowlands into the hills to the south. By mid-century the
first of many Hispanic cattle ranches were interspersed with former
croplands in a patchwork that spread throughout the area. Those
ranches represented the primary form of land use for three hundred
years, until the cattle were replaced by banana plantations. In the wide
reaches between the ranches tiny hamlets of Indian, Spanish, African,
and mestizo farmers raised a wide variety of edible crops.

By the time of independence in the early 1820s the land was already
controlled and settled by a local elite of Spanish ancestry. In this the
region more closely resembled El Salvador than any other Central American country: there was no landholding vacuum for the foreign companies to fill. The ranchers maintained homes in Santa Marta and nearby
Cienaga, and some became involved in international trade. In contrast
with all the Central American countries, this local elite created the Colombian banana export industry in the 1870s and maintained control of

most of the country's banana land thereafter. They were involved with the financing of a railroad that would link Santa Marta with Sevilla on the Magdalena River in 1890. An equally ambitious project was an irrigation canal, built between 1873 and 1886, that tapped the river at Sevilla and transported its water as far as Cienaga. The canal ultimately irrigated 60 percent of the entire banana zone. In 1891 the local growers were able to send 45,000 stems of bananas to New York. Yet the Colombian growers knew that their profits from trans-Caribbean shipments could be increased by marketing their fruit to a far bigger operation—the United Fruit Company.

In 1894 Keith arrived from Costa Rica, began buying land in Santa Marta, and set up a branch of his export operations. United's administrative headquarters rose in the old port after the company was founded in 1899, but its hospital and other facilities were built closer to the new plantations, in Sevilla. As its operations prospered, the company hired estate managers, bookkeepers, commissary agents, and labor supervisors from the ethnically mixed literate population of the region's towns. As elsewhere, United favored the English-speaking Jamaicans, but the resulting urban commercial boom also attracted immigrants from other coastal settlements along the Caribbean shore, Colombia's mountainous hinterland, and countries as far away as Italy and Lebanon.

Their desire to sell their bananas to United led the local banana growers ultimately to adapt the production and marketing strategies of the foreign company. Within a few years they found that the booming market could absorb more bananas than their existing holdings could produce, so the aristocratic families of Santa Marta, Barranquilla, and other nearby towns moved aggressively to purchase public lands and Indian *ejidos,* or common lands. By 1920 most of those lands had changed hands and many private landholders were growing bananas. United Fruit was their primary purchaser, exporting nine million bunches per year to New Orleans and Liverpool.

As the industry prospered, other private investors, many from Bogotá, the national capital in the interior, and even some from as far away as France, joined the scramble. An indeterminate number of subsistence farmers were displaced in the process; they moved into the hilly region to the east, or into Aracataca, a town near Santa Marta, where they might find work with the new plantation owners. As workers migrated into the area, labor brokers representing both the private landlords and the company blended them with the local workers, hiring them to clear old vegetation, dig irrigation channels, and plant the endless rows of banana stalks.

Other American companies, from Goodyear to Colgate, followed United Fruit into Santa Marta in later years. Their executives built grand houses, a social club, and a hospital. Many of them were new to South America, and the local elite did not often include them in social functions. Members of the local elite were happy, however, to use the telegraph to Bogotá that United installed and the shipping and commercial services that the company provided throughout the Caribbean and to New York and Europe.

Communications with the wider world provided local society with more news than United Fruit might have wanted. Newspapers in Santa Marta carried news from other United plantations around the Caribbean perimeter, including the dramatic news of Sandino's rebellion against the oligarchs and the Americans in Nicaragua from 1926 on. In November 1928 company plantation workers petitioned Thomas Bradshaw, the American manager of United's operations in Colombia, demanding a major pay increase. When he ignored them, they responded by refusing to work on the next scheduled banana harvesting day. At the request of Bradshaw and major private growers, the army attacked the striking workers, massacring perhaps as many as three thousand of them in Cienaga and other towns.[75] Although the strike and massacre became the most notorious event in the region's popular memory, the growers' purposes were achieved. Production and marketing returned to normal in the months before the Depression hit.

The 1930s were a turbulent decade. In addition to the economic shock, Panama disease hit the plantations, further destabilizing the industry, and a Sigatoka epidemic in 1936 crippled production on several old plantations. Many workers were laid off. Sporadic violence plagued town and countryside, as displaced workers organized a second major strike in 1934 and invaded several estates. Despite it all, the region's banana production exceeded its previous levels before the end of the decade.

Trouble was greater during the war that followed, for the company's ships did not visit the Colombian shore from 1941 to 1947. The local landed aristocrats, the same few families whose ancestors had run cattle in the area for three centuries, were resourceful. They formed their own marketing corporations, along the lines of Colombia's highly successful coffee marketing system, and they took over the company's plantations, keeping them in production.

When United returned in 1947, the Colombian government required the company to allow the "tenants" to remain on its lands and continue producing bananas for it to purchase. Bogotá was forcing United to move toward the multiproducer system that had been in place at the beginning of its operations throughout the Caribbean region. By 1953 United had turned over to Colombians 17,290 acres of irrigated lands, and in 1964 it withdrew entirely from land management operations. The extent of lowland Colombia planted in bananas increased only modestly, from 112,500 acres in the mid-1950s to 125,000 acres in the early 1960s. Total banana exports rose from 162,000 tons in 1938 to a peak of around 200,000 tons in the 1950s and early 1960s.[76]

Most of the production increase came from the old Colombian estates, which specialized in supplying bananas to the revitalized German market. As the next chapter shows, Colombia's nationally controlled export system was centered on its leading product, coffee, which was transforming the Andean mountain slopes south of the banana belt. The same social network of Colombian exporters—wealthy families with personal connections in New York and several European cities—was presenting the Yankee fruit company with serious competition, more so here than in any Central American country.

United Fruit did not leave Colombia when it retired from operating plantations, for it still had a profitable marketing system, and the company was benefiting from a more diverse geographical range of sources. In 1955, although United planted only 6 percent of Colombia's banana acreage, it still handled 58 percent of its exports. Thereafter its share of Colombian exports gradually fell, reaching 32 percent in 1973 and 20 percent in 1984.[77] As an offshore presence it had only indirect influence on land use in the Santa Marta lowlands. The areas that it had developed into irrigated croplands were left haphazardly to former plantation workers and wartime squatters. The irrigation channels were left to silt and weeds. Many small plots were returned to food crop production, and some 17,290 acres again became old-style, low-productivity cattle ranches. When the company's commissaries left, they created a vacuum of food production that was filled by large producers of rice and small producers of vegetables and beef. The area's highlands also attracted immigrant squatters who were fleeing civil war. The region settled in to a period of recession, de-linkage from the international economy, and chronic social conflict. Moreover, the last remnants of natural areas were vanishing, although this could be only partially charged to the changing role of foreign corporations.[78]

One other environmental change—pesticide pollution—was about to appear in the region: in Colombia, just as around the globe, the consequences of chemical-intensive market agriculture in the 1960s were accelerating. As banana planters adopted the new international strategy of intensive production of Cavendish bananas, the accompanying heavy application of pesticides produced dangerous pollution downstream. Pesticide pollution from acreage that United Fruit had retained and turned to the production of African oil palms joined the stream running toward the coast. The great swamp became increasingly stagnant and noxious.[79]

In sum, United Fruit's capacity to dominate the banana industry was more limited in Colombia's coastal lowlands than it was in Central America. The company's expansion in Colombia was more gradual and was integrated into a land tenure system that had been transforming the lowland ecosystem into a landlord-dominated patchwork of farming and ranching for generations before the Americans arrived.

In contrast to Colombia, neighboring Ecuador was an entirely new frontier for the multinational banana industry in the 1940s. It had previously exported a few stems of bananas, but only down the coast to Peru and Chile. Because Ecuador lacked a concentrated production area, it was still free of Panama disease, so the American fruit companies, this time led by Standard Fruit Company (which had been outflanked by United in Colombia), made a massive move into the country. By the mid-1950s Ecuador had become the world's largest exporter of bananas, and many patches of its hitherto largely intact rainforests had been cleared.

United Fruit first explored Ecuador's possibilities during the Depression. In 1933 United purchased one former cacao plantation of 96,000 acres at Tengel, but it planted only about one-eighth of that land in bananas. But in the long run United was content to remain second in Ecuador. The shipping problems of World War II prevented either United or Standard Fruit from developing their Ecuadorian operations until peace returned.

Major export production began in the Guayas lowlands in 1947, the hinterland of the ancient port of Guayaquil on the Gulf of Santa Clara. The production area then quickly spread inland toward Quevedo, a frontier town founded in the 1850s that had seen booms and busts in rubber, cacao, and balsa wood. In the 1950s banana production expanded along the south coast as well, anchored by a new port, Puerto

Bolívar, which was hacked out of mangrove marshes. The south coast, where United dominated purchases, was dry, and the fruit was grown on irrigated plantations.

This was in sharp contrast to the very wet north coast, which was upriver from the port of Esmeraldas; over 100 inches of rain fall annually in this region, and there is no dry season.[80] The northern rainforest supported a unique biota with perhaps the greatest biodiversity on the planet, including many species found nowhere else. Some of its soils were rich fresh alluvium; others were volcanic soils that were equally rich in nutrients.

Prior to the era of the multinationals, agricultural settlements in the area were sparse and the regional economy was sleepy. Some hacienda owners grew cacao and coffee on old, partially disused plantations while they lived elegantly in Guayaquil, Paris, and Madrid. Previously there had been only one railroad, which ran directly east from Guayaquil into the highlands, then north to Quito. The lowlands had neither a railroad nor all-weather motor roads. Most of the region still supported virgin forest, but political planners and economic investors did not value the rainforest for itself. The Ecuadorian government, eager for rural development and foreign investment after 1945, built roads up the central valley to encourage smallholder migration inland; the new highways were largely financed by U.S. government aid and World Bank funds. Government forest was available for clearing in 124-acre plots, and it could be purchased on easy terms. Between 1948 and 1951 smallholders cleared 25,000 acres of primary forest for new plantations. These pioneers preferred clean weeding, to keep jungle growth under control until the bananas were tall enough to shade the weeds. The short-term consequence, especially on hilly terrain, was rapid erosion, which had also been a serious problem in the hills of Jamaica after 1870. As one commentator on Jamaican agriculture noted, "A similar prospect faces Ecuador, but the industry is as yet much too young and heady with optimism to have given any attention to such matters."[81]

United and Standard never dominated the banana industry in Ecuador. The United States had no political control in the country and could not promote the interests of U.S. companies. The international market after World War II was competitive, and Ecuador's markets diversified rapidly to include western Europe. By the late 1950s European exporters were as strong as the American companies. United's local subsidiary, Compañia Bananera del Ecuador, grew or purchased only one-fifth of the country's banana exports. One Swedish firm operated the major plantations in the Esmeralda area, and German, Belgian, and older Chilean interests were responsible for the rest of the great boom.[82]

In striking contrast to the other banana producing countries of tropical America, the great majority of Ecuador's banana exports were grown by small-scale private producers. Export firms either contracted with individual growers or bought the crop from small producers; they did not manage the land directly. Consequently, until the early 1960s increased production was achieved almost entirely by increasing the acreage on many smallholdings by clearing additional forestland, rather than by intensifying production on land already under cultivation. United Fruit in particular provided information about cultivation and disease control to growers and bought and marketed their fruit.

Productivity increased more slowly in Ecuador than in other countries. This meant that epidemic banana diseases spread more slowly there than in areas where corporate plantations ruled the land. Panama disease first appeared in Ecuador in 1936, but it did not become widespread until the 1950s. Sigatoka was a far more severe threat. It first appeared in 1949 and was fairly severe and widespread by 1952. Spraying with copper sulfate was an inefficient and costly process on small and hilly properties. By the 1960s Sigatoka had made a major contribution to the end of expansion in Ecuador's banana industry.

In Ecuador the degradation of natural forest as a consequence of expanding banana production was explosively rapid. Production stabilized after fifteen years of growth. By the early 1960s banana yields began to drop and costs rose, primarily because of disease. The number of acres under cultivation peaked in 1965, at about 296,400 acres. During the 1970s the country's banana acreage fell dramatically, to just over 148,200 acres in 1980. Productivity was gradually rising, however, especially on the larger estates that sold directly under contract to foreign firms: in the same decade exports fell only from 1,364,000 tons to 1,318,000 tons. European demand leveled off in the 1970s as the growth of personal income slowed, but the insatiable American market began to absorb a larger percentage of Ecuador's exports.[83]

By the late 1970s Standard Fruit had about 19,760 acres of bananas under multiyear contract, which provided it with about one-third of Ecuador's exports. In contrast, United's local subsidiary controlled less than 10 percent of the market. By the late 1970s the Ecuadorian consortium Noboa controlled nearly 40 percent of national exports. The era of domination by North American companies had been fairly brief and limited in extent, but still crucial.

The international market could not support an endless rise of exports from Ecuador: the expansion of banana production ended after three decades. The environmental impact of this rapid expansion, however, was permanent. By 1970 approximately half of former forestlands had been cleared, and the entire lowland rainforest region of Ecuador had been opened to settlement and agriculture. Banana production was the spearhead of infrastructure development and, consequently, immigration and the growth of towns and small farms. Soil erosion, severe in some places, resulted from the practice of clean weeding on hilly terrain. Although the acreage under bananas was more widespread and dispersed in Ecuador than in the plantation enclaves of Central America, the cleared acreage was still considerably concentrated in strips along roads, rail lines, and rivers, which intensified the environmental damage in those areas.

In the 1960s United and Standard once again centered their major new production efforts in Central America, where they began growing varieties of the Cavendish banana. In one sense the adoption of the Cavendish marked a return to the beginning, since by planting a new type of banana the industry was able to shift back to the same Caribbean lowlands where corporate production had begun seven decades earlier. In other ways the further expansion of cultivated acreage in the banana belt of Central America opened a new chapter in the history of banana production. The maturation of the corporate agrochemical industry in the same years provided commercial fertilizers and pesticides that the delicate Cavendish banana required to achieve its full potential. The corporations were gradually learning to diversify not only their supply regions but their range of marketable crops as well.

INTENSIFICATION AND DIVERSIFICATION: NEW STRATEGIES IN THE OLD BANANA LANDS

In the Central American fiefs of the banana multinationals, exports increased little during the 1950s, and each of the major banana producing countries experienced widely varying export patterns from one year to another. The most dramatic events were political, as the foreign multinationals and the host governments maneuvered for control of the banana wealth. After World War II political conditions shifted so sharply that they threatened the power of the landed oligarchies and their foreign supporters. The most turbulent banana politics in all of Central America occurred in Guatemala in the decade after 1945. Events there revealed the raw political power of the corporate giants, especially United Fruit.

Under the leadership of presidents Juan José Arévalo Bermejo and Jacobo Arbenz Guzmán, Guatemala made the most determined land reform efforts of any Central American country in the immediate postwar years.[84] The country was as socially and economically polarized as any in the region. Two percent of the population owned 72 percent of the land, while 50 percent of the population owned 4 percent of the land. Rural per capita income was only about ninety dollars per year. Malnutrition was widespread, and it worsened as coffee and banana lands expanded at the expense of food production.

Arévalo, elected president in 1945, was determined to turn uncultivated lands into food producing acreage. As a first step in that direction he designed a law of forced rental, which required the oligarchs to rent unused land at low rates. In 1951 Arbenz succeeded Arévalo. Arbenz went a step further, supporting peasant unions against the great landowners. In the same year the National Peasant Union Federation was forged, unifying twenty-five regional peasants' unions. In 1952 Arbenz's government passed a more aggressive agrarian reform law that was designed to break up big estates and return land to food production. It nationalized unused lands, compensating their owners with twenty-five-year bonds carrying 3 percent interest. The greatest holder of uncultivated land was the United Fruit Company. United had previously rejected a renegotiation of its contract with Arévalo, so in 1953 Arbenz announced the nationalization of 234,000 acres of United's uncultivated land. Using an assessment based on official tax records, Arbenz offered the company one million dollars in compensation (and thereby implicitly challenged the accuracy of those records). United Fruit, outraged, demanded sixteen million dollars, but did verify that it was producing bananas on only about 5 percent of its vast land holdings.

Arbenz was planning to build a new electrical power system for the capital, independent of United's system, which until then was the only source of power for Guatemala City. He also planned new roads and railroads independent of the company's systems. Clearly, the company would have to either adjust to a reduced role in the country or retaliate. In 1953 the national labor union federation forced the government to increase the pace of reform by organizing strikes in United's electric company and railroad; the government's response was to nationalize them. This went too far for the Americans.

By 1953 the Cold War was fully entrenched in Washington, and the new Eisenhower administration fully supported U.S. interests in Central America. Indeed, the New York law firm of John Foster Dulles, the secretary of state, had represented United Fruit; Allen Dulles, the secretary's brother and the new head of the Central Intelligence Agency, was on United's board of directors.

The CIA organized a group of exiles under Carlos Castillo Armas, a former colonel in the Guatemalan army, on a United Fruit banana plantation across the border in Honduras. In a coup in 1954 Castillo Armas threw Arbenz out and took power for the military and its gringo supporters. United recaptured a quarter of a million acres of land, although it agreed to raise the government's cut of profits from 10 percent to 30 percent and to give up 100,000 acres for land reform. These concessions would never have been made to the liberal governments of Arévalo or Arbenz; under the new oligarchic regime of Castillo Armas the promised land distribution was never implemented.[85]

Under its refurbished alliance with the Guatemalan government, United Fruit was assured of continuing control over the country's agricultural lowlands. In 1955 United planted 52 percent of Guatemala's banana lands and exported 75 percent of its bananas. A decade later it still accounted for 52 percent of the acreage under bananas. United prospered, and Castillo Armas and his successors maintained oligarchic control of the fertile lowlands. Interminable civil war followed as the campesinos and the Indians of the highlands, whose poverty forced them to provide much of the labor on the coffee, banana, and cotton lands below, struggled against the regime that the United States had helped put into place.[86]

In the late 1950s the multinational corporations finally won the struggle against Panama disease. Standard Fruit developed the Giant Cavendish banana, while United Fruit developed the genetically similar Valery. The Cavendish varieties bruised more easily than the Gros Michel did, and the old system of shipping whole stems of fruit was no longer viable. Each hand of bananas had to be carefully cut from the stem and boxed for shipment, so the companies integrated packing operations at each plantation or collection point.[87] The first exports of boxed fruit left Central America in 1959, and the first from Ecuador were shipped in

1963. By 1965 nearly all Latin American banana exports were boxed. Jamaica, the original banana island, followed suit only later.[88]

To complicate matters, the new varietal fruit was more susceptible to pests than its predecessor. It needed greater amounts of pesticide and more commercial fertilizer than had the Gros Michel banana.[89] As production intensified, the risk of soil and water pollution and workers' diseases escalated.[90]

By growing the new banana variety in Guatemala, the United Fruit Company was able to return to the lands that it had cultivated before 1930, near Morales in the Motagua river valley on the Caribbean. By intensifying its cultivation techniques, United soon brought production back to its record 1930 levels.[91] Annual exports averaged 162,000 tons between 1948 and 1952 and rose to 198,000 tons in 1960. This increase resulted almost entirely from an intensification of productivity, since the acreage planted in bananas from one year to the next did not vary greatly, averaging about 40,000 acres from the mid-1950s well into the 1960s.[92]

This use of land and employment initially seemed to indicate that production of the Cavendish varieties would result in an agroeconomic system that would be far more sustainable than was the system that supported the Gros Michel banana. But the costs were high: intensification required ever-increasing amounts of commercial fertilizer and pesticides, which were supplied by American agrochemical giants led by Dow Chemical Company and Monsanto Chemicals. This produced a drain on Guatemala's dollar reserves. Moreover, negative effects on the health of the work force and the health of the land and water were accumulating.

In 1964 United closed its production in Guatemala's Pacific lowlands, selling its territories there to private entrepreneurs who turned them into highly productive cotton farms. The heavy use of pesticides on the cotton resulted in the poisoning of workers and the polluting of downstream waters that flowed into estuarine and coastal ecosystems.[93]

Next door to Guatemala was Honduras, the classic Banana Republic. The banana economy of the north coast gave Yankee corporations hegemony over the country's political and economic system. American consumers continued to dominate Honduras's foreign trade in the early 1950s, eating 75 percent of Honduras's banana exports. In return, the United States provided two-thirds of Honduran imports and 85 percent of foreign investment. Direct investment by U.S. interests rose from $62 million in 1950 to $110 million in 1959.[94]

The two giants, United Fruit and Standard Fruit, entirely controlled the commercial production and export of the country's bananas. After their sojourn on the Pacific the two companies returned to the north coast of Honduras with the Cavendish banana. Their plantations and railroads once again dominated the fertile alluvial river valleys. The area planted in bananas on the north coast rose dramatically from 70,000 acres in the mid-1950s to 170,000 acres in the early 1960s, much of it land that had produced Gros Michel bananas a generation before. The work force for the two corporations populated San Pedro Sula and other towns. Their port facilities at Puerto Cortes, Tela, and La Ceiba and their steamships supplied the major markets of North America and Europe with the delicate yellow fruit.

In the 1950s the market for Central America's bananas began to shift away from the total American dominance of the previous decade. As Europe's consumer economy recovered, its banana purchases rose rapidly, while American consumption grew only slowly. If the giant American corporations were to maintain their position, they would need to expand their sales in Europe. By 1966, 75 percent of Guatemala's banana exports were going to western Europe, mostly on United's ships. Honduran exports presented a similar picture. Of 371,000 tons sent out in 1951, nearly all, 352,000 tons, were shipped to the United States. In 1960 the total export figure was 360,000 tons, but of that, only 296,000 tons went to the United States, a significant reduction. Production remained relatively stable, but a rising percentage was diverted from North American to European markets.[95]

In Honduras the political triangle of the American companies, the local labor force, and the national government fostered less violence than the same structure did in Guatemala. For fifteen somnolent years, between 1933 and 1948, Tiburcio Carías Andino was president. He did little to develop his country's economy. His successors in the 1950s made more energetic efforts, and they tolerated a more active grassroots labor movement, which focused on the foreign banana companies. In 1954, 40,000 workers launched a spontaneous strike at the companies' docks at La Ceiba. The workers finally gained token concessions from Standard Fruit, consisting of a 4 percent to 8 percent increase in wages, plus a two-week annual vacation.[96] The fruit companies had developed a concentration of plantation labor and thus were the catalyst for the rise of the rural labor movement, but they had no intention of losing political control.

For a while in the early 1960s Honduras followed Peru's military

regime by moving leftward, legislating new land reforms and national-
izing the timber industry. In 1961 the president, Ramón Villeda Morales, followed Arbenz's example and drafted an agrarian reform law to
take back the large acreage that United and Standard controlled but
were not using. Exercising pressure through the U.S. State Department,
which feared a repeat of Fidel Castro's nationalization of American-
owned lands, United forced Villeda Morales to cut back the effort. His
challenge was the beginning of the end of his career. Two years later an
army coup installed a new president, Osvaldo López Arellano. At his
inauguration the president of Standard Fruit and the vice president of
United Fruit sat in places of honor. López Arellano rolled back the former reforms, and, in the years of Lyndon Johnson's presidency, new
private American capital flowed into Honduras. The Chase Manhattan
and National City Banks, long closely associated with United Fruit, took
control of Honduras's banking system.[97]

Honduran landlords, in alliance with the American fruit corporations
and backed by both governments, maintained control of fertile agricultural land, using it to produce export crops for profit rather than a more
varied set of food crops for domestic consumption. By 1973 the oligarchy had crushed reforms and organized the National Federation of Agriculturalists and Cattle Ranchers and the Council of Private Business,
both aided by American investors and fruit companies.[98]

Then Hurricane Fifi struck in September 1974, killing 800 people,
leaving 300,000 homeless, and ravaging the fruit lands. Fifi devastated
the entire north coast—railroads, roads, bridges, plantations. Almost all
plantations were flattened by the winds and the 20- to 30-foot floodwaters that only slowly receded.[99] Even the multinationals were badly
hit, and they were in no mood to tolerate any challenge to their power.
Public scandal broke out in 1975 when Eli Black, president of United
Brands, the parent company of United Fruit, committed suicide in New
York. An investigation revealed that United had paid a $1.25 million
bribe to the Hondurans and had promised more. In the face of these
revelations President López Arellano resigned, but in 1978 General Pol-
icarpo Paz García seized power in Tegucigalpa and initiated reprisals
against the peasant movements. In 1980 he gained new U.S. military
aid, especially to patrol the Nicaraguan border against the new Sandinista regime next door.[100] Nothing basic changed in the kingdom of
banana politics as the Cold War rolled on.

The long process of domestication of the Honduran coastal rainforests continued. The acreage under bananas was more or less stabilized at around 49,400 acres in the late 1970s, for now the companies, using Cavendish banana stock, no longer had to move rapidly from one newly cleared forest to another to avoid disease. In this new era banana plantations had two additional sources for expanded acreage. One was former banana lands that were returned to production; the other was land taken out of food crop production. Accurate figures have not yet been compiled to describe this mosaic of change more exactly, but it seems clear that the rate of destruction of primary forest was considerably lower than it had been in the first third of the century.

Costa Rica provided a sharp contrast to Guatemala and Honduras, at least in the political relations between the government and the American corporations. Costa Rica evolved after 1945 into a stable, moderate political regime determined to manage its economic growth with some degree of equity. It might not have turned out that way, for the country's economy was heavily influenced by United Fruit and other foreign companies, and the Costa Rican Communist Party was the strongest in Central America, its strength centering among the banana workers. As Walter LaFeber comments,

> Costa Rica prided itself on its distribution of wealth, but the equality was remarkable only when compared with the grossly unequal distribution in the rest of Central America. In truth, key sectors of the society were foreign-controlled; the profits from its large amounts of exports rolled out of the country. . . . Large areas of the country were controlled by oligarchs who refused either to cultivate their land or allow others to do so.[101]

As early as 1943 President Rafael Calderón Guardia engineered social reform legislation that provided an eight-hour workday and a social security system and guaranteed labor the rights to form unions, bargain collectively, and strike. Calderón's regime declined into incompetence and corruption by the late 1940s, and he was defeated in the election of 1948. The government tried to annul the election and reinstate Calderón, which triggered an uprising led by the charismatic José (Pepe) Figueres Ferrer, a social democrat. In 1948 the larger landlords openly opposed Calderón's land-reform coalition, which was defeated by Figueres and his allies in a revolution of the moderates.

Figueres gained popularity when he denounced the power of United Fruit and other foreign companies. He was a pragmatist, however: soon after he swept into office in the 1953 presidential elections, he negotiated a new contract with United that both socialists and conservatives could support. It reiterated United's access to land and water resources, its ownership of harbor facilities in Limón and railroads in the old banana lands outside Limón, and its right to build new lines. The contract also tripled Costa Rica's share of profits from the banana industry, enforced minimum wage laws on company plantations, and turned a token 12,350 acres of company land back to the government.[102]

In 1955 United planted 58 percent of the country's total banana acreage and controlled 99 percent of Costa Rica's banana exports.[103] In the late 1950s United returned to its old plantations on the Sarapiquí lowlands outside Puerto Limón, slowly closing down its plantations in the Pacific lowlands around Quepos and Golfito or shifting them from bananas to African oil palm. New corporate acreage came in part from newly cleared forest, but the largest number of acres under cultivation was on land that had once produced the Gros Michel banana.[104]

In Costa Rica as a whole, corporate banana acreage slowly expanded from the 1950s through the 1970s. The companies kept an average of 40,000 acres in banana production from the mid-1950s into the 1960s, and then, after 1970, expanding production in the Caribbean lowlands raised annual acreage to an average of around 62,500 acres. Export markets were volatile; shipments fluctuated between 355,000 metric tons in 1954, including 289,000 to the United States, and 273,000 tons in 1960, of which 260,000 tons went to the United States.[105]

In the 1960s, as production increases in Ecuador tailed off, Costa Rican banana prices rose steadily, spurring banana production. Total national production tripled between 1963 and 1967; most of the increase was in fruit cultivated by smallholders, United's "associate producers." Almost all the acreage opened or reopened to bananas in the Caribbean lowlands was owned by the local producers and was part of United's purchasing system. For the company this system reduced its costs and risks, but for the smallholders it was not a straightforward bonanza. Part of what they delivered to United Fruit came at the expense of food production. In addition, smallholders who were attracted into the commercial banana system faced the danger of price slumps. The possibility of new profits also meant higher risks on the volatile international market.

In the midst of these transformations the banana corporations began experimenting with new strategies for managing their sources of fruit. Beginning in the early 1950s both companies began selling or leasing their unused lands to local governments or private producers.[106] In 1952 United launched an experiment in Costa Rica called the Higuerito Project, dividing up large plantations into small parcels that were managed individually by its former workers.[107] Each farmer was given a ten-year lease at a nominal rate, then the company transferred title to the farmer after the contract expired. The company managed disease control and transported the fruit, and it kept exclusive purchase rights for the bananas produced, at its price.

United's cultivated acreage in Costa Rica averaged 42,000 acres between 1947 and 1951. The highest figure, 45,925 acres, was in 1953. That was gradually reduced to about 25,000 acres in the mid-1970s: 17,500 acres managed by the company plus some 7,410 acres managed by associate producers. Standard Fruit cultivated a smaller number of acres—19,250 in 1953—and maintained all its land under direct ownership until 1965. Then it began diversifying ownership: its average between 1972 and 1976 was 10,870 acres under company control and 8,173 acres under associate producers.[108] By then both companies' subsidiary producers included former company employees, larger private companies, and even several local cooperatives.

Despite these major changes in the pattern of ownership of acreage under production, the companies still controlled the system. As one skeptical observer described the system years later, "The associate producers are under the administrative control of the superintendent . . . and they act according to the advice of the company; the infrastructure and the development expenses of production all are handled by the company, and they depend totally on the company for the sale of their fruit."[109] The company provided credit, technical advice, seeds, fertilizer, machines, chemicals, aerial spraying, irrigation equipment, and packaging. Advance guarantees of price were usually below 25 percent, often as interest-bearing loans. Producers thus bore the risk of plant diseases and hurricanes.

The companies' control was partially remodeled in structure, but not threatened in substance. Their political power was still formidable, and they were assured of the support of the U.S. government. They were direct beneficiaries of the Cold War and Washington's determination to maintain economic control in Central America. Their struggles with national governments and labor movements, however, were increasing.

In the 1970s the banana belt countries in Latin America began to make more serious cooperative and regionwide efforts to loosen the power of the American corporate banana empires. In 1974 Costa Rica, Guatemala, Honduras, Nicaragua, Panama, Colombia, and Ecuador formed the Union of Banana Exporting Countries (UPEB), emulating the dramatic moves made by OPEC a year before against foreign corporations. At that time only seventeen cents of every dollar in banana sales went to the producer countries. UPEB wanted to instate a one-dollar export tax on every forty-pound crate of bananas. United Brands, Del Monte, and Castle and Cooke (the owner of the Standard Fruit Company since 1969), which together handled 90 percent of those countries' banana exports, refused to pay the dollar tax. Panama backed off, lowering its demand to twenty cents on the dollar. Ecuador dropped its new demand entirely. In Costa Rica outgoing President Figueres threatened to nationalize the companies' lands; in response the companies threatened to leave the country. Under that pressure Figueres's successor Daniel Oduber dropped his demand to twenty-five cents on the dollar. Guatemala and Nicaragua subsequently dropped out of the cartel, which collapsed. Costa Rica finally succeeded in collecting a one-dollar tax on each carton of bananas—but not until 1981.[110]

In the short run it seemed that the effort to create a regional strategy strong enough to oppose northern power had broken down in the traditional rivalries between each country and its neighbors. In the longer run it became clear that a new era of banana production began in 1974 with the formation of UPEB. Country by country the organization altered the relations between companies and governments and changed the operating costs and market competitiveness of each corporation. Perhaps the most important shift toward governmental control of banana income was the change from long-term contracts with foreign corporations to specified taxes on each carton exported.

In Panama the total banana acreage averaged 37,500 acres in the 1970s and early 1980s. Exports fluctuated considerably, between 420,000 and 658,000 tons. United's subsidiary, the Chiriquí Land Company, owned all export acreage until 1962, when it began its associate producer program; by 1984 the small-scale producers owned 32 percent of the banana lands in production. Two state corporations were founded between 1974 and 1975, but they too had to export through United's monopoly. Yet there were marginal changes in the political terms of the business. After the 1974–1976 "banana war" over the export tax, United sold all of its 105,000 acres of land to the Panamanian government, then leased back 39,250 acres, which produced an average of 400,000 tons of bananas per year.[111]

The corporations also increased their efforts to diversify crops and growing locations. Crops other than bananas could grow on the cleared alluvial lands. The most successful experiment involved intensifying cultivation of cacao, which had been introduced centuries earlier from its evolutionary birthplace in the lower reaches of the Andes. The cacao tree grew widely in the moist lowland forests in southern Mexico and to the south, dispersed through woodlands with many other species. The chocolate-producing beans, growing in large pods directly from the tree trunk, had been harvested and traded for centuries by the indigenous Mesoamericans.[112] In the early 1900s the British transplanted cacao to West Africa and successfully grew it in single-species plantations, replacing wide areas of natural moist forest especially on the Gold Coast, present-day Ghana. The burgeoning chocolate industry of Europe (and the spurt in sugar production that accompanied it) was responsible for the elimination of an area of African rainforest by translocating and cultivating the cacao tree, a species native to the rainforests of the Americas.[113]

Cacao was a transitional crop in the decline of the company's original Caribbean coastal operations. In 1932 United owned 24,809 acres in Costa Rica and 14,277 acres in Panama where, guided by English-speaking Jamaican foremen, company workers interplanted cacao trees with diseased banana trees. The Central American climate was not favorable for extensive cacao cultivation: it was too wet, and fungi prospered in concentrated plantings. Nonetheless, by 1966 cacao had become Costa Rica's fourth largest export. Commercial crop diversification was gradually emerging, in response to both economic and ecological pressures against total reliance on one crop.

The corporate agenda for diversification focused on tropical fruits, especially citrus and pineapple. Oranges had been a familiar commodity, sold to boats trading along the Caribbean coast of Central America, before they were elbowed out by bananas; they now returned in escalating amounts, introduced to new countries on a commercial scale by the fruit multinationals after a series of corporate mergers that began in the 1950s. For example, the Dole Corporation began to export fresh or processed pineapples from Standard's old plant in La Ceiba, Honduras. Workers protested the heavy use of pesticides for pineapples there, launching a protracted controversy between labor and management.[114]

In the 1960s the fruit companies in Honduras and Costa Rica also began to grow oil palm, which was used in the production of margarine and salad oil, on former banana lands, importing the palm from its ancestral home in equatorial Africa. Globalization of tropical horticulture research was in full swing.

CONCLUSION: THE BANANA
MULTINATIONALS' ENVIRONMENTAL LEGACY

By the 1970s the bananas that Americans peeled and consumed were still imported entirely from Latin America, and 95 percent of them came from five countries: Colombia, Costa Rica, Ecuador, Guatemala, and Panama. Three American companies—United Fruit, Standard Fruit (which had been absorbed by Castle and Cooke) and Del Monte (which was now controlled by Reynolds Tobacco)—handled 78 percent of all imports. In 1971 United and Standard still controlled 83 percent of the market between them. Del Monte began importing bananas only in 1969, but by 1984 it shipped 450,000 tons, 19 percent of the market.[115]

Yet there was space for other companies as well in the 1970s. They increased their share of the American market from 8 percent in 1971 to 22 percent in 1984; this share was dominated by Pacific Fruit, the American marketing subsidiary of Noboa, the Ecuadorian consortium, which shipped to New York, and Turbana, a subsidiary of the Colombian consortium UNIBAN, which shipped to Miami.

Bananas arrived at twenty American ports. Over half entered through three ports: New York (21 percent in 1984) for eastern markets, Long Beach (17.5 percent) for the West Coast, and Gulfport-Mobile (15 percent) for the Mississippi Basin. The leading companies maintained national sales networks at each site; these networks were linked to jobbers and chain stores after 1958, when a court order forced United to divest its monopoly of ripening and marketing facilities.

The dominance of United, Castle and Cooke, and Del Monte was based on a series of new production technologies that they introduced between the late 1950s and mid-1970s, making their large-scale production systems more cost-efficient than those of their competitors. Then they reached a plateau, making few important innovations thereafter. Most significant was the adoption of the Cavendish banana. New procedures were implemented to grow and market the new variety: boxing the fruit, placing polyethylene sleeves on the bunches before they ripened to control parasites, using overhead cableways to speed them to processing sheds in the fields, and low volume aerial spraying for Sigatoka. As a result, yields per acre tripled on Central American corporate plantations, from 37 to 108 tons per acre. These innovations spread slowly to independent producers in Colombia and, finally, Ecuador, where widely diverse growing conditions kept yields much lower. Yields on individual farms in Ecuador began falling off after three to five years, and they declined rapidly after ten to fifteen years. Persistent planting on the same acreage required the liberal application of chemical fertilizers and other soil supplements.[116]

Total production costs rose much faster in Central America and Colombia, to higher levels than those in Ecuador. This was largely because of two factors. First, export taxes rose in the Central American countries. Colombia, which still imposed no export tax, saw its share of exports rise from 5 percent in 1973 to 20 percent in 1984. Second, Black Sigatoka, a new disease that affected Cavendish varieties, hit the large monocrop plantations, demanding costly new programs for disease control.

Corporations alone did not drive the market for bananas or the use of land to meet market demand. International consumption of the fruit evolved during the 1970s, although the United States continued to provide the world's largest market. In the aggregate, American consumers behaved differently from Europeans and Japanese. On those two continents consumption grew rapidly when incomes began to rise, then leveled off. But demand continued to grow steadily in the United States; even in the 1970s consumption rose faster in the United States than in Europe or Japan, rising from 26.5 percent of total global sales in 1973 to 36 percent in 1983.[117]

Americans were eating nearly twenty-five pounds of bananas per person per year by the 1970s, a higher rate than anywhere in Europe or Japan. Ninety-five percent of all U.S. households purchased bananas. One authority surmised that this reflected the "greater diet and health consciousness of recent years that favours consumption of fresh fruit and vegetables." Because bananas had become such a standard presence on American tables, by the 1970s any international production glut was dumped on the American market, even at depressed prices. An economist would conclude that demand in the United States, which imposes no duties, internal taxes, or quantity restrictions on banana imports, had become unusually supply-led.

This enormous scale of concentrated corporate power had grave consequences for the ecological destinies of the region. In the seventy-five years that American fruit companies dominated the Caribbean Basin's tropical lowlands, the region underwent several stages of environmental change. The first and most fundamental stage was the transformation from rainforest to clearings for plantations. Then, beginning in the 1920s, the early plantations underwent reversion to subsistence farming and secondary woodland. The 1950s ushered in an era of intensified, chemical-based stable banana production. Corporate agrocapitalism was the driving force of ecological change, both on the plantations and in the surrounding lands from which the corporations drew labor and resources. Furthermore, in several Central American countries, the companies dominated governments, allowing the U.S. government to maintain its strategic hegemony over the Caribbean Basin without colonialism.

Did the companies' management of land and resources improve as experience increased? Did their plantations become more sustainable, or less? By the 1960s bananas grew on more stable acreage for longer periods than they had in the era of the Gros Michel banana and Panama disease, but this was accomplished only with accelerating applications of chemical fertilizers and pesticides. When aerial spraying began in the 1950s, the toxic chemicals traveled far from the fields for which they were intended. The toxification of soil and downstream water was not monitored at all in the early years of intensive agrochemical use. This was a new era for the industry, one with inexorably evolving consequences in the form of serious damage to workers' health.

Although crop diversification, another trend of those years, helped stabilize the region's agroecology and export economies by moving away from reliance on a single crop species, some major alternative cash crops, like oil palm, were also grown in massive, one-crop plantations. Export crops were grown at the expense of food production for local needs, which drove campesinos onto marginal lands, mostly hill forests, or into cities, destabilizing ecosystems and societies.[118]

One by-product of the corporate agrosystem was settlement and land clearance throughout the lowlands, a process that then accelerated beyond the immediate range of the corporate economy. This transformation rested as much on consumer demand as on corporate resources. Consumers in the mass markets north of the banana lands benefited from availability of the tasty and nutritional fruit, as their diets expanded beyond what temperate climates could provide.

Banana corporations represented the highest degree of American ecological imperialism, matched only by Firestone Rubber in Liberia in their capacity to control entire countries. Another perennial crop, coffee, became even more widespread in Latin America. Its economic scale was greater, and its consumers were more demanding—it played a decisive role in the destruction of forest in higher elevations of the region.

CHAPTER 4

The Last Drop

The American Coffee Market and the
Hill Regions of Latin America

Every plant of civilization creates a state of strict bondage.
                                        Fernand Braudel, 1979

COFFEE IN THE AMERICAS:
COLONIAL TRADE AND CONSUMPTION

Of all the tropical crops sold on world markets, the first in value is coffee. By the 1960s coffee had the second highest value of any internationally traded commodity, surpassed only by petroleum. It is grown across hill regions throughout the tropical and subtropical world—anywhere on the planet that does not suffer winter frosts. Of all the social and environmental consequences that have been the result of the commercial growth of tropical crops, the most varied have been the result of coffee production.

Coffee contrasts with sugar cane and bananas in many ways. It is versatile in its habits, growing in a wide range of natural settings and soils throughout the world's warm uplands, needing only moderate rainfall and temperatures that do not fall below freezing. Unlike sugar and bananas, coffee is a perennial crop. It exploits ecological zones that are different from the lowland rainforests that sugar and bananas have replaced. Coffee groves can be grown on steep slopes where other cash crops cannot be easily sustained, but they often cause heavy erosion or the gradual depletion of soil nutrients. A tree begins to bear fruit in the third or fourth year; production rises for several years, then slowly falls for the useful life of the plant, anywhere from twenty to forty years. As a perennial coffee also presents economic difficulties, for a plantation cannot adjust its production annually to meet market demand.

Coffee is grown on many scales of operation and in many combinations of crops. It is as economically competitive when harvested from peasants' small plots for a cash supplement to their subsistence crops as it is on large landed estates with slave or sharecropper or wage labor. In further contrast to sugar, it has not necessarily been tied to the radical disruption of social and subsistence systems that have been the consequences of slavery—although slavery was an essential element of coffee production in Brazil.

The coffee tree evolved as an understory tree in the hill forests of Ethiopia in northeastern Africa. Early in its domestication it was planted in groves in Yemen. From there Arab traders introduced it to southern Europe in the thirteenth century. Market demand developed first in the Mediterranean countries, spreading from east to west, then northward through Europe, where large-scale consumption began during the Renaissance.[1] Eighteenth-century France in particular provided a thriving market. In the last decades of the Ancien Régime, coffeehouses in Paris and elsewhere became a cultural and political institution as public locations where political thought was allowed to thrive uncensored. Marketing organizations grew up to supply the rising enthusiasm.

Coffee culture was transferred to the North American colonies in the same period. By the early 1700s in cities along the eastern seaboard, a shared pot of coffee was becoming an important middle-class convention, marking sociability and hospitality. A French, rather than a British, element of lifestyle had taken root in the American colonies. The search for sources of coffee took North Atlantic consumer culture into tropical America. Ultimately the United States became the world's greatest consumer of coffee.

While England was stimulating its mania for tea through a vast expansion of imports from Asia, France experimented with coffee production on its Caribbean holdings from the 1720s on, so as to reduce its reliance on sources from the Arab world. Europe was well on its way to dictating the ecological destinies of hill lands suited for growing the mildly narcotic drinks, as well as lowlands suited for sugar cane, which provided the great sweetener. Colonial sugar plantations had rooted western Europe's importers of tropical products firmly in the Americas. The hill regions of the Caribbean islands and the Latin American mainland both promised profitable results.

Chronologically, coffee was the second major export crop produced in the Caribbean Basin for European and North American consumers. On the Central American mainland it had far surpassed sugar by the late nineteenth century as the largest vehicle for foreign capital investment and the largest source of profits for the landed elites who controlled newly independent national governments. Before 1800 coffee was grown in the Americas mostly on French-owned plantations in Saint-Domingue (which became Haiti in 1804), with slaves as the labor force. Establishment of sugar plantations had already cleared Haiti's lowland vegetation; the establishment of coffee farms cleared the higher hillsides and disrupted watersheds. Some forty million pounds of coffee were grown in the colony and shipped to France in 1789, the final year of the Ancien Régime. In 1791, in the wake of the French Revolution, slave revolts broke out in Haiti, and the control structure of coffee production collapsed. The dense populace reverted to subsistence farming, and Haiti's hilly landscape continued its downward slide toward becoming the Caribbean's most devastated environment.

During the Napoleonic Wars, European markets for goods brought in by sea were severely disrupted; the British navy's tight blockade of the French coast helped see to that. After 1815 coffee consumption rose steadily in Europe and the United States, its cultural extension. American thirst generated the largest single market, reaching almost 750 million pounds annually by 1900, or over thirteen pounds per year for every person.[2] As northern coffee consumption increased, sources for coffee in the Americas diversified, and Ladino landed gentry and urban exporters together harvested a bonanza of hard currency.

In the present century the growth of coffee has had an enormous impact on Latin America, covering the largest area of any plantation crop in the region. In 1960 coffee trees covered over 18 million acres, in contrast with 11.5 million acres of sugar cane and only 1.75 million acres of bananas. Among all crops in Latin America, only wheat and maize covered a greater acreage.[3] About two-thirds of Latin America's coffee production is exported to Europe and North America. In the mid-1960s the United States alone consumed over 40 percent of the world's coffee, importing slightly more than all of western Europe combined. Coffee is responsible for 15 to 25 percent of Latin America's foreign exchange earnings each year, ranking behind only petroleum.

A survey of Latin America's coffee history must focus on southern Brazil, the world's dominant producer since the 1830s and the scene of one of the greatest environmental tragedies in the history of the Americas. Coffee built modern Brazil, in a symbiosis between the Portuguese-Brazilian landed elite and international market demand led by the United States.

BRAZIL: COFFEE PLANTERS DEVOUR THE FOREST

In contrast to their investments in sugar, Europeans and North Americans were almost entirely confined to purchasing coffee at coastal ports. With insignificant exceptions they did not own or manage coffee lands. Those who bought coffee felt no responsibility for the land. Indeed, they rarely paid much attention to the systemic effects of their investments, or even knew much about local agrarian settings. Thus it might seem that trends in the United States were remote from the landscape of southern Brazil. When this region was integrated with the world economy, however, it was transformed, in a pattern that would not have occurred without the demand of European and North American markets.

Well before 1900 American buyers became Brazil's dominant coffee purchasers, indirectly but fatefully helping to destroy indigenous Indian populations in the regions where coffee was planted and to sustain African slavery on the plantations. The American thirst for coffee was also indirectly responsible for the immigration of more than one million Europeans into Brazil after 1888, and it generated capital for the railroads and infrastructure that made Brazil the most powerful country in Latin America. American purchases of coffee were also the key to the extension of frontier zones, as coffee trees were grown on increasingly marginal land. Social and political conflicts and ecological deterioration inexorably resulted. The wave rolled on for a century, as the Brazilian plantocracy squeezed maximum short-term profits from the deforested land. It continued until inexpensive virgin land was no longer available.

Far south of the Amazonian basin and stretching inland beyond the coastal rainforest, southern Brazil's landscape ranges from subtropical to temperate. The coastal rainforest reaches southwest beyond the Portuguese colonial capital, Rio de Janeiro, which was built around one of the few fine harbors along the entire coastline. The colonial court that gathered in eighteenth-century Rio brought together the wealthy and powerful from all parts of colonial society, both inland and along the coast. After Napoleon's armies conquered Lisbon in 1807, John VI, the prince regent of Portugal, fled into exile in Rio, escorted by the British navy. Returning to Lisbon in 1821, he left his young son Pedro in charge, but the crown prince declared Brazil independent a year later and had himself crowned as Brazil's emperor. From that time until Pedro's son, Pedro II, was deposed in 1889, Brazil was led by rulers who were determined to bring the country—or at least its wealthiest citizens—into the era of progress and prosperity enjoyed in Europe.

The slaveholding landlords who spent part of their time at court turned their attention to turning the natural resources of Rio's back-country into wealth for themselves and power for their country. Coffee *fazendas,* or slave estates, flourished from the 1820s on in the Paraíba River valley, Rio's hilly hinterland.[4] The upper Paraíba valley has fertile soil of decomposed granite, and it enjoys a moderate maritime climate, with adequate rain during the growing season, followed by a dry season convenient for the harvest.

Through the mid-nineteenth century plantations spread rapidly up the steep hillsides. Land was virtually free for purchase by any speculator, Brazilian or foreign, who had connections to the imperial court in Rio. Labor was the greatest single cost for the owners of coffee estates, even though the workers were slaves imported from Africa.[5] The early estates were highly risky ventures; many failed within a few years, particularly those started by speculators who had little knowledge of the land and established the coffee trees on poor soils.

Soil on the sloping hills was rapidly eroded by conventional techniques of planting and tilling.[6] Woodcutters felled forest trees straight down, even on steep slopes. Lianas grew among the trees' crowns, binding them together, so when a giant tree toppled, it dragged down many others with it. Workers burned the jumble of felled trees and then planted coffee seeds or seedlings in rows between the large trunks that were left to provide good drainage in times of heavy rain. The ashes provided nutrients for the seedlings for their first couple of years. The fires often swept out of control, invading adjacent stands of forest. Each August a pall of smoke hovered over the region.

In the scramble for quick profits, the *fazendeiros* paid little attention to the quality of tree stock, planting clusters of whatever coffee seeds could be obtained from their neighbors. Mulching and harvesting were done haphazardly by the slaves, who had no incentive to work efficiently. In consequence, soil fertility was neglected, and many trees bore profitably for only twenty years or so.

By the 1850s, even in a time of prosperity, massive difficulties began to be evident on the *fazendas* of the Paraíba valley. Estate owners faced rising costs and unreliable profits on volatile international markets, as well as declining productivity from the first generation of coffee trees. The planters' early euphoria was changing to worry and gloom over their prospects. A few planters began to acknowledge the devastation; one criticized his peers for "mining the land without art or science."[7] Few paid any attention to the critics, however, for it was less expensive and less labor intensive to move to virgin territories, which were available for almost nothing by a government eager to conquer the forest.

Richard Burton, the indomitable British traveler, went through the Paraíba valley in 1867 and reported that it was "cleaned out for coffee. . . . The sluice-like rains following the annual fires have swept away the carboniferous humus from the cleared round hilltops into the narrow swampy bottoms. . . . Every stream is a sewer of liquid manure, coursing to the Atlantic, and the superficial soil is that of a brick-field."[8]

The last years of the century brought demoralization to the Paraíba coffee zone. The devastation of the soil and the dropping productivity of aging trees on old plantations, combined with the abolition of slavery in 1888 and the competitive wages demanded by free labor, led landowners to desert most of the old estates. "Under the beating rains of summer and the annual rough harvests and weedings, defertilized and aged coffee bushes no longer produced fruit and were abandoned. Some were used for firewood, others were cut down, and the rest withered away."[9] Hundreds of thousands of coffee trees were abandoned as planters migrated to new lands farther west. A secondary growth of grasses fit only for cattle replaced the coffee trees, and ranches gradually replaced the old *fazendas*. As the coffee planters moved to virgin land, the familiar sequence of roughly cleared forests, crude tilling methods, and rapid erosion of hillsides was extended. This pattern continued for another half-century.

THE RISE OF THE SÃO PAULO PLANTERS

From Rio's backcountry, coffee planters spread inland and southwestward, into the Paulista West. This was the hinterland of the city of São Paulo, which until the mid-1800s had been a small town on the escarpment above the coast southwest of Rio. In the last half of the century, coffee transformed São Paulo into Latin America's primary center of capital, technology, and political power.

São Paulo city stands on the heights of a dramatic escarpment, roughly two thousand feet high, looking down to the coastal lowlands. The state of São Paulo is a vast rolling plateau, its hillsides less steep than the Paraíba watershed. The region falls off toward the west, drained by several rivers that flow into the Paraná River. Large areas of the plateau support a purple soil called *terra roxa,* which is rich with iron oxides but dangerously subject to laterization, a process that turns it into barren hardpan if its vegetation is stripped carelessly away.

For thousands of years, nomadic hunters had roamed the São Paulo hill region. Roughly a thousand years ago they were succeeded by the semisedentary Tupi-Guarani farming culture. After 1530 Portuguese adventurers conquered, slaughtered, or enslaved the tribes. As historian Warren Dean writes, "Everywhere the Europeans acted rapaciously in their first contacts with the primitive inhabitants of the new world. In Brazil they were hunted for slaves to work on the coastal plantations. Raid after raid decimated them and shattered their culture."[10] Under pressure from these *bandeirantes* most of the survivors fled into the backlands. The Europeans managed to assimilate a few captured Indians into plantation life. "As servants and auxiliaries the Tupi taught [the Portuguese] how to dominate the wilderness; as concubines they bestowed upon them a mestizo population."[11]

In the early 1800s the São Paulo coffee frontier was penetrated and settled by smallholder squatters or *caboclos,* people who had been marginalized in the social struggles of colonial coastal Brazil. Dean describes the scene:

> In between the decamping aborigines and the nodes of town life on the edge of the plateau stretched a broad territory, still insecure and unclaimed, where only scattered army posts intruded. Into this were drawn people who sought a refuge from the oppressiveness of colonial rule. The landless could find land. The young and able were free of the draft, a terrible scourge because of intermittent war with Spain in the River Plate. Criminals were beyond the reach of the law. In fact the law often exiled them to the frontier. . . . The escaped slave headed for the frontier often—the hired slave hunter was called for good reason the "captain of the forest."[12]

The squatter settlers worked the land by the slash and burn techniques that they learned from the Indians' multicropping system. They planted crops with a digging stick in the fertile soil. Unlike the Indians, though, they harvested little more than maize, which was a large portion of their diets.

In the early 1800s there were only a few tiny towns in the Paulista West. They were surrounded by forest and linked precariously to each other by trails and mule trains. Around the town of Rio Claro, for example, was a landscape that had been partially domesticated by temporary human settlements in earlier years. In hilly areas, scrub pasture and second-growth woodlands grew on red soils that were still fertile, even after two hundred years of the sporadic cultivation of corn, rice, beans, sugar, and citrus. Other areas contained open fields on thin sandy soil, which supported only scattered brush, stunted trees, and a few cattle.

In the mid-1800s the landscape of the Paulista West was transformed into estate holdings. Outsiders from the coast or elsewhere gradually gained title to these lands, either by purchase or through crown grants. Coastal plantation owners, merchants, bureaucrats, and professionals used cash surpluses generated by the economy to invest in new lands. Acquiring virgin land was vital, since the owners depended on fertile new soils to maintain production. New landowners evicted most small-holders, subordinating many to tenancy.

The granting of land had begun in the colonial era, and the grants were still issued by the viceroy or governor. Grantees were required to begin cultivation or the title lapsed, which many titles did. By 1818, 98 percent of Rio Claro land was held in grants. New grantees immediately began land speculation. Many never lived on their lands. Many sold portions of their grants to sugar speculators. Those who stayed practiced the most casual farming methods as long as they had difficulty establishing title to specific locations.

The first plantations in the Paulista West were sugar estates, founded by speculators from the older sugar belt along the coast. Coffee beans were more stable than semirefined sugar, however, and they could be transported on mule back along the winding trails to the coast more successfully. Large plantings of coffee trees began in the 1840s. Soils in the region varied widely in quality, and the early planters did not understand the relation between soil and coffee production. Many coffee trees were planted in inappropriate locations and failed. The planters were convinced of only one thing: virgin forested land meant undepleted soil fertility. Within twenty years coffee trees had entirely displaced sugar cane in the Paulista West, and coffee remained the region's dominant crop until the 1930s. Its international position received a great boost after 1870, when the British Empire's Asian sources of coffee for European markets were crippled. A blight which first appeared in the

British colonies of southern India and Ceylon in the late 1860s devastated coffee production there, forcing the colonial planters to replace coffee bushes with tea. That blight never spread to the Americas.

By the 1860s the planters of the Paulista West had reached the farthest limit of profitable coffee cultivation for the era. Winding trails, rarely over six feet wide, were the only transport lines; mules had to ford streams or cross rivers on unsteady ferries. A major expansion of the region available for coffee estates came with the first British-financed railroad in 1865. Groups of plantation owners built branch lines with their profits. Planters thus controlled railroad profits as well; their companies gave their stockholders contracts to supply wood for railroad ties, fuel, and construction materials. Greater mobility allowed planters to move to São Paulo; most did so, turning their plantations over to hired administrators, who forwarded coffee to brokers in Santos on the coast below, who in turn sold the coffee to exporters.

Labor problems loomed large throughout the era. The speculative mining of Nature that occurred in Brazil during the early plantation period was based on a system of extreme human exploitation: the groves were worked by African slaves. In the rainy season they hoed the soil several times to uproot weeds and to keep the surface loose to absorb rain. As picking time neared they cleared the soil under the plants so that some workers could strip the berries from the entire branch and others could gather them from the ground. After the harvest, they raked old stems and leaves back under the bushes.

In 1850 Brazil abolished the import of slaves from Africa, so the planters began experimenting with wage labor on the coffee plantations. The planters hired European workers who might stay on the plantations for a few years, until they learned local farming techniques. The Brazilian government paid their passage, using public funds to underwrite the coffee planters' largest expense. By the 1870s a rising tide of farm workers was immigrating from southern Italy, forced from their ancestral homes by long-term soil degradation resulting from their own agricultural system, and brought to São Paulo by Brazilian recruiters. Brazil was their point of entry to a new and more hopeful life.

In 1888 the Brazilian government declared the total abolition of slavery. Most slaves happily left the *fazendas,* but there were many European laborers to replace them. By 1914 more than a million immigrants from southern Europe had arrived in São Paulo, drawn by the magnet of coffee and swelling both rural and urban populations of the region.

Under severe financial pressure from the unstable labor market, planters continued to minimize the care of the land. The old processes of mismanagement were encouraged more than ever by international demand in the last years of the century. The consumer economy of the United States was becoming the key to the ecological transformation of southern Brazil, although almost no Americans understood anything of the consequences of their caffeine intake.

AMERICAN MARKETS FOR THE BROWN TREASURE

The Brazilian plantocracy never encouraged foreigners to purchase coffee lands; Brazilians had both the capital and the political power to keep the Europeans and North Americans largely confined to the trading houses of the coast. Brazilians did have to work with the foreign buyers in the port cities through which the stream of coffee flowed. Rio de Janeiro was the only Brazilian coffee entrepôt until 1848, when English and German buyers also began trading in Santos as production rose in the Paulista West. In the 1870s coffee trading in Rio reached its zenith. Exporters handled the production of over four thousand plantations, which sent over four million sacks of coffee beans, each weighing sixty kilograms (132 pounds), through their warehouses yearly.[13]

Each planter had an agent, or factor, in Rio, who received and graded the coffee, using seven to nine grades to meet their foreign buyers' increasingly precise demands. Factors sold the graded coffee to sackers, who blended and sacked the beans and then sold them to exporters, or brokers. Most factors were wealthy and their homes were elegant, adorned in the European style. From the 1850s through the 1880s there were anywhere from one hundred to two hundred coffee factorage and sacking firms in Rio. Foreign buyers developed long-term working relations with the local brokers. The Brazilian government limited the number of brokers to seventy, and allowed no foreigners to become brokers. In response many brokers hired foreign assistants.

Trouble was brewing for the Rio exporters. Their source plantations began to spiral into ecological decline, and planters began to move their operations to the hinterlands of São Paulo and Santos. By 1900 Santos permanently replaced Rio as the world's largest coffee export city. In 1900 through 1901, Santos handled 2,945,000 bags of coffee, and Rio handled 2,413,000.[14] In Santos, factors and sackers were more often the same individuals, in contrast to the system that had flourished in Rio. The Santos system was narrowly controlled by the local oligarchy, whose members were well on their way to dominating national politics.[15]

The growth and decline of the coffee-growing regions were rapid and the consequences were far-reaching. The continuation of this pattern was assured by the international coffee market, which turned the coffee berries into gold for those who controlled them. The growth of European and American demand through the nineteenth century was the driving force for the expanding market. A few leading importers, most of them based in London and New York, controlled international prices. In conjunction with the wide fluctuation of coffee production from one year to the next, they produced a series of booms and panics that made coffee as wildly speculative as any commodity that ever left the tropics.

London had dominated transatlantic coffee shipping ever since the eighteenth century, when it succeeded in monopolizing coffee exports from the West Indies. By the mid-1800s London specialized in the premium mild coffees of Central America, the Caribbean, and southern Asia, especially Ceylon. But British consumers had cast their lot with tea as their primary source of caffeine. Their demand for coffee never ranked with that of their stepchildren across the North Atlantic.

After mid-century, New York, Hamburg, and Le Havre dominated the international market for the strong Brazilian coffee blends. New Yorkers had begun importing coffee early in the city's expansion, selling it in shops that also featured tea and spices. The heady aroma that floated from the facilities of commercial coffee roasters was familiar on Manhattan's streets from the 1790s on.[16] In 1864 the New Yorker Jabez Burns perfected a more efficient coffee roaster, boosting lower Manhattan's ability to process large amounts of beans. Simultaneously, the pump of consumer demand was being primed by adventurous Yankee businessmen who were traveling around Latin America looking for investment opportunities. Some of them headed inland from Santos on the new railroads and brought back enthusiastic reports from the *fazendas*.[17]

By 1880, of the ten leading coffee exporters in Rio, two were New Yorkers: Hard, Rand & Company, and Arbuckle Brothers. These two were among the biggest of the ten. Their power to manipulate coffee purchases reflected events in the commercial heart of New York City. From the 1870s on, as the American demand for coffee expanded in line with a flourishing industrial economy, a series of coffee booms and busts showed how volatile the market could be, and how much it could be manipulated by insiders. Stakes were high: through the 1870s as many speculators lost their shirts as prospered. Coffee wholesaling was closely tied to the New York Stock Exchange, and major traders like Arbuckle attempted to corner international as well as domestic markets.

High international coffee prices in the 1870s stimulated coffee production in Brazil and various other countries. Coffee from Java was still important in American markets, whereas trade with Santos was just starting up. In 1881 the notorious New York "Syndicate" or "Trinity" of O. G. Kimball, B. G. Arnold, and Bowie Dash canceled all imports of coffee from Java, and its price collapsed on the New York exchange. The price of Brazilian coffee fell with it, however, from $.1625 to $.095 in under a year. Several firms went bankrupt; collective losses were somewhere between five and seven million dollars.[18]

The New York Coffee Exchange was founded that year in an attempt to bring coherence to the trade. Its historian described it as "a central location to standardize sales, collect data on market conditions, and further develop the futures contract."[19] It was so successful in rationalizing the trade that a year later it was replicated in Le Havre for the French import market, and by 1890 Amsterdam, Hamburg, London, Antwerp, and Rotterdam had followed suit. Similar systems emerged more slowly in the ports of coffee producing countries: it was not until 1914 that a formal coffee exchange was set up in Santos.

As global coffee trade became more streamlined, it became even more volatile. Major competitors gained access to a communications breakthrough in the 1870s: the international telegraph. Rapid-fire manipulation of prices became possible, based on the telegraphed news of crop conditions and supplies from countries like Brazil. In 1887, predictions of a bad crop in Brazil led a cartel in New York, New Orleans, Chicago, Brazil, and Europe to drive the wholesale price up to nearly twenty-five cents per pound. Then they received revised news—a bumper crop was coming after all—and the New York price immediately fell by one-third. In the spring of 1888 several major European firms collapsed.[20]

By the end of the 1880s Arbuckle Brothers had emerged as the most powerful trader on the New York Coffee Exchange. They had dozens of competitors, but no one else imported even half of Arbuckle's volume. By 1900 the New York firms imported 676 million pounds of coffee, 86 percent of the country's total. In 1900 Baltimore was still a close rival, but its coffee exchange collapsed after 1903, unable to compete with New York for control of eastern markets. However, New York could not control the entire country's coffee imports, since by 1900 the national retailing system was simply too big and diverse for any city to dominate. New Orleans increasingly controlled the coffee markets of the lower Mississippi region; between 1900 and 1920 its trade rose from 44 million to 380 million pounds—from 5 to 29 percent of national consumption. The San Francisco exchange, which marketed coffee to the western states, expanded exponentially as the city recovered from the earthquake and fire of 1906. In 1913, 36 million pounds of coffee were imported; by 1919 the figure had risen to 160 million.[21] All sections of the country and all sectors of society were participating in a caffeine binge that seemed to have no limits, and southern Brazil was its major supplier. In 1920 the New York Exchange imported an astounding 767 million pounds of coffee, but that was only 59 percent of a steadily expanding national total. The increasing centralization of control was one way in which the international system attempted to manage the boom and bust cycles that were typical of tropical crop production.

By 1890 Brazil was growing only half of total U.S. coffee imports, but São Paulo still had vast areas of native forest that could be brought into production. By 1900 the region was producing record crops nearly every year: in 1902 its *fazendas* produced 15 million bags. The next year the figure rose still further to 20 million as additional areas of São Paulo's hinterland came into production; these were areas that had been cleared of forest five to seven years earlier. Trade in Santos was demoralized by the glut and prices collapsed. From their high of nineteen cents per pound in 1890, they crashed to five cents in 1903. Many estate mortgages were foreclosed, especially in the old area of Rio's hinterland, and some estates began passing into European hands.[22]

In response to these precarious economic swings, the state government of São Paulo, which was dominated by the coffee planters, decided to intervene massively in the market. In the harvesting season of 1903 it agreed to buy the next crop and hold it for sale until market conditions improved. It labeled this strategy "valorization"—equalization of prices—so as to give each year's crop similar value. Both the fiscal and ecological consequences of the policy would be far more vexing in subsequent years than anyone imagined at the time. Valorization committed the São Paulo government to occasional massive purchases in Santos, and for that it needed large infusions of cash whenever overproduction drove international prices down. The valorization mechanism encouraged maximum expansion of coffee production by guaranteeing planters a profitable price without fixing any limits to government purchases. Coffee production was also rapidly rising elsewhere in response to the high prices of the 1890s. In 1902 the global crop was 19 million bags; another bumper crop in 1907 produced 24.3 million bags, including Brazil's crop of 20.2 million.

To support the valorization strategy, in 1907 the São Paulo state government tried to borrow heavily from the Rothschilds in Paris, who had been Brazil's bankers for sixty years. The Rothschilds refused to enter the highly speculative game, so São Paulo approached the banker Herman Sielcken of Hamburg and New York. Sielcken raised enough cash for the São Paulo government to buy two million bags at seven cents a pound if necessary. Then the state was deluged by the biggest crop in history, and the government had to buy nine million bags. The price was still only just over six cents a pound by late 1907.

Other high stakes gamblers, including John Arbuckle, joined Sielcken. Now the Rothschilds decided to enter the bailout, but they proposed several conditions that would affect future coffee production and land use: the Brazilian government must prohibit estate owners from planting new coffee trees and levy fines on those who did, and it must guarantee not to export over nine million bags from the next crop, or more than ten million in later years. In 1908 the São Paulo government borrowed seventy-five million dollars from its New York and European creditors, who set up a committee of seven to sell the coffee when it would not upset profitable prices. The committee included representatives from São Paulo, Antwerp, New York (Sielcken), London, Le Havre, and Paris. This system promised to stabilize the Brazilian market, but it placed Brazil's export economy under foreign domination. In the following years North Atlantic bankers and brokers controlled nearly 90 percent of Santos's exports. The Houston-based Anderson-Clayton Company began operations in Santos in about 1910 and by the 1960s had become the leading coffee exporter. The foreign creditors even began expanding their loans to the *fazendeiros* themselves, and they foreclosed on some bankrupt plantations.[23]

It was not long before domestic American politics intervened, derailing the attempt to restrict the expansion of Brazilian coffee production. In 1912 Senator George Norris, the famed crusader against cartels and monopolies, charged the bankers with conspiring to restrain trade. The resulting congressional debate produced a 1913 law that empowered the U.S. government to seize coffee imported in restraint of trade. This effectively killed all American participation in future valorization systems and assured that violent price and production swings would continue.[24]

A severe international coffee glut threatened the markets again in 1913. The European bankers granted São Paulo two more loans, for a total of $60.5 million. They were forced to repeat the procedure in 1918 and 1922. All of the loans were gradually repaid and the coffee released on international markets. Little was done to control coffee production in southern Brazil, however, and the extent of degraded land continued to expand.[25] Ironically, although the international bankers' attempts to restrict coffee production had been made purely to support the long-term financial interests of producers and traders, had the policy continued the effect would have been to restrict the acreage under coffee, an environmentally beneficial result. Stabilizing demand, and thus planning for production, would have avoided wild speculation and frontier expansion.

The expansion of coffee acreage had long-term consequences for the landscape of southern Brazil. Large areas of Rio's hinterland were degraded, and the São Paulo hills were well on their way. Severe erosion followed forest clearance.[26] The coffee frontier continued moving inland and southward, claiming additional forestland as the international market drove it on. Cheap land with virgin soil was still so readily available that planters, having solved their labor crisis by importing larger numbers of Italian workers, could move entire operations to new locations. The heavy costs of forest clear-cutting were less expensive than the costs of intensive labor and revised land management techniques, which were necessary to sustain production on old lands.[27]

The cataclysm that was about to occur in Europe produced a decisive shift in the international market for Brazilian coffee. In the early stages of World War I Germany's imports from the Americas were cut off by its enemies' navies, giving the United States an opportunity to dislodge a major competitor from the lands to the south. By the end of the war, Brazilian coffee was exported largely to the United States. In 1919 American imports of coffee totaled 1,338 million pounds from all of Latin America, a figure that represented a remarkable 11.7 pounds for every American.

American coffee consumption continued to rise throughout the prosperous 1920s, the low-income 1930s, and the high-income 1940s.[28] In the 1920s Brazilian landowners responded to that enticing market by continuing to clear forest for access to new coffee soils. In 1929 and 1930, as the Great Depression descended on the global economy, exports to the industrial countries began to sag, and prices fell similarly. In 1931 the Brazilian government established new price supports for coffee, and workers suffered wage cuts or were thrown out of work.

Among coffee producing countries, only the Brazilian government restricted new planting during the Depression. Its efforts were futile. An additional law requiring *fazendeiros* to uproot a portion of their trees failed to reduce production because the planters destroyed only their oldest trees, concentrating their subsequent work on their younger, more productive groves. Some planters used payments received for uprooting trees to establish new groves on the sandy soils of the western São Paulo tableland. The planters, who continued to cut down shade trees, would find that these poor soils supported coffee production for no more than twenty to thirty years. Other planters replaced their groves with cotton or sugar cane, or chose to graze cattle on the degraded soils.[29] New small-scale coffee growers attempted to work the less fertile soils in the interspaces among the old estates, but the large *fazendas,* which had adequate capital for the heavy initial investment for clearing and infrastructure, continued to destroy additional forest on the coffee frontier. The scourge spread across the land.[30]

In November 1937 the São Paulo government changed its policy to one of dumping coffee on international markets. This strategy pushed international prices to their lowest levels in the twentieth century, since all of Brazil's competitors, including the second largest producer, Colombia, refused to restrict production or exports. Both supply and demand were proving virtually impossible to manage under the existing arrangements. In the 1930s Brazil was forced to destroy vast amounts of picked coffee, a total of almost 80 million bags. The government attempted price supports in 1937, but this only aided foreign competitors.

By then war was brewing again in Europe. In the relatively prosperous year of 1936 Germany had imported 14,821,488 pounds of Brazilian coffee, and France had bought 20,850,865 pounds (in contrast, the United States bought slightly over one billion pounds).[31] After Hitler's armies invaded Poland in late 1939, European markets for Brazilian coffee were closed for six years. Under these difficult conditions, the major European coffee consuming countries finally united their efforts, and in 1939 created a cartel, the International Coffee Agreement, which adopted a new system of quotas. Europe's quota system could hardly function, though, without the cooperation of the world's largest coffee buyer, the United States. In November 1940 Washington joined the agreement by setting quotas for American coffee purchases from fourteen producing countries. In 1941 the United States went further, setting price ceilings, as it did for many commodities. A year later it presided over a new Inter-American Coffee Agreement, which would guarantee a wartime supply of New World coffee to the United States. This system lasted through the war years, until 1946. It stabilized the purchasing and marketing of Latin American coffee, buffering the rural economies of Brazil and its competitors against wartime disruptions, and further consolidated the United States's dominant position in the market.[32]

INSTANT COFFEE AND THE FAST FOOD CULTURE

With the end of the war, a new era began for the American consumer economy. Less damaged than European economies, the U.S. economy dominated world trade for the next twenty years. Peacetime promised limitless security and affluence for an ever-widening segment of a booming population.[33] The automotive industry, its capacity bloated by the intense wartime production effort, turned to the mass marketing of family cars, feeding consumer dreams of speed and mobility.[34] The advertising industry blossomed, projecting visions of a new consumer utopia to an industrial and suburban population. Supermarkets and shopping malls trumpeted a cornucopia of consumer abundance, instantly accessible. Exotic products including bananas and other tropical fruits became commonplace on market shelves.

This was the culture that invented fast food. Technological breakthroughs in food processing made food and drink more convenient than ever for the mass of consumers. More highly processed foods, laced with sugar and preservatives, pervaded the American diet.[35] One of the most profitable inventions was instant coffee. Coffee that was powdered for mass consumption had to have a strong taste, and strong coffee was a Brazilian specialty. So the world's biggest and fastest expanding coffee market focused its drawing power on Brazil.[36]

In the 1950s the American consumption of coffee soared upward; both total and per person consumption increased. In 1961 the United States imported 22,500,000 bags, or 3 billion pounds, of coffee beans. Latin America supplied 85 percent of the total. A 1963 survey reported that the average American over age ten drank 3 cups daily, for a national total of 441 million cups daily. It concluded that "coffee and the coffee break are today an intimate part of the American way of life." The value of coffee beans was second only to petroleum products among U.S. imports.[37]

The end of the war in 1945 led to a rapid depletion of international stocks, and coffee prices shot up, tripling between 1946 and 1952. By 1949 Brazil's massive surplus of coffee was exhausted. Most coffee trees in São Paulo were old and badly damaged by then, as were the soils on which they grew.[38] Other parts of Brazil rapidly increased production, especially the southern state of Paraná, where coffee groves fast replaced the natural forest. The forest of Paraná was unique, dominated by *Araucaria*, or Paraná pine. This tall conifer was not a true pine, but the physical properties of its lumber were similar to pine, and the forests of Paraná were harvested intensively to meet Europe's urgent need for reconstruction after the war.[39]

Fortunately for the state's economy, coffee grew well in the soils and climate of the *Araucaria* zone. By the late 1950s, although the natural forest was greatly reduced, it had been successfully replaced by this other tree crop. This transformation was a continuation of the old practice of opening virgin soils for coffee production, but unlike Rio and São Paulo states, the contours of Paraná were less steep, and coffee was a stable crop. In 1959 Paraná passed São Paulo as the leading coffee-producing state in Brazil.

In response to endlessly expanding markets, world production hit an unprecedented level in 1958, at 45,780,000 bags of coffee, and even that figure was slightly exceeded in the following year. Brazil's contribution in 1959 was 25,500,000 bags. Coffee exports contributed roughly half of Brazil's total foreign exchange earnings. In comparison, Colombia, the world's second largest producer, marketed 6,500,000 bags that year, only one-fourth of Brazil's production. Those were the years when the American market totally dominated trade; it imported nearly 20,170,000 bags of coffee in 1958, and 81 percent of that was from Latin America. That year American firms imported 7,500,000 bags from Brazil, 37 percent of its total. By comparison, its Colombian imports were 4,200,000 bags, or 21 percent. Americans consumed a half-billion cups of coffee every day.[40]

Yet not all was well for the coffee producers. World coffee prices remained dangerously volatile. In 1957 coffee purchased unroasted at dockside in New York cost 51.85 cents per pound; by 1961 the price had fallen to 35.14 cents per pound. In 1958, groping for effective stabilization mechanisms as the price skidded, the principal importing and exporting countries founded the Coffee Study Group, which launched a global survey of coffee production and trade. A year later international coffee politics suddenly intensified, when Fidel Castro swept into power in Havana and threatened to export his revolution throughout Latin America. When John Kennedy became president in 1961, he launched the hemisphere-wide Alliance for Progress, partly as a Cold War strategy to thwart Castro in politically and socially unstable countries.[41] That August, at the hemispheric conference at Punta del Este, Uruguay, which launched the Alliance for Progress, Kennedy's representative announced that the United States would join a long-term intergovernmental program to stabilize coffee price levels. The new Democratic administration thus overturned the Eisenhower regime's opposition to governmental intervention in international commodity pricing.

Stabilizing the global market had the potential to help stabilize production and reduce its environmental impacts. But did it, in fact? In 1962 the world's major coffee exporting and importing countries signed the International Coffee Agreement, which established comprehensive, centralized international control of coffee stocks. Under the agreement, no more coffee would be released onto global markets than would maintain prices at that year's levels. More significant for coffee production and the lands on which the trees grew, the signers of the agreement vowed to promote coffee consumption internationally and work to reduce tariffs and quota limitations.

At its heart the new system was designed to adjust production to demand. This would prove to be very difficult. As the British expert J. W. F. Rowe noted at the time, most overproduction was in Brazil, which would have to pay its planters to reduce their yields. Funds for that would have to come from the United States. Rowe predicted accurately that this would not happen and that much coffee, especially in Brazil, would still have to be destroyed. The familiar, absurd pattern would be perpetuated in which "many men and much [sic] natural resources will continue to be employed in producing coffee for destruction."[42] Support for the existing system was simply too powerful among the planter politicians of southern Brazil and their friends in Washington, and American and European consumers were willing to approve any system that supported their drinking habits.

Kennedy's government saw the 1962 agreement from a different perspective from Rowe's, and officials carefully built political support for the new regulating system. On the morning the agreement was signed, the president's press release noted that the U.S. market was responsible for 50 percent of the world's coffee trade—441 million cups daily! In 1961 85 percent of that coffee had come from Latin America: 3 billion pounds, or 22,500,000 bags. Stretching the analysis a bit, the press release presented statistics showing that this trade was responsible for 662,000 jobs in the United States. Two-thirds of them were related to producing goods for export to the thirty-seven countries that produced coffee for the American market (over 16 percent of all U.S. exports in 1961), and one-third was directly related to processing the imported coffee. The White House calculated that 1,146 American communities, in all fifty states, were linked to that economic activity.[43]

Rowe certainly was correct in pointing to the Brazil–U.S. link as the most powerful element in global coffee trade. Across the social spectrum, Americans were addicted to a beverage that continued to devour the forest ecosystems of southern Brazil's hill region. Was there any hope that coffee production could be made more sustainable, more environmentally benign? By the 1960s the supply of new and inexpensive coffee land was no longer limitless, and land values were rising steadily. The financial equation was beginning to lead Brazilian coffee growers to intensify production practices on their lands by increasing their use of agrochemicals.

A United Nations survey in 1962 encouraged the estate owners to adopt input-intensive methods. It reported that modern techniques—including closer planting of trees, introducing more productive stock, and contour planting for soil retention—had begun in the 1930s. More fertilizers, both manure and chemicals, were beginning to appear, but soil enrichment of any sort was still used on only a small percentage of new plantations. By 1958 only 13 percent of Brazil's coffee lands were fertilized with chemical fertilizers and 29 percent with organic manures. Most chemical fertilizer was used on older plantations to prolong their productivity. By that time three-fourths of the soils under coffee, especially in Paraná, were sandy. These soils were especially deficient in nitrogen, but U.N. agronomists estimated that the planters used only 14 percent of the nitrogen fertilizer that should be used under those conditions.[44]

In a complementary strategy, the Brazilian government in 1953 had imposed systematic controls, favoring crop diversification in São Paulo. By the late 1950s the state was in the midst of an agricultural revolution, as production of cotton, oranges, sugar cane, and soya escalated, mostly for export. As agricultural land became more profitable under the new capital- and chemical-intensive methods, it also became more expensive. Land ownership in São Paulo became even more concentrated, and mechanization and export cropping proceeded at the expense of food production. Landowners either reduced workers' wages or laid them off. Unemployment increased and food shortages developed, leading to growing labor tension and even food riots.[45]

The Paulista planter aristocracy dominated national policies concerning cattle and Amazonian development. This in turn led to Brazil's Amazon development strategy, as an escape valve for rising social tensions. By the 1970s large numbers of landless laborers, whose forbears had migrated into the southern region in search of work on the coffee estates, began to join the exodus to western Amazonia.

American food distributors and their customers had been the primary source of the enormous profits that brought São Paulo and its ideology of hell-bent exploitation of the land into its commanding position in Brazil. The drink that kept American workers on the job, fueling the productivity of an economic empire, denuded the hills of southern Brazil. Over a wide region the species diversity of the original forest was replaced first by one species, the coffee tree imported from northeast Africa, and then by an eroded patchwork where scrub cattle grazed until modern agribusiness took over in the 1950s.

Warren Dean's ironic conclusion about the coffee era in São Paulo is fitting:

> Coffee enlarged the fortunes of [the big planters] and secured the plantation system. Plantations, on the other hand, were not essential to the development of an export trade in coffee. Unlike sugar, coffee does not have an unrelieved history of large-scale cultivation. The plant responds to extra labor inputs and skillfulness of tending with greater output and higher quality berries. Thus in Jamaica, Puerto Rico, and Colombia in the nineteenth century coffee was the salvation of a smallholding peasantry. The exporters of Santos, therefore, necessarily directed their coffee to a mass market unable to pay for better quality and inured to an undistinguished product. A great paradox: the freeholding peasants of the Caribbean raised their superior coffee for an affluent European middle class, while their factory- and farm-working counterparts in the United States drank the product of slave-driving latifundists.[46]

The counterpoint between social and ecological change was stark in southern Brazil; it was less easy to define in Colombia.

COLOMBIA: FRONTIER FARMERS, MOUNTAIN FORESTS, AND EXPORT MARKETS

The American and European coffee thirst became so great in the nineteenth and twentieth centuries that even Brazil's massive production became insufficient to quench it. New York and the other major import centers turned for additional supplies to the northern regions of South America, on the other side of Amazonia from Brazil to the Andean hill lands of Venezuela and Colombia, former Spanish colonies that had been independent from the early 1820s.

After 1900 Colombia became, and remains, the second largest producer of coffee for the U.S. market. There, just as in Brazil, American impact on the land was indirect. Just as in Santos, foreigners remained in coastal ports as coffee buyers and rarely bought or managed coffee-producing lands. But the Colombian coffee society, which American purchasers helped shape, contrasted sharply with that of southern Brazil. When coffee plantations were first established in Colombia in the 1830s there was no slave system to provide labor. Instead, the hill zone was settled by a complex, shifting mix of landlords and squatters; both could organize coffee production successfully. The social and ecological outcomes that this mixed land use produced were also very different.

In Colombia small growers played a major role in replacing ancient forest with the coffee tree, because coffee was an ideal cash crop for frontier squatters. The more profitable the harvest was, the stronger the alliance of landlords and urban traders became. As the country's major cash crop, coffee became the focus of social conflict between landlords and peasants that chronically disrupted production and frustrated the English-speaking buyers on the north coast. In each case—whether extensive estate or tiny grove—one ecological consequence was the same: the elimination of natural forest cover on the mountainsides of the northern Andes. It seems reasonable to assume, however, that another fundamental ecological change differed from large plantations to small coffee holdings: the large monocrop groves eliminated many other species of both flora and fauna that were natural to the forest, whereas the smallholdings tended to preserve many of them in remaining patches of woodland or in the variety of crops that peasants intermixed with their coffee groves.

The northern Andes of Colombia and Venezuela stretch northeast in a great arc, from the Ecuador border nearly to Caracas on the Caribbean coast.[47] The cordillera lies just north of the equator, so elevation rather than latitude produces a temperate climate. At these latitudes coffee grows at elevations of 3,000 to 6,500 feet. The first experiments in commercial production in the northern Andes began in northwestern Venezuela in the 1830s, where prosperity was slowly emerging after the ravages of over a decade of warfare. Cacao had been the primary export crop before 1810. As coffee prices began to rise, coffee production rose as well. Production tripled in the 1830s, mostly from the clearance of virgin forest at elevations above the cacao zone, and coffee prices continued to rise until the late 1830s. Sugar cane, cattle hides, and indigo were exported to Europe along with coffee and cacao; coffee provided one-third to one-half of Venezuela's total export value in those years.[48]

From the start, growers in the northern Andes specialized in the mild *café suave* for European and American speculators who provided loan capital but charged high interest rates. Rising competition from Ceylon and Brazil drove prices slowly down after the late 1830s, but the links between the coffee market and domestic affairs were tightening. Coffee prices crashed after 1842, and in 1848 the damaged Venezuelan planters rose in rebellion against their government. The cycle of civil violence tied to the coffee cycle had begun. Continuing agricultural depression through the 1850s triggered the Federal Wars in 1858, which disrupted the rural economy. Production returned to its pre-1858 levels only after 1870, when a new golden age for coffee began in the Andean region.[49] By then Colombia was on the way to passing its neighbor's production levels. Coffee groves had gradually spread from the narrow Andean belt of Venezuela southwestward into the much more extensive mountain ranges of Colombia.

Colombia is the only country in South America that has coastline on both the Atlantic and Pacific Oceans. (See appendix, map 6.) It is divided into four distinct biogeographical zones. The northernmost is the wide savanna of the Caribbean lowlands. Behind this coastal plain rises the Andean region, which dominates the western third of the country in three parallel chains of ridges towering 10,000 to 18,000 feet high, carved by the Magdalena and Cauca rivers. Just west of this range lie the Pacific lowlands, which contain one of the planet's wettest and biologically most diverse rainforests. Finally, the entire southeastern half of Colombia, beyond the Andean chain, is a remote, vast segment of Amazonia. Even now this region supports primarily a sparse Indian population, and its borders with Brazil and Peru are only vaguely demarcated.

In the colonial era agricultural estates clustered in the lowland hinterland of Cartagena, Barranquilla, and Santa Marta, which were the most important ports on that stretch of the Caribbean. In this seasonally flooded savanna, which extends east into Venezuela, cattle ranching dominated the landscape, supplemented by the cultivation of tobacco, sugar cane, cacao, and wheat.[50] From there settlement spread slowly south toward the mountains, concentrating first in the department of Norte de Santander, just west of the Venezuelan border.

The modern coffee zone, the northern Andes, has no pronounced seasons; the climate varies by elevation. The region contains three settlement zones: the *tierra caliente,* or coastal lowlands (1,000 to 3,000 feet), the *tierra templada,* or middle hills (3,000 to 6,500 feet), and the *tierra fria,* the zone of high mountain settlement (6,500 to 10,000 feet).[51] The forested mountainsides of the temperate middle hills were the coffee frontier—and experienced the worst environmental damage—from the mid-1800s on. Three north-south cordilleras constituted formidable barriers, hindering interregional travel and trade until the 1870s. In other words, the Colombian Andes presented many local frontiers that were settled one by one. Unpopulated areas, or *baldíos,* were abundant until nearly the end of the century. The Colombian government saw them as a challenge to development and a welcome outlet for the social tensions that developed in older settled areas. The environmental history of the Colombian Andes was thus inseparable from the country's socio-economic and political history; in turn, its economy was inseparable from the global coffee market and, in particular, the consumer economy of the eastern United States.

Before the Spanish conquest Indian communities were concentrated in the hill zone. These tribes cultivated mixed food crops on small plots of land. In the late 1600s and 1700s the Spanish conquerors gradually established haciendas in the river valleys, planting their crops in the rich bottomland soils. Much of the coffee produced before 1850 was grown on private estates that dated back to the seventeenth century. Marco Palacios, Colombia's leading coffee historian, concludes that

> [t]he establishment of the coffee hacienda did not take place at the expense of communal lands and the minifundia holdings [in the interior], as had been the case in other parts of Latin America, where commercial agriculture had come into sharp conflict with peasants and local communities. Colombian coffee-growers were able to claim, perhaps justifiably, that the consequences of their activities had been to further the advance of civilization in a wild and hostile environment.[52]

Coffee spread south into the hills of Cundinamarca around Bogotá, the new capital, from 1850 on, largely through the efforts of frontier peasant settlers. The heavy bags of coffee beans were shipped down the Magdalena River and sold to eager buyers from the northern world in the Caribbean ports of Santa Marta and Cartagena. In the 1870s mer-

chants from Bogotá entered coffee speculation; investors in Medellín
began competing with them in the 1880s. The rural elite, owners of large
estates, entered coffee production in the same years, using knowledge
they had gained in tobacco production. Together they became a class of
absentee owners and exporters. In the hills above Bogotá, quinine plantations were established in the 1870s; when quinine failed, the fields
were transformed into coffee groves on the higher slopes and cattle
ranches below. Newly consolidated cattle haciendas drove peasants off
their lowland farms, creating a floating labor market. The dispossessed
peasants became either sharecroppers on the estates—where their labor
was badly needed, at the lowest possible cost—or small family (*colono*)
farmers on the hill frontiers.

The Colombian government, eager to turn the land to the production
of marketable commodities, encouraged frontier settlement by giving
baldío land to any settler who would cultivate it. Dispossessing the indigenous populace of the mountains, the government sold wide areas of
Indian communal lands in the highlands to coffee speculators large and
small. The increasing immigrant population also grew various other
crops, including subsistence foods, tobacco, and cacao. They cultivated
marginal hillsides, gradually exhausting the land as nutrients were depleted and soil was eroded.

The national legislature generally supported small settlers, praising
the peasants as hardy frontiersmen. But when export booms occurred—
in the 1870s, for example—the resulting wealth was captured by merchants, financiers, commercial farmers, and land speculators, not the
smallholders. When land prices rose, the government happily sold *baldío*
land to the highest bidders, strengthening the power of urban speculators in Bogotá and Medellín.

The international marketing system for Colombian coffee brought
competitive buyers from Europe and the United States into the picture.
American purchasers helped determine the investments and markets that
fueled Colombian coffee production and settlement in the middle Andean hills. Foreign buyers set up their offices in the north coast ports as
the nineteenth century wore on. Exports grew rapidly from 1870 to
1897, then stagnated until 1909. At the turn of the century U.S. purchases clearly exceeded Europe's, and the U.S. market totally dominated
Colombia's exports for the following six decades. From a market share
of 16 percent of coffee exports in the mid-1860s, American purchases
rose to 72 percent in the period between 1903 and 1907.[53]

After 1900 the role of New York investors became steadily more important, as coffee importers adopted a policy of prepaying for annual crops. Colombian exporters attempted to open their own offices in Manhattan, but the New Yorkers successfully prevented them from doing so. In turn the Colombians prevented the New Yorkers and their European competitors from dominating the shipping houses in the Colombian ports—at least until 1920.

Under such powerful economic incentives, new transport technology began to open access to the hinterland, just as it was everywhere in Latin America. In the 1870s steamboats began plying the Magdalena and Cauca Rivers.[54] Gradually railroads replaced them, funded to a large extent by and for the coffee industry. By 1920, 800 miles of rail lines had been built in Colombia. A dramatic breakthrough came in 1915 with the completion of the Pacific Railroad, which ran from Cali in the far southwestern hills to the Pacific port of Buenaventura. The newly opened Panama Canal, pride of American engineers and politicians, had decisively reduced the transport costs from North Atlantic ports to the west coast of tropical America, and Colombia's luxuriant Pacific coastal rainforest belt was now available for exploitation.

Reflecting those infrastructural changes was the great coffee boom that developed in the central cordillera after 1910 and spread into the Antioquia region from Medellín south. Antioquia, known nationally for the entrepreneurial spirit of its people, was primarily responsible for a 450 percent increase in Colombia's export earnings between 1870 and 1918. In Palacios's words, the area "contained the most fertile and ecologically most propitious conditions for the cultivation of coffee, perhaps of anywhere in Latin America."[55] By 1920 coffee produced 70 percent of the country's export revenues.[56] Thanks largely to Antioquia, national exports rose from one million 60-kilo bags in 1913 to three million in 1930.[57] When Brazil's valorization strategists held coffee off the market, Colombia happily filled the gap, and its rising production kept international prices from rising and frustrated speculators in Santos. By the 1920s, the more difficult stages of the settlement of western Colombia were completed.

On the middle slopes between the Cauca River and the high mountain ranges, peasant settlements with their variety of crops produced a patchwork landscape of farm and forest; coffee was the cash crop that made their existence barely viable. Squatter *colonos* seldom had secure titles to their land, so they were vulnerable to takeover by the wealthy. In some areas colonization was dominated by the landed elite, although

Antioquia was a rather more open, egalitarian frontier society than were the older centers. Farming techniques on the small *colono* coffee holdings were land and labor intensive. The peasants used little manure or fertilizer, and they planted and replanted coffee trees in random relation to soil and contour. They planted trees in low density, interplanting other crops, which gradually exhausted the soil.[58] They did maintain shade trees over their coffee groves, in contrast to the plantation owners in Brazil, who felled the shade trees. The roots of the shade trees increased stabilization of the soil, and their crowns promoted microspecies diversity. Intercropping with subsistence crops also provided an element of stability.

During World War I transatlantic shipping was disrupted and European purchases of Latin American coffee were almost totally curtailed. At the end of the war, when European buyers returned, coffee prices leaped upward. Then in mid-1920, in a brief but sharp depression, prices collapsed. All of the Colombian exporters in New York went bankrupt, and American importers took control of the trade. The concurrent "Dance of the Millions," when New York banks foreclosed on many of the great Cuban sugar cane estates, was strikingly similar. Colombia's banks suspended operations and had to borrow heavily from New York and European banks. The Bank of New York and Battery Park National Bank seized the coffee stocks of two major Colombian traders. Importers like the American Coffee Company, a subsidiary of the Great Atlantic and Pacific Tea Company, began to buy green coffee directly from producers on the land, cutting out Colombian traders. E. A. Kahl, a coffee trader in San Francisco who knew Colombia well, was also deeply involved in these maneuvers as the West Coast manager of W. R. Grace and Company.[59] From then on into the 1950s American importers were dominant in the Colombian coffee trade. Coffee made up 60 to 80 percent of Colombian exports, and 80 to 90 percent of that went to the United States.[60]

Colombia's export economy grew rapidly after 1921 with the help of an accelerated inflow of North American capital. Investments in oil, plus loans to national and state governments and banks totaling $200 million in the decade between 1920 and 1929, developed industry, communications, energy, public services, and transport.[61] This trend was reinforced by the expanding world demand for coffee. Colombian coffee exports tripled between 1915 and 1929, and their value increased over 400 percent. Total government revenues from coffee exports quadrupled between 1919 and 1929.[62] Major credit for the new dynamism went to FEDECAFE, the National Coffee Federation, which was founded in 1927. Historian David Bushnell concludes that the trade association

> has worked with commendable efficiency to regulate internal prices, assure supplies of credit, control the quality of the Colombian product, and much else besides; and all those involved in growing and selling coffee were invited to belong. In practice, the federation was dominated by the larger growers and the coffee merchants, who naturally derived the principal benefit from its services. At the same time, though, the mere fact that the small grower was himself an independent operator did give him a sense of having a stake, even if a modest one, in the existing system.[63]

Vast tracts of hitherto "worthless" public land attracted large-scale entrepreneurs, especially in the newer western coffee zone, and elite speculators increased pressure on resident *colonos*. The boom and bust cycles of the global economy continued to plague the suppliers of primary commodities. When the Depression hit in late 1929, it reverberated immediately into the mountains of Colombia. By January 1930 the international price of coffee fell by 50 percent, destroying the financial base of many marginal coffee farmers. The European preference to import goods from colonies in Africa and Asia whenever possible further cut into the market for Latin American coffee, leaving Colombia even more at the mercy of the North American market.

Colombia's coffee zone was a perennial breeding ground for social violence. Under the pressures of the Depression, many dispossessed *colonos* attacked and occupied the larger estates. The Colombian government attempted to mediate between landlords and peasants, purchasing 240 estates in the heart of the coffee zone to subdivide for peasants. In those locations small coffee *fincas* replaced large estates. An agrarian reform law in 1936, which initially seemed to favor settlers, was used by landlords to dispossess marginal or unruly workers. Endemic social upheaval prevented any effort at careful, sustained management of the land.

World War II and events in the years following did little to alleviate either social tension or the consequent stress on the land. In 1945 peace returned to the international arena, but not to Colombia. Three years later one of Latin America's longest civil wars began; Colombians bluntly call it La Violencia. Widespread violence lasted for over a decade. By the time the war sputtered to a halt, some 200,000 people had died, and 800,000 were left homeless.[64] This epic but confused civil war had many facets. It was not just a peasant war: the conflict pitted region against region, urban area against rural, liberal against conservative, and more. Class violence was more severe in the coffee zones of the mountains than on the lowland haciendas, and its intensity surpassed the fighting of the 1930s. Many peasants left particularly bloody areas for mountain frontiers that were more remote, squatting without formal title on the public lands of newly opened frontiers. Guerrilla organizations flourished in hill frontier regions.

Few observers of the bloodshed in those years were concerned about the impact of the social and political catastrophe on the agricultural and forest ecosystems where it played out. Conclusions must be tentative, but some insights are possible, and they reveal the indirect impact of American coffee buyers on Colombian society and the country's landscape. In 1948 the American T. Lynn Smith reported at the Inter-American Conference on Natural Resources and Conservation that soil erosion was acute in the temperate zones north of Bogotá, as well as in large parts of the Andean zone of Antioquia. The result was either a major drain of population off the land or "hopeless resignation to abject poverty and misery." Smith laid the blame on the landlords, arguing that in colonial times the Spaniards had forced Indians off valley lands to establish cattle ranches. The Indians had retreated into the hills, where they grew wheat and potatoes. The steep slopes, gradually stripped of vegetation and soil, were "converted into badlands absolutely beyond reclamation, and the destruction is continuing at what is probably an accelerating rate."[65] Those hill areas, of course, comprised the zone of mixed cropping and coffee estates.

In the postwar years Colombia's coffee production and exports continued to expand. In 1959, a global boom year, Colombia produced 6,500,000 bags of coffee. The United States imported 4,255,000 bags, 21 percent of its total coffee imports. Another 1,077,000 bags went from Colombia to Europe, primarily West Germany.[66] By 1970, of the 11,250,000 acres of land in Colombia's coffee zones, approximately one-fourth was in coffee.

FEDECAFE, the national coffee organization, searching for new efficiencies in handling coffee, turned to a program of modernizing warehousing and credit, the commercial aspects of the coffee industry. The national economy as a whole was moving toward industrial diversification, and industrial investment by foreign concerns was increasing. Large-scale mechanized farming was gradually replacing traditional low-yield cattle ranching in the country's lowlands. In the 1950s the national elite emphasized industrialization and efficiencies of large-scale operations, which meant the consolidation of land ownership into fewer, larger properties.

Foreign coffee experts, whose advice was funneled largely through the International Coffee Organization, were nearly unanimous in their belief in the virtue of modernization, and they saw the large-scale coffee growers as agents of badly needed change. In the conventional wisdom of the time, they perceived the peasant smallholders as inefficient and backward, stolidly resistant to innovation.[67] Major Colombian growers began making the transition toward intensive production methods and, by 1960, technological changes were visible on the coffee plantations; after 1970 they became common.[68] Farmers began to increase the density of trees per acre by seven to twelve times; they used more productive tree varieties and, at last, began to employ contour planting and soil stabilization. They also increased applications of chemical fertilizers and pesticides. Land consolidation and more systematic management of larger groves somewhat stabilized land use on larger coffee *fincas,* but the cost of this improvement was increasing levels of agrochemical pollution. In the long run this reduced species diversity on and around the modernized estates. In contrast, smallholders could not afford the greater capital expense of chemical fertilizers and pesticides, which protected the species on their holdings from chemical pollution.

The ongoing struggle between landlords and *colono* peasants reflected the larger picture of national politics in those years. Between 1931 and 1971 the Colombian government distributed 27 million acres of *baldío* land to individuals and land companies. In certain instances landlords sold some land to peasants, but generally this was the least fertile, most marginal land. Other landlords turned tilled land into cattle pasture to eliminate the presence of unruly workers. Landless peasants moved to the cities, provided seasonal labor on coffee, banana, and cotton estates, or continued the migration to upland frontiers, putting pressure on the ecology of the hill lands. Forest loss and soil degradation continued to spread in these areas, a cycle that would continue until the underlying social problem was solved.

Americans provided the largest market for Colombian coffee exports until the end of the 1960s, when rising European purchases roughly equaled American totals. Yankee housewives and factory workers depended on Hills Brothers and Maxwell House, whose agents bargained with Colombian exporters; agents and exporters dealt with the large coffee growers of the core zone and the squatters on farther, marginal land as well. Northern marketers and consumers had no direct responsibility for the devastation of the Colombian coffee lands. Yet the steaming mugs on American breakfast tables were connected with the machetes and hoes on the remote north Andean mountainsides. Each was an element of the complex causal web in which international trade helped to perpetuate social violence and its environmental consequences. Other variations on this theme were played out closer to American homes, in Central America.

CENTRAL AMERICA: COFFEE GROVES ON THE HILLS

The third region where American coffee purchases produced major social and environmental impacts was Central America, the arc of land that connects the two American continents. After the region struggled free of Spanish rule in the early 1820s, it was split into five republics: Guatemala, El Salvador, Honduras, Nicaragua, and Costa Rica. Here, in contrast to Brazil and Colombia, Yankee buyers entered the coffee business late, nearly a century after European entrepreneurs established their position, and Americans dominated the trade only during and immediately following the two world wars. From the American perspective Central American supplies of coffee were hardly more than an afterthought when compared with the flow from Brazil and Colombia. In 1935, for example, U.S. importers bought 8.5 million 60-kilogram sacks of coffee from Brazil, 2.8 million from Colombia, and only 405,000 sacks from El Salvador, their largest Central American supplier. In a small country, however, that flow could dominate the economy and play a decisive role in determining how its land is used.

Coffee became the opening wedge of modern market agriculture in Central America in the 1830s. There, just as in South America, Africa, and Asia, coffee groves grew best in the middle hills, at elevations between 2,000 and 5,000 feet, where the moderate, healthy climate had supported most of the isthmus's population since long before the Spanish conquest. Each of the five Central American countries had its own distinct social hierarchy and pattern of land tenure. The ownership of coffee groves varied from being centered in a few large plantations in Guatemala and El Salvador to being dispersed among many smallholdings in Costa Rica. Environmental change initiated by coffee production varied according to the tenure system employed and the secondary effects it had on the land. Thus foreign demand for coffee had differing consequences from one Central American country to an-

other. In all of them the long-term transformation of the hills from biologically rich forestland to a patchwork of farmland featuring coffee
trees was closely tied to the European and North American craving
for caffeine.

About three-fourths of the region's land surface is locked in cordilleras, in sharply dissected hill lands and intermontane valleys and plateaus. Rising above the Caribbean and Pacific coastal lowlands, the central mountain spine is responsible for dividing weather and rainfall
patterns into distinct zones that determine vegetation patterns and influence potential human uses. Most of the region experiences a dry season from November through April and then a long rainy season from
May through October. The highest mountainsides of Guatemala, in the
northwest, know winter frosts, but elsewhere the climate is frost-free all
year. Rainfall varies dramatically, however, producing a range of environments from Costa Rica's saturated rainforests to local arid pockets
on the Pacific side that are as dry as northern Mexico. The mountain
zones tend to be moist throughout the year.

In the moderate hill climate, soils are as varied as the topography.
Weathered volcanic ash in the main mountain valleys and on the Pacific
slopes constitutes one of the richest agricultural soils on earth. It is very
erosive on slopes, however, and it quickly degrades when the stabilizing
forest cover is removed. Elsewhere soils are much poorer. On the eastern
hill slopes, in central Guatemala, Honduras, and Nicaragua, soils are
old, thin, and rocky. These soils are suitable for the traditional subsistence cultivation—small plots (*milpas*) of maize, beans, and squash—
but they cannot successfully be turned to large-scale commercial cropping. On valley floors, in contrast, alluvial soils are generally rich, providing some of the most desirable lands in the region for agriculture and
pasture.[69]

For centuries before the Spanish conquest, the Indian population concentrated in the moderate climate of the middle hills. Small communities,
the *ejidos,* shared their surrounding croplands and woodlands communally. Private property was a European invention, imported to the
Americas as a basic component of cultural and ecological imperialism.

In the 1500s Spaniards spread gradually southward from Mexico.
Military bands roamed the region searching for gold and silver and Indian slaves to mine the precious metals.[70] Their campaigns and their
diseases decimated the Indian population, which collapsed by some 90
percent within two generations. The total population of the region did
not reach the levels of 1500 until about 1800; by that time secondary

forests in the middle hills had reclaimed much of the land that had been converted into *milpas*.

The Spanish found little that interested them in Central America. They established a few haciendas on the Pacific slopes of El Salvador and Nicaragua, where the drier climate was similar to that of their Iberian homeland and suitable for their cattle and horses. They maintained a small export trade in cacao and indigo, which were the primary market crops before the conquest. Indigo, a natural deep blue dye used by Europe's burgeoning cloth industry, was the only natural product exported from Central America in large amounts in the colonial era.[71] From about 1600 on the Spaniards neglected the region, leaving more cattle than humans on the land as they failed to support the original lines of conquest. After the Spaniards retreated, the small population left behind was sharply divided between the culturally Hispanic or Ladino communities and the remnant Indian communities. The Creoles, the landlord class of Spanish origin, dominated the land and the economy. They were supported by the mestizos, a somewhat larger class of racially mixed workers in towns and on ranches, and the largest group, the campesinos, the culturally and economically marginal farmers and farmworkers. This social hierarchy largely determined the impact of investment from northern Europe in the nineteenth century, which reintegrated the region into the transatlantic economy and began to transform land use patterns.

For the final two centuries of the colonial era the region was a backwater, of no economic interest to Madrid or Mexico City and strategically significant only for crossings across southern Nicaragua and Panama to the Pacific and the viceroyalty of Peru. Just as in Mexico and South America, the Spanish Empire ended in Central America in the early 1820s, after more than a decade of sporadic civil wars. An exhausted economy was the most immediate fruit of independence. The elites of the new capital cities hoped to attract European investment, especially from England, which had emerged from the Napoleonic Wars as Europe's dominant economy. Primary products from the land were the only possible candidates for new exports, and from the 1830s on coffee proved to be the most viable.

In several countries of Central America, coffee ultimately became one of the two or three major exports. Grown in the hills of the central cordillera, it not only replaced the natural forests but also had a critical impact on the remnant Indian tribal communities, gradually depriving them of their subsistence base. In this regard coffee has been unlike sugar cane and later export crops including bananas and cotton, all of which grow primarily in lowlands where Indian populations had been very sparse since their decimation in the colonial era.

Coffee estates, or *fincas,* in Central America were generally owned by local Ladinos. Few Europeans or Americans actually owned coffee lands, except for Germans in Guatemala. The international marketing systems from the start were controlled by the importing countries in western Europe and North America. In this regard the coffee system resembled that of other plantation crops, whose marketing was controlled to a large extent by foreign exporters.

In Central America coffee became a dominant export crop under two very different social and political regimes: the relatively equitable landholding pattern in Costa Rica and the domination of the landlord elite in Guatemala and El Salvador. The long-term effects on the land were somewhat different under the two systems. A patchwork of hill forests was cleared and replaced by coffee, reducing forest cover in the region. Soils eroded more or less rapidly, depending on cultivation methods, but throughout the region the rows of coffee trees were interplanted with taller trees whose crowns provided mottled shade that helped produce the smooth, aromatic coffee prized in European markets and whose roots helped anchor the soil and reduce erosion. As a result, soil loss throughout the Central American hill zone was less disastrous than it was in the hinterland of Rio and São Paulo, and coffee plantations in Central America proved to be more permanent in the locations where they were first established. The Central American coffee economy did not move inexorably farther into virgin forest frontiers, leaving devastated lands in its wake.

In another contrast with southern Brazil, Central America did not have a history of slave labor. In El Salvador and Guatemala, where the colonial landlord class reinforced its wealth and power through coffee planting, some peasants were integrated into the labor force of the *fincas* and some were forced onto steeper, less fertile hillsides where they grew their food crops. In Costa Rica, where a colonial landlord class had never developed and hill land was rather more equitably owned, coffee trees could be grown successfully on smallholdings as a cash crop in conjunction with food crops. This system, similar to that in Colombia, tended to preserve a greater diversity of plant and animal species than was possible on the large *fincas.*

In the balance, coffee cultivation systems in Central America were less harmful to the land, and more sustainable over long periods in particular locations, than they were in Brazil. They were, however, highly varied agroecosystems, so it is dangerous to generalize about the region as a whole. In only one of those countries, El Salvador, did American buyers dominate the export market for any long period.

EL SALVADOR: COFFEE OLIGARCHS AND AMERICAN BUYERS

Through the first eighty years of production, before World War I, the entire crop of Central American coffee was grown largely for European buyers, who wanted milder, smoother tasting coffees than those available in Brazil. The United States entered this regional market only in World War I. When the naval war cut off shipment of Central American coffee to Europe, access to the American market enabled the region to avoid economic disaster. European buyers returned to the region during the 1920s, but beginning in the Depression years the United States dominated Central American coffee purchases for roughly thirty years. In 1950 the United States imported 100,000 metric tons of coffee from El Salvador, Costa Rica, and Nicaragua combined, ten times Europe's purchases from those three countries. Europe's revitalized markets—primarily that of West Germany, which could not draw from colonial sources in Africa and Asia, as did France and Great Britain—exceeded American purchases from Costa Rica in 1954, El Salvador in 1959, and Nicaragua in 1964.[72] For almost a half-century, then, the American market sustained coffee production in the region; it was also a mainstay of American strategic hegemony.

El Salvador, the region's smallest and most environmentally degraded country, is significant because of two linked circumstances. The first was a voracious hunger for land, which promoted the region's most extreme social polarization, between a tiny landed aristocracy and a dense rural population of landless, desperately poor laborers.[73] The second was the role of the American coffee market. Of all the Central American countries, only in El Salvador did American coffee purchases grow to be larger than European purchases during the 1930s. The American purchase of coffee was the primary source of the Salvadoran oligarchy's wealth and power. Today El Salvador sustains a population of about 5 million on 8,236 square miles, about the size of Massachusetts. Yet it produces the third largest volume of coffee for export of all countries in the Americas.

Lying entirely on the Pacific coast of the cordillera, El Salvador has three bioclimatic zones: a coastal plain, a belt of volcanic slopes, and an interior zone of geologically old mountains with thin, poor soils. The most suitable zone for coffee is a wide belt of well-drained, basic soils stretching from 1,500 to over 4,500 feet on the upper slopes of valleys and the central plateau, precisely the area where communal Indian villages were concentrated. On at least half of that land, groves were planted on steep slopes, inviting serious soil erosion.

Coffee production began in the 1820s, after the Central American provinces gained their independence from Mexico. From the start, the *fincas* in El Salvador were dominated by a tiny circle of wealthy landowners, the so-called Fourteen Families, who controlled not only land but banking and commerce, politics and the army.[74] This was a direct legacy of Spanish colonialism: in the 1600s and 1700s their ancestors had gained large land grants from the Spanish crown, on which they grew and harvested indigo.

The newly independent landlords looked for other crops that might supplement or replace indigo as their means of obtaining European goods and hard currency. As early as 1846 the Salvadoran government encouraged large-scale capitalist coffee production by passing laws such as one that exempted growers of 5,000 trees or more from taxes, military service, or export duties on their production.[75] These laws promoted the elimination of natural and second-growth forest over wide areas. Forest was cleared most rapidly by fire. Landowners gave tenants the right to burn, clear, and till the land for three years if at the end of that time no forest remained. From about 1850 the hill forests suffered a vast number of fires each dry season. One British traveler described the sight: "We were surrounded by fires on all sides. . . . The mountains around us seemed to be illuminated and glowing red. . . . Along a certain section of the road, where it passed over a well-wooded hill, the smoke enveloped us while we traveled to such an extent that it was difficult to breathe or even to see clearly."[76]

With the national wealth flowing into a very few hands, the coffee oligarchy dominated the government and the levers of law. For years, though, these landowners were stymied by the colonial legacy, which guaranteed local Indian *ejidos* communal ownership of their ancestral lands: these hill lands were precisely the best setting for export coffee production. The oligarchy's vision of Progress saw Indian cultures as hopelessly backward, lacking any trace of individual initiative, entrepreneurial drive, or desire for profit. The best that could be done for them was to force them into the dynamic new capitalist export economy. As one writer of the 1850s argued, "The only method of improving the situation of the Indians, of taking them out of the state of misery and abjection in which they exist, is to create in them the needs they will acquire by contact with the Ladino class, accustoming themselves to work by which they can fill them, thus becoming useful to national agriculture, commerce and industry."[77]

In the 1880s new laws abolished communal property, replicating a process that was happening throughout the colonial world. This accelerated the colonial inroads on Indian subsistence systems on hill lands and produced a rural proletariat that was dependent on wage labor. This was precisely what the agrarian capitalists needed, as an editorial in a San Salvador newspaper observed enthusiastically in 1880:

> On the one hand we see our virgin fertile lands that are calling for the application of capital and labour to reap the wealth that is promised; while on the other, we see the majority of the inhabitants of our villages content to grow crops of maize and beans that will never raise this miserable people above their sorry position. . . . [T]he government is determined to transform the Republic, to make each one of the villages, yesterday sad and miserable, into live centres of work, wealth and comfort.[78]

Taxes on coffee profits made possible a major improvement in the country's roads. By 1900 all-weather roads linked the east and the west through the highland valleys, and north-south roads provided connections between the hills and the expanding Pacific coast ports. Railroads quickly followed; a British firm built El Salvador's first railway to the Pacific coast in the late 1880s.

Much of the credit for El Salvador's expanding economy went to immigrant planters, Germans and others, whose achievements were giving El Salvador the reputation for being the most industrious and productive society in Central America. The most successful was Herbert de Sola, a Sephardic Jew, who entered the coffee export business in 1896; his family firm was Salvador's largest, controlling 14 percent of the country's coffee exports. The coffee elite had a variety of backgrounds.

> Immigrants with capital, international connections, and expertise came to El Salvador from many places in Europe and the Americas. No single immigrant group was large enough to form its own cultural enclave as the Germans did in Guatemala. The British, French, Germans, Italians, North Americans, Spaniards, Lebanese, and Jews who were attracted by the coffee boom, mixed with the Salvadoran elite, adopted Spanish as their primary language, married Salvadorans, and became naturalized citizens of El Salvador.[79]

Given their national ties to European markets, these immigrants were in a strategic position to open coffee export houses. They traded to a diverse set of markets, a diversity that could not be matched elsewhere in Central America.

This trend entailed serious social and ecological costs. Most of the labor on the *fincas* had to be extracted from Indians since no other workers were available. Few Indians would agree to a life so different from their traditional shifting cultivation unless their subsistence were so severely undermined that they had no choice but to look for low-paid wage labor. This was precisely the problem that had constrained the Hispanic rural economy since the sixteenth century. In the early years of coffee production, the *finca* owners maintained the colonial tradition of hiring squatter *colonos,* who worked the estate in return for the use of a small plot of land on which to grow food. But the traditional slash-and-burn method of cultivation practiced by the *colonos* was not compatible with large-scale, permanent coffee plantations. Many of the larger *fincas,* especially in the western hills, ultimately adopted a system of building permanent villages where the owners supplied food and other necessities to long-term workers, allowing them little or no land for their own crops.

By 1900 El Salvador had suffered grave ecological damage. Most of the country's forest cover had been stripped away from the mountains, and the crop soils had been leached of their nutrients. The disruption of the *ejido* lands and the consequent undermining of Indian subsistence were increasing the landless labor force, which threatened the landscape with slash-and-burn cultivation and the political system with the discontent of the dispossessed. El Salvador was well on its way to earning its modern reputation of being the "basket case" of Central America.[80]

This was the setting when Americans began penetrating the country's coffee economy after 1898, under the umbrella of American strategic dominance of the entire region. After the American military eliminated Spain from its last Caribbean colonies in 1898, Washington made it plain that it would intervene in the region's affairs by whatever diplomatic or military means it deemed necessary, whenever its strategic or commercial interests seemed at stake. The American military intervened six times between 1911 and 1925 in Honduras, next door to El Salvador. In adjacent Nicaragua Washington openly supported a revolution in 1909 and backed that up with military occupation beginning in 1912.

The United States intervened much less openly in El Salvador, but its interests were increasingly clear. As one State Department officer plainly stated, "Any student of modern diplomacy knows that in these days of competition, capital, trade, agriculture, labor and statecraft all go hand in hand if a country is to profit."[81] The United States happily moved into the market breach caused by World War I. In the postwar decade when European buyers returned, coffee constituted more than half of El Salvador's total exports. But inflation increased during the decade, and farm labor suffered. Staple foods became difficult for the campesinos to obtain: between 1922 and 1926 the market price for maize rose by 100 percent, and the price of beans rose by 225 percent. This provided a growing market for grain imports from the United States.[82] As long as American grain was available for those who could afford it, landlords had no incentive to improve or even maintain production of basic grains in local economies at the expense of coffee—and no incentive for concern about peasants beyond their function as plantation laborers. Social stress in the coffee economy intensified during the late 1920s, when world coffee prices steadily fell, reducing profitability and the demand for labor. Many small growers were squeezed out of business even before 1929.

During the 1920s El Salvador's coffee was still exported mostly to England and Germany. The upheavals of the Depression and World War II extracted a heavy toll from Europe's global trading system. During the Depression Great Britain chose to follow a policy of "Imperial Preference," in order to maintain its colonial economy. London favored the import of coffee from its East African colony of Kenya rather than the Americas, in order to maintain its imperial economy in East Africa. In Central America London's buyers maintained their former level of purchases only in Costa Rica. By the mid-1930s Germany's purchases from El Salvador had fallen to less than half their pre-Depression levels, and American purchases finally established pre-eminence: in 1936 over 70 percent of El Salvador's total coffee exports were shipped to the United States.[83]

The estate owners responded to the onset of the Depression almost immediately by cutting back production and employment on the *fincas*. The result was bloody social conflict between those who controlled and those who worked the land. In 1931 and 1932 the most widespread peasant rebellion in Central America since independence a century before wracked the coffee-clad hills of western El Salvador. General Pio Romero Bosque, president since 1927, allowed El Salvador's first open elections in 1930, and mass protest movements emerged, as they had in the 1920s throughout Latin America. The coffee planters in response formed the Asociación Cafetalera de El Salvador, to protect the industry from any governmental attempt to limit the transfer of *milpa* lands into coffee production or to regulate wages and working conditions on the *fincas*. Then, in December 1931, an army coup overthrew the relatively moderate Romero and placed Maximiliano Hernández Martínez in power. The coup triggered peasant uprisings in the coffee plantation region of the western hills. The rebellion was led by the scion of a landowning family, Agustin Farabundo Martí, who had become a Trotskyite, joining the new Central American Socialist Party in 1925. Martí knew anti-Yankee organizers in New York, including the relatives of Augusto Sandino, the leader of the peasant revolutionary movement next door in Nicaragua, which was challenging American-run banana plantations.[84] But fatally for the rebellion, there was a wide gap between urban Marxist organizers and the campesinos whom they intended to liberate. The urban men vacillated, and in 1932 Hernández's army slaughtered 30,000 machete-wielding peasants and their allies. The first great challenge to the oligarchy was bloodily suppressed. For another thirty years there was no other serious political challenge to the oligarchy and no other serious threat to their insistence on growing coffee rather than food. In the interim, the population on the already overcrowded land rose steadily.

The eminent botanist Paul Standley, working from the Field Museum of Natural History in Chicago, conducted forest ecology surveys in the Salvadoran hills in the 1930s. He saw the ecological consequences of the country's polarized land tenure system. Describing the squatters' impoverishment, he wrote, "In the valley of Sija woody plants have been exterminated so that . . . the only available fuel is grassroots. Tortillas are not made because they require too much fuel; instead the people subsist on boiled tamalitos blancos which need less fuel for their preparation."[85]

In the aftermath of World War II, Standley's younger contemporary William Vogt pursued the implications even further. Vogt, then chief of the conservation section of the Division of Agricultural Cooperation of the Pan American Union, was the leading American conservationist and agricultural development planner of the 1940s for Latin America. He concluded from a 1946 survey of El Salvador that, "As a result of the combination of overpopulation and resource destruction, there now remains within the country approximately only 25 percent of a hectare of cultivable land per person, and much of this has had its productive capacity gravely injured."[86] Vogt saw one significant hope. Since land use in El Salvador's agricultural system was very inefficient, the country might yet stabilize long-term productivity and come closer to meeting the basic needs of its population if it could move toward more equitable production. The challenge was becoming a matter of political will and ecological understanding in both El Salvador and the United States. Vogt's observations also implied one possible contradiction between social equity and environmental stability: the large labor-intensive *fincas* seemed to be more sustainably managed than the precarious campesino plots. At the end of his 1946 tour of Central America, Vogt concluded that El Salvador's oligarchic *fincas* were more carefully and intensively worked than the smaller plantations that characterized Costa Rica, where there was less terracing and ground cover, and yields were steadily falling.

Vogt also observed that on the slopes of Mount San Vicente in El Salvador, the large *finca* owners were managing their own soils well, but they were facing a serious problem of erosion from deforested slopes higher up the mountain.[87] He did not pursue that point explicitly, but suggested obliquely that the destructive operations above were caused by squatters forced to practice *milpa* slash-and-burn cropping on marginal lands because great landlords controlled the best agricultural lands below. That pattern, pervasive among dispossessed farmers throughout El Salvador and many other parts of Latin America, was essentially a political problem: the environmental issue was rooted in social inequity. Vogt, no matter what his personal views might be, was a senior employee of an intergovernmental organization, and he was in no position to challenge this political issue directly in an official report. Instead he proposed that peasants planting on slopes with grades of over 50 percent be resettled on remaining government landholdings on the coastal lowlands. Like other postwar agronomists, he also urged the accelerated use of commercial fertilizers to help maintain soil quality on the coffee plantations: "An active campaign should be carried on to induce as many people as possible to use fertilizer, and government advice should be given on proper fertilizer types. The first step toward increasing fertilizer imports would seem to be the removal of all import duties on them."[88] From that vantage point Vogt could not anticipate the problems that resulted when, beginning in the 1950s, that strategy was adopted throughout the region and commercial fertilizers and pesticides were used in excess.

Julian Crane, an American agronomist who surveyed the area in the same year, reinforced Vogt's warnings. He reported that few growers actually used careful soil conservation techniques. Their terraces did not follow the contours of the land, and on many *fincas* the interplanted trees and bushes were not dense enough to ensure soil retention. Crane warned that serious and widespread soil erosion had begun and could undermine the country's primary source of wealth.[89]

The national economy and the oligarchy were still supported mainly by coffee exports. By 1950 El Salvador's coffee was shipped almost totally to the United States: of 66,400 metric tons exported, 62,300 went to the United States, and only 3,200 tons went to Europe. The European share recovered partly during the 1950s. By 1956, of 67,000 tons total production, 37,700 tons went to the United States, and 29,600 to Europe, mostly to West Germany.[90]

A systematic United Nations survey of El Salvador in 1958 concluded that land use could be intensified and production increased, especially on the small peasant plots. Production figures indicate how powerfully tied to coffee the Salvadoran landscape and economy had become. By 1955, coffee accounted for 25 percent of the country's gross national product, 30 percent of the government's revenue, and 90 percent of its exports. For that it devoured 25 percent of all arable land, or some 2,316 square miles. Existing coffee plantations covered 338,390 acres in productive trees. The *fincas* also included 172,900 acres that were not growing coffee. This was a critically important figure, revealing how much land remained out of food production at the same time as dispossessed campesinos were encroaching on mountain forests merely to survive.[91]

By the 1950s coffee production had reached 1482 kilograms per acre in El Salvador, one of the world's highest yields. El Salvador's system was very different from Brazil's because of differences in land and labor. Unlike plantations in Brazil, those in El Salvador did not move every few years onto virgin land. They were, and are, permanent, because even in the late nineteenth century nearly all arable land had been settled; little new land was available in that small, crowded landscape. Brazil's large *fazendas* were dependent on the abundant numbers of low-paid laborers who could work the estates intensively. In Brazil, newly cleared coffee lands were seeded. In contrast, on the *fincas,* once the yield of older plants began to fall, they were replaced on the same slopes by new seedlings transplanted individually from nurseries. Manure and mulch were commonly applied to the terraces to maintain productivity and inhibit erosion. Again in contrast to Brazil, in El Salvador coffee was grown under mottled shade provided by a variety of indigenous trees, which held the soil in place and in some cases actually returned nitrogen to the soil. In addition, deep-rooted yuccas were planted between the rows of coffee bushes.

The character and consequences of coffee production in El Salvador were indicated in the 1958 survey. By then coffee was grown on a combination of large estates and peasant plots, but the major growers totally dominated coffee processing. Large *fincas* controlled the best soils and optimum elevations, and their owners practiced more intensive weeding and harvesting. The large owners also had better access to credit and marketing and could afford the most labor per acre. In consequence they had higher yields. The use of fertilizer and soil conservation was greater in the western hills, where the large *fincas* were concentrated, than in the eastern hills, where many campesinos had their own small groves. The estate lands of El Salvador were in some ways ecologically more stable than the estate lands in South American countries. Beyond that core acreage, however, environmental stress resulted from the survival struggle of dispossessed campesinos that had been forced off the good agricultural soils by the landlord elite. Politics remained responsible for the poor health of the land.

From the 1950s to the 1970s the oligarchy, and their military allies who protected their control of the land, were largely unchallenged. Military strongmen ruled the country from 1948 on, protecting the oligarchy's interests. One percent of El Salvador's people controlled 70 percent of the land and nearly all fertile agricultural soils. The Alvarez clan owned large *fincas* and a coffee exporting business; the Regalado family owned *fincas* and an instant coffee processing plant; the Quiñónez family owned coffee estates but also diversified into industry and export trade.[92]

American strategic interests throughout Central America undergirded this system in the 1950s as the Cold War intensified. The Eisenhower regime pursued a program of training and equipping the military forces of the region's oligarchic governments. American economic investment also increased under the safety of that umbrella. In El Salvador in 1948, $35 million of the country's total economic exports of $46 million went to American buyers. The value of coffee exports doubled in the following four years; nearly all of the coffee went to the United States.[93]

The instability of such a highly exploitative system was no secret. In 1948 Albert Nufer, U.S. ambassador to the region, observed,

> El Salvador's economy, which is based on a single crop, coffee, is necessarily unstable. This, together with the fact that the bulk of the population exists on a bare subsistence level, creates conditions favorable to periodic political

disturbance; has at times detracted from the effectiveness of El Salvador's cooperation in international affairs; and affords fertile soil for the seeds of communism.[94]

The ambassador was preoccupied with the Cold War, but there was more to the situation than that. Salvadoran landlords, firmly in control of the best arable land, expanded sugar and cotton production as well as coffee, further reducing food croplands.[95] By 1949 some 100,000 displaced Salvadoran campesinos had migrated to Honduras, looking for tiny *milpa* plots in the poor soil of the northern hills or wage labor with the Yankee banana companies on the Caribbean shore. The recession that hit the Americas beginning in 1957 drove down coffee prices dramatically: by 1962 El Salvador's predominant cash crop sold for merely half of what it had five years earlier, causing a further loss of cash income for the seasonal estate workers. By the early 1960s the number of Salvadoran migrants had swollen to a quarter-million.

The trend toward social polarization on the land accelerated further under Kennedy's Alliance for Progress. The program, which was launched in 1961, was designed to encourage a more moderate middle class and a gradual reduction of social polarization in Latin America, but most of its funds were controlled by the old elite. Aid to El Salvador amounted to $63 million by 1965, the largest of any Central American country. Under President Lyndon Johnson the United States wanted stability above all and was willing to cooperate with the oligarchy to that end.[96]

The flow of landless workers from El Salvador across the border into Honduras continued to grow. Honduras functioned as an escape valve for El Salvador's social pressures, but its hill forests paid a rising price. A British analyst observed that

> across the heavily-populated central highlands . . . the erection of temporary huts and the cultivation of maize and sorghum on any piece of available land, however unsuitable, continues everywhere. On the most inaccessible steep and rocky slopes, a straw hut, a scratched patch of earth, and the bent backs of a squatter family tending their maize are a common sight.[97]

By 1969, 300,000 Salvadorans, one-eighth of the population, were in Honduras. That July a riot at a soccer match escalated into a week-long war between the two countries; in the convulsion, several thousand died and 100,000 were left homeless. The Honduran government used the situation to expel as many Salvadorans as it could. Something like 200,000 workers and their families staggered home to El Salvador, but their own country could not absorb them without serious land reform, which the regime would not tolerate.

Economic and living conditions steadily deteriorated through the 1970s. Almost half the land on large estates was in pasture or lay fallow. Guerrilla operations against the landlords slowly expanded, and death squads organized by oligarchs began kidnapping and murdering hundreds of campesinos. After the 1979 revolution in Nicaragua, when Sandinista forces overthrew a similar oligarchy dominated by the Somoza family, the Carter administration finally pressed the Salvadoran government to initiate serious land reform. A 1980 plan envisioned that the United States would pay the cost of purchasing and dividing estates over 1,250 acres, and then subdividing farms over 250 acres. A few estate owners sold their land at inflated prices and moved to Miami, but this effort was doomed to failure: the regime would not cut away seriously at its own base of wealth and power. After the far right, led by Roberto D'Aubuisson, won rigged elections in 1982, the government in San Salvador cancelled all pretense of land reform.[98]

Meanwhile the Cold War's pressures were accelerating. American military aid to El Salvador, which had totaled $6 million in 1980, rose to $82 million in 1982 under President Ronald Reagan. Economic aid, controlled by the oligarchy for its own ends, rose from $58 million to $185 million.[99] The civil war was stalemated, and it continued to drain blood and wealth and devastate the land for another decade.[100] Production was disrupted on many coffee estates. Short-term laborers could not be found for the autumn harvest, and during the rest of the year the less dramatic but environmentally important work of protecting the soil was neglected.

As the stalemate continued, El Salvador's land and natural resources continued to be dominated by the coffee-growing oligarchy, which also controlled the country's politics, its army, and its export economy. The Salvadoran system was supported economically and strategically by the U.S. government—thus the United States held a major share of ultimate responsibility for the festering social and ecological wounds of the country.

CONCLUSION: TOWARD A SUSTAINABLE TREE CROP?

America's consumption of coffee always had a more indirect environmental impact than its consumption of sugar or bananas. In the coffee cycle from production to consumption, Americans played two roles: as purveyors of the world's largest market, and as consumers of the black brew. They played little or no role in the actual management of the land. Nonetheless, the American market was the engine that drove coffee-centered agroecosystems in Brazil, Colombia, and El Salvador.

Coffee production began to transform hill lands throughout tropical and subtropical Latin America in the 1830s. As a dominant cash crop for international markets, coffee strengthened the hold of landed oligarchies in some countries and was the key to successful peasant pioneer farming on the forest frontier in others. The United States was central to this transformation, since Americans had become the world's greatest coffee consumers by the late 1800s. Their virtually exclusive source of supply was Latin America until the 1950s, when American purchasers began moving into African production areas as well.[101] In contrast to sugar cane and bananas, but much like rubber, coffee did not have to be quickly processed and transported to market. Coffee could be produced by small farmers as competitively as by landlords or corporate plantations. Peasant households that grew coffee as a cash crop in conjunction with a variety of subsistence crops were financially viable. This more complex, multispecies strategy supported the continuing presence of a wider spectrum of flora and fauna than was possible under the one-crop system of large estates.

When intensified production (based on new varieties and denser planting of coffee plants) emerged in the 1950s, along with more sustainable management of hill soils, the larger producers throughout Latin America were in a better position to adopt the innovative methods than the marginal farmers were. Brazilian growers at last began to nurture shade trees in the coffee groves in the 1950s, echoing the system long used in tiny El Salvador. Thirty years later, new varieties of coffee trees whose product did not require shade from the intense sun began to displace the older shaded groves throughout the Americas, so as to increase production on existing acreage. Throughout recent decades production has continued to rise as growers have intensified the application of commercial fertilizers and pesticides, a strategy that eliminates adjunct species and places chemical residues in the soil and downstream waters.

Finally, as large-scale coffee production advanced, it displaced subsistence farmers, who were forced either to squat on forestlands or to migrate to the burgeoning cities. In Brazil by the 1960s and 1970s the production area stabilized somewhat and land management improved, but farm workers were displaced into cities or onto the Amazonian frontier, where an even greater ecological disaster was growing. In Colombia conditions on the land remained notoriously unstable, as the struggle between landed and landless continued to roil. And El Salvador drifted into civil war, as Central America's most poverty-stricken campesinos organized against their landlord government and its strategic backer from the North with increasing effectiveness.

None of this mattered to coffee advertisers in the United States, who convinced their public that Juan Valdez, the resourceful and contented independent coffee farmer, would tend his small groves in perpetuity to satisfy his Yankee consumer's need for caffeine and sociability. Northern coffee traders and consumers fueled both social conflict and environmental stress through their purchases. Even if American traders spent long years in the coastal marketing offices of Latin American producers, they had no concern for what was happening to the landscapes of the supplying countries. Their sole interest was to buy the coffee beans at competitively low prices and in assured supplies. American consumers knew virtually nothing of the ecological or social circumstances that supported their daily rituals: a first morning cup at home, a mid-morning coffee break at the workplace, and a final cup with dessert in the evening.

CHAPTER 5

The Tropical Cost of the Automotive Age

*Corporate Rubber Empires
and the Rainforest*

Take away from us the motor vehicle, and I do not know
what would happen. The damage would be more serious
and lasting than if our land were laid waste by an invader.
We could recover from the blowing up of New York City
and all the big cities on the Atlantic seaboard more quickly
than we could recover from the loss of our rubber.

Harvey Firestone, 1926

INTRODUCTION: THE ERA OF INDUSTRIAL RUBBER

The commercial cultivation of sugar cane and bananas had devoured
the coastal lowlands of the Caribbean, Central America and northern
South America, Hawaii, and the Philippines. Coffee estates had eroded
the mid-elevation hill regions of tropical and subtropical America. This
process was continued by the corporate rubber plantations, which extended the domestication of tropical rainforest ecosystems into new
regions: Indonesia and Malaya in Southeast Asia and Liberia in West
Africa. The industry also made abortive efforts in Amazonia and other
tropical American rainforest regions.

The rubber industry, and the global consumer demand that it created
and satisfied, attacked the moist tropical ecosystems on two fronts.
Somewhat similar to coffee, rubber could be commercially grown either
on vast one-crop plantations or as the primary cash-earning commodity
on multicrop smallholder farms. Varieties of the best source of rubber,

Hevea brasiliensis, were developed that raised productivity fully ten times over that of natural trees. Rubber could also be harvested directly from wild trees in its Amazonian homeland without seriously damaging its surroundings, but intensification of production, particularly on the corporate estates, became a hallmark of the industry and one of the most dramatic triumphs of tropical agronomy.

However vast the clearings of natural forest for rubber were, the acreage would have been far greater in the long run if the rubber products industry had not developed a second source to complement it: synthetic rubber refined from petroleum, which came on the market during the supply crisis of World War II. This technological breakthrough, catalyzed by the military emergency, transformed the global rubber economy. Since 1960 roughly two-thirds of global rubber production has been derived from synthetics; the other third has been harvested from lands that once sustained rainforests. In this segment of tropical forest clearance, the United States led the way, driven by innovations in automotive engineering and marketing. America's impact on the production of rubber was unmatched for any other tropical monocrop except bananas.

Rubbery substances derived from the latex of various tropical trees, bushes, and vines had long been in use, but in hot weather they tended to melt and in cold settings they became brittle. In 1837 the American inventor Charles Goodyear invented the vulcanization process, which stabilized latex products over a wide temperature range, opened up a vast new range of possibilities for the industrial era, and gave Goodyear's company an early lead in developing product lines and markets. American rubber consumption rose slowly until about 1890. At first the new product was used primarily by the clothing industry in New England's mill towns to produce wet weather boots and clothes. Toward the end of the century this market was superceded as rubber was used increasingly for bicycle and then automobile tires and a burgeoning range of other commercial and industrial uses. Around 1900 heavy industry—especially the new automotive industry, in which American markets quickly became dominant—began creating an insatiable market for the latex.

Unsure of where sources of latex might be reliably found, commercial adventurers from Europe and the United States searched the world's tropical lowlands throughout the century. In Africa Europeans tried collecting the milky sap of several species in the genus *Landolphia,* but these rainforest vines were generally destroyed by the tapping. They also experimented with the Kickxia tree (*Funtumia elastica*), a large forest tree whose latex they collected by cutting deep lateral gashes in the trunk, but this species of tree also often died in the process. Both experiments ended after 1910.[1]

A very different source of latex grew naturally in Mexico and Central America: guayule (*Parthemum argentatum*), a shrub that thrives in semi-arid settings at elevations of 3,000 to 5,000 feet. Its latex is found in solid particles dispersed throughout the woody fiber. Workers harvested it by regular clipping or by uprooting it when it was at least five years old and then separated the latex by pulping the stalks. In 1904 the pioneer United States Rubber Company staked a three-million-acre stand of guayule in Coahuila in northern Mexico, in a concession gained in the final years of President Porfirio Díaz's courting of northern investments. The young Bernard Baruch and his associates were involved in that experiment until it collapsed in 1911 with the onset of the Mexican Revolution and the massive entry of Southeast Asian rubber onto the world market.[2] Thereafter, industrial efforts never succeeded in producing guayule latex in major quantities.

The lowland wet forests of Southeast Asia revealed several promising species that British, Dutch, and French colonial botanists studied. In British Malaya the rambong tree (*Ficus elastica*) produced latex in its aerial roots, but it gave very low yields. The jelutong tree (*Dyera costulata*), which towers as high as 170 feet in the jungle, was another possibility, but its latex had a heavy resin content and was difficult to purify. A third possibility was the getah grip of the *Willughbeia* genus, a vine that climbs high into its host trees. It was tapped by ringing the stem, but like the lianas of the African rainforest, this vine was usually killed in the process.[3]

The rapacious aspect of the research damaged all of these species, but because none of them proved to be commercially viable on a large scale, no permanent harm was done to the plant and animal communities in which they grew. The *Hevea brasiliensis,* a tree endemic to the Amazonian rainforest that had been already harvested for decades, proved to be the best source of latex. Rubber exports from Brazil, the United States' primary supplier, rose from 200 tons in 1830 to 17,000 tons in 1890.[4] After 1890, as the world demand for rubber burgeoned, *Hevea* latex rapidly eliminated all others from international trade, and the tree was taken to Africa and Asia, where dense one-species plantations replaced rainforest over large areas.

AMERICAN SPECULATORS IN AMAZONIA

Until the start of World War I in 1914, Americans used natural *Hevea* rubber from Brazilian Amazonia almost exclusively.[5] The U.S. market was the single largest from the start; thus American consumers generated a fateful link to the rainforest. The Yankee buyers who served their interests followed a procurement strategy similar to that used by their counterparts in the coffee business. They purchased commodities from Brazilian suppliers in coastal ports on the periphery of the production regions. They made few efforts to produce the products themselves, which would have entailed direct responsibility for managing the land.

Beginning in the 1820s British and American explorers and speculators engaged in a strategic race in the Amazon basin, mapping the vast unknown territory and searching for any product that they could commandeer, including rubber. The first American steamboat explored the upper Amazon in 1826. In 1849 two U.S. Navy officers, Lewis Herndon and Lardner Gibbon, conducted a navigability survey of the main river. Herndon was the brother-in-law of Matthew Maury, head of the National Observatory in Washington and chief booster of U.S. trade with Amazonia. In hyperbolic prose typical of the age, Maury reported that Brazil "has arrayed herself against the improvement and the progress of the age, and she has attempted by intrigue so to shape the course of events that she might lock up and seal with the seal of ignorance and superstition and savage barbarity the finest portions of the earth."[6] Global progress would result from increased international trade, and Americans of imperial ambition would lead that historic trend, Maury trumpeted.

By the 1850s explorers had probed nearly all the major tributaries of the Amazon, searching for the occasional fairly dense stand of *Hevea*. Along the vaguely defined border between Brazil and Bolivia, on the Madeira branch, were the finest of all *Hevea* forests. (See appendix, map 7.) George Church, an American adventurer, worked with the Bolivian government to build a railroad into its portion of the Amazonian lowlands. Backed by British capital, he began constructing the notorious Madeira-Mamoré Railway in 1872, but his workers collapsed in large numbers from jungle diseases. Church went bankrupt, but he was not yet finished. He went next to Philadelphia, whose large pool of unemployed laborers might be willing to go to civilization's farthest frontier for a pittance. In 1878 he again left for South America, this time with Irish, German, and Italian workers. In the brutal working conditions of the jungle, their ethnic rivalries turned into brawls, and those who did not die raced away from what had become a green hell. Next Church hired landless peasants from Ceará in northeastern Brazil, but by 1881, 500 out of 1,400 had died from yellow fever. That marked the end of the first ignominious Yankee effort to tame the Amazon.[7]

The Bolivian powerbrokers were obsessed with the desire for a link to the Atlantic. They were determined to gain free passage down the Amazon, an idea that the Brazilian government disliked. In 1866 the two governments agreed on the Treaty of Ayacucho, which drew an arbitrary line across terra incognito, giving the remote jungle region of Acre to Bolivia.

Then in 1877 northeastern Brazil suffered one of its most severe droughts. Desperate for any form of survival, 100,000 dispossessed Cearense workers flooded up the Amazon, many of them into Acre, whose Indian tribes had never before seen more than a handful of Brazilians. The rootless peasants provided a new opportunity for American speculators to dabble in rainforest politics. The "Bolivian Syndicate," whose member investors included J. P. Morgan, the Vanderbilt family, and a cousin of Teddy Roosevelt, attempted to raise capital to back the Bolivian side.[8] Brazil was not about to allow its competitors to grab land that Rio coveted, however. In 1903 Brazil defeated Bolivia in a brief war and annexed the wide, remote region of Acre, which was the home of the finest stands of natural *Hevea* in existence.

Over many millennia in the Amazonian rainforest, several closely related species of *Hevea* had evolved. The most productive was *Hevea brasiliensis*. The *Hevea* trees were widely dispersed, with only a few growing in each acre of forest. This prevented the parasites, which had co-evolved with the tree, from concentrating their attacks. This natural defense was destroyed when humans planted the trees in dense groves.

Extracting the precious white *Hevea* latex and shipping it out of the jungle required the skills and tenacity of people who could survive the extremely difficult living conditions of the basin. Outside speculators had failed in their efforts to gain direct control of forest tracts, and they had no hope of participating directly in latex extraction. The latex was tapped by *seringueiros*, hardy men who knew the obscure trails through the forest. Demand for the *seringueiros'* work began to accelerate after Goodyear's invention. By the 1860s the industrial world was beginning to penetrate even the most remote areas of Amazonia.

The flow of immigrant workers from poverty-stricken Ceará began to increase. They were controlled by *seringalistas,* powerful men who grasped the ownership of large or small forest tracts from the indigenous tribes of the forest by legal or illegal means. Indians were displaced, destroyed, or occasionally forced to collect rubber. The owners supplied the tappers with food, tools, and loans, and bought the crude rubber they harvested at improvised trading posts along the main flow of the Amazon and its tributaries, far beyond the reach of civilized existence. This was a brutal life; the tappers were locked into servitude to the owners by debts and the threat of violence. No government could reach far enough into the interior to restrain the exploitation.

In turn the *seringalistas* sold the collected crude rubber to *aviadores*, investors or their agents in Belém, the largest city near the mouth of the Amazon and capital of the vast state of Pará. By 1880 foreign buyers, both British and American, had set up offices in Belém to purchase large orders of what they dubbed "Pará rubber" from the merchant houses there.

International markets for Pará rubber expanded rapidly after the late 1880s, led by the newly booming tire industry. "The bicycle craze proved to be a mere preview of things to come; it was the rise of the automobile that definitively transformed rubber manufacturing into a major component of the world's most sophisticated industrial complex."[9] In 1900 the Amazon basin produced 25,000 metric tons of rubber; by 1909 that figure rose to 40,000 tons. Demand rose even faster, so prices doubled in that decade to almost three dollars per pound.

Market prospects like these were enough to give the jungle itself market value, for whoever owned the land might hope to control the profits. The remote interior of Amazonia underwent a boom in speculative land sales in the 1890s, as soon as the Brazilian government adopted simplified land registration procedures. The large *aviadores* of Belém exploited their contacts in the interior to amass huge parcels—at least on paper—in the first of Amazonia's destructive land scrambles.[10]

With their title papers in hand, speculators in Belém cashed in on gullible buyers at home and abroad. Like their brothers in the western United States in the same years, some of these agents were legitimate, others total frauds. They advertised land for sale in many newspapers and trade journals; the first American ad appeared in 1901 in New York's *India Rubber World*.

Some of the companies in Belém came to be controlled by foreigners, who had larger capital reserves than local people did. One of the largest foreign speculators, Comptoir Colonial, a French firm organized in

1899, bought 300 square miles of rainforest with 2,500 functioning trails and 250,000 *Hevea* trees, plus assorted trading posts, huts, boats, and three steam launches. Foreign speculation like this never succeeded in controlling the upriver networks, which were dominated by the new Portuguese-speaking land barons.

The obstacles that the foreigners faced did not result from any lack of grandiose ambition. In the dawn of the new century a group of American rubber manufacturers organized the United States Rubber Company, dreaming that they could monopolize Amazonian production. Assuming that a big enough barrel of cash would enable them to dominate the trade, they planned to raise $50 million and to buy out Amazon Steam, the only steamboat company plying the river. They hoped the Pará state government would pay their navigation subsidies in rubber lands, not cash. Their Brazilian competitors, much better placed politically, prevented that from happening. The plans of these ambitious Yankee investors failed because they knew nothing about the jungle or its people.[11]

American and European speculators never gained any effective control over the harvesting of Amazonian jungle rubber. Portuguese was the language of domination in the jungle; Brazilians systematically manipulated and frustrated the northerners. After the British-owned Brazilian Rubber Trust collapsed, a manager commented in exasperation that only Chinese or Japanese labor would work under discipline for wages—no foreign firm could make the Brazilian *seringueiros* work on its terms. As Barbara Weinstein writes,

> Dismayed at the "primitive" character of the Amazon's extractive economy, European and American corporations made intermittent attempts to play a greater role in the production of rubber, but to no avail. Although these corporations had financial resources at their disposal far surpassing those of the typical Brazilian patrao, they soon discovered that capital alone would not permit them to preempt the local trader or *seringalista*. Since the middlemen—the group the foreigners hoped to eliminate—frequently dominated local politics, the British and American estate managers could expect little cooperation from the municipal authorities.[12]

In the face of inefficiency, corruption, and ethnic antagonisms in the business of collecting wild rubber, British strategists attempted to grow *Hevea* in dense plantations. They never succeeded in conquering the tree's fatal disease, South American leaf blight, a fungus that had co-evolved with *Hevea* in the forest. *Hevea* trees had survived over the millennia by growing widely dispersed among other species; capitalist concentration of production demanded the opposite.[13] The leaf blight was as impossible to control on plantations as was Panama disease in concentrated banana groves.

When foreign business interests learned how to cultivate *Hevea,* they succeeded not in its Amazonian home but in Europe's colonies in Southeast Asia, where climate conditions were favorable for intensive plantation of rubber trees and its worst disease did not follow it. Moreover, in Southeast Asia colonial investors could dominate political conditions and the work force was much easier to control. In the early 1870s the British succeeded in taking *Hevea* seeds out of Brazil, first to Kew Botanical Garden in London and from there to their colonies of Ceylon and Malaya. They established their first full-scale plantations in 1900, and the young trees began to produce latex in commercial amounts in 1910. The resulting transformation of world rubber markets was sudden and decisive.

By 1912 sales of Brazilian rubber on the world market collapsed, and the entire network of Brazilian penetration into the interior of Amazonia fell to pieces. Entrepreneurs moved into other extractive products, most particularly Brazil nuts and rosewood lumber. The rubber workers remained in semisubsistence farming and rubber tapping along the riverbanks. The forest remained largely intact, although the population of Pará state was thereafter double or triple what it had been in 1870. The demands of global markets forced many Indians into the money economy. Their rhythms of life had begun to be undermined—the fate of the rainforest that had supported them. As soon as the British demonstrated that rubber plantations in Southeast Asia were viable, American companies joined them, happy to be out of the Brazilian quagmire. They were following four centuries of European adventures in the extraction of Southeast Asia's natural wealth.

AMERICAN RUBBER CORPORATIONS ON SUMATRA

In 1511, when the Portuguese explorer Albuquerque stormed the Malayan port of Malacca, Southeast Asia's richest entrepôt, he initiated the West's efforts to control the riches of tropical Asia. Securing his hold on Malacca, he immediately moved east, to the fabled Spice Islands, or the Moluccas, a cluster of tiny volcanic islands whose forests produced the world's supply of cloves, nutmeg, and mace. (See appendix, map 8.)

The Portuguese were superceded in the first years of the seventeenth century by the Dutch East India Company. Incorporated and financed by the merchants and bankers of Amsterdam, the company's ships established a base at Batavia (now Jakarta), on the northwest coast of Java, and cruised the East Indian coastal waters in search of spices for European tables. The company's profits came first from purchasing spices from local merchants; the next step was to control the actual production of spices.[14]

Inevitably the Dutch merchants became entangled in a shifting relationship of cooperation and rivalry with the local aristocracy throughout the islands. Between them they organized the harvest of cloves and nutmeg from the natural forest. Cloves were endemic to Ternate, Tidore, and only a few other small islands of the Moluccas. The clove is easy to grow and harvest; it flowers at age twelve and continues producing for seventy years and more.[15] The sixteenth-century traveler Pigafetta, entranced by the clove forests, wrote, "Almost every day we saw a mist descend and encircle now one and now another of those mountains, on account of which those cloves became perfect. Each of those people possesses clove trees, and each one watches over his own trees although he does not cultivate them."[16]

Nutmeg was the other great prize; its natural range was limited to Ambon and the Banda Islands. It fruits after ten years, and bears to age sixty or more. When the Europeans first arrived, the rival sultans of Ternate and Tidore completely controlled the export of the two spices, selling them to Javanese, Gujarati, and Chinese purchasers. The Dutch struggled to monopolize the trade and to monitor its supply for Europe, limiting its availability so that prices remained high. Indeed, they went to any length to control the market. By the mid-1600s they had banned clove and nutmeg production outside the Banda Islands and Ambon. They organized annual expeditions of fleets of *proas,* or indigenous war boats, to destroy the trees on other islands, reducing total production by three-fourths. They then forced the growers to buy all their foods from the company at high prices. In this way they partially depopulated Ambon and entirely destroyed the people of the Banda Islands, replacing them with imported slaves.[17]

The Dutch East India Company maintained its European monopoly through much of the eighteenth century, but it frequently struggled with overproduction or excessive inventories in the Netherlands. European consumption of spices was steadily increasing: they were in fact becoming a common ingredient in middle-class meals. Nonetheless, price and supply cycles bedeviled the merchants. In 1735 the company destroyed

1,250,000 pounds of nutmeg in its Netherlands warehouses to keep prices from collapsing.[18]

The long-term impact of spice production on land and vegetation on the Banda Islands and Ambon is difficult to assess; it must have included reversion of some food-producing lands to secondary natural vegetation. In more recent times, nutmeg has become a valuable smallholder cash crop on several islands, integrated into the multicrop plots of peasants.[19] More significant was the fact that spice production represented the first and perhaps most blatant example of monopoly profits in European markets, causing the destruction of Asian populations or forcing them to work the land. This was repeated with many variations in colonial Indonesia.

Through the 1780s the Dutch East India Company was content to remain along the coast of Java. From Batavia they co-opted the Javanese aristocracy and the Chinese exporters into profitable secondary roles in their export empire. This coalition forced the peasants to deliver exportable crops, especially coffee, which was grown on government lands in the hills of Java.

This was the high tide of mercantilism. The Dutch established an effective monopsony: total control of the export of the profitable products. Although London was rising to challenge Amsterdam's supremacy as the source of development capital for the tropics, the Dutch East India Company prevented England's East India Company from sailing farther east than Calcutta. The English finally penetrated beyond the Strait of Malacca to the south coast of China by the year 1793, when they established trading relations with the Chinese merchant cartel in Canton. By then the Dutch East India Company was in a state of financial collapse.

From 1795, when Napoleon's armies conquered the Low Countries, until 1820, the British took effective control over Dutch interests in the Indies. Stamford Raffles, the British proconsul, developed Singapore into a hub from which Britain could issue its great modern power to exploit Southeast Asia's resources. The British also introduced principles of private property and free trade to the Dutch Indies.

When the British handed the Indies back to Amsterdam in 1820, Dutch imperialists made an ecologically fateful change in strategy. In what they called the "cultivation system," they took direct control of the agricultural operations for the large-scale production of new export crops, centering their strategy almost exclusively on Java. They expanded coffee from its eighteenth-century beginnings in the volcanic hills of Java and introduced sugar plantations on a large scale in the lowland areas of eastern Java.[20] The cultivation system did away with land tax and tribute and, instead, forced peasants to grow export crops on a stipulated percentage of the lands. These commercial crops often took terraces out of rice production. The government's Netherlands Trading Company was nearly the sole supplier of the country's exports.

In the late 1860s the Dutch courted broader competition by turning toward a greater diversity of crops. This move was closely related to the global maritime transportation revolution: the Suez Canal opened in 1869, and in the early 1870s steam navigation arrived in the Indies. To encourage capitalist investment in clearing forest for agriculture, Batavia passed a new agrarian law in 1870, removing the barrier to long leases of land: the term of leases could now be extended up to seventy-five years.[21]

In the same period a long-term shift in global food prices began. Prices for primary commodities had been high since mid-century, but after the early 1870s they went into a steady decline until the late 1890s. Coffee and sugar prices suffered sharp drops between 1877 and 1878, and 1883 and 1884. Hence the Dutch intensified their search for new crops—and Javanese peasants, their numbers rising and their income and land shrinking, became increasingly impoverished and desperate.[22]

Until late in the century, Dutch resources of capital and manpower were too limited to reshape land use in the Outer Islands significantly. They took on that challenge in an era of economic liberalism in their homeland, and they were ideologically ready to encourage foreign investment. British, Swiss and German companies put their capital into tobacco; the British concentrated on tea; and the Americans turned to rubber.

RUBBER PLANTATIONS CONQUER NORTH SUMATRA'S WILDERNESS

At the end of the eighteenth century, American voyages into the Pacific had reached south of the Philippines and into the East Indies. Here American captains and their sponsors on the New England coast were drawn into the current of several centuries of Europe's romantic fascination with tropical Southeast Asia. The avaricious eagerness of western imperial powers eventually transformed the ecology of the region. Although the colonial grip of the Dutch and British limited the Americans to a subordinate role until after World War II, the impact of American industrial wealth came to be directly felt on the island of Sumatra.

Shortly after 1900 U.S. rubber purchasers began to fear that the British might establish a monopoly of global supplies through their new colonial plantations in Ceylon and Malaya, possibly in conjunction with Dutch interests in the East Indies. American rubber companies therefore began searching for their own production sites in Southeast Asia in 1907. The political umbrella offered by U.S. control of the Philippines might have saved American companies the trouble of negotiating a secondary position in European colonies, but the 1902 law that restricted the purchase of public lands to 2,630 acres evidently discouraged them from lengthy exploration. Rubber planters made some brief experiments on Mindanao, but they found the growing conditions to be poor. So they looked to new frontiers.

Sumatra became the center of U.S. agricultural operations. Here, in sharp contrast to Latin America and even the Pacific Islands, American influence had to conform to patterns of power long since defined not only by several centuries of European imperialist rivalry but also by preceding centuries of local dynastic power and conflict and Chinese-dominated international trade.

Sumatra is a dramatic and massive island of 182,812 square miles. It is 1,085 miles long and an average of 185 miles wide, lying across the narrow, shallow Strait of Malacca from the Malay Peninsula. The island hangs from the Barisan mountain range, which falls sharply southwest into the open depths of the Indian Ocean. To the northeast, toward the Java Sea, the mountains fall more gradually into a vast plain that becomes a wide coastal mangrove marsh before subsiding into the sea. A series of short rivers link the hill forests with the sea.[23] Until the onset of plantation agriculture in the late nineteenth century, the northeastern lowlands supported a thin population. Tribal communities subsisted in the higher mountains, practicing swidden agroforestry. Below them Muslim Malay farmers cultivated rice paddies. Local sultans, their capital towns located near the mouths of the short rivers, skimmed tax revenues from the export of forest products, but they had little effective control over the land and its people.

Europe's first commercial interest in Sumatra, from the early 1500s on, centered on the archipelago's finest pepper, grown in Aceh, the northwesternmost region of Sumatra. Acehnese farmers grew pepper vines on the coral trees in the forest, and had been exporting the peppercorns to China, the Arab world, and the Mediterranean for fifteen centuries and more. But in the 1400s, at the height of China's prosperity under the Ming emperors, the Chinese demand for pepper brought unprecedentedly high prices to Sumatra's coastal markets. In response the farmers cleared patches of forest and grew pepper on stakes as a monocrop. The vines were in prime producing condition after seven years, but were exhausted after fifteen. Then the land reverted to secondary growth often dominated by *Imperata* grass, a dense coarse grass that inhibited the return of secondary forest or the growth of more useful crops. The Chinese had essentially the same impact on land and vegetation as the Portuguese, Dutch and American traders did nearly a century later. Through the nineteenth century, the Dutch sponsored pepper cultivation for European and U.S. markets, watching it spread to many areas of Sumatra.[24] Pepper was Sumatra's first major export crop; coffee was the second.

Yankee traders first arrived in Sumatran coastal waters in the 1790s, when they began to use the northeast coast of the island as a stop on the run to Canton. There they discovered Sumatran coffee. Dutch entrepreneurs were beginning to experiment with coffee on the volcanic soils of mountain slopes, where it was grown by swidden farmers, integrated with their upland rice, maize, and sweet potatoes.[25] Called Mandheling coffee, it was exported beginning in 1829 from Padang on the southwest coast and shipped by clipper to Boston, where its bouquet was preferred over the coffee grown in the hills of Java. The Mandheling trade continued briskly until the last years of the century, when the coffee groves were devastated by blight. The disease started to attack the region's coffee in the late 1860s; it eventually destroyed groves in the Nilgiri Hills of South India and in the uplands from Ceylon east through Southeast Asia.

On coffee plantations where Arabica coffee was severely diseased, Dutch planters first switched to Robusta coffee and interplanted it with tobacco. Then a second blow fell, when Indonesian coffee was undercut by Brazilian competition and prices fell precipitously. By the 1890s the planters desperately needed a new crop that would prosper on Sumatra and would have promising markets in Europe and North America.

They experimented with tobacco, tea, rubber, coffee, sisal, agave, and palm oil. In the low hills in the hinterland of the old port of Medan, where nearby volcanoes had deposited fertile soils and the gentle slopes guaranteed good drainage, they found their answer. In 1863 Jacobus Nienhuys planted the first export tobacco here, on the Deli River. This became the famous Deli leaf, the world's most desired cigar wrapper. The first shipment arrived in New York in the early 1870s, to great American interest, as an alternative to wrapper leaf from the hills of western Cuba. American imports were shipped under Dutch control through Amsterdam and Rotterdam. The highest figure for U.S. imports was in 1920, when Americans bought 9,823,000 pounds of tobacco for $17,616,066. Amounts and values declined steadily thereafter, until in 1959 the amount was only 19,756 pounds, costing $131,466.[26]

Dutch pioneers did the initial work of taming tropical Nature and its human inhabitants in Indonesia. Land clearing in Sumatra was made possible in part by American tobacco purchases. In contrast with the densely settled tobacco region on Java, Sumatran tobacco plantations took over largely natural forests, which were under minimal control by the sultans. Development of Dutch estates was threatened by ethnic conflicts between Batak hill tribes and Muslim lowlanders. The sultans saw the European interest as an opportunity to extend their authority, and with Dutch support they mounted pacification expeditions against the Batak hill tribes; the process was complete by the 1890s.

The Dutch planters, at least nominally members of the Reformed Church, set about to impart European values of social production into what they saw as degenerate, slothful cultures. Tys Volker, writing for the planters' association, noted that "[t]he conditions prevailing in these overwhelmingly Batak districts were, to put it frankly, bad. The natives were degenerated and enslaved to gambling and opium, even women and children being gambled for."[27] Through its tobacco plantations the expansionist Dutch regime brought to the island what it projected to the world as peace, human dignity, and prosperity. The planters conquered the wilderness, established orderly agriculture, and civilized the towns.

> The visitor to the modern "greater Deli," witnessing the intense activity of this region and the present day run for the extreme South, can hardly imagine that this region, where in every respect welfare and prosperity are prevalent, where the native population is very well-off, where no pauperism exists, was 65 years ago nothing but untrodden primeval forest, with here and there settlements of native Bataks and Malays [who have] come as colonists.[28]

By 1900 tobacco cultivation had expanded so far that it spread beyond good tobacco soils, and the new plantations were proving unprofitable. Planters began looking for alternatives and asked the colonial government's department of agriculture for advice.[29] The agronomists suggested rubber, specifically *Ficus elastica,* a tree that had first been grown in groves on Sumatra in 1864 but had never fulfilled planters' hopes. In 1876 the Dutch had begun experimenting with *Hevea* on Java, maintaining close contacts between the Dutch colonial botanical gardens at Buitenzorg (now called Bogor) and the British center at Kew Gardens, which was the source of the *Hevea* seeds. The success of those dense groves convinced the Dutch to begin their first large plantation of *Hevea* in 1906 on Sumatra. On that lightly populated island large amounts of land could be commandeered for growing rubber. Successful rubber production needed massive capital, large acreage, and long leases—and a seven-year wait for the first latex. This necessitated that the local aristocracy and the Dutch administrators in Batavia establish a legal basis for land contracts.

The colonial Residency of East Sumatra consisted of several autonomous local sultans and rajas, under loose Dutch overlordship from Batavia. These local lords could negotiate leases for agricultural land directly with western firms. The standard lease was for seventy-five years, and the payments to the sultans were high, reinforcing their power and wealth over the peasantry. For a few decades the alliance between local aristocracy and foreign corporations enabled the fast clearance of forestlands and highly profitable rubber exports. By 1925, 2,470,000 acres were under concession.[30] Virtually all land that foreign investors thought was worth cultivating was leased to them; very little was left to the peasant population for meeting its own subsistence needs. This disregard for the rural population worked against both the planters and the sultans when organized protests by food-deprived peasants in the 1930s began to disrupt the estates, finally crippling them in the 1940s and 1950s.

The environmental consequences of the new plantation system would prove to be equally broad. The acreage planted to rubber would represent the acreage of natural forest cleared. This, however, was only the core of the transformation. The web of transport and settlement infrastructure that arose among the plantations, and the work force of Javanese and Chinese coolie laborers who were imported to clear the forest, plant the seedlings, and tend the trees, produced impacts that rippled outward from the groves across the Deli region. The population of the east coast region rose from 568,400 in 1905 to 1,693,200 in 1930.[31] This increase was caused almost entirely by the new export agriculture; it inevitably put much greater pressure on the region as a whole, both in the lowlands and the hills, than did the plantation lands themselves.

Immediately after 1900, with the land concession system in place and the industrial market for the product burgeoning, the forests of the Deli lowlands were ready for massive clearance. From 435 acres under rubber in 1902, the figure grew exponentially, to over 320,000 acres actually cleared of forests and planted in rubber groves by 1914.[32] The allure of the rubber market was greater than the Dutch planters could finance, so they began searching for additional western capital, to turn Sumatran soils to greater commercial production. They soon found a major American firm that was ready to pull out of Brazil.

The United States Rubber Company was becoming alarmed that its major tropical sources of *Hevea* would soon be controlled by its European competitors, who could manipulate the price on Amsterdam and London markets to their own profit. U.S. Rubber first attempted to centralize purchasing, with agencies in Belém and Manaus, London, Singapore, and Colombo, but this effort was insufficient.[33] So, in 1907, searching to develop its own supplies in tropical Asia, the company sent out Stuart Hotchkiss, scion of an old family of Massachusetts rubber processors, to survey the potential of the Deli region. Acting on his recommendation in 1910, U.S. Rubber purchased a fifty-two-year lease of a 14,511-acre Dutch estate, the New Asahan Tobacco Company, located one hundred miles south of Medan, which had repeatedly tried and failed to cultivate Deli wrapper on soils unsuitable for tobacco.[34]

By 1913 U.S. Rubber had added several other estates for a total of 75,947 acres. Suddenly it was the largest single holding in the world designated for rubber cultivation. At its greatest extent, just over 100,000 acres, or 150 square miles, were held by the company's new subsidiary, the Dutch American Plantation Company. "Hoppum," as the company was referred to throughout the rubber world, was incorporated in Amsterdam for administrative convenience. Dutch investors bought shares in Hoppum, although U.S. Rubber maintained American financial control; the supervisory staff in Medan were a mixture of Dutch and Americans.

In 1911 Hoppum planted 14,000 acres of *Hevea* trees, or a massive twenty-two square miles; by 1913 the planted area was over 32,500 acres. A year later Hoppum built the world's largest rubber processing plant outside Kisaran on the coast southeast of Medan. That year war broke out in Europe. Responding to escalating wartime prices, Hoppum converted an additional 14,200 acres from forest to plantation in 1915. By that time 14,000 imported Chinese and Javanese indentured workers toiled under 90 European and American supervisors. By 1916 the United States Rubber Company had sunk nine million dollars into clearing the lowland forests of Sumatra.

The Panama Canal opened in 1914, and the first Sumatran rubber shipments to the United States were made the following year. U.S. Rubber could now ship its product directly to the United States from Deli, rather than through the older European entrepôts of Batavia and Singapore. In an intricate game of cooperation and competition between the British and Dutch on the one hand and the Americans on the other, the largest American rubber firm was beginning to hope that it could control the entire process, from clearing the rainforest to producing the rubber to transporting it to North America for final manufacture and retail sale.

Three other U.S. companies soon joined the Sumatran adventure, led by Goodyear, the United States's largest tire producer, which began purchasing crude rubber at Medan in 1916. In 1917 Goodyear leased a 16,700-acre concession southeast of Medan that was covered almost entirely with primary forest. In three years it was cleared and planted in long straight rows of *Hevea*. As one American commentator bluntly stated, "Capital development . . . turned the East Coast from a jungle into a vast commercial garden by 1925."[35]

The U.S. Rubber Company controlled 110,000 acres of the region: 88,000 acres in Sumatra and 22,000 more in Malaya. Stuart Hotchkiss, chief of Goodyear operations, described the corporation's technically intensive management: "Preparatory to establishing a rubber plantation, it is of course necessary to make an exhaustive study of the country from the technical standpoint of soil conditions, rainfall, freedom from wind, transportation and labor supply."[36] His team brought in plant geneticists and soil specialists; they organized careful surveys of soils, built bunds to inhibit erosion, and manured intensively to maintain soil fertility. Their package of western techniques also included removing all stumps from cleared fields and clean weeding the rubber groves. This thoroughness in the early years guaranteed a degree of soil depletion that never occurred in pre-European land tilling systems. By the 1920s the plantations were obliged to supplement the soil's natural nutrients with chemical fertilizers.

The entire system rested on an elaborate strategy of labor control. The Dutch first relied on indentured Chinese coolies for their tobacco plantations in the 1870s; this system expanded directly into the first generation of rubber plantations. After 1920 most indentured laborers on the estates were Javanese landless peasants, imported on contract in large numbers. Batak tribals of the North Sumatran hills were prohibited from settling in the plantation region, although they had begun expanding beyond their easily tilled valley lands several decades before and had begun migrating toward the new international economy. They knew the land, and thus they could not be reliably controlled, in contrast to imported contract labor.[37]

Labor conditions in the early decades were notorious, as they were on many forest frontiers of the new global economy. The conquest of the tropical forest extracted a heavy toll of life and health from the coolie laborers. The colonial planters organized an essentially industrial labor discipline. In the early years they imported only men, whom they housed in barracks. The laborers were called out every day at dawn, and they worked as long as the sun shone, cutting and burning the forest, planting seedlings in the fires' ashes, weeding the young plantations as long as sunshine reached the understory, and tapping the mature trees. The planters controlled all aspects of their workers' lives: they provided markets, mosques for the Javanese laborers, even athletic fields and prostitutes for any men who had energy left after a day of grueling work.[38] The Chinese were alien to that landscape, and few could hope to escape these rigors until their contracts were completed. Those who attempted to flee were pursued by the indigenous Karo Batak, whom the planters rewarded for capturing the escapees. Coolies who were caught were lashed severely and returned to their barracks.

After the 1920s, when the Dutch plantations allowed Javanese men to bring their wives to Sumatra, the managers reluctantly allocated small plots to the worker families to use for kitchen gardens. How much this extended the area of forest clearance is unclear—this is one of the shadowy peripheral impacts of the plantation system.[39] Both Hoppum's estates and Goodyear's Wingfoot plantation established somewhat better working conditions and living facilities for their laborers than the Dutch did. A Congressional investigation of tropical plantation labor in the mid-1920s resulted in a warning to the American companies not to emulate the systematic brutality of their European compatriots. Like their American counterparts in the banana business, U.S. rubber companies provided better housing than the Dutch did, and they subsidized the workers' food. Perhaps most important for their own interest, the U.S. companies provided basic medical care. Malaria could devastate a labor force; it was particularly important to bring that disease under control. Clearing the jungle produced widespread malaria where little had previously existed; the sun could now penetrate to the ground, and stagnant pools of water proliferated. The incidence of malaria was highest in newly planted groves; the older, cleaner estates reduced malaria among the workers by almost three-fourths.

After World War I, crude rubber prices in Singapore, Amsterdam, and London fell from a wartime high of over $1 per pound to $.115 in the summer of 1921. The British rubber corporations in Malaya and Ceylon, which had built up large stocks from their first generation of trees, were faced with possible fiscal disaster. Winston Churchill, then the British colonial secretary, appointed James Stevenson, president of Johnnie Walker Distillery, to head a review commission. The Stevenson Plan of 1922 restricted production on Malayan rubber estates and prohibited the planting of new higher yielding trees.

The other rubber interests did not follow suit. The Dutch refused to join the system of production controls. In the United States, Henry Ford's new assembly lines were producing an automobile production boom. Moreover, Goodyear's newly introduced balloon tires, which gave a more comfortable ride to the mobile middle class, required 30 percent more rubber than the old high-pressure tires. In combination, these factors resulted in rising international rubber prices: by early 1923, rubber had reached $.35 per pound.

American plantations on Sumatra were coming into full production in the early 1920s, the era of Ford's Model T, but American demand was expanding so rapidly that U.S. tire companies had to buy most of their rubber from other suppliers, through their purchasing offices in Batavia and Singapore. By mid-1925 the international price had reached $1.23 per pound. The Stevenson Plan restrictions continued to be enforced in Malaya, however, especially the ban on new plantings.

American importers were determined to free themselves of European-controlled sources. In addition, American attitudes were generally hostile to any regulation of free markets. Herbert Hoover, then secretary of commerce, denounced the Stevenson Plan's restrictions as severe violations of free trade. Goodyear's Hotchkiss, on the spot in Sumatra, was guardedly in favor of the Stevenson strategy, for in 1923 U.S. Rubber had reported losses of $128 million from the collapse of unregulated prices. Rubber company executives shared Hoover's view. Their resistance to the British strategy paid off, for American imports of crude rubber rose from 692 million pounds in 1923 to 888 million pounds two years later.[40]

In 1927 Goodyear leased another huge estate—28,600 acres—185 miles southeast of Medan. Except for a small area that had been developed by a former Japanese lessee, the acreage was all in virgin jungle. Goodyear mobilized 16,000 workers to clear that forest and create Wingfoot Plantation. Ultimately Wingfoot boasted 40,028 acres, all in bud-grafted trees. At Wingfoot the corporation carried on sophisticated research and developed soil management techniques such as terracing on loose volcanic soil.

By 1927 the total ecological impact on Sumatra was immense: over 536,000 acres of natural forest had been cleared and planted in *Hevea,* producing 63,510 tons of rubber for export. Of the total, 46 percent went directly to the United States; another 24 percent were moved to Singapore, where a major portion was bought by American purchasers.[41] The Holland American Plantation Company cultivated 70 square miles in the mid-1920s, and employed a labor force of up to 20,000 workers. In 1933, at the height of their operations, American companies in Sumatra controlled 218,393 acres, including 131,000 acres that were actually planted. This represented a capital investment of nearly $40 million.[42]

From the start the Dutch and Americans in Indonesia cooperated closely in the research that intensified production on the estates. Their research facilities worked intensively to find a chemical or biological control for brown bast disease and soon eliminated it. Hoppum cooperated with the research undertaken by the Dutch planters' associations, especially on the phytopathology of *Hevea.*

The Dutch colonial department of agriculture at first insisted on clean weeding, in the tradition of European agriculture. On Java rubber was grown mostly in the hills up to 2,000 feet elevation; lowland soils were unavailable, since they had been fully dedicated to intensive peasant rice farming for many years. Disastrous soil erosion resulted during the rainy season, so the Dutch quickly abandoned clear weeding and introduced leguminous creepers. In later years they allowed the growth of mixed weeds, controlling their growth by slash weeding twice a year.[43]

In a botanical breakthrough of major importance, Hoppum pioneered the bud grafting of high-yielding varieties on older, hardy rootstock. Planting the high-yielding grafts began on a large scale in 1925. To better realize the full genetic potential of the new trees, Hoppum also imported large amounts of American fertilizers. By 1925 the United States supplied 75 percent of the sulfate of ammonia imported into Sumatra. These new trees more than doubled latex yield, from 1,235 kilograms per acre to well over 2,470. This was a decisive step toward the extraordinary increase in productivity that the growers ultimately achieved—more than ten times that produced by the first *Hevea* trees. Intensifying production, rather than clearing more forest, had become the corporations' major strategy.

Genetic and chemical innovations alone could not solve all the problems on the estates. Planters also initiated a system of water management for the plantations that needed seasonal irrigation. Thus in the same decade the planters became increasingly concerned about the condition of the forested watersheds in the higher mountains above their groves. The planters' associations began to demand that the Dutch colonial government restrict tribal swidden systems in the forest, although the planters had slashed and burned vastly greater acreages of forest than had the indigenous farmers. Ironically, the rubber planters emerged by the early 1920s as the first forest conservationists in Indonesia, but as with most western foresters and conservationists, these technocratically oriented men charged indigenous tribes (elsewhere they blamed marginal peasants) with the destruction of the ecosystem.

The boom years of the 1920s also saw a great expansion of smallholder rubber farms. Consumer demand for rubber and tobacco encouraged the opening of small-scale mixed farming on the upland plateau above the Medan lowland estates. Sumatran farmers, like their counterparts across the straits in Malaya, learned that they could grow *Hevea* trees as their major cash crop just as competitively as the estate planters could by integrating a few acres of rubber into the varied subsistence production of their annual crops. Spotty settlement in the hill forests became the first major ecological change in the hill lands of central Sumatra. Rough estimates indicate that smallholder operations had cleared 370,500 acres by 1920; the figure rose rapidly to 1.24 million acres by 1930. In 1936 the first systematic census counted 1.78 million acres of rubber trees on small farms. A second census at the end of the decade indicated that probably over 2.47 million acres had been cleared by smallholders. These farmers tapped their own trees and usually processed the latex into brown sheets of crude rubber, which they sold to Chinese middlemen.[44]

During the Depression rubber was as much at the mercy of the collapsing market as any tropical crop. Prices in New York hit their lowest point, $.027 per pound, in June 1932, as supplies piled up in warehouses.[45] Although they were faced with precipitous price drops, the corporations chose not to reduce but to increase their production because rubber from the new bud-grafted trees that they had planted in the mid-1920s was just reaching the market.

In order to meet this crisis, the major producers formed the International Rubber Regulation Commission in 1934. By now there was a much higher degree of common interest between the Europeans and Americans, and common policies could be enforced more effectively. The commission soon imposed cutbacks in production even on American acreage in Sumatra. The commission allowed no new planting of any sort and, for bud-grafted trees, limited replanting to 20 percent of existing acreage.

By the mid-1930s, as the Depression's worst effects weakened and consumer markets began to expand again, U.S. imports slowly responded, rising from 427,000 tons in 1932 to 496,000 in 1936.[46] By 1941 American firms produced 20 percent of all Sumatra rubber, which accounted for 14 percent of U.S. imports from the Dutch East Indies. These were the highest yielding years of all. The U.S. companies continued to ship until March 1942, when Japanese armies destroyed the Wingfoot Plantation's headquarters.

In addition to the economic roller coaster, the Depression years produced wrenching social and environmental disruptions in the Deli region. The planters laid off many workers in the early 1930s, forcing them off the plantations and onto adjacent lands. On or off the plantations, they became squatters, struggling to raise enough food to keep from starving. They cleared small patches of forest or cut down rubber trees in their search for cropland. Conflicts flared between estate managers and squatters, and land use on the periphery of the estates was uncoordinated and changeable. Long-term farming of private plots was out of the question.[47]

By the time of the Japanese invasion in March 1942, Sumatra was running an annual trade deficit of at least 120,000 tons of rice. In the naval and commercial uproar of the following months, rice imports ended and large-scale starvation threatened. Japanese policy encouraged peasants to occupy the tobacco and rubber estates, cut down the older rubber trees, and grow their own food. Many plantations were taken over by warlords and labor unions. Three years of war and Japanese occupation, followed by four years of struggle for Indonesian independence, left the plantations badly battered and their former workers in turmoil. A very different era of rubber production would emerge in the 1950s.

THE SEARCH FOR ALTERNATIVE SOURCES OF SUPPLY

Unlike any of the other primary export products from tropical trees and plants, rubber came to be considered a "strategic material" in the minds of American military and foreign policy planners. The term *strategic materials* arose during World War I. It denoted those raw materials that were considered critical for military preparedness and whose sources had to be controlled if a country was to survive international conflict. The United States and other major industrialized countries willingly put their full military and diplomatic machinery behind corporations that mined, pumped, or produced the strategic resources. The materials designated as strategic were primarily metals, but they included petroleum and rubber. From World War I, therefore, rubber imports were assigned a strategic priority not given to any other tropical crop.

Since the 1890s the United States had insisted on an "open door" policy in global trade, or open international access to natural resources. In this the U.S. Department of State backed the free trade policy of the British Foreign Office. After World War I, British support for this policy was eroding, replaced by "Empire preference," a strategy of purchasing vital commodities first from colonial possessions and attempting to limit the investments of other powers in its colonies. The United States, Germany, and others had penetrated the British Empire's sources of minerals and other materials during the war, to the alarm of British imperial strategists. In 1917 the Dominions Royal Commission asserted, "We regard it as vital that the Empire's supplies of raw materials and commodities essential to its safety and well-being should be, as far as possible, independent of outside control."[48]

In the volatile international economy of the early 1920s British policy included price supports for rubber produced within the Empire. Under the Stevenson Plan the British planters in Southeast Asia, who controlled three-fourths of world production, adopted a strategy to restrict production, which would reduce stockpiles left over from the war and thereby raise prices that were sagging under the weight of overproduction. The policy imposed prohibitive export duties on the producer countries and limited shipments to a prescribed percentage of production.

This strategy was anathema to Americans, for whom free trade was gospel. It challenged the American rubber companies' efforts to buy rubber at low prices and to expand their own production. By the early 1920s Americans were purchasing 85 percent of the world's cars and three-fourths of global rubber exports, of which 80 percent was used for automobile tires. The boom market, combined with the Stevenson restrictions on production and sales, rapidly drove up U.S. retail rubber prices. In 1925 the price of raw rubber on the American market shot from $.45 per pound in May to $1.21 in July.[49]

The official American response to British efforts to control the rubber supply was sharp and combative. In 1926 William C. Redfield, who had been secretary of commerce under President Woodrow Wilson, published *Dependent America*, in which he argued that the United States was dangerously dependent on the import of thirty critical materials; most were metals, but his list included rubber. Herbert Hoover, who was secretary of commerce at the time, had launched a five-year crusade against foreign cartels, including the British rubber industry. His department encouraged rubber conservation at home and the development of non-Southeast Asian sources, and he personally urged the Dutch not to cooperate with their British competitors.[50]

Harvey Firestone was already working to break British domination of the world rubber economy. During the war he had presided over the Rubber Association of America, which allotted the rubber that the British had allowed the United States to import from Southeast Asia.[51] Later he observed in his characteristically blunt fashion that

> [w]hen the war broke out, the United States was building two great industries. When the war was over, we had built them. . . . I mean the automobile industry and the tire making industry. An automobile without a tire is useless; and so is a tire without an automobile. And yet these two great industries depend absolutely upon the will of foreign countries for their lives. They depend on rubber, and no rubber is grown in the United States.[52]

Firestone was unwilling to tolerate such a situation. In 1923 he appealed to Congress for support in identifying tropical locations outside Europe's colonies in Southeast Asia that would be appropriate for growing plantation rubber. Firestone argued that in this case strategic concern and corporate interest were identical: "If our business were to perform a public service, it was our duty to keep open the way to the sources of raw material."[53] Congress agreed, establishing a global Rubber Survey, for which it appropriated $500,000 to finance surveys of other countries.

That May, Firestone ordered his manager in Singapore to organize teams of specialists to study possibilities in the American colony of the Philippines, on the islands of Luzon, Basilan, and Mindanao.[54] In January 1926 he personally lobbied Congress to force the Philippine congress to set aside the 2,500-acre limit to foreign land purchases, which it had established over two decades earlier to stop the ambitions of American sugar barons. Firestone insisted that rubber was a different matter.

> If America is to attain any degree of independence in its source of supply of rubber as well as other materials, which are now in the hands of foreign monopoly, our government must give proper encouragement to capital and must assure the industries interested that it will lend its utmost assistance in protecting our investments. . . . Surely it is practicable to recommend that our government take active steps to remove those laws in the Philippine Islands which are an effective barrier against large-scale development of rubber plantations there and to enact such laws as would encourage the investment of capital in the Philippine Islands.[55]

The Philippine congress, in a nationalist mood, did not bend to the pressure, fearing that if great American corporations were to control large tracts of the islands directly, their drive toward independence could be slowed. The bill languished in committee, and the acreage limitation on foreign holdings held fast. The type of coalition that American sugar interests held with Filipino landlords on Negros was not feasible or attractive for Firestone, for he had no interest in working through local middlemen.[56]

Firestone's team also considered Chiapas, the southernmost region of Mexico, where the climate seemed appropriate and properties were available. An upheaval in Mexico City in 1923, one of the last stages of the long revolutionary war there, forced the team to flee to Guatemala. They returned in 1925, when stability was reestablished in Mexico City, and leased a 35,000-acre plantation that was already growing 350 acres of *Hevea* and several thousand acres of the native latex-bearing tree Castilloa. Although soil and climate conditions seemed promising, it was difficult to mobilize a disciplined labor supply from among the local Indians, and the political scene was still unpredictable. Chiapas was not what Firestone wanted.[57]

THE AFRICAN PLOY: FIRESTONE IN LIBERIA

Firestone next turned his attention to Liberia, where an early American experiment in growing Brazilian *Hevea* rubber had paralleled European efforts in Southeast Asia at the turn of the century. In 1910 an American entrepreneur had established a 2,000-acre plantation called Mount Barclay. He abandoned the operation in 1914, but even a decade later, although overgrown with secondary vegetation, the acreage still had healthy trees, which might well be tapped.

Liberia was one of the most improbable of all the arbitrarily imposed Western colonies in Africa in the nineteenth century. In 1816 the American Colonization Society was incorporated by an alliance of northern white clergymen and businessmen and southern slave owners; their aims were, primarily, to return freed slaves to their "ancestral homeland" and, secondarily, to Christianize the region and to begin American trade with West Africa.

On the west coast of Africa, between the Ivory Coast and Sierra Leone, the American Colonization Society purchased 43,000 square miles of land on Cape Mesurado from local ethnic groups in the 1820s and established a base, calling it Monrovia.[58] What was to become Liberia lay on 350 miles of Atlantic coastline. (See appendix, map 9.) The shoreline had no deep-water ports. The coast was marked by lagoons and the tidal flats of a series of small rivers. Soils were mostly very sandy and supported a dense mangrove forest. Inland was primary forest dotted with many patches of "low bush," secondary scrub vegetation that was characteristic of the shifting cultivation practiced by the indigenous population.[59] The rivers that flowed down from the rolling hills in the interior were navigable for only a few miles inland before shallows and rapids made floating impossible even for small craft. Even the immediate inland reaches were navigable only during the rainy season, from June to October.

Inland are the Nimba mountains, which rise to 5,748 feet. Over sixty inches of rain falls in these hills, supporting a rainforest in which many species of flora and fauna thrived. This zone stretches inland for as much as 150 miles. In the north lay savannas, an extension of the Sahel, where elephant grass had taken over abandoned farmland, preventing the forest from returning.

Numerous ethnic groups had emigrated from the broad plains of the continent's interior over the previous several centuries.[60] They grew rice interplanted with cassava and a variety of vegetable and fruit crops, moving gradually from one location to another. Groups who controlled the hills discouraged outsiders from traveling along the forest trails. Even a century later, by the 1920s, there was no railroad to the interior and few good roads had been built. It was difficult to move far from the coast into the hilly hinterland.

Facing this prospect, the immigrant freedmen from the United States, known as Americo-Liberians, settled only along the coast, despite the

constant threat of malaria. In addition to Monrovia they established
other towns: Sinoe, Grand Bassa (now Buchanan), and Cape Palmas. By
the end of the immigration in 1867, they numbered 12,000. In 1847
they declared the Republic of Liberia. Their leader, the mulatto Joseph
Roberts, became president, and the newly invented country was dominated thereafter by American mulattos. Their backgrounds were varied,
but none knew African crops or farming methods or wanted to eat African foods. Their American past held them together and apart from
those they encountered: they assumed their cultural superiority to the
people they confronted. Americo-Liberians' national motto was "The
love of liberty brought us here." But that liberty, it gradually became
clear, was for themselves as a group, not for the various African peoples
whose homelands fell within the country's politically determined borders. Their effective domination of the entire country, especially the hinterland away from the coast, would ultimately depend on international
capitalist investors.

Among the indigenous African tribes along the coast, the Kru, the
Mandinka, and the Grebo were traders and entrepreneurs who had long
been immersed in the international money economy. They already had
connections to British ship captains, who bought palm oil and supplied
well-paying jobs, especially as sailors on European ships. They also harvested and sold dyewoods and raffia palm fibers. In the 1850s they
added coffee and sugar to their portfolio. Liberian coffee was considered
the finest on international markets; coffee trees native to Liberia were
planted in Brazil to produce coffee for the U.S. market.

Coastal and hinterland tribes had a long history of rivalry, for they
lived in different cultural as well as ecological zones. The coastal tribes
had participated in inland slave raids for European buyers, and they did
what they could to maintain a monopoly of trade with inland areas,
keeping foreigners from adventuring beyond the coastal littoral. In contrast, the tribes of the interior, such as the Vai and the Gola, were shifting
agriculturalists. Aside from some connections to inland trade routes they
did not live in a money economy, and they had no conception of private
property. The land was used collectively by household and village
groups for sustenance; it was not owned by individuals. Land surveys
had never been carried out.

After 1830 when settlers tried to buy land from the inland tribes,
their local kings sold or leased the land several times over, not understanding what the outsiders meant by purchase. The Americans faced

uncertain descriptions of land, the claims of rival tribes, and vague language on sale deeds that did not distinguish between individual rights and sovereignty. The hinterland became a zone of intensified interethnic conflict. The American Colonization Society tried to prohibit the settlers from directly purchasing land from the hill people, but speculators among the settlers often evaded the prohibition, in hopes of growing coffee or other crops for export.[61]

A nation state was in gestation, and its infancy would be turbulent. Politics were largely the business of the American immigrants. In 1869 the True Whig Party won the presidential election, and it stayed in power for most of the following one hundred years. Civil service jobs were created for powerful families, who were mostly mulattos of American ancestry. Cultural policy projected their values. For assimilation into ruling circles, Africans had to use English and give up communal landholding.

The government in Monrovia maintained control of coastal agricultural and trading interests. Its ambition was to conquer the interior with the usual weapons of foreign investment, including an American railroad. Through that investment they hoped to dominate the African ethnic communities and their chiefs who still held full control over the hinterland. The government dealt with its hill region through a system of indirect rule, negotiating with local chiefs in much the way the British were learning to do in their colonies of Gold Coast and Nigeria farther east. It taxed inland Africans for development funds and forced native chiefs to sign away title to numerous tracts of land.

In response the tribes of the hinterland launched a series of ethnically based riots and rebellions from the 1880s on. These were fueled between 1880 and 1900 by a long international depression, a period in which many Americo-Liberian plantations collapsed and powerful coastal merchants were ruined. In response to the turmoil, most American buyers left the African trade, turning to Latin America as the United States displaced the remnants of Spanish imperialism there. As one consequence, Liberian coffee exports were crushed after 1880 by booming Brazilian competition.

In the colonial scramble in central and western Africa in the last years of the century, Monrovia lost border areas to the British in Sierra Leone and the French in Ivory Coast. The borders were established in 1885 at the Berlin Conference of Europe's imperial powers, but even then they remained very indistinct. In 1906 the Liberian Rubber Corporation, a subsidiary of the British firm Dunlop, opened the first interior rubber plantations.[62] German commercial interests also moved into Liberia, replacing the departing Americans.

Fearing that Europeans might entirely displace American interests in Monrovia, Booker T. Washington, Liberia's most prominent booster in the United States, convinced President Theodore Roosevelt to force Europeans to guarantee Liberian independence. In early 1909 his secretary of state, Elihu Root, wrote to Roosevelt, "Liberia is an American colony. . . . Our nation rests under the highest obligation to assist them toward the maintenance of free, orderly, and prosperous civil society."[63] The Liberian government had already requested U.S. support to maintain its independence from the European empires.

In 1912 American bankers succeeded in taking over a British loan when the Liberian government defaulted, a strategy they were using in the small Central American countries where U.S. interests were eager to consolidate their control. After that the United States effectively controlled the Liberian economy, successfully competing against the British-owned Bank of West Africa. Americans were not interested in a formal empire anywhere in Africa, but control of one area of Africa's wet tropical zone might well suit American commercial and industrial interests.

Liberia remained a backwater into the 1920s, but gradually the government established control over inland areas by penetrating the hills economically. One observer put it succinctly: "As Liberia's economic resources have multiplied, the settler sphere of influence has expanded over the whole country, a regular administration has been established in the hinterland," and a century-long dream in the immigrants' minds began to take tangible shape.[64]

In April 1924 Firestone's team studied Liberia, focusing on the neglected rubber plantation. They found promising conditions:

> The land for the most part is well drained, much of it consisting of gently sloping hills with intervening wide, winding depressions. Forests cover almost the entire area, but there is comparatively a small amount of "big bush" or virgin jungle. This is due, for the most part, to the rotating system of cultivation practised by the natives for centuries. . . . This system has not robbed the soil of its fertility, and at the same time has made the work of clearing for rubber plantations less expensive because secondary-growth timber is much easier to remove than virgin jungle.[65]

Moreover, the surveyors found fine health conditions, giving them a major competitive advantage over the disease-ridden plantations in Southeast Asia.

Firestone's team immediately hired five hundred laborers and set them to work on the old 2,000-acre Mount Barclay plantation fifteen miles inland from the coast. They cleared the brush from between the lines of rubber trees and began tapping. This small operation was only a pilot project: Firestone envisioned supplying a major portion of the booming American rubber economy from Liberia. This entailed elaborate and diplomatically delicate negotiations with the Liberian government. The U.S. government stepped in on Firestone's behalf. The American consul managed the discussions, and Washington hinted that major financial support might be available to strengthen the Monrovia regime.[66]

In 1926 the Liberian government granted Firestone Tire and Rubber Company an enormous concession: one million acres of land for ninety-nine years. In return Firestone would build port and harbor facilities, roads, hospitals, sanitation systems, and hydropower plants. Firestone would also provide medical staff, a sanitary engineer, a mechanical engineer, an architect and builder, a soil expert, and a forester. Moreover, the company loaned the government five million dollars to pay off foreign debts. This arrangement was clearly in the tradition of private chartered companies in the European colonies of Africa: these corporations were appointed by the regime to provide the accoutrements of organizational and technological modernity; in return, the companies were guaranteed wide-ranging power and enormous profit. Some observers saw dangers in this. The International Society for the Protection of Natives protested the agreement before the League of Nations, but to no avail.[67]

Harvey Firestone projected that producing profit from such a vast estate would require $100 million in capital costs and a work force of 35,000 native laborers. The first trees were tapped in 1934, and rubber soon produced over 50 percent of Liberia's exports in value. By the mid-1930s Firestone was the country's principal employer, with over 10,000 employees; by 1946 the figure had grown to 25,000.

This single foreign concession transformed labor patterns and rural society over an entire geographical region. Previously the hill cultures had been subsistence farmers, uninterested in wage labor. As one observer noted, "Work was largely seasonal and intensely social; work was performed collectively for family or village ends. In general, a non-individualistic ethic resulted from the traditional kinship system."[68]

From the beginning Firestone used the Liberian government to solve his labor recruitment problems. Laws administered by the department of interior enhanced the powers of local chiefs, assigning them recruitment quotas and paying them for selecting and sending workers to the plantations. A Firestone agent walked into the forested interior with a government representative, from one village to the next, to negotiate quotas, pay the chiefs and transport the workers to the plantations. The minimum work period was two months, and this was often extended.

Firestone's officers deliberately recruited among all the interior tribes, observing a policy of social homogenization. They paid each chief a "dash," or gift, in the traditional manner, for allowing men to work for the outsiders; the workers would return a portion of their wages to their village or clan. The negotiations covered all aspects of wages, living conditions, food, and medical care. The arrangement was more flexible and noncoercive than labor recruitment in the French and Belgian colonies of central Africa at the same time: Firestone workers could leave at any time, and the chiefs might require them to return home for farm work or other responsibilities.[69] Firestone himself described the recruitment process rather complacently:

> When an agent has assembled a group of natives—let us say about 200—they start for the plantations accompanied by a "messenger" who represents their chief by supervising the welfare of his people. This trip along a forest trail, in some instances several hundred miles long, is a great adventure. Many of the men never traveled that far from home before.[70]

The new system, which merged the power of the corporation and the authority of the local government, was open to abuse. In later years, an American investigation drew a rather different conclusion, but rationalized the system as the unfortunate cost of social and economic modernization.

> The recruitment practices for concessions are not nearly as extreme as those exposed during the forced-labor scandal of the late 1920s, or, indeed, as some present-day abuses. However, there is no denying the coercive features of recruitment. The chiefs . . . levy fines (and, we are told, more drastic penalties) on their recalcitrant subjects.
> Despite the feudal cast of the system with its abuses and defects, it probably gave initial impetus to the creation of a wage-earning labor force. The dislocations have undoubtedly been unpleasant and painful for many, but the disruption of tribal patterns in one way or another is an inevitable consequence of development.[71]

The scale of the rubber corporation's effort was overwhelming for a country of Liberia's size. Firestone's labor force was ultimately 50 percent larger than any other group of wage laborers in the country. The main plantation, headquartered at Harbel, was 140 square miles in extent. It employed 21,000 workers by the early 1960s, 3,000 of them skilled and semiskilled, the rest tappers. Its senior staff numbered 180 and was comprised mostly of Americans and Europeans.

Workers were recruited from throughout the country, especially the central and western provinces. Only the men were brought to the vast plantation at Harbel. There they lived in dormitories and ate food supplied by the company. They were not allowed to maintain the village way of life, and, consequently, turnover was high. A secondary plantation, on the southeastern side of the country on the Cavalla River, across the national border from the French colony of Ivory Coast, was organized along different lines. It employed 3,000 workers; most of these were long-term workers, and they lived on the plantation with their wives, who grew their own rice on small plots. These laborers were able to maintain their traditional patterns of social life.[72]

Labor troubles were frequent and unpredictable among the workers. Their clans and villages, even their linguistic identities, were being transformed as they were grouped into a national wage labor force. Periodic resistance over payment of the government's hut tax had occurred among the coastal Kru. Inland, a traditional pawning system, in which an impoverished tribal could indenture himself or a relative to a chief until a debt was paid, often placed men in servitude for years. In places there was even a continuation of some semislavery, just as there was elsewhere in nearby European colonies.

In rural Liberia government officials often abused the traditional porterage system by conscripting men to carry them and their supplies as they toured the interior or supervised roadwork. Worst was forcible recruitment to supply labor for the private farms of district commissioners. Under President Charles King's administration in the 1920s, the abuses went as high as the vice president.

In 1930 the League of Nations sent the Johnson-Christy Commission to Liberia to investigate allegations of forced labor and slavery, allegations that were substantiated. King broke off diplomatic relations with the United States in anger at the challenge to his authority, but he was forced to resign in late 1930 and was replaced by Edwin Barclay. The United States reestablished diplomatic relations in 1935, but Barclay continued to repress unrest, among his own Americo-Liberian critics as well as the country's ethnic minorities.[73] Firestone operations continued to prosper throughout the period, using the country's power hierarchies and social conflicts for its own ends. Although exact figures are not

known because the written record is indistinct, a vast acreage of the
country was transformed by the rubber company as agricultural fields
and natural and second-growth forest gave way to massive groves of
Hevea trees.

AN ABORTIVE EMPIRE: FORDLANDIA IN AMAZONIA

While Harvey Firestone was sending his troops ashore in West Africa,
his friend Henry Ford was pursuing dreams of tropical empire in Amazonia. Ford centered his attention on an area that had been productive
during the rubber boom a generation earlier, the basin of the lower
Tapajós River, one of the Amazon's major southern tributaries. Tapajós
was the source of the trees that Henry Wickham had taken to Southeast
Asia a half-century before. Both banks of the river had concentrations
of *Hevea* trees. Brazilian planters had made efforts in that area from the
1870s on, and the rubber boom of the 1890s produced an increasing
concentration of estates. Americans in Belém had become aware of the
lower Tapajós beyond Santarém around 1900. Raymundo Pereira Brazil
became dominant in Itaituba, located upriver from Santarém at the foot
of major rapids, exercising his power with ruthless violence over the
tappers, who were either impoverished landless peasants from the northeast or Mundurucu or Apiaca Indians from Pará state. Barbara Weinstein, historian of the rubber boom, concludes, "The violence and dislocation that accompanied the commercialization process left large areas
nearly depopulated and the Apiaca tribal culture in tatters."[74]

The rubber economy along the stretch of the river from Itaituba to
Santarém subsided into somnolence after 1910, but the memory of its
productive years was not lost. In 1923 J. C. Alves de Lima, Brazil's
consul general in the United States, approached Henry Ford, looking for
a powerful corporate ally to exploit the region's resources, but Ford
expressed no immediate interest. There were rumors of other buyers in
the wings, especially British interests. In 1925, when prices were high,
he approached Ford again, offering a vast estate free of rent, with tax
remission and police protection.

In 1927 Ford's agent struck an agreement with Pará's governor,
Dionisio Bentes, for a concession of 2,500,000 acres, nearly as large as
Connecticut, with a twelve-mile frontage along the river. Ford could
import equipment and export rubber duty-free; after twelve years a 7
percent tax on profits would be imposed. Ford could dam the river, build

railroads and airports, operate banks, stores, schools, hospitals—he had few restrictions.[75]

The Tapajós was a clear blue river, as much as seven miles wide. The plantation site was on a 50-foot bluff, backing into low rolling hills. The Americans named the tract Fordlandia and called its new head-quarters complex Boa Vista. There were troubles from the start. Endemic yellow fever, malaria, and hookworm made elaborate sanitation works necessary. The workers, desperately poor northeasterners, opposed the import of West Indian workers, and they rioted in protest at the food served in the cafeteria.

A more fundamental concern was that the land was unsuitable for a monocrop plantation. The site was so hilly that Ford could not mechanize its operations. He hoped for immediate income from the sale of timber from the many hardwood tree species that his workers were clearing. His managers installed the most modern sawmill in all of Brazil. They took samples of new hardwood species to U.S. importers, but the unfamiliar species dulled Yankee saw blades and tended to crack. In 1933 Ford gave up this effort and dismantled the sawmill. A profitable industry based on Amazonian hardwood timber could not be created overnight.[76]

Ford's team had hoped for an annual production of 20,000 tons of rubber, but labor troubles presented obstacles. By 1929, 1,440 acres had been cleared and planted; by late 1931 only 3,300 acres were under cultivation. Worse still was the trouble with the *Hevea* seedlings themselves. The trees fared badly. They were imported stock from Southeast Asia, but they were hit hard by leaf blight after five years, as soon as the canopy closed. As Ford's chroniclers put it,

> If Boa Vista was a "green hell" for its human inhabitants, it was quite as infernal a habitat for the Hevea. This tree was subject to root diseases, leaf maladies, fruit and flower blights, injuries caused by phanerogamic plants, brown bast, abnormal nodule structure, cortex nodules, abnormal exudations of rubber pad, chlorosis of the leaves, and numerous other hazards.[77]

In 1931 Archibald Johnston took charge of Fordlandia. Johnston was a dynamic manager but no botanist. Ford and Johnston decided to bring in the botanist James Weir from the Rubber Research Institute in Malaya. Weir saw the severe disadvantages of the location, and he proposed that the entire operation be moved downriver. In 1934 Ford traded 700,000 acres of Fordlandia for a new site on a 400-foot-high plateau eighty miles downstream. The site, which was close to Santarém, was named Belterra. The new plantation was accessible to deep-water ships all year. Fordlandia became a research station. The soil at the new site was richer, and the land was drier and level, more suitable for the standardized procedures of an industrial plantation.[78]

In five years 12,300 acres had been planted at Belterra. Workers budgrafted Malayan and Liberian stock onto local rootstock that was more resistant to disease. They systematically and repeatedly sprayed the trees against leaf blight. Despite these precautions, trouble again developed: the new trees attracted twenty-three varieties of insect predators.[79] Watching the accumulating devastation, Weir proposed to headquarters in Dearborn, Michigan, that the entire operation be moved out of the home ecosystem of *Hevea* and its parasites into Central America. The proposal echoed the strategy that the banana corporations were pursuing in desperate defense against Panama disease. His proposal was ignored, and Weir resigned in January 1938, just in time to miss the onset of a three-year drought, which made the trees grow spindly. When good rains came again in 1940, leaf wilt hit with epidemic force. Tropical Nature was proving more powerful than Henry Ford's empire.

Brazilian political conditions and the strategic interests of the American government came into play in the 1930s, when a revolution installed Getulio Vargas as president. Skeptical of the privileges enjoyed by foreign corporations, Vargas insisted on renegotiating all aspects of the Ford agreement. This was a time-consuming process, but one that Ford could live with, since Vargas's demand was made during the worst years of the Depression, when demand for rubber was low. In the late 1930s Vargas developed a vision he called "The March to the West," in which Brazil acquired global greatness through the mobilization of Amazonia's riches. At the time Germany was buying 80 percent of Brazil's rubber. With war in Europe and the Pacific a growing possibility, Washington began building up the nation's rubber reserve and maneuvering to oust Germany from Brazil. The Inter-American Affairs Agency, under major influence from Nelson Rockefeller, proposed to Vargas $100 million in development capital, including $5 million to develop rubber, which would be administered by a Rubber Development Corporation. The United States would buy all surplus Brazilian rubber, at thirty-nine cents a pound. In 1940 Congress authorized the U.S. Department of Agriculture to work with Ford and Brazil's new Northern Agricultural Institute to hasten development of a vast rubber industry that would be fashioned after those of Southeast Asia and Liberia.[80]

It did not matter how pressing the Brazilian junta's dreams of grandeur were or how urgent the military necessities of Washington and Berlin were: the difficulties of producing *Hevea* rubber in large amounts in its ancestral forest were insurmountable. In 1940 the United States spent $318 million to purchase natural rubber, but only 3.percent of it was derived from Latin America. The rest was either produced on American plantations in Sumatra, Malaya, and Liberia or purchased from European growers in the markets of Singapore and elsewhere.

By the time the United States entered World War II in December 1941, prospects for Ford's Amazonian empire were dim. By that time Belterra had 3,651,500 young rubber trees; the first tapping in 1942 yielded 750 tons of latex. Ford was still hoping for an annual production of 38,000 tons, but the diseases worsened:

> In 1942 Johnston . . . reported that Belterra had been attacked by the greatest multitude of caterpillars ever seen in the area—they came "in swarms like locusts and laid their eggs only on the new shoots at the top of the trees. At that height they cannot be seen until it is too late, then they swarm down the tree eating all before them." The trees were completely defoliated, but soon they put out new shoots that in turn were besieged by the most severe attack of leaf disease in the history of the plantation.[81]

During the war, synthetic rubber became fully established in American industry, which sharply reduced the urgency of maintaining militarily secure Latin American sources of natural rubber. In 1943 Edsel Ford, the founder's son, who had been enthusiastic about the Brazilian project, died. Two years later his son Henry Ford II became president of the company. He made several moves to tighten financial management and reduce costs. The experiment on the Tapajós River was an obvious target. In November 1945 Ford turned over its entire Brazilian operation to the Brazilian government for $244,200, about the amount that the company owed to its work force as severance pay. Ford had invested somewhere between twelve and twenty million dollars over the years; its Brazilian assets in 1945 amounted to six to ten million dollars.[82] Like so many failed plantations, Fordlandia was converted into a cattle ranch, and Belterra became an experiment station of the Brazilian department of agriculture.

STRATEGIC CRISIS AND THE RISE OF SYNTHETIC RUBBER

In the late 1930s, as war loomed again in Europe and the Pacific, diversification of rubber sources became an urgent strategic concern of the

U.S. government. Direct confrontation with Japan over Southeast Asia's strategic materials began to accelerate. Japan wanted to import petroleum and rubber from the Dutch East Indies, but Japanese leaders feared an American and British embargo, especially of aviation fuel, unless Japan left China. The American consul general in Batavia cabled Washington, asserting that 92 percent of the U.S. supply of natural rubber was at stake.

The U.S. government had been attempting to stockpile rubber from Southeast Asia for some time, but Great Britain had been only partially cooperative with American goals. At the end of 1939 the United States had less than a three months' supply of rubber on hand, and it attempted to expand purchases from the International Rubber Regulation Committee. Nazi Germany had begun its invasion of adjacent countries, and the British-controlled committee began to loosen its restrictions. Nonetheless, by May 1940 the United States still had only five months' supply of tin and three months' supply of rubber in reserve.

In June 1940 the Reconstruction Finance Corporation was empowered to create satellite purchasing corporations for strategic materials. It created four of them, including the Rubber Reserve Company. By early 1941 stockpiling had accelerated. In July 1941 President Franklin D. Roosevelt created the Economic Defense Board under Vice President Henry Wallace. In mid-December, even after the Japanese attack on Pearl Harbor, it had acquired only 30 percent of its rubber target, and less than that of various minerals.[83]

Firestone's production in Liberia was steadily accelerating, but it never accounted for more than 7 percent of the enormous American demand. Only a qualitative breakthrough in rubber production could solve the dilemma. Fortunately for the war effort—and in the longer run for the remaining rainforest reserves of the tropical world—a synthetic rubber derived from petroleum became available as the war continued, transforming the entire industry.

From the 1830s on, European chemists had been attempting to synthesize rubber from a wide variety of source materials.[84] Early efforts produced an elastic synthetic from isoprene, which could be distilled from turpentine. During World War I, the Allies' blockade suppressed German imports of tropical natural rubber and Germany, desperate for rubber, managed to produce methyl rubber from butadiene, but the substance lacked stability.[85] Tires made of solid methyl rubber lost their shape when the vehicles were parked for any length of time. The Weimar regime, which had been producing 150 tons of methyl rubber a month, dropped the effort to synthesize rubber from petroleum.

German efforts to find a synthetic had revived by the late 1920s as the country attempted to become strategically independent of imported natural rubber, and in 1926 German scientists produced polymerized rubber from butadiene. In 1929, I.G. Farben, a German company, made a synthetic rubber that it called Buna S. The name was derived from three materials used to make the compound: the initial syllables of butadiene and natrium, plus *s* for styrene. I.G. Farben and Standard Oil of New Jersey had signed a contract to develop synthetic petrol jointly; the terms of the contract included a provision for information sharing. As a result, I.G. Farben shared its information about Buna S with Standard Oil. This was a stroke of great good fortune for the company and for American strategic interests.

After the Nazi regime took power in Germany, it imported natural rubber from Brazil and elsewhere, but it wanted independence from tropical products. By 1933 trials with Buna S were still not encouraging: treads stripped from their casings when tires made from the substance were used heavily. The Nazis pushed German companies for improvements of Buna S, and by 1939 the substance had improved enough to meet military requirements. Buna S was used for many wartime purposes.

As international military tensions rose during the 1930s, Roosevelt's strategic planners watched German and Japanese developments, realizing that the United States would be just as vulnerable as its potential enemies should its supply of natural rubber be disrupted. As early as 1934 planners at the U.S. Department of State and the Army and Navy Munitions Board argued that the United States must maintain a large strategic stockpile of rubber.[86] Congress, under severe budgetary constraints during the Depression, was not interested in paying for large amounts of rubber. It was only in June 1939, with the Japanese army already occupying large areas of China and Hitler's military machine in full operation, that Congress allocated $100 million for all strategic stockpiles, including metals and other materials as well as rubber. By the end of that year American reserves stood only at 125,800 tons, hardly three months' supply. Germany had occupied Poland, and Japan was threatening Southeast Asia.

In June 1940 Jesse Jones, the powerful chairman of the Reconstruction Finance Corporation, urged Congress and the oil and rubber corporations to launch a crash program to perfect synthetic rubber—an effort that would require a high degree of cooperation among them. Firestone's earlier collaboration with Ford was a precedent.

As early as 1934 Firestone had attempted to use the DuPont Company's synthetic rubber, which it called neoprene, to make airplane tires for the Army. These tires wore out quickly, so the company looked to Germany's Buna S. Firestone made experimental tires with the compound in the summer of 1938, and in May 1939, Firestone produced a buna rubber from its own, somewhat different formula. Although I.G. Farben held the patent to Buna S, Standard Oil Company of New Jersey held a portion of the rights. Standard was able to buy the sole rights from the Germans, which it then shared with Firestone.

In the summer of 1940 Firestone unveiled synthetic tires at the New York World's Fair. In July, Harvey Firestone Jr. conferred in Washington with the Council of National Defense. In a radio broadcast that month he asserted in an eloquent mix of patriotism and self-promotion,

> Events abroad have swept into the discard many previous conceptions of military strategy and tactics. Speed is the very essence of modern warfare. And the realization of this significant fact emphasizes again the vital importance of rubber, the material that makes such speed possible. . . . The army tank, once a cumbersome, unwieldy vehicle which waddled along no faster than a man could walk, now races along its rubber track blocks at forty miles an hour. No longer does the infantry, footsore and weary, plod twenty-five miles a day. It covers twice that distance in a single hour in its rubber-tired cars and trucks.[87]

Standard Oil continued to improve its synthetic compound, now with help from Congress. In 1942 Congress passed a bill encouraging corporations to make synthetic rubber from grain alcohol. President Roosevelt vetoed it, favoring rubber from a combination of petroleum and coal, and set up the Baruch Committee to oversee the accelerated research program and the use of federal funds. At a cost of $700 million, in two years the companies reached full-scale production of synthetic rubber made from petroleum and coal, making one million tons of rubber per year.

Britain struggled with severe shortages after German air raids in 1940 and 1941. In 1942 they lost an important source of natural rubber when the Japanese suddenly conquered Malaya. The only natural rubber supplies left available for Churchill's compatriots were from Ceylon and India. In desperation Britain turned to the United States for wartime supplies of synthetic rubber. The British received their first American synthetics in late 1943; by 1944 75 percent of their rubber products were made from synthetics. Many products, including clothing, could not use the synthetic, but until May 1945 the pressure to broaden uses of the synthetic and reduce the usage of natural rubber was heavy.

At end of the war Britain rapidly reconverted to natural rubber, a process that was complete by December 1945.[88] Until 1947 the British government purchased rubber from its Southeast Asian colonies to deliver to the United States; these shipments helped to pay its wartime debts and to accumulate dollars for reconstruction. That flow helped stabilize rubber production in the British colonies and prepared the plantations for the boom era of the 1950s.

After 1945 the global rubber economy rose steadily with the reindustrialization of Europe and Japan and the continuing expansion of the industrial economies of the United States and elsewhere. A growing percentage of synthetic rubber was used in international industries, particularly in America. Between 1948 and 1973 world demand for rubber rose 6 percent per year. Natural rubber production grew by 3.3 percent per year, but synthetic rubber increased nearly three times as fast, by 9.3 percent per year.[89] The production of synthetic rubber first passed natural rubber in 1962; by 1973, when the Organization of Petroleum Exporting Countries (OPEC) raised oil prices by 70 percent, it had reached a stable two-thirds of total global rubber production.

The increasing use of synthetic rubber meant that the steadily rising global demand for rubber had a cumulative effect on tropical lands that was far milder than it would have been. Ironically, in this case warfare had the long-term impact of limiting the destruction of a major tropical ecosystem.

The rubber industry in the United States, with its limited supply base of natural rubber, pushed for further rapid development of synthetic rubber. Until the mid-1950s most production of petroleum-based rubber was in the United States. By 1973, when global production reached 7,295,000 tons, 40 percent was produced in the United States and Canada.[90] The American rubber industry pursued backward integration: by the 1960s five tire companies controlled more than 55 percent of American production of the synthetic, and only one-fourth of synthetic rubber was produced by the petrochemical industry. Western Europe and Japan began large-scale production only after 1960, and then it was pursued mostly by petrochemical companies.

Supplies were influenced by the U.S. government's policy of contin-

uing rubber stockpiling throughout the 1950s and 1960s and into the
1970s. The American stockpile rapidly increased between 1951 and
1954, during the Korean War, reaching its highest level in 1954 at
1,250,000 tons. It was gradually phased out between 1959 and the mid-
1970s.[91] The American government, fearing renewed shortages of natural rubber during the Korean War, also decided to maintain a large
domestic synthetic rubber industry under private ownership. In other
words, rubber production continued to be influenced by the strategic
materials debate, a circumstance that revealed a distinctive American
attitude toward tropical resources in relation to U.S. hegemony.

The primary market for rubber, synthetic and natural, was the booming civilian automotive tire industry, the core of the American Dream.[92]
Two-thirds of all rubber imported and produced in the United States
was used by the auto industry. No economy or consumer culture has
been so gripped by that industry as the United States. In 1950, for every
1,000 people, there were 265 cars in the United States, 139 in Canada,
21 in West Europe, and 1 in Japan. By 1973 there were 481 in the United
States, 355 in Canada, 216 in West Europe, and 134 in Japan.[93]

NATURAL RUBBER GROVES AFTER 1945

Natural rubber, not its petroleum-based competitor, is what determines
land use today in the tropical lowlands. Global production, after its
immediate postwar low of 851,000 tons in 1946, quickly revived to
1,890,000 tons in 1950. By 1973, just at the onset of the OPEC era, the
figure had risen to 3,493,000 tons.[94] Much of this was produced on
acreage that had already been growing rubber trees, but additional acreage was also achieved by clearing more primary forest.

Of course, these figures must be understood in terms of natural
rubber's markets and consumers. The United States remained a major
consumer, but it was not always the largest. In 1973 Canada and the
United States purchased 757,000 tons of natural rubber from the tropical world. Western Europe, with its far greater direct sources in the
postcolonial tropics, surpassed this figure, buying 921,000 tons. Japan's
purchases from Southeast Asia had risen to 335,000 tons as Japan's
consumer economy became a major source of pressure on tropical resource systems.[95]

The automotive industry was far and away the largest consumer of
natural rubber, especially in the United States. In 1970, 400,000 tons

of natural rubber went into auto, truck, and bus tires; 168,000 tons were used for other products. In contrast, the European Economic Community consumed 384,000 tons of natural rubber for tires and nearly as much, 317,000 tons, for other purposes. Japan's pattern was similar to Europe's. The auto industry, still led by America, was the most insatiable consumer of all.[96]

Throughout the postwar years the geographical pattern of natural rubber production has remained stable: over 90 percent has been produced in tropical Asia, about 6 percent in equatorial Africa, and only 1 percent in Latin America.[97] Malaya became an even more dominant producer, its production rising from around 700,000 tons in the mid-1950s to over twice that in the mid-1970s. Indonesia's production, which equaled Malaya's in the mid-1950s at slightly over 700,000 tons, rose much more slowly, not quite reaching 850,000 tons twenty years later. By contrast, the production of estate rubber in Liberia doubled in those years, but only from 40,000 to 80,000 tons, merely 2 percent of the global supply.[98]

Peninsular Malaya's preeminence as the world's largest producer of natural rubber continued because of three factors: expansion of the acreage under rubber (replacing both forest and other crops), introduction of young trees of higher yielding varieties, and more intensive cultivation.[99] By 1980 most Malayan rubber estates were owned by Malayan nationals, especially ethnic Chinese, who had taken over the old European and American estates. Europeans controlled only 12 percent of the estate land, and American tire manufacturers retained direct control of between 4 and 5 percent.

Smallholders had emerged as the primary rubber producers in Southeast Asia. By 1980 they worked 80 percent of the region's total rubber acreage. In Thailand 95 percent of the country's rubber acreage was farmed by smallholders; in Indonesia the figure was 80 percent, in peninsular Malaya 65 percent, in Sri Lanka 53 percent. Production statistics on their lands were significantly lower since smallholders were almost always less efficient than were the large-scale estates: 56 percent of rubber production in peninsular Malaya, 70 percent in Indonesia, and 90 percent in Thailand.[100]

From early in the century the United States had provided the Malayan rubber economy with corporate investment and consumer markets. By 1923 the U.S. Rubber Company held 22,000 acres on the peninsula, and by 1941 its plantations covered 31,000 acres.[101] After the bloody hiatus of World War II, U.S. Rubber reopened its Malayan plantations, taking up where it had left off in 1948, during the final days of British colonialism. The company did not stay long, however.

In 1948 Communist guerrilla organizations opened a war of attrition against British rule in Malaya, known as the Emergency, which lasted for twelve years. They were supported especially by many of the 300,000 Chinese squatters on the forest fringe, some of whom had planted rubber during the 1920s. Others had fled from the cities during the Japanese occupation in World War II. The guerrillas concentrated on disrupting plantation operations. They murdered over one hundred European managers and many Indian and Chinese staff. The insurgency was gradually contained during the 1950s, but production on the estates suffered.[102]

The Federation of Malaya achieved independence in 1957, and in 1963 the rainforest states of Sabah and Sarawak on Borneo merged with Malaya to form the Federation of Malaysia. The Malaysian government encouraged smallholders as well as corporate estates, leading corporations to shift their focus from land management to the control of export markets, a strategy similar to that of the fruit companies in Latin America. Plantation acreage gradually declined, while smallholder acreage increased to half the total acreage.

In 1960 Malaysia provided 35 percent of total global rubber production, or 706,000 tons, of which 413,200 tons were produced on estates and 292,800 tons were tapped by smallholders. Estate production was the more efficient, since acreage under the two cultivation systems was just about equal. Estates held 1,834,523 acres; smallholders worked 1,832,693 acres. Rubber continued to dominate the country's agricultural acreage, occupying two-thirds of Malaysia's total cultivated land.[103]

The long-term environmental legacy for the Malay Peninsula was vast. Wide areas of lowland forest were cleared for rubber groves, and an intensified population of both Malay and Chinese coolie laborers were installed on the land. The foreign corporations contributed greatly to Malaysia's growth as the country became a major player in world markets and to strengthening the power of its aristocracy.[104]

The American investment in direct management of rubber plantations on the Malay Peninsula ended in the 1950s during the Emergency, when U.S. Rubber sold all its holdings there. By 1973 the only remaining American holding was Uniroyal Malaysian Plantations, which managed 27,500 acres—in comparison with 550,000 run by British firms and 120,000 run by Singaporean Chinese. The Malaysian industry was dominated by five British corporations, which had been there, embedded in colonial society, since the early 1900s.[105]

This was by no means the end of U.S. importance for Malaysian rubber, however. American rubber companies continued to buy large amounts of rubber from agents in Singapore, the world's largest entrepôt for the rubber economy, where sales from Indonesia, Malaysia, and Thailand were concentrated.[106] Singapore's ascendancy dated from the very start of the plantation era. In 1911 Chinese traders organized the Rubber Association of Singapore to standardize the management of the rubber trade in Southeast Asia. The association is preeminent in the region today and is therefore influential in the movement of world supplies of natural rubber.

The marketing system that moved rubber from the Malay countryside to global markets had become a virtual Chinese monopoly by the late 1950s. Malay villagers sold their semiprocessed sheets of rubber to local Chinese packers, who controlled three-fourths of smallholder production; the packers took the rubber to Penang or Singapore. There the great integrated marketing firms remilled, packed, and exported the rubber. Chinese firms had gradually eliminated British firms by then. They dealt with Dunlop, Michelin, Goodyear, and other major western buyers; some of them had their own agents in London and New York.[107]

British and other estate rubber producers in Malaysia and Indonesia also sold their stocks on the Singapore rubber exchange. Brokers, who were not allowed to trade on their own account, made connections between suppliers and purchasers in the West. In the 1970s "the main office of each broker was often intensively busy; in a veritable cacophony of voices each member of the firm, equipped with earphones and mouthpiece, sat around a table: here immediate contact could be made with all buyers and sellers, and personal consultations could be had with colleagues."[108]

In the western world the major rubber purchasing and distribution exchanges were in London, Amsterdam, and New York. These organizations were oriented more to consumers than to suppliers. New York was a massive distribution hub for the whole of North America. The New York exchange, and Amsterdam's as well, had direct links to Jakarta after Indonesia became independent in 1949. Few consumers had any idea of the ecological cost of the natural rubber goods that they purchased: the insatiable American consumer market was the end of a chain with many links, from production through trade and transport to the final retail sale outlets.

After 1945 American rubber companies recognized that they could not diversify their production locations as much as they wished. The leaf blight continued to dictate that natural rubber had to be grown outside tropical America, and Africa and Southeast Asia were the only alternatives. In Southeast Asia, American investment before World War II had been far larger in the Dutch East Indies than in British Malaya. American corporations in Indonesia fared better than did their Dutch counterparts under the new nationalism of the 1950s, but the political transition was long and painful.

INDONESIA: NATIONALIST POLITICS AND THE PLANTATIONS

Indonesia declared independence in 1945, but the Dutch refused to recognize the new nation and attempted to reassert their control over the next four years. During this period the young government struggled to transform its colonial economy and the peasant unions struggled to overthrow the sultans who had collaborated with the Dutch. In persistent, bloody fighting between 1946 and 1948, most of the sultans and their immediate supporters were either killed or dispossessed, and their palaces were ransacked.

By the early 1950s there were approximately a half-million squatters on the estates, many of whom claimed the right to stay based on occupancy rights in traditional *adat* law. Many had settled on the estates during the Japanese occupation; others had arrived during the struggles in the late 1940s. By 1957 they occupied at least 115,000 hectares in East Sumatra.[109] They flooded some lands for rice production, thus damaging hydrological systems.

American companies were reluctant to reopen their operations under Dutch rule, which was tenuous at best in the fighting against Indonesian nationalists. In addition, they would have to return to overaged stands of trees, since there had been little planting of new stock for several decades. Production figures for 1951 were half of prewar totals.

A price boom during the Korean War caused international prices to triple in 1951. American firms, seeing a major opportunity to increase production to meet wartime demands, reopened their Sumatran plantations in 1950 and 1951; the first was Goodyear's Wingfoot Plantation. The Americans immediately began the major job of replanting the old groves with higher-yielding varieties.

Sukarno, president of Indonesia between 1949 and 1965, was ambivalent toward foreign investors. Sukarno wanted the continuing income, but he also wanted greater long-term control over the plantations. Many of the original leases were running out, and the government in Jakarta proposed to renew them for only thirty years. The Dutch planters resisted the proposed new dispensation, so in 1957 the government confiscated all Dutch estates. The Indonesian government was not as hostile to the Americans as it was to its former colonial managers. During the early 1950s all U.S. companies in Indonesia were reincorporated.

In 1958 political turmoil once again determined the flow of rubber production. Indonesia plunged into civil war, and most estates on Sumatra were seriously damaged as rebels tried to cut off the government's income. By then the major American rubber companies had found reliable alternatives: they bought their rubber directly from middlemen in the world's great sales emporium, Singapore, which handled production from Indonesia and Malaysia. U.S. companies were no longer interested in struggling with the political conditions on the estates and in Jakarta. By the early 1960s U.S. Rubber had left Indonesia and Goodyear's operations were being liquidated.

In 1965 revolutionary upheaval exploded again. Several months of nationwide chaos left some 500,000 dead. Sukarno was packed away, replaced by a military command that was headed by General Suharto and trained in the United States. The Suharto government, in sharp contrast to the militant nationalism of Sukarno's regime, welcomed foreign investment.[110] No American rubber producers were interested. They had opted out of the financial risks and management headaches of running the plantations. They were no longer responsible for incursions into the rainforests of Southeast Asia.

Environmental changes, which had initially been caused predominantly by lowland forest clearance for plantations, were now increasingly entangled with the broader trend of population and land use in post-1945 Sumatra. The senior American specialist on Sumatra in those years, Karl Pelzer, wrote in 1957 that "[t]here is, at this time, no shortage of land in North Sumatra, but there is a scarcity of land which is easily accessible, well drained and protected against destructive floods or the encroachment of tidal salt water."[111] Over the years the corporations had commandeered most of the best agricultural land in lowland Sumatra. Little cropland was available for the rapidly rising population, much of it a consequence of the rubber magnates' recruitment from Java and beyond in earlier years. Rubber trees, the cash crop for many peasants, spread inexorably throughout the forest in thousands of tiny patches, in a way that was somewhat similar to coffee planting in Colombia. In higher hill areas of southeastern Sumatra, smallholder coffee has continued to play that role in recent years, as the ancient forest cover has been replaced bit by bit.[112]

In spite of, or perhaps because of, the political difficulties of the 1950s on Java and Sumatra, Indonesia's rubber industry had gone through a period of expansion.[113] Over 700,000 tons of rubber were exported every year through 1958. A new production zone was emerging on Indonesia's rainforest frontier in Kalimantan, the vast Indonesian segment of Borneo, where social conflict between landlords and peasants had not yet developed. The island became an area of smallholders, as the government sent large numbers of surplus farm laborers there from Java.

After 1965 General Suharto's authoritarian regime ushered in a new era of political stability and economic growth favorable to the export sector. The rubber economy saw rapid expansion, almost entirely at the expense of primary forest on the formerly undeveloped Outer Islands, especially Kalimantan.[114] By 1973 the country's total exports were 886,000 tons. The acreage utilized comprised 1,148,550 acres on large estates and over four times as many, 4,547,270 acres, on smallholdings. In this system productivity was low: 944 kilograms per acre in Indonesia in 1973, in comparison with 879 in peninsular Malaysia.[115] The smallholdings caused further land clearance since more forest had to be felled and burned in order to maintain production, but the profits gained benefited a broader spectrum of the population than just the plantation elite.

Indonesian rubber relied on Singapore as its main market, and Malaysia's port of Penang as well. In a system similar to the peninsular Malaysian operations, Indonesian Chinese traders purchased semiprocessed sheets of rubber from the growers and exported them to Singapore and Penang for further processing and sale to purchasers from Europe and North America. American and European rubber buyers were thus ultimately partners in the global economic web that was responsible for the accelerating destruction of Borneo's rainforest.

One other tropical source of natural rubber, Liberia, was still important for American markets. Although Liberia's production in the 1960s was only about 2 percent of the world's natural rubber supply, it provided closer to 7 percent of U.S. imports of natural rubber. Americans believed it was a showpiece of the contribution of Yankee enterprise to the development of tropical economies and societies, reassuring any who cared to notice that their global impact was a boon to humanity. The symbolic significance of the Firestone Tire and Rubber Company loomed larger than its actual impact on that small country.

LIBERIA: FIRESTONE'S HEYDAY AND DEMISE

Harvey Firestone had fared well during World War II in his Liberian venture. Warfare did not surge over that region of the globe, but the struggle in North Africa gave Firestone an important role in strategic American operations. He formed a subsidiary, the Liberian Construction Corporation, which was the only civil engineering firm in the country. He built Robertsfield Airport, Liberia's first major airfield, down the coast from Monrovia, which the U.S. Air Force used extensively during the war.[116] After the war the construction company completed the first all-weather highway to the interior border of Liberia. This was the first major project financed by U.S. development aid to Liberia, and it extended Firestone's reach through many aspects of the industrialization of Liberia's economy and society.[117]

In 1960 Firestone had 69,000 acres of mature trees and 18,000 acres of young preproducing trees on his two great estates. Harbel plantation, the largest rubber plantation on the globe, spread over 74,000 acres, and the smaller Cavalla plantation added 13,000 more. Together they produced 80 million tons of crude rubber each year. Their production averaged 12,000 pounds per acre, equal to the highest in the world. By the early 1960s Firestone's research division was producing new tree varieties that gave close to 30,000 pounds per acre per year; especially productive was its famous "Harbel No. 1" variety.

From 1956 to 1960 Firestone's net profits were $95 million. In the decade of the 1950s this one corporation paid 26 percent of the Liberian government's total tax income. The scale of its operations was dramatized by a sign at the entrance to the Harbel plantation that proclaimed that the plantations contained "12,400 housing units, 2 hospitals with 200 beds, 7 club houses, 2 golf courses, 18 schools and churches, a 4,200-kilowatt hydro-electric power plant, 400 miles of road, a modern telephone system, the United States–Liberia Radio Station, a brick plant and modern laboratories and service facilities. This includes the largest continuous rubber plantation and the largest latex concentrating plant in the world."[118]

Production—and, ultimately, resource management—depended on political stability. As in so many other cases in the developing world, the interests of the foreign agroindustrial corporation and the host regime converged. In Liberia's postwar years much of Firestone's success depended on William Tubman, who was president from 1943 to 1971. Tubman believed that rapid economic growth was an essential underpinning for the work of modernizing Liberian society. Furthermore, he thought that development would extend the government's control throughout the country, as well as improve relations with ethnic groups who were not Americo-Liberian.

Major new concessions to American firms began in 1947, when Tubman granted a lease of up to 150,000 acres to the Liberia Company, a corporation organized for the occasion by Edward Stettinius, who had visited Liberia during the war and had seen the country's natural resource potential. After Stettinius's death, Juan Tripp became president of the company; Tripp was also president of Pan Am World Airways, which dominated international air travel in Central America. The Liberia Company created the 25,000-acre Cocopa Plantation in the interior, and began planting rubber in 1956. By the mid-1960s it was producing coffee and cocoa, as well as 5,500 acres of rubber. Like Firestone's operation, the Liberia Company also incorporated lumber operations with its land clearing operations: by 1960 it was milling an impressive 200,000 board feet of lumber annually for use on the plantation and sale to markets around the country.

In the early 1950s President Tubman launched an "open door" economic policy, encouraging foreign companies to invest in the country. By the mid-1960s he had given forty major concessions and many smaller ones to foreign corporations, all for the exploitation of Liberia's land and mineral resources.[119] Several of the earliest and most massive contracts went to members of the inner circle who controlled strategic interests in the United States, including the production of rubber.

In 1954 the major tire manufacturer B. F. Goodrich gained a massive 600,000-acre concession for agriculture, mining, and logging. Goodrich established a 58,000-acre development between Monrovia and the iron mines of the Bomi Hills; by 1968 that plantation had 11,000 acres in rubber. A plantation of this size entailed a massive infrastructure, an infrastructure that Goodrich would construct—a major element of the Liberian government's interest. By 1961 Goodrich had paved forty-three miles of new roads and constructed warehouses, shops, a 180-kilowatt power plant, housing, schools, and a twenty-four-bed hospital. It had plans for a $400,000 rubber processing plant that would process the latex collected by local farmers—including of course the Monrovia-based landlords.

Tubman's team also saw the usefulness of diversifying the countries to which it was linked through corporate contracts, and they began cultivating European firms. In 1952 another enormous 600,000-acre land concession was granted to the German-owned African Fruit Company. Unlike the concessions to the American rubber companies, this one was along the coastal lowlands and was intended for banana production. Panama disease soon struck the German operation, so this concession was converted to rubber. By 1963 5,000 acres were planted in rubber groves, under the direction of a manager who had worked for fourteen years for Firestone.[120]

During these years independent Liberian producers also rapidly expanded their rubber holdings: they rose from 150 to 2,300 farms between 1941 and 1960. Most of these owners were members of the Americo-Liberian elite, government officials, and their friends. High international rubber prices during World War II and the Korean War helped them gain economic eminence. By 1960 their annual output had increased to over 14 million pounds. Firestone, whether willingly or otherwise, played a critically important role in this trend. It distributed over 10 million trees, similar to its own number; it gave surveys and advice to new plantations, including management plans; it lent the services of its technical specialists; and it extended credit for start-up operations. In turn, the Liberian growers marketed all their production through Firestone.[121]

By the terms of all concessions, foreign companies were granted extensive "reserve areas," within which were intensive "development areas." Development areas were required to be developed within several years, but the land rent of six cents per acre on development land was a steal: the rate had not been changed since the first concessions were granted just after 1900. Firestone paid a royalty on the amount of rubber produced; others were expected to pay income tax after initial tax-free periods, usually of fifteen years. Each concession could legally import duty-free all equipment and supplies. As for its infrastructure, rail lines were entirely within the concessions and were used only for company business. New paved roads were open to the public, benefiting national development more generally.

Perhaps most important for its impact on Liberian society, the concessions contained tribal lands that had been appropriated by the government for development; the contracts stipulated that the government would compensate the tribes for the use of the land. In a social setting of long-standing ethnic rivalries, this system—funded by the international rubber economy—was an invitation to abuse by the Americo-Liberian elite.

Integrating the country into the global corporate web thus drove the economy inland, penetrating regions that previously only Firestone had entered. The oligarchy was widening its base, and the gap between it and the majority poor was also widening.[122] Economic integration of the country was Tubman's path toward ethnic integration as well. Tubman, although of Americo-Liberian background himself, understood that the deep cultural and ethnic divisions in Liberian life must at least be mitigated if the country was to have a viable future. He cultivated good relations with inland Africans, cautiously widening the cultural basis of Liberian nationalism. Whether this was an attempt to assimilate or to dominate the indigenous African communities was open to debate.

Here, too, Firestone played a major role in transforming the country, although the role was, ultimately, not that which it had intended. In 1960, 35,000 Liberians worked on rubber plantations, over 40 percent of the country's total labor force. Firestone employed 21,000 of them, a figure that had been constant since 1950. Firestone divided the tasks on its plantations by ethnic identity. By structuring established tribal divisions into its corporate labor management, the company actually accentuated the ethnic distinctions and hierarchies of Liberian society. One of Firestone's managers wrote, "Tribe loyalties and distinguishing talents endure. Belles, for example, excel as builders; Krus as boatmen and fishermen; Mendes as policemen, Buzzis as technicians, Bassas and Gios as farmers, Mandingos as traders. Rubber growing requires all these skills and many more."[123]

Despite Tubman's interest in maintaining positive ties to inland tribes, the Americo-Liberian members of the government distrusted the other ethnic groups and critics within its own ranks. The dominance of the elite depended in part on the system of labor recruitment, in which tribal leaders were rewarded for furnishing workers for the plantations. Labor troubles continued to simmer. A series of strikes erupted in 1961; government troops arrested the organizers. In 1966 new strikes hit Firestone and Goodrich, as well as the vast new iron mining complex in the Bomi Hills.[124]

Tubman's long era as president ended with his death in 1971. In the following years the increasing split between the landed elite and the vast majority of the population took Liberia into a period of increasing instability and interethnic tension. In 1980 armed factions began battling for control of Monrovia and its hinterland. A military coup led by Master Sergeant Samuel Doe overthrew the settler-dominated government. Once in power Doe favored his own ethnic group, the Kru. In response, American-educated Charles Taylor invaded the country from the Ivory Coast with an insurgent force in 1989, launching a six-year civil war. Doe was executed in 1990. Five other armed factions, also based on ethnic groupings, emerged in the course of the war. Until 1994 all factions tacitly agreed not to destroy Firestone or the other plantations, for any rubber that any faction could export would help finance its military operations.

Taylor established his fortress inland from Monrovia at Gbarnga, up the road from the Firestone center at Kakata. When he finally attacked Monrovia, fighting quickly engulfed the Firestone plantations. Groves and facilities were largely destroyed in the chaos that descended on the artificial nation maintained by the industrial world's hunger for a tropical crop. A tenuous peace was negotiated in 1995. In 1989, the country's population was 2.6 million. During the six years of fighting, 150,000 people, mostly civilians, died, 800,000 fled the country, and 1 million more were forced from their homes.

Liberian society was shredded, the land lay in ruins, and the plantations were paralyzed. The country's agroecological system was crippled. The rubber industry, dominated by the American rubber manufacturers, had left a complex and ambiguous legacy. It had made decisive contributions to raising incomes and health and literacy rates among its plantation workers, and it had established one of the most stable corporate monocropping systems in the tropics. Yet it had also contributed to the ethnic and class tensions that ultimately tore Liberian society apart by displacing subsistence communities as it eliminated natural forests and supporting a one-class governing elite. In the early years of Tubman's presidency, he and his Americo-Liberian circle had gambled that turning the country's economy and natural resources over to foreign corporations would mitigate Liberia's ethnic divisions while reinforcing their own wealth and power. That gamble ultimately failed. The ecological fallout of the civil war and its antecedents has still not been assessed in any detail.

LATIN AMERICA: THE FAILURE OF DIVERSIFICATION

The search for sources of jungle rubber in Central and South America almost ceased after *Hevea* production collapsed in Amazonia after 1910. Yet it was not many years before a second round of field research began.

Neither American corporate captains nor their counterparts in the government were happy about the British domination of international rubber supplies and prices. In 1922, when the British Stevenson Plan threatened to distort prices for American buyers, U.S. Secretary of Commerce Herbert Hoover, who was on the warpath against foreign cartels, and the American rubber industry were ready to revive exploration in tropical America. Goodyear and its European competitors as well made attempts at rubber growing in the wet Caribbean lowlands.[125]

Other kinds of corporations tentatively joined the experimentation. United Fruit's agronomists considered planting *Hevea* as a successor to the bananas that had been ravaged by Panama disease. Harry Whitford, chief of the congressional Rubber Survey, urged United to pursue this possibility. But the company's directors, enamored of their one delicate crop, refused to support a risky and untried diversification strategy.[126]

Experimentation accelerated somewhat in the late 1930s in fragmentary efforts to diversify the sources of the strategically vital material. Ultimately, affected by the rise of petroleum-based rubber and the twists of bureaucratic priorities in Washington, the production of natural rubber failed to take root in Latin America's rainforests.

After the attack on Pearl Harbor the American rubber emergency deepened every month, and the government finally intensified its search for new sources of *Hevea* rubber in tropical America. It hoped finally to establish a plantation industry based on blight-resistant varieties.[127] Robert Rands, who had worked for many years in Sumatra, headed the project as a senior pathologist in the U.S. Department of Agriculture. In November 1942 he hired Richard Schultes, one of the rising stars in tropical botany, to head a search for disease-resistant and highly productive rubber stock. Their destination was a Bolivian area of Amazonia adjacent to the Brazilian border, where unusually dense groves of *Hevea brasiliensis* had been reported a half-century before.

For the next five years, Schultes and his colleagues combed the Colombian and Peruvian tributaries of the Amazon, recording several new species of *Hevea* as well as the disease-resistant *brasiliensis*. They collected tons of seeds from promising trees and established new plantations in several countries. Their base of operations was at Turrialba, in the hills of Costa Rica, where an inter-American agricultural research center had been set up. By 1947, with the war behind them, they had increasingly conclusive evidence that *Hevea* could be grown on a commercial scale in the Americas. At last it seemed reasonable to hope that Brazil and its neighbors could compete successfully with Southeast Asia for the production of plantation rubber. The total cost to the U.S. government for the exploration and research had been less than three million dollars.

Cold War politics stood in the way. In 1943 the *Hevea* project had been transferred from the Department of Agriculture to the Department of State. The State Department did not have an expert on natural rubber. Although men as powerful as Paul Litchfield of Goodyear gave firm support to continuing the project through to commercial production, Rey Hill, director of the program in the State Department, had learned that most of the work force at Turrialba were active in the Popular Front, which State considered to be proto-Communist. Harold Stassen, director of the Foreign Operations Administration, was appointed to survey the situation. He cancelled the entire program in December 1953, dismissing the arguments of the natural rubber industry and declaring that Latin American countries were politically unstable and that synthetic rubber was about to become adequate for all the industry's needs. Wade Davis despairingly described the consequences:

> The forest slowly reclaimed the . . . research gardens established by the rubber program. Soon after the program was terminated, agents dispatched by the State Department to Turrialba shut down the station and left with all the records. Within a year nearly all the rubber trees at Turrialba . . . had been cut to the ground. The clonal garden that had once served as a repository for the germplasm of an entire continent was replaced by a field of sugarcane.[128]

This twist of McCarthy-era reasoning was undoubtedly an enormous economic mistake. Ironically, in biotic terms, the cancellation of the *Hevea* program was a boon, sparing the moist forests of countries like Colombia and Costa Rica from a transformation into single-species rubber plantations. On the other hand, the cancellation deprived Brazil in particular of an opportunity to develop large-scale production, prosperity, and stable land use in the rainforest. The rubber tappers continued their rounds of the Brazilian forest, and cattle ranchers and landless peasants began making massive inroads, which the industry has been unable to resist.[129]

By the early 1970s less than a third of world rubber production came from natural rubber, and petroleum-based synthetics seemed destined to dominate the industry. A major shock jolted the global rubber economy in 1973, when the member countries of OPEC imposed a sudden steep increase in the price of petroleum.

In 1973 the world rubber economy suffered its first severe exogenous shock: the oil crisis and subsequent sharp rise in crude oil prices. For an industry whose major component—synthetic rubber—depends so heavily on petrochemical feedstocks, the sudden drastic increase in crude oil prices in 1973–74 represented a major change in cost structures and production economics. The other component of the industry—natural rubber—was less affected directly, but was still subject to all the indirect effects of the oil crisis: acceleration of world inflation, changes in consumer expectations, and rising doubts about the long-term future of world elastomer demand in the energy-intensive automotive sector.[130]

The price of natural rubber also rose, but it was less than half of the new price of synthetic rubber. OPEC had introduced a new, unpredictable factor into the rubber economy and a new level of demand for *Hevea* rubber. In addition, the superior properties of natural rubber became decisive in tire markets in the 1980s, when radial tires, first created by Michelin's technicians, came to dominate the market. By placing cords at ninety degrees to the spin of the tire, then adding a steel belt beneath the tread, Michelin produced a tire that lasted longer, handled better, and increased fuel conservation.

By the early 1990s natural rubber had risen again to well over one-third of global rubber production:

> There is today no product that can match natural rubber's resilience and tensile strength, resistance to abrasion and impact, and capacity to absorb impact without generating heat. Today the tires of every commercial and military aircraft . . . are 100 percent natural rubber. . . . The enormous tires of industrial machinery are 90 percent natural. Nearly half of the rubber in every automobile tire originates on plantations located thirteen thousand miles away.[131]

CONCLUSIONS: THE MOTOR CAR IN THE JUNGLE

What can be concluded about the ecological consequences of American capital and consumption of natural rubber? Certainly, corporate plantation rubber was as powerful a weapon as bananas for the conquest of the rainforest. Large-scale corporate investment was driven in turn by an equally fundamental aspect of industrial society: its markets. Rubber came to have thousands of uses, but its engine was the automotive industry and its cultural counterpart, the dream of personal mobility. Strategic motives were also central to the evolution of the American rubber firms. In the race for control of sources and profits, American firms had become entangled in an elaborate rivalry with European empires, especially Great Britain in Southeast Asia. The strategic value of rubber marked it off from sugar, fruit, or coffee and heightened the rivalries for its growth and production.

Rubber-induced ecological change in the tropical forest took two contrasting forms, reflecting the contrast between corporate and smallholder production, a contrast also present in the production of coffee and bananas. European and American corporations carved out separate spheres of influence. The Southeast Asian estates in particular—both those established by foreign corporations and, later, those controlled by local elites—mobilized massive labor forces, reconstructing entire societies and concentrating alien populations in rainforest zones.

In almost every case, foreign corporations determined land use by choosing the monocrop; foreign management controlled cultivation systems. In order to create the plantations they clear-cut the forest, burning the biomass or, in some cases, selling valuable hardwood timber. At first the newly cleared land was prone to erosion, the soil washed away by the beating monsoonal rains. Estate management improved rapidly, however, and soil erosion came under much better control as experience increased. In the more competitive era after 1945, agronomists produced new varieties of rubber trees that dramatically increased yields. Existing acreage in the groves could meet rising market demand, thus reducing the pressure to expand onto other acreage. In order to sustain higher productivity, estate managers resorted to increased applications of commercial fertilizer and pest controls. In the longer run these agrochemicals threatened to pollute subsurface and downstream water supplies.

The development of smallholdings in Southeast Asia and, later, in Liberia followed a contrasting system. In a pattern resembling the production of coffee and bananas, small-scale producers integrated rubber trees with the varied food and fiber crops that they already grew. Small rubber groves were more dispersed and had fewer monolithic impacts on ecosystems, and these groves had more stable interrelations with the peasant agroecosystems because they did not displace food cropping to any critical extent. Those groves were considerably less productive, however, and the farmers were slower to adopt intensive methods. For any given amount of rubber produced, smallholders required greater acreage. The same was true of coffee and bananas. Thus smallholders may have had a greater tendency to expand into land that was newly cleared or had been previously cleared for crops. At the same time they were much slower to induce the accumulation of agrochemicals in soil and water.

Large American firms like U.S. Rubber and Goodyear did not become directly involved with smallholder production in Southeast Asia, but Firestone took a leading advisory role in Liberia, in a strategy similar to that of British firms in Malaya and Ceylon. The American connection to smallholder production was more indirect, but momentous nonetheless. American buyers purchased much smallholder rubber from middlemen in Singapore and, later, Monrovia, although on a smaller scale. The immense market for rubber that was created by military and domestic consumers in the United States not only spurred the creation of vast American plantations; it also sustained the massive expansion of the small producers.

In the early 1970s some proponents of synthetic rubber expected that the entire natural rubber industry would soon die out. The action taken by OPEC in 1973 and the innovations introduced by Michelin dramatically reversed that course. By the 1990s natural rubber had regained a large share of global rubber production, and the rubber groves—both corporate estates and small farmers' modest groves—prospered.

Thousands of miles separated the rubber groves of South America, Southeast Asia, and West Africa from the American consumer. Although the distances those miles spanned were great, they linked the fragile economies and cultures of those countries to the American automotive age, and they provided a horizon beyond which consumers saw no need to look.

PART TWO

Pasturelands

CHAPTER 6

The Crop on Hooves

Yankee Interests in
Tropical Cattle Ranching

> Tropical agricultural economies are mostly weak, in part be-
> cause what they have to sell—coffee, sugar, cotton, rice—is
> in oversupply. Beef, however, is not in oversupply. It can be
> produced indefinitely, moreover, without exhausting the
> land, provided one takes care of the grass cover.
>
> *Bob Kleberg, King Ranch, 1969*

INTRODUCTION

The European introduction of domestic livestock into the Americas was
probably an even more radical shock to New World ecosystems than
the introduction of European crops. When cattle, horses, sheep, and
goats spread across the land, they were mobile and fecund, running wild
and multiplying at a staggeringly fast pace. Livestock voraciously consumed native vegetation, and native plant and animal communities were
reduced or eliminated. Indigenous grasses were replaced by hardier European species, which grew from the seeds that had hitchhiked across
the Atlantic on the livestock. Unlike most plant crops, however, the
mobile cattle—and the Old World grass seeds that traveled with them—
ranged across the land, ignoring all human boundaries.[1] Throughout
the five centuries of European control, cattle were a powerful and ubiq-
uitous adjunct of the extraction systems that operated on the frontiers.

Yankees entered the livestock industry of the subtropical New World
earlier than they began commercial crop production, but ranching was
always tightly linked to agricultural subsistence as well as the agricultural market. Beginning in the 1820s, in what was then northern Mexico, an intricate fusion of Anglo and Hispanic cultures and economies

emerged to exploit the land and its living systems. This collaboration produced smoother and stronger links between the United States and Latin America than those produced by the commercial cultivation of crops.

Yankee cattle interests in the tropics were rooted in the hacienda culture of Spanish colonial Mexico, which Anglo settlers encountered in south Texas when they began drifting beyond Louisiana after 1820. These settlers were the forerunners of the ranchers who supplied the Chicago beef packing industry after 1860. As the era of industrial ranching began in the late 1800s, a counterpoint evolved, both within the U.S. and internationally, between the lean, range-fed Hispanic cattle, and corn-fed, lot-fed modern cattle breeds.

From the mid-1800s onward, new breeds of cattle raised for international markets were introduced into the wet tropical lowlands in commercial concentrations, turning moist forest ecosystems into low-grade pasture that could be grazed only for short periods. The result was the permanent degradation of wide regions, where the vegetation was reduced to a low-level stasis and varying amounts of soil eroded away.[2]

YANKEE CATTLEMEN AND THE
RANGELANDS OF NORTHERN NEW SPAIN

The transformation of the subtropical American rangelands began across the Atlantic, on the Iberian peninsula in late medieval times. It was rooted in Spain's cattle culture, which centered in the rolling highlands of Castile and Extremadura. Ranching evolved there on grasslands that were parched each long summer, when the moist winter winds from the Atlantic had died away. The grasses and the Criollo cattle breed that evolved there had to be tough and drought resistant in order to live in the demanding climate. So did the caballeros, the gentlemen ranchers whose life style became one of the most prestigious and powerful in Spain.[3]

In the Americas after 1492, newly transplanted cattle, introduced onto Caribbean islands by Columbus's men, overwhelmed grasslands and probed into woodlands.[4] Ranching became a tradition on the central lowlands outside Havana, where cattle were raised to supply the export trade in hides and tallow. These products were sent back to Spain by the shipload to supplement western Europe's increasingly inadequate supplies of cattle and pasture.[5] Some Cuban range was lost to sugar in the nineteenth and twentieth centuries, but other ranches remained, playing a continuing role in forest clearance. In the early 1920s Americans became involved in this business with investments linked to their sugar interests, when Armour Meats built a packing plant in the Havana area.[6]

The great ranching saga evolved in Mexico, where cattle spread in every direction from Spain's early colonial base in Tenochtitlán. Faced with few natural enemies, the cattle multiplied massively by 1550, running half wild in the savanna lands of northern Mexico. Cattle traveled with the conquistadors into southern Mexico and Central America's Pacific lowlands, where they remained after their masters left.[7] The indigenous people, already under siege from European epidemic diseases, had no way of protecting their croplands from the ravages of the feral cattle. Many Indians deserted their lands and faced death by hunger as well as disease, thereby making it easier for the Creole landlord class to consolidate the haciendas in the later colonial period.

By the late 1600s permanent haciendas were founded in the Central American lowlands, providing cattle products for local use and regional trade. Large areas of pasture were gradually cleared in the rolling lowlands around Lake Nicaragua and Lake Managua. British traveler John Bailey described the area in 1850.

> One of the principal sources of wealth at present consists of cattle, [especially] on the eastern side of the lakes, and reaching . . . within a few leagues of the river San Juan—a space containing many hundred square miles, but without towns, and with little more population than is required for attending the herds. This tract affords admirable pasturage . . . besides furnishing what is required for the consumption of the inhabitants of the more populous districts, many thousands are annually driven off to the fairs of San Miguel in Salvador . . . and also Guatemala.[8]

From Mexico City, Spanish colonial interests turned north into the Mesa del Norte, the mountain slopes and intermontane valleys and tablelands between the Sierra Madre Occidental and the Sierra Madre Oriental. (See appendix, map 10.) There the volcanic soils supported pine, oak, and mesquite forests on the steeper slopes. In the bottomlands agricultural Indians had grown the classic Mesoamerican triad of crops—maize, beans, and squash—for centuries before the Spaniards arrived. In the wide regions that received less than twenty inches of rain, the natural grasslands faded away into drought-resistant shrubs, especially mesquite, which was nutritious for browsing cattle, and then into the northern desert of Sonora and Chihuahua. Even there livestock could find moister grasslands on the higher mountains and by springs and perennial streams as well.[9]

As the Spaniards and their cattle moved north in the mid-1500s, they overwhelmed the descendants of the imperial Aztecs and Toltecs, whose numbers had been decimated by up to 90 percent by the mid-1500s, leaving wide areas of deserted fields.[10] The grasses of the high plateau fed exploding numbers of cattle, which systematically overgrazed the land within a few decades. In the mountains of Zacatecas and Guanajuato cattle were linked to the European economy by silver mining. The steers supplied draught power, and tens of thousands were slaughtered each year to provide food for the men who worked the mines. Their hides and tallow were exported to Europe for use in industry and warfare.[11] The carrying capacity of the pasture declined rapidly. When easily accessible lodes of silver were played out, the Spaniards moved north, and the number of cattle in the region fell to a far lower level. These were sustained on the tired land for another two centuries and more.[12]

Spaniards and their livestock spread more slowly into the lower semi-deserts and ranges farther north, where they confronted hotter temperatures and scantier rainfall. This was a border region for Spaniards and the agricultural Indians: both considered the area the dividing line between civilization and savagery. The area was the home of the Chichimec Indians, tough nomadic hunter-gatherers who knew how to survive in a region too arid for settled farming.[13] War between the Chichimec and the Spanish began in 1546, when the tribe began attacking the mule trains that took the invaders north from Mexico City to the mines. The Chichimec defense of their homeland was slowly worn down, and by the early 1600s the Spanish had fortified a series of outposts in the north. Ultimately colonial Mexico reached northward through the deserts of Sonora and Chihuahua into the present-day states of California, Arizona, New Mexico, and Texas.

By the early seventeenth century miners had introduced cattle throughout northern Mexico, establishing ranches that survived the decline of the mines.[14] When the silver mines began to play out, Mexico became the backwater of the Spanish Empire, and the international market, even for cattle products, fell steeply. Urban populations and their markets shrank, and rural society fell into somnolence. Landed estates became more nearly self-sufficient. The population was sparse, and cattle required little labor, unlike agricultural crops. Creole landlords, or hacenderos, worked the cattle and small plots of grain with the help of local Indians.[15]

In the northern borderlands most outposts that survived for any length of time were Catholic missions, run first by Jesuit and then Franciscan friars who had a far more powerful organization to support them than any individual hacendero could summon. In 1785 one visitor to a mission ranch in Texas wrote, "The only wealth that this mission has enjoyed since its erection has been that derived from the herds of cattle. . . . With only this wealth the mission was able to sustain and even grow and perpetuate itself without difficulty. . . . All the missions had considerable property of this kind."[16]

In colonial Texas the Spanish founded the Presidio of San Antonio de Bexar (the modern city of San Antonio) in 1718. They organized the cattle industry along the San Antonio River and taught the local Indians Christianity and horsemanship. By 1780 smaller outposts were created in the Rio Grande–Nueces valley and as far east as Nacogdoches, on the fringe of the pine forests of the Mississippi lowlands. Along the more humid coastal lowlands of Padre Island, on bluestem prairies and salt marshes, a secular society of private ranches gradually extended northward from its earlier home along the Veracruz and Tamaulipas coast.[17]

The Spanish land grants on the northern range resulted in continual conflict between ranchers and the Indian communities over the use of grazing lands and untilled fields.[18] Many cattle escaped from the undermanned Mexican haciendas and multiplied. Thousands of cattle and horses were established in Texas before Spanish colonial settlers arrived. In 1780 the total number of cattle in Texas was estimated at somewhere between fifty and one hundred thousand. Cattle became late colonial Texas's primary export: the hacenderos sent herds west to California, northeast to Louisiana, and south to Coahuila. In the early nineteenth century, after the United States took Louisiana, the Texas breeding zone sent Longhorn cattle to stock farms in Tennessee, Kentucky, and even Illinois and Ohio. The integration of Hispanic and Anglo rangeland economies had begun.

In the long depression of the late eighteenth and early nineteenth centuries, Mexican authorities neglected the northern frontier region. After the 1790s, political turmoil was endemic in Mexico, and Texas and Coahuila became a virtually autonomous, self-sufficient backwater region. Toward the west and north the numbers of Mexicans were effectively limited by counterattacks from Apaches and Plains Indians.[19]

By then the region's semiarid grasslands had suffered serious long-term consequences. Cattle and sheep had overgrazed and trampled the grasses, compacting and eroding the soils in a process of devegetation and desiccation. Moist riverine tracts, where most Indian vegetables were grown, were severely affected. Native grasses were replaced by tough woody plants such as chaparral and the Old World grasses that had been imported with Spanish cattle. Especially prevalent was the variety that came to be known as Kentucky bluegrass. As historian David Weber notes, "Old World grasses had adapted for centuries to close cropping and bare or compacted soil, and evolution had equipped them with seeds hardy enough to survive a journey through the digestive system of ambulatory quadrupeds, or with barbs or hooks that enabled them to hitch a ride."[20]

These changes shaped the land in unknowing preparation for a new invasion from the northeast, as Anglo-American farmers and cattlemen spread into east Texas after Louisiana became part of the American empire. Jefferson's dream of an American imperium in mid-continent was to be established as much by bovine interlopers as by human conquerors.

The cowboy culture and ranching economy of the Great Plains evolved from the fusion of Hispanic cattle ranching practices with a northern European livestock economy. American farmers and cattlemen had managed northern European cattle breeds in conjunction with mixed crop agriculture in the woodlands and pastures of the eastern United States. The European cattle were not well adapted to arid grasslands, and the American farmers had little experience with drought or with drought-resistant species of grass.

In the 1820s, as soon as Mexico was free of Spain, Yankees began moving west from the southeastern states and New Orleans. In Louisiana they initiated intensive land and commercial speculation and cultural rivalry with the resident French and Spanish. They moved into east Texas against the wishes of the Mexican government. In the following quarter-century Texas became a region of cultural fusion, with American political and commercial systems ultimately gaining control. In the frontier region Yankees mixed with Hispanics and Indians, especially the agricultural Choctaws of the lower Mississippi.[21] They swept all the others into the culture of commercialization, and fundamentally changed life on the land.

Politics increasingly shaped the use of Texas's grasslands in the early 1800s. A modicum of political stability returned to Mexico City after

1823, when Spain recognized Mexico's independence, and by the end of 1824, 272 land titles had been granted to Americans in Texas. The Mexican government was distant from the northern frontier region: in 1825 Texas was still part of Coahuila, whose capital was in distant Saltillo. Moreover, the Mexican economy had failed to develop strong links with the North. The vacuum gave the gringos room to maneuver: individual speculators and adventurers moved far ahead of the political frontier.

At first the gringos followed individual strategies against their Mexican rivals, giving the Indians guns to rustle Mexican livestock.[22] By the 1830s they had launched an open rebellion, and in 1836 Sam Houston declared the region independent. Texas entered the United States as a territory in 1845, precipitating war with Mexico three years later. When the United States won, it took possession of a vast region, roughly the northern half of Mexico. Yankee ranchers began to settle the western Texas rangelands in the 1850s. Texas was moving toward the brief but spectacular Longhorn era, when for a few years its ranchers exploited their grazing lands as never before, in response to a great new hunger for beef that radiated from Chicago and the eastern states.

In sum, even in the colonial era the arid rangelands of northern Mexico were linked into a wide market economy, although only weakly. This was a preindustrial economy that had none of the long-distance efficiencies that emerged in the 1860s. That second transformation of American cattle lands was to prove far more powerful and far-reaching than the first.

INDUSTRIAL CAPITALISM ON THE RANGE

From the early nineteenth century on, Great Britain and the United States integrated the grasslands of western North America into the global economy as a primary source of beef and mutton. In the late 1800s Americans began moving south beyond Texas, into the cheaper grazing lands of northern Mexico. In 1900 American interests aggressively entered Argentina, processing and shipping its beef to England with a system developed in the midwestern United States. Significantly, Americans did not attempt to market South American beef in the United States since the Great Plains proved capable of satisfying the American market and generating major exports as well, until far into the twentieth century. But the East Coast's bankers and Chicago's meat packers took major roles in domesticating the planet's grasslands far beyond U.S.

borders. In this work they joined an international group of breeders of hybrid beef cattle.

THE BEEF PACKING INDUSTRY AND THE WORLD'S PRAIRIES

Tropical crop plantations were systems largely fabricated on the spot. The modern beef industry was not; it was devised in London and Chicago and the ranches of the western United States and then exported south. The mechanization of the meat trade began in Cincinnati in the 1830s, when increasing numbers of livestock were dressed and shipped; hogs especially were processed in Cincinnati, transforming abundant corn harvests into pork. By the early 1860s Chicago passed Cincinnati to become the continent's great center of beef processing. Railroads provided the key. Chicago's railroads to the East Coast began running in 1856.[23] In 1862 the young city on Lake Michigan slaughtered a million cattle for the first time. Processing such vast numbers was a technical and organizational challenge. In 1865 the world's largest meat packing operation, the Union Stock Yards, was opened. Refrigerated storage rooms and mechanizing slaughtering processes were introduced in the early 1870s, greatly increasing the industry's capacity. One commentator called these innovations "the brutal and inventive vitality of the nineteenth century."[24]

The industrialization of cattle processing created a need for total vertical integration. Cattle had begun to be mass-produced; processing was being mechanized and organized into industrial assembly lines; refrigerator cars and refrigerated storehouses extended the shelf life of the commodity.

Names that later spread internationally into Latin America now appeared. The early struggles of these entrepreneurs shaped their aggressive push into southern nations. One was Gustavus F. Swift, who began life in 1839 in New England. He worked first as a local butcher and then as a cattle buyer; in 1875 he went to Chicago. He soon began using refrigerated cars to transport his beef, and in 1882 he made his first shipment from Chicago to New York.

Swift and his competitors, determined to dominate the national industry, decided to eliminate the independence of local suppliers in the east by reducing their role from that of butcher to that of salesman of chilled meat. Swift's major competitor was Philip D. Armour, a meat packer and grain trader from Milwaukee. Armour, the most aggressive speculator of them all, had joined the Gold Rush in California in 1851, but later returned to the Midwest. Like Swift, he too moved to Chicago in 1875. Chicago was no less lively than San Francisco had been: "[T]urbulence and confusion pervaded the Chicago grain market, where the price of the world's bread was decided. [The beef trade was a] vortex of cracks and crashes."[25] Armour bought grain elevators in Chicago, and in 1890 his purchases had a capacity of nine million tons, 30 percent of the city's total. He also made a heavy investment in California citrus, to exploit the possibilities of refrigerated shipping to the East Coast.[26]

Entrepreneurs such as Swift and Armour were creating a national grid of speculative investment. In the west they saw a massive rangeland supply base. In the late 1860s and early 1870s, in the aftermath of the Civil War, railroads were laid from Chicago to the Pacific Coast, crossing through bison country and over mountain ranges; by 1870 one train left Chicago every fifteen minutes. Men and cattle walked hundreds of dusty miles to meet them. In 1867 Joseph G. McCoy, a Chicago businessman, laid out a safe trail from San Antonio, Texas, to the nearly deserted settlement of Abilene, Kansas, which was on the new Kansas Pacific Railroad. This route, called the Chisholm Trail, linked the Longhorns with the national processing and marketing system. That fall McCoy shipped 35,000 steers from Abilene to Chicago. As William Cronon, a historian of Chicago and its hinterland, writes, "Called into being by the same urban markets that had sent the hunters scurrying across the plains in the first place, the new herds would be tied to the cities by the same iron rails that had turned the plains into a slaughterhouse."[27] As cattle replaced bison, a single economic cycle replaced varied ecological cycles.

The development of the cattle industry led directly to a new chapter in the international competition between England and the United States after 1800. England's investment in the beef industry of the western United States was its last great effort to exploit North America as a market frontier. The British had a passion for beef, especially when it was richly marbled. Although some demand could be supplied by the newly perfected Shorthorn crossbreed, pasture acreage in England, Scotland, and Ireland was too limited and expensive to satisfy the burgeoning urban population's hunger. Only imports from distant lands would suffice.

London's Smithfield Market became the focal point of both import and domestic trade for the British Isles. In the 1860s live cattle and salted beef began to be shipped to England from the United States, but the supply was still inadequate and expensive. In 1875 New Yorker John

Bates shipped the first chilled beef to England, in ice-cooled rooms in the holds of British steamers. This market boomed instantly, and by the end of 1876 three million pounds of fresh beef were crossing the Atlantic each month.[28] British financiers responded aggressively: during the 1870s British firms made major investments in railroad construction in the western United States,[29] immediately following the Indian wars and the slaughter of bison on the Great Plains.

THE TRANSITIONAL LONGHORN ERA

In 1860 there were already 4.5 million cattle in Texas.[30] As soon as the War Between the States was over in 1865, demand for beef from the eastern United States and Britain caused an acceleration of Longhorn beef production in the old hacienda system in the U.S.–Mexican border region. Facing rising costs and competition from other western states, Texan ranchers had to modernize the production and marketing of their cattle.

Cattle had been driven from Texas to Louisiana and even Cincinnati since the 1840s, and to California in the 1850s. The scale of the drives expanded massively when the railroads were hammered into the land, although the technique of driving the cattle long distances did not change. In 1867 the first steers were driven to Abilene and then shipped by rail to Chicago. According to a count made in 1869, 350,000 cattle walked the Chisholm Trail to Abilene; by 1871, 700,000 head had traveled the same route to market. Between that year and 1885 the herds multiplied and spread explosively, and twelve states, now cleared of bison and their Native American coinhabitants, were filled with cattle. Five and one-half million beasts moved to market and to stock ranges in the north during this period.[31]

The era of the long drives and the vast Longhorn herds was a romantic interlude in the region's history that lasted only twenty years. Despite its brevity, it permanently disrupted a great grassland ecosystem. By the mid-1880s cattle ranching was grossly overexploiting the region's resources. A sudden crash ended the era in the winter of 1886–87, when the worst blizzards of the century destroyed millions of cattle.

In the northeastern United States corn-fed, stall-fed hybrid cattle were replacing the demand for Longhorn stock. New techniques of livestock and pasture management were being perfected on the short-grass prairie from Indiana to Iowa, some of which could be transplanted to the far less expensive lands in Mexico and beyond.

Simultaneously, another competitor for the prairie, at least the moister sections of it, was moving in: settled farming. Cropping required more labor and water than ranching, and it displaced cattle onto poorer pasture. This groundswell of change steadily raised the cost of land until it was no longer financially viable to graze cattle. By the last years of the century, the ranchers had to be more efficient. They had to find cheaper rangeland for raising young beef, or feeder cattle, then fatten them in intensively managed pastures and feedlots close to packing-houses and transport to markets.

Many Texas ranches did not fare so well in the hard years after the end of the long drives. Many failed and were purchased by larger, more integrated, and better-capitalized corporate ranches. Texas ranches gradually consolidated into fewer, larger spreads and began a long pro-cess of modernization and capital intensification. The largest of them was the King Ranch. In 1853, shortly after the United States annexed Texas, Richard King bought an old hacienda on Santa Gertrudis Creek south of Corpus Christi. Sprawled across the mesquite-covered plains, this was the first portion of what ultimately became a 1,200,000-acre family ranch that was a symbol of modern scientific cattle and pasture management.[32] The King Ranch, probably more than any other entity, was to play an innovative role in bringing a widening variety of Latin American habitats under the hoof. In the early 1900s the King Ranch developed the only new breed of the century in the United States, the Santa Gertrudis, a complex cross between Brahman and Hereford. The new breed was designed to thrive in hot lowland settings, resist their diseases, and produce maximum beef.

The ecological costs of the excesses of extensive ranching throughout the region were massive. In the 1930s the U.S. Forest Service conducted the first general survey of the western range. The surveyors found that the original capacity of native range vegetation had been halved; by 1930 it was still carrying 60 percent more animal units (a cow and her calf) than its estimated capacity. Of 728 million acres of range in the West, 589 million suffered serious erosion and silted streams. The east-ern stockmen still did not understand the limitations of arid grasslands.[33]

By the early 1890s, in a fundamental shift in perception, Americans had concluded that their western frontier was closed. What merely thirty years earlier had looked like utterly limitless prairie resources now seemed sharply limited. Government lands had been sold in massive amounts to private speculators and dirt farmers. Settled farming and barbed wire fences were rapidly encroaching on the open prairie, the

ranchers' former domain. And land values were inexorably rising. The
beef industry in response showed that it had no need to be limited by
national borders, and it began to look south to the great savanna lands
of Latin America for new sources of supply and profit.

The extraordinary pampas of Argentina and Uruguay became a
source of profit for the beef industry. There, as in so many other colonial
and neocolonial countries in modern times, international capital, technology, and markets transformed natural ecosystems and strengthened
the power of national elites.

THE CHICAGO MEAT PACKERS
AND THE ARGENTINE PAMPAS

Chicago's imperial relation to the western grasslands of the United States
was extended globally, and nowhere more extensively than in Argentina.
Although the conquest of Argentina's wide lands and its indigenous
people was primarily the work of a British-Argentine alliance, American
interests played an important role as well. The corporate entrepreneurs
of Chicago did not purchase or manage ranch lands in Argentina, but
they did invest in the beef processing technology. From 1900 on they
were vital to the process that linked Argentina's soil to Britain's dinner
tables.

The pampas, one-fifth of Argentina's land surface, is a flat plain of
ancient granite covered with hundreds of feet of sediment, fine clay,
sand, and dust. No major rivers run through the pampas, but during
the seasonal rains huge shallow lakes cover the lush grasses of the prairie. The pampas is the country's social and economic heartland.

For centuries the only human inhabitants of the pampas were the
Araucanians, nomadic hunting tribes who had mastered European
horses and weapons by the 1560s. The transformation of the pampas
began in the sixteenth century, when cattle introduced by the first Spanish explorers escaped and multiplied at astounding rates, faced with no
natural diseases or predators other than the packs of wild dogs (another
European introduction) that roamed the plain.[34] The colonial population expanded very slowly around the Río de la Plata, an estuary on the
Atlantic coast, for the early Spanish found little that interested them
there. Only in 1776 did Madrid found the Viceroyalty of Río de la Plata,
with Buenos Aires as its capital.

Colonialists began capturing the wild herds of the pampas for the
slowly expanding urban market. During the colonial period the cattle

were slaughtered primarily for leather and tallow, just as they were in Mexico; most of the meat was usually left at the site. The first solution to that waste was a *saladero,* a meat-salting plant for whole carcasses, which was constructed around 1800.

European-American expansion across Argentina was blocked by the Araucanian defense, for the indigenes could move fast and strike their enemies decisively on the wide savanna. Conquest of the Araucanians became a national obsession in Buenos Aires and its hinterland. Finally, in 1879 and 1880, President Julio Roca led the "Conquest of the Desert," a war of obliteration against the indigenous culture.[35]

Industrial technology and capital were ready to move in and complete the domestication of the land. The first British railway had been built from Buenos Aires on the coast far inland to Córdoba in the 1860s; more lines were completed across the pampas by the late 1880s. Just as it did in North America, the new transport system helped to create a great concentration of landholdings. The 1876 Land Law, designed to facilitate settlement of the pampas, provided 250-acre lots for family farming. It was difficult to make that size homestead viable in the wide reaches of the pampas, and speculators and rich landlords soon took control of most acreage. (Many parts of the western United States were turned over to large landholders in the same years in much the same process.) Between 1880 and 1910 millions of acres were transferred into private hands. The new ranchers built elegant homes on their *estancias,* and Buenos Aires became the Paris of South America, its population rapidly swelling beyond its 300,000 of the 1880s.[36]

This transformation depended almost exclusively on the insatiable consumer market for beef, which reflected the new prosperity of the urban middle class of western Europe. Europeans now demanded tender, fat-marbled meat. Their own cattle breeders had learned how to provide that quality and encourage a taste for it. By 1900 Argentine ranchers had adopted new cattle breeds from Europe, especially the Shorthorn, which demanded richer pasture.[37] Achieving a revolution in pasture management, they planted natural grasslands with alfalfa and wheat and began fencing the pampas. They established intensive feed pastures near the point of export, Buenos Aires. Men who controlled the beef industry now controlled the country's politics and cultural life in the capital as well.

The settlement and domestication of the pampas required a large new labor force. At the turn of the century a wave of immigrants arrived from Europe; most were marginal and tenant farmers from poor northern Italy and Spain. These men and their families were the real conquerors of the native pampas. They became tenant farmers, breaking the soil and replacing native grasses with alfalfa and wheat. Many became a permanent part of the rising Argentine population; others were seasonal Italian and Spanish laborers called *golondrinas,* or swallows, who crossed the Atlantic annually for the grain harvests. The domestication of the grasslands was remarkably rapid. Between 1872 and 1895 the cultivated area of the pampas increased fifteen times, to 10 million acres. Argentine exports included wheat as well as cattle; wheat shipments to Europe were regularly above one million tons in the 1890s.

The export of beef increased steadily. On-hoof shipments dominated until 1900, when England banned live animals because of a massive outbreak of aftosa, known commonly as hoof and mouth disease, in South America. Frozen beef was thought not to carry the dreaded epidemic, so immediately packinghouses came to dominate the trade, providing frozen beef and bypassing Smithfield and other European slaughterhouses. The first frozen meat shipments from Argentina to Europe were made in 1876. After 1900 that method expanded exponentially. From 0.2 percent of Argentina's beef exports in 1897, frozen shipments rose to 51 percent in 1907. In 1908 the transport of chilled beef was perfected. Chilled beef was shipped at the freezing point instead of being thoroughly frozen, and when it arrived at Smithfield it was of much better quality than frozen beef was.[38]

Here was where the Americans were competitive. In the late 1880s Swift had chased cattle southwest from Chicago, building branch factories on the range in Texas and elsewhere.[39] Moving into the Argentine business was only one more step. Chicago firms entered the industry in Buenos Aires immediately when Britain banned the import of live beef in 1900. The Yankees were not ranchers but industrialists whose firms specialized in slaughter, packing, and shipping. They had no need to develop markets for Argentine beef in the United States, but American capital reinforced the scale of European consumption.[40] The growth of U.S. investment in that industry was steady for the next thirty years. By 1929, at the onset of the Great Depression, more than one-third of the total American investment in manufacturing in Latin America, $82 million, was in Argentina, mostly in meat processing.[41]

Ecologically the pampas was transformed. By 1960 Argentina's pastureland (for cattle and sheep) amounted to 307,151,910 acres, or 44.8 percent of national land. However, only 34,449,090 acres, or 11.2 percent of total pasture, were sown to alfalfa and carefully managed; the rest was in degraded pastures. Alfred Crosby summarizes the biotic change: "Today only a quarter of the plants growing wild in the pampa are native, and in the well-watered eastern portions, the 'natural' ground cover consists almost entirely of Old World grasses and clovers."[42]

The entanglement of American corporations in this transformation of natural grasslands to domesticated pasture was restricted to the competition for profits from processing and marketing. Although the Chicago meat packers did provide essential capital and technology, American investors and consumers remained at a great distance from the ecological changes that the meat packers were fostering. They saw those changes, which served the urban appetites of Europe and South America, purely as Progress.

Except for Argentina, American cattle interests did not penetrate into South America on a significant scale before World War II. The United States imported no cattle or beef from South America. The U.S. Department of Agriculture refused to risk importing fresh beef for fear that it carried the scourge of aftosa, which was endemic in every country south of the buffer zone of lower Panama, where the terrain was so rugged as to be almost impenetrable. Cooked and packaged meat was allowed to enter, but the domestic industry filled the demand for those products in U.S. retail markets.

Uruguay's livestock industry was developing in ways similar to Argentina's, and exports to Europe were growing. The cattlemen of Montevideo modernized more slowly, refusing to switch from dried beef to chilled beef until well after 1900. Changes in the old ranching territory of Rio Grande do Sul in nearby southern Brazil were similarly lethargic. Yankee beef packers were satisfied with investment possibilities in Buenos Aires in the first part of the century, and they made little investment in Montevideo or southern Brazil.[43]

Farther north still, beyond the northern fringes of the Amazon basin, lay another great grassland, the llanos of Venezuela and Colombia, just inland from the southern shore of the Caribbean Sea. This vast sea of grass undergoes an annual alternation of flood and drought, making permanent settlement difficult, but cattle can be managed successfully. In 1926 Colombia alone was estimated to have 10 million livestock in this region, including 6.5 million cattle.[44] Managing the estates was difficult, for cattle diseases of the wet lowlands were a plague, and they inhibited for many years the rise of modern cattle and pasture management.[45]

By 1900 Americans had begun to invest cautiously in Colombia and Venezuela in a variety of sectors. Total U.S. investments of all sorts were only between $2 million and $4 million in 1913. They accelerated during World War I, reaching $30 million in 1920. By late 1929 the figure had increased to $280 million.[46] Little of this was in livestock. The huge cattle ranching and processing industry had some export possibilities, but it was too traditional in its methods of handling the Criollo stock to interest Chicago. There was not one modern packinghouse in the country. One experienced observer of Colombian cattle operations wrote in the early 1920s that "[a]bsolutely no care is bestowed upon the animals. . . . The most careful owners only give salt once a month and every now and then take out a few maggots. . . . Hardly any attempt is made to prevent the pest of ticks."[47] Modernization of ranching and beef processing on the llanos accelerated only in the 1960s, when Venezuela and Colombia began probing export possibilities.[48]

The environmental consequences of traditional ranching on that scale were grim. In 1946 William Vogt reported widespread severe erosion in the adjacent hills. Because ranches controlled most good lowland soils, peasants were forced onto steep and marginal slopes, where they inevitably did disastrous damage. Vogt's was one of the first reports that explicitly addressed the social polarization of ranching as the root cause of environmental damage.[49] Damage was especially intensive in the Cauca and Sinu river valleys, where ranchers still practiced the old ways almost exclusively, running Criollo cattle in open, unmanaged pastures on good river-bottom soils. If this system had ever been relatively benign, the population pressures of mid-century altered that decisively.

Into this fabric a few Yankees wove their threads. These individual Americans were drawn south into an expatriate life on the tropical frontier. It is difficult to find descriptions of small-scale operations in the region, but it seems that these men were drawn especially to ranching. One account, written by the American geographer Raymond Crist, gives a close-up picture of such an operation, the ranch of a Mr. McRae. "[A]n American engineer with a little capital and all his time to invest," McRae had settled in a hilly area of rainforest southwest of Lake Maracaibo, Venezuela, by about 1940.[50] On Venezuela's forest frontier land rights could be gained and maintained only if the land was put to human use. McRae bought the right to run an old 800-acre ranch with its buildings and cattle. Fortunately for him, the ranch was on fine alluvium, rich in humus and nutrients and well drained, far superior to the soils of the nearby llanos. He recruited labor from among the tribal people who had been clearing patches of land along a nearby river, providing them with food or the right to grow their food in return for cutting and burning the forest vegetation. They planted hills of maize to divide with him, intercropping it with other foods and pasture grasses, which ultimately took over each patch of land.

As more forest was cleared, mosquitoes bred along the densely wooded fringe, bringing malaria to the workers, who also contracted various intestinal parasites that did not thrive in the mature forest. McRae had three hundred cattle, of which he sold up to one hundred each year in Maracaibo, where the expanding oil fields had generated a big market for foods from the forest border. He harvested milk from his cows, turning it into white cheese for his workers and the urban market. He kept hogs, feeding the razorbacks the whey from the cheese making, or letting them forage in the nearby forest.

McRae struggled to maintain tolerable quality in his pasture, paying workers to remove weeds and plant Guinea grass, which was "higher than the backs of the steers when they are turned in."[51] In this fashion he had "improved" five hundred acres of his spread, first adopting the traditional native system of cropping, then adding a few inexpensive elements of modern pasture management to it. His most important source of income was using his pasture to fatten lean steers from the llanos. He bought them in the lowlands, had them driven across the hills to his richer pastures, and sold them six months later for twice their original value. His own cattle were Hereford crosses, superior to the herds from the llanos.

Crist, McRae's guest and chronicler, concludes his account by enthusing, "it is not only possible to cut down tropical rainforest and keep it at bay by planting grass, but it is possible to do this privately, without government subvention and, at the same time, very profitable [sic]."[52] He adds that financial success also depends on an assured urban market and efficient transport facilities such as the nearby railroad to Maracaibo. McRae represented to Crist a vision of utilizing the otherwise latent hill forests of the entire Andean cordillera as a source of food for nearby urban populations, lifting them out of immemorial poverty.

> The contrast is indeed very great between this intensive cattle ranching where the original natural landscape has been wholly substituted by a man-made one, and the extensive type in the Llanos, where the natural landscape is exploited as found, without any change at all. . . . Access to an expanding

market has spelled growth and development for many an area which would otherwise have only half heartedly supported a miserable population.[53]

Difficult issues arose from the fusion of two beliefs: that rich soil and lush forest were wasted unless they were turned into "productive" and "improved" pasture, and that effective pasture management and marketing could constitute progress in meeting great human need. Yankees who held both beliefs thought that such improvements could lift entire communities out of an unproductive, backward, wasteful, and passive use of land, and they were usually unaware or indifferent to the actual effect their entrepreneurship had on environmental and social systems. Crist's account, which was published in the early 1940s, foreshadowed the vastly greater scale of ranching modernization in the tropics that emerged in the following decade.

RANGELAND SCIENCE AND THE COMMERCIALIZATION OF TROPICAL RANCHING

In the early 1800s a new era of cattle breeding emerged in Europe, producing hybrid cattle adapted either for meat or for milk. Their commercial development was dependent on the new science developed from the eighteenth-century European revolution in pasture management.[54] A branch of this movement flourished in the United States as the 1800s advanced, moving gradually west from the intensively managed cattlelands that had supplanted eastern woodlands to the great prairie beyond Chicago.[55] Its proponents flourished in stockmen's associations and its theories were propagated in periodicals and at county fairs.

The experiments in stock breeding were transferred from Britain and the United States into Latin America beginning in the mid-1800s, when British sugar planters in Jamaica experimented with powerful, disease-resistant Zebu stock from India in an effort to improve the performance of Criollo cattle as draft animals.[56] Far more important in the long run was the effort to increase beef production. The potential productivity of the vast natural grasslands that stretched to the horizon seemed to be limitless, if only a meatier animal could be bred. Durham bulls were imported into Chile from the 1840s on and were spread by the ranchers' organization, the Agricultural Society.[57] By 1900 a series of crosses of the lean Criollo with Hereford, Shorthorn, and Angus cattle of northern European ancestry had been achieved.[58]

Equally important for the long-term transformation of Latin American grasslands into intensively managed pastures was the work of pasture specialists who imported hardy African grass species. Argentina and Uruguay, aided by a great influx of northern capital and labor after 1880, led the way in replacing the natural pampas with alfalfa pasture. By the early 1900s little remained of the indigenous savanna ecology of the pampas, but the new pastures were the world's most productive for beef.[59]

Outside the pampas there was little incentive or capital available for change in range management until after 1945. In the 1950s American technology helped the cattle industry expand rapidly in the llanos. The King Ranch's Santa Gertrudis breed was introduced into several South American countries in the 1950s, along with European breeds, including dairy cattle.[60] These crosses achieved much better beef production than the Criollo cattle could, but they were less hardy in the harsh climate of the llanos.[61] Pasture management also modernized rapidly in the 1950s, since the introduced breeds demanded exotic forage such as African star grass. During the 1950s the export industry was still largely undeveloped, but observers saw much potential for it.[62]

The lowland rainforest required an infusion of intercontinental science before it could be sustainably grazed on a commercial scale. The species of grass that made the invasion of lowland forests possible was introduced from Africa into several specific niches. The six primary species of *Gramineaceae* grasses that were introduced and that became widespread in wet tropical America (Guinea, Pará, molasses, jaragua, Kikuyu, and Pangola) coevolved with ungulate mammals in woodland margin habitats of Angola, Rhodesia, and the Transvaal. Easily propagated in tropical America, these grasses were highly aggressive, spreading rapidly over wide regions. Moreover, the introduced species were more palatable and nutritious to livestock than were the native grasses that they displaced.[63]

Guinea grass thrives on well-drained slopes. As early as the 1600s sugar planters introduced it into coastal Brazil to support their cattle. In the 1680s British sugar planters naturalized Guinea grass for their cattle on Barbados. It appeared in the lowlands of Colombia before 1800. It was introduced on Jamaican sugar plantations in the 1740s, then transferred to Mississippi and to southern Mexico and Central America in the mid-1800s, where it encouraged the expansion of the cattle industry.

The second widespread African exotic is Pará grass, which complements Guinea grass by growing best on poorly drained bottom lands of the hot tropics. It had appeared in Brazil by the early 1800s and had spread to Venezuela and Colombia by mid-century. One writer reported, "In the warm and temperate lands where it was so difficult to maintain clean pasture they are now established easily by means of these two grasses, which destroy all other competing plants."[64]

Jaragua grass, which disperses very easily by seed, was carried to Brazil on slave ships, but did not spread to northern South America or the Caribbean Basin until after 1900. In 1906 it had reached Colombia, then it spread rapidly into the Andes, Central America, and the West Indies in the 1920s. Jaragua thrives best in areas with a dry season of five months or more.

In contrast, Kikuyu grass, originally from the slopes of Mount Kilimanjaro, flourishes in cool, higher elevations. A twentieth-century arrival, it spread explosively after about 1950 in Ecuador, Colombia, Mexico, and as far north as San Francisco Bay. It thrived in upland Costa Rica from the late 1920s on, where it provided excellent pasture grass for dairy herds.

As James Parsons, professor of geography at the University of California, Berkeley, concludes, "The African grasses stand up better to grazing and have higher nutritive values than native American species. In this respect the invasions can be considered advantageous, although botanists may mourn the disappearance of native members of the flora that it may cause."[65] Africanization crowds out native grasses, replacing species diversity with a commercial system of radically reduced variety, but it makes much increased livestock grazing economically possible. In contrast with the earlier European practice of cutting and burning off the vegetation, the new system had major advantages. The vast area of unsystematically burned and grazed grassland that was not turned into managed pasture continued a process of gradual degradation. At least the productivity of the new system of intensive pasture management was far higher and more sustainable than its predecessor had been. The introduction of pasture management into Mexico and other areas of Latin America was a long process, shaped by local politics as much as anything.

YANKEES IN NORTHERN MEXICO

American penetration of the Latin American cattle industry, and its slowly expanding role in the industry's modernization, began in the wide arid rangelands of Chihuahua and Coahuila states in northern Mexico. The grassland area of northern Mexico was much drier than the pampas

or the llanos; it would give only modest rewards for intensified investment and management. This was a harsh and fragile environment, with
uncompromising limits to its carrying capacity. The occasional rains fall
between June and October; the land is increasingly desiccated until the
next June. The high dry pastures sustain drought-resistant native grama
grasses and chaparral shrubbery, especially mesquite, which can help
reduce cattle losses in times of severe drought. In extreme drought nopal
and other edible cacti still survive. Up to 30 percent of the livestock
might be lost in a dry year.[66]

Yankee ranching investment in northern Mexico emerged in the early
1800s, when Texans began to play a major role in shaping the use of
the land. The northeastern states of Mexico and Texas were one political
unit, with its capital in Saltillo, until Texas broke away in 1836. Yankees
and Englishmen, brandishing far more investment capital than Mexico
could muster after the long decades of depression, quickly began buying
out the properties owned by the old hacenderos.[67]

These operations remained tentative and highly risky during the long
period of political unrest in Mexico in the mid-1800s. Then, in the last
decades of the century, presidents Benito Juárez and Porfirio Díaz
launched an aggressive policy to attract foreign capital into the country.
Their goal was to generate more rapid economic expansion.[68] Beginning
in 1885, Yankee investors poured capital into Mexican mines, railroads,
logging companies, ranches, and telecommunications systems. The anti-
clerical Mexican government expropriated lands owned by the Church
and many traditional *ejido* common lands, turning some of them, especially in the north, into vast new *latifundia*. Their new owners included American and European land speculation companies. Those factors in combination created a new interlocking Mexican-foreign
hacendero elite. Two of the most enormous and most internationally
visible ranches, one owned by a Mexican grandee and the other by an
Anglo empire builder, are illustrative of the politics of the land over the
following decades.

The most massive Yankee ranch in northern Mexico was owned by
George Hearst, the founder of the publishing empire. When Hearst met
President Díaz in 1884, he decided to buy a thousand square miles of
land in Veracruz, Campeche, and Yucatán, plus a million-acre ranch
named Babicora in Chihuahua. He bought the spread from rancheros
worn out by fighting Geronimo, paying twenty cents per acre.[69] Babicora
sprawled across four high plateaus separated by mountain ranges. Its
water was supplied almost entirely by artisian wells.[70]

Hearst and his son William Randolph appointed Jack Follansbee supervisor of Babicora. Suave and languid, Follansbee became eminent in Mexican aristocratic circles and popular on the New York circuit.[71] In 1903 the young Hearst drove with his bride to Mexico City, where they were received with honors by the aged President Díaz, who was now a good friend of Follansbee. The Hearsts visited Babicora, where 48,000 cattle roamed on its million acres. Some of the land was rented to Mexican tenants, who grew beans and corn, but most of the plains were pasture for Shorthorns and Herefords, managed by hundreds of vaqueros. The cattle were sold in El Paso markets each year. By 1910 Hearst's Mexican properties were valued officially at $4 million, and in fact were probably worth much more.[72]

In the same years, Luis Terraza, Hearst's greatest competitor for power on the northern rangelands, was the classic example of a politically powerful cattle baron who used British and American links to build and maintain his power.[73] At age twenty-two he owned a herd of Criollo cattle and had inherited his father's butcher business. On that basis he married into a Mexican-British landlord family, then rose rapidly in state politics. In 1860 Terraza was elected governor of Chihuahua. In the struggle to oust the French force that occupied Mexico City in the mid-1860s, he allied himself with Juárez. After 1866, when the new Juárez government confiscated Church lands and *ejidos,* it resold many at trivial prices, along with *baldios* or putatively government-owned lands. Many lands remained abandoned until the final bloody suppression of Indian resistance in the north. Apache raids on haciendas were effectively ended around 1880—almost the same time that indigenous resistance was finally crushed on the grasslands of the United States and Argentina. In the midst of this turmoil Don Luis Terraza, now a Mexican political insider, purchased several old estates at fire-sale prices.

Terraza became the largest beef exporter in Mexico after Díaz's northern railroads were built in the 1880s to Brownsville, Laredo, and El Paso. In an era when the rangelands north of the border either were becoming increasingly expensive to manage or were cultivated for crops, northern Mexico was a relatively inexpensive place to raise feeder cattle. After two years the cattle were shipped north for fattening on American corn in American feedlots. Terraza and a few lesser hacendero entrepreneurs were the first to gather the profits of breeding and raising Mexican heifers for fattening on Yankee ranches. By the turn of the century Terraza was the greatest of all *ganaderos;* by 1910 he owned 7 million acres in Coahuila, 10 percent of Mexico's largest state (in comparison, the King Ranch, the biggest in Texas, was 1.2 million acres). With his son-in-law, Enrique Creel, Terraza branched into banking, textile mills linked to newly irrigated cotton lands, flour mills, and other Mexican industries. Terraza also became Mexico's leading experimenter with crossbreeding cattle, anticipating post-1918 breakthroughs.

The revolution exploded in 1911 with the downfall of Díaz, and the great *ganaderos* were prime targets for Pancho Villa's army in the north.[74] Terraza's family was killed, his rural palaces were gutted, and his prime herds slaughtered. His empire had lasted less than a generation, but it provided the model for the future of Mexico's cattle export industry and the use of Mexico's enormous acreages. The revolution seethed for nearly fifteen years before civil order was restored in the mid-1920s.[75] During those years the cattle population of northern Mexico was slaughtered en masse by marauding armed bands crossing the land. By 1923 three-quarters of the cattle that had grazed on the plains of northern Mexico at the turn of the century were lost.[76] In central Coahuila, on the lands around the old colonial town of Parras, the haciendas were virtually wiped out by the long, spasmodic violence.[77] It was one of those moments—by no means rare in modern history—when warfare reduced domestic populations so much that pressure on the vegetation was at least temporarily reduced.

The Yankee stake in Mexican ranching, like all Yankee investments in Mexico, was also badly damaged by the revolution. In Coahuila in 1910 the majority of ranches were owned by Yankees, partly as a drought reserve for Texan herds because most of the Texas range was degraded and Mexican acreage was much cheaper. Gringos had also begun investing heavily in breeding stock for the Mexican haciendas.[78] In Chihuahua as well many haciendas large and small were owned by Englishmen and Americans, including Hearst and the Cudahy meat packing firm. Yankee smallholdings were worth over $3.8 million, including lands worth $2.9 million that were owned by Mormon immigrants from Utah.[79] Many of these were destroyed or temporarily crippled by Villa or his opponents. Little was left after the war except the knowledge of how to rebuild and expand on experience.

Hearst's Babicora hacienda was equally in peril during these chaotic years, in part because of Hearst's participation in the expropriation of Indian communal lands under the Porfiriato. Local peasants' organizations had emerged around 1900 in self-defense against the new landlords and Apache raids from the north. In May 1908 fifty campesinos rode to Babicora, protesting what they insisted was the grabbing of 22,230 acres of communal land and water rights. Hearst's men relented and realigned their fences.[80] Several years later Villa attacked the ranch, took 60,000 cattle, and killed one of the ranch's vaqueros. Hearst's newspapers denounced the Mexican revolutionaries. In the *San Francisco Examiner* on 8 July 1916, Hearst demanded that "the United States Government exercise the fundamental functions of all governments and protect its citizens; that it prevent the Mexicans from murdering any more of our citizens and that it punish Mexico for the murders and outrages already committed upon our citizens and our soldiers."[81] His belligerent invocation of the American imperium was not entirely necessary at the time, for most Yankee properties survived through the 1920s. That was a favorable decade for Yankee ranchers, and Hearst continued to enjoy the international high life. In 1921 he and his equally flamboyant mistress Marion Davies went to Mexico City to meet the new president, Alvaro Obregón, who agreed to protect the Hearst estates, including his lands in lowland Campeche.

But the arrogance and high visibility of the Yankee capitalists left them vulnerable to rising Mexican political wrath. Obregón's successor Plutarco Calles confiscated several parts of Babicora, distributing them to peasants. Hearst also began to worry about his mines and timber and chicle lands in Guanacevi and San Luis.

In 1935, under the reformist president Lazaro Cárdenas, a new law was passed that limited individual holdings to 100,000 acres. The government expropriated 175,000 acres of Hearst's arable land, and in 1940 it took 117,000 more. The rest remained under the management of Hearst's team, who maintained it as the most productive ranch in northern Mexico. Breaking up an estate that was run in sophisticated ways—including effective water use and pasture management—and turning some of the best lands over to subsistence farming may well have caused environmental deterioration. Any ill effects, however, are difficult to measure against the rights and needs of campesino families.

Other states in Mexico's arid north saw a similar picture. By the late 1920s many *ganaderias* in Coahuila, east of Babicora, were held by U.S. interests. The ranches at Piedras Negras were worth $2 million. When Frank Tannenbaum of the Brookings Institution in Washington surveyed the economy of rural Mexico in the late 1920s, he found that foreigners owned some one-fifth of all Mexico's private lands, primarily in the northern and coastal states, where population was sparse and land cheap, and where the old Hispanic elite was less entrenched than in the high lands of central Mexico. In Chihuahua foreigners owned 42.7 percent of private lands; in Sonora 27.1 percent, and in Coahuila 22.7 percent. Most must have been ranchland. Americans owned just over half of the foreign-held acreage, followed by Spaniards, British, Germans, and French.[82]

These figures reflected a rapid expansion of American interests and the beginning of the modernization of the Mexican cattle industry in the mid-1920s as well. The import of breeding stock and the export of beef cattle constituted the key element of modernization, an exchange that was almost exclusively with the United States. The expropriation of some U.S. interests, including mines and ranches, in the 1930s under President Cárdenas did not seem to change the industry much. Although exports faltered during the early years of the Depression, the export of range-grown cattle into the southwestern United States for feedlot fattening continued. Mexican exports, which went almost entirely to the United States, rose strongly in the months before the United States entered World War II, from a low of 60,000 cattle in 1934 to a high of 754,000 in 1939.[83]

Between 1930 and 1944 the greatest increase in Mexico's cattle production was in the north. This region had the largest percentage of large private ranches, most of them between 50,000 and 175,000 acres. Many northern ranchers who were producing cattle for the U.S. companies were originally from the United States or had spent much time there. The bilingual alliance was becoming steadily stronger.[84]

How important were American beef markets for the changing pattern of use of northern Mexico's arid lands? From 1921 (when statistics were first reliably recorded) to 1949 U.S. beef imports from Mexico varied from under 1 percent of U.S. consumption to a high of 5 percent in 1939, almost entirely from the northern region of the country.[85] That was only a small fragment of U.S. consumption, but because that demand was concentrated in the fragile northern drylands of Mexico, it had significant long-range ecological consequences. Over the years the ranching system in which foreigners became so deeply involved suffered a gradual elimination of vegetation, on both flatlands and hillsides. Erosion, especially sheet erosion caused by wind, removed varying amounts of the thin topsoil, making it ever more difficult to reconstitute and improve pastures even when more funds and modern pasture management became available. In 1954 the first systematic soil survey of Mexico and Central America reported serious erosion in northern Mexican grasslands.[86]

Since the United States refused to import South American beef because of the danger of aftosa, American suppliers had long centered their interest on Mexico. In the immediate aftermath of World War II Mexico suddenly faced a major crisis in its cattle industry, when aftosa began to ravage Mexican herds. The U.S. banned live cattle imports in 1947 as a result. By 1949, when only 21,000 head were imported, Mexican beef canneries had begun selling canned beef to the U.S. Department of Agriculture, which it shipped largely to British markets. In 1949, 149 million pounds of processed beef passed through Yankee hands on that route.[87]

The eradication of aftosa necessitated improvements in stock management. From the late 1940s on, thousands of breeding bulls were shipped to northern Mexico from the United States.[88] Mexican breeders used that stock to extend their work south into Central America. Yankee cattlemen could now buy Mexican feeder cattle when periodic droughts depleted the ranges in the western United States—thus Mexican cattlemen were now dependent on range conditions in the western United States. A severe drought in the southwestern United States in 1956 led Mexico to begin large exports to the United States again four years later.

Chihuahua and Coahuila, the largest beef-producing states, underwent a big expansion of beef production and export, and they began to supply the burgeoning Mexico City market as well. Consequently, pasturage increased. In 1930 the pasturelands in Mexico that contained twelve acres or more totaled 155 million acres, including 32 million acres in Chihuahua. Cárdenas's land reform campaign of the 1930s organized many *ejidos* at the expense of big ranches. As a result, by 1940 ranchlands had fallen to 111 million acres. The turnaround began in the late 1940s, and in 1950 over 125 million acres were once again in large pastures, including 35 million in Chihuahua.

Anti-gringo sentiments remained high during the aftermath of the 1930s, and attacks on foreign-owned estates continued through the war years. In 1947 the Palomas Land and Cattle Company was nationalized, and many small segments were given to the resident campesinos; other portions ended up in the hands of President Miguel Alemán's friends. In Chihuahua, Hearst's Babicora Ranch was fully nationalized after he died in 1951. In 1954 the Mexican government paid Hearst's estate a bargain price of about $2 million for the final 125,000 acres of his holdings and turned the ranchland into fifty-acre plots for agricultural colonies.

Profits and costs continued to rise after 1945. Little additional pastureland was available in northern Mexico, so ranchers increasingly turned to stock improvement, accelerating the trend that had begun in the late nineteenth century with the introduction of Hereford and Short-horn bulls. In 1910, 17 percent of northern Mexican cattle had been crossbred; by 1930 that figure rose to over 50 percent.

Northern Mexico's feeder calves were hardier, healthier, and hungrier than stock north of the Rio Grande. Consequently, by the 1950s there was a rising demand for them in the southwestern United States. In 1960, 318,000 feeder cattle were shipped across the border; two years later that figure jumped to 740,000. Chihuahua and Sonora increasingly aimed beef production for U.S. markets, using improved breeding, range, and water management to increase the quality of their stock. By the late 1960s, 65 percent of Chihuahua's cattle were Hereford crosses. Cattle production in Sonora presented a similar picture of mixed breeds on irrigated pastures. Coahuila favored the Charolais, the white French crossbreed.

In the early 1950s, although only 3 percent of Mexico's pastureland was improved with hardier grasses, many of the large ranchers began to benefit from contracts with Yankee beef purchasers and raised the capital to modernize. More ranches began sowing their pastures to the drought-resistant black grama grass, which by 1970 covered large portions of the plateau from Mexico City to Juárez.

Ranchers also had better access to a U.S.-financed research program, sponsored by the Rockefeller Foundation and the U.S. Department of Agriculture, that focused on improving breeds and pasture. In 1941, a Rockefeller Foundation Survey Commission traveled around rural Mexico. The commission found that about one-third of Mexico was still in native grasslands that could only be productively used for grazing. The commission's report praised excellent herds of Holstein and Jersey dairy cattle near Mexico City and Querétaro, which had been developed from American and Canadian bloodlines. On the northern ranges the commission noted many fine herds of Hereford and Angus, which were maintained for markets to the north. In contrast, most of Mexico City's beef, still raised in the traditional manner, was lean and tough.[89]

The larger operations had the technical and financial capacity to re-constitute severely damaged grasslands and, in some places, the political power to control water resources. Thus, on the intensive commercial ranches many pastures were improved, although at the long-term cost of depleting both surface and underground water resources. Yankee capital and Yankee markets were a major driving force behind that trend.

Beyond the reach of intensive management of the large commercial ranches were the *ejidos*. The reforms of the 1930s had given the Indian communities title to the land, but had left them with access to few other resources, including water, and little technical support. The pastures remained mostly unfenced commons, and the village communities did little or nothing to improve the pasture. The villagers still relied on random breeding. Most of the *ejidos* were badly degraded and poverty-stricken.[90] In the area around Parras, for example, Indian campesinos were marginalized, squatting on poor dry soils on the fringes of the remunerative private estates. Cattle grazing expanded into hill forests, degrading them more than ever.[91]

The impact of the cattle industry in transforming rangeland and forest did not stop at the eastern shores of the Pacific, but followed in the immediate wake of the Hispanic and Anglo cultures as they crossed the great ocean. Introduced on one Pacific island after another, along with goats and other Eurasian ungulates, cattle had an even more systemic impact on the fragile and biologically restricted island ecosystems than they had on continental landmasses. Hawaii is a relatively well-documented case.

AMERICAN CATTLE CROSS THE PACIFIC

The first goats arrived on the Hawaiian Islands in 1778 with Captain Cook. Their population began to explode, and they began to reduce the native vegetation immediately. The first cattle began to reinforce their destructive work in 1793, when Captain George Vancouver presented Kamehameha I with several breeding pairs as a handsome gift. The king declared that all cattle were his personal property, so there was little anyone could do to hinder them from running wild. They invaded the native grasslands and woodlands of the volcanic slopes; their aggressive tempers became a danger to the human population as well.

Cattle ranching in Hawaii was started by some of the early settlers from New England. The greatest of the ranches was the work of John Palmer Parker, the sailor son of a whaler from Newton, Massachusetts. Like many New Englanders of his generation, Parker was caught up in the romance of global sailing: he sailed first as a clerk on a clipper traveling to the Northwest for furs. Parker arrived at Kawaihae on the Big Island in 1809 to take on sandalwood that Hawaiian commoners were hauling down from the forests of Waimea.

Through his resulting contacts with Kamehameha I, Parker was able to marry the king's granddaughter in 1816, an action that combined romance with access to land. Other aspiring *haoles* gained new properties through marriages to *ali'i* women in the years that followed, and turned them into ranches. Several had the additional panache of official aristocratic status, and they lived that role to the hilt—but before they could practice ostentatious, elegant living, they had to make money.

In the late 1820s beef replaced sandalwood as the major item of sale for the *haoles,* especially salted beef, which was purchased as provisions by the whalers. It was just as well that cattle came to have high commercial value, for in their wild state they were causing nothing but trouble. In the few years since Vancouver's gift in 1793, the tough Criollo cattle had gone through a classic irruption, multiplying rapidly and spreading into the forests where they exceeded the pigs in battering the native vegetation. In the leeward lowlands, where the woodlands were xerophytic and open and where water was scarce, cattle ravaged the Hawaiians' irrigated sweet potato and taro gardens.

The king hired Parker and a few other riders in the 1820s as "bullock hunters," paying them to catch wild steers, but there were no fully trained cowboys who could effectively herd and pasture the wild cattle. Certainly a man born in suburban Boston lacked the full range of skills. In 1832 Parker hired three well-known vaqueros from Mexican California to train local riders to conquer and manage the wild Waimea herds. The Hawaiians called their teachers *paniolo* (a mispronunciation of the word *Español*), so Hawaiian cowboys themselves became known as paniolo, whatever their ethnic background might be.[92] Reflecting the broad trend of social history in the islands, the paniolo became a multiracial mix of Hawaiians, Japanese, Chinese, Filipinos, and Yankees.

Although they shared the essential working traits of their mainland counterparts, Hawaiian paniolo in the long run were somewhat more settled than mainland cowboys; from one generation to the next they were better integrated into the society of the islands and more firmly established on the land. Parker and his successors and their wives were paternalists, providing jobs that were held for generations and housing and other support to their employees. Like their mainland counterparts, the paniolo were hired workers for an industry that transformed the biological systems of the land into economic entities whose species composition was determined (more or less efficiently and deliberately) by their contribution to the market value of one commodity—beef.

It took the paniolo many years to make much progress. One observer reported as early as 1836, "Those parts of the plain adjoining Hamakua are . . . wooded, having a parklike appearance, with numerous herds of wild cattle and many wild boars, which are either caught in pit falls, shot or speared by the natives."[93] The deeply scarred rubble surface and tangled forest growth of the old volcanoes thwarted the paniolo. By the late 1850s there were an estimated 8,000 tame cattle but still 12,000 wild head in the Waimea area. When Parker first arrived, the Waimea plateau was under a wide forest of endemic tree species dominated by the ohia.[94] As the ranching system expanded and the cattle were increasingly domesticated, the forest was steadily depleted, turned into pastureland. Ohia was cut extensively to supply material for pens and stockyards.

A turning point in the effort to establish a modern ranching culture on the islands came in the Great Mahele of 1848, the royal proclamation that established private property, followed by the 1850 law that allowed foreigners to own land in fee simple. Indeed, one scholar of the ranching system suggests that the cattle business was in part responsible for the Great Mahele. So much poaching had gone on since the late 1820s that wild cattle populations had declined steeply. Ranching could no longer thrive on new infusions of wild steers, so the cattlemen pressured the king to establish a system of private property, which would allow long-term commercial ranching to function.[95]

One of the first foreigners to gain a private parcel was Parker, whose wife received a grant of 640 acres in 1850 from Kipikane, cousin of the king. High in the rolling Waimea hills, the grant provided a homestead surrounded with grazing land interspersed with forests of endemic maile, mamane, and ohia. The Parker Ranch led the way for commercialization of the cattle industry in the islands. In the 1840s Parker began building cattle corrals. In 1851 he introduced Angus and Herefords to upgrade the meat production of his herds for the newly escalating beef market created by the gold rush in California. The founder's grandson Sam inherited the estate in 1868. Born to wealth and adventure, Sam held innumerable parties at the manor house that attracted the bulging wallets of Honolulu. Sam's love of the high life took him to Honolulu much of the time, and he let the ranch gradually decline toward ruin. Cattle began going wild again; breeding was no longer controlled, and no efforts were taken to manage pastures against overgrazing. Yet the natural forest continued to retreat before the inexorable demand for lumber to build sluices, fences, and farm buildings in the later years of the century.

With the Parker family in disarray, Alfred Wellington Carter, a leading Honolulu lawyer, was appointed manager of the ranch in 1900. Born in 1867, Carter was the son of a whaler who had become a Honolulu merchant. The son's career epitomized what the *haole* elite of Honolulu had made possible. He worked at various jobs, including one at the Bishop Bank, then was appointed clerk at the Hawaii Supreme Court. The judges sent him to Yale Law School, from which he graduated in two years in 1893. Returning to Honolulu, he opened a law partnership with his cousin, an older brother of the governor of the islands, and then with Lorrin Thurston, the leading organizer of the 1893 overthrow of the monarchy. With his dynamism and his inner-circle connections, Carter was the Parkers' choice to bail out the ranch. His long stewardship was strikingly successful in financial terms.

Facing a bankrupt cattle operation but with access to plenty of cash through his Honolulu network, Carter began to modernize the ranch. Like the sugar planters on the islands, Carter had access to an international network of agricultural associations that provided the most up-to-date information on cattle and pasture management. In the following years he turned the ranch into a biologically cosmopolitan showcase of plant and animal varieties.

The pastures of the Parker Ranch had deteriorated badly and were increasingly arid, but Carter had the capital to invest in large-scale innovative pasture management. He had an aqueduct built to take water thirty-five miles from the Kohala mountains to the Waiki'i meadows. Then his men experimented with exotic pasture grasses. They planted Rhodes grass from South Africa, Yorkshire fog and cocksfoot from England, paspalum from Australia, Kentucky bluegrass, and assorted clovers, brooms, vetches, ryes, and pigeon peas. Kikuyu grass, introduced in the 1920s, was one of the most successful.

The herds were still mostly wild; only 5,000 cattle were tame. Under Carter's direction the paniolo rounded up most of the wild cattle and began a new program of breeding with Hereford bulls from the mainland. This required new paddocks and many miles of fencing, which they had constructed by 1908, using mamane, an endemic wood, from the upland forests. To control spreading plant pests (German ivy, thistles, burrs, o'i, air plants, cactus, lantana, and guava) and insect pests (cutworm and fruit fly), the Parker Ranch began the heavy use of new poison sprays. There was no way at that time to assess what the environmental costs of these decisions might be.

Carter pushed reforestation as well, using introduced species. His workers planted windbreaks, using 200,000 eucalyptus seedlings from Australia as well as Monterey cypress and Japanese cedar. He worked closely with the American Forestry Association, later joining its board of commissioners. He became a major supporter of the effort to set up the islands' Bureau of Forestry and helped designate forest reserves on the Big Island, gaining a reputation as a champion of the conservation strategies of his time.

In the broadest picture, ranching in Hawaii depended on available markets for the beef. In the early days the cattlemen had provided hides and salted beef to the whalers. The California gold rush created a bonanza market on the U.S. mainland after 1848, but that was short-lived. Before long California ranches expanded to provide all the cattle products needed there. Hawaiian beef was then raised mostly for Hawaiian markets. By the 1930s ranching used 35 percent of the islands' 6,435 square miles and supplied 77 percent of the islands' beef consumption. Much of this was produced in Honolulu's hinterland on the island of Oahu.

A 1982 census of the islands' ranches counted 242,000 head of cattle on 400 ranches of all sizes. Many of those cattle were run as a secondary aspect of sugar operations.[96] From the early years, ranching's connections to sugar plantations were close and complex. As the director of the state's experiment station noted in 1937, "ranching has always been an adjunct to a sugar plantation for the purpose of utilizing waste land and supplying the plantation with meat."[97]

The history of cattle ranching on the islands includes stories of high living and financial risk. Rose Ranch on Maui was famous, or perhaps notorious, for its owner's lavish lifestyle. James Makee arrived in the islands in 1856, jumping ship to escape a mutiny on his whaling ship. Settling in Honolulu, he set up shop as a general merchandiser and gradually moved into ranching in the city's hinterland. Accumulating profits rapidly, he was soon able to purchase the 35,000-acre Ulupalakoa Ranch on Maui, which he renamed. Although Makee successfully raised cattle and grew sugar, he was better known for his lavish parties; in the 1870s they were often held in honor of King Kalakaua.

The smaller island of Lanai presents a very different case. Here the entire island was set up as one ranch by Mormon immigrants in 1866. That first ranch was short-lived, for the Mormons left Lanai in 1878. The new owners attempted to grow sugar, but the operation failed around 1900, which was by then a familiar story. Lanai reverted again to a cattle ranch run by the Baldwin and Gay Company, the owners of Koele Ranch on Maui. Sanford Dole bought the island in 1922 to turn it into the world's greatest pineapple plantation, but ranching continued as a sideline on Lanai until the mid-1950s.[98]

Wide ranchlands covered Molokai, a dry island that could not support crops without elaborately long irrigation systems from the windward hills. The largest ranch, 53,000 acres of arid scrub pasture, was inherited in 1873 by Bernice Bishop, the most powerful Hawaiian woman in the islands. After consolidating it into a working ranch, the Bishops sold it to Honolulu businessmen in 1897, who tried to grow irrigated sugar cane, but failed. Not surprisingly, it reverted to cattle production again. By 1980 it specialized in Santa Gertrudis steers bred from King Ranch stock in Texas.

The saga of Hawaiian ranching caught many people's fancy, but it had critics as well. In the late 1950s historian Fred Beckley wrote disparagingly of "the whims and dictation of King Sugar and his son Pineapple, as well as his nephew, Island Cattle Ranches, and their high-priced beef. They are but tentacles of the 'Big Five' octopus of King Sugar's oligarchy."[99]

In any event, by the mid-1900s ranch management gradually became far more complex than it had been in the uproarious, unstable years of the late nineteenth century. Financial pressures forced ranchers to manage their cattle, pastures, and water more efficiently. In the 1920s, and especially after 1945, they found themselves interacting with an increasingly complex range of state agencies and research offices. By the early 1950s organizations monitoring or advising on pasture, forest, and watershed conservation included the state Agriculture and Forestry Department, the Public Lands Commission, the University of Hawaii, and the Hawaii Sugar Planters' Association's Experiment Station. Belatedly, in 1960, following their mainland counterparts, the ranchers organized themselves into a formal network, the Hawaii Cattlemen's Council, to provide a communications network and a lobby for ranching interests.

Ranching operations continued to expand. A 1964 land census revealed that 1,286,000 acres were in pastures in the islands, slightly over half the entire farm acreage. By 1971 there were approximately 60,000 cattle on all ranches, supplying half of Hawaii's consumption. Of the rest, half was imported from California and half from Australia and New Zealand.[100]

The long-term environmental consequences of cattle ranching in the Hawaiian Islands remain controversial and inadequately studied. They particularly affect two areas: pasture management and the upland forest watersheds. The degradation of pasture vegetation became widespread over the years. Localized small-scale erosion became evident in many open pastures around the islands, where the pressure of cattle hooves and teeth exceeded the capacity of roots and rain to regenerate the

vegetation and hold the soil. The damage may have been particularly
severe in dry forest zones, on old lava flows and on higher leeward
slopes. Very little remains of that original forest, and it is difficult to
reconstruct a picture of what grew there before Captain Vancouver
dropped anchor.[101]

The amount and type of pasture management practiced on the
ranches varied greatly over the years. Some of the largest and most prosperous ranchers played leading roles in managing their cattle lands and
planning for future use. Most ranchers, however, only belatedly abandoned the established practice of rotating their herds among only two
to four pastures and letting the cattle consume all the grass in each
pasture. They began to adopt methods that conserved pastureland and
that remain in use today: strip- or block-grazing, using twenty-five to
fifty pastures, moving cattle as often as daily. This more intensive management allows the cattle to graze on fresh grass daily, which cuts the
amount of feed imported from the mainland and reduces costs. Managed
in this way, the pasture can support twice the number of cattle and
overgrazing is greatly reduced.[102]

Hawaiian ranching has developed in a unique setting of forests and
pastures growing on young volcanic soils at dramatically varying elevations. In watersheds and upland forests, cattle—along with other introduced mammals, from the Polynesian pig to the Eurasian goat, sheep,
and horse—have had a transformative impact over the past two hundred
years. Many native plant and animal species were driven to extinction
or severely reduced by the introduction of alien species of pasture grass,
trees, and animals.

The financial and technological aspects of cattle raising were intimately linked with the rest of the islands' economic power structure.
Cattle ranching, like many aspects of Hawaiian life in the modern era,
was a bridge that helped Americans reach across the Pacific to the world
of tropical Asia.

AMERICAN COLONIAL RANCHING
IN THE SOUTHERN PHILIPPINES

One more American experiment in cattle ranching took place in the
Philippines, where Spanish colonists had introduced cattle to the grasslands of central Luzon, transplanting them from the hacienda system of
colonial Mexico. Criollo cattle did not spread rapidly on Luzon, since
the market for beef and leather was strictly limited. Few Filipinos ate

beef, and the Spanish community in Manila, which numbered only a few thousand souls, was almost the only market. Criollo cattle had difficulty grazing on the tough Philippine grasses, especially when the patchy savannas were burned in dry weather, reducing the species variety. Moreover, herds on the island were restricted by a rinderpest epidemic in the 1880s.[103]

Another example of the colonial expropriation of land and the displacement of local culture was created by an American on Mindanao, the southernmost island of the Philippines. Mindanao was home to intensive rice production in its lowlands, vast reserves of rainforest on its mountainous slopes, and rolling grassy uplands on the Bukidnon plateau. The climate of the plateau is cool enough to sustain cattle that are susceptible to rainforest diseases.

Shortly after World War I, Dean Worcester, who had been the colonial secretary of the interior until 1913, founded an experimental ranch in the Bukidnon grasslands, on acreage purchased from a Filipino landlord. On his Diklum Ranch he imported the Philippines' first Nellore bulls from India, which were more resistant to rinderpest than Spanish cattle. He encouraged several other American friends to do the same. By 1940 the Bukidnon plateau had several successful ranches, which had displaced local subsistence farming. Local men were trained as cowboys. In the name of economic development, Worcester thus brought capitalist agriculture and ranching into the formerly remote upland areas of Mindanao, starting the process of binding the region into the national and international economy.[104] The market for beef continued to be largely limited to those with Western tastes, most of whom lived in Manila.

These cattle operations did not initiate a broader process of ranching development in the Philippines, and in that sense beef production there was only a footnote in the global history of domesticated livestock. More important was the link that ranching provided for agricultural industry: beef was one commodity through which American speculators established themselves in the Philippine Islands.

Japanese forces occupied Mindanao in early 1942, taking Worcester's ranch to supply their logistical needs. When the Philippines became independent in 1946 and title to the land was available, Worcester's ranch was sold, as were some other old American ranches, to rich Filipinos. These owners used the ranches as playthings, and they rarely visited them from their homes in Manila and other coastal cities. American holdings on the plateau were linked to the expanding network of corporate fruit plantations, which were moving or expanding into Southeast Asia from Central America and Hawaii. Del Monte's pineapple plantations on Lanai in the Hawaiian Islands had been threatened with destruction by epidemic disease in the early 1920s, so the company organized a subsidiary, Philippine Packing Corporation, on Mindanao in 1926. The company began growing pineapples for export on 20,000 acres of rented land in Bukidnon, using laborers from Luzon who were already familiar with its operations in California and Hawaii.[105] By the late 1930s Philpack was exporting nearly $2 million of canned pineapples annually. After the wartime interregnum it reestablished and expanded its Bukidnon operations in both fruit and ranching.[106] By the 1960s Bukidnon was surpassing Lanai as the foremost producer of pineapples for U.S. markets.

This was the extent of American experimentation with cattle culture in the ecological settings of the southern Pacific and Southeast Asia. Worcester's venture was essentially the probe of a few politicians and entrepreneurs; it established no broad trend. American colonialism never stretched beyond the Philippines, and Western colonialism in the Asian tropics was dying in the 1940s. Moreover, the economies of the western Pacific Rim provided no market for beef before World War II. Perhaps more fundamental, the only lands of any extent that might have conceivably been converted to ranching—apart from those already densely settled by rice growing farmers—were the lowland forestlands, where aggressive entrepreneurs usually could find ways to displace the tribal populations. The technical knowledge needed to establish ranching in hot, humid lowlands was just emerging after World War II, and, by that time, European and North American investors had sources enough elsewhere.

Although brief, the experiment with beef production in the Mindanao highlands did share some characteristics with ranching in other tropical countries. It transformed subtropical grasslands; it contributed to the decline of former communal subsistence use and the destruction of indigenous cultures. Beyond this, it provided a point of economic entry, opening lands to the production of commercial export crops. After 1945, following more than four centuries of preparation on grasslands beyond the Old World, the cattle industry was primed to establish export-scale commercial operations in the lowland wet forests of tropical America. Ranching embraced a unique complex of political power, control of extensive tracts of land, and cultural prestige. The ranchers' product moved on its own locomotion; it could eat its way into the forest.

Once again, trends in the economy and culture of material consumption in the United States were to have a profound effect on the ecological fortunes of its southern hinterland.

PENETRATING THE LATIN AMERICAN RAINFOREST

When World War II was over, American families produced a baby boom and participated in an unprecedented rush for affluence and all its attributes. Like instant coffee, beef became one of the most prominent symbols of the speedy life on wheels that affluence could buy. Beef of all cuts appeared on family dining tables, and hamburgers became the raison d'être of new fast-food restaurants, especially chain outlets like White Castle and McDonalds. The increase of supermarkets and growth in the packaging industry fed the demand. By the 1950s the United States, Canada, Europe, and the Soviet Union, which made up less than 40 percent of global population, consumed 80 percent of the world's beef. The United States, with one-twentieth of the world's population, was responsible for nearly half of the entire global consumption of cattle flesh. In 1960 an average American consumed under 100 pounds of beef per year, but in 1976 that figure had risen to well over 150 pounds— nearly a half pound of beef every day for every American—before starting to recede in the early 1980s.[107]

The trend toward rising consumption of beef and rising prices of domestic production coincided with declining supplies of home-grown beef, as pasture costs rose inexorably in the western states. This led American meat packers to begin looking outside their borders for low-priced beef. In the late 1960s the United States, long an exporter, became the world's largest importer of beef. At the beginning of the import era in the late 1940s its imports of beef averaged 35,000 tons annually, in contrast with western Europe's imports of 480,000 tons (mostly from southern South America, Australia, and New Zealand). By 1970 American imports skyrocketed to 527,000 tons, while western European imports only doubled to 945,000 tons.[108] The trend continued until about 1980. The American appetite for beef had important consequences for the economies of several Latin American countries and their lands as well, both savannas and forests, as those regions became economically dependent on the new market.

The United States was the only major meat producer whose herds had not been attacked by aftosa. The U.S. Department of Agriculture feared that the dread disease would enter the country with fresh beef from

South America, so it banned the import of live cattle and fresh or frozen beef in 1970. The restriction did not include processed meats, so Argentina and Uruguay continued to ship this product to American markets. Experts at the U.S. Department of Agriculture forged an agreement with the two southern countries on standards for processed beef: the beef had to be cooked in approved plants that met U.S. conditions for sanitary processing, and it had to be shipped directly to the United States. In 1964, at the insistence of the domestic beef lobby, Congress set import quotas for beef, veal, and mutton. The effect on Argentina and Uruguay was striking. The two Plata countries provided one-half of total U.S. beef imports in the 1950s, but by 1970 that figure fell to only one-quarter. Argentina's share dropped from one-third to under one-tenth.[109]

American meat processors and hamburger chains intensified their search for new sources of disease-free beef. During the 1950s and 1960s most additional U.S. imports were from a new source region, Australia. This major development was spearheaded by the aggressively corporate King Ranch, which bought large amounts of land there after 1950. The costs of transport across the Pacific were rising, however, and the economics of long-distance bulk transport worked to the advantage of lands closer to home.

The rising demand for beef in Latin America and the United States produced a major expansion of Latin American rangelands from the 1950s on. By the 1960s livestock was Latin America's third most valuable export commodity, behind petroleum (largely from Mexico and Venezuela) and grain (largely from Argentina).[110] American imports would have to be drawn from Central America, though, because aftosa was still endemic among herds in South America.

Beginning in the late 1950s Central America became a supplier for American markets. Its cattle were raised on grass rather than grain, making the beef very lean, suitable for only one sector of the U.S. beef market: the fast-food trade. Central American beef began to make its way into hamburgers, frankfurters, chili, T.V. dinners, baby foods, luncheon meat, salami, and other processed meats for humans, to say nothing of dog and cat food. Hamburgers accounted for more than one-third of the fast-food industry in the 1970s.

LAYING SIEGE TO THE CENTRAL AMERICAN RAINFOREST

Development of the industry in moist forest zones of Central America posed a series of problems that were not present in the grassland countries. The biotic complexities of rainforest ecosystems were an effective barrier against commercial ranching until the 1950s. Lowland pasture diseases such as blackleg, anthrax, and splenetic fever had been a hindrance to livestock, much as malaria and yellow fever had been to humans. In addition, roads remained poor except where corporate plantations had taken hold.

One source of innovation for the establishment of ranching in the Caribbean lowlands of Central America came from cattlemen farther up the coast, in the Mexican lowlands that stretch from Tamaulipas south to Tampico, Veracruz, and Tabasco. These ranchers led the way in adopting new techniques that made their operations financially successful. In colonial times and through the 1800s Mexican cattlemen had maintained small herds of Criollo cattle on the coastal savannas and riverine marshes; the cattle provided leather and tallow for Mexican markets. During the revolution, most of the herds were decimated, but thereafter their numbers rose steadily again. After the war, as roads improved and new railroads were built, the market for beef in Mexico City grew stronger. This provided a reason to improve the size and productivity of the herds.

In the 1930s and early 1940s there was a considerable increase in the number of cattle in the wet lowlands of the Gulf Zone. Ranchers introduced new Brahman bulls in 1932 and began to improve their pasture. By the 1920s Pará and Guinea grasses were displacing large areas of native species.[111] Both traditional and improved pastures had ecological disadvantages. Where intense pasture management was achieved by the introduction of African grasses, economic productivity rose at the expense of species diversity. Where cattle were run in traditional ways, grasslands were degraded and suffered the invasion of woody shrubs as well as the exotic grasses.

In Mexico's Caribbean coastal lowlands American rubber, banana, and sugar plantations introduced commercial cattle operations as early as 1910.[112] Cattle were never the leading product of the plantations, but a few managers became familiar with techniques that mitigated the problems of maintaining beef cattle in the disease-infected lowlands. To resist the cattle diseases of the hot, moist lands, they had to introduce crossbreeds. From 1924 on they used Brahman stud bulls extensively for their resistance to ticks and adaptability to the coastal climate. Their meat was less tender and marbled than that of the Shorthorn and Hereford crosses of the arid uplands, so it was not favored in the United States, and lowland beef exports to the north remained modest. Nonetheless, the Gulf coast of Mexico provided a corridor for tests of new cattle and ranching technology that made the subsequent penetration of the Central American lowlands possible.

The American banana corporations in Central America were also an important source of innovative cattle and pasture management for the Caribbean lowlands. When Sam Zemurray began organizing large-scale banana production on Honduras's north coast around 1910, he paid attention to pastures as well as plantations, partly to provide beef for his workers. His employees worked with local ranchers to introduce other aspects of modern pasture and cattle management. Corporate ranching greatly escalated the scale of operation, and corporate ranchers had access to international innovations in cattle breeding and veterinary medicine. By 1929, when United Fruit bought out Zemurray, it inherited over $2 million in livestock, herded on 117,272 acres of managed pasture that were seeded with nutritious exotic grasses such as Guinea grass.[113]

None of this had widespread impacts on the rainforests of the Caribbean lowlands until the 1950s, when market demand was transformed by the rise of the American hamburger industry. Traditional ranching in Central America was far from the corporate enclaves. Ranching in the Petén forest region of northern Guatemala was typical: scattered, semiwild cattle had roamed the area from colonial times, especially in the 10 percent of the region in which small savannas dotted the forest. Farmers kept a few cows and steers in many tiny clearings, grazing on the ragged grass at the edge of the forest. Small ranches were scattered across the region, making patches on the land; the largest of these operations ran a few thousand head of cattle. The owners marketed their scrub cattle by driving them north into Yucatán or into British Honduras and selling them for their leather and meat. They also supplied beef to mahogany loggers beginning in the 1860s. These were backcountry operations, poorly run; by the early 1900s most of them were failing. Only in the 1960s did a new cattle boom hit the Petén, but the region remained densely wooded: even in 1970 between 70 and 80 percent of the land was still in forest.[114]

A similar pattern of land use evolved in the lowlands of the north coast of Honduras before the banana era.[115] By the late 1800s small towns lined the meandering rivers that drained the forest, and scattered crop and ranch lands radiated out from the settlements. Some of the larger landowners grew coconuts, rubber, fruit, and other products to sell to ships docked at the little coastal ports. Other landowners pre-

ferred to run cattle, raising them in the old colonial style for their cow-
hides, which found buyers from Europe. By the mid-1800s they were
also shipping live cattle to Cuba to supplement the sugar island's herds.
Until pastures and croplands were efficiently fenced with barbed wire,
the hardy, aggressive Criollo cattle ran semiwild, wandering off the
Honduran pastures onto croplands and into the forest, damaging them
both repeatedly. In the hinterland of San Pedro Sula, the largest town
in the region, a 1908 survey showed that about 50,000 acres had been
cleared for crops and 25,000 acres were in pasture.

Cattle ranchers in this region still had little knowledge of the new
techniques of cattle management. Anyone who wished to expand commercial operations faced formidable obstacles. On the wet Caribbean
lowlands cattle were tormented by sunburn, ticks, and disease—the defenders of the natural forest. Moreover, market infrastructure was primitive. Only local markets existed, and cattle walked to market, losing
weight and quality along the way. Slaughterhouses or abattoirs were
local monopolies and were heavily taxed. Change was slow. One American expert who toured neighboring El Salvador at the end of the 1950s
described the slaughterhouses as "small, poorly illuminated, unscreened
structures of some antiquity. Tools, facilities, and techniques are rudimentary; and disposal of waste usually involves a rear wall, buzzards,
and dogs."[116] Typically there was no refrigeration in open markets, and
no packaging.

As one commentator succinctly put it, "Before the export boom of
the 1960s, cattle managed Central America's pastures."[117] Criollo cattle
survived with little care even on rough pasture, but they were poorly
adapted to the demands of modern markets. They gained weight slowly
and their frames carried a low percentage of meat; their meat was tough
and stringy; and they had low reproduction rates. They overgrazed the
unmanaged pastures, leaving only low-nutrition weeds and lowering the
pastures' long-range carrying capacity. Native grasses survived with little care, but, like the Criollo cattle, they had low productivity. Malnutrition, insect infestation, disease, and infertility were standard on the
small ranches.

In the 1950s cattle began replacing trees in massive numbers, as new
developments in livestock technology as well as modern meat processing
methods brought a revolution in animal husbandry, pasture management, transportation, slaughtering, and marketing to Central America.
The new technologies and investments led to consolidation of larger
properties, which in turn led the way toward more intensive operation.

The social costs were high, for the increasingly powerful ranchers forced many smallholders off their ancestral lands.[118] The American role in that trend was selective, but in most of Central America it was the decisive force. In the new era of widening U.S. investments, Americans strengthened close links to local landed oligarchies, supporting them and their methods of working the land as long as Yankee standards for beef quality were achieved.

In the two decades after the mid-1950s, beef exports from Central America soared from 20,000 tons a year to almost 150,000 tons, nine-tenths being dispatched to the United States. Central America provided only 5 percent of all beef imports to the United States in the early 1960s; from there it tripled, reaching 15 percent in the late 1970s. Nicaragua increased sales to the United States by five times between 1957 and 1967; Honduras increased its sales by twenty-four times.

By the 1970s beef had become Central America's fourth largest earner of foreign exchange, behind coffee, cotton, and bananas. Revenues from beef exports rose from $9 million in 1961, when the Alliance for Progress was launched, to over $100 million in the early 1970s.[119] The area domesticated for pasturelands more than doubled in the thirty years after 1950. The expansion occurred primarily at the expense of primary forests.

Ranching patterns in the rainforests of the Caribbean lowlands evolved partly out of centuries-old economies in the seasonally dry Pacific coastal lowlands, which were subject to periodically severe drought. Ranchers burned their pastures on Pacific slopes before the rains began in order to reduce weeds and brush, to encourage new grass to grow vigorously, and to kill tick eggs and other parasites. This strategy damaged the physical and chemical properties of the soil.[120]

Some pasturelands, in locations like central Nicaragua where the dry season was not too long, were more productive. These lands provided a base for the long-distance movement of cattle from pastures to urban markets. For this, hardy Criollo stock was excellently adapted. But the slow-growing, lean Criollo gave ranchers low profits, rarely over three or four dollars per animal in the 1950s. Hacenderos were reluctant to spend money to improve cattle and pasture management until greater profits were promised by a new scale of investment capital and improvements in cattle breeding, pasture management, and marketing technology appeared.

By the 1930s many local ranchers knew that arsenic dips kill ticks. Moreover, vaccines against blackleg and anthrax were becoming available, as well as worm medicine for internal parasites. More important still were new breeding programs. Zebu or Brahman crossbreeds were well known, and most hacenderos knew that light-colored breeds like Zebu and Charolais would prosper in the moist forest. Zebu bulls had been introduced into Central America in the early 1900s, but for better draft power, not beef.[121] The Zebu-Criollo cross was faster maturing and also beefier, and it had a lower rate of calf mortality than Criollo cattle did and high resistance to pests and heat. In the 1950s Santa Gertrudis bulls were introduced from Texas, along with artificial insemination. Costa Rica led the way in adopting these changes: by 1955 half its national herd consisted of the Zebu-Criollo cross; by the early 1970s that figure was over 90 percent.

Another element of the package was intensified pasture management. In the dry season all grasses increase their cellulose content; the grasses native to Central America become unpalatable to cattle because they have a much higher cellulose content than introduced grasses. The protein content of many native grasses is under .5 percent; that of planted pastures is up to 8 to 10 percent. In the wet season grasses increase in water content and protein, and decrease in cellulose; they are then more nutritious, especially from April to June. Beginning in the 1940s commercial ranchers began to sow their pastures with high-yielding grasses from tropical Africa and South America, including Pará, Guinea, Jaragua, Pangola, and, later, African Star. In the 1960s chemical fertilizers were introduced, especially on ranches that fattened cattle for slaughter. In Costa Rica the fertilized acreage rose from 5,434 acres in 1955, mostly in dairy operations, to over 100,000 acres in 1972.[122] This work was initiated not only by corporate managers and governmental aid advisors, but also in part by small communities of American Quakers and Seventh Day Adventists in the high hills above Guanacaste. Beginning in the late 1940s these communities introduced a modern system of pasture improvement and rotation for dairy cattle. Herbicides were introduced more slowly, from the mid-1960s in Costa Rica, and even later elsewhere.[123]

These changes were part of a package that brought new pressures to increase production. By 1972 Costa Rica had built four packing plants to slaughter beef for export to the United States. The plants could process 200,000 head per year, but because of the long dry season on the Pacific side, they were closed from December to April. Considerable capacity was thus wasted. One advisor concluded, "An expansion in feeder cattle production for fattening in the Caribbean area is needed to supply slaughter cattle more in line with current export slaughter capacity."[124]

All Central American beef destined for Yankee markets had to be slaughtered in their home countries according to U.S. standards. Beginning in 1957 the U.S. Department of Agriculture worked in tandem with local officials and slaughterhouse operators to set up modern packing plants. The first was opened that year in Nicaragua. By 1960 Honduras and Costa Rica each had a USDA-approved plant as well. By 1965 Guatemala had two, Honduras had four, and Nicaragua and Costa Rica each had one. El Salvador's first USDA-approved plant was on line by the early 1970s; by 1978 the five republics boasted a total of twenty-eight approved plants. The sixteen major ones had a capacity of nearly 900,000 head per year. The hamburger connection was set in place.[125]

Operators of the plants could control most of the profits from sales to the United States. Investors in the new plants included several American corporations with holdings in other food industries. Borden Foods, the milk products conglomerate, bought the Henderson Packing Plant, Costa Rica's first plant, in 1965. In Honduras the Tela Railroad Company, a subsidiary of United Brands, managed 14,000 acres of improved pasture plus 34,000 acres of extensive rangeland. The cattle added financial value to the high percentage of the land that United Brands had not planted in bananas. The company built a packing plant to process the cattle from its own estates, plus others on the north coast. Remarkably, by the late 1970s sales of United Brand's Honduran beef were bigger than its banana sales. Not to be outdone, the other food distribution giant, International Foods, also bought two plants in Honduras.

Other multinational fruit corporations followed United in their diversification campaigns, turning more marginal land into cattle production. By the 1960s Del Monte, by then a subsidiary of R. J. Reynolds, the tobacco conglomerate, ran cattle on 99,000 acres of concessions in Guatemala and Costa Rica. Standard Brands, which by then had been absorbed into Castle and Cooke, had extensive ranching concessions in Honduras and Costa Rica. Even Goodyear Tire turned its old rubber plantation in Costa Rica into a cattle ranch.

Individual American entrepreneurs as well as corporations profited from the new ventures. Leroy Denman, of the King Ranch, spent fifteen years in Guatemala when the ranch introduced Santa Gertrudis cattle into Central America in the 1950s. Rudolph Peterson, former president of the Bank of America and head of the United Nations Development Program, bred cattle in Panama. Another Yankee speculator, Toby Orr, was head of the Peace Corps in Costa Rica in the late 1960s. Costa Rica, the most politically moderate and stable and the most prosperous of the Central American republics, had long been eager for American investment. By 1972 about twenty Americans were operating ranches there.[126]

These men were vital channels for the changes that were industrializing Central American agriculture and reducing the rainforest. Yankee multinationals marketed virtually every element of the whole spectrum of modern improvements for cattle operations, including animal feeds with veterinary supplements, introduced grasses, pasture fertilizers, barbed wire, and more. "The companies that sold tubes of refrigerated semen also dispensed worm medicines, fly sprays, tick dips, vaccines, vitamin/mineral supplements, and other imported ingredients for improved animal health and sanitation."[127] Fort Dodge Laboratories in Kansas set up processing and packaging of veterinary products in Costa Rica, Honduras, and El Salvador. Ralston Purina marketed veterinary products and feeds in Guatemala and El Salvador. A subsidiary of Cargill Foods took enriched animal feeds into Guatemala. W. R. Grace introduced frozen bull semen into Nicaragua, plus fertilizer and improved grass seeds.

Yet another dimension of the new industry further strengthened American domination in Central America: vertical integration of operations from production to sales. The fruit companies had pioneered that system shortly after 1900 since bananas, their vehicle of prosperity, were so fragile. Those decades of experience enabled the companies to diversify dramatically in the 1960s. United Brands owned a packing plant, a railroad and docks in Honduras, a fleet of refrigerator ships for beef shipments, and until 1977 a major meat packing and distributing business in the United States. Morrell Meats, by then associated with United Brands, began diversifying in the region in 1960; its subsidiary John Morrell and Co. expanded beef production on owned or leased Central American lands. R. J. Reynolds, the tobacco giant, owned the Sea-Land piggy-back containership company as well as Del Monte, which provided American consumers with Ortega beef tacos, Chun King beef chow mein, and Patio beef enchiladas.[128] From its corporate headquarters in Panama, the Latin American Agribusiness Development Corporation (LAAD) moved into food processing and added cattle. Its stockholders made up the inner circle of American corporate power in Central America, including Bank of America, Chase Bank, Borden Foods, Castle and Cooke, Cargill Foods, Ralston-Purina, Caterpillar, John Deere, and Monsanto Chemicals.[129]

In conditions of such prosperity and reliable control, related industries that attracted foreign investments sprang up, placing yet more pressure on the forest resource. The two American lumber giants Weyerhauser and Crown Zellerbach built cardboard factories in Central America, especially for the banana companies' use. The list grew longer by the year through the 1970s, as American corporations dominated the region.

Inevitably the American corporate network worked closely with the Central American landed elites, strengthening their joint hold on land, commerce, and politics. In the Latin American ranching culture a man who owned land and cattle had both social standing and political power. By the 1950s local ranchers and oligarchs were active participants in the corporate expansion, matching the gringos in their level of economic involvement. Widely varying international corporate structures had been designed; joint ventures were also popular. Shareholders of Mataderos de El Salvador, one of two meat packing plants in that country, were mostly members of the coffee oligarchy. In 1971 the Agrodinamica Holding Company was incorporated as an international investor in Central American cattle. Sixty percent of its capitalization came from Latin American investors; the other 40 percent came from foreigners. The venture was launched with an $8 million loan from the Inter-American Development Bank.

Ironically, the new profitability extended the life of archaic systems in some areas. The more conservative owners of the old haciendas on the Pacific slope, who still ran Criollo cattle and practiced extensive grazing, expanded their acreage into marginal and untitled lands at the expense of campesinos and their food crops.[130] As the cattle economy expanded, so did social conflict. By the early 1970s class conflict had become violent. The titles held by campesinos were often ill defined, which made them easier for aggressive ranchers to expropriate. As their lands were stripped away, the campesinos lost their ancestral means of subsistence. Alternatively, ranchers used tenant farmers to clear the forest fringe. Smallholders who survived kept a few head of cattle to provide draught power, meat, and milk.

In contrast with the small-scale peasant, who struggled to make the most of his smallholding, many a "prestige rancher" let his cattle wander across unimproved pasture; this usually meant inefficient and wasteful land use. Many large-scale landholders felt little incentive to intensify their cattle raising methods, especially when they believed that there was still plenty of untouched forest available beyond their existing estates.

Thus those who controlled the largest amounts of agricultural land were those with the least motivation to use it efficiently. Moreover, their privileged position in the political structure made them unlikely to encounter serious opposition.

Costa Rica provides a vivid example of the linkage between Central American ranches and the U.S. beef industry. In 1950 cattle land in Costa Rica accounted for only one-eighth of the country, whereas it amounted to more than one-third by the early 1980s. In 1960 the country's cattle herds totaled around 950,000 head, but by 1980 they had reached 2.3 million. Between 1960 and 1980, beef production more than tripled, yet during that period the consumption of beef in Costa Rica actually declined by more than 40 percent, to a mere 35 pounds per person per year, or under one-third of what an average American consumed. The extra output was exported, a total of around 45,000 tons a year by the late 1970s—more than two thirds of total output. Central America as a whole exported an average of one-third of its total output.[131]

Costa Rica's beef exports, all of which went to the United States, steadily increased from an average of 17.5 million pounds between 1959 and 1963 to 50 million pounds in 1972. Indeed, Costa Rican ranchers had difficulties getting adequate domestic sales. In the existing state of the Costa Rican economy, the purchasing power of the urban middle class, which had some disposable income, was not adequate to match rising production. Per capita domestic consumption averaged 27 pounds per year between 1959 and 1963; it went up to 30 pounds in 1965, but then fell severely to 18 pounds in 1968.[132]

The improved breeding stock that Costa Rican ranchers imported in the 1950s was mostly Brahman, with a few Santa Gertrudis, Charolais, Angus, Brangus, and Hereford bulls brought in from the United States, plus experimental Indo-Brasil stock imported from Mexico. The innovations were concentrated in Guanacaste and Puntarenas, on the dry side of the country, although livestock operations were beginning to grow on the Caribbean side, where industry specialists saw untapped potential.

Costa Rica had the most equitable land-holding system of all the Central American republics, but even there the power of the international market to shape land tenure was evident. Beginning in the late nineteenth century the profits from coffee production made it possible for landlords to force small farmers into the status of agricultural laborers. By the 1950s the landlords as a group were in a financial position to bring beef cattle rapidly onto land that had once been in food production or forest. Commercial beef production in Costa Rica came to be dominated by only about 2,000 ranchers, who held an average of 1,853 acres each and controlled over half the agricultural land in the country.

Nicaragua offers a contrasting case. Under the dictator Anastasio Somoza, Nicaragua was much slower to modernize its ranching. Most of the country's cattle were raised on Pacific coastal lands, close to population centers, on flat or rolling terrain and rich volcanic soils. A two-tier industry emerged in Nicaragua. The Somoza family controlled approximately half of the country's ranch lands. What pasture remained was largely broken into small commercial ranches; most of these operations ran between 100 and 500 head apiece, hardly enough to encourage innovation. Somoza did some upgrading, breeding Criollo stock with American Brahman sires for the export market, but made few other improvements.

Improved transportation on new all-weather roads and more efficient processing in U.S.-designed slaughterhouses allowed the ruling family and a few other ranchers to expand their operations, penetrating into formerly remote areas. Nearly all of the country's exports went to the United States. Between 1959 and 1963 the annual average was 20.7 million pounds; that figure rose steeply to 65.9 million in 1972.[133]

In the early 1980s the regionwide growth of beef exports finally began to reverse, when the consumption of beef began to fall in the United States. Although overall American beef consumption fell only slightly, the drop was enough to cause major cuts in imports from the south. Beef exports from Central America peaked at 162,000 metric tons in 1979, representing 40 percent of the region's total production. By 1980 the total dropped to 110,000 tons (31 percent), and by 1985 to an estimated 61,000 tons (19 percent). Production totals fell from 400,000 tons in 1979 to 318,000 tons in 1985.[134]

By then severe and permanent damage had been done. Although the connection between North American hamburgers and Central American forests was greatly reduced after 1980, its thirty-five-year history produced irreversible changes in the equation of social power, which determined the fate of the forest. Large amounts of forest had been cleared.

YANKEE INTERESTS IN SOUTH AMERICA

In all of Latin America, Amazonia underwent the most massive expansion of rainforest ranching in those years. The American presence in

Amazonia was significant, but it was more limited, a minor force on the forest frontier. It centered in Brazil. Brazil's massive cattle population provided beef almost exclusively for its growing domestic market. In colonial Brazil, cattle ranches were an adjunct of the sugar plantations along the northeast coast. Farther inland, in the arid *sertão* plateau, vast sprawling ranches began to evolve in the 1600s. Then, in the eighteenth century, cattle surged into the state of Minas Gerais following the gold rush and slave raids. Cattle were a phenomenon of the moving frontier, providing animal labor and processing scrub vegetation into animal protein for the settlers, while degrading newly cleared lands. Ranchers formed a powerful political elite in the countryside, ruling over a poverty-stricken peasantry.

In the nineteenth and early twentieth centuries the urban centers of Brazil, primarily Rio de Janeiro and São Paulo, generated a steadily expanding market for beef. This provided some opportunity for American meat packers. After World War I Americans began investing in Brazilian packing plants, but on a smaller scale than in Argentina. By 1929 the three major U.S. meat packers—Wilson, Swift, and Armour Meats—constructed and operated packing plants at the ports of Rio Grande and Rio de Janeiro.[135] This was a tiny fragment of the national picture: it enhanced Brazil's industry, but did not shape it. Until after World War II Americans played no significant role in the penetration of the mighty Amazonian rainforest by the cattle industry, because commercial cattle ranching in the Amazon lowlands began on a significant scale only after 1950.

In the 1950s it was a very different matter, as the Brazilian government and its associated oligarchy of coffee magnates and cattle ranchers turned their interest toward Amazonia as the next frontier of national greatness. Brazil's cattle herd doubled between 1945 and 1968, when it reached 90 million head. By then only two commercial beef producing countries had larger herds: the United States, with somewhat over 100 million head, and the Soviet Union, with slightly under 100 million.[136] Moreover, Brazil's herds were still mostly in older ranch areas south of Amazonia, where the Criollo cattle ranged widely across unimproved pasture. Almost none of the ranching complex was geared to the capital-intensive export market and its modern methods. In 1970 Brazil exported only 2 percent of its total beef production, and this figure was about to decrease: the country was heading toward importing beef for its burgeoning market, as the United States had done earlier.[137]

When Brazil launched its Amazonia development program in full scale in 1966, American companies quickly entered the risky arena; among them were Swift, Armour, United Brands, and International Foods.[138] The new American ventures were among the largest operations and were often linked with Brazilian partners. The King Ranch of Texas was in the forefront of corporate cattle breeding, veterinary medicine, and pasture management. Although a minor element in Brazil's overall cattle complex, the Texan ranch was at the forefront of expansion, eating the rainforest in the most scientific way.

By that time the King Ranch was known internationally for its huge capital resources, efficient corporate structure, powerful land-clearing machinery, and careful range management. Its fame was above all based on its work in cattle genetics. The ranch, the largest and most technically advanced in the continental United States, was determined to produce a new breed that combined the rapid beef production of Europe's finest breeds (Aberdeen Angus, Shorthorn, and Hereford) with the Criollo's hardiness and the Zebu's resistance to disease. This was a long and expensive process, but it was successful when in 1940 the U.S. Department of Agriculture officially accepted the Santa Gertrudis cross as a new American breed. It was the only new American breed developed in the twentieth century.

By the early 1950s the ranch's owner, Bob Kleberg, grandson of the founder, began an international search for grazing lands and economies that could help him break out of the increasing cost crunch of the American cattle economy. He was ready to challenge the tropics, to increase his fortune by showing the world that it was possible to intensify beef production in the arid and the humid tropics. Kleberg was a distinctively American sort of technocratic idealist: he was confident that Yankee (in this case, Texan) energy and know-how, if applied in sufficiently large amounts, could solve any of the world's problems—and do it profitably. In 1969 *Fortune* magazine quoted Kleberg's view of the tropics:

> In these parts of the earth are to be found the last immense reserves of cheap undeveloped or underdeveloped land capable of sustaining livestock in numbers large enough to provide whole populations with beef . . . the hot climates where much of the human race lives on the rim of famine.[139]

In the 1950s Kleberg and carefully chosen Australian secondary partners bought the world's largest ranching complex, over ten million acres in the arid range lands of western Queensland, making his family the largest landowners in the world. Clearing the scrub vegetation, they planted Mitchell grass, an indigenous Australian grass that was easily propagated, very drought-resistant, and highly nutritious. To overcome perennial semidrought and turn the land green, they drilled dozens of deep wells, 300 to 600 feet down, and bulldozed new catchment basins for the occasional rain. Even so, the system required sixty acres of pasture to support each animal unit.

Kleberg dreamed of moister, lusher pastures, and he found them in the moist forest belt of eastern Queensland, Australia's only rainforest, which was already being replaced by corporate sugar plantations. This was to be his primary testing ground for large-scale cattle raising in the wet tropics. His chief engineer described the battle against tropical Nature's troops: "Alligators actually charge you. So do snakes. You can suffocate from the flies. Any animal that is unable to sting, bite or shoot noxious effluvium at you will chase, hiss, spit, harass, and otherwise abuse you."

This was a challenge worthy of the machismo of the toughest Texan. In 1962 Kleberg leased 51,000 acres on the Tully River and turned it over to Lowell Wilkinson, who had been his specialist on heavy equipment for thirty-five years. A description in *Fortune* was ominous: "No one has been more ingenious than 'Wilkie' in rejiggering and beefing up the fleets of bulldozers and the root plows and the choppers and rollers that have enabled the King Ranch to master the mesquite and the other ravenous scrub on the south Texas lands."[140]

Within five years of Kleberg's arrival in the Australian wetlands, 50,000 acres of primary rainforest were gone. The massive trees that had provided its crown had been uprooted by the irresistible bulldozers. The forest was immediately replaced by a carefully selected blend of grasses from Brazil, New Guinea, Africa, and Queensland. This new pasture supported 15,000 Santa Gertrudis cattle: one on every three acres, in contrast to one on every sixty acres of arid land. They gained weight faster than any other cattle in the country; within less than three years they weighed well over 1,000 pounds apiece and were ready for market.

This experience could be applied in the American tropics as well. Kleberg had also been looking for properties in the traditional ranching countries of Latin America, and in 1952 he began purchasing old ranchlands in Cuba. By 1959 he was running 7,600 cattle there, a modest number in itself, but he used that herd for breeding Santa Gertrudis bulls to cows elsewhere around the country. This experiment ended in 1960, when Fidel Castro expropriated the King *estancia* as a vivid symbol of gringo imperialism. Kleberg lost about $2 million on the venture.[141] In retrospect he mused,

> After my experiences in Cuba I had this clear idea: that I would take the King Ranch into the tropics, both wet and dry, with a straightforward commitment to show the less developed countries how to create a profitable supply of cheap animal proteins. My aim is to promote the mass production of tropical beef protein at low cost. Tropical agricultural economies are mostly weak, in part because what they have to sell—coffee, sugar, cotton, rice—is in oversupply. Beef, however, is not in oversupply. It can be produced indefinitely, moreover, without exhausting the land, provided one takes care of the grass cover.[142]

He was surely right about the dilemma of monocrop export economies and agroecosystems, but it was too early to tell whether the beef industry was as sustainable in the tropics as he believed.

In 1963 Kleberg moved into Venezuela, buying properties to produce beef for the Caracas market, since the United States would accept only canned beef from South America, and canned beef had a limited market. American oilmen had already been prospecting in the rainforest inland from Venezuela's Caribbean coast. Kleberg found a junior partner in a friend, Gustavo de los Reyes, scion of one of the old Cuban ranching families, who was now in exile. Together they formed the Companía Venezolana de Ganadería, with King holding 80 percent of the equity. In the late 1960s they found suitable land in the rainforest beyond San Felipe in northwestern Venezuela, inland from the highway that ran from Caracas to Maracaibo. When Kleberg saw the forest, he said, "Good God, this is the way it must have looked in Columbus' time."

Kleberg's exclamation illustrated a paradox that was familiar in the tropics: the reverence for the grandeur of primordial tropical Nature was instantly transmuted into the challenge to overpower it, to transform and domesticate it. Using techniques perfected on the Tully River hacienda, Wilkie's bulldozer wranglers cleared 31,000 acres of rainforest in three years. They drove two fifty-ton tractors through the forest, linked to each other with a heavy chain that dragged a three-ton eight-foot hollow steel ball between them, uprooting even giant trees as they ground forward. They then immediately fenced the land and seeded the raw soil by hand, before the debris was cleared. In this area, which received 50 inches of rain each year, the grass grew as much as 3 inches each day. The corporation's emphasis was on speed: cattle were grazing the new pasture within six months. After several centuries of traditional Iberian cattle ranching, Venezuela's lowland rainforest had entered the global realm of corporate technology and finance.

Kleberg was also moving into the much more modern ranching system of Argentina, and there too he introduced innovative operations that only his scale of operations could achieve. In the early 1950s President Juan Perón, in an action emblematic of his distinctive brand of populism, set out to curb the power of the cattle barons of the pampas. He placed price ceilings on domestic beef, a popular move with his voters, and sharply raised the taxes on beef exports. By 1955, when the oligarchy forced him out of office, Argentina's beef exports (still largely to Europe) had fallen by half, leaving an opening for other countries. The King Ranch decided to enter Argentine beef production and pasture management, which the Chicago meat packers had always avoided.

Kleberg formed a corporation with Juan Reynal, scion of one of the old ranching families and a friend met in international polo circles. They bought two old *estancias* totaling 43,000 acres in Santa Fe state, the heart of the pampas, and established King Ranch Argentina. Argentine ranchers already raised the world's most productive cattle, and the highest quality beef, in this region, using Aberdeen Angus and Shorthorn stock. Kleberg was determined to show that he could mix competitively with the best in the world—but he had more in mind than that.

Several hundred miles farther north was the Gran Chaco, a region of oppressive summer heat, ticks, cattle disease, and annual winter flooding, where poor back-country ranchers had run lean Criollo stock since early colonial days and a few ranchers had recently introduced the meatier Herefords. The productivity of the Chaco was far lower than that of the pampas, and the obstacles to profitable grazing far greater, but the land was also far cheaper. Kleberg was convinced that with the investment funds and modern machinery at his command, he could make this area productive too, for the beckoning international market. Around 1960 he bought Aguay, a 36,000 acre tract where "the flat grayish land is undergirded three feet down by basaltic rock and, in the brittle shadeless brush, ostrich mingle with the cattle and sheep."[143] Six years later he consolidated his position in Corrientes by buying a second ranch, Oscuro, which contained 85,000 acres of scrub forest.

Year-round water was the key to production in the dry subtropics. Kleberg's team drilled deep wells, put up windmills to power them, created ponds with a bulldozer, and built a dam to create a new reservoir. Enough money and machinery could accomplish anything, it seemed.

Kleberg's team quickly cleared 15,000 acres of the partially degraded Chaco woodland, replacing it with exotic grasses. The King ranches on the pampas were used as a breeding base for Santa Gertrudis cattle, which were then trucked north to Aguay and Oscuro for fattening on the less expensive range—this was the real innovation in Argentina. By 1970, 5,000 steers were taken to market annually. In cattle management Kleberg and his associates had proved their methods to be better than anything Brazil had achieved, giving the King Ranch a great competitive advantage on that front. But could they clear the magnificent forest quickly and cheaply? This had traditionally been done by squatter families living on the frontier, who could clear a maximum of five acres per year. Wilkie's pair of fifty-ton tractors could do the same work in an hour. High technology could attack the forest much more efficiently, leaving the squatters with no role at all, at least on the corporate frontier.

The power of the King Ranch extended into the Amazon basin. Swift had long been active in Brazil, but only in meat processing. By the early 1950s Swift was increasingly interested in raising cattle as well, to assure a steady supply to the slaughterhouses; moreover, land was a safe investment in inflationary times. Swift organized International Packers Ltd. as its Latin American subsidiary. He then merged the company with Deltec International, a large South American financial house, adding Brazilian partners and their capital and thereby increasing his political influence. They still needed a corporate partner for ranch management. The head of International Packing, Thomas Taylor, was a friend of Kleberg. Kleberg had liked the looks of Amazonia's reliable rains and cheap land when he had surveyed Latin American in 1952, and the steadily growing demand for domestic beef in Brazil's cities increased the region's attractiveness. King Ranch Argentina and Deltec joined in a fifty-fifty partnership to buy old estates and manage them on more competitive modern lines.

Kleberg began acquiring land near the Paraguay border, in the old coffee lands of São Paulo, where under his own name he bought two tracts called Mosquito and Formosa, and, jointly with International Packers, 71,000 additional acres farther northeast, closer to Rio. On the new pastures the Santa Gertrudis cattle reached a marketing weight of 1,000 to 1,200 pounds in two and one-half years, in contrast to the three and one-half to five years required on more traditional ranches. Using artificial insemination, the King combine achieved a calving percentage of over 90 percent, in contrast to the less than 70 percent that older stock produced.

By the late 1960s Kleberg dreamed of even bigger feats, in Amazonia itself. He bought 180,000 acres in Pará in the eastern Amazon rainforest, 300 miles south of Belém, and began negotiating with the government of Pará for 120,000 more. He calculated he could clear 100,000 acres and plant them with African grasses in twelve years. This would revolutionize ranching in the wet tropics, and make it abundantly clear that the only limit to clearing the rainforest was the amount of corporate capital that could be mobilized. Kleberg saw a certain nobility in this, contrasting his system of corporate sustainability with his vague understanding of traditional methods:

> The forest is not eternally fertile. Where the Indians had farmed the land, without replenishing the soil with fertilizers, the humus was exhausted and legumes must be introduced to restore the nitrogen to the soil; it is the right combination of perennial grasses and legumes that makes cattle pastures productive.[144]

The thought that centuries-old methods of agroforestry might be sustainable did not seem to cross his mind; he might have observed that the ancient system could not provide for the massive protein requirements of a growing population, or for the profitability of modern corporate technology.

In the same years the Rockefeller family was moving into Amazonia. Nelson Rockefeller began his tropical beef ranching in Venezuela in conjunction with his oil interests. He then plunged into Amazonia in 1956, buying a major share in the Brazilian-owned Bodoqueña Ranch, which comprised a virtual territory of its own: more than one million acres in Mato Grosso state on the Brazil-Bolivia border. The ranch supported 50,000 Criollo cattle, extremely inefficiently. Rockefeller planned to replace them gradually with 250,000 head of Santa Gertrudis from his brother Winthrop's ranch in Arkansas. He also set up a new company called IBEC Research Inc., which would conduct research on intensive rainforest ranching and hold training seminars and extension services for Brazilian ranchers. His beef would not be exported, but would be sold in urban markets like Rio and São Paulo. For an operation of that scale Rockefeller needed a slaughterhouse, which would put him into competition with the four existing major packers, Swift, Armour, Wilson, and Anglo. At this time, however, American companies were entering the era of corporate mergers: old adversaries were beginning to form partnerships overseas, buying major holdings in each other's operations. In 1968, when Swift and Armour merged their Brazilian interests, Rockefeller invested jointly with them, purchasing a 180,000-acre ranch in the older ranching territory of Lower Amazonia, near Paragominas in Pará state.[145] Like Kleberg's King Ranch, Rockefeller's personal corporation played an important role in the intensification of cattle ranching in the wet tropics, in counterpoint with local partners and rivals.

CONCLUSION: THE NORTH AMERICAN CATTLE INDUSTRY AND THE ECOLOGICAL COST OF TROPICAL RANCHING

The web of circumstances that has linked North American cattle interests to the depletion of tropical America's forests has been spun for half a millennium. Cattle moved the agricultural frontier of modern capitalism forward, and determined the social and environmental impacts that were felt on the frontier. For four centuries cattle were a crucial component of settlement in tandem with crops, especially on forest frontiers, helping squatters survive and establishing landlords' ownership claims.[146] Then in the twentieth century modern crossbreeds appeared. The product of the scientific revolution in cattle management, they were bred for a wide range of tropical ecological settings, both arid and moist.

Until the mid-twentieth century the presence of cattle in the moist tropical forest was limited by disease and lack of appropriate pasture. But a host of changes, in both the livestock industry and the wider economy, accelerated the reduction of the forest belt. Ranchers benefited financially from rising international markets and used their profits to consolidate their hold on political power and the land. Subsistence farmers were displaced into cities or onto marginal (usually forest) lands, causing further environmental damage as they daily struggled for survival.

The new capabilities accelerated into the rainforest from the 1950s on, propelled by new technologies, capital, and markets, much of that provided by the United States. In this era of industrial ranching and processing, as North American pasturelands and production costs rose inexorably above those south of the U.S. border, it became convenient to use Latin American lands—whether arid savanna or moist forest—as a less expensive adjunct to the American beef industry. Chicago was the center of the global beef system, which transformed the natural rhythms of grassland and forest into the economic rhythms of the international marketing system. This provided new goods for those people anywhere who had purchasing power, but it destroyed or radically altered rural preindustrial cultures, and replaced or degraded natural environments.

In the semiarid grasslands, from the Great Basin of the United States southward as far as the Argentine pampas, people who raised cattle replaced native species with more aggressive exotic African species. Improvements to pasture and breeds appeared, but those who instituted them tended to monopolize land and water, and social and ecological costs increased.

The sharpest irony of the new cattle breeding was that for adaptation to dry land climate and vegetation, the old Criollo breed was most viable. Its relegation nearly to extinction by the faster nutrient cycling of the hybrids was the mark that modernization and specialization of the ranching tradition was nearly complete.[147] Before that happened, however, the Criollo herds contributed to the increasing scarcity and, for some species, extinction of wildlife in Mexico and Argentina. This aspect of ranching history is rarely considered in the literature, but it was a major consequence of the domestication of natural grasslands.

The invasion of corporate cattle ranching into the moist lowland forests of tropical America is a recent chapter in the environmental history of ranching. Massive rainforest clearances for cattle production began only in the 1950s. Nevertheless, the entire development of ranching, starting in the colonial era, was preparation for that more recent onslaught in the rainforests of the New World.

PART THREE

Forestlands

CHAPTER 7

Unsustainable Yield

*American Foresters and Tropical
Timber Resources*

In a comprehensive and unified program of conservation,
designed to replace scarcity with abundance, forestry and
forest lands commonly occupy a key role. They may provide
a continuing flow of products to satisfy human wants; and
they may ensure the protection of soil, water flows, and
local climate, without which food and agriculture in many
lands will continue to deteriorate. They may, then, hold the
whole task of conservation together.

> *Norris Dodd, Director-General of FAO, 1948*

INTRODUCTION: TROPICAL TIMBER
EXPLOITATION IN THE TWENTIETH CENTURY

The global loss of tropical forests mounted slowly for several centuries,
then began a rapid acceleration during the 1940s. The increase occurred
for many reasons; the most important undoubtedly was the expansion
of agriculture in all of its forms. Export crops and beef production degraded or replaced incalculable extents of tropical forest and wetland
and savanna, as if the forest itself had no biological or even economic
value. The benefits of these industries to investors and consumers have
been enormous, constituting the primary driving force behind this great
ecological transformation. But the value of the forest itself has also risen
on local and global markets, primarily in the form of timber products.
As the tropical timber products industry became industrialized, wood
products joined foods as a major commodity that northern economies
could harvest from tropical lands,[1] and as light railways, heavy-wheeled
vehicles for grading roads and hauling timber, and more efficient mul-

tipurpose sawmills became available to meet rapidly increasing global demand, forests retreated before the logger as well.

The United States provided markets for tropical hardwoods beginning in the eighteenth century. In the twentieth century the market for tropical hardwoods accelerated, but as a portion of total U.S. hardwood consumption, it was always minute. Domestic hardwoods like oak, maple, and walnut provided as much as 99 percent of each year's market. In terms of harvests in some tropical countries, the American market for tropical hardwood produced major ecological impacts. To make the picture more complex, the flow of timber between the United States and the tropics was reciprocal, for Pacific and Caribbean markets were important for American conifer lumber from the late nineteenth century on, when the U.S. timber industry began looking for foreign customers in order to diversify its markets and stabilize its operations.

Americans played four major roles in the expanding scale of tropical forest exploitation: as investors and consumers, and as loggers and foresters. Logging companies measured their effectiveness largely in terms of the expanding scale and efficiency of the extraction of wood products. A foreign mahogany logger was aware of his lack of knowledge, but he could recognize a tall, straight mahogany trunk even if he found only one per acre—and that was enough for him. Professional foresters saw their effectiveness increasingly in terms of managing the forests for a sustainable yield of wood products. Although foresters studied tropical ecosystems, coming over the course of decades to understand their complexity, fragility, and limited extent, most of their time was spent studying commercially important species, since no species had any "value" unless it was recognized by the buyers of finished products. Even more than agronomists and ranch managers, they struggled to understand how to maintain the forest for future human use. By the 1950s some of them had begun to wrestle with the social and ecological issues that are imbedded in forest use.

These foresters faced a profound dilemma, which even today is unresolved. Was it possible, by introducing more systematic exploitation of timber resources, to establish sustainable forestry in the tropics and contribute to social welfare into the future? Or would modern timber technology be yet another power in the hands of those who wanted quick profits at the expense of entire ecosystems? Through the work of pioneering American tropical foresters, we can glimpse what the forests of Southeast Asia and Latin America were like at various times, how the patterns of human pressure on them escalated, and how these ecological technicians envisioned the future of domesticated tropical eco-systems.

THE YANKEES' TROPICAL WOODLOT:
TIMBER EXPLOITATION IN THE CARIBBEAN BASIN

Timber had been a profitable export from the Caribbean Basin since the time of the first Iberian settlements. When American loggers and timber buyers began working the hardwood forests of the Caribbean Basin in an extensive way in the 1880s, they entered a three-hundred-year-old competition among Europeans for capturing treasures like dyewoods and mahogany. Two major forest types were exploited over the centuries. One was lowland moist forest, which contained the precious dye and cabinet woods that grow as individual trees in the midst of many other species. The other was the higher, drier pine forest, useful primarily for inexpensive building lumber. The two stories had different histories, and each history had a distinctive American role.

HIGH-GRADING IN THE LOWLAND FORESTS

High-grading—felling only the finest trees—was practiced by the first Portuguese to intrude on the Bahia coast of Brazil in the early sixteenth century. These loggers were interested only in brazilwood, which they exported to Europe as a source of red dye. The dye was highly valued in the clothing industry, which was expanding to meet the demand generated by a rising and prospering population.[2] By the end of the 1500s high-grading had reduced the forest along the coasts and riverways to economic insignificance. Constrained by the only timber transport method then available, a team of oxen, loggers rarely penetrated far from waterways or into steep hilly areas. The full diversity of the deeper forest remained.

During the same era, European dyewood hunters, or Baymen, discovered logwood, an equally valuable source of red dye, growing along the Caribbean littoral. A hardwood of the lowland moist forest, logwood grew prolifically from Campeche and Yucatán in Mexico through coastal Belize to the Miskito coast of Honduras and Nicaragua. In the 1600s, despite the Spanish navy's attempts to suppress them, British and other non-Spanish privateers generated a large-scale export of logwood for the cloth mills of northern Europe. This trade lasted for over 300 years.[3] The Baymen's anarchic ways served them well in the turbulent political conditions that prevailed until 1670, when Spain and Britain agreed by treaty that Belize would become the British possession of British Honduras.[4]

Even thereafter political instability was so severe and working conditions were so harsh that the loggers took what they could easily find and sailed away. Logs had to be floated to the coast in the rainy—the very rainy—season.[5] One early traveler observed,

> During the wet season, the land where the logwood grows is so overflowed, that they step from their beds into water perhaps two feet deep, and continue standing in the wet all day, till they go to bed again; but nevertheless account it the best season in the year for doing a good day's labour in. . . . When a tree is so thick that after it is logged, it remains still too great a burthen for one man, we blow it up with gunpowder.[6]

The size of the logwood tree did not affect the extraction of dye, so the loggers took all available trees, large and small, ultimately depleting accessible supplies almost totally. The loggers were itinerant and the work was very difficult—modern ideals of sustained-yield forestry were beyond imagining.

As easily accessible stands of logwood quickly declined, the Baymen began using oxen for hauling and Garifunas (escaped African slaves from the British Caribbean islands) for laborers, thereby expanding the reach of their operations. Exports to Europe rose from 700 tons in 1800 to 35,000 tons in 1896. In Jamaica logwood supplies actually increased during the nineteenth century, because the species turned out to be an aggressive invader of deserted crop lands. When slavery was abolished in Jamaica in 1834, large areas of fertile hill lands reverted to secondary woodland, which contained logwood. By 1897, at the beginning of the era when banana planters recleared those lands, logwood was Jamaica's most valuable export, exceeding sugar and coffee.[7]

The era of logwood exports to Europe ended suddenly in the late 1890s when chemical dyes totally replaced dyewoods throughout Europe. Only 3,600 tons of logwood were exported from British Honduras in 1913.[8] This was just one of numerous examples of industrial products replacing depleted tropical resources on international markets.

In the first century of the colonial enterprise, dyewoods were almost the only timbers exploited for European use. European navies changed that in the seventeenth century, as they began using mahogany in European and Caribbean shipyards. Havana was the major shipyard for the colonial Spanish fleet, and in the 1600s its forested hinterlands began to be combed for mahogany, an effort that continued well into the 1800s.

A major increase in the demand for mahogany occurred in the mid-eighteenth century, when it became the most fashionable furniture wood in Europe. Hepplewhite and Chippendale styles, whose elegant lines and elaborate detail required a fine-grained, easily tooled wood, were perfected by craftsmen working with mahogany.[9] In more recent centuries, mahogany, or caoba (as it is known wherever it grows), has epitomized the commercial wealth of the rainforests of Central America and the Caribbean islands. Like most tropical hardwoods, mahogany grows scattered in mixed-species forests, not in easily accessible single-species stands. Mahogany logging inevitably was a matter of high-grading. Sawyers with their oxen searched the forest for single large trees of high commercial value, carving out logging trails as they went. Each great tree that fell shattered numerous smaller trees in its path. After the woodsmen left a logged mahogany forest, as many as a hundred other species remained standing, as did young, twisted, or old mahogany trunks. The best seed trees of mahogany were felled, and as the oxen dragged them to a nearby river for floating away, they damaged still more trees and tore the soil along the paths and riverbanks. Mahogany does not regenerate easily or grow rapidly; it can take up to one hundred years for a tree to mature. Thus, although a degraded mahogany forest was still ecologically stable, its quality as a sylvan community of species was damaged.

British loggers led the way in this phase of forest exploitation, searching the entire Caribbean coast from Campeche on for mahogany, Spanish cedar, and other precious cabinet woods. By the late 1700s the scale of mahogany extraction had become far greater than the dyewood trade had ever been. The logging was carried on in a setting of legal confusion: titles to land were cloudy and contract systems were rudimentary. Quarrels were frequent among the mahogany cutters, most of whom worked the forests without bothering to establish formal rights. During the last half of the nineteenth century, first small-scale Yankee loggers and then larger-scale Yankee timber companies became a major force on the islands and mainland coasts of the Caribbean. Their operations became the major pressure on the mahogany and pine forests outside the British possessions, intricately interweaving the U.S. forest economy with that of the Caribbean Basin.

The first Americans to appear were the hardwood purchasers, who were not lumbermen but shippers—middlemen between the loggers in the rainforest and the manufacturers of fine furniture in American cities from New Orleans to Boston. In the first decades of U.S. independence they imported mahogany mostly from Cuba, by way of their commercial offices in Havana, but also from Honduras and British Honduras. The East Coast markets thus provided profits for Cuban and Spanish speculators who cleared mahogany forests in central Cuba to grow the white gold of sugar.[10]

As urban affluence expanded in the United States during the nineteenth century, an increasingly prosperous middle class demanded more tropical hardwoods for furniture, paneling, and other uses. Craftsmen used several rainforest species in their fine cabinetry, but mahogany dominated the market. Yankee timber importers began searching for mahogany stands and logging concessions throughout the region.

At first the Yankee entrepreneurs and speculators were a miscellaneous lot who made short-term investments in small concessions and organized the logging themselves; their operations are difficult to trace. Probably representative of them was Walter Wilcox, best known as a writer of wilderness camping books, who operated in the rainforest of Cuba. Shortly after Cuban independence, when American investments in Cuba became safer than they had been under Spanish rule, Wilcox bought a timber concession on the Bay of Pigs on the south coast, in an area of largely intact mangrove swamps and hardwood forests, where a few scattered local farmers scratched out a minimal subsistence. Wilcox saw himself as a resourceful frontiersman: a year after his first reconnaissance visit on a sailboat hired in the port of Cienfuegos he returned "with a force of carpenters and laborers and a cargo of lumber and tools. A place was cleared in the forest for a house, docks were built, gardens laid out, wells dug." He added almost parenthetically, "In all that time we were not molested by the natives."[11]

Wilcox was typical for his time in his contradictory attitudes toward the forest. One feeling was admiration verging on awe at the forest that he was cutting. Echoing the prose of many other northern writers after their first exposure to its grandeur and mystery, he wrote in 1908 for the *National Geographic* that

> the number of species of trees is very great, and, while including such splendid varieties as mahogany, sabicu, ebony, and Spanish cedar, there are many other hardwoods, probably 150 in number, some of which are very rare or quite unknown to experts in tropical timbers. . . . The mahogany and cedar are imposing trees, the latter sometimes reaching a diameter of seven feet.

Their massive branches, hung with purple and yellow orchids, bromeliads, ferns, and other parasitic plants, are the resort of parrots and other birds of brilliant plumage.[12]

For that audience, lovers of natural history, he presented a photo of teams of oxen hauling the felled mahogany logs to the coast. In a photograph on the next page, he showed a farmer proudly observing a field of corn; his caption blandly read, "Six months before this picture was taken the field was covered with a dense tropical forest."[13] This was still the era when the forests seemed so vast that it was civilizing work to clear them for one's own profit and for the local peasants' corn crops as well.

Other early operations were run along the Caribbean coast of Mexico, including what was probably the first long-term operation by a firm specializing in tropical hardwood imports. The Ichabod Williams family firm of New York, whose lumber operations specialized in tropical hardwoods throughout the company's long life from 1838 to 1966, became specialists in negotiations with local authorities, contracts with local labor, and shipment of logs to their sawmill in Bayonne, New Jersey.[14]

When easily accessible supplies in Mexico were depleted and the first series of land concessions ran out toward the end of the nineteenth century, several American companies began searching the Central American rainforests, starting across the border in Guatemala. The region was crudely cosmopolitan. Mexican businessmen from Tabasco, as well as Englishmen and Lebanese from British Honduras, competed with the Yankees as investors. The loggers they hired were very skillful with ax and saw, but they were also a motley, itinerant collection of men who were far from home for long periods of time. Many of them were working off debt peonage incurred in other parts of Central America and Mexico. On their occasional recreational forays into muddy frontier towns, they drank, brawled, and whored. A recent observer in the mahogany region of northern Guatemala describes "a pervasive tone of immorality in the entire operation."[15] Like the rootless loggers in the commercially penetrated forests of many other countries, they had no stake in the health of the forest, which they attacked like commercial game hunters. In that turbulent setting the largest of the Yankee firms, the American-Guatemalan Mahogany Company, founded in 1907, cut over 16 million board feet of mahogany in twenty-three years, mostly in the Usumacinta River basin.[16] Companies like this enabled U.S. mahogany imports to double between 1900 and the late 1920s.[17]

Farther around the Caribbean coast, into the Miskito coastal forests of Nicaragua, the George D. Emery Company of Boston was the most important producer of timber products. The company experienced initial success, but ultimate frustration. Its history illustrates the formidable difficulties that affected profit making in the timber industry at the turn of the century. In 1894 Emery negotiated two leases with the Nicaraguan government that gave him the timber rights in previously untouched forests along rivers flowing into the Caribbean. Because of the level of his investment and the extent of his marketing, Emery accelerated the high-grading of the best hardwoods in the region.[18] Casa Emery, as it came to be known, was soon exporting about 1,000 mahogany and Spanish cedar logs monthly to Boston, an unprecedented scale of operations. Its work force of 1,300 was mostly drawn from the region and included local Miskito Indians and other indigenes, but some one hundred Americans were imported for the more highly skilled jobs.[19] In 1905, using newly available dynamite, Emery began deepening river channels to smooth travel and log floating.[20] Dynamite was used in the same way by Emery's competitors as well. The channel blasting and the logging operations along the riverbanks had downstream effects: siltation and the disrupted flow of water damaged lowland riverine systems near the coast by increasing flooding and damaging fisheries.

No timber concession was ever granted except through political maneuvering, and none was secure against changing political winds. Casa Emery's concessions had been granted by a friendly regime in Managua, but Central American governments were notoriously unpredictable and faction-ridden. Timber operators, in contrast to banana growers, could easily be replaced; high-grading for maximum short-term profits was the inevitable result. In 1909 Emery became entangled in a Nicaraguan presidential campaign, one in which the U.S. government was enmeshed as well. Emery backed the losing candidate, and the new government retaliated by revoking his concession, ending his fifteen years of logging on the Miskito coast. Washington attempted to intervene through diplomatic channels, on the usual principle of defending the sanctity of American investments abroad, but this time it did no good. Finally Emery sold out in 1911 to Ichabod Williams, whose sources of supply were diverse, enabling him to continue his business for a full century.

Casa Emery initiated the flow of a much higher level of capital and milling technology into mahogany extraction than the rainforest had ever experienced. As in many other fields of resource extraction, the scale of American capitalism shaped major changes. The aftermath of World War I brought a momentous change to the forests, one that originated in Detroit. After a severe but brief postwar depression in the timber industry, mahogany logging investments expanded in the 1920s, and what was most needed was access to forests that were even more remote. Motor-driven tractors appeared, along with large skidders and log-wagons—equipment that far surpassed oxen: tractors could operate with ease on hilly terrain and could haul logs several miles from the cutting site to the river.

The new scale of investment and technology was evident downriver as well. At log collection points near the mouths of rivers, more sophisticated sawmills began to appear that were capable of milling a wider variety of species and utilizing a higher percentage of each log. The situation was parallel to expanded-scale technology in the sugar refineries. The imported sawmills were too expensive and too efficient for local millers: they could neither afford them nor compete with them. Ladinos were beginning to produce mahogany furniture, but their efforts were largely stymied by the financial and organizational power of U.S. and European industry. Two highly qualified American observers noted that "there is a small but steadily increasing local industry producing mahogany lumber, mainly from inferior material unsuitable for export, but inefficiency of plant and limited shipping facilities have hitherto precluded it from competing to any material extent with the highly organized lumber manufacturing industry in the United States."[21] Local operators could function only on the fringes of the northerners' corporate power.

EXPLOITING THE CARIBBEAN PINE FORESTS

A very different dimension of the logging business appeared in the pine forests that grew on drier land and poorer soils in the interior highlands of Mexico and Central America.[22] Little is known about the relationship between subsistence life and commercial pine extraction before the nineteenth century, although the issue must have been significant as far back as early colonial times. The Spanish were actively interested in the pine belt, for several species of pine provided not only low-cost building materials for local use but also pitch and tar for naval stores, just as the pine forests of the Atlantic coast provided for the American colonies. In the 1700s the Spanish colonial regime of Peru relied extensively on the Central American pine forests to supplement the Peruvian uplands as a source of material for shipbuilding and naval maintenance at its shipyards in Guayaquil.[23]

By the nineteenth century these uses depleted pine forests around the Caribbean. These semiarid forests were also grazing grounds for local livestock, since soils were too poor for prosperous crop production. The villagers annually burned the undergrowth in the dry season to encourage the stronger growth of new fodder. In the process they destroyed new pine seedlings; moreover, many of their fires burst out of control, severely damaging more mature trees.[24]

Some pine forests were protected from commercial exploitation by their remoteness from transport arteries. In these areas, however, methods of logging were primitive and wasteful: only a relatively small portion of each tree was milled. Partly as a result of this, the production of export lumber remained limited until well into the twentieth century, despite the fact that several of the densely populated islands of the Caribbean imported pine lumber from the southeastern United States for the construction of their expanding coastal towns.

The risks faced by potential U.S. investors in Caribbean Basin timberlands were great, as the Casa Emery case demonstrated. It was difficult to gain and harder to keep logging concessions from local governments. The boundaries of the concessions and their certainty of tenure against the rights of local landlords and peasants were unpredictable, and concessions were likely to be revoked abruptly. Of course, a wealthy or politically powerful corporation could play the game of influence as well as the local regime. The banana companies were the only ones in that league.

American tropical fruit companies began large-scale forest clearing on the Caribbean coast around 1900. In the early years of their operations, they simply removed the primary forest, making no effort to harvest timber for commercial profit. In 1923 the Vaccaro brothers, soon to found the Standard Fruit Company, became the first to harvest timber as one stage of their effort to vertically integrate the entire banana production process.[25] Three years earlier, in 1919, when pine was scarce in the southeastern United States, a Louisiana lumbering family purchased a concession giving it the rights to 80,000 acres of pine forest behind Bragman's Bluff on the Miskito coast of Nicaragua. The family intended to export pine lumber to New Orleans. The declared value of the new venture was $50,000. The Vaccaro brothers, whose banana empire was well established in the adjacent lowlands of Honduras, were looking for land in Nicaragua. They purchased the small firm in 1923 and christened it Bragman's Bluff Lumber Company. They renegotiated the original concession with Managua and gained the right to import their machinery duty-free. In return the company agreed to pay a small export tax on lumber.

The new owners quickly invested $5 million to construct port facilities at Puerto Cabezas and one hundred miles of private railroad to serve both lumber and banana operations. They imported a modern sawmill from Louisiana to supplement the three existing small mills along the coast, and they began exporting pine boards in 1925. This was the first step toward realizing Standard Fruit's long-range ambition to operate in Cuba, Puerto Rico, and other Caribbean countries.

The Vaccaro brothers' joint investment in Standard Fruit and Bragman's Bluff amounted to $8 million.[26] That investment totally dominated Nicaragua's Caribbean coast in the 1920s. Harold Denny, a *New York Times* correspondent, traveled throughout Nicaragua in 1929, investigating the civil war and American corporate involvement. He described Puerto Cabezas, one of two main ports on the Miskito coast—the other was Bluefields—as a Yankee enclave with rough environs.

> Puerto Cabezas is even more American than Bluefields. It is an industrial village of some 1,200 population, situated on a broad, flat plain overlooking the Caribbean. It looks and is precisely like a lumber mill village in some southern state in North America. . . . [Standard Fruit] owns the town and everything in it. The inhabitants, American families from American villages, live in quantity production wooden houses rented from the company, buy their clothing and groceries from the company's store, and find their relaxations in a club built by the company. . . . From the margin of the American settlement the native town of Bilway, 100 feet wide and two miles long, stretches parallel with the seashore. It is a filthy street of Chinese and German stores interspersed with half-breed bars and brothels. The population is largely "*mestizo,*" a mongrel of Mosquito Indian and Jamaican negro, and the languages range from bad Spanish and degenerate Mosquito to Oxford English.[27]

In sum, it was both a typical self-contained company town and a typically unstable, rowdy town on the frontier of the exploitation of tropical Nature. It was extremely difficult to maintain orderly operations during the civil war that engulfed Nicaragua in the following years. The Caribbean coast was frequently in revolt against the remote capital. Sandino periodically attacked the fruit companies and their subsidiaries from his base in the rugged interior along the Honduran border between 1926 and 1934, when he was trapped and assassinated by Somoza's men in Managua.[28]

In that setting difficulties arose over the duration and territorial extent of the concession that had been granted to Bragman's Bluff. Neither the company nor the government was careful about the ownership claims of local smallholders. Some years previously the Miskito Indians living in the area had confirmed their title to the lands they tilled in one of their periodic negotiations with the distant government. Campesino communities had survived in close symbiosis with the pine forests for many years; many of their settlements dated back to pre-Columbian times. Reacting to the fruit company's 1923 concession, the Miskitos angrily told the government that it had casually given away their ancestral lands to the company. The government ignored the Indians. Conflicts of this type—between Indians and foreign capitalists, and between Indians and national governments—were frequent in locations where detailed cadastral surveys had never been done and land records were chaotic.

A more serious blow to Standard's banana operations, one that probably reduced the pressures on the Miskitos, was the attack of Panama disease and Sigatoka on its plantations along the Caribbean coast. These diseases crippled the company's Nicaraguan operations. In 1935 Standard began preparing to move from Nicaragua to Mexico and the Pacific lowlands. They exported their last Nicaraguan bananas in 1942, and in the same year they liquidated the Bragman's Bluff Lumber Company. Standard kept control of the port facilities but leased the pine forests to the Robinson Lumber Company of New Orleans, which was willing to take the political risks of working with the Somoza regime. Robinson cut large amounts of pine lumber, making no attempt to replant any of it or to protect the growing stock that remained.[29]

If efficient management and profitable pine lumber export industry was to develop in the Caribbean Basin, it would likely be in Honduras, where the most extensive and economically most significant stands of pine in Central America are found. Honduras even in the mid-1980s had reserves of 27,000 square kilometers of pine forests.[30]

The first Honduran pine lumber was shipped from the Miskito coast to the timber-starved islands of the Caribbean around the end of the nineteenth century. By the 1920s the timber industry was tightly linked to the corporate strategies of the American banana companies, and pine lumber had begun to play a major role in the Honduran export economy. Soon the largest Central American timber operations were in Honduras. In 1926 its primary export, coffee, was valued at $8 million. Timber exports nearly equaled bananas. That year Honduran exports of mahogany and pine totaled $1.5 million, while banana exports totaled between $1.5 million and $2 million.

The country's corporate and political structure and its available timber resources were only part of the reason that American companies chose to focus their efforts in Honduras. Changing investment patterns, forest resources, and lumber markets in the southeastern United States were equally important, since they determined which pine forests were exploited and how intensive the exploitation was. The destinies of yellow pine and Caribbean pine were inextricably linked throughout the first half of this century.

Just as wheat had been exported from the U.S. eastern seaboard to the Caribbean as early as the mid-eighteenth century, construction lumber was exported beginning in 1829.[31] The great expansion of this export industry came after 1865, in the aftermath of the U.S. Civil War, as the southern lumber industry gradually rebuilt and expanded its scale.[32] The forests of the New England and Great Lakes states were severely depleted by 1880,[33] and the Mississippi Valley from Minneapolis and Chicago to New Orleans was entering an era of industrialization. Many northern lumber firms and loggers moved into the southern pine and cypress belt, which stretches 1500 miles from Virginia to eastern Texas, in a burst of land speculation that was equal to any in the western states in those years.[34]

Markets both domestic and international were eager for the strong, handsome lumber of the longleaf or yellow pine. The most important export market was Europe, where Germany in particular began purchasing large amounts of pine from the American South, but the Caribbean Basin also emerged as a significant market.[35] The Southern Pine Association, a trade association formed by American loggers in the 1890s, had found Latin American markets for 10 percent of their total production by 1900.[36]

Lumber firms produced 20 billion board feet of southern pine in 1909. The insatiable appetites of World War I accelerated cutting, and the ecological results were devastating. A 1919 survey declared that 92 million acres—nearly half of the region's pine acreage—was cutover land and that most of these acres were deserted, not fit for crops or cattle.

As the yellow pine forests declined, southern lumber firms began studying Caribbean Basin forests as a potential source for future supplies.[37] U.S. capital was first invested in Central American timber operations during the early 1920s. Yankee loggers could see the great difficulty of setting up financially viable operations where lumber could be transported only by the railroads owned by the banana companies or in the maddeningly shallow rivers. They also faced the legendary political turbulence of the region, which only companies the size of the fruit giants could hope to influence or withstand. A few small entrepreneurs were operating in Nicaragua by 1930, and when Sandino's revolutionary forces turned on gringo companies, the loggers joined the chorus of U.S. interests calling for protection from revolutionary nationalism. The fruit companies were powerful enough to invoke the help of the U.S. Marines—the loggers largely had to fend for themselves.[38]

The trend did not last long, for by the late 1920s the pine forests in the southern United States had begun a remarkable recovery under new techniques of fire control and forestry management.[39] The pressure to look beyond U.S. borders for additional supplies rapidly diminished, and when lumber markets began to recover slowly after the early Depression years, U.S. companies returned to exporting pine lumber to Latin American and European markets.

What effects did the American lumber exports have in recipient countries? In British Honduras, despite its considerable pine reserves, little was logged apart from small amounts that were exported west into Mexico. Most building lumber used there was yellow pine imported from the American South, which gave a better finish and was available in convenient sizes.[40]

Other countries with extensive pine forest resources, especially Honduras, were inhibited by powerful U.S. competition from attempting to improve the biomass production of their forests or increasing their economic value. For countries with inadequate conifer resources of their own, the United States was an important source of lumber. Imports drained national coffers, however, or increased the pressure to expand export cropping in payment.

To a trained eye, timber extraction in the hardwood and pine zones of Latin America appeared inefficient and wasteful. Surveying the forests of the region in 1929 for the Pack Forestry Foundation, Tom Gill concluded that there was little regeneration of logged tracts, and that local foresters (such as they were) seemed passively complacent about the situation.

> Today . . . logging is a thoroughly primitive, unsatisfactory, and haphazard process. Methods are slow and wasteful, and because of the highly selective character of logging, the costs vary from merely high to prohibitive. . . . There is no steady flow of ties or logs or any other product. For that reason industry has been very loath to consider seriously so uncertain a source of supply.[41]

It was into this setting that modern professional forestry from the North was introduced. U.S. foresters were rapidly learning how to counteract the devastation caused by rampant, unmanaged logging in the forests of temperate North America. Only a few were actively interested in the tropics as yet. These pioneers found grounds for urgency, but they were optimistic that modern scientific forestry and management practices could transform the forest into a resource that could profit the forest products industry and the welfare of tropical societies alike. Whether in this vision the future still held a species-diverse wealth of natural forest or vast expanses of tree farms—that controversy still had to be formulated sharply.

AMERICANS AND THE ORIGINS OF THE FORESTRY PROFESSION IN LATIN AMERICA

Spanish foresters had left only a slight footprint on the colonial landscape. In Spain itself government agents had been at work since the 1700s to manage upland timber for commerce, to reserve certain hardwood species as a royal monopoly, and, in principle, to protect upland watersheds. Spain's New World and Pacific colonies passed similar laws in the 1700s and 1800s, but U.S. observers after 1898 agreed that these were "paper laws," as Tom Gill called them—edicts existing only on paper. There was little or no enforcement of those laws while Spain was in the Americas, but they were the formal precedent for later American initiatives. The need for better management was urgent, for the forests throughout the region had been severely depleted in the nineteenth century.[42]

American foresters first turned their professional interest south into the Caribbean in the aftermath of the Spanish-American War, when the United States permanently took over Puerto Rico. The island's tropical forests were the only ones in Latin America that were directly administered by the United States. The U.S. Forest Service recognized that it was almost totally ignorant of the physical and biological properties of Caribbean forests, and in 1911 it established the U.S. Tropical Forest Experiment Station, a research station in Río Piedras, just outside San Juan, to carry out research in the Luquillo Forest Reserve. This marked the beginning of formal U.S. studies of the rainforests of the Americas, but until the 1940s the research developed very slowly. As only a branch of the Forest Service's Southeastern Experiment Station in the United States, the Puerto Rican station had no direct voice in Washington during budget debates, and Yankee hardwood companies around the Caribbean were so unstable that they made little effort to lobby for its research program.

Substantial research began in the 1920s at Río Piedras and Luquillo. It had to begin with taxonomic studies to identify and catalog the vast number of tree and shrub species in the exotic woodlands. Research was designed to broaden the range of marketable species, and for that it was important to understand life cycles and regeneration conditions—this was the beginning of the study of rainforest ecology. From the start this work was closely linked with research at the wood technology laboratory at Yale University. Samuel Record, the leading tropical wood technologist in the Americas, designed and directed the research agenda at the laboratory, and he published the results in the journal *Tropical Timbers,* which served the needs of tropical biological science and the timber trade alike.

In those years professional management of the Luquillo National Forest began on a modest scale. That forest became an important experimental model for tropical moist forests, offering students experience with a variety of tropical conditions.[43] Through the fledgling institute in Puerto Rico, American foresters were able to develop connections to the emerging international forestry network. In Trinidad, not far from Puerto Rico, was a British research institute, the Imperial Forest Research Institute, which was founded in the 1920s as the empire's American research base for tropical forest science.[44] The center in Trinidad was linked to the Empire Forestry Association, a worldwide network established by the British in 1921. The association published a journal, the *Empire Forestry Review,* and sponsored international conferences, through which it disseminated information and ideology. The *Review* and its American counterpart, the *Journal of Forestry,* which was published by the U.S. Forest Service, began publishing in the early 1920s.

In 1928 the Pack Forestry Foundation sent Tom Gill on a survey tour of the forests of the Caribbean Basin, instructing him to bring back a report detailing their extent and composition, how they were being used, their potential for a modern logging industry and silvicultural management, and how extensively they had been damaged. For many months Gill traveled throughout the Caribbean and the mainland of Mexico and Central America. He explored a vast rainforest reserve, much of it largely untouched by the outside world. Only a small, scattered population of peasant farmers and remnant Indian tribes subsisted in the forest. He found few roads, railroads, or other signs of industrial-era penetration. Such logging as he found was mostly small and local in scale. Loggers used rough axes and handsaws to fell the trees, and bullocks hauled the logs from the forest to antiquated sawmills whose machinery wasted a large portion of each log. The loggers were totally unsupervised by government officials or trained foresters, and such forestry laws as existed on paper in a few countries were never enforced on the ground.

The industry was still primitive in contrast to the massive wood products corporations that had been established in the United States. Gill found this both good and bad. He observed that logging south of the border had not ravaged the forest resource as it had in the United States, but neither had it been utilized to meet the needs of Latin American society or to help lift local populations out of deep poverty. The industry had not even been able to meet local demands for construction timber: users imported yellow pine from the southeastern states and redwood and Douglas fir from the northwest coast of the United States, using precious foreign exchange. A more modernized industry could entirely avoid that embarrassing symptom of underdevelopment.

Gill's recipe for the future was to modernize timber processing by building capital-intensive, highly efficient mills that could process more species and waste a smaller portion of each log. Gill recommended that governments invest in better transport facilities, so as to take timber products inexpensively to distant markets. These improvements could be dangerous, he knew: modernization would allow the faster penetration of forests but would not guarantee better management.

The Caribbean countries also needed accelerated research in order to understand how tropical forest ecosystems function. Better biological knowledge was the prerequisite to improved silviculture—management of the forest—which could assure the sustained yield of all marketable species. Essential to good forest management were proper and enforceable laws, forestry agencies to enforce them, and the development of clear legal titles to forested land, whether in private or government hands.

In sum, Gill believed that the pressures of modern life necessitated strong laws, developed by trained scientists and managers and backed by committed governments, to manage this most precious renewable resource so as to meet immediate economic needs and also to nurture it for the long biological future. Local people could not do this—they just

lived from day to day in their poverty—nor could those who were working the forest at the time, since they were concerned only with each
season's profit.

Gill's book includes lyrical descriptions of the forest's beauty and
mystery, impatience with and warnings about the existing Ladino management of the forest, and confidence that modern forestry could both
use and preserve this great resource without losing it to the Promethean
power of modern machines. His writing also reveals a paternalism verging on condescension toward local forest people and their knowledge
and management of the resource. He saw that *conuco*—slash and
burn—cropping techniques produced erosion on hillsides, but he could
not distinguish between the ancient sustainable system of multicrop rotation practiced by the indigenous Indians and the destructive maize-
beans *milpa* plots of peasants who had been dispossessed from lowland
farms by landlords, either local or foreign.

At that stage of his career, Gill was primarily concerned with expanding wood products for commercial markets; he understood little,
and inquired little, about the many nontimber forest products in local
use. Like all foresters of his generation, he looked from the top down
and from the outside in. His knowledge of trees and love of the forest
were exemplary; his knowledge of and curiosity about the local cultures
and their use of the forest were rudimentary. Gill's worries about the
likely future deterioration of the tropical rainforest were totally appropriate. In his later years, before his death in 1971, he lived to see and
protest a steady acceleration of forest clearance in all three tropical continents.

In the 1930s the small group of Americans at Río Piedras began to
develop liaisons with foresters working in the independent countries of
Latin America. No formal international organization yet existed to facilitate those contacts—such organizations developed more readily in
parts of the tropics that were still under colonial rule. Because the foresters at Río Piedras were employees of the U.S. Forest Service, however,
they were not bound by the fiscal constraints of private companies. In
addition to their research on forest biology and timber products, they
could address the broader issues of forestry law and administration in
each country and promote the training of competent forest managers.
Their agenda was therefore far broader and more ambitious than that
of their counterparts who worked in private industry. Corporations did
not own forestland, and their contracts were short in term and insecure.

Contacts with Mexico led the way, aided by long-established connections with the father of Mexican natural resources management, Miguel de Quevedo. Thirty years of his work finally resulted in the Mexican government passing forest laws in 1936 (which were based on American law) and establishing its first forestry training program.[45] Aside from this, Latin American countries had no real administrative or technical capacity to design or enforce forestry laws before the 1950s.[46] Government timber inspectors were usually untrained, and often corrupt.

By the early 1940s the British and American scientists, working together, had carried out some detailed ecological studies, which led to a few experiments in which exotic tree species were planted and assessed for their possible commercial value. The researchers were not given even minimal resources to enable them to study such basic matters as watershed protection or the impact of forest fire. Surprisingly, they were not even able to initiate studies of forest economics.[47]

The efforts of forest scientists and administrators had little impact against the increasing incidence of high-grading and the expansion of croplands before World War II. In 1940 Gill's ten-year-old conclusions were still valid: little effective forest management existed in the American tropics. Nevertheless, the groundwork was being laid for what would emerge with postwar peace. The tiny fraternity of American tropical foresters was able to accomplish far more in a far more remote tropical setting in the south Pacific.

AMERICAN COLONIAL FORESTRY AND
TIMBER HARVESTS IN THE PHILIPPINES

American forestry operations in Southeast Asia before World War II present a striking contrast to events in the Caribbean Basin for two reasons. First, a complex trade in tropical hardwoods controlled by the Chinese and Europeans had existed throughout the region for centuries before the Americans arrived. Second, in 1904 American foresters were given the direct responsibility of constructing a forestry service for the islands; in the Caribbean, Americans had similar control only in Puerto Rico. The Philippine Islands played a pivotal role in the history of tropical logging and silviculture in the United States and Southeast Asia, for it was there that U.S. foresters and timber firms learned the methods of systematic tropical logging.

By the 1920s the alliance forged between American foresters and loggers and their Filipino counterparts and protégés had produced a forest economy that was as modernized as any in tropical Asia. The Philippines became a stage that showcased the tropical foresters' great gamble with technological and political power. The advanced technology of timber extraction that was developed in the Philippines turned the islands into one of the first great tropical timber exporters, but it also prepared the way for the tragic devastation of the islands' vast forest cover that began after 1946, the year of Philippine independence. The interplay of American rule and Filipino society resulted in reckless and often illegal deforestation after 1950. In recent years the natural wealth of these forests has been squandered, and the biotic treasures of the islands have been decimated.[48]

Export markets drove the exploitation of the Philippines' lowland forests. Although the islands were net importers of timber in 1900, by the 1920s that trend had been reversed. Hardwood timber was shipped to many markets, primarily in the United States. By 1960 the Philippines were the single largest forest products exporter in Southeast Asia. Little of the forest being cut was growing back as a timber resource; the nation was steadily borrowing from the future, with sobering consequences. The roots of the tragedy lay in the power of the country's landowning elite, which controlled the export of timber as well as sugar and other plantation crops.

SOUTHEAST ASIA'S TIMBER ECONOMY BEFORE THE AMERICAN ERA

When the Philippine Islands fell to the United States in 1898, America inherited one of the great treasures on the planet. Much of lowland Southeast Asia is covered by a richly diverse rainforest dominated by the *Dipterocarpaceae* family of giant hardwoods. In other areas are seasonally dry monsoon forests, which have a different biological composition dominated either by deciduous species or by extensive stands of pine. In brackish coastal lowlands are some of the most extensive mangrove ecosystems in the world.[49] The evergreen dipterocarp rainforest represents a species composition that is almost entirely different from that found in the humid tropics of Latin America and Africa, but both types of rainforest can contain several hundred tree species in a small acreage.[50] Its exquisite biotic complexity dazzled but baffled early western observers, who saw it as both intimidating and a challenge to conquer.[51]

Southeast Asia had long produced a harvest and international trade of tropical timber products that far exceeded that of either Latin America or Africa. The hardwood trade was highly competitive, and penetrating it proved to be a difficult challenge for western interests. For many centuries before westerners first arrived in the early 1500s, there was a lively international trade in both specialty woods and many nontimber forest products throughout the region.[52] Hardwoods and aromatic species such as sandalwood and sappanwood had their major market in the regionally powerful markets of China. Many nontimber products were exported as well. Tribal communities of the forested highlands harvested animal skins, bird feathers, and medicinal herbs, exchanging them with traders from the lowlands and coasts at semipermanent riverside or coastal locations. These products were then exported, in a complex exchange of goods and money.[53]

European penetration of the Southeast Asian economy began in 1511 when Albuquerque conquered the trade-based kingdom of Malacca on the Malayan mainland across from Sumatra. The Portuguese were interested primarily in interdicting the Asian-Arab trade in pepper and spices, which were harvested in the native forests of Indonesia's equatorial islands. The Portuguese made no attempt to penetrate the hardwood trade or to change the pattern of land use in the region. That began to change when they were displaced by the Dutch East India Company.

The Dutch began their conquest of Java in 1619, and from then until 1949 they maintained an extractive empire in Indonesia. They built ships using teak from the forests of eastern Java; as early as 1755 they employed 650 men at their shipyards in Batavia. They purchased the timber from local Javanese and Chinese traders whose small boats sailed the north coast of the island. By the 1700s they began purchasing large tracts of inland teak forest from Javanese rulers. After the Napoleonic Wars, in a forward surge of colonial administrative power, they began exploiting the great teak forests directly. The decimation of the forest continued until 1849, when the colonial regime imported three German foresters in the first step toward developing sustainable timber production.[54]

Teak was a product that promised sustained timber harvests. Unlike almost all other Asian hardwoods, teak thrives in single-species plantations. In the teak forests of British India, both along the Malabar Coast and in upper Burma, rotational growth and logging in managed one-species teak plantations was beginning to be assured by the midnineteenth century. In the multispecies dipterocarp forests the situation was much more difficult. When the Americans began extracting rainforest hardwoods from the Philippines shortly after 1900, they were not so fortunate as to find teak growing there.

Lauan—Philippine mahogany—had been exported from the Philippines for centuries before the Spanish conquerors arrived in the 1570s. In a pattern typical of many parts of Southeast Asia, local men cut the trees and Chinese merchants exported the timber, much of it heading to markets in southern China. The immensity of the forest resources on the Philippine Islands was evident to the Spanish colonial rulers, but they were able to exploit that wealth only fragmentarily. At the end of the Spanish era in 1898, primary forests covered fully two-thirds of the islands' territory, and three-quarters of that were dipterocarp forests.[55] Mature lauan trees are the great commercial timber wealth of the Philippines, but once logged they regenerate very slowly. Hence loggers operated largely in the shrinking virgin forests.

The Spanish regime placed most of its attention on Manila's hinterland, on the island of Luzon. European officials frequently struck up alliances with the men they called *caciques,* those who already held power in the towns and countryside well before the Spaniards arrived. In joint control of the land, these two groups proceeded to transform large lowland areas of Luzon into haciendas that produced sugar and other crops.[56] Many of the other islands retained much of their forest cover through the 1800s.

Spanish law stipulated that all untilled land belonged to the state.[57] In the Philippines this meant that virtually all forestland came to be government owned, a principle that was codified in the 1863 law that established the Inspección de Montes, or Forestry Bureau. The main function of the Inspección was to systematize the Crown's claims to forestlands and to stipulate which areas would be more valuable as arable land than as forested public domain.[58] In its few years of work, the bureau did little to administer or even to study the islands' forests, whose composition was still largely unknown except to the tribal groups who subsisted in them. Furthermore, the bureau did little to regulate or improve commercial logging. By 1898 logging was still primitive and localized. Trees were cut by light, blunt axes, then hauled by carabao (water buffalo) to rivers, then the logs floated to sawmills downstream. There were only five or six power-driven sawmills in the country, all of them in the environs of Manila.

A considerable amount of the country's lumber trade took the form of small interisland log shipments on sailboats. Much of this was handled by resident Chinese traders, who controlled a large portion of the local market economy around the islands.[59] The Chinese had been exporting hardwoods to China and beyond for centuries, both salt-water-resistant species for ships and wharves and lauan for elegant cabinetry and building purposes.[60] In the last years of the old century this trade was temporarily disrupted, first by warfare in the Philippines after 1896, and then by endemic political upheaval in China. Under the American regime after 1900 the Chinese traders returned to prosperity and used that strength as an important base for their rise to a powerful position in the timber economy throughout Southeast Asia. The Chinese exporters were gradually joined by Spanish and British entrepreneurs, who controlled exports to Europe. The first U.S. link to the islands' timber wealth appeared in the 1890s, when Philippine companies began importing redwood and Douglas fir for their building projects in Manila.

American companies with early interests in the Philippines included those with links to British logging operations on Sabah, in the northernmost region of Borneo.[61] Like much of the international trade of the southwest Pacific at the height of the imperialist scramble, this was a high-risk business. No American company or logger survived for long until U.S. rule was formally established in the Philippines after 1898. That political change brought the stability and control that timber operators needed if they were to make any major return on their investments.

THE BUREAU OF FORESTRY AND THE LOGGERS

In the decades after the Spanish American War, the exploitation of forest wealth in the Philippines was distinctively shaped by American logging and forestry practices and by the ways the U.S. regime's Bureau of Forestry functioned within the overall American colonial system centered in Manila. The U.S. government was almost totally unprepared to take on colonial rule in the tropics. It was familiar with the colonial systems of the Dutch, British, and French, and it knew something about the region's centuries-old international trade in tropical hardwoods—but it knew little about the forest ecosystems that it was about to manage and exploit.

Forestry in the United States at the turn of the century was still in its infancy, but it was being rapidly shaped by Bernhard Fernow and then by his successor, Gifford Pinchot.[62] George P. Ahern, protégé of Fernow and Pinchot, became the creator of modern forestry management and timber exploitation in the Philippines.[63] Son of a New York labor organizer, Ahern went to the U.S. Military Academy at West Point. He might never have reached the Philippines had it not been for the U.S. Army. When his days at West Point were over, he was posted to Minnesota, where the white pine forests were being decimated. In the following years he saw firsthand the ecological and cultural damage wrought by the march of European-American civilization across the continent. From Minnesota he moved to South Dakota, where he was translator for the defeated Indian chief Sitting Bull. There and in Montana he spent several years as an explorer, geologist, and hunter. His social and cultural sympathies were wide, he was technically versatile, and his experience of wanton deforestation had sobered him. In the mid-1880s he began planning forest reserves in Montana, and it was here that he came into contact with Fernow and Pinchot.[64]

In 1898 Ahern was sent to Cuba during the Spanish-American War. When his leg was injured, he was posted to the fledgling military administration of the Philippines. The Americans now controlled one of the great rainforests of the planet, and they had much to learn about it. Pinchot, as head of the U.S. Forest Service in Washington, arranged for Ahern to be assigned the job of creating a forestry bureau in the new colony. His task was to learn as rapidly as possible the rudiments of Southeast Asian forest biology, assemble a team to work with him, and design a system of forestry laws.

In 1901 Ahern wrote to Pinchot, urging him to visit the islands and tour their forest resources with him. Pinchot was delighted to have his first view of the tropical abundance, because, as he later wrote, "of experience in tropical Forestry I had exactly none. But I had learned something about Forestry in Burma and in British India from Dr. Brandis"[65] (the founder of British colonial forestry, with whom Pinchot had studied in England). Pinchot arrived in Manila in October 1901, after crossing imperial Russia's vast forest region on the Trans-Siberian Express. Ahern met him and took him immediately to Malacanan Palace, the new home of William Howard Taft, the governor of the islands. Taft had arranged for his official yacht, a 1,400-ton gunboat, to take Pinchot and Ahern on a month-long survey tour of the islands, and he promised to implement whatever regulations they proposed. Pinchot delighted in the comfort and authority of the ship, writing to his mother, "This is the proudest way to travel in my experience. A vessel 212 feet long, with a crew of 78 men, to go where you like when you like."[66] He loved the life of a proconsul, surveying his realm of rainforest and its people in efficiency and comfort.

On their first stop, Mindoro Island, where U.S. timber operations would soon begin, they walked for a day "through almost distressingly interesting tropical forest, where every tree was new and strange."[67] The two men visited every major island, taking copious notes on the forests, the local economy, and the people. Their fascination focused on scores of tree species that they had never seen before. They delighted in the beauty and grandeur of the trees—yet at the same time they were calculating their potential value as timber. In southern Negros, south of the region of new sugar plantations, they hiked into a forest that Pinchot called "the most luxuriant I have yet seen, and in by far the best silvicultural condition. On the lower slopes it consisted of old trees from 130 to 150 feet in height, frequently with from 90 to 100 feet of clear trunk, standing in a selection forest in which all age classes were represented."[68]

The two men began to design a system of sustainable timber exploitation. Existing logging operations in the rainforest could not have been further from sustainable. Pinchot recorded in his diary that on the southernmost island, Mindanao, they sought out one well-known sawmill. The operation was owned by the Philippine Lumber and Development Company,

> whose manager, Mr. Bourns, had much pull at Manila (but not with Taft). We expected to find bad work, and we found it. Everywhere we went the untouched forest was in a superb condition. [Yet] I have never seen a more complete slash. . . . Everything was destroyed as far as logging had gone. Unquestionably the kind of logging now going on will lead to erosion of the most serious character on a surface so steep as to be totally unfit for agriculture.[69]

It was urgently important to stop such logging operations, and the only way to do that was to design strict forest laws and to train a generation of foresters who would have the authority to control both the ravaging work and the corrupt influence in Manila that protected it. Returning to Manila, Pinchot and Ahern designed a set of laws that Taft's regime officially adopted in 1904. The carte blanche that Taft had given them was backed by President Roosevelt's complete trust. This was the fulfillment of the Progressive dream: full authority had been placed in the hands of those who knew best what was necessary to meet human and biological needs. Pinchot outlined the forestry system in a long letter to Taft. In the preface he stated,

> The internal condition of the forests, the degree of governmental control, the efficiency and spirit of the Insular forest service organized by Captain Ahern,

and the general economic situation, combine to present the best opportunity for successful and profitable forest administration of which I have knowledge. . . . A great development of forest industries in the Islands is evidently at hand. If this development is not to be accompanied by serious, extensive, and permanent injury to the forests, preparation by study and experiment must begin at once.[70]

Pinchot returned to Washington, leaving the future of the Philippine forests in Ahern's hands. From then until he returned to the United States in 1914, Ahern was the creator and shaper of modern forestry for the islands. He was committed equally to rapidly modernizing the timber industry of the country and to making the forest wealth serve the long-term needs of the Philippine people. Both ambitions were, at best, only ambiguously fulfilled.

Ahern was confident that modern scientific forestry and the rapid expansion of timber exports could overcome the pervasive poverty of the islands. One urgent priority was to modernize timber operations so that the islands would no longer have to rely on imported lumber for domestic needs. In 1917, looking back on his years there, he reminisced that "communities living in sight of virgin forests imported lumber from abroad. Near such forests were people living in houses of thatch and bamboo."[71] The Philippines had been importing building timber since the nineteenth century despite the great riches of its forests. Like many of the rapidly expanding ports of the southern Pacific rim, Manila was being built with timber from the U.S. Pacific Northwest.[72] For Ahern and the men he hired to work with him (including Filipinos who had already been serving in the Inspección de Montes under the Spanish), reversing that pattern was a matter of establishing competent laws, organizing their effective administration, and linking that system to the most up-to-date, large-scale logging technology.

The forestry law adopted in 1904 carried over major elements of its Spanish precedent, including the provision that declared almost all the forested land to be government property. It created the Bureau of Forestry and gave it great powers, including the authority to decide which forests would be more appropriate as agriculture and which would be retained permanently in forest cover.

The bureau also had the authority to regulate commercial logging by granting timber concessions. If a company applying for a concession could demonstrate that it had adequate capital, machinery, and management for the task, it could receive a license for ten to fifty years. To encourage the expansion of the industry, the bureau looked in particular for large firms possessing the most advanced technology and the strongest capitalization, and it granted most of its large concessions for long terms. It also granted short-term leases, usually of one year, which were meant to provide lumber for local use. In both cases the bureau was required to specify conditions for cutting and marketing, although in practice its inadequate staff and limited funding often left that supervisory work undone. Foresters were also charged with the collection of stipulated stumpage fees and other timber taxes.[73]

The felling laws directed timber firms to clear-cut the forest on good agricultural land below elevations of 500 feet. On land inappropriate for agriculture, foresters would select marketable trees for felling, imposing a minimum diameter of 40 centimeters (14 inches) for hardwoods. Stressing maximum growth rates more than maximum biotic diversity, the laws indicated that all commercially valuable trees over 75 centimeters in diameter should be cut. If the species was not considered commercially useful, loggers were allowed to remove all trees regardless of size.[74]

The Bureau of Forestry immediately forged close working relations with logging companies, especially American firms that were interested in expanding their operations to the Philippines. Often the bureau carried out detailed field studies and planning for these firms. The results were impressive: major American firms began operating in the islands almost as soon as the forestry laws were in place.

Ahern and Pinchot knew their commercial counterparts well. Their contacts with the timber industry in the American northwest immediately yielded fruit when the Insular Lumber Company, the first modern lumber company in the Philippines, was launched in 1904. Headed by W. P. Clark, a leading manufacturer of sawmill equipment in Seattle, Insular took advantage of the new law to gain a 115-square-mile timber concession in the lauan forests of Negros, which was beginning intensive forest clearing for sugar plantations. Thereafter, sugar expansion and lumber operations were closely linked, and their alliance was far more efficient than were those anywhere in Latin America. As one forester observed with pride six years later, "The operations are an exact copy of the lumbering operations of a large company in Seattle, Washington, and the sawmill, of 100,000 board-feet daily capacity, is as thoroughly fitted up with up-to-date appliances and as well run as almost any mill in America. . . . All this is a new venture, believed to be utterly impossible a few years ago."[75]

The technological transformation was immediate and dramatic. On tour several years later, the leading American forester and ecologist Barrington Moore, although skeptical of some of the aspects of forest management that he saw, wrote, "In utilizing the forests the most astounding progress has been made from a lumbering point of view."[76] In contrast with existing logging methods in the islands, which used only rough axes for cutting and carabao for hauling, Insular and other American-backed firms rapidly made the lumber technology in the islands the most up-to-date of any in the tropical world. In the early years, American supervisors controlled every aspect of logging operations, as "boss loggers, superintendents of logging railways, sawyers and saw filers, and yard bosses."[77] All other workers were local, including those trained for various semiskilled jobs. By 1911 Insular employed 800 Filipino and Chinese laborers, who worked under only 18 American supervisors.

Another U.S. firm that began operating at this time was the Cadwallader-Gibson Company, which launched a long-lasting operation on Manila Bay in 1904. It was almost equally as significant as the Insular Lumber Company was in the evolution of American technology in Philippine tropical forestry. Cadwallader-Gibson worked closely with the bureau over the years to refine the system of logging laws and to train Filipino recruits at the nearby national school of forestry, which was founded in 1910.[78]

Under Ahern's direction the bureau also cultivated close relations with Filipino loggers, teaching and encouraging them to expand and modernize their operations. In this work, the foresters were entirely in tune with the general tenor of American colonialism in Manila, where entrepreneurs from the United States and their local counterparts evolved much closer working relationships than those that developed in many other colonial systems. In forestry as in plantation agriculture, one broad consequence of these ties was the strengthening of Manila's elite, allowing them to dominate land use after independence.

The domestic timber trade had evolved long before the Americans arrived. It had its own structure, which shaped American intentions as much as the new resources influenced its expansion. In 1916 one member of Ahern's team characterized the industry as falling into three categories according to size and complexity of operation.[79] First and smallest were the shops of the local retail trade throughout the islands. These firms cut and finished their lumber by hand. Reflecting the overall character of the commercial economy, all of these firms were Filipino or Chinese. Second in scale were the small power mills, with stocks of thousands or tens of thousands of feet of rough and milled lumber.

These were more varied in scale, owned by Spaniards, Filipinos, or Chinese, as well as a couple of larger firms owned by Americans or Europeans. Third were the large specialized mills, mostly owned by Americans or British, although one was owned by Spaniards, one by Chinese, and one by a Filipino-Spanish partnership. The American foresters' goal was to modernize the Filipino firms; the entrepreneurs' goal presumably was to maximize profits with minimal governmental control over their operations.

The evolution of the Filipino-American lumbering connection and its role in transforming lowland forests into agriculture are illustrated by an important early concession, the 1905 grant to the Mindoro Lumber and Logging Company. Mindoro, the seventh largest island of the archipelago, lies only ten miles across the Verde Island Passage from the southern coast of Luzon.[80] At the turn of the century only the narrow plains of the eastern and northeastern coast had been developed; mountainous Mindoro was still relatively untouched. Mindoro had not shared the economic expansion that some islands experienced in the nineteenth century. Its total population in 1903 was only 28,300, most of it clustered around several small ports. The mountainous interior was home to various swidden-farming tribes that had not had much contact with the lowlanders.[81]

The eastern lowlands of Mindoro receive between 80 and 100 inches of rain annually, mainly in July and August, and it has no severe dry season. The soils of the region are rich clays. It was an excellent setting for wet rice cultivation. The area's forests were easily accessible to the nation's major urban market, Manila. Northern Mindoro thus was one of the country's most attractive targets for loggers. The 1905 license to the Mindoro Lumber and Logging Company gave it the exclusive right to commercial logging on a tract of eighty-five square miles along the east coast.[82] The tract was mostly virgin lowland dipterocarp forest, with some mature second-growth trees. Its total population was 650. No land survey had been done and none of the inhabitants held formal land titles. Thus the company had no legal problem in operating as it wished.

Mindoro Lumber was a subsidiary of a Manila milling company; thus it is likely that it was a Filipino operation with direct connections to Ahern's forces. Mindoro Lumber became an important actor in the category of medium-sized firms that produced lumber for the rapidly expanding Manila market, a dimension of the timber industry that was controlled by Filipinos and Chinese, not foreigners.

The Mindoro Lumber Company's sawmill processed mostly lauan, but it handled smaller amounts of several other species as well. The company still relied on carabao to haul the logs to the water, but it also used some newly imported American equipment, including heavy American axes and a portable sawmill. The lumber was shipped to Manila by small steamer or sailboat. Manila's construction market was booming, and the company had no trouble finding buyers.

Firms like Mindoro Lumber prospered, and their expansion was reflected in the rapid rise of national timber production figures. Nonetheless, conflicts between the Bureau of Forestry and Filipino commercial interests soon became evident. The landed and commercial elite resisted any system of sustained-yield logging, and their opposition quickly found a political voice in the national legislature. The lower house, which was made up entirely of elected Filipinos, annually opposed any additions to the bureau's budget, making it impossible for the bureau to establish operations in the richly forested islands.[83]

In those years Dean Worcester was the secretary of the interior for the colonial government and the most influential American in the islands. In 1915 he criticized local lumbermen for wanting only quick profits and resisting restraints on their access to the forest.[84] He knew that they had power as a lobby, and he worried—prophetically—about their capacity to circumvent the bureau's regulatory powers. Moore, on an inspection tour five years earlier, had found that the legislative constraint on the forestry budget was accompanied by strong pressure to maximize timber harvests, presumably for both private profit and public revenue.[85] As Moore well understood, a race was developing between those who favored the expansion of the timber industry and those who supported sustained-yield forest management: the long-term fate of the forest would depend to a considerable degree on the changing balance between the two. The result of the combination of these forces was a rapid expansion of cutting.

Until the 1920s Philippine timber primarily supplied domestic markets. Ahern's ambition was to make the Philippines an exporter of timber, and to make the timber industry an important contributor to the islands' net balance of trade, by marketing Philippine timbers to the burgeoning ports of Hong Kong, Nagasaki, Shanghai, Sydney, and Singapore. Both Ahern and Clark saw that the markets of the western Pacific promised great demand for Philippine lumber. Insular Lumber, Clark's company, successfully introduced lauan timber to international markets as Philippine mahogany. By 1920 lauan and similar species, particularly red lauan, were replacing American redwood in western Pacific ports.

Timber exports expanded very slowly. One major stumbling block was the lack of standardized timber grading rules; until they could be devised and implemented at logging sites and mills, no foreign customer could be assured that size and quality were reliable. The bureau formulated a system in 1914. In 1915 the Philippine Lumber Manufacturers Association was founded, and their first substantive act was to adopt the uniform grading rules for its logging operations.

More fundamental still was the need for systematic knowledge of the composition and commercial uses of dipterocarp forests and working plans for timber exploitation. Without a link to the profits that came from timber cutting, the bureau could not finance the scientific studies necessary for creating a systematic forest botany of the scarcely known and exceedingly complex forest types of the Philippines.[86]

By the early 1920s the timber export trade was divided equally among three groups: Filipino firms, American firms, and a mixture of other western and Asian firms, primarily British. By 1920 most Philippine mahogany exports were destined for the United States, for paneling, doors, and furniture in West Coast markets. A similar though less extensive trade developed with businesses in the northeastern states, including furniture makers in Michigan who began purchasing red lauan from New York importers in the 1920s.[87] In addition, Asian markets for red lauan expanded in these years, as the tropical wood replaced redwood for furniture and flooring. The chief markets were Shanghai and Hong Kong. Timber from several other species also competed well in Asia, presumably reflecting Chinese familiarity with tropical timbers.[88]

For building construction within the country, and increasingly for wood pulp, the Philippines continued to import softwoods. These imports were still dominated by redwood and Douglas fir from the northwestern United States; they accounted for approximately 85 percent of the country's total import value between 1915 and 1918. In addition, railroad ties were imported from Australia, although these imports were steadily being reduced by the increased Philippine production.[89]

The ultimate issue was whether the expansion of production in the dipterocarp forests could be sustained. For many years foresters, in their enthusiasm for the challenge, tended to estimate that fellings could be greatly accelerated without permanent damage to local soil and vegetation patterns. This was a dangerous stance, for these foresters knew little about the biotic cycles of the rainforest. Only a few were alert to the danger. As early as 1910 Moore warned of the danger of rapid cutting when loggers knew so little about the forests' rate of regeneration. He challenged the government's habit of putting pressure on the Bureau of Forestry to maximize production and revenue while minimizing its management and research budget.[90] Unfortunately, voices such as this were rarely heard in the general enthusiasm for the new wealth.

The harvesting of the Philippine forests took more than one form. Government policy encouraged clear-cutting of lowland forests on land that seemed flat enough to warrant conversion to rice production. Moore argued that it was foolish to destroy any forest if its land was not needed for crops. In forests on steep slopes or higher elevations, which were not marked for conversion to rice, foresters used a selection system to harvest the timber, marking each mature tree for cutting. Because the bureau had a severely limited staff, this system was slow—too slow to satisfy the market for timber. Soon the system was changed to diameter-limit cutting, which allowed loggers to take every commercially useful tree that was over 40 centimeters in diameter. The system was extremely wasteful, because in areas without sawmills loggers left behind everything felled except the main trunks of large trees. Foresters gradually learned that the diameter-limit system led to severe forest depletion and little regrowth because smaller trees were burnt by the sun when the upper canopy was disrupted: the number of new seedlings in clearings was reduced to an estimated one-eighth of the natural rate in undisturbed forest. The foresters' early optimism that dipterocarp forests would respond to cutting just as temperate forests did was being eroded.[91]

All in all, the work of the Bureau of Forestry presented contradictory implications for the fate of the Philippine forests. Its research in forest botany and its design of appropriate timber harvesting systems led to efforts at sustained-yield logging, including the first afforestation programs. Political and budgetary constraints and the foresters' enthusiasm for expanding export production focused early research on commercial matters, however, which constrained the study of forest sustenance, as Moore noted.

Mindanao provides an example of how the system worked on the forest frontier. Mindanao has always been a special case in Philippine life. The major port of Davao, on the south coast, was founded by the Spanish only in 1849. Until the end of Spanish rule the Moro populace controlled major population and agriculture areas, and the interior mountains were left to the tribals. Mindanao remained a remote frontier until the 1920s, and the American colonial government in Manila made only slow progress in extending its reach to the island. In the 1920s the depletion of timber supplies in Cebu, Negros, and central Luzon led to the first major wave of commercial logging on Mindanao. In 1914, according to Worcester, there were more lumber mills in the port of Zamboanga than in any other location in the islands. Loggers there were especially determined not to tolerate any restrictions or regulations from the Bureau of Forestry.[92] To solidify their resistance, they organized a lumbermen's association in 1914, a year before the national association appeared in Manila.

A new competitor appeared in the Davao region in the 1920s: the first Japanese logging operations.[93] The Japanese had begun to settle in the hinterland of Davao around 1900, first as small traders and then as abaca planters. Timber operations were only a small component of their commercial network before World War II.[94] In the 1930s Japanese investors established new abaca plantations in the mountains above the city of Davao where there had been little previous cultivation, even shifting agriculture, called *kaingin* in the Philippines, which hill tribes throughout the islands had practiced for centuries. Abaca laborers felled the taller forest trees and allowed the remnant to die from insolation— exposure to the sun. They planted the abaca plants with dibbles and did only light weeding. When the plants were mature, the harvesters cut and stripped the leaves without further digging. The total effect of this process was to reduce the forest to a remnant, although the practice did little soil damage.

These plantations were largely abandoned during the Pacific war. Some of the area was then used for secondary *kaingin;* the rest began reverting to natural forest. After 1945 the plantations were subdivided into small subsistence farms. Only the flatter sites were actually farmed, and some of the steeper slopes became covered with a mat of coarse grass. Then, in the mid-1950s, adjacent local areas were cleared of their primary forest, especially for local logging, which was still very limited and inefficient.[95] The Davao region was ripe for the large-scale Japanese timber operations that began in the 1960s.

As this example illustrates, the fate of the forest was coming to rest on the interplay between local peasant populations and the tree harvesters. In recent years this has become a crucial problem, in the Philippines and elsewhere. The inception of the problem can be found in the first application of the laws and management policies of modern forestry and in the foresters' perceptions of subsistence farming. When the Bureau of Forestry was given power over nearly all the forested land in the Philippines, it was granted jurisdiction over the peasants' access to forest products. Foresters thus took on major social responsibilities, but without adequate preparation for this dimension of their work.

The law required foresters to designate forest parcels to meet the villagers' needs for building timber and fuelwood. In the early years of the century, when rural pressures on forestland in many areas were not yet severe, this was not a difficult task.[96] Far more difficult and controversial was the struggle to define and regulate the boundaries between government forestland, individually owned agricultural land, and the remnant of pre-Hispanic communal land.[97] The colonial regime's fundamental Forestry Organic Law of 1904 provided a legal mechanism for landless peasants to settle on newly cleared land; it was administered by the Bureau of Lands. The law also required that the Bureau of Forestry certify that any land newly designated for agriculture was better suited for cropping than for forest. Between them the two bureaus had to confront the truly difficult issue of *kaingin,* which extracted a wide variety of forest products in a complex pattern.[98] Forest reserves in the western tradition were defined as lands in which no forest clearances for agriculture were permitted, but for shifting cultivators many of the forests designated as public lands were the location of the soil and organic nutrients they needed to grow food for their survival.

Until very recently, most foresters trained in the European and North American tradition broadly condemned shifting cultivators for wantonly destroying the forest. Their understanding of agriculture was derived from the settled farming of temperate lands; their denunciations of *kaingin* agriculture arose from a lack of knowledge about the wide variety of swidden systems. Moore, writing in 1910, expressed views characteristic of the accepted wisdom among foresters.

> Caingins are . . . destructive and wasteful in the extreme. To make a Caingin,
> . . . the Filipino plants a haphazard crop of gabi (a kind of edible root), corn,
> or tobacco. He makes no pretense of plowing, or even scratching the ground,
> but merely pokes a hole with a stick and puts in the seeds. Neither does he
> attempt to keep out the weeds. The result is that within a couple of years the
> area is so overgrown that it has to be abandoned. He then moves on and
> destroys another valuable piece of forest. At Port Banga, on the Island of
> Mindanao, it is estimated that from $75,000 to $100,000 worth of timber
> was destroyed by Caingins in a single year.[99]

Worcester, who knew the islands far more intimately,[100] agreed that *kaingin* cultivation was destructive, but he saw the political machinations behind it. His understanding of the situation represents the frustrations of foresters ever since that time. He knew that peasant families settled in the forested hills not only because the rising population had forced them off other land: "In many instances the maker of the unlawful caingin is a poor native employed by a rich one. If detected he is left to pay the penalty for his wrong conduct; otherwise the land cleared is eventually incorporated with that of the rich neighbor who hired him to violate the law."[101]

What Worcester observed was the system of debt peonage, which had developed during Spanish colonial times. During the eighteenth century, when the population expanded and the amount of arable land increased, *cacique* landowners increasingly hired landless laborers to clear forest and share the resulting crops with the owners. The system usually involved loans from owners to tenants at usurious interest rates, which bound the tenants to their patrons. Spanish efforts to mitigate the exploitation were rarely effective.[102]

Essentially nothing had changed by the early twentieth century; indeed, as the pressures of rural population and market-oriented agriculture rose, the stakes also began to rise, toward today's heightened struggle for control of state-owned forests. Worcester described the challenge to the legal system and effective management and emphasized the importance of the resource administrators' legal authority, but he did not discuss the rural socioeconomic system that produced the pressures.

The foresters had ample reason for alarm, for logging and agriculture had already done irreversible biotic damage to the dipterocarp forest, damage that made it susceptible to *Imperata cylindrica*, or cogon grass. Throughout Southeast Asia when the rainforest vegetation was cut and burned but not immediately allowed to return to natural forest, the land was taken over by cogon, whose dense cover and intricate root systems suppressed other vegetation. Moreover, although fire cannot destroy cogon, the grass burns readily and intensely, destroying tree seedlings. Once cogon takes over, neither peasants nor cattle nor foresters can effectively use the land, and it has often been abandoned. Moore estimated that the cogon lands, "at present absolutely useless," already covered 30 percent of the total area of the Philippine Islands in 1910.[103]

These trends—political, economic, social, and ecological—were all tied to the global economy, whose relative prosperity during most of the

1920s encouraged export production of plantation crops and timber. The following decade brought a severe downturn in the Philippine export economy, and with it a change in the pattern of pressures on the land.

THE TRANSITION TO FILIPINO CONTROL

By the 1930s forestry policy and management were no longer the exclusive preserve of the Americans. The colonial administration emphasized educating and training Filipinos and turning actual planning and administration over to them as rapidly as possible. Americans rarely questioned the character of the power structure that they were creating and reinforcing in the dependent country. They built the colonial administration and the transition to self-rule on an alliance with the landed and commercial elite—the sugar barons and others. The forestry profession reflected this reality and adjusted to it.

In 1910, very early in the colonial years, Ahern set up a college of forestry at Los Baños, not far outside Manila, where his team began training Filipino foresters. Some of the first graduates of the basic course there were sent on to Yale Forestry School, the alma mater of Pinchot, for advanced training in American forestry management. By the mid-1920s nearly all foresters in the islands were Filipino: the entire five-hundred-man hierarchy of guards, rangers, and foresters was made up of nationals, except for five Americans at the top. In 1936 Arthur Fischer, the last American chief of the bureau, turned his office over to his Yale-seasoned protégé and friend, Florencio Tamesis. From that time forward Americans were only consultants. No other tropical colony moved local men into authority over forest resources so fast.

The American trainers had done their job systematically. Their local protégés had adopted the skills, values, and perspectives of the forestry fraternity. They knew how to harvest timber from the lauan forests efficiently and market it internationally. They were sure that this made a major contribution to the nation's economic growth. They argued that this was the only way to generate the revenue that would carry the industry beyond mere high-grading. And despite the enormous remaining task of scientific study of rainforest biology, they were convinced that they had the tools to accomplish it. Not surprisingly, their conception of competence precluded a full understanding of the forest peoples and their lifeways.

Internationally the new work of modern forestry was a profession with high social prestige. In tropical countries especially, foresters were recruited almost exclusively from high status backgrounds; the social perspectives of their class fit well with the profession's belief in the prerogatives of expertise. Filipino foresters were almost exclusively recruited from the landed class, with its links to Manila society. These young men understood the realities of urban and international markets and assumed that urbanization and rising standards of consumption were the pattern of progress. Except for those who specialized in laboratory analysis or sawmill technology, they loved being in the deep forest, discovering new species of trees, shrubs, and vines. They were paternalistic or hostile to the agrarian poor and at best condescending to the tribal cultures of the mountain forests.

When the global economy contracted sharply in 1930, markets for tropical primary products went into a state of collapse. The economy of the Philippines was no exception, and timber exports declined with other commodities. The worldwide depression did not affect the overall pattern of ownership in the timber industry. The political setting did change significantly in 1935, when a new constitution brought the islands Commonwealth status and internal autonomy, one step short of total independence. The new government, dominated by the landlords, set about legislating to defend Filipino commercial interests against foreign competition, especially the Chinese. The special ties with U.S. lumber interests were carefully preserved, however: under the new legislation, only Filipino or U.S. firms could be given long timber leases. Investment by other foreigners was limited to 40 percent of a firm's capital. In 1939, as the Depression was lifting but the Pacific was drifting toward war, investment in the Philippine sawmill industry, which had an estimated $15.5 million capitalization, came from several nations: 42 percent was U.S. capital, 26 percent was Filipino, 12 percent was Chinese, 7 percent was British, and 4 percent was Japanese.[104]

By that time the logging industry stood fifth in capital investment in the country, fourth in the value of its production, and second in the size of its labor force. It had become a major force in the national economy, in part because the Bureau of Forestry had spent years developing foreign markets for tropical timbers. The market for Philippine timber grew most rapidly in Europe, where red lauan and many other specialty woods were gaining popularity. The United States remained the largest single market, one the bureau continued to cultivate. A booklet issued by the bureau in 1939 reminded its potential buyers that when Americans bought Philippine lumber, they were "helping not only the Filipinos, but also the American lumbermen in the Philippines and the American machine manufacturers in the United States."[105]

The symbiosis between American and Philippine lumber industries was shattered by World War II. During the Japanese occupation of the islands, the Philippine economy, including agriculture and forestry, and urban life were totally disrupted. Many Filipino foresters joined the resistance against the Japanese occupation, and forest administration and control dissolved. The last year of the war was the most destructive. As the Japanese forces retreated, they destroyed nearly all the sawmill machinery in the country. They left Manila and other cities badly battered. In the process of withdrawing from the Manila area, the Japanese burned the records of the Bureau of Forestry and leveled the college of forestry at Los Baños.[106]

The war left a legacy of severe social disruption on forested land. The upheavals of the war dispossessed masses of peasant squatters, who were still looking for new land after the war was over. In 1948 Tamesis summarized the dilemma of social policy that the foresters faced.

> Forest destruction increased after the liberation. Illegal clearings to alleviate the food shortage destroyed valuable forests. On account of the tremendous demand for timber, illegal cutting and timber smuggling became widespread. The great number of unlicensed firearms left over from guerrilla warfare makes enforcement of forest law difficult, especially in the more remote regions.[107]

The most pressing task after the end of the war was the islands' final transition to independence, which was accomplished in 1946. The rebuilding of the country and its economy began simultaneously, starting with ravaged Manila. The devastated timber industry revived rapidly. Approximately one hundred cast-off U.S. military sawmills were installed, old lumber was recycled, and new supplies were milled.[108] The small-scale local lumber industry recovered especially fast: most of the rebuilding of Manila passed through the hands of ninety Chinese dealers, who charged high prices. In the nationalistic mood of the time, local resentment against those timber dealers fueled legislative efforts to dislodge ethnic Chinese from their dominant position in the nation's retail trade.[109]

Gradually, as the political system and economy stabilized, the forest wealth of the Philippines was tapped again. The islands became the great supplier of timber products to Southeast Asia, a leading source of export earnings for the government, and a source of enormous wealth and power for individuals, many of whom began logging illegally. Market demand rapidly outstripped administrative control in the forests, for the forestry administration could not be reestablished in the countryside until the early 1950s.

GLOBAL MARKETS AND THE DEFORESTATION
OF THE PHILIPPINES AFTER 1945

In the course of the 1950s the Philippines regained their prewar position of Southeast Asia's largest producer and exporter of hardwood timber. This position was based on the islands' market economy, which was one of the most developed in the tropical world, and its forestry system, which had been one of the most advanced in the colonial world. Southeast Asia dominated global tropical forest production throughout the post–World War II era.[110]

The 1950s saw a sharp decline in production costs of lauan plywood and veneer, and Philippine lauan exports dominated the Southeast Asian industry through the 1960s.[111] Although Americans were no longer in charge of industry or government policy, U.S. interests continued to concentrate in the Philippines until the late 1960s, when they moved for a short while into Borneo. In 1949 forest products were 1.3 percent of the country's total exports; a decade later, by 1959, they had become 15 percent of total exports.[112] Major profits were flowing into entrepreneurial pockets—but the country's forests were being rapidly depleted. The Bureau of Forestry recovered very slowly from its wartime decimation, and it had little power to control the issuance or management of timber concessions.

The College of Forestry at Los Baños was slow to recover after the war. Although a new generation of forestry recruits went to Yale for training, especially in wood technology, from 1946 on,[113] the college itself was effectively revived only in 1957, with major assistance from the Division of Forestry and Forest Products of the United Nation's Food and Agricultural Association (FAO) and the U.S. International Cooperation Agency (the forerunner of USAID).[114]

In the mid-1960s the timber supply in Philippine forests began to decline precipitously as its virgin forests began to disappear. The gamble taken by the American foresters in the previous generation—that more efficient, larger-scale logging technology could both utilize and sustain the Philippine forests—had apparently failed. Timber merchants with powerful political leverage in Manila and a burgeoning squatter population with political patrons in the countryside were the twin forces that were driving a disastrously rapid deforestation of the Philippines.

For many reasons the Bureau of Forestry was politically unable to raise stumpage fees and other timber taxes to reflect rapidly rising world prices. Consequently the government began to lose large amounts of potential revenue, money that went instead into private pockets.[115] Management of the country's forestlands was also becoming more fragmented because several government agencies had influence over land use planning.[116]

The world market for lauan grew insatiably and profits soared for those who logged the timber, whether legally or illegally. Equipped with a new generation of more powerful logging and milling machinery, Filipino and foreign loggers dramatically increased their operations after 1960. Even Palawan island, a frontier 350 miles from Manila and the last great island forest in the Philippines, began to reel under the blows of ax and saw.[117] The race to cut the last easily accessible lauan forests accelerated rapidly after 1965, when Ferdinand Marcos was elected president of the republic. Marcos's rule was effectively a dictatorship, and his policies of "crony capitalism" bled the country dry: he rewarded his friends with vast short-term timber concessions, and they profited from the islands' natural resources.[118]

Trade statistics from these years dramatically register the shrinkage of timber supplies. The late 1960s saw a steady decline in timber production, exports, and earnings. Between 1968 and 1969, and 1974 and 1975, log production fell from 11.58 million cubic meters to 8.44 million. Exports in the same years fell from 8.65 million cubic meters, with a value of $232 million, to 4.6 million cubic meters, with a value of $198 million. Logs and lumber exports, after more than doubling in the mid-1960s, fell from 4 billion board feet in 1970 to under 1 billion in 1985. By 1985, purchasing power from earnings had fallen to 13 percent of the 1970 level.[119]

By the mid-1970s 13.1 million acres of the Philippines were listed as treeless ex-forestland; much of this was critical watershed. Moreover, logging roads led to the destruction of far more than just trees: they allowed squatters to penetrate the region. Squatters slashed and burned patches of forest, planted survival crops that they tended for a brief time, and then turned the degraded land over to cattle.[120]

The loss of forest cover is difficult to assess precisely, because several surveys since the 1950s have presented widely varying figures. It is significant that Bureau of Forestry statistics for the amount of land that has been deforested are regularly much lower than those from other sources. A somber trend is clear. David Kummer, in the most systematic analysis, concludes that the nation's forest cover shrank from 50 percent of its total surface in 1950 to 44 percent in 1957, 35 percent in 1969, and to a mere 22 to 24 percent in 1987.[121] The figures express a seemingly irreversible depletion of forest stock. By 1976 the Bureau of Forestry had reforested only 52,000 acres.[122]

This growing crisis was reflected in the constant changes made by the government to the terms of timber concessions and the regularity of the violations made by the timber corporations. In 1959 Nicolas Lansigan, head of the Society of Filipino Foresters, attacked the lumber barons publicly, concluding, "While some lumbermen are decidedly of the desirable type who are frankly worried about the fate of the forests and the future of their investments . . . many are plain timber miners of the cut-and-get-out variety."[123]

The complaint illustrates the running tension between foresters and loggers. Lansigan's criticism also reveals the strain that was typical between foresters and villagers. The tension was generated by the slash-and-burn squatters, who were supported in increasing numbers by local landlords who used them to gain control of government forestlands.

> And the kaingineros! They are now the lords of the forests. Many of them have taken the "land-for-the-landless" policy as the green light to squat at the nearest forest land. . . . Forest officers have grown tired hailing them to court. . . . Since that ill-fated day one President on the spot released some kaingineros from jail, the situation has never been the same. Squatters are literally sticking out their tongues at the poor forestry men doing their duty.[124]

Forestry management had become deeply entangled with social and political controversies, but the foresters had made no effort yet to distinguish traditional agroforestry systems from the effects of social displacement, or production forestry from rainforest conservation.

AMERICAN FORESTERS AND TIMBER
CORPORATIONS AFTER INDEPENDENCE

In their new postwar and postindependence role in the Philippines, Americans had no political or administrative power, but as consultants they could continue to monitor and perhaps marginally influence the trend of forest exploitation. The Truman administration saw the value of maintaining close professional ties between the two countries, as well as encouraging the further expansion of Philippine exports of primary products to American markets. In 1951 American timber specialist Winslow Gooch was sent to the Philippines to conduct a two-year study of the country's forest resources. The study was sponsored by the Mutual Security Agency (the U.S. bureau that replaced the Economic Cooperation Administration after the Marshall Plan ended in 1951) and was directed by Tamesis.

Gooch's final report to the agency was a highly specific survey of timber supplies, logging companies, forest laws, forest products of all kinds including nontimber products, and useful information for potential concessionaires. It showed a vital, varied, and internationally competitive wood products industry among the Filipinos themselves. Gooch also noted that the Bureau of Forestry and other agencies were having some trouble enforcing forest laws against illegal operators and exporters.[125]

Of the few American foresters who visited the country in these years, the most prestigious was Tom Gill. The Philippine government and the U.S. International Cooperation Agency co-sponsored Gill's tour of the islands in 1959. He was commissioned to assess the quality of logging and forestry operations throughout the islands, and he was appalled at what he saw. Addressing the Philippine Lumber Producers Association in Manila at the end of his tour, Gill reported, "Some weeks ago I flew over and visited Cebu, Bohol and Negros. Parts of these islands made me think I was back again in Korea, North China, or the man-made deserts of Mexico. For I saw thousands upon thousands of hectares of cut-over, burned-over and abandoned land, pock-marked with red and yellow scars of bare earth at the mercy of sun, wind and rain."[126]

Irresponsible lumbermen bore half the brunt of his critique; landless squatters and their political patrons bore the rest. "The legitimate landless Filipino, sincerely looking for a place to make a home, is being rapidly replaced by professional squatters organized very often by someone higher up. . . . The result is . . . a land grab that could go down as one of the most notorious in history—a nation being robbed of the very thing that makes existence possible—the soil and the productivity of the soil."[127]

Gill's sympathy for his colleagues in the forestry service was reflected in his recommendations for reform. He advised the Philippine government to greatly increase the Bureau of Forestry's budget, to reflect its value to the treasury and to the nation, and to strengthen its power so that it could prosecute the loggers and squatters who violated the forestry laws. He maintained that timber leases should be awarded only to the most efficient and responsible loggers and that the leases be awarded on a long-term basis, long enough to make it worth the loggers' while to invest in the next generation of trees.[128] Although his formulas were plausible, they did not address the root of the trouble: the broader political and economic forces that were at work in a politically polarized society. His recommendations did not suggest that foresters and villagers should cooperate in managing the resource: his advice was entirely paternalistic.[129]

One of the major purposes of Gill's tour was to encourage American timber corporations to invest in the Philippines. Gill hoped that more enlightened cooperation would develop between American timber corporations and Filipino loggers. This hope was largely fulfilled in at least one joint venture, the Paper Industries Corporation of the Philippines, or PICOP, the largest and most modern paper manufacturer in the islands. The firm's roots stretched back into the 1930s, when Andres Soriano, a Spanish immigrant, first invested in Philippine industry and built the family fortune primarily by producing San Miguel beer.[130] In 1935 Soriano joined a group of Filipino investors in Manila to found the country's first paper manufacturing firm, largely to replace imported packing materials in the sugar industry (another instance of the modernization of a tropical forest industry being linked to a major export crop).

In 1951 the Soriano family invited the world's largest paper company, the International Paper Corporation of Washington state, to become a partner in developing a paper industry in the Philippines that would use native wood stock. The American firm agreed, but it took a decade of research before they believed they had the technology to produce reliable paper pulp from the hardwoods available on the islands. PICOP was launched as a joint venture in 1963. By 1974 PICOP was capitalized at $72 million and controlled 80 percent of the paper pulp industry in the islands. By 1980 it was the largest forest products company in all of Southeast Asia and was praised internationally. One leading forestry expert praised it for its "mastery of papermaking from mixed tropical hardwoods; major commitments to plantation forestry, unequalled anywhere in Asia, and silvicultural research; dedication to community and social development; underwriting tree farming, food production and seeking to break dependence on shifting agriculture."[131]

Unfortunately, PICOP's innovative management was expensive. Moreover, social turmoil and government corruption of the Marcos years prompted most American timber firms to withdraw from the Philippines, including International Paper.[132] In the 1970s International Paper owned 40 percent of PICOP; by 1980 International Paper had cut back its participation in PICOP to 10 percent.[133] PICOP began incurring heavy annual losses, and in 1980 it began turning to the government for major subsidies, in effect becoming a semipublic corporation.

By the 1980s direct U.S. investment in the Philippine timber economy was minimal. The major American connection with deforestation in the islands in recent years has been indirect. America has supplied a steady market for forest products. Hardwoods harvested by Japanese firms in Mindanao and elsewhere are processed into plywood, sawnwood, and veneer in South Korea, Taiwan, or Singapore, and then sold in Japan and the United States.

The Philippines today is probably the most ecologically degraded large country in the tropics. During the colonial era American resource managers in the Philippines developed a greater degree of actual control over the forests than they did in any Latin American country (although it was perhaps weaker than the control exercised in the more authoritarian European colonial systems). Paradoxically, the control American foresters had may have been the worst possible degree of power over Nature for the fate of the living ecosystems of the archipelago.

THE TIMBER ECONOMY IN TROPICAL AMERICA AFTER 1945

Latin America experienced a similar postwar acceleration in the timber industry, although it was slower and more tentative than the postwar growth in the Philippine Islands. Slower growth was a reflection of the region's corporate technology, forestry administration, and government support for forest exploitation, which was less developed there than it was in the Philippines. Put another way, international market demand was not as interested in Latin America's forest resources.

There were two dimensions to the changes in forest exploitation and management that occurred after the war in Latin America: breakthroughs in processing technologies and multinational corporate systems, and the belated development of professional forestry. Biology and policy were combined in an attempt to meet local people's needs as well as profit from distant markets. Surprisingly—a shred of hope for the forest's biological survival—there were some indications that a forestry system designed to meet the needs of local populations might also encourage a more biologically diverse approach to silviculture, one that might even blend modern science with traditional knowledge.

The demand for forest resources generated by the international market for industrial products grew inexorably. The market was seductive: it promised ever-rising profits, and it was backed by an ideology of socioeconomic development that had not yet learned to recognize that the planet's natural resources had limits. None of this was uniquely American, for the world of modern timber corporations and the world of the forestry profession shared the unrestrained optimism of those years.

Although World War II was not fought on New World soil, the natural resources of all the Americas were mobilized for the war effort; nearly the entire planet was drawn into the vortex. Agriculture was accelerated to the maximum extent possible given the limited civilian work force. Many forests both temperate and tropical were cleared for temporary food production, but by 1945 they had been abandoned, leaving diminished soil and damaged vegetation.[134]

The story was similar for the production of lumber. All combatant nations drew on available timber resources for materiel. The American military sponsored a search in tropical woodlands for strategic timber species such as exceptionally light balsa, which was used for airplane parts, and mahogany, which was transformed into boats and gliders.[135] The number of tropical species used in northern markets increased, adding another element to the complex ecological legacy of global warfare.

Probably most fundamental for the long term, World War II brought further acceleration of technological scale. Between 1943 and 1945 three U.S. firms—Ichabod Williams from New York, Freiberg Mahogany of Cincinnati and New Orleans, and Weis Fricker of New Orleans—introduced trucks and other mechanized equipment for hauling timber in the Guatemalan Petén and in British Honduras. Together the three Yankee firms hauled out fifty million board feet of hardwood timber between 1943 and 1948. In 1948 the border between Guatemala and British Honduras was closed—politics once again determined the loggers' fortunes.[136] This was a clear example of how urgent wartime priorities, and their associated profits, increased corporate capability to extract natural resources in peacetime.

As the war neared its conclusion in 1945, Allied planners knew that Europe and East Asia faced a monumental task of rebuilding that would continue to place heavy demands on the planet's natural resources.

Northern Europe's conifer forests could not provide for all of Europe's timber needs, and the Soviet Union, home of the world's greatest conifer forests, was crippled. Canada and the United States had only a limited capacity to expand their harvest of yellow pine, Douglas fir, and other conifers. High consumption levels in the United States were also driving the timber cutting.

In 1949 Marcel Leloup, director of the Division of Forestry and Forest Products of the FAO, discussed the critical international shortage of forest products and cited the market supported by consumers in North America: "The *per capita* consumption of saw timber is one cubic metre, five times greater than in Europe. The region uses 65 percent of the total world consumption of pulp, although the population is only 8 percent of that of the world." South America, where consumption was very low and the timber industry was underdeveloped, had the largest reserve of unexploited forest.

The United States still imported far more timber from the Philippines than from Latin America.[137] The entire U.S. market for tropical hardwoods was modest from the Yankee perspective: tropical species were less than 1 percent of U.S. hardwood consumption. American timber imports from Latin America rose from 974,000 cubic feet in 1948 to 1,291,000 cubic feet in 1956, only a gradual increase.[138] But, just as in earlier years, the U.S. demand for specialty hardwoods was very significant for the tropical exporters themselves and the particular tracts that they high-graded.[139]

The trade in softwood species was more complex. Faster growing softwoods include pine and many species native to the biologically complex rainforest. Softwoods are valued primarily for inexpensive building lumber and as the major source of paper pulp. The paper industry gradually learned how to use more softwood species for the production of pulp, and as it did, it found clear-cutting of the rainforest to be increasingly valuable. Planners turned their eyes to the tropical horizon and found a major potential source of paper pulp in the pine forests of southern South America.

The era of massive tropical timber exports was only beginning in South America in the late 1940s. In striking contrast to the Philippine timber economy, Latin American timber production and export expanded only slowly until the 1960s, when rapid industrialization and economic expansion began. Latin America continued as a small exporter of hardwood logs and coniferous sawnwood. Even then, two-thirds of the trade in timber products was from one Latin American country to another. One major exception was the European market for Paraná pine.

The country with the most accessible reserves of marketable timber was Brazil, whose southern states in the temperate zone well beyond Amazonia's rainforest had great stands of Paraná pine, or Araucaria. This species, which was not a true pine, had evolved only in the far southern lands that in geologically remote times had been linked to Australia, not the tropics. The harvest of Paraná pine was a great windfall for Brazil's export economy, but by the late 1950s Brazil had lost most of its Araucaria forest ecosystem. This devastation occurred at least two decades before the more massive onslaught on the Amazon rainforest began in earnest.[140]

There was obviously major potential for increased timber production throughout the forest region of Latin America, but there were many hindrances to the expansion of the industry as well. Old mahogany firms, both American and European, continued to provide specialty hardwoods. They faced familiar difficulties in dealing with local authorities, however, for through the 1950s tropical timber management remained in its infancy, and governments continued in their old bureaucratically irregular ways. An FAO study in 1959 concluded that although Latin America had ample resources, "the relative unattractiveness of investment in an industry which may not immediately yield great profits" had resulted in a severe shortage of development capital.[141]

The forest products industry in North America began to respond to this opportunity. Major northern timber corporations had accumulated the scale of investment capital and the technical and managerial capacity needed to begin risking major investments in the tropics. They also had achieved greater "efficiency," extracting a wider range of forest species and processing a higher percentage of each tree. Because Yankee companies were able to use more of the harvested trees, they could outcompete local operators. Local firms exported only the best logs, wasting most of the rest of the cut. Even then, their production was by no means negligible: in 1950 seventy-three local sawmills together produced 48.6 million board feet annually for use within Guatemala. Such inefficient utilization of timber harvests could benefit no one.

Waste on such a scale was intolerable to the generation of foresters working in the Americas in the 1950s. Among them were Leslie Holdridge and his colleagues, who were the most experienced American experts in Central America at the time. They were intent on increasing the efficiency of lumber operations:

Only a small part of the potential productivity of the land is being utilized by the present wood-working industries of the country. Increased use depends on many factors, such as the improvement of transportation facilities, management of forest lands to reduce loss from fire, control of utilization practices that destroy the productive capacity of the forests, the establishment of more efficient manufacturing methods, and the development of marketing organizations to promote the sale of manufactured products.[142]

They urged the mill owners to build modern sawmills that were designed to make fuller use of the harvested trees than hand axes and saws could. They also promoted the manufacture of plywood and veneer, made possible by sophisticated new machinery, which would not only raise efficiency but also increase the species that could be milled. In the years that followed, their more professional approach was adopted very slowly by the logging industry.

Politics continued to make systematic forest utilization a difficult science to practice. In the mahogany belt of the Petén, the Guatemalan government was still unstable, and efforts to develop the country's mahogany industry on a more orderly basis broke down in 1956. As Bruce Lamb, the leading authority on mahogany, explained years later, this was

> due to intrigue over how to measure the logs. The Guatemalan Forest Service set a flagrantly inflated basic stumpage price. The Robinson Lumber Co. [based in New Orleans] tried to offset this by defining a log measuring system that Guatemala could not accept. The survey effort for Petén and the legislation authorizing industrial units went down the tubes. And Guatemala went back to the old chaotic system of giving its mahogany timber away for the largest pay-off. Whose fault? I hesitate to say.[143]

A similar condition prevailed in the pine belt of eastern Nicaragua, where Somoza ruled largely for the benefit of his family and friends. Lamb commented that the Nicaraguan Longleaf Pine Company, controlled by Robinson Lumber Company, "liquidated a lot of pine timber without making any effort to establish or protect natural growing stock to replace what they had cut. They just paid off Somoza. Maybe that was all that was practical."[144]

At the other end of the spectrum were the small local loggers, who provided for local needs using lower quality woods. In the gradual economic expansion of the 1950s they increased in number, always in the shadow of the larger export firms. Reasonably good information is available from Honduras, where the largest pine woodlands in Central America were found. In the early 1960s there were some 111 small mills functioning in the country, producing 575,000 cubic meters of timber yearly. A few of them were able to participate in the export trade, exporting one-third of their production, mostly mahogany and cedar, to markets in Europe. The rest milled pine as construction lumber for local and domestic markets. Their work was very inefficient and technically primitive; labor productivity was very low and a high percentage of each log was wasted.[145]

Throughout Central America small Yankee expatriate firms competed with the local sawmill operators. Like the individual Americans who had migrated to warmer climates for small-scale farming or trade, their numbers and cumulative impact are difficult to trace. Gill did not overlook them, though. Toward the end of his long career, he described them with fervor:

> Ever since forestry graduates first emerged from our colleges, men have been going out to work for foreign powers or private companies, or to teach or, precariously, to start enterprises of their own. Outgrowth of conditions where not only their work but life itself was often a gamble, the stories of these men are among the most stirring sagas in American forestry. . . . They left behind something that has come to be recognized as inherent in the American forestry tradition—a willingness to try anything once, and a positive genius for dealing with the unexpected.[146]

Gill could not resist the indulgence of praising this national myth: that the dynamic, resourceful, courageous Yankee had introduced a new and valuable quality into the saga of resource exploitation in the tropics.

GROWTH OF SOFTWOOD MARKETS

The rapidly expanding northern consumer markets of the postwar boom years included an insatiable demand for brown kraft paper for packaging. Most of the pulp for this product was supplied by the boreal zone coniferous forests of Canada, Scandinavia, and Finland. Similarly, but on a far smaller scale, the new affluent urban middle class in Latin America demanded packaging. By the 1950s there was a severe and increasing shortage of paper products in Latin America. It was filled by imports from the north, since the domestic industry was not yet technologically modernized to meet the expanding demand. A major market was beckoning to American timber products corporations.

The modern pulp industry had emerged in the late nineteenth century to meet the expanding market for paper and packing materials. It developed especially in the northern European conifer zone. Until the

1960s, when major tropical sources came on line, the northern boreal coniferous forests of Europe and North America provided nearly the whole global supply of paper pulp. In 1918 production was 10 million tons of pulp; by the late 1930s it had risen to 25 million tons. Eighty percent came from Sweden, Finland, Norway, Germany, the United States, and Canada. This accounted for 7 percent of the global wood harvest, and most was processed from trees that were not good for lumber.

Because pulpwood has a greater value-to-weight ratio than milled lumber, the FAO thought that increased pulp production would help finance better forest management, particularly in Latin America, and might reduce the harvest of primary forest. In 1946 the agency recommended an increase in pulp production in all countries, partly to eliminate imports into South America and Africa.[147] By 1947 pulp production had recovered to prewar levels, and it almost doubled between 1946 and 1955, from 25.7 million to 49.7 million tons, an annual growth of over 7 percent. As one FAO expert observed, "Expansion and modernization plans were continually being announced from all regions of the world."[148]

The consumption of wood pulp in Latin America increased similarly, far outstripping production in the region. Latin American economies had to purchase more than half of their wood pulp with precious foreign exchange. In 1937 the region produced 27,000 tons and consumed 233,000 of pulp. In 1948 it produced 170,000 tons but consumed 345,000 tons. The consumption gap continued to widen: in 1955 the region produced 320,000 tons and imported 840,000.[149]

U.S. pulp and paper operations arrived in Latin America in the 1950s, effecting a dramatic change in the region's wood products industry. American paper companies moved into the region in part to provide packaging for the American fruit companies, which had begun packing their Cavendish bananas in cardboard boxes. Thus, the exploitation of tropical forests by American corporations in many instances began as an adjunct to large-scale export crop operations.

The paper companies preferred not to become embroiled in the dismal struggles over ownership or enmeshed in the management of disputed local lands. The long-term trend was to stay at a distance from local circumstances. By 1981 only seven U.S. timber firms were operating in all of Central America—in Costa Rica, Guatemala, Panama, and Honduras—and none was using local supplies. The two companies that continued to operate in Honduras were Gould Paper and Robinson

Lumber.[150] As a result the actual work of forest exploitation throughout Latin America remained largely in the hands of local firms, especially in the pinelands.

Some local firms formed associations with U.S. partners, who had been recruited for the investment capital and consumer markets that they could provide. The most notable example of what could be accomplished when a local firm collaborated with a North American timber corporation was Carton de Colombia, which became Latin America's most modern integrated paper and paperboard producer. The company was founded in 1944 by the Container Corporation of America in a fifty-fifty partnership with Colombian investors. The company's goal was to replace imported paper pulp with local supplies and to make products primarily for domestic markets. It was the first company to enter Colombia that had resources adequate to the challenge of opening a major tract of the country's primary rainforest.

In 1952, logging and sawmill equipment that was becoming obsolete in the United States was shipped by Container Corporation to Colombia, where it constituted the industry's most advanced technology in northern South America. Several years of cooperative planning with the Colombian government resulted in 1960 in the creation of Pulpapel, a joint venture between Container Corporation and the government, to launch large-scale clear-cutting and replanting in the forests of the Magdalena River valley. Its packaging papers soon met almost all of Colombia's domestic need, including cartons for the banana export industry.[151]

A similar story emerged in the pine region of southern Brazil in the 1950s, when two American multinational corporations moved into the region to join the development of the pulp and paper industry. In 1953 Westvaco Corporation purchased Rigesa Celulose from an old local family in Valinhos outside São Paulo. The new owners of Rigesa built an automated paper mill to produce cardboard boxes and brown paper bags for domestic Brazilian markets, especially that of booming São Paulo. Quickly expanding beyond their local supplies, they surveyed the pine region farther south, in Santa Catarina, for sources of pulpwood. There they purchased land that had been stripped of its stands of native Paraná pine early in the century. Rigesa replanted the pine, and in the years before the new trees were mature enough to harvest, the company relied on recycled corrugated boxes, waste wood from local sawmills, and miscellaneous fellings on private lands in the region.[152]

Five years after Westvaco pioneered Yankee paper technology in southern Brazil, another Louisiana firm, Olin Mathieson, purchased a pulp mill from the Itajai Pulp and Paper Company in Santa Catarina state. By the end of the 1960s the new Olinkraft facility was producing 160 tons of kraft paper, newsprint, and specialty papers daily. From its headquarters in São Paulo, Olinkraft also purchased or leased 110,000 acres of old Paraná pineland, which it replanted, some with the original species, but most with loblolly pine (also called southern pine), whose silviculture the company understood from its main operation in the United States.[153] Reforestation and modernized production of paper production went hand in hand. It is too soon to tell whether local soils can sustain the venture and whether the local poor will be displaced, but by the 1970s, waste wood and paper were being used more efficiently, and employment in the mills had tripled in little more than a decade.

Whether they employed a rusty rural band saw or a modern corporate sawmill, by the 1940s loggers were turning the forests of Latin America into timber products at an accelerating speed. Very little land had been reforested. Efforts at sustained-yield management of hardwoods and softwoods had only just begun, as had integrated wood products processing. These circumstances, plus those of new market openings and rising costs, demanded more highly trained and technically competent forest managers.

FORESTERS AS DEVELOPMENT PLANNERS

American roles in the trend of forest control and exploitation were complex and paradoxical. The U.S. presence had evolved in colonial and neocolonial settings and matured with the American rise to domination in world trade and politics. The forestry industry embraced the scientific orientation toward the twin demigods of growth and modernization, using them as touchstones as they developed forestry policy in Latin America and the Philippines. In its belief in mechanization, expansion, and greater efficiency, forestry policy reflected its practitioners' experience in the temperate zone of North America.

Foresters had to work within the institutional and social frameworks of tropical countries. After 1945, as tropical governments became more assertive, foresters tried to channel national development policies toward sustainable timber management, integrated with agriculture. All too often political, economic, and demographic pressures were far stronger than foresters' ecological knowledge of the tropics. Too often foresters gambled with a stake that many now regret: the tools of timber extraction raced far ahead of the wisdom to use them with restraint.

Moreover, most foresters understood little about rural tropical populations and their traditional ways of living with forests. Whether implicit or explicit, the social policy embraced by professional foresters was only rudimentary. It began with a genuine concern to provide for local consumption needs, primarily in terms of meeting construction timber requirements. Foresters believed that settled farming was the best method of sustenance agriculture. Until at least the 1960s foresters were nearly unanimous in condemning all forms of shifting agriculture, not distinguishing between ancient tribal agriculture and the damage caused by dispossessed lowland peasants as they were forced into mountain forest watersheds.

Most foresters did not trace the dilemma of the dispossessed peasants back to its source, in the politics of plantation monocropping. Only an occasional forester ever pointed to the system of land tenure, in which a few powerful people controlled most of the land, as a primary impetus of forest degradation. Nor was there much mention at all of this class hierarchy as a major source of high birth rates among the rural poor, the population pressure which foresters and wildlife conservationists routinely agreed was becoming a major pressure on forest resources.

Foresters were trained to study tree communities, not human communities. Here, as in all other areas of tropical resource utilization, specialization and professionalization, although necessary, promoted a deadly separation of technical from social and political understanding. Thus they unwittingly contributed to accelerating the transformation of tropical Nature into commodity patterns, biologically simplified, ecologically unstable, socially polarized, and culturally degraded.

That was not the whole story. By the 1950s a few tropical foresters with the requisite combination of biological knowledge plus social awareness and imagination began warning that the forest resources of the tropics could not be indefinitely preserved unless the whole range of social factors could be integrated in management strategies. These foresighted individuals understood local subsistence as well as tree growth and distant markets, but they had little political voice until a groundswell of change in political consciousness began to appear internationally in the late 1960s.

The United Nations was very important for the development of the forest industry, and it also became a major pathway for U.S. influence. The Food and Agriculture Organization was founded in 1945 especially to provide food for a war-worn world. At the urging of a small group that included Pinchot's protégés in the United States, forestry was added to its portfolio. In 1943 President Roosevelt convened a conference on international food, which was midwife to the FAO. He was convinced to include forestry in the agriculture agency's agenda by Gill, Lyle Watts, director of the U.S. Forest Service, Henry Graves, long-time dean of the Yale school of forestry and a former director of the U.S. Forest Service, plus members of the national Lumber Manufacturers' Association.[154]

In March 1944 a Technical Committee on Forestry and Primary Forest Products was established to plan that aspect of FAO. Graves was appointed its chair, and among the eleven other members were Watts, Gill, and Walter Lowdermilk, whose work on global soil erosion had pioneered soil conservation efforts in the pre-war years. An inner circle of American internationalists was coalescing, together with their European counterparts. Their collective view of the role of forests in the postwar global development agenda would be very weighty.

The FAO's forestry division was born with a sense of urgency to use all forest products to maximum efficiency. Little additional lumber supply was available from the U.S. and Canada in the late 1940s. North American foresters were acutely aware that tropical regions could play a greatly expanded role in international trade and thus economic development, and that tropical countries could not afford to leave their forest resources "underutilized" while draining foreign exchange to pay for imports.

FAO foresters saw vast areas of badly managed and severely depleted forest stocks, including regions of the United States. Equally important, they looked at the tropical forest zone as one of the greatest untapped resources for humanity's future use. In 1949 Egon Glesinger, a Polish forest economist who migrated to the United States during the war, and who was the second-ranking officer in the FAO Forestry Division, published a widely read global survey of forests and the timber industry, *The Coming Age of Wood,* in which he declared that "Earth's last frontier has by no means disappeared; 5000 million acres of virgin forest—in tropical and sub-tropical regions of Africa and Latin America, and in Alaska, Manchuria, and Siberia—constitute the largest and most exciting frontier left to man."[155]

The fledgling state of professional forestry in Latin America was indicated by the fact that when the FAO's forestry division was founded, Gill and Watts, not Ladinos, represented the region.[156] FAO launched its forestry consultations in Latin America in 1948 at a conference in Teresópolis, Brazil, on the edge of the Serra dos Orgãos National Park north of Rio de Janeiro. Participants considered forestlands to be a dimension of a nation's productivity, but that did not preclude discussion of conservation under the rubric of sustainable production. Participants agreed that many forests were badly depleted and poorly managed, with a resulting "havoc" of erosion; they also agreed that other vast areas of forest were virtually untouched and should be brought under active management for socioeconomic development. As one conference resolution put it, "Latin-American forests should be utilized in accordance with modern scientific and mechanical concepts, and in such ways as to raise the standards of living of local populations to a level compatible with human dignity."[157]

The emphasis of the conference was entirely on productive utilization of resources. The idea that some natural regions should be preserved—and protected—in their original character was still just beyond the ideological horizon. The Teresópolis resolutions asked for "rational expansion of forest products industries drawing on the long accumulated wealth of virgin forest tracts, so as to take the utmost advantage of present export possibilities," and "increased efficiency at all stages of production."[158]

There were scattered references to preserving forest cover so as to protect watersheds: "[I]n order to avoid wasteful cutting of forests, particularly protection forests around centers of population and in mountainous regions, countries of Latin America should endeavor to regulate the cutting of wood for fuel and charcoal, basing this cutting on principles of sound forest management." This principle was linked primarily to the region's growing demand for industrial energy supplies. In a recommendation that would begin to be challenged as one-sided a decade later, the conference encouraged "a greater use of hydroelectric power, wherever this is economically justified."

Acceleration of timber production was also necessary to reduce Latin America's dependence on imported wood products and to expand the region's ability to export. Participants repeatedly emphasized that timber products should be exported only after processing, so that producer countries could capture the values of employment and accelerated technology, thereby using their natural resources to begin to emerge from dependency on the industrialized economies. To accomplish this governments would have to encourage the flow of up-to-date technology from industrialized countries, "permitting a logical exchange of trade and a mutual betterment in countries' standards of living," a process that could be backed by the World Bank and the International Monetary Fund. The seeds of another generation's controversies were being unwittingly planted.

American foresters also preached the gospel of sustained-yield forestry. This philosophy was succinctly summarized by Hardy Shirley at the Inter-American Conference on Conservation of Renewable Natural Resources, held in Denver in 1948, the same year as the Teresópolis conference. Shirley, the assistant dean of forestry at Syracuse University, was another American forester who was gaining influence in inter-American forest resource development. In a talk titled "Obstacles to Sustained-Yield Forestry," he asserted that

> abundant resources, together with an energetic populace skilled in exploiting natural wealth, afford nations strength, prestige, and high living standards. But nations rich in resources, just as some wealthy individuals, may use up their heritage with little thought for future needs. Other nations resemble the miser in having abundant resources which they use but little. Neither spendthrifts nor misers make good citizens, nor do prodigal or miserly nations make their rightful contribution to a world society.[159]

Shirley condemned the wastefulness and technical crudeness of highgrading. Restating what had been the mainstream tenet of American official forestry ever since Pinchot's early years, he described the "perpetuation of a renewable resource through wise use," adapted carefully to the specific conditions at each locale.

> Sustained yield of necessity varies in intensity with terrain, timber quality, and markets. It must be adjusted so that operations can be made profitable. Sustained yield, therefore, implies intensive forest use on fertile, well-developed forests near wood-using centers; it means very conservative forestry on steep mountain slopes subject to erosion; and it means rudimentary forestry on remote, inaccessible lands, [a] practice that will maintain useful forest growth.[160]

Shirley was unreservedly confident that large-scale timber extraction and processing would provide the solution. He praised the major strides that had been made in the use of heavy-duty machinery, including truck-mounted sawmills. The greatest problem he saw, especially in Latin America, was the high portion of hardwoods in natural forests, when the accelerating market demand was for pulp. A more capital-intensive industry could speed the transformation of natural forests to softwood plantations on a scale that would be large enough to meet the world's demand for paper stock. The paper industry also presented a major opportunity for Latin American economies to become competitive in international markets. "Export markets should be built up. Developing the potentially very large domestic market is even more important. But good markets in themselves may be either a boon or a hindrance to sustained-yield forestry."[161]

Shirley's technocratic confidence, its priorities dominated by the market for timber products, typified the stance of foresters immediately after the war.[162] He assumed that long-term material needs could be met and environmental health could be maintained by production forestry, if the scale of production was large enough. He and most of his contemporaries did not approach forests as intricate ecosystems worth preserving intact for an entire range of ecological value, transcending social value. In particular, they assumed that rainforest ecosystems were so utterly vast that their full range of species did not need defenders in international development forums.

The overall thrust of American forestry aid in Latin America was toward the rapid development of the region's varied timber resources. Virtually no one warned that the strategy had dangers. In the immediate postwar years U.S. technical assistance for forest management spread throughout Latin America, not only through FAO channels, but also through the International Cooperation Agency (the forerunner of the Agency for International Development), for which forestry aid was a major emphasis. The push for development prescribed the formulation of competent policy.[163]

The pattern was set in 1946, when a team of U.S. foresters who had been sent to Chile submitted a report that became a model for subsequent U.S. assessments.[164] Chile, twice the size of California and 2,650 miles long from the deserts of its northern border with Peru to the icy south of Tierra del Fuego, had 40 million acres of forests, which constituted 22 percent of Chile's land. Most of the forest cover was in the cool, moist south. The American team reported that much of it had already been degraded to varying degrees, primarily by ill-advised clearing for agriculture.[165] In the optimistic vein that characterized the dispersion of most American development aid after the war, they reported that production could easily and sustainably be tripled in those already damaged forests. Scientific forestry could achieve a major expansion of timber exports and make an important contribution to the national economy. In sum, said the foresters, Chile's forests should be integrated into the global economy. The team urged the installation of integrated sawmill complexes to expand veneer and plywood production, which would use much of what smaller mills wasted.

The story was similar in southern Brazil. In the urgent postwar search for coniferous timber resources to rebuild Europe, Watts proposed that the FAO send a survey mission to southern Brazil, knowing that his close associate Gill would head it as FAO's representative for Latin America. In 1947 Gill and his team surveyed the Paraná pine belt. They estimated that despite years of severe overcutting, Paraná pine still covered well over 24.7 million acres. The loggers in southern Brazil were part of the most highly developed forest industry in South America. In the early decades of the century the area had been equipped with German machinery. Paraná pine had been shipped to Argentina, Uruguay, Britain, and South Africa; the United States had imported a pittance. Gill thought that these circumstances gave the timber industry a base for very rapid growth, and he believed that with the help of the FAO its efficiency could be improved in major ways. He proposed a World Bank loan for new equipment and other financing, which would constitute "an example to all nations of the role FAO is capable of assuming as an integrating factor in the world economy."[166]

The natural pine forest regions of Latin America were one thing to manage, the rainforests were quite another. Their great variety of trees, most of which could not be identified by anyone except the tribal inhabitants of the forests, defeated any attempt to extract the value of more than one or two timber species in any given area. Throughout this period foresters had little success in establishing managed forests for sustained timber production in the wet lowland zones of Latin America. Research on moist forests had just begun, but foresters were optimistic about the possibilities for the "rational exploitation" of the rainforest along "scientific" lines.[167] The images of rationality and science were compelling when juxtaposed with their converse: the wastefulness, inefficiency, political corruption, and administrative weakness that existed throughout the region. Unfortunately, tropical foresters had simply not accumulated enough experience to anticipate the silvicultural complexities and social pressures that continue to make their goal so elusive. The confidence of the generation made many advances in tropical resource management possible, but it also delayed full confrontation with the social issues of the forests.

Afforestation strategies were also an element of the FAO's vision of development. The American team that visited Chile in 1946 reported that replanting of logged forests in Chile had already reached 353,210 acres, of which Insignis pine accounted for 58 percent and eucalyptus 31 percent. This became the dominant pattern of reforestation following the war: replanting would concentrate on one or two fast-growing species that would provide paper pulp. These efforts did not establish a true forest with varied species of flora and fauna, but a one-species crop: any species that was plantation-grown displaced entire natural forests. Both natural forests and (more extensively in Chile) previously degraded lands were being replaced by softwood monocultures. The trend began to accelerate rapidly in the 1950s, and became dominant throughout the tropics in the 1960s.

Experiments with tree replanting began in the early 1900s, when U.S. timber firms in Central America experimented with planting several commercially valuable hardwood species. Through the 1930s most experiments were initiated by private U.S. companies. Until the burgeoning post-1945 demand for construction timber and paper pulp focused attention on softwoods, most experiments tested various species of hardwoods and softwoods. By the 1950s, only a tiny number of tropical species—slowly growing hardwoods or fast growing softwoods—were known to silviculturists as a species that would grow well in one-species plantations and that were also in high demand on international markets.

The earliest efforts at reforestation may have been made by the Emery Company on its Nicaraguan concession. To comply with a clause in Nicaragua's forestry law (one that was usually ignored), Emery established experimental mahogany stands. The abrupt end of its concession in 1909 ended that effort.[168]

In the late 1920s the United Fruit Company's research center at Tela, Honduras, took up experiments with hardwood reforestation under its first director, Wilson Popenoe. Popenoe made similar sustained efforts at Antigua, Guatemala. By 1960 mature cypress plantations were established on various sites.[169] In the 1950s United Fruit Company also put over 2,000 acres in teak, which had been experimentally introduced from Southeast Asia early in the century. Teak did exceptionally well on its banana plantations near Quepos and Golfito, which were on Costa Rica's Pacific coast, where the seasonally dry climate was similar to that of teak's homeland. The company also experimented with more than twenty other species, including hardwoods from central Africa and India.[170]

United's experiments were the work of its director of tropical research, Vining Dunlap, who like his mentor and predecessor Popenoe took a biologist's interest in tree plantations that went beyond immediate corporate calculations of profitable trade possibilities. In 1950 Dunlap hosted the American forester Hugh Raup on a tour of United's reforestation efforts in Honduras. The work was centered at Tela and especially nearby Lancetilla, where an old natural forest had been long protected because it was the watershed for the town of Tela. Raup praised Dunlap's high-class research team, who had fifty-four species of seedlings under trial, led by mahogany, primavera, cedar, and teak—6,300 acres of teak.[171]

Raup reported that United Fruit had also undertaken the replanting of pine in the hills of Honduras, mostly on old pasture that had been repeatedly burned. The company planted 3,300 acres of pine in 1950 and planned 12,000 more for the following year to prevent fire and grazing. Raup concluded that the project was very successful and had incurred only low costs, but he suggested that the company experiment more with mixed-species plantations, since little was known about which combinations flourished well together.[172]

In these years managed forest or reforestation projects relied on authoritarian controls over peasant subsistence. Dunlap's strategy was to exclude local livestock, prevent fires, and allow natural pine regeneration, allowing reversion toward a more natural forest.[173] When left to itself, the pine forest reseeded very well indeed, and Dunlap was encouraged. In a crucial sense, however, Dunlap's experiment was of limited significance. Pinelands usually supported a heavy peasant population, in contrast to most moist forests. Dunlap could decree an end to grazing local animals on United's land, but on government forestlands the problem was as much social as silvicultural. The reforestation of the southern pinelands in the United States had required a massive public education campaign about the destructive impact of annual fires; a similar effort in Honduras would have been much more difficult. Yet Dunlap did make an important point: the natural biotic processes of recovery could work effectively if the social issues could be successfully addressed.

Working with the sugar company's researchers, in 1960 a team of forest biologists from the research center in Puerto Rico carried out a survey of reforestation work throughout Latin America. The team, headed by Lamb, found a wide variety of multispecies trials that supported efforts to repair or enrich existing forests. In some, foresters and agronomists were encouraging natural regeneration of selectively felled hardwoods like mahogany and Spanish cedar, although little was yet known about the soil and light conditions needed by the hardwood seedlings. The report highlighted the work of the United Fruit Company, whose work it termed "probably the most extensive experimental reforestation in Central America."[174] Investors at company headquarters in Boston, where a rapid return on capital was the standard of value, did not share the interests of the agronomists and foresters. In the 1950s the policy makers for United Fruit ordered the forestry work at Tela to be gradually phased out. Once again corporate priorities—in research as well as marketing—were narrow and shortsighted.[175]

More ominous for the integrity of the rainforest, the corporations began to replace the natural rainforest with pine and eucalyptus tree farms, a trend spurred by rising demand in northern markets for paper products. In the Colombian rainforest in the 1950s Carton de Colombia and its American partner, the Container Corporation of America, were attempting to reduce imports of long-fiber pulp for the local paper industry. Other companies in several countries followed suit, planting several species of pine or eucalyptus, on various soils and various elevations and rainfall patterns.[176]

In Honduras, U.S. consultants aided the expansion and intensification of local pine timber industries. Honduran pine lumber had been shipped from the Miskito coast to timber-starved islands of the Caribbean since the end of the nineteenth century, but large-scale logging operations were constantly threatened by the political turmoil that centered on a long-lasting border dispute between Nicaragua and Honduras. By the mid-1950s other operations had been tried and abandoned, as geographer James Parsons reported: "At present there is no forester, no fire prevention crew, and no inventory of the merchantable timber still standing on this low-lying Caribbean coast of Nicaragua and Honduras. . . . Pine lumbering will soon drop off to insignificant levels." Most of the mature, high quality trees were gone and nothing was being done to foster a new generation.[177]

Surprisingly though, by 1960 coniferous lumber was third in value among the exports of Honduras, behind bananas and coffee. Exports to the Caribbean, which were largely controlled by local firms, were responsible. In addition, by 1960 Honduras was shipping nearly 200,000 cubic meters of mahogany and cedar annually to markets in Europe.[178] But when the International Cooperation Agency sent the forester Virgil Heath to assess the state of Honduran pinelands in 1964, he was aghast at how primitive the country's timber industry still was: "Good forest management practices are completely lacking. Timber sales are made by long term concessions, but evidently once they are made, there is no administration of the sale. Proper silviculture practices are completely ignored. The poor logging practices contribute to an unbelievable waste of timber."[179]

The degraded stands of single species had become highly vulnerable to disease, weakened by the pressure of logging, over-tapping for resin, and annual fires, as Heath reported: "Repeated burning is a way of life in Honduras. . . . Indiscriminate burning is done to kill insects, clear land in a shifting agriculture economy, and to provide grass for cattle. . . . The present beetle epidemic [is] due to an over aged stand of timber continually weakened by fire."[180] In the early 1960s the Honduran pine forests were attacked by a massive infestation of beetles, which killed many thousands of trees. Heath recommended cleanup fellings of old and damaged trees, plus strict regulation of villagers' access to fodder grasses that grew beneath the pines in the open woodlands.

Heath's recommendations made good silvicultural sense, but they provided little hint as to how the Hondurans might go about reconciling local land use with export timber production. Dunlap had been able to remove local users from United Fruit's private lands, but Heath was studying government lands where peasants exercised traditional rights. The next move had to come from Tegucigalpa, but the Honduran government had little effective presence in the remote countryside.[181]

The insatiable demand for profits on international markets continued to grow, and the trend inevitably forced forest managers and development planners to raise fundamental questions. Was the future of tropical forests to be dominated by one-species tree farms? What role should be given to tropical silviculture? For whose benefit should the forests be managed?

TOWARD SUSTAINING BIODIVERSE RAINFORESTS

The term *sustained yield* meant many things to many people, and the debate over sustained yield of tropical forests was highly contentious. The ecologist's meaning—preservation of rainforest ecosystems in all their diversity—was not even a common goal in the first two postwar decades. Crucial research on ecosystem management, such as watershed protection or the social aspects of forest protection, had barely begun. The fledgling research institutes struggled with miniscule budgets, and rainforest ecosystems were so exquisitely complex that it would take years of additional work by forest biologists and ecologists just to develop an adequate taxonomy, or even to standardize terminology for the research, to say nothing of understanding how entire interlocking life systems function.

Until the late 1960s few people, even the best informed, felt any sense of urgency about the threat to the diversity of life in the wet tropics. The natural forest regions of the tropical Americas were still vast, and nearly all development specialists except for a few foresters saw them as the adversary to be conquered. In the greatest rainforest of all, the Amazon basin, extensive permanent field agriculture and large-scale logging were launched only in the late 1950s. Even in Central America, where U.S. fruit growers had made heavy inroads into the forests for commercial cropping and transport infrastructure, the forest zone beyond the plantations was still nearly impenetrable in the 1950s. Leslie Holdridge, who was emerging as the preeminent tropical forest ecologist of his generation, first explored the Sarapiquí rainforest region between Costa Rica's central valley and the banana zone in the early 1950s. He found no paved roads; transport was possible only by small boats along a few rivers. Only a few peasant huts and clearings along the streams interrupted the majestic forest.[182]

Holdridge often stated later that his generation of foresters was too sanguine in their expectation that the forests of Latin America could easily be made to produce abundantly forever. His younger colleague Gerardo Budowski put it more bluntly in 1970, when he looked back on his early years around 1950:

> As a University student in Caracas, I believed, like everyone else—in fact I may even say today that I was "obsessed"—that the greatest potential of my country was in those vast areas of "virgin forests" mapped in solid green that were sparsely settled and just awaited the drive of ambitious government planners to be opened to civilization.[183]

As a young forest biologist in 1940, Holdridge had sketched what was then a novel approach to sustainable rainforest management: he argued that sustainability would be possible only if the fixation on single-species plantations were replaced by locally varied systems of mixed farming and agriculture, taken in part from traditional subsistence farming. In characterizing the vast zone that lay between fertile alluvial lowlands and high mountain slopes, he repeated conventional wisdom:

> This is the zone where land-use evils first come into focus, where the farmers recall the "good old days" of fertile soils, the soil expert frowns at the soil erosion in progress, the forester points out the felling of the forests as the source of the evil, and most all unite in pointing at the system of "conuco" or shifting agriculture as a prime evil which must be abolished at all costs.[184]

A change of far-reaching social and biological priorities required many steps, however. As an alternative approach Holdridge presented the case for what later came to be known as agroforestry or agroecology. He argued that intercultivation, already practiced in several areas, was "the most practical and least expensive of methods for establishing forest plantations."

Holdridge was supported by his senior officer, Arthur Bevan, director of the research station at Río Piedras, who argued in a 1943 article that prevailing approaches to tropical forestry neglected local needs, and thus they would never be sustainable. Despite the denudation of hill forests by peasants struggling for survival throughout the region, "no serious consideration has yet been given to short rotation quick-growing forest crops suitable for fuel, stakes, posts, and other materials needed for local consumption and for the improvement of the standard of living of the peasant or peon class which makes up by far the greater portion of the population of these countries."[185]

Both European and American agronomists and foresters in the Caribbean Basin had begun to introduce the Burmese system of *taungya* in the 1930s, which British foresters in India had been adapting for many years. In the *taungya* system, which evolved in teak forests, local tribals or peasants planted the commercial species, and for the first two to four years they planted their food crops between the rows of teak seedlings. When the tree canopy was dense enough to suppress the understory crops, the workers moved to a new location and repeated the process. Until the 1960s there were only a tiny number of forestry plantations of this sort in the tropical Americas.[186] Challenging the prevailing priorities of his profession, Bevan insisted that the needs of local people must be met first, and only after that should the international markets be considered.

The work of the experiment station at Río Piedras was key in the development of forest management strategies that could protect biological diversity. In close contact with its European counterparts around the Caribbean region, the institute began research on sustained-yield management of commercially accepted species.[187] In Puerto Rico itself the foresters' strategy was to work within the biological structure of existing forests, in part because local markets had always used a wide variety of wood species on a small scale for housing construction, furniture, wagons, boats, and many other purposes.

In 1947, Frank Wadsworth, the future director of the experiment station, surveyed the impact of silviculture in the region. He stressed the need to maintain forests until they could be studied, pointing out that in the rainforest "perpetual cover, mixed composition, and all-aged structure" should be protected. Wadsworth insisted that a complete understanding of the region, including "knowledge of local environments, forest structure and composition, qualities of tree species, and social and economic factors" was essential for silviculture.[188] He charged foresters to encourage the use of all species with any market demand for local and urban use—the article went on to enumerate ninety-eight species.

Wadsworth knew enough about rainforest silviculture to understand its difficulties. He pointed out that there were many problems in this approach: each species was widely dispersed through the forest; it was difficult to supervise cutting; the regeneration of fast-growing light-loving species was rarely successful in shady areas.[189] Moreover, the practice of silviculture was a process of mediation: "Silvicultural practice is a compromise between the biological requirements for optimum future wood production and the economic requirements of the logging industry. This compromise must provide a present yield as well as an improved resource for the future."[190] He could already see the trend toward clear-cutting and one-species plantations, but that would occur with the establishment of large-scale industrial operations and the growth of international markets, especially for pulp and paper products.

An active debate began in the late 1940s in international forestry circles over the relation between tropical forestry and local subsistence. Those who took the issue most seriously saw great virtue in the oldest, least highly monetized and modernized farming systems, those of Indian shifting agriculturists. The debate was inhibited in the 1950s by the rush to modernize the timber export industry.

Forest biologists who were challenging the prevailing assumptions of their profession had some important support from other conservationists from the late 1940s on. In 1947 William Vogt wrote an article in *Unasylva*, the FAO's forestry journal, which in both tone and substance was startlingly at odds with most of what was being written by foresters at the time. Titled "Latin-American Timber, Ltd.," a deliberately indignant pun, Vogt's article began, "Every sector of the human race enjoys—or suffers from—its own superstitions. There are few superstitions as deeply grounded as the belief that Latin America is rich in timber resources."[191] Vogt, who knew the region from Mexico to northern South America as well as any North American of his time, granted that "the region between the Rio Grande and Cape Horn includes one of the greatest remaining extensions of forest," but he reminded his readers that most of that forest grew on steeply sloping lands that were highly susceptible to erosion, had nutrient-deficient soils, or suffered harsh aridity. He calculated that only about 5 percent of Latin America's soils could support intensive agriculture, and most of that was river-bottom alluvium.

Vogt argued that between twenty and forty million Latin Americans were already displaced from their lands, not because of political conflicts but because of terminal land degradation, dating back as far as the early days of the Spanish conquest. He proceeded to describe highland forests that had been stripped to serve the silver mines of colonial Mexico, the woodlands of densely populated El Salvador that had been chopped away for firewood, the highland oak forests of Costa Rica that were being degraded as the new Pan American Highway was being built, the Andean hill forests of Venezuela that had given way to agriculture under Spanish rule. In each case he pointed to the disruption of hydrological systems. Irrigation water in upland Mexico was increasingly scarce. Man-made erosion was crippling the capacity of the Lempa River in Guatemala and El Salvador to provide hydropower. Floods in the Venezuelan Andes were exacerbating the annual flooding of the llanos. And agricultural expansion at the expense of forests on the Andean slopes of southern Chile had led to such soil loss that plans for reforestation were jeopardized.

No other writer of the late 1940s sounded such an urgent alarm. An outsider to the forestry profession, Vogt raised a broad conservation perspective. In the immediate postwar years he was the most trenchant critic of forestry management as well as governmental development policies generally.[192] His writings only obliquely suggested that the political factor of landownership was a source of massive landlessness, but few other North American writers at the time even hinted that tensions between rich and poor were causing ecological stress in Latin America. By and large, Yankee commentators and resource managers simply took for granted the power structures of Latin America—and the ways that North Americans reinforced them—until the late 1960s.

The pioneer critics saw Latin America's natural resources not as a series of separate commodities but as interlocking elements of living systems. This more inclusive view was associated with a greater awareness of how entire societies related to the land. A year before Vogt published his article in *Unasylva*, in 1946, he wrote a more detailed survey of Costa Rica for the Pan American Union in Washington. He noted that because little was known about the lowland rainforests they seemed to have little economic value. He warned that all Central American forests should be managed for multiple use on a long-term sustainable basis. Consistent with his emphasis on the impact of deforestation on hydration systems, he emphasized that forest preservation was vital for watershed protection. He then vehemently stated that a complete lack of trained foresters had led to a total lack of land management. In that void "lumber companies usually have the ethics of pirates and if they can make money quickly will completely disregard the welfare of the land."[193]

There was one ray of hope, Vogt argued, one basis for aggressive action: the fledgling Centro Americano Tropical de Investigación (Interamerican Institute of Agricultural Sciences) at Turrialba, Costa Rica. He urged that CATIE (the acronym by which it came to be internationally known) organize its research and training programs on the basis of interdisciplinary teams composed of a forester, a soils expert, a land-use biologist, a wildlife manager, a hydrologist, a grazing expert, and a specialist in conservation aspects of agricultural extension. He was ahead of his time, but his influence undoubtedly helped to create the position of senior forester at Turrialba, which Holdridge shaped in the following decade.

The debate over the underlying assumptions of tropical forestry blossomed again in the 1960s, centering on the FAO's appointment of the Australian R. F. Watters to study the great variety of shifting agriculture systems in tropical America. Watters's report was a major step toward integrating forestry with social policy.[194] Through such studies as this, awareness of the value of biological diversity and traditional indigenous management systems grew slowly among professional foresters in this period.[195]

An indication of the changing terms of debate among foresters was the FAO's conference on Latin American forestry, held in 1964 in Curitiba, in the heart of Brazil's Paraná pine region.[196] Lengthy discussions of the problems of sustained-yield forestry in various zones led to a set of recommendations to the governments of the Americas. The recommendations stressed the importance of integrating forestry planning with the full spectrum of land use planning for entire countries. In particular, they insisted that the random migrations of squatters and private loggers be controlled to protect viable soils in remaining forest zones.

It was no accident that this meeting was held in Brazil: foresters from across the globe were beginning to be aware that one of history's greatest ecological tragedies, the rampant stripping of Amazonia's forest cover, was underway. Until that time the worst case of tropical deforestation had been in the Philippine Islands, where the forest had been under American forms of management for the first half of the century.

POSTSCRIPT: THE FRONTAL ATTACK ON THE RAINFOREST

From the mid-1960s on there was a rapid global acceleration of markets for tropical timber products, as more economies, led by Japan, gained affluence. The growth of the timber market in Southeast Asia was led by the Philippines, which under American tutelage had developed a timber industry and forestry establishment that were backed by the government and were fully competent to accomplish the rapid reduction of rainforest resources. Could this exploitation possibly be done in such a way that resources could be sustained? PICOP was an encouraging example, but its efforts were limited by its growing dependence on the Philippine government.[197]

The Marcos regime made it extremely difficult for foreign corporations to operate legally and competitively in the Philippines. In the 1970s a few multinational companies operated there, including Georgia-Pacific, Boise-Cascade, International Paper, Weyerhauser, and the largest Japanese competitor, a subsidiary of Mitsubishi.[198] But, all in all, by the 1980s direct U.S. investment in the Philippine timber economy was minimal. The major American connection with deforestation there in recent years has been indirect, taking the form of markets for forest products harvested by Japanese firms in Mindanao and elsewhere and manufactured in Asia for the American market. The connection between the world economy and deforestation in the Philippines remains vital, but it is by no means a simple one.[199]

In Indonesia and Malaysia political stability was not fully established until the 1960s. This delayed major logging operations there until the late 1960s, just as the reduction of Philippine resources became severe. Malaysia and Indonesia were ready to fill the gap. Southeast Asia remained the dominant region for the production of tropical hardwoods and mixed-species pulpwood until the 1990s.

By the 1960s the timber products industry was moving aggressively into the major rainforest zones of Latin America. Rainforests presented far greater challenges for timber operations than did less complex forest ecosystems in less perpetually wet settings. By the early 1960s the industry had accumulated considerable experience, primarily in the banana areas of Central America and Colombia and the pine zone of the Caribbean basin and southern South America.

By then the timber industry's capital, technology, and managerial skill were adequate to confront the enormous challenges of timber extraction and shipment from major rainforests. Large corporations were prepared to clear-cut wide areas and replant them with one-species plantations, if they could gain a political mandate. Governments, steeped in the new ideology of maximum development of forest resources, seemed prepared to grant them large-scale, long-term concessions.

Amazonia was the great challenge for the modern, large-scale, integrated timber products industry. The industry did not penetrate the Amazonian rainforest on a large scale until the 1960s. In the 1950s American firms as well as their European and Japanese counterparts had begun studying how to overcome the almost total lack of economic infrastructure in most of Amazonia, but until the Brazilian government and massive foreign aid began providing it in the 1960s, the largest foreign venture was a veneer and plywood plant built by an American firm near the mouth of the great river near Belém.[200]

In this setting forestry planners were caught in the intensifying tensions among three goals: short-run acceleration of timber yields, sustained-yield timber management, and conserving rainforest ecosystems as a biologically diverse whole. The mainstream of American forestry practice had not prepared its men adequately to meet this challenge. In 1989 two experts on the subject, Louise Fortmann and Sally Fairfax, offered a critique of American forestry.

> [I]ts primary tenet is a commitment to technical expertise as the goal and criterion for public and private decision making. From it arise three other principles: (1) the tenet of large scale, comprehensive government planning for resource management; (2) the related doctrine emphasizing fibre production for commercial operators; and (3) the view of forestry as a predominantly biological undertaking.[201]

Most foresters, they argued, believe that since resource management is primarily a technical problem, experts (not politicians or local people) should make the decisions: "[N]on-professionals are not considered to be foresters or managers. . . . The forester recognises neither the local user's knowledge about local conditions nor his/her definition of the resource and priorities concerning its management."[202] In their bias toward biology, and specifically trees, they overlook the social and political institutions that shape their work. They find Third World property systems obscure and confusing, and they prefer private or government control.

The consensus described by Fortmann and Fairfax was beginning to be challenged in an intensifying debate within international forestry circles over the ultimate goals of their work. Gill and other American foresters working in the tropics after the war were among the first to raise the issues of the debate. They charged that the Forest Service as a whole, and the higher authorities in Washington whom it served, had been unwilling to pay much attention to tropical forestry and resource management. Gill had been frustrated for many years about the general indifference of American foresters working in the United States to developments in the rest of the world, especially the tropics. In 1948 he launched the International Society of Tropical Foresters, running it virtually single-handedly from his home in Washington. By 1960 its membership had passed three hundred and included nearly every name of any importance in tropical forestry. Several American members in Latin America represented U.S. corporations, including United Fruit in Honduras and Champion Paper in southern Brazil. A large number of Latin Americans were also members by that time, as were many nationals of India and Southeast Asia.[203] The list included officers of private-sector corporations and foresters in the employ of governments and international agencies.

In 1960 the U.S. government and the U.S. timber industry offered for the first time to host the World Forestry Congress, inviting the world's foresters to Seattle for the organization's fifth meeting. Several American members of the International Society of Tropical Foresters had lobbied hard for this support. Gill chaired the planning subcommittee on problems of tropical forestry. In a plenary address to the congress, he commented that for American forestry, this was the belated end of a "trail of indecisive detours and bewildering back-trackings." By hosting the conference, the U.S. forestry community had set "the official seal of approval" on "America's participation in international forestry."[204]

In the Pacific, the international network of foresters had been institutionalized through the forestry division of the Pacific Science Association. The association, founded in Honolulu in 1920, held triennial conferences in cities around the Pacific, giving scientists in many fields the opportunity to develop together international agendas of research and policy planning. The forestry division was established almost immediately after 1920. Its agenda covered the laws and technology of tropical timber extraction, concern about sustained-yield timber management, and concern about the damage to watersheds caused by prevailing logging technology. American foresters in Hawaii made an important contribution to the forestry division's agenda. These men had pioneered the work of government forest services in watershed preservation and management in the Hawaiian Islands, working in conjunction with the Hawaiian Sugar Planters' Association. For them, the practice of forestry was intended to be economically profitable and environmentally stabilizing.

This pattern was equally evident at the Tenth Pacific Science Congress in 1961 in Honolulu. Revived in 1949 after a wartime paralysis, its congresses continued the prewar tradition of comparing the latest technology of tropical timber management and debating the development priorities of government policies. At the Honolulu congress the Standing Committee on Forestry described its broadening research agenda for tropical forests, which included strategies of natural regeneration of tropical forests and the particularly difficult challenge of reforesting logged areas that had become dominated by Imperata grass.[205] This agenda did not address the preservation of tropical forest ecosystems for their biodiversity or their contribution to controlling global atmospheric warming—these overarching issues began to be of concern to specialists and the public only in the early 1970s. The agenda of the science congress was, however, moving toward that more inclusive scope.

Together, concerned foresters and their conservationist allies in other fields faced an enormous task of slowing down the attack on the world's tropical forests. On one front was the steady incursion of subsistence farming and local agricultural industry, which supplied crops and meat to a rapidly expanding population in tropical countries. On the other front was the aggressive corporate agricultural industry, which exported monocrops to markets in ever more affluent North America.[206]

By 1970 the record of tropical forestry represented seven decades of work by a tiny handful of men who had produced only a deeply ambiguous achievement. They had created a system of science and management dedicated in principle to the sustained yield of forest resources, but, in so doing, they had participated in a wider process that unleashed the forces of technological and corporate power in the rainforest, power that was backed by a development ideology that saw the exploitation of tropical resources largely in terms of short-range payoffs. The science of tropical timber management had grown out of experience in relatively simple temperate forest ecosystems. Sustaining the yield of marketable commodities from the fragile cornucopia of the tropical forest was far harder to achieve.

Conclusion

The Ecological Cost of the American
Appetite in the Tropical World

The arrival of man has invariably increased . . . the degree
of instability in these [eco]systems. With the advent of modern man this increase has frequently assumed catastrophic
proportions.

F. R. Fosberg, 1963

In 1914 the gigantic, newly completed Panama Canal stood as the em-
bodiment of the American venture of speculation, technocracy, consumption, and strategic power in the tropics. The first ship that passed
through its enormous locks that summer seemed to confirm to the American public that their civilization could accomplish any task it chose,
anywhere in the world, no matter what the scale. Although decadent
and corrupt Europe had failed to sever the Central American isthmus,
they believed that no task of conquering tropical Nature was too great
for Yankee ingenuity, determination, and integrity, backed by the rising
power of Washington.[1]

The great cut was fifty miles long; it had taken ten years to build, at
a cost of $352 million, with a work force totaling hundreds of
thousands. More than 6,000 workers died from disease and accidents,
but new discoveries in tropical medicine had virtually eradicated malaria
and yellow fever from the Canal Zone. Engineers had created the largest
structure of the industrial age; planners and managers had overcome
organizational problems of unprecedented complexity, coordinating
several thousand different firms. Yet the canal was completed within
budget and six months ahead of schedule.

The locks themselves had taken four years to create out of more than
4.4 million cubic yards of ferroconcrete; no other structure equaled that

amount until Boulder Dam was constructed more than fifteen years later. Twelve chambers, each 110 feet by 1,000 feet, were built, using five million sacks and barrels of portland cement shipped from New York. The concrete was mixed with sand and gravel; the sand was found first on the San Blas Islands, ninety miles east of Colón on the Caribbean coast, but in one small victory against Progress, local Indians prevented the builders from desecrating their shoreline.

Filling and then emptying the locks required immense amounts of water, so the engineers dammed the Chagres River to create Gatun Lake, turning peninsulas into islands and eliminating rainforest and rural communities from entire valleys and mountainsides. They transformed an entire region of tropical Panama to meet the requirements of a global network of trade and security, which the United States would dominate only five years later, after Europe's imperial regimes met on the battlefields of northern France and wore each other down.

In the long perspective from the century's end, a skeptical interpretation of the consequences of the American ecological imperium might convey a starkly unambiguous assessment of the damage that resulted from the ventures launched by Yankee entrepreneurs. This view holds that until the advent of the modern global trading system, all of Nature's unfathomable complexity and exuberance was embraced by the virgin forests; now monocrop plantations, farmsteads, ranches, and tree farms scar tropical lands. According to this view, corporate America has been the greatest driving force in this accelerating biotic impoverishment, leading to the loss of species and the destabilization of soils and cropping systems. Only intensive use of agrochemicals could temporarily stabilize the production of agricultural commodities. Tribal and peasant communities that had lived harmoniously on the land were dispossessed and transformed into wage labor forces; they were often moved far from their ancestral homes to locales of which they had no knowledge. These populations were reduced to poverty in the service of northern affluence and induced to damage natural systems for their own survival. The skeptical view frames this record as a morality tale for the new millennium. Villains and victims are clearly defined, but according to this view, the story may yet conclude with a healing alliance between oppressed people and crippled Nature.

How adequate is this image in the light of the historical record? Not entirely adequate, surely, because it suffers from several limitations. For one, the image of pristine tropical Nature submitting to Yankee entrepreneurship and technocracy borrows from the American myth of wilderness, which assumes that unexplored lands are empty of people. In reality, tropical forests had supported human settlement and undergone concomitant biotic change for ten thousand years or more. The change resulted from the establishment of swidden fields, peasant farms, and towns along the rivers. Moreover, money economies had partially transformed rural lands into pastures and fields for commodity production. Many years later, it is now often difficult to determine how radically the natural systems of the tropical forest had been transformed when the first Americans arrived to begin their work.

Second, early American entrepreneurs in the tropics encountered the always complex and sometimes paradoxical legacy of 400 years of European interaction with local populations. When the United Fruit Company began purchasing forest acreage on the Caribbean coasts of Panama and Costa Rica, its managers found few people living there. The indigenous Indians had already been forced out by raiding Miskitos from the Nicaraguan coast; they in turn were instigated by British schemers on a remote, obscure fringe of London's empire. A quarter century later, when Firestone negotiated its million-acre contract in Liberia, it became entangled with an intricate rural mix of local ethnic groups and re-immigrant American Africans; the second-growth vegetation that Firestone cleared for its rubber plantations had already experienced multicropping, managed fires, and human settlement. Similarly, in the Sumatran rainforest Goodyear found Malay farmers and Batak tribal communities competing for the use of forest resources. For six centuries and more, even before the Portuguese and Dutch appeared in the Strait of Malacca, Chinese traders had bargained for Sumatran products at the place where the rows of rubber trees would ultimately grow.

Third, transformations from subsistence farming into capitalist agriculture and integration into international networks dominated by Europeans or Americans entailed the willing cooperation of national elites who profited mightily and consolidated their control over both societies and landscapes. Central American dictators and Filipino landlords alike prospered from the alliance. Fourth, a few biotic transformations that resulted from the Yankee's century in the tropics now seem to be relatively stable; their crops are growing productively in juxtaposition to locally consumed products and natural areas, and their pests and predators are controlled by biological means and multicropping strategies.

However, when all this is said, there remains an irreducible core of truth in this critique of the Yankee adventure. American initiatives created, supported, or refined a wide spectrum of extraction systems. On one end was the total (and in hindsight, reckless) elimination of natural systems in favor of single crops such as sugar, bananas, and rubber, which yielded maximum profits on volatile international markets. On the other were the patchworks of multicrop peasant plots in Colombia and parts of Central America and smallholder rubber farms in Southeast Asia. In the process, these forces transformed entire societies and state systems. In competitive cooperation with fledgling national regimes, the Americans penetrated regions that local governments had dreamed of dominating but had neither the capital, the concentrated labor force, nor the industrial technology to achieve by themselves. Together the two forces transformed tribal, peasant, and former slave populations into farm and factory wage labor forces. Moreover, especially in the case of bananas, if productivity or profitability declined or crop disease dictated, big Yankee investors simply abandoned their lands and moved away, leaving unemployed workers to improvise a frayed patchwork of subsistence cropping, in the midst of neglected areas reverting to secondary woodlands.

The appetites of affluent Europeans and then Americans provided the engine of consumption that pulled tropical resources north. Cane sugar raised their calorie intake and sweetened their increasingly processed diets. Bananas provided novelty and nourishment. Coffee fueled their industrial energies and provided sociability. Rubber gave them precious mobility and military might. Beef imparted social prestige and hearty suppers. The production areas south of the Hispanic border and across the Pacific guaranteed lower prices for American consumers, even for commodities like sugar and beef, which could be produced in temperate climates as well. In sum, the American consumer economy blossomed by drawing on and reducing the abundance of tropical Nature in many parts of Latin America, the Pacific basin, and beyond.

The northern world developed many appetites: consumers' appetite for products; advertisers' eagerness to create those appetites; executives' and shareholders' hunger for profits; speculators' passion for conquest and power; governments' reach for hegemony over sources of goods; and tropical elites' appetite for power and control of peripheral regions within their domains. The appetite that was at all environmentally supportive was the biologists' search for crop viability—in the right hands it could lead in the direction of stability.

In the beginning the American appetite was for conquest: conquest of precapitalist social relations, land tenure systems, and cultures; conquest of unruly, underexploited tropical Nature itself. In two centuries of the preimperial era, maritime traders from Boston to Savanna imported sugar and then coffee, gaining knowledge of the tropical crops that would sell in their northern homeland.

Then came the filibusters in the mid-nineteenth century. Many were social misfits, outside the law wherever they went as they attempted to carve out petty kingdoms around the Caribbean basin. The United States had begun to export not just its manufactured goods but its social pressures as well.

The decisive, formative era of the American ecological empire was ushered in by the naval victories of 1898. Some had staked out their estates even earlier. After 1898 a host of land speculators moved beyond the merchants and adventurers into direct control and management of tropical landscapes. Zemurray, Firestone, and other corporate planters created sugar, banana, and rubber plantations. Corporate ranchers like Hearst raised or purchased cattle. Lumbermen extracted the finest mahogany trees, opening the forest to further penetration. The agrocorporate investors hired a spectrum of engineers and managers to implement their dreams of conquest and transformation. None of them understood the complexity and fragility of tropical Nature; few were even cautious enough to suspect the grave dangers of their ignorance.

Corporate competition led time and again to consolidation of the estates into fewer and larger units, as the producing and marketing giants integrated their complex routes that led from the points of production to the consumers' households. The New York banks, the Sugar Trust, the New York Coffee Exchange, and the great octopus, United Fruit, led the way toward centralization of power and profits in their various spheres. During the first half of the twentieth century, and in many ways even up to the present, their strategic production and marketing decisions were made in terms of competitive success in the metropolis, not social or environmental viability in the tropics.

Ironically, most of the great corporate estates were created in countries that were not under colonial American administration. Nonetheless, the American agroimport companies were the environmental spearheads of the nation's system of successful sustained competition with Europe. The companies were supported, although sometimes reluctantly, by the U.S. government's military, diplomatic, and overseas commercial agencies. The web of American power shaped tropical governments, societies, and landscapes in the process of extracting profitable commodities. Even domestic U.S. politics had widespread impacts on tropical lands. The most prominent example is tariff laws and import quotas, passed with little reference to their consequences for land use beyond American borders.

In order to create a labor force to reshape tropical lands, the companies and their counterparts among the local elite organized an unprecedented intercontinental movement of Africans, Asians, Latin Americans, and southern Europeans. The transformations of tropical ecosystems were linked to ethnic disruption and mixing and, consequently, the intensification of ethnic consciousness on a vast scale. In the process these migrants gained money, skills, literacy, medical improvements and often a new class-consciousness. Labor resistance began to erupt, led by workers such as Papa Isio in Negros, Sandino in Nicaragua, and Martí in El Salvador.

After World War II the entire system of extracting tropical crops became much more institutionalized and intensive. Host governments slowly increased their administrative effectiveness and capacity to influence the work of foreign corporations. First the booming markets in the United States, then the recovered economies in West Europe and Japan, as well as massive domestic markets in large tropical countries such as Brazil and Mexico, all contributed to the pressure. Advances in science and technology reinforced the accelerating trend, including many technical efforts toward intensification or stabilization of commodity production, profits, labor management, and land management. The science of tropical agronomy produced more productive and hardier varieties of major crops. The most dramatic improvements were made to natural rubber; moreover, no other tropical crop elicited such close cooperation between government and industry.

Rubber and oil intersected. Petroleum's promise as the core resource for the good life had complex ecological ramifications. These included the new dominance of synthetic rubber, which reduced market pressure on natural rubber. On the other hand, although petroleum-based fertilizers and pesticides increased the yield of market crops, they did so at heavy social and environmental costs.

Even the Cold War cast its shadow on the exploitation of tropical wealth. New agencies of governmental development aid, such as the U.S.-led Alliance for Progress and international agencies such as the World Bank and the United Nations Food and Agriculture Organization contributed to the ideology of rapid growth. American bilateral alliances for the anti-Communist struggle reinforced U.S. penetration of tropical resource areas in many countries including Guatemala, El Salvador, Nicaragua, Cuba, and the Philippines. As Cuba demonstrated, Yankee strategic and ecological hegemony could not always be maintained.

Workers' ability to organize and challenge their masters grew, not just on the plantations but as a major element of society in general. Hawaiian Japanese sugar workers, Central American banana plantation workers, and many of Fidel Castro's supporters all emerged from scenes of corporate agriculture to lead the labor movement in their countries. Their agendas focused on financial issues, working conditions, and health safety. Only health safety was an environmental issue in any direct way.

As for the tropical lands themselves, by the 1960s some were degraded almost beyond recognition, whereas others had been turned to agricultural lands that were sustained artificially with petrochemicals, which intensified pollution of soil and streams and eliminated an unmeasured spectrum of living species. One form of stabilization, crop diversification, was emerging, although that trend was more often motivated by volatile market factors than by knowledge of what would assure biological stability.

Among the foresters engaged in extracting tropical resources before the 1970s, only a few argued that some forests should remain basically as they were. Even most of those men sanguinely thought they could harvest timber products without reducing the forest ecosystems beyond biotic recognition. In the late 1940s a few prophetic voices—Tom Gill, Leslie Holdridge, Frank Wadsworth—began to warn that tropical Nature could not be treated so cavalierly and, moreover, that local people's needs and priorities must be addressed alongside market demands from the North, if agroecological systems were to be sustained.

This study ends in the 1960s, when a new era of environmental management began to emerge, both within the United States and internationally. Tropical forest protection gained increased support in the 1970s, as American government agencies became much more active in promoting environmentally alert management programs, working through the U.S. Forest Service's international office, the Peace Corps forestry program, and the Agency for International Development.

Research into sustainable tropical agroecology strategies also emerged that emphasized biological controls of plant diseases and integrated pest management systems. Organic farming networks defended older ways of weeding and fertilizing. Research centers, frequently supported by private foundations, built upon the field knowledge of men like Paul Standley and Richard Schultes. Agricultural universities slowly expanded these lines of research, although that ran against the long-dominant influence of corporate agriculture. A few corporations, both agricultural and pharmaceutical, joined the effort to produce genuinely sustainable tropical farm crops and forest products in the tradition of Wilson Popenoe and Vining Dunlap, at least in instances where environmentally benign production could be profitable.

In the 1960s the American environmental movement also began to stress the importance of international and tropical issues on its lobbying and educational agendas. This reflected a new infusion of awareness through linkages with political campaigners who opposed American global power; they in turn began to identify environmental issues as vital to their agendas. Among wildlife conservationists, this represented the dawning of an understanding that tropical Nature cannot be successfully defended except through strategic links with local populations in every location—a massive organizing agenda. The converse of that work, the campaign against environmentally indiscriminate consumerism, is only now beginning to emerge. In the end, one must wonder: can any story be told satisfactorily when its resolution is not yet known and its portent for the future is so uncertain? This global struggle has no neat Aristotelian plot, with a clear catharsis for the audience at the end of the evening; indeed, there are ominous portents. We now share the earth and seas with those who administer the Global Agreement on Trade and Tariffs and the World Trade Organization—this is an era of global free trade dominated by great corporations. There is something close to a consensus among policy-making elites that rapid material and capital expansion, and tighter integration of the world economy, constitute the route to a better future. In that climate voices which warn of dangerous environmental consequences are marginalized.

This book cannot attempt to engage that debate directly, yet it suggests a few conclusions from the historical record. The era prior to the introduction of intensive chemical agriculture was in many ways less ecologically destructive, even in concentrated monocrop plantations, than the subsequent era of agrochemicals. During our century, over a wide spectrum of situations, smallholder production was more species-varied and socially equitable, if not more environmentally stable, than corporate monocropping. In some instances, when agricultural corporations used their powerful research facilities to diversify cropping systems in specific locations and to adopt biologically benign inputs, the resulting crops were both profitable and genuinely sustainable. This was all too rare. Even now, as long as corporate Free Trade is ascendant, and as long as little heed is paid to its ecological consequences, the health of the tropical world is gravely endangered.

Appendix

Map 1. West Indies: Lesser Antilles

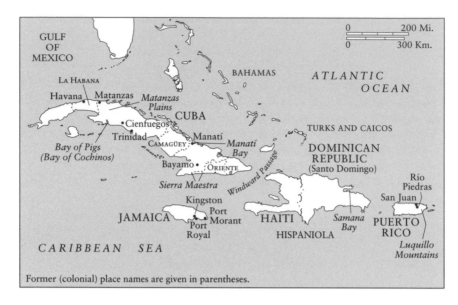

Map 2. West Indies: Greater Antilles

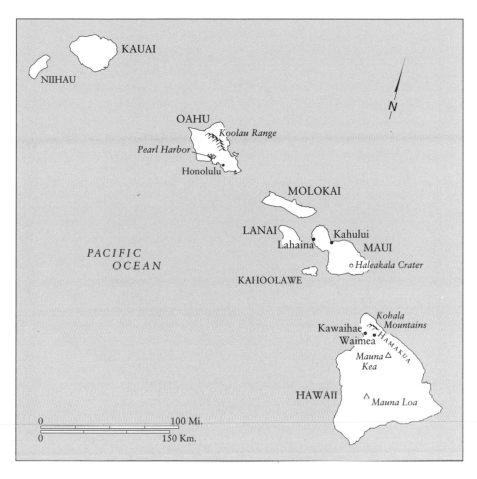

KAUAI

NIIHAU

OAHU

Koolau Range

Pearl Harbor

Honolulu

MOLOKAI

LANAI

Kahului

Lahaina

MAUI

PACIFIC
OCEAN

o Haleakala Crater

KAHOOLAWE

Kohala
Mountains

Kawaihae

HAMAKUA

Waimea

Mauna △
Kea

HAWAII

△ Mauna Loa

0   100 Mi.

0   150 Km.

Map 3. Hawaii: The Eight Major Islands

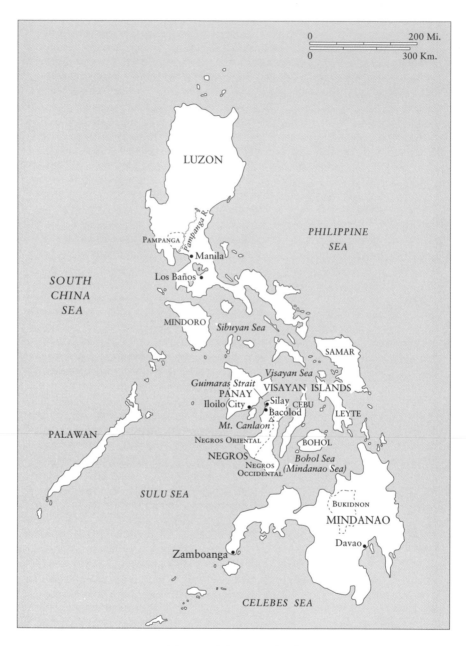

Map 4. Philippine Islands

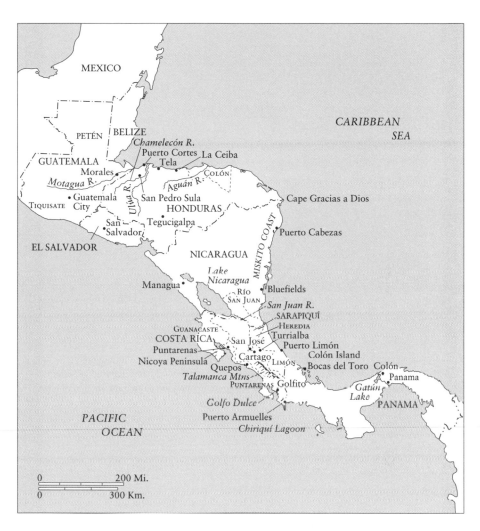

MEXICO

CARIBBEAN
SEA

PETÉN · BELIZE
Chamelecón R.
Puerto Cortes · La Ceiba
GUATEMALA · Tela
Morales · COLÓN
Motagua R. · Aguán R.
· Guatemala · San Pedro Sula · Cape Gracias a Dios
TIQUISATE City · HONDURAS
San · Tegucigalpa
·Salvador
EL SALVADOR · Puerto Cabezas

NICARAGUA

Lake
Nicaragua
Managua · Río · ·Bluefields
SAN JUAN
San Juan R.
·SARAPIQUÍ
HEREDIA
GUANACASTE · Turrialba
COSTA RICA · ·San José · Puerto Limón
Puntarenas · Cartago · Colón Island
Nicoya Peninsula · LIMÓN · ·Bocas del Toro · Colón
Quepos · Panama
Talamanca Mtns · Gatún
PUNTARENAS · Golfito · Lake
PANAMA
Golfo Dulce
PACIFIC · Puerto Armuelles
OCEAN · Chiriquí Lagoon

0   200 Mi.
0   300 Km.

Map 5. Central America

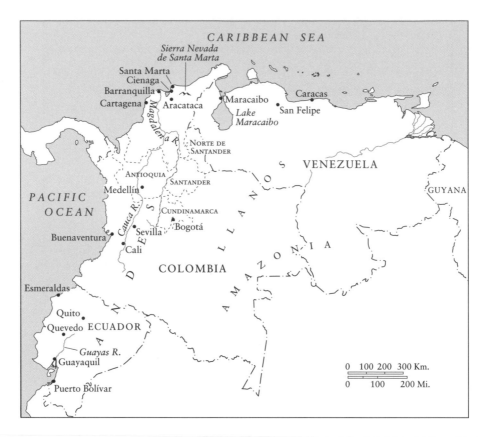

Map 6. Ecuador, Colombia, and Venezuela

Map 7. *Brazil, Uruguay, and Argentina*

Former (colonial) place names are given in parentheses.

Map 8. Indonesia and Malaya

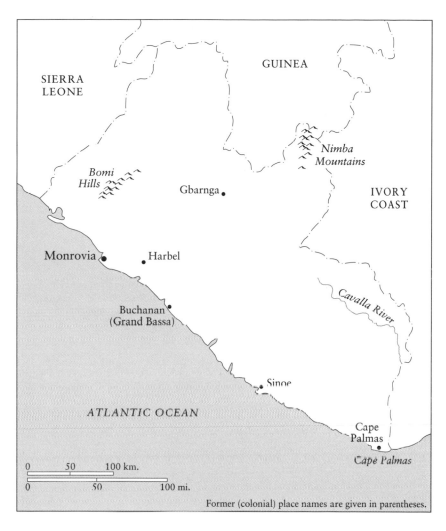

SIERRA
LEONE

GUINEA

Nimba
Mountains

Bomi
Hills

Gbarnga

IVORY
COAST

Monrovia

Harbel

Buchanan
(Grand Bassa)

Cavalla River

Sinoe

ATLANTIC OCEAN

Cape
Palmas

Cape Palmas

0   50   100 km.

0   50   100 mi.

Former (colonial) place names are given in parentheses.

Map 9. Liberia

Map 10. Mexico

Notes

INTRODUCTION

1. From the first page on it is impossible to overcome the trap of an imperial language which history has set for us. Although the term *America* is properly usable for anyone in South and North America, it has been appropriated in the English language to refer to the United States. By *American* I will mean North American, or more precisely someone from the United States. I shall use it interchangeably with *Yankee* or *gringo* when the context invites the more brash or more pejorative terms, especially in regard to Latin America.

2. I use the geographical or ecological term *tropics* very loosely in this account, to mean roughly the region between the Tropics of Cancer and Capricorn. The term encompasses a vast variety of biotic settings: wet regions and arid, mountains and flatlands and coastal zones, and the monsoon belt with its oscillation between wet and dry seasons. Together they have been the heartland of the Western empires. Refinements and extensions in my use of the term will appear in each chapter. I will use *tropical America* and *the American tropics* as geographical terms for the tropical zone of the New World as a whole.

3. The few recent environmental historians bold enough to attempt something approaching global overviews encompassing the past half millennium include Alfred W. Crosby, Jr., *The Columbian Exchange: Biological and Cultural Consequences of 1492* (Westport, Conn.: Greenwood Press, 1972); Alfred W. Crosby, Jr., *Ecological Imperialism* (Cambridge: Cambridge University Press, 1986); Donald Worster, "The Vulnerable Earth: Toward a Planetary History," in Donald Worster, ed., *The Ends of the Earth* (Cambridge: Cambridge University Press, 1988), 3–20; and Clive Ponting, *A Green History of the World: The Environment and the Collapse of Great Civilizations* (New York: Penguin, 1993). A new generation of important syntheses by John McNeill, Elinor Melville, John Richards, Michael Williams and others will be appearing shortly.

4. For this fledgling field of analysis, see for example Fernand Braudel, *The Structures of Everyday Life: The Limits of the Possible,* vol. 1 of *Civilization and Capitalism, 15th–18th Century* (New York: Harper and Row, 1979); Neil McKendrick, John Brewer, and J. H. Plumb, *The Birth of a Consumer Society: The Commercialization of Eighteenth Century England* (London: Europa Publications; Bloomington: Indiana University Press, 1982); Joan Thirsk, *Economic Policy and Projects: The Development of a Consumer Society in Early Modern England* (Oxford: Oxford University Press, 1978).

5. William Cronon, *Nature's Metropolis: Chicago and the Great West* (New York: Norton, 1991).

6. For broad trends in American consumerism, see for example Neva R. Goodwin, Frank Ackerman, and David Kiron, eds., *The Consumer Society* (Washington: Island Press, 1997); Daniel Horowitz, *The Morality of Spending: Attitudes toward the Consumer Society in America, 1875–1940* (Baltimore: Johns Hopkins University Press, 1985); William Leach, *Land of Desire: Merchants, Power, and the Rise of a New American Culture* (New York: Pantheon Books, 1993); Stanley Lebergott, *Pursuing Happiness: American Consumers in the Twentieth Century* (Princeton: Princeton University Press, 1993); William Leuchtenburg, *A Troubled Feast: American Society since 1945* (Boston: Little, Brown, 1973); Susan Strasser, *Satisfaction Guaranteed: The Making of the Mass Market* (New York: Pantheon Books, 1989); Richard S. Tedlow, *New and Improved: The Story of Mass Marketing in America* (New York: Basic Books, 1990).

7. Numerous studies of the postwar years are relevant. For example, social critics such as Leuchtenburg, *A Troubled Feast;* David Halberstam, *The Fifties* (New York: Villard Books, 1993); and Christopher Lasch, *Culture of Narcissism* (New York: Norton, 1978) discuss the shapes and consequences of the cultural changes expressed in mass consumerism. Economic historians have quantified the rising amounts of specific commodities absorbed by the American economy in those years. One source that is particularly relevant to this study is Joseph Grunwald and Philip Musgrove, *Natural Resources in Latin American Development* (Baltimore: Johns Hopkins Press, 1970). Occasionally a writer combines both roles. J. K. Galbraith, *The Affluent Society* (New York: New American Library, 1958) comes to mind. But none of them makes sustained explicit connections to the processes of social and environmental change at the sources of these commodities. The present study is only a beginning of that effort, since it centers more on environmental change at the tropical sources of American imports.

8. For glimpses into that tradition, see G. B. Masefield, *A History of the Colonial Agricultural Service* (Oxford: Clarendon Press, 1972); Richard Grove, *Green Imperialism: Colonial Expansion, Tropical Island Edens and the Origins of Environmentalism, 1600–1860* (Oxford: Oxford University Press, 1995).

CHAPTER 1. AMERICA'S SWEET TOOTH

1. For a fuller analysis of the key role of cane sugar in the rise of the modern world system, see the eloquent exposition in Sidney W. Mintz, *Sweetness and Power: The Place of Sugar in Modern History* (New York: Viking, 1985).

2. Gordon Wrigley, *Tropical Agriculture: The Development of Production* (New York: Praeger, 1969).

3. For complete detail, see G. C. Stevenson, *Genetics and Breeding of Sugar Cane* (London: Longmans Green, 1965).

4. Andrew Watson, *Agricultural Innovation in the Early Islamic World* (Cambridge: Cambridge University Press, 1983).

5. Anthony Reid, "Humans and Forests in Pre-Colonial Southeast Asia," *Environment and History* 1 (1995): 93–110.

6. Braudel, *The Structures of Everyday Life*, 224–227; Mintz, 74–138.

7. Noel Deerr, *The History of Sugar*, 2 vols. (London: Chapman and Hall, 1949–50); J. H. Galloway, *The Sugar Cane Industry: An Historical Geography from Its Origins to 1914* (Cambridge: Cambridge University Press, 1989), chaps. 3–7.

8. For a succinct survey of that link, see W. R. Aykroyd, *Sweet Malefactor: Sugar, Slavery and Human Society* (London: Heinemann, 1967).

9. Crosby, *Ecological Imperialism*, 79–103.

10. James J. Parsons, "Human Influences on the Pine and Laurel Forests of the Canary Islands," *Geographical Review* 71:3 (July 1981): 253–271.

11. Stuart B. Schwartz, *Sugar Plantations in the Formation of Brazilian Society: Bahia, 1550–1835* (Cambridge: Cambridge University Press, 1985); Peter L. Eisenberg, *The Sugar Industry in Pernambuco, 1840–1910: Modernization without Change* (Berkeley: University of California Press, 1974), chaps. 1–2; Warren Dean, *With Broadax and Firebrand: The Destruction of the Brazilian Atlantic Forest* (Berkeley: University of California Press, 1995).

12. Wrigley, 205–210.

13. Schwartz, chap. 5. For the Caribbean plantation system see George L. Beckford, *Persistent Poverty: Underdevelopment in Plantation Economies of the Third World* (Oxford: Oxford University Press, 1972).

14. Charles R. Boxer, *The Dutch Seaborne Empire: 1600–1800* (New York: Knopf, 1970).

15. For a broad history of the Caribbean since 1492, which discusses the political economy of sugar in detail, see Eric Williams, *From Columbus to Castro: The History of the Caribbean, 1492–1969* (New York: Harper & Row, 1970).

16. Crosby, *The Columbian Exchange*, 68–69.

17. See the classic study of island biogeography, R. H. MacArthur and E. O. Wilson, *The Theory of Island Biogeography* (Princeton: Princeton University Press, 1967).

18. Robert C. West and John P. Augelli, *Middle America: Its Lands and Peoples*, 2d ed. (Englewood Cliffs, N.J.: Prentice-Hall, 1976), 61–63.

19. For the rise of Amsterdam, see Simon Schama, *The Embarrassment of Riches: Amsterdam in the Golden Age* (New York: Knopf, 1987); and Boxer, *The Dutch Seaborne Empire*.

20. Grove, *Green Imperialism*, 68.

21. David Watts, *The West Indies: An Environmental History* (Cambridge: Cambridge University Press, 1987), 176–211.

22. Watts, 219.

23. Watts, 219–223.

24. Grove, 67–70.

25. J. S. Beard, *The Natural Vegetation of the Windward and Leeward Islands,* Oxford Forestry Memoirs (Oxford: Clarendon Press, 1949), 31–33.

26. Watts, 216–217, 281–292.

27. Philip Curtin, *Two Jamaicas: The Role of Ideas in a Tropical Colony, 1830–1865* (Cambridge, Mass.: Harvard University Press, 1955), 19–22.

28. Early colonial efforts at resource conservation began in the 1700s on this and other similar tropical islands. See Grove.

29. Curtin, 110–118.

30. Sydney Haldane Olivier, *Jamaica, The Blessed Island* (London: Faber and Faber, n.d. [1935?]), 311–312.

31. Olivier, 312–313.

32. Curtin, 11, 19–22.

33. R. W. Logan, *Haiti and the Dominican Republic* (London: Oxford University Press, 1968).

34. For the cumulative impact on vegetation cover, see Leslie R. Holdridge, "The Pine Forests of Haiti," *Caribbean Forester* 4:1 (1942): 16–21; Schiller Nicolas, "Forestry and Forest Resources in Haiti," *Caribbean Forester* 1:2 (1940): 7–9, and 1:3 (1940): 16–22. See also Harold A. Wood, *Northern Haiti: Land, Land Use, and Settlement* (Toronto: University of Toronto Press, 1963). Gerald Murray, in "The Evolution of Haitian Peasant Land Tenure: A Case Study in Agrarian Adaptation to Population Growth" (Ph.D. diss., Columbia University, 1977), points to another cause, intensive hardwood logging by foreign companies in the 1800s. For the sobering recent picture, see Laurence A. Lewis and William J. Coffey, "The Continuing Deforestation of Haiti," *AMBIO* 14:3 (1985): 158–160. Martinique is another, smaller French island for which the ecological consequences of sugar and other export crops have been studied in detail. See Clarissa Therese Kimber, *Martinique Revisited: The Changing Plant Geographies of a West Indian Island* (College Station: Texas A&M University Press, 1988).

35. Smith, *The Forests of Cuba*, 12.

36. The following description is derived from West and Augelli, 131–147.

37. This account will omit tobacco, Cuba's other great commercial crop. Although tobacco has consistently been Cuba's second most important export, and although American markets were central until Fidel Castro came to power in 1959, tobacco was never more than 5 percent of Cuba's total exports by value. Even at its height it was vastly overshadowed by sugar in both acreage and value.

38. For a detailed analysis of Cuba's soils, see Hugh H. Bennett, *The Soils of Cuba* (Washington, D.C.: Tropical Plant Research Foundation, 1928).

39. West and Augelli, 115–118.

40. West and Augelli, 121.

41. Allan J. Kuethe, "Havana in the Eighteenth Century," in *Atlantic Port Cities: Economy, Culture, and Society in the Atlantic World, 1650–1850,* ed. Franklin W. Knight and Peggy K. Liss (Knoxville: University of Tennessee Press, 1991), 13.

42. John R. McNeill, *Atlantic Empires of France and Spain: Louisbourg and Havana, 1700–1763* (Chapel Hill: University of North Carolina Press, 1985), 132–133, 173–176.

43. Kuethe, 33.

44. Leland H. Jenks, *Our Cuban Colony: A Study in Sugar* (New York: Vanguard Press, 1928), 23.

45. Richard Pares, *Yankees and Creoles: The Trade between North America and the West Indies before the American Revolution* (Cambridge, Mass.: Harvard University Press, 1956), 92–121; Samuel Eliot Morison, *The Maritime History of Massachusetts, 1783–1860* (Boston: Houghton Mifflin, 1941); and McNeill. For the intricate commercial politics which linked New England with London and the West Indies, see Bernard Bailyn, *The New England Merchants in the Seventeenth Century* (New York: Harper and Row, 1955).

46. For the role of the British Navy, see Robert G. Albion, *Forests and Sea Power* (Cambridge, Mass.: Harvard University Press, 1926). Graeme Wynn, *Timber Colony* (Toronto: University of Toronto Press, 1981), tells the story of the forest clearance of New Brunswick. Richard W. Judd, *Maine, the Pine Tree State, from Prehistory to the Present* (Orono: University of Maine Press, 1995), surveys the similar impact on the forests of Maine.

47. McNeill, 15–16, 106–113. Farley Mowat, Canada's most eloquent chronicler of the colonial European mentality, has described the staggering depletion of the North Atlantic's fishing resources in that era. Farley Mowat, *Sea of Slaughter* (Boston: Atlantic Monthly Press, 1984).

48. Linda K. Salvucci, "Supply, Demand, and the Making of a Market: Philadelphia and Havana at the Beginning of the Nineteenth Century," in *Atlantic Port Cities: Economy, Culture, and Society in the Atlantic World, 1650–1850*, ed. Franklin W. Knight and Peggy K. Liss (Knoxville: University of Tennessee Press, 1991), 49.

49. Richard W. Van Alstyne, *The Rising American Empire* (New York: Norton, 1974), 147–148.

50. Quoted in Van Alstyne, 81.

51. Salvucci, 40–57.

52. Quoted in Van Alstyne, 152.

53. Van Alstyne, 153–154.

54. Van Alstyne, 147–169; Basil Rauch, *The American Interest in Cuba, 1848–1855* (New York: Columbia University Press, 1948).

55. Braudel, 226.

56. Deerr, 2:483–485.

57. J. H. Parry and Philip Sherlock, *A Short History of the West Indies*, 3d ed. (London: MacMillan, 1971), 231.

58. Rebecca J. Scott, *Slave Emancipation in Cuba: The Transition to Free Labor, 1860–1899* (Princeton: Princeton University Press, 1985).

59. Esteban Montejo, *The Autobiography of a Runaway Slave* (Harmondsworth: Penguin, 1970).

60. Edwin F. Atkins, *Sixty Years in Cuba* (New York: Arno Press, 1980), 67.

61. Atkins, 82–84.

62. Atkins describes Cienfuegos in some detail on 48–55.

63. Atkins, 105.

64. Thomas Barbour, *A Naturalist in Cuba* (Boston: Little, Brown, 1945), 15.

65. Atkins, 7–11, 77–81.

66. Deerr, 2:461–463; Matthew Josephson, *The Robber Barons: The Great American Capitalists, 1861–1901* (New York: Harcourt, Brace and World, 1962), 381–382.

67. Quoted in Van Alstyne, 167.

68. Mira Wilkins, *The Emergence of Multinational Enterprise: American Business Abroad from the Colonial Era to 1914* (Cambridge, Mass.: Harvard University Press, 1970), 155.

69. Earl E. Smith, *The Forests of Cuba,* Maria Moors Cabot Foundation Publication 2 (Petersham, Mass.: Harvard Forest; Cienfuegos, Cuba: Atkins Garden and Research Laboratory, 1954), 13, 34–35.

70. Jenks, 153.

71. Jenks, 205.

72. Jenks, 207.

73. Smith, 11–13, 20–38.

74. Jenks, 281–87.

75. Lester D. Langley, *The Cuban Policy of the United States: A Brief History* (New York: Wiley, 1968), chap. 5.

76. Harry A. Franck, *Roaming Through the West Indies* (London: T. Fisher Unwin, 1921), 76–77.

77. Tom Gill, *Tropical Forests of the Caribbean* (Washington, D.C.: Charles Lathrop Pack Foundation, 1931), 90–91, 159–163.

78. Franck, 78.

79. Franck, 78.

80. Donald R. Dyer, "Sugar Regions of Cuba," *Economic Geography* 32 (1956): 179.

81. This account summarizes Mark Smith, "The Political Economy of Sugar Production and the Environment of Eastern Cuba, 1898–1923," *Environmental History Review* 19:4 (1995): 31–48.

82. Dyer, 177.

83. Quoted in J. Fred Rippy, *Globe and Hemisphere* (Chicago: Regnery, 1958), 155.

84. Parry and Sherlock, 258–259.

85. For the regional context see Dana Munro, *The United States and the Caribbean Republics, 1921–1933* (Princeton: Princeton University Press, 1974); Bryce Wood, *The Making of the Good Neighbor Policy* (New York: Columbia University Press, 1961); Irwin F. Gellman, *Good Neighbor Diplomacy, 1933–1945* (Baltimore: Johns Hopkins University Press, 1979).

86. Parry and Sherlock, 267.

87. Dyer, 181.

88. Dyer, 181–183.

89. Williams, *From Columbus to Castro*, 479.

90. Edward Boorstein, *The Economic Transformation of Cuba* (New York: Monthly Review Press, 1968), 181–212.

91. Medea Benjamin, Joseph Collins, and Michael Scott, *No Free Lunch: Food and Revolution in Cuba Today* (San Francisco: Institute for Food and Development Policy, 1984), 123–124.

92. Benjamin, Collins, and Scott, 125.

93. Benjamin, Collins, and Scott, 120.

94. John Vandermeer and Ivette Perfecto, *Breakfast of Biodiversity* (Oakland, Calif.: Institute for Food and Development Policy, 1995), 120–125.

95. Michael Kudela, "Los problemas actuales de la silvicultura cubana," *Silvaecultura Tropica et Subtropica* (Prague) 4 (1976): 59–76, and Michael Kudela, Richard Hochmut, and Roman Leontovyc, "Proteccion forestal en Cuba," *Silvaecultura Tropica et Subtropica* (Prague) 4 (1976): 97–112. For the beginnings of reforestation and watershed stabilization in pre-Castro years, see Gerardo Budowski, "La conservacion de los recursos forestales de Cuba," *Agrotecnia* (Havana) (May–June 1954): 71–79.

96. For an overview, see Lawrence Mosher, "At Sea in the Caribbean?" in *Bordering on Trouble: Resources and Politics in Latin America*, ed. Andrew Maguire and Janet Welsh Brown (Bethesda, Md.: Adler and Adler, 1986), 235–269. Of the many studies of the Alliance for Progress, almost the only one which explicitly addresses its environmental implications is Walter LaFeber, "The Alliances in Retrospect," in *Bordering on Trouble: Resources and Politics in Latin America*, ed. Andrew Maguire and Janet Welsh Brown (Bethesda, Md.: Adler and Adler, 1986), 337–388.

97. Watts, 86–127.

98. Patrick Bryan, "The Transition of Plantation Agriculture in the Dominican Republic, 1870–84," *Journal of Caribbean History* 10–11 (1978): 82–105.

99. Quoted in Bryan, 88.

100. Quoted in Bryan, 88.

101. Bryan, 89.

102. Murray, 15–21; Melvin M. Knight, *The Americans in Santo Domingo* (New York: Vanguard Press, 1928), 129–143.

103. Paul Vogt, *The Sugar Refining Industry in the United States: Its Development and Present Condition* (Philadelphia: University of Pennsylvania Press, 1908).

104. Martin Murphy, *Dominican Sugar Plantations* (New York: Praeger, 1991).

105. Grunwald and Musgrove, *Natural Resources in Latin American Development*, 352–362.

106. West and Augelli, 145.

107. Luzviminda Bartolome Francisco and Jonathan Shepard Fast, *Conspiracy for Empire: Big Business, Corruption and the Politics of Imperialism in America, 1876–1907* (Quezon City: Foundation for Nationalist Studies, 1985), chaps. 19, 23.

108. West and Augelli, 127–130.

109. Guadalupe Jimenez Codinach, "An Atlantic Silver Entrepot: Vera Cruz

and the House of Gordon and Murphy," in *Atlantic Port Cities: Economy, Culture, and Society in the Atlantic World, 1650–1850,* ed. Franklin W. Knight and Peggy K. Liss (Knoxville: University of Tennessee Press, 1991), 149–167.

110. West and Augelli, 323–325.

111. Grunwald and Musgrove, 352–362.

112. Grunwald and Musgrove, 352–362.

113. George C. Abbott, *Sugar* (London: Routledge, 1990).

114. Janet D. Momsen, "Crisis in the Caribbean Sugar Industry," *Geography* 56: 253 (1971): 338–340.

115. Grunwald and Musgrove, 356.

CHAPTER 2. LORDS OF THE PACIFIC

1. John McNeill, "Of Rats and Men: A Synoptic Environmental History of the Island Pacific," *Journal of World History* 5:2 (1994): 299–349; Reid, "Humans and Forests in Pre-Colonial Southeast Asia," 93–110.

2. See K. N. Chaudhuri, *Asia Before Europe* (Cambridge: Cambridge University Press, 1990), on the fifteenth- and sixteenth-century trading world.

3. J. Beaglehole, *Exploration of the Pacific,* 3d ed. (Stanford: Stanford University Press, 1966).

4. Morison, *The Maritime History of Massachusetts;* Bailyn, *The New England Merchants in the Seventeenth Century.*

5. Mira Wilkins, "The Impacts of American Multinational Enterprise on American-Chinese Economic Relations, 1786–1949," in *America's China Trade in Historical Perspective,* ed. Ernest R. May and John K. Fairbank (Cambridge, Mass.: Harvard University Press, 1986), 259–260.

6. For the closely parallel near-extinction of the fur seals of both northern and southern Pacific shores, see McNeill, "Of Rats and Men," 319–320, and his sources.

7. Raymond H. Fisher, *The Russian Fur Trade, 1500–1700,* University of California Publications in History, vol. 31 (Berkeley: University of California Press, 1943).

8. Beaver and fur seal, less dense and warm, were preferred by wealthy buyers in south China.

9. This resulted from the linking of the North American and Eurasian frontiers of capitalist trade and settlement through the three-century exploitation of the fur-bearing animals of boreal forest zones and their indigenous cultures. For the Canadian fur trade and its impact, see John S. Galbraith, *The Hudson's Bay Company as an Imperial Factor, 1821–1869* (Toronto: University of Toronto Press, 1957). Eric Wolf presents an overview of the cultural transformation of the Canadian Indians under the westward-advancing slaughter of fur-bearers in *Europe and the People Without History* (Berkeley: University of California Press, 1982), chap. 6.

10. There are two races of the Pacific sea otter. The northern race breeds from northern Japan around the Arctic shores and as far south as Vancouver Island. The rugged coast of Washington and Oregon interrupts their range; the southern race predominates along the California coast. For the fullest zoological

treatment of the otter, see Joseph Grinnell et al., *Fur-bearing Mammals of California*, 2 vols. (Berkeley: University of California Press, 1937).

11. Quoted in James R. Gibson, *Otter Skins, Boston Ships and China Goods* (Seattle: University of Washington Press, 1992), 56.

12. Quoted in Gibson, 57.

13. Adele Ogden, *The California Sea Otter Trade, 1784–1848* (Berkeley: University of California Press, 1941), chap. 5.

14. Gibson, 59.

15. Under more effective official protection in the twentieth century, the numbers of sea otters have climbed slowly upward again. See Grinnell.

16. The classic accounts of the whaling era, all written before World War I, include Alexander Starbuck, *History of the American Whale Fishery* (Waltham, Mass.: the author, 1878); and Walter S. Tower, *A History of the American Whale Fishery* (Philadelphia: University of Pennsylvania Press, 1907).

17. From a beginning in Norwegian whaling that dated back to at least the eighth century, it spread to Portuguese fishermen in the Bay of Biscay, who first captured seasonally migrating whales in its relatively shallow waters. Then, by the sixteenth century, as this stock declined, the Portuguese cruised the open northern ocean in the wake of Sebastian Cabot, as far as the New England coast. In the early 1600s, as national rivalries of the mercantilist era expanded, the English monopolist Russia Company surveyed the Spitzbergen and then Greenland whaling grounds, but it was soon outflanked by its Dutch competitors, the aggressive entrepreneurs who had led Europe's expansion into the great northern fishing fields for two centuries already. For the early centuries of international competition and depletion of the resource, see Tower, chaps. 2, 3. For the broader decimation of wild species in the Canadian maritime provinces, see Mowat, *Sea of Slaughter*.

18. Gavan Daws, *Shoal of Time: A History of the Hawaiian Islands* (Honolulu: University of Hawaii Press, 1968), 166–173.

19. Daws, 170.

20. Gibson, 284–287.

21. Gibson, 281–282.

22. Tower, chap. 6; Daniel Yergin, *The Prize* (New York: Simon and Schuster, 1991).

23. Quoted in Van Alstyne, *The Rising American Empire*, 126.

24. For overviews of island ecosystems globally, see Sherwin Carlquist, *Island Biology* (New York: Columbia University Press, 1974); MacArthur and Wilson, *The Theory of Island Biogeography*. For outlines of Pacific island ecology and its disruptions by human cultures, see F. R. Fosberg, ed., *Man's Place in the Island Ecosystem* (Honolulu: Bishop Museum Press, 1963).

25. J. C. Ripperton and E. Y. Hosaka, *Vegetation Zones of Hawaii*, Bulletin 89 (Honolulu: Hawaii Agricultural Experiment Station, 1942); Charles P. Stone and M. J. Scott, eds., *Hawaii's Terrestrial Ecosystems: Preservation and Management* (Honolulu: University of Hawaii Press, 1985); Sherwin Carlquist, *Hawaii, a Natural History: Geology, Climate, Native Flora and Fauna Above the Shoreline*, 2d ed. (Honolulu: SB Printers, 1980), 275–333.

26. E. S. Craighill Handy and Elizabeth Green Handy, *Native Planters in*

Old Hawaii: Their Life, Lore and Environment (Honolulu: Bishop Museum Press, 1972).

27. P. V. Kirch, "The Impact of Prehistoric Polynesians on the Hawaiian Ecosystem," *Pacific Science* 36:1 (1982): 1–14; H. D. Tuggle, "Hawaii," in *The Prehistory of Polynesia,* ed. J. D. Jennings (Cambridge, Mass.: Harvard University Press, 1979).

28. I. A. E. Atkinson, "A Reassessment of Factors, Particularly *Rattus rattus L.,* That Influenced the Decline of Endemic Forest Birds in the Hawaiian Islands," *Pacific Science* 31 (1977): 109–133.

29. James O. Juvik, Sonia P. Juvik, and Lawrence S. Hamilton, "Altitudinal Resource Zonation versus Vertical Control: Land Use Conflict on Two Hawaiian Mountains," *Mountain Research and Development* 12:3 (1992): 211–226; Sonia P. Juvik and James O. Juvik, "Valuations and Images of Hawaiian Forests: An Historical Perspective," in *Changing Tropical Forests: Historical Perspectives on Today's Challenges in Asia, Australasia and Oceania,* ed. John Dargavel et al. (Canberra: Australian National University, 1988), 377–392.

30. Linda W. Cuddihy and Charles P. Stone, *Alternation of Native Hawaiian Vegetation: Effects of Humans, Their Activities and Introductions* (Honolulu: University of Hawaii Press, 1990), 17–36; Kirch, 1–14.

31. For a discussion of the precolonial timber trade, see chapter 7.

32. Mark Merlin and D. Van Ravenswaay, "The History of Human Impact on the Genus *Santalum* in Hawaii," in *Proceedings of the Symposium on Sandalwood in the Pacific,* ed. Lawrence Hamilton and C. Eugene Conrad (Honolulu: USDA Forest Service, 1990), 46–60; Peter Brennan and Mark Merlin, "Biogeography and Traditional Use of *Santalum* in the Pacific Region," in *Sandalwood in the Pacific Region,* ed. F. H. McKinnell (Honolulu: Pacific Science Association, 1992), 30–38.

33. Shobha N. Rai, "Status and Cultivation of Sandalwood in India," in *Proceedings of the Symposium on Sandalwood in the Pacific,* ed. Lawrence Hamilton and C. Eugene Conrad (Honolulu: USDA Forest Service, 1990), 66–71.

34. Dorothy Shineberg, *They Came for Sandalwood: A Study of the Sandalwood Trade in the South-West Pacific* (Melbourne: University of Melbourne Press, 1967), 7.

35. Ernest S. Dodge, *Islands and Empires: Western Impact on the Pacific and East Asia* (Minneapolis: University of Minnesota Press, 1976), 62–65.

36. Douglas L. Oliver, *The Pacific Islands,* rev. ed. (Honolulu: University of Hawaii Press, 1975), 107, 247–249.

37. Gibson, 278–280.

38. Dodge, 60–65; Daws, 49–52.

39. Gibson, 288.

40. Gibson, 253–258; the quotation is on 257.

41. Alfred W. McCoy, "A Queen Dies Slowly: The Rise and Decline of Iloilo City," in *Philippine Social History: Global Trade and Local Transformations,* ed. Alfred W. McCoy and Ed. C. de Jesus (Manila: Ateneo de Manila University Press, 1982), 301.

42. David E. Stannard, *Before the Horror: The Population of Hawaii on the*

Eve of Western Contact (Honolulu: Social Science Research Institute, University of Hawaii, 1989), 48–53.

43. Statistics are compiled from Robert C. Schmitt, *Demographic Statistics of Hawaii: 1778–1965* (Honolulu: University of Hawaii Press, 1968), 42, 223; Robert C. Schmitt, *Historical Statistics of Hawaii* (Honolulu: University of Hawaii Press, 1977), 1–25; Don Woodrum, *This Is Hawaii* (Honolulu: Book Publishers Hawaii, n. d.), 12.

44. Daws, 120.

45. Juvik and Juvik, 221.

46. Thomas K. Hitch, *Islands in Transition: The Past, Present and Future of Hawaii's Economy* (Honolulu: First Hawaiian Bank, 1992), 75–76.

47. Hitch, 73.

48. John W. Vandercook, *King Cane: The Story of Sugar in Hawaii* (New York and London: Harper and Brothers, 1939), 67–69.

49. For the details of Spreckels' career, see Jacob Adler, *Claus Spreckels: The Sugar King in Hawaii* (Honolulu: University of Hawaii Press), 1966.

50. Isabella Bird Bishop, quoted in Daws, 226.

51. Quoted in Adler, 48.

52. Quoted in Adler, 35.

53. Daws, 208, 311–312.

54. Daws, 311–313.

55. Daws, 311–312.

56. Lawrence Fuchs, *Hawaii Pono: "Hawaii the Excellent": An Ethnic and Political History* (Honolulu: Bess Press, 1961), 243–244.

57. For Amfac's history in sugar and its later diversified investments, see George Cooper and Gavan Daws, *Land and Power in Hawaii* (Honolulu: University of Hawaii Press, 1985), chap. 6.

58. Fuchs, 245.

59. Hitch, 81–82.

60. Hitch, 83.

61. Vandercook, chap. 12.

62. Daws, 181.

63. Statistics are from Fuchs, 24–25.

64. Daws, 304–306, 314–316.

65. Hitch, 72.

66. Vandercook, 72.

67. Vandercook, 71.

68. Hawaiian Sugar Planters' Association, *Sugar in Hawaii* (Honolulu: Hawaiian Sugar Planters' Association, 1949), 25.

69. Quoted in A. R. Grammer, "A History of the Experiment Station of the Hawaiian Sugar Planters' Association, 1895–1945," *The Hawaiian Sugar Planters' Record* 51, nos. 3–4 (1947): 185.

70. Grammer, 207–209.

71. Hitch, 77.

72. Donald Worster, personal communication.

73. Vandercook, 134.

74. Grammer, 185.

75. Grammer, 217.

76. Hitch, 77–79. The efficiencies of drip irrigation came only in the 1970s, when the plantations began using that system on a large scale.

77. Ralph Sheldon Hosmer, "The Beginning Five Decades of Forestry in Hawaii," *Journal of Forestry* 57 (1959): 84.

78. Grammer, 207.

79. Hosmer, 83.

80. Woodrum, 337.

81. Schmitt, *Demographic Statistics,* 359–361.

82. Schmitt, *Demographic Statistics,* 359–361.

83. Much detail on recent years is taken from Fuchs, 385–395.

84. Fuchs, 379.

85. For the struggle and triumph of the labor movement in those years, see Cooper and Daws, chap. 5.

86. Fuchs, 386.

87. Woodrum, 339.

88. Schmitt, *Historical Statistics,* 344, 346.

89. Fuchs, 385–386.

90. This would not have been possible without close cooperation with the Hawaiian Sugar Planters' Association, for a variety of pineapple diseases began to appear even in the earliest years of mass plantations. Agents of the HSPA searched the entire Pacific basin for disease-resistant varieties and biological controls of the pests. Moreover, pineapples demanded more iron for their growth than the volcanic soil could provide. In 1916 the industry's soil chemists devised an iron sulphate spray, which overcame that crisis.

91. Ralph S. Kuykendall and A. Grove Day, *Hawaii: A History, from Polynesian Kingdom to American State,* rev. ed. (Englewood Cliffs, N.J.: Prentice-Hall, 1961), 236–239, 263.

92. See Woodrum, 344, for acreage statistics.

93. In 1975 Dole closed its pineapple production on Molokai and Del Monte cut its operation back to eighty-five workers. Cooper and Daws, 201, 210.

94. Cooper and Daws, 201. See also Hitch, 99ff.

95. Elyse Tanouye, "Goodbye Big Five," *Fortune* 103 (1983): 36–39.

96. Schmitt, *Historical Statistics,* 359–361.

97. See especially Carlquist, *Hawaii,* 275–333, for an overview of the zones that were reduced or displaced.

98. W. L. Shurz, *The Manila Galleon* (New York: Dutton, 1959).

99. Benito F. Legarda, Jr., "Foreign Trade, Economic Change and Entrepreneurship in the Nineteenth Century Philippines" (Ph.D. diss., Harvard University, 1955), chaps. 4, 7; Norman G. Owen, ed., *The Philippine Economy and the United States: Studies in Past and Present Interactions,* Papers on South and Southeast Asia, No. 22 (Ann Arbor: University of Michigan, 1983).

100. See table in John A. Larkin, *Sugar and the Origins of Modern Philippine Society* (Berkeley: University of California Press, 1993), 49–50, for export data on sugar, abaca, tobacco, coffee, and coconut products from 1846 through 1920.

101. See Larkin; Dennis Roth, *The Friar Estates of the Philippines* (Albuquerque: University of New Mexico Press, 1977).

102. Larkin, 9.

103. See Dennis Roth, "Philippine Forests and Forestry: 1565–1920," in *Global Deforestation and the Nineteenth Century World Economy*, ed. Richard P. Tucker and J. F. Richards (Durham, N.C.: Duke University Press, 1983), 30–49.

104. Legarda, 278–279.

105. Gibson, 252.

106. Larkin, 14–17.

107. For the classic study of traditional tribal hill agriculture, see Harold Conklin, *Hanunoo Agriculture* (Rome: Food and Agriculture Organization, 1955), which describes nearby Mindoro Island. His tale is similar to that of the Negros highlands.

108. For the social history and political economy of Iloilo, see McCoy, "A Queen Dies Slowly," 297–358. McCoy asserts that the British, with their background in the industrial organization of cloth mills, approached the problem of a labor force for Negros sugar plantations with the same strategy of creating industrial labor, rather than peasant smallholdings for sugar production, as was done in the more traditional agrarian society of Pampanga.

109. Quoted in McCoy, "A Queen Dies Slowly," 323.

110. Dean Worcester, *The Philippines, Past and Present* (New York: MacMillan, 1914), 2:897–899; Carlos Quirino, *History of the Philippine Sugar Industry* (Manila: Kalayaan Publishing Co., 1974); Larkin, chaps. 2–3.

111. Quirino, 19.

112. Larkin, 61; Robert E. Huke, *Shadows on the Land: An Economic Geography of the Philippines* (Manila: Bookmark, 1963), 311.

113. For details of the Negros sugar system, see McCoy, 317–326.

114. Bartolome Francisco and Fast, *Conspiracy for Empire*, chaps. 17, 24, 29.

115. Quoted in Bartolome Francisco and Fast, 225.

116. McCoy, 324–325.

117. Quirino, 47–48.

118. Frank Golay, "Taming the American Multinationals," in *The Philippine Economy and the United States: Studies in Past and Present Interactions*, ed. Norman G. Owen (Ann Arbor: University of Michigan, Center for South and Southeast Asian Studies, 1983), 132.

119. Golay, 160.

120. Norman G. Owen, "Philippine-American Economic Interactions: A Matter of Magnitude," in *The Philippine Economy and the United States: Studies in Past and Present Interactions*, ed. Norman G. Owen (Ann Arbor: University of Michigan, Center for South and Southeast Asian Studies, 1983), 177–198.

121. Quirino, 53–54, 61–64.

122. Huke, *Shadows on the Land*, 314–315.

123. This and following material are taken from Herbert S. Walker, *The*

Sugar Industry in the Island of Negros (Manila: Bureau of Science, 1910), 14–21, 133–136.

124. Walker, 15.

125. Walker, 17–18.

126. Robustiano Echauz, *Apuntes de la Isla de Negros* (Manila: Tipo-lit, 1894), 21.

127. Walker, 136.

128. Walker, 133–135.

129. Quirino, 50.

130. Larkin, 58.

131. Quirino, 53, 61; Golay, 157.

132. The following account is derived from Larkin, 150–171.

133. Walker, 138–141.

134. Quoted in Larkin, 170–171.

135. Gary Hawes, *The Philippine State and the Marcos Regime: The Politics of Export* (Ithaca: Cornell University Press, 1987), 83; Larkin, 175–176.

136. McCoy, 317–323.

137. Larkin, 150, 203, 239.

138. Golay, 25.

139. Larkin, 237–247.

140. Frank H. Golay, "Economic Collaboration: The Role of American Investment," in *The United States and the Philippines,* ed. Frank H. Golay (Englewood Cliffs, N.J.: Prentice Hall, 1966), 102–120.

141. Hawes, 176.

142. Hawes, chap. 3; Robert Pringle, *Indonesia and the Philippines: American Interests in Island Southeast Asia* (New York: Columbia University Press, 1980).

143. Alfred W. McCoy, *Priests on Trial* (New York: Penguin, 1984), 56.

144. McCoy, *Priests on Trial,* chap. 2.

145. U.S. Department of State, *Draft Environmental Report on the Philippines* (Washington, D.C.: U.S. Department of State and U.S. Man and the Biosphere Secretariat, 1980), 67.

146. Hawes, 83–84.

147. *Washington Post,* 21 September 1986; Violeta Lopez-Gonzaga, *Voluntary Land-Sharing and Transfer Scheme in Negros* (Bacolod: Social Research Center, La Salle College, 1986); Frank Lynch, *A Bittersweet Taste of Sugar* (Quezon City: Ateneo de Manila University Press, 1970); McCoy, *Priests on Trial.*

148. Huke, 296.

149. Steven Berwick, field notes, 1987.

150. McCoy, *Priests on Trial,* 160.

CHAPTER 3. BANANA REPUBLICS

1. Grunwald and Musgrove, *Natural Resources in Latin American Development,* 364.

2. Curtin, *Two Jamaicas,* 118.

3. Quoted in Curtin, 106.

4. Olivier, *Jamaica, the Blessed Land,* 314–316, 377. See also Monica Schuler, *"Alas, Alas, Kongo," A Social History of Indentured African Immigration into Jamaica, 1841–1865* (Baltimore: Johns Hopkins University Press, 1980).

5. Kimber's *Martinique Revisited* offers a detailed history of ecological change in Martinique.

6. Quoted in Ansell Hart, "The Banana in Jamaica: Export Trade," *Social and Economic Studies* (Kingston) 3:2 (1954), 213.

7. Hart, 216–219. Export statistics are on 220–224.

8. Olivier, 307.

9. See Grunwald and Musgrove, 365, for subsequent U.S. consumption.

10. West and Augelli, *Middle America,* 388.

11. For the dominant position of British capital, see Herbert Feis, *Europe: The World's Banker, 1870–1914* (New Haven: Yale University Press, 1930).

12. Their outrageous careers are treated in detail in Lester D. Langley and Thomas Schoonover, *The Banana Men: American Mercenaries and Entrepreneurs in Central America, 1880–1930* (Lexington: University of Kentucky Press, 1995).

13. Merritt P. Allen, *William Walker, Filibuster* (New York: Harper Brothers, 1932).

14. Samuel Crowther, *The Romance and Rise of the American Tropics* (Garden City, N.Y.: Doubleday Doran, 1929), 114.

15. Thomas L. Karnes, *Tropical Enterprise: The Standard Fruit and Steamship Company in Latin America* (Baton Rouge: Louisiana State University Press, 1978), 102–108.

16. Mary W. Helms, *Middle America: A Cultural History of Heartland and Frontier* (Englewood Cliffs, N.J.: Prentice-Hall, 1975); Bernard Nietschmann, *Between Land and Water: The Subsistence Ecology of the Miskito Indians, Eastern Nicaragua* (New York and London: Seminar Press, 1973); Craig L. Dozier, *Nicaragua's Mosquito Shore: The Years of British and American Presence* (Tuscaloosa: University of Alabama Press, 1985).

17. For the industrial romance of railroads in the United States, see Leo Marx, *The Machine in the Garden: Technology and the Pastoral Ideal in America* (Oxford: Oxford University Press, 1964).

18. Watt Stewart, *Henry Meiggs: Yankee Pizarro* (Durham: Duke University Press, 1946); Charles D. Kepner, Jr., *Social Aspects of the Banana Industry* (New York: Columbia University Press, 1936; reprint, New York: AMS Press, 1967).

19. Philippe Bourgois, *Ethnicity at Work: Divided Labor on a Central American Banana Plantation* (Baltimore: Johns Hopkins University Press, 1989), 27–28.

20. Pierre Stouse, "The Instability of Tropical Agriculture: The Atlantic Lowlands of Costa Rica," *Economic Geography* 46 (1970): 78–97.

21. Watt Stewart, *Keith and Costa Rica* (Albuquerque: University of New Mexico Press, 1964), 65; David McCullough, *The Path Between the Seas: The Creation of the Panama Canal, 1870–1914* (New York: Simon and Schuster, 1977).

22. The environmental consequences of building the canal were of two sorts. First was the presence of the Canal Zone itself and its associated radiating development. Second, many engineers, managers, and laborers settled permanently in Panama and Costa Rica when construction of the canal was completed. Their collective impact on land and resources is difficult to trace.

23. Stewart, *Keith and Costa Rica,* 149–160.

24. Frederick Upham Adams, *Conquest of the Tropics: The Story of the Creative Enterprises Conducted by the United Fruit Company* (Garden City, N.Y.: Doubleday Page, 1914), 152–162.

25. Quoted in Stewart, *Keith and Costa Rica,* 140.

26. Adams, 50.

27. Crowther, 303; Adams, chap. 14.

28. Kepner, 17–18.

29. Olivier, 301.

30. Aviva Chomsky, *West Indian Workers and the United Fruit Company in Costa Rica, 1870–1940* (Baton Rouge: Louisiana State University Press, 1996).

31. O. Henry, *Cabbages and Kings* (New York: Doubleday, Page, 1912), 21.

32. West and Augelli, 427–437.

33. John Soluri, "Landscape and Livelihood: An Agroecological History of Export Banana Growing in Honduras, 1870–1975" (Ph.D. diss., University of Michigan, 1998), provides the first fine-grained study of the northern corporate economy in the rainforest in Central America, its antecedents, and its impacts. This segment draws heavily on his research. For land use patterns and local social hierarchies before the company era, see chaps. 1–2.

34. West and Augelli, 433–435.

35. Karnes, 71–86.

36. Walter LaFeber, *Inevitable Revolutions: The United States and Central America* (New York: Norton, 1983), 44–45. There was simultaneous saber rattling in Nicaragua, where Wall Street and the State Department assisted a client, Adolfo Díaz, in overthrowing the anti-American President José Santos Zelaya in 1909. Once in office, Díaz refinanced the Nicaraguan government's debts on the basis of loans from New York banks, an early step in the process of displacing the British financial underpinnings of Central American regimes. For the role of the United Fruit Company in these machinations from its base in the coastal town of Bluefields, see Dozier, chap. 9.

37. Quoted in Harold M. Denny, *Dollars for Bullets: The Story of American Rule in Nicaragua* (Westport, Conn.: Greenwood Press, 1980), 142.

38. Karnes, 77–78.

39. This section is derived from Soluri, 91–98.

40. It is difficult to calculate how much land was or had been in banana production, since Standard held some acreage directly and other land through subsidiaries; at any given time only about 10 percent of the company's concessions was actually in banana production.

41. Soluri, 99–106.

42. For more fully differentiated details see Paul Standley, "The Flora of

Lancetilla," *Bulletin of the Field Museum of Natural History—Botany*, 5:10 (1931): 8–49.

43. Quoted in Soluri, 142.

44. This section is derived from Soluri, 106–115.

45. This section is derived from Soluri, 115–122.

46. See the discussion in William Durham, *The Soccer War: Scarcity and Survival in Central America* (Stanford: Stanford University Press, 1979), and its application to the north coast in Soluri, chap. 3.

47. LaFeber, *Inevitable Revolutions*, 59–64.

48. Soluri, 114.

49. Wilson Popenoe, *Manual of Tropical and Subtropical Fruits* (New York: Hafner Press, 1920).

50. Louis Adamic, *The House in Antigua* (New York: Harper and Brothers, 1937), 6–7.

51. Stouse, 91.

52. See Bourgois's incisive survey of each ethnic group.

53. Crowther, 255.

54. Karnes, 84. See that passage for other forms of pressure and subterfuge.

55. Paul J. Dosal, *Doing Business with Dictators: A Political History of United Fruit in Guatemala, 1899–1944* (Wilmington, Del.: Scholarly Resources Books, 1993), chap. 9.

56. Grunwald and Musgrove, 372.

57. Chomsky, 209–243.

58. Kepner and Soothill, 77–87.

59. Kepner and Soothill, 80–81.

60. Kepner and Soothill, 82.

61. Crowther, 318–319.

62. Quoted in Joseph S. Tulchin, *The Aftermath of War: World War I and U.S. Policy Toward Latin America* (New York: New York University Press, 1971), 31.

63. See Denny, chap. 14, for Washington's fear of the possible spread of Bolshevism southward from Mexico.

64. Munro, *The United States and the Caribbean Republics*, 380. See also Herbert Feis, *The Diplomacy of the Dollar, 1919–1932* (New York: Norton, 1950).

65. Quoted in Tulchin, 237, 239.

66. Karnes, 60–61, 90.

67. They often dabbled in local political intrigues on the side, as well. For a vividly rendered and mordantly humorous fictional depiction of their role, see O. Henry, *Cabbages and Kings*.

68. Kepner and Soothill, 133–147.

69. Chomsky, chap. 9.

70. Grunwald and Musgrove, 372.

71. Grunwald and Musgrove, 371.

72. Grunwald and Musgrove, 365.

73. Grunwald and Musgrove, 372–376.

74. William L. Partridge, "Banana County in the Wake of United Fruit,"

American Ethnologist 6 (1979): 491–509; Catherine LeGrand, "Living in Macondo," lecture at the University of Michigan on 26 January 1996. Also see Catherine LeGrand, *Frontier Expansion and Peasant Protest in Colombia, 1850–1936* (Albuquerque: University of New Mexico Press, 1986), 7.

75. The most vivid account available in English is in Gabriel García Márquez's novel *A Hundred Years of Solitude* (New York: Avon Books, 1970).

76. Grunwald and Musgrove, 372, 374.

77. Grunwald and Musgrove, 374. This percentage gradually shrank over the following twenty years as new areas were planted by local landowners in conjunction with the German purchasing firm of Weichert and other continental European companies. See United Nations, Food and Agriculture Organization, *The World Banana Economy, 1970–1984: Structure, Performance and Prospects* (Rome: Food and Agriculture Organization of the United Nations, 1986), 12–15.

78. Partridge, 498.

79. Partridge, 502.

80. James J. Parsons, "Bananas in Ecuador: A New Chapter in the History of Tropical Agriculture," *Economic Geography* 33 (1957): 201–216.

81. Parsons, 206.

82. In Ecuador, unlike anywhere in Central America, United and Standard also faced competition from W. R. Grace, the American corporation that had dominated lowland Peru's development since the late 1800s. By the 1950s Grace shipped six shiploads of bananas monthly to New York, carrying 6,000 tons of the fruit. For the dominant role of Casa Grace in the economic development and land use patterns of Peru's Pacific coastal lowlands, which fully equaled United's role in the lowlands of several smaller countries, see Eugene W. Burgess, *Casa Grace in Peru* (Washington, D.C.: National Planning Association, 1954).

83. United Nations, *The World Banana Economy*, 16–19.

84. For Arévalo's view of the story, see Juan José Arévalo, *The Shark and the Sardines* (New York: Lyle Stuart, 1961).

85. LaFeber, *Inevitable Revolutions*, 111–126.

86. Guatemala's troubles were not entirely political. The weather itself occasionally cursed the land. In 1954–55 hurricanes caused widespread flood and wind damage; half of Guatemala's production was destroyed in 1954–1955.

87. For the new cardboard industry, an important aspect of the region's expanding timber products industry, see chap. 7.

88. Grunwald and Musgrove, 366–368.

89. For the history of the pesticide industry, see Edmund P. Russell, "War on Insects: Warfare, Insecticides, and Environmental Change in the United States, 1870–1945" (Ph.D. diss., University of Michigan, 1993).

90. For an analysis of the consequences of input-intensive production, see Vandermeer and Perfecto, *Breakfast of Biodiversity*.

91. West and Augelli, 410.

92. Grunwald and Musgrove, 372, 374.

93. Robert G. Williams, *Export Agriculture and the Crisis in Central America* (Chapel Hill: University of North Carolina Press, 1986).

94. LaFeber, 94–97, 128.

95. Grunwald and Musgrove, 374–376.

96. LaFeber, *Inevitable Revolutions*, 132–133.

97. LaFeber, 177–181.

98. LaFeber, 183. Contract growers and associated producers by the early 1980s constituted almost half of the two companies' acreage. The concession era had ended in 1975; a new export tax was imposed instead. Some diversification of crops resulted: bananas were 51 percent of all Honduran exports in 1971, but fell to 30 percent by 1983. They still provided 21,000 jobs, including 12,000 for field workers. United Nations, *World Banana Economy*, 22–24.

99. Frank Ellis, "The Banana Export Activity in Central America 1947–1976" (Ph.D. dissertation, University of Sussex, 1978), 105.

100. LaFeber, 262–264.

101. LaFeber, 100.

102. LaFeber, 99–105; Ellis, 87.

103. Grunwald and Musgrove, 372, 374.

104. The geographer Pierre Stouse assessed in the late 1960s that the larger-scale estates may have been more stable, economically and environmentally, than small private producers. Stouse, 91–95.

105. Grunwald and Musgrove, 372, 374; United Nations, 19–22.

106. Tom Barry, Beth Wood, and Deb Preusch, *Dollars and Dictators* (New York: Grove Press, 1983), 15–31.

107. Ellis, 102.

108. Ellis, 101–104.

109. Barry, Wood, and Preusch, 17.

110. LaFeber, 207–209; Barry, 18–19.

111. United Nations, *World Banana Economy*, 24–26.

112. Murdo J. MacLeod, *Spanish Central America: A Socioeconomic History, 1520–1720* (Berkeley: University of California Press, 1973), chaps. 1–2.

113. For the international industry and major markets, see V. D. Wickizer, *Coffee, Tea and Cocoa* (Baltimore: Johns Hopkins University Press, 1977).

114. Barry, Wood, and Preusch, 15–31; Lori Ann Thrupp, "Pesticides and Policies: Approaches to Pest-Control Dilemmas in Nicaragua and Costa Rica," *Latin American Perspectives* 15:4 (1988): 37–70; and Lori Ann Thrupp, "Sterilization of Workers from Pesticide Exposure: The Causes and Consequences of DBCP-Induced Damage in Costa Rica and Beyond," *International Journal of Health Services* 21:4 (1991): 731–757.

115. United Nations, 8.

116. United Nations, 61–65.

117. United Nations, 40–42.

118. For an overview of this process, see Daniel Faber, *Environment under Fire: Imperialism and the Ecological Crisis in Latin America* (New York: Monthly Review Press, 1993).

CHAPTER 4. THE LAST DROP

1. Braudel, *The Structures of Everyday Life*, 249–260.

2. Michael F. Jimenez, " 'From Plantation to Cup': Coffee and Capitalism

in the United States, 1830–1930," in *Coffee, Society, and Power in Latin America,* ed. William Roseberry, Lowell Gudmundson, and Mario Samper Kutschbach (Baltimore: Johns Hopkins University Press, 1995), 38–64.

3. Grunwald and Musgrove, *Natural Resources in Latin American Development,* 320–330.

4. Stanley J. Stein, *Vassouras: A Brazilian Coffee County, 1850–1900* (Cambridge, Mass.: Harvard University Press, 1957).

5. For the slaves' story, see Mary Karasch, *Slave Life in Rio de Janeiro, 1808–1850* (Princeton: Princeton University Press, 1987).

6. A detailed description of the process and its impact is in Dean, *With Broadax and Firebrand,* 178–190.

7. Quoted in Stein, 214.

8. Quoted in Stein, 217.

9. Stein, 221.

10. This section is derived from Warren Dean, *Rio Claro: A Brazilian Plantation System, 1820–1920* (Stanford: Stanford University Press, 1976). Quotation is on 2.

11. Dean, *Rio Claro,* 2.

12. Dean, *Rio Claro,* 3.

13. Joseph E. Sweigart, *Coffee Factorage and the Emergence of a Brazilian Capital Market, 1850–1888* (New York and London: Garland Publishing, 1987), 12–16.

14. William H. Ukers, *All About Coffee* (New York: Tea and Coffee Trade Journal Company, 1922), 484.

15. Stein, 58 n. 21.

16. Ukers, 531.

17. Jimenez, 52–53.

18. Mark Pendergrast, *Uncommon Grounds: The History of Coffee and How It Transformed Our World* (New York: Basic Books, 1999), 63–76.

19. Sweigart, 27–37; the quotation is on 37.

20. Ukers, 527–529.

21. See the table in Ukers, 484.

22. Stein, "Epilogue."

23. Joseph L. Love, *São Paulo in the Brazilian Federation, 1889–1937* (Stanford: Stanford University Press, 1980), 42–50.

24. For efforts by the U.S. Department of Commerce to undermine Brazil's valorization system in the 1920s, see Joseph Brandes, *Herbert Hoover and Economic Diplomacy: Department of Commerce Policy, 1921–1928* (Pittsburgh: University of Pittsburgh Press, 1962), 130–135.

25. Ukers, 530–534.

26. Warren Dean, "Forest Conservation in Southeastern Brazil, 1900–1955," *Environmental Review* 9:1 (1985): 55–69.

27. See Warren Dean, *The Industrialization of São Paulo, 1880–1945* (Austin: University of Texas Press, 1969), for the transformation of the coffee belt into modern agribusiness in the twentieth century.

28. Don D. Humphrey, *American Imports* (New York: Twentieth Century Fund, 1955), 278, table 42.

29. Pierre Monbeig, *Pionniers et Planteurs de São Paulo* (Paris: A. Colin, 1952); Preston E. James, "Trends in Brazilian Agricultural Development," *Geographical Review* 43: 3 (1953): 313–318.

30. See Verena Stolcke, *Coffee Planters, Workers and Wives* (Oxford: Macmillan, 1988), 43–57.

31. Instituto Cubano de Estabilizacion del Café, *Segunda Conferencia Panamericana del Café* (Havana: Instituto Cubano de Estabilizacion del Café, 1937), 211–219.

32. Love, 52.

33. For samples of a wide literature on the culture and economics of this era which is relevant to our analysis, see Richard Wightman Fox and T. J. Jackson Lears, eds., *The Culture of Consumption: Critical Essays in American History, 1880–1980* (New York: Pantheon Books, 1983); Goodwin, Ackerman, and Kiron, eds., *The Consumer Society;* Kenneth T. Jackson, *Crabgrass Frontier: The Suburbanization of the United States* (Oxford: Oxford University Press, 1985); William E. Leuchtenburg, *Paradox of Plenty: American Society since 1945* (Boston: Little, Brown, 1975); Paul Wachtel, *The Poverty of Affluence: A Psychological Portrait of the American Way of Life* (New York: Free Press, 1983).

34. James J. Flink, *The Automobile Age* (Cambridge, Mass.: MIT Press, 1988).

35. See Harvey A. Levenstein, *Paradox of Plenty: A Social History of Eating in Modern America* (Oxford: Oxford University Press, 1993); and, especially, Harvey A. Levenstein, *Revolution at the Table: The Transformation of the American Diet* (Oxford: Oxford University Press, 1988).

36. Pendergrast, 257–287.

37. United Nations, Food and Agriculture Organization, *World Coffee Trade* (New York: UNFAO, 1963), 7–10; quotation is on 7.

38. Stolcke, 77–79.

39. John McNeill, "Deforestation in the Araucaria Zone of Southern Brazil, 1900–1983," in *World Deforestation in the Twentieth Century,* ed. J. F. Richards and Richard Tucker (Durham, N.C.: Duke University Press, 1987), 15–32.

40. Pan American Coffee Bureau, *Annual Coffee Statistics: 1958* (Washington, D.C.: Pan American Coffee Bureau, 1958), 14, 18–20, 27.

41. LaFeber spells out some of the environmental implications more explicitly in "The Alliances for Progress," in *Bordering on Trouble: Resources and Politics in Latin America,* ed. Andrew Maguire and Janet W. Brown (Bethesda, Md.: Adler and Adler, 1986), 337–388.

42. J. W. F. Rowe, *The World's Coffee* (London: Her Majesty's Stationery Office, 1963), chap. 9. Quotation is on 190.

43. Anonymous, *The International Coffee Agreement* (Washington, D.C.: U.S. Government Printing Office, 1963).

44. United Nations, *World Coffee Trade,* 39–40, 77.

45. Stolcke, 242–246; James, "Trends in Brazilian Agricultural Development," 302–327.

46. Dean, *Rio Claro,* 49.

47. For the northern Andes as an ecological region, see Dennis V. Johnson,

ed., "The Northern Andes: Environmental and Cultural Change," *Mountain Research and Development* 2:3 (1982): 253–336.

48. John V. Lombardi and James A. Hanson, "The First Venezuelan Coffee Cycle, 1830–1855," *Agricultural History* 44:4 (1970): 355–368.

49. Lombardi and Hanson, 365–368.

50. Carl Sauer, *The Early Spanish Main* (Berkeley: University of California Press, 1966).

51. LeGrand, *Frontier Expansion*, chap. 1.

52. Marco Palacios, *Coffee in Colombia, 1850–1970: An Economic, Social and Political History* (Cambridge: Cambridge University Press, 1980), 63. The material that follows is derived largely from LeGrand's and Palacios's outstanding studies.

53. Palacios, 212.

54. Gabriel García Márquez gives a vivid account of the devastation to the riverside forests which was caused by the steamers' appetite for fuelwood, in the final chapter of his novel *One Hundred Years of Solitude*.

55. Palacios, 23.

56. James J. Parsons, *Antioqueño Colonization in Western Colombia*, rev. ed. (Berkeley: University of California Press, 1968).

57. David Bushnell, *The Making of Modern Colombia: A Nation in Spite of Itself* (Berkeley: University of California Press, 1993), 169.

58. Palacios, 227–242.

59. Jimenez, 53–54.

60. Palacios, 212.

61. J. Fred Rippy, *The Capitalists and Colombia* (New York: Vanguard Press, 1931), 152–176.

62. LeGrand, 93–96.

63. Bushnell, 173.

64. See, for example, Bushnell, 201–222.

65. T. Lynn Smith, "Land Tenure and Soil Erosion in Colombia," in *Proceedings of the Inter-American Conference on Conservation of Renewable Natural Resources* (Washington, D.C.: U.S. Department of State, 1948), 155–160. Nearly twenty years later Smith expanded this analysis at length in *Colombia: Social Structure and the Process of Development* (Gainesville: University of Florida Press, 1967). Quotations are on 155.

66. Grunwald and Musgrove, 326.

67. United Nations, Food and Agricultural Organization, *Coffee in Latin America: Productivity Problems and Future Prospects* (New York: United Nations, 1958).

68. Bushnell, 223–235.

69. See especially West and Augelli, *Middle America*, chap. 2. Also James J. Parsons, "The Miskito Pine Savanna of Nicaragua and Honduras," *Annals of the Association of American Geographers* 45:1 (1955): 36–63; William M. Denevan, "The Upland Pine Forests of Nicaragua: A Study in Cultural Plant Geography," in *University of California Publications in Geography* 12:4 (1961): 251–320; H. Jeffrey Leonard, *Natural Resources and Economic Devel-*

opment in Central America (New Brunswick, N.J.: Transaction Press, 1987), 16–26.

70. MacLeod, *Spanish Central America,* chap. 1.

71. MacLeod, chap. 1.

72. See statistics in Grunwald and Musgrove, 328–329.

73. For a political analysis of the region's coffee elites in this period, see Jeffery M. Paige, *Coffee and Power: Revolution and the Rise of Democracy in Central America* (Cambridge, Mass.: Harvard University Press, 1997). See also David Browning, *El Salvador: Landscape and Society* (Oxford: Clarendon Press, 1971), chaps. 3–5; Alastair White, *El Salvador* (New York: Praeger, 1973).

74. Guatemala developed a closely similar pattern of oligarchic coffee production, with similar destruction of traditional Indian communal life and lands. See David J. McCreery, "Coffee and Class: The Structure of Development in Liberal Guatemala," *Hispanic American Historical Review* 56:3 (1976): 438–460. By 1900 coffee was Guatemala's major export crop. Coffee acreage varied between 145,000 and 260,000 acres, on land cleared from hill forest by Indian peon labor. By 1900 German estate owners and coffee processors were dominant there: they owned half of the crop and exported 80 percent of it to their homeland. Ukers, 219. Except during the two world wars, the United States was never the major purchaser of Guatemalan coffee.

75. Browning, 155–173.

76. Quoted in Browning, 158.

77. Quoted in McCreery, 456.

78. Quoted in Browning, 173.

79. Robert G. Williams, *States and Social Evolution: Coffee and the Rise of National Governments in Central America* (Chapel Hill: University of North Carolina Press, 1994), 183.

80. For the long-term consequences, see especially Durham, *The Soccer War.*

81. LaFeber, *Inevitable Revolutions,* 17–18, 60–64. The quotation appears on 60.

82. Ukers, 217; LaFeber, *Inevitable Revolutions,* 70–71; Durham, 33–36, 40–43, 57–59.

83. Instituto Cubano de Estabilizacion del Café, 217.

84. LaFeber, 72–74.

85. Quoted in William Vogt, *The Population of El Salvador and Its Natural Resources* (Washington, D.C.: Pan American Union, 1946), 17.

86. Vogt, 1.

87. Vogt, 17–18.

88. Vogt, 27.

89. Julian Crane, "Coffee is Gold for El Salvador," *Agriculture in the Americas* 7:4–5 (1947): 69–72.

90. Grunwald and Musgrove, 328.

91. United Nations, Food and Agricultural Organization, *Coffee in Latin America: Productivity Problems and Future Prospects* (New York: United Nations, 1958), 2:105–109, 124–126.

92. LaFeber, 174–175.

93. LaFeber, *Inevitable Revolutions*, 91, 129. Also see Robert T. Aubey, "Entrepreneurial Formation in El Salvador," *Explorations in Entrepreneurial History* 6 (1969), 59–75; Gerald E. Karush, "Plantations, Population and Poverty in El Salvador," *Studies in Comparative International Development* 13 (1978): 59–75.

94. Quoted in LaFeber, 131.

95. For their American commercial partners, see Roger Burbach and Patricia Flynn, *Agribusiness in the Americas* (New York: Monthly Review Press, 1980).

96. LaFeber, *Inevitable Revolutions*, 172–176; Walter LaFeber, "The Alliances in Retrospect," in *Bordering on Trouble: Resources and Politics in Latin America,* ed. Andrew Maguire and Janet Welsh Brown (Bethesda, Md.: Adler and Adler, 1986), 337–388.

97. Browning, 256.

98. Laurence Simon and James Stephens, Jr., *El Salvador Land Reform, 1980–81* (Boston: Oxfam America, 1982); Joseph Collins, *Nicaragua: What Difference Could a Revolution Make? Food and Farming in the New Nicaragua,* rev. ed. (San Francisco: Institute for Food and Development, 1985); Martin Diskin, *Agrarian Reform in El Salvador: An Evaluation* (San Francisco: Institute for Food and Development Policy, 1985); Harlan Davis, "Aid to the Small Farmer: The El Salvador Experience," *Inter-American Economic Affairs,* 29 (1975): 43–47; Leonard, *Natural Resources and Economic Development in Central America.*

99. LaFeber, *Inevitable Revolutions*, 286.

100. Cynthia Arnson, *El Salvador: A Revolution Confronts the United States* (Washington, D.C.: Institute for Policy Studies, 1982); Tommie Sue Montgomery, *Revolution in El Salvador* (Boulder, Colo.: Westview, 1982); Marvin Gettleman et al., eds., *El Salvador* (New York: Evergreen, 1982); John Womack, Jr., "El Salvador and the Central American War," *Socialist Review* 12 (1982): 9–30.

101. For the context and impact there, see Timothy C. Weiskel, "Toward an Archeology of Colonialism: Elements in the Ecological Transformation of the Ivory Coast," in *The Ends of the Earth: Perspectives on Modern Environmental History,* ed. Donald Worster (Cambridge: Cambridge University Press, 1988), 162–169.

CHAPTER 5. THE AUTOMOTIVE AGE

1. For the exceptionally brutal and destructive colonial extractive system in the Belgian Congo, see Robert Harms, *River of Wealth, River of Sorrow* (New Haven: Yale University Press, 1981); Samuel H. Nelson, *Colonialism in the Congo Basin, 1880–1940* (Athens: Ohio University, 1994).

2. Glenn D. Babcock, *History of the United States Rubber Company: A Case Study in Corporation Management* (Bloomington: Bureau of Business Research, Indiana University, 1966), 83–85.

3. Colin Barlow, *The Natural Rubber Industry: Its Development, Technol-*

ogy and Economy in Malaysia (Kuala Lumpur: Oxford University Press, 1978), 16–19.

4. Exports of natural rubber (in thousands of tons):

	South America	Africa
1830	0.2	—
1849	0.4	—
1850	1.6	—
1860	3.0	—
1870	7.3	—
1880	10.2	0.5
1890	17.0	2.8
1900	28.0	16.0

Source: Barlow, 16.

5. For world production of rubber, 1900–1919, including Brazil, Africa, Central America, and Asia, see Barbara Weinstein, *The Amazon Rubber Boom, 1850–1920* (Stanford: Stanford University Press, 1983), 218.

6. Reported in *The National Intelligencer,* quoted in Susanna Hecht and Alexander Cockburn, *The Fate of the Forest: Developers, Destroyers and Defenders of the Amazon* (New York: Harper Perennial Books, 1989), 75.

7. Hecht and Cockburn, 77–78.

8. Weinstein, 177, 206f; and Hecht and Cockburn, chap. 5, give vivid details.

9. Weinstein, 165.

10. Weinstein, 172.

11. Weinstein, 171. For other abortive American investment attempts, see Dean, *Brazil and the Struggle for Rubber,* chap. 3.

12. Weinstein, 264.

13. See the detailed analysis of this disease and the long history of plant pathologists' failure to defeat it, in Dean, *Brazil and the Struggle for Rubber,* chap. 4.

14. They followed a similar development penetrating inland for teak timber in eastern Java. See Peter Boomgaard, "Forest Management and Exploitation in Colonial Java, 1677–1897," *Forest and Conservation History* 36 (1992): 4–14.

15. For brief accounts of production and trade of these spices, see Bernard H. M. Vlekke, *Nusantara: A History of Indonesia* (The Hague: van Hoeve, 1965), 89–93, 203–204; Reid, "Humans and Forests in Pre-Colonial Southeast Asia," 93–110.

16. Quoted in Victor Savage, *Western Impressions of Nature and Landscape in Southeast Asia* (Singapore: Singapore University Press, 1984), 78.

17. J. H. Parry, *The Age of Reconnaissance: Discovery, Exploration and Settlement, 1450 to 1650* (London: Weidenfeld and Nicholson, 1963), 41–42, 254. For the European markets for Asia's spices in medieval and early modern times, see Braudel, *The Structures of Everyday Life,* 220–222.

18. Boxer, *The Dutch Seaborne Empire,* 199.

19. Rubber has recently been cultivated extensively elsewhere in Indonesia, including 68,000 hectares on Java, as a profitable smallholder crop. See Wolf Donner, *Land Use and Environment in Indonesia* (Honolulu: University of Hawaii Press, 1987), 72.

20. Robert E. Elson, *Javanese Peasants and the Colonial Sugar Industry: Impact and Change in an East Java Residency, 1830–1940* (Singapore: Oxford University Press, 1984). Teak timber, their other lucrative export crop from Java, provided the origins of Europe's forestry system in the tropics. See Boomgaard.

21. See summary in J. A. M. Caldwell, "Indonesian Export and Production from the Decline of the Culture System to the First World War," in *The Economic Development of Southeast Asia: Studies in Economic History and Political Economy*, ed. C. D. Cowan (New York: Praeger, 1964), 72–101.

22. Robert van Niel, "The Effect of Export Cultivations in Nineteenth-Century Java," *Modern Asian Studies* 15:1 (1981): 25–58.

23. Donner, 10–15; Anthony J. Whitten et al., *The Ecology of Sumatra* (Yogyakarta: UGM Press, 1984), chap. 1.

24. James W. Gould, *Americans in Sumatra* (The Hague: Martinus Nijhoff, 1961), 23–25.

25. Donner, 234.

26. Gould, 28–30. Competition from Philippine leaf tobacco was important by then, and in any case, Dutch capital had begun moving into the United States.

27. Tys Volker, *From Primeval Forest to Cultivation* (Medan: Deli Planters Association, 1924), 87.

28. Volker, 7.

29. T. A. Tengwall, "History of Rubber Cultivation and Research in the Netherlands Indies," in *Science and Scientists in the Netherlands Indies*, ed. P. Honig and F. Verdoorn (New York: Board for the Netherlands Indies, Surinam and Curacao, 1945), 344.

30. Clark E. Cunningham, *The Postwar Migration of the Toba-Bataks to East Sumatra*, Southeast Asia Studies Cultural Report Series (New Haven: Yale University Press, 1958), 11.

31. Cunningham, 11.

32. Malcolm Caldwell, *The Wealth of Some Nations* (London: Zed, 1977), 87–88.

33. For the corporation's activities see Babcock.

34. Volker, 77; Gould, chap. 3.

35. Cunningham, 12.

36. H. Stuart Hotchkiss, "Operations of an American Rubber Company in Sumatra and the Malay Peninsula," *Annals of the American Academy,* 112 (1924): 154. Of a total 3,500,000 acres of rubber in Asia, 2.5 million were in British territory, .9 million in the Netherlands East Indies, and the rest in Indochina.

37. For the Batak migrations, especially the flood of them in the 1950s, see Cunningham.

38. Ladislao Szekely, *Tropic Fever: The Adventures of a Planter in Sumatra* (Kuala Lumpur: Oxford University Press, 1979).

39. For the fullest analysis of labor's living conditions, see Ann Laura Stoler, *Capitalism and Confrontation in Sumatra's Plantation Belt, 1870–1979* (New Haven: Yale University Press, 1985).

40. Babcock, 176–179.

41. Volker, 173.

42. Gould, 95.

43. Details are in Tengwall.

44. Tengwall, 349–350.

45. Babcock, 353.

46. Babcock, 357.

47. Stoler, 136, 161.

48. Quoted in Alfred E. Eckes, Jr., *The United States and the Global Struggle for Minerals* (Austin: University of Texas Press, 1979), 34.

49. Eckes, 46.

50. Brandes, 106–128.

51. Harvey S. Firestone, *Men and Rubber: The Story of Business* (Garden City, N.Y.: Doubleday, Page, 1926), 258–259.

52. Firestone, 253.

53. Firestone, 259.

54. Firestone, 259–260.

55. Firestone, 262–263.

56. Stephen D. Krasner, *Defending the National Interest: Raw Materials Investments and U.S. Foreign Policy* (Princeton: Princeton University Press, 1978), 101–103.

57. Firestone, 262.

58. Following details are taken from J. B. Webster and A. A. Boahen, *The Growth of African Civilisation: The Revolutionary Years, West Africa since 1800* (London: Longman, 1968).

59. For Liberia's biogeography see Torkel Holsoe, *Third Report on Forestry Progress in Liberia, 1951–1959* (Washington, D.C.: International Cooperation Administration, 1961), 1–10.

60. For an ethnographic survey, see Yekutiel Gershoni, *Black Colonialism: The Americo-Liberian Scramble for the Hinterland* (Boulder, Colo.: Westview, 1985), 1–6, 67–95.

61. Robert Clower et al., *Growth Without Development: An Economic Survey of Liberia* (Evanston, Ill.: Northwestern University Press, 1966), 159–164.

62. Dean, *Brazil and the Struggle for Rubber*, 69.

63. Quoted in Firestone, 264.

64. W. W. Schmokel, "Settler and Tribes: Origins of the Liberian Dilemma," in *Western African History*, ed. Daniel F. McCall, Norman R. Bennett, and Jeffrey Butler (New York: Praeger, 1969), 153–181. The quotation is on 174.

65. Firestone, 267.

66. Krasner, 104–105.

67. Brandes, *Herbert Hoover and Economic Diplomacy*, 119.

68. Clower et al., 157.

69. Charles M. Wilson, *Liberia: Black Africa in Microcosm* (New York: Harper and Row, 1971), 132–134. For the contrast with European colonies,

see Jean Suret-Canale, *Afrique Noire de la colonisation aux indépendances,*
1945–1960 (Paris: Editions Sociales, 1977); Suret-Canale, *Afrique Noire, L'ère*
coloniale, 1900–1945 (Paris: Editions Sociales, 1962); and Catherine Coquery-
Vidrovitch, *Le Congo au temps des grandes compagnies concessionnaires,*
1898–1930 (Paris: Mouton, 1972).

70. Quoted in Wilson, 133.

71. Clower et al., 158.

72. Firestone's domination of the national economy was indicated by its
other institutions too. In the mid-1930s Firestone set up a bank in Monrovia,
the Bank of Monrovia, which became the country's only commercial bank and
handled all government accounts. Gradually growing friction led Firestone in
1955 to sell it to First National City Bank of New York.

73. J. Gus Liebenow, *Liberia: The Evolution of Privilege* (Ithaca: Cornell
University Press, 1969), 65–70.

74. Weinstein, 52, 182–191. The quotation is on 189.

75. Allan Nevins and Frank E. Hill, *Ford: Expansion and Challenge, 1915–*
1933 (New York: Scribners, 1954), 231–238; Randolph Resor, "Rubber in Brazil: Dominance and Collapse, 1876–1945," *Business History Review* 51:3
(1977): 360–366.

76. Mira Wilkins and Frank Ernest Hill, *American Business Abroad: Ford*
on Six Continents (Detroit: Wayne State University Press, 1964), 176.

77. Wilkins and Hill, 173.

78. Dean, *Brazil and the Struggle for Rubber,* 76–77.

79. Hecht and Cockburn, 97–100.

80. Hecht and Cockburn, 100–103.

81. Wilkins and Hill, 182.

82. Dean, *Brazil and the Struggle for Rubber,* 105.

83. Eckes, 80–83, 93–102; Alfred Lief, *The Firestone Story* (New York:
McGraw Hill, 1951), 250–251.

84. W. J. S. Naunton, "Synthetic Rubber," in *History of the Rubber Indus-*
try, ed. P. Schidrowitz and T. R. Dawson (Cambridge: Heffer, 1952), 100–109.

85. Firestone, 253.

86. This chronology is based on Jonathan Marshall, *To Have and Have Not:*
Southeast Asian Raw Materials and the Origins of the Pacific War (Berkeley:
University of California Press, 1995), 33–53.

87. Quoted in Lief, 251–252.

88. S. A. Brazier, "The Rubber Industry in the 1939–1945 War," in *History*
of the Rubber Industry, ed. P. Schidrowitz and T. R. Dawson (Cambridge: Heffer, 1952), 316–326.

89. Barlow, 408.

90. Barlow, 109, 415.

91. Barlow, 94.

92. From the enormous literature on that aspect of American consumerism
in the postwar era, see for example, James Flink, *The Car Culture* (Cambridge,
Mass.: Harvard University Press, 1975); and his *The Automobile Age.*

93. Enzo R. Grilli, Barbara Bennett Agostini, and Maria J. 't Hooft-

Welvaars, *The World Rubber Economy: Structure, Changes, and Prospects* (Baltimore: Johns Hopkins University Press, 1980), 21.

94. Barlow, 408. Further tables are in Grilli, Agostini, and Hooft-Welvaars, 186–187. Also see H. J. Stern, *Rubber, Natural and Synthetic* (New York, 1967); Neal Potter and Francis T. Christy, Jr., *Trends in Natural Resources Commodities, Statistics of Prices, Outputs, Consumption, Foreign Trade and Employment in the United States, 1870–1957* (Baltimore: Johns Hopkins University Press, 1962).

95. Barlow, 412.

96. Grilli, Agostini, and Hooft-Welvaars, 48.

97. Grilli, Agostini, and Hooft-Welvaars, 27.

98. Grilli, Agostini, and Hooft-Welvaars, 19–20.

99. Major sources include Grilli, Agostini, and Hooft-Welvaars; Barlow; International Rubber Study Group, *Statistical Bulletin,* annual volumes; FAO, *Trade Yearbook,* annual volumes.

100. Grilli, Agostini, and Hooft-Welvaars, 16–17.

101. Babcock, 172, 395; Hotchkiss, 158.

102. Barlow, 78–81.

103. Clifton R. Wharton, Jr., "Rubber Supply Conditions: Some Policy Implications," in T. H. Silcock and E. K. Fisk, eds., *The Political Economy of Independent Malaya: A Case-study in Development* (Berkeley: University of California Press, 1963), 131–132.

104. For further details see S. Robert Aiken and Michael R. Moss, "Man's Impact on the Tropical Rainforest of Peninsular Malaysia: A Review," *Biological Conservation* 8 (1975), 213–229; Harold Brookfield, Lesley Potter, and Yvonne Byron, *In Place of the Forest: Environmental and Socioeconomic Transformation in Borneo and the Eastern Malay Peninsula* (Tokyo: United Nations University Press, 1995).

105. Barlow, 202, 205.

106. Most Indonesian rubber sales from the 1950s onward continued to be to the United States and western Europe. Japan purchased most of Thailand's rubber. China traded rice for most of Sri Lanka's rubber exports. Barlow, 414.

107. Barlow, 313–317.

108. Barlow, 332–333.

109. Karl Pelzer, "The Agrarian Conflict in East Sumatra," *Pacific Affairs* (1957): 152.

110. Richard Robison, *Indonesia: The Rise of Capital* (Sydney: Allen and Unwin, 1986).

111. Pelzer, 159.

112. Stephen Brechin, personal communication.

113. Indonesian government statistics, in Charles A. Fisher, *South-east Asia: A Social, Economic and Political Geography* (London: Methuen, 1964), 319–321.

114. For background on the early years of Kalimantan's incorporation into global markets, see Lesley Potter, "Indigenes and Colonisers: Dutch Forest

Policy in South and East Borneo (Kalimantan), 1900 to 1950," in *Changing Tropical Forests: Historical Perspectives on Today's Challenges in Asia, Australasia and Oceania,* ed. John Dargavel et al. (Durham, N.C.: Forest History Society, 1988), 127–154.

115. Barlow, 106–107.

116. Lief, chap. 21.

117. Clower et al., 156. Other private foreign construction firms began competing for Liberian government contracts in the early 1950s.

118. Clower et al., 156. The company's sawmill at Harbel produced about 720,000 board feet of lumber in 1961, all for the plantation's use.

119. Clower et al., 172–195. The greatest resource which the government could trade upon was the rich iron deposit of the Bomi Hills. By 1966 iron exports were worth $112 million, compared with $30 million in rubber exports.

120. Several other European firms also entered Liberian rubber production during these years. In 1959 the Liberian Agricultural Company, a consortium of Italian bankers, was formed. It gained a concession of 600,000 acres for rubber, timber, oil palm, sugar and cocoa. Another new corporation, created for the occasion in 1960, was a Dutch-German consortium, the Salala Rubber Corporation. This one could only command a modest 100,000 acres, for plantation agriculture and forestry. It planned the usual panoply of roads, bridges, forest clearing, and also intended to process rubber from many nearby Liberian rubber planters, but perhaps not willingly. As the major assessment of the industry commented, "The company has been hampered considerably in its operations by the demands made upon it by independent farmers. Since a large proportion of these private farmers are also government officials (or their relatives), the company has found it politically expedient to accede to their demands." Clower et al., 195.

121. Clower et al., 167–168.

122. Quoted in J. Gus Liebenow, 71–84.

123. Wilson, 137.

124. Liebenow, 216–217.

125. Krasner, 100–101.

126. Brandes, 122.

127. The following account is distilled from Wade Davis, *One River: Explorations and Discoveries in the Amazon Rain Forest* (New York: Simon and Schuster, 1996), 296–371.

128. Davis, 369.

129. Among the many commentaries on the social and policy history of Amazonian Brazil in recent years, see for example Stephen G. Bunker, *Underdeveloping the Amazon: Extraction, Unequal Exchange, and the Failure of the Modern State* (Urbana and Chicago: University of Illinois Press, 1985). For a commentary on the Brazilian effort to grow Hevea in concentrated plantations, see Dean, *Brazil and the Struggle for Rubber,* chaps. 8–9.

130. Grilli, Agostini, and Hooft-Welvaars, 7.

131. Davis, 370.

CHAPTER 6. THE CROP ON HOOVES

1. See Crosby, *The Columbian Exchange,* chap. 3; Crosby, *Ecological Imperialism,* chap. 8.

2. For an ecological baseline, see Robert Orr Whyte, *Tropical Grazing Lands: Communities and Constituent Species* (The Hague: Junk, 1974).

3. C. J. Bishko, "The Peninsular Background of Latin American Cattle Ranching," *Hispanic American Historical Review* 32 (1952): 491–515; Karl W. Butzer, "Cattle from Old to New Spain: Historical Antecedents" (paper presented at the Latin American Geographers' Meeting, Merida, Mexico, January 1987); David E. Vassberg, *Land and Society in Golden Age Castile* (Cambridge: Cambridge University Press, 1984); Julius Klein, *The Mesta: A Study in Spanish Economic History, 1273–1836* (Cambridge, Mass.: Harvard University Press, 1920).

4. For an excellent survey and bibliography of New World ranching, see Richard W. Slatta, *Cowboys of the Americas* (New Haven: Yale University Press, 1990), especially chap. 2.

5. McNeill, *Atlantic Empires of France and Spain,* 170ff.; Kuethe, "Havana in the Eighteenth Century," 13.

6. Max Winkler, *Investments of United States Capital in Latin America* (Boston: World Peace Foundation, 1929), 191.

7. Robert Wasserstrom, *Class and Society in Central Chiapas* (Berkeley: University of California Press, 1983), especially chap. 6; MacLeod, *Spanish Central America,* chap. 1; Carl L. Johannessen, *Savannas of Interior Honduras* (Berkeley: University of California Press, 1963), 36–47.

8. John P. Bailey, *Central America: Describing Each of the States of Guatemala, Honduras, Salvador, Nicaragua, and Costa Rica* (London: Saunders, 1850), 121, quoted in Elbert E. Miller, "The Raising and Marketing of Beef in Central America and Panama," *Journal of Tropical Geography* 41 (1975): 59.

9. Terry G. Jordan, *North American Cattle-Ranching Frontiers: Origins, Diffusion, and Differentiation* (Albuquerque: University of New Mexico Press, 1993), chap. 5.

10. Charles Gibson, *Aztecs under Spanish Rule* (Stanford: Stanford University Press, 1964).

11. MacLeod, chap. 1.

12. P. J. Bakewell, *Silver Mining and Society in Colonial Mexico: Zacatecas, 1546–1700* (Cambridge: Cambridge University Press, 1971), 68–73. Vast flocks of sheep went through a similar irruption cycle of rapid breeding with no natural enemies. By the late 1500s they displaced both indigenous agriculture and its vegetation and moisture base before declining to long-term steady numbers on degraded lands. Elinor Melville, *A Plague of Sheep* (Cambridge: Cambridge University Press, 1994), chaps. 4–6.

13. Richard J. Morrisey, "The Northward Expansion of Cattle Ranching in New Spain, 1550–1600," *Agricultural History* 25 (1951): 115–121.

14. Robert C. West, *Sonora: Its Geographical Personality* (Austin: University of Texas Press, 1993), 58–59.

15. For the classic work on the later hacienda system, see François Chevalier, *Land and Society in Colonial Mexico: The Great Hacienda,* trans. Alvin Eustis (Berkeley: University of California Press, 1963).

16. Quoted in Sandra L. Myres, "The Spanish Cattle Kingdom in the Province of Texas," *Texana* (Fall 1966): 245–246.

17. Jordan, 147–158.

18. For a summary of the political function of the grants, the way they were designed for the aridity of the land, and the contrast to U.S. land law, see Paul F. Starrs, *Let the Cowboy Ride: Cattle Ranching in the American West* (Baltimore: Johns Hopkins University Press, 1998), 45–49.

19. Myres, 233–246; see also Odie B. Faulk, *The Last Years of Spanish Texas, 1778–1821* (London: Mouton, 1964).

20. David J. Weber, *The Spanish Frontier in North America* (New Haven: Yale University Press, 1992), 309–313; quotation is on 311.

21. Richard White, *The Roots of Dependency* (Lincoln: University of Nebraska Press, 1983).

22. David J. Weber, " 'From Hell Itself': The Americanization of Mexico's Northern Frontier," in *Myth and the History of the Hispanic Southwest* (Albuquerque: University of New Mexico Press, 1988), 105–115.

23. Cronon, *Nature's Metropolis,* 82; Arthur M. Johnson and Barry E. Supple, *Boston Capitalists and Western Railroads: A Study in the Nineteenth-Century Railroad Investment Process* (Cambridge, Mass.: Harvard University Press, 1967).

24. Siegfried Giedion, *Mechanization Takes Command* (New York: Oxford University Press, 1948), 218.

25. Giedion, 226.

26. Cronon, *Nature's Metropolis,* 248.

27. Cronon, 218.

28. Jeremy Rifkin, *Beyond Beef: The Rise and Fall of the Cattle Culture* (New York: Dutton, 1992), 88.

29. Ralph W. Hidy and Muriel E. Hidy, "Anglo-American Merchant Bankers and the Railroads of the Old Northwest, 1848–1860," *Business History Review* 34 (1960): 150–169; A. W. Currie, "British Attitudes toward Investment in North American Railroads," *Business History Review* 34 (1960): 194–215.

30. Raymond Dasmann, *Environmental Conservation* (New York: Wiley, 1984), 182.

31. See the classic account in Walter P. Webb, *The Great Frontier* (Boston: Houghton Mifflin, 1952).

32. Tom Lea, *The King Ranch,* 2 vols. (Boston: Little Brown, 1957).

33. Dasmann, *Environmental Conservation,* 190–191.

34. For the geographical and historical setting see Emilio Coni, *Historia de las vaquerías de Rio de la Plata, 1555–1750* (Buenos Aires: Editorial Devenir, 1956); Tulio Halperin-Donghi, *Economy and Society in Argentina in the Revolutionary Period* (Cambridge: Cambridge University Press, 1975); James R. Scobie, *Argentina: A City and a Nation* (London: Oxford University Press, 1971), chap. 1; James R. Scobie, *Revolution on the Pampas: A Social History of Argentine Wheat, 1860–1910* (Austin: University of Texas Press, 1964); Peter

Smith, *Politics and Beef in Argentina: Patterns of Conflict and Change* (New York: Columbia University Press, 1969); Oscar Schmieder, "Alteration of the Argentine Pampa in the Colonial Period," *University of California Publications in Geography* 2:10 (1927): 303–321.

35. For a survey of this changing era, see Richard W. Slatta, *Comparing Cowboys and Frontiers* (Norman: University of Oklahoma Press, 1997), chaps. 3, 5, 8.

36. Scobie, *Argentina*, chap. 5.

37. John E. Rouse, *The Criollo: Spanish Cattle in the Americas* (Norman: University of Oklahoma Press, 1977), 94–95, 120–121. These were developed by some of the same breeders who had developed the hybrid sheep that were conquering the colder plains of Patagonia in the same years.

38. Scobie, *Argentina*, 120.

39. For further details of the mechanization of beef production, see Giedion, 214–229.

40. The main destination was the United Kingdom; much also went to western Europe; very little was shipped to the United States. Grunwald and Musgrove, *Natural Resources in Latin American Development*, 427.

41. Rippy, *Globe and Hemisphere*, 41.

42. Alfred Crosby, "Ecological Imperialism: The Overseas Migration of Western Europeans as a Biological Phenomenon," in *The Ends of the Earth*, ed. Donald Worster (Cambridge: University of Cambridge Press, 1988), 114. See his source, Schmieder, 310–311.

43. Slatta, *Cowboys*, 16–17, and personal communication to the author.

44. Rouse, *World Cattle*, 448, 452–456.

45. Rouse, *World Cattle*, 457; Slatta, *Cowboys*, 14–17.

46. Rippy, *The Capitalists and Colombia*, 152.

47. Quoted in Rippy, *The Capitalists and Colombia*, 33–34.

48. Rouse, *The Criollo*, 124.

49. William Vogt, *The Population of Venezuela and Its Natural Resources* (Washington, D.C.: Pan American Union, 1946), 13ff.

50. Raymond E. Crist, "Cattle Ranching in the Tropical Rainforest," *The Scientific Monthly* 56 (1943): 521.

51. Crist, 525.

52. Crist, 527.

53. Crist, 547.

54. J. D. Chambers and G. E. Mingay, *The Agricultural Revolution, 1750–1880* (New York: Schocken Books, 1966), chaps. 2–3, 7; Christabel S. Orwin and Edith H. Whetham, *History of British Agriculture 1846–1914* (London: Longmans, 1964), chap. 5.

55. Cronon, *Nature's Metropolis*, chap. 5; Jordan, chap. 2.

56. Rouse, *World Cattle*, 358–359; Rouse, *The Criollo*, 196.

57. Slatta, *Cowboys of the Americas*, 17.

58. Rouse, *The Criollo*, 281–283.

59. Schmieder; Scobie, *Revolution on the Pampas*, chap. 5.

60. See Rouse, *World Cattle*, 361, 389–90, 451, for Brazil, Argentina and Venezuela.

61. Rouse, *World Cattle,* 449; Rouse, *Criollo,* 125.

62. Rouse, *Criollo,* 459.

63. James J. Parsons, "Spread of African Pasture Grasses to the American Tropics," *Journal of Range Management* 25 (1942): 12–17. Quotation is on 12.

64. Parsons, "Spread of African Pasture Grasses," 14.

65. Parsons, 17.

66. Thomas Sheridan, *Where the Dove Calls* (Tucson: University of Arizona Press, 1988); Philip Wagner, "Parras: A Case History in the Depletion of Natural Resources," *Landscape* (Summer 1955): 19–28; A. Starker Leopold, "Vegetation Zones of Mexico," *Ecology* 31 (1950): 512–513.

67. Andrew J. W. Scheffey, "Natural Resources and Government Policy in Coahuila, Mexico" (Ph.D. diss., Univ. of Michigan, 1958), 39–50, 249–260.

68. For the impact of those policies on the northern arid lands, see Miguel Tinker Salas, *In the Shadow of the Eagles: Sonora and the Transformation of the Border during the Porfiriato* (Berkeley: University of California Press, 1997).

69. Lindsay Chaney and Michael Cieply, *The Hearsts: Family and Empire— The Later Years* (New York: Simon and Schuster, 1981), 40–41; W. A. Swanberg, *Citizen Hearst* (New York: Scribner's, 1961), 29; Oliver Carlson, *Hearst, Lord of San Simeon* (New York: Viking, 1936), 13–14.

70. Carlson, 117.

71. Swanberg, 190.

72. Swanberg, 207.

73. Florence C. Lister and Robert H. Lister, *Chihuahua: Storehouse of Storms* (Albuquerque: University of New Mexico Press, 1966), 149–155.

74. John Womack, *Zapata and the Mexican Revolution* (New York: Knopf, 1969).

75. Manuel A. Machado, Jr., *The North Mexican Cattle Industry, 1910– 1975: Ideology, Conflict, and Change* (College Station: Texas A & M University Press, 1981), chaps. 1–2.

76. See the table in Machado, 125.

77. Wagner, "Paras," 19–28.

78. Machado, 125–126: table, "Cattle Imported to Mexico, 1920–33." Most of these investors were from the United States; a few were from Colombia, Guatemala, Cuba, and elsewhere.

79. Winkler, 252–253. See also Robert W. Dunn, *American Foreign Investments* (New York: B. W. Huebsch and Viking Press, 1926), 105–106.

80. Ana Maria Alonso, *Thread of Blood: Colonialism, Revolution, and Gender on Mexico's Northern Frontier* (Tucson: University of Arizona Press, 1995), 166–167.

81. Swanberg, 298.

82. Frank Tannenbaum, *The Mexican Agrarian Revolution* (Washington, D.C.: Brookings Institution, 1930), 358–369.

83. Mervin G. Smith, "The Mexican Beef-Cattle Industry," *Foreign Agriculture* 8:11 (1944): 256. Also see Machado, 127–129, 132–134, 135: tables on cattle exported from Mexico.

84. Smith, "The Mexican Beef-Cattle Industry," 249.

85. Humphrey, *American Imports,* 273.

86. Mark Baldwin, "Soil Erosion Survey of Latin America," *Journal of Soil and Water Conservation* 9:4 (1954): 161–162.

87. Humphrey, 274; Machado, 95.

88. Statistics are in Machado, 96. Data in the following paragraphs are from Machado, 95–117.

89. E. C. Stakman, Richard Bradfield, and Paul C. Mangelsdorf, *Campaigns against Hunger* (Cambridge, Mass.: Harvard University Press, 1967), 162–176.

90. One instance in a village of dry rural Chihuahua is recounted in detail in Sheridan.

91. A. Starker Leopold, "Adios, Gavilan," *Pacific Discovery* 2:1 (1949): 4–13.

92. For details on Paniolo culture, see Lynn J. Martin, ed., *Na Paniolo o Hawai'i* (Honolulu: Honolulu Academy of Arts, 1987); and Joseph Brennan, *The Parker Ranch* (New York: Harper & Row, 1974), 51–63, 145–148.

93. Brennan, 66–67.

94. Brennan, 65.

95. Brennan, 79–81. Material in the following paragraphs is also derived largely from Brennan.

96. Virginia Cowan-Smith and Bonnie Domrose Stone, *Aloha Cowboy* (Honolulu: University of Hawaii Press, 1988), 125.

97. Quoted in Cowan-Smith and Stone, 125.

98. Cowan-Smith and Stone, 128–133.

99. Quoted in Daws, *Shoal of Time,* 334.

100. Hawaii Department of Agriculture statistics, tabulated in Schmitt, *Historical Statistics of Hawaii,* 345, 348; Woodrum, *This Is Hawaii,* 259, 261.

101. Carlquist, *Hawaii, A Natural History,* 275–333.

102. Cowan-Smith and Stone, 126–127.

103. Roth, *The Friar Estates of the Philippines,* 30–62; Marshall McLennan, "Peasant and Hacendero in Nueva Ecija: The Socio-Economic Origins of a Philippine Commercial Rice-Growing Region" (Ph.D. diss., University of California, 1973), 26–35.

104. Ronald K. Edgerton, "Frontier Society on the Bukidnon Plateau, 1870–1941," in *Philippine Social History: Global Trade and Local Transformations,* ed. Alfred W. McCoy and Ed. C. de Jesus (Quezon City: Ateneo de Manila University Press, 1982), 361–390.

105. Edgerton, 375.

106. Burbach and Flynn, *Agribusiness in the Americas,* 197–198.

107. D. B. Agnew, *The Outlook for Hamburger Livestock and Meat Situation* (Washington, D.C.: U.S. Department of Agriculture, 1979), 26–28; Norman Myers, "The Hamburger Connection," *Ambio* 10:1 (1981): 3–8; Norman Myers, *The Primary Source: Tropical Forests and Our Future* (New York: Norton, 1984); Douglas R. Shane, *Hoofprints on the Forest: An Inquiry into the Beef Cattle Industry in the Tropical Forest Areas of Latin America* (Philadelphia: Institute for the Study of Human Issues, 1986); James R. Simpson and Donald E. Farris, *The World's Beef Business* (Ames: Iowa State University Press, 1982). Relevant tables are in Grunwald and Musgrove, 423, 428; and Lovell S. Jarvis, *Livestock Development in Latin America* (Washington: World Bank, 1986), 88.

108. Grunwald and Musgrove, 428; Jarvis, 88.

109. Grunwald and Musgrove, 415–416. Latin American exports in 1970 were 100,000 tons of canned beef per year; half of that went to the United States from Argentina.

110. For statistics, see Grunwald and Musgrove, 422.

111. R. C. West, N. P. Psuty and B. G. Thom, *The Tabasco Lowlands of Southeastern Mexico* (Baton Rouge: Louisiana State University Press, 1969), 118–119, 158–159.

112. J. Fred Rippy, *Latin America in the Industrial Age* (New York: Putnam, 1944), 86.

113. Winkler, 51–52.

114. Norman B. Schwartz, *Forest Society: A Social History of Peten, Guatemala* (Philadelphia: University of Pennsylvania Press, 1990), 10–14, 104–108.

115. Soluri, "Landscape and Livelihood," 33–37, 102–108.

116. John Thompson, "Production, Marketing and Consumption of Cattle in El Salvador," *The Professional Geographer* 8:5 (1961): 20; quoted in Robert G. Williams, *Export Agriculture and the Crisis in Central America* (Chapel Hill: University of North Carolina Press, 1986), 80.

117. Williams, *Export Agriculture*, 78.

118. For the debate over the impact of the hamburger connection, see Billie R. DeWalt, "The Agrarian Bases of Conflict in Central America," in *The Central American Crisis: Sources of Conflict and the Failure of U.S. Policy*, ed. Kenneth Coleman and George Herring (Wilmington, Del.: Scholarly Resources, Inc., 1985), 43–54; Myers, "The Hamburger Connection," 3–8; James Nations and Daniel Komer, "Indians, Immigrants and Beef Exports: Deforestation in Central America," *Cultural Survival Quarterly* 6:2 (1982): 8–12; James J. Parsons, "Forest to Pasture: Development or Destruction?" *Revista Biologica Tropicale* 24 (1976): 121–138; Shane, *Hoofprints on the Forest*.

119. Commercial ranching was one of the favorite development strategies of Cold War economic planners in agencies such as USAID and the World Bank. Q. Martin Morgan, *The Beef Cattle Industries of Central America and Panama* (Washington, D.C.: U.S. Department of Agriculture, 1973).

120. Miller, "The Raising and Marketing of Beef," 61.

121. Rouse, *The Criollo*, 172; Williams, *Export Agriculture*, 79; Miller, 68.

122. Williams, 223 n. 37.

123. Williams, 95.

124. Morgan, 16.

125. Miller, 64; Williams, 87–90, 99, 205.

126. J. C. Tanner, "U.S. Cattlemen Buy Spreads in Central America to Exploit Good Grazing, Growing Demand for Beef," *Wall Street Journal,* 27 July 1972, p. 30.

127. Williams, 95, 109.

128. Barry, Wood, and Preusch, *Dollars and Dictators*, 20; Williams, 110.

129. Williams, 106–107.

130. Williams, 106; Miller, "The Raising and Marketing of Beef in Central America and Panama," 59–69.

131. See also P. S. Bartlett, *Agricultural Choice and Change: Decision-*

Making in a Costa Rican Community (New Brunswick, N.J.: Rutgers University Press, 1982); DeWalt, 18–23; George Guess, "Pasture Expansion, Forestry and Development Contradictions: The Case of Costa Rica," *Studies in Comparative International Development* 14 (1979): 42–55; S. H. Moreno, *Cuando Se Acaban Los Montes* (Panama City: Smithsonian Tropical Research Institute, 1983); Myers, *The Primary Source;* Nations and Komer.

132. Morgan, 15–18.

133. Morgan, 8–10. Morgan, an American advisor, typical of U.S. officials at the time, did not mention the Somoza family estates in his report, thus grossly distorting the Nicaraguan reality.

134. Edward C. Wolf, "Managing Rangelands," in *State of the World 1986,* ed. Lester R. Brown (New York: Norton, 1986), 70–72.

135. Winkler, 88.

136. Grunwald and Musgrove, 410.

137. Rouse, *World Cattle,* 384; Grunwald and Musgrove, 418, 422, 425, 426.

138. In this vast new field for multinational corporations' speculative ventures, other major players included Grace and Gulf & Western, along with European and Japanese companies including Volkswagen and Mitsui. Myers, *The Primary Source,* 138.

139. For the Australian chapter in the King Ranch saga, see Charles J. V. Murphy, "The Fabulous House of Kleberg," *Fortune* 89 (1969): 112–119, 218–219, 224–225. The quotation is on 114.

140. Murphy, "The Fabulous House of Kleberg," 224.

141. The Latin American operations of the King Ranch are surveyed in part two of Charles J. V. Murphy's series, "The King Ranch South of the Border," *Fortune* 89 (1969): 132–136, 140, 142, 144.

142. Quoted in Murphy, "The King Ranch," 134.

143. Murphy, "The King Ranch," 142.

144. Murphy, "The King Ranch," 144.

145. Gerard Colby, *Thy Will Be Done: The Conquest of the Amazon: Nelson Rockefeller and Evangelism in the Age of Oil* (New York: Harper Collins, 1995), 298–302, 608, 618–621, 632–634, 883.

146. Silvio R. Duncan Baretta and John Markoff, "Civilization and Barbarism: Cattle Frontiers in Latin America," in *The Frontier in History: North America and Southern Africa Compared* (New Haven: Yale University Press, 1981), 587–620.

147. Rouse, *The Criollo,* 167.

CHAPTER 7. UNSUSTAINABLE YIELD

1. A similar process in Europe had accompanied the High Middle Ages; probably the greatest loss in Western Europe's forest cover occurred during the agricultural clearances of the eleventh and twelfth centuries. See H. C. Darby, "The Medieval Clearances," in *Man's Role in Changing the Face of the Earth,* ed. William L. Thomas (Chicago: University of Chicago Press, 1956), 183–216, for an authoritative summary. This process extended to Europe's frontiers in

the nineteenth century, although this time it was more chaotic and less controlled by social constraints. See Richard P. Tucker and J. F. Richards, eds., *Global Deforestation in the Nineteenth Century* (Durham, N.C.: Duke University Press, 1983). The process was perhaps at its most intense in the woodland regions of the United States. See Michael Williams, *Americans and Their Forests: A Historical Geography* (Cambridge: University of Cambridge Press, 1989); Thomas Cox et al., *This Well Wooded Land: Americans and Their Forests from Colonial Times to the Present* (Lincoln: University of Nebraska Press, 1985).

2. F. W. O. Morton, "The Royal Timber in Late Colonial Bahia," *Hispanic American Historical Review* 58:1 (1978): 41–61.

3. For the trade, from the perspective of Europe, see Arthur M. Wilson, "The Logwood Trade in the Seventeenth and Eighteenth Centuries," in *Essays in the History of Modern Europe,* ed. Donald C. McKay (New York: Harper Brothers, 1936).

4. Stephen L. Caiger, *British Honduras, Past and Present* (London: George Allen and Unwin, 1951), 50–59.

5. See A. R. Gregg, *British Honduras* (London: Her Majesty's Stationery Office, 1968), chap. 8, for a description of the logging camps.

6. William Dampier, quoted in Narda Dobson, *A History of Belize* (Trinidad and Jamaica: Longman Caribbean, 1973), 55.

7. Olivier, *Jamaica, The Blessed Land,* 292.

8. Caiger, 135, 139.

9. Sources include William F. Payson, *Mahogany: Antique and Modern* (New York: E. P. Dutton, 1926).

10. Various sources cursorily mention the wanton clearance of mahogany for sugar in the Cuban lowlands and, after 1920, in the eastern hills. In most cases it seems that commercial marketing of the timber was either not financially feasible, because transport systems were primitive, or simply not in the sugar speculators' minds. See Gill, *Tropical Forests of the Caribbean,* 90–91; the competition with Honduran and British Honduran exports is mentioned by Mosher, "At Sea in the Caribbean?," 240–245; Dobson, 134; and Caiger, 141.

11. Walter D. Wilcox, "Among the Mahogany Forests of Cuba," *National Geographic* 19 (1908): 485.

12. Wilcox, 486.

13. Wilcox, 488.

14. John C. Callahan, *The Fine Hardwood Veneer Industry in the United States: 1838–1990* (Lake Ann, Mich.: National Woodlands Publishing Company, 1990), esp. 124.

15. Schwartz, *Forest Society,* 111.

16. Leslie Holdridge, F. Bruce Lamb, and Harold Mason, *Forests of Guatemala* (privately printed, 1950), 60–61, briefly discuss the history of several Yankee firms in that area until 1930, when markets collapsed.

17. See import statistics in F. Bruce Lamb, *Mahogany of Tropical America: Its Ecology and Management* (Ann Arbor: University of Michigan Press, 1966), 10–21.

18. Belize experienced a mahogany-felling bonanza as well. Its exports ex-

panded from 6 million board feet in 1899 to over 16 million in 1914, with steadily rising prices. Caiger, 140.

19. Parsons, "The Miskito Pine Savanna of Nicaragua and Honduras," 55.

20. Gregg, 90.

21. Paul C. Standley and Samuel J. Record, *The Forests and Flora of British Honduras*, Botanical Series, vol. 12 (Chicago: Field Museum of Natural History, 1936), 30.

22. For detailed descriptions, see William M. Denevan, "The Upland Pine Forests of Nicaragua: A Study in Cultural Plant Geography," *University of California Publications in Geography* 12:4 (1961): 251–320; Johanneson, *Savannas of Interior Honduras;* and Parsons, "The Miskito Pine Savanna of Nicaragua and Honduras."

23. Denevan, 298.

24. Parsons, "The Miskito Pine Savanna of Nicaragua and Honduras," 51–52.

25. Its major consumer now is the Dominican Republic; Europe stands second. The following account is taken primarily from Parsons, "The Miskito Pine Savanna of Nicaragua and Honduras," 54–61; and the somewhat different detail in Karnes, *Tropical Enterprise,* chap. 9.

26. Denny, *Dollars for Bullets,* 61.

27. Denny, 78.

28. LaFeber, *Inevitable Revolutions,* 64–69.

29. After World War II Robinson reorganized as the Nicaragua Longleaf Pine Lumber Company, or NIPCO, and constructed the region's network of permanent logging roads. Karnes, chap. 10.

30. James D. Nations, *Tropical Moist Forest Destruction in Middle America: Current Patterns and Alternatives* (Austin, Tex.: Center for Human Ecology, 1980), 20.

31. Frank H. Wadsworth, "The Development of the Forest Land Resources of the Luquillo Mountains, Puerto Rico" (Ph.D. diss., University of Michigan, 1949), 113.

32. In a more modest parallel development in the Old Southwest centering on the lower Mississippi, cypress logging expanded and found Caribbean markets as well. John Hebron Moore, *Andrew Brown and Cypress Lumbering in the Old Southwest* (Baton Rouge: Louisiana State University Press, 1967).

33. Susan Flader, ed., *The Great Lakes Forest: An Environmental and Social History* (Minneapolis: University of Minnesota Press, 1983).

34. James E. Fickle, *The New South and the "New Competition": Trade Association Development in the Southern Pine Industry* (Urbana: University of Illinois Press for the Forest History Society), 1980.

35. A closely parallel pattern appeared in the late nineteenth century along the Pacific coast of the Americas, as Douglas fir and to a lesser extent redwood came to dominate the construction industries of Chile and Peru. Roger E. Simmons, *Lumber Markets of the West and North Coasts of South America,* Special Agents Series, No. 117 (Washington, D.C.: Department of Commerce, Bureau of Foreign and Domestic Commerce, 1916).

36. Fickle, 199–200, 204.

37. Gill, *Tropical Forests of the Caribbean,* 272.

38. Mira Wilkins, *The Making of Multinational Enterprise: American Business Abroad from 1914 to 1970* (Cambridge, Mass.: Harvard University Press, 1974), 98.

39. Stephen Pyne, *Fire in America: A Cultural History of Wildland and Rural Fire* (Princeton: Princeton University Press, 1982).

40. Standley and Record, 33.

41. Gill, *Tropical Forests of the Caribbean,* 18.

42. Tom Gill, "America and World Forestry," in *American Forestry: Six Decades of Growth,* ed. Henry Clepper and Arthur B. Meyer (Washington, D.C.: Society of American Foresters, 1960), 285.

43. Frank H. Wadsworth, "An Approach to Silviculture in Tropical America and Its Application in Puerto Rico," *Caribbean Forester* 8:4 (1947): 252–254.

44. For the tropical mainland British foresters also worked in British Honduras and British Guinea on the South American mainland near northern Amazonia, see Arthur Bevan, "A Forest Policy for the American Tropics," *Caribbean Forester* 4:2 (1943): 49–53.

45. For the nineteenth-century background of Mexico's modern forestry operations, see Herman W. Konrad, "Tropical Forest Policy and Practice During the Mexican Porfiriato," in *Changing Tropical Forests: Historical Perspectives on Today's Challenges in Central and South America,* ed. Harold K. Steen and Richard P. Tucker (Durham, N.C.: Forest History Society, 1992), 123–133. For the emergence of formal training and expanded forestry law in the 1930s, see Enrique Beltran, "Forestry and Related Research in Mexico," in *Forestry and Related Research in North America,* ed. Frank H. Kaufert and William H. Cummings (Washington, D.C.: Society of American Foresters, 1955), 254–271; Miguel Caballero, Victor Sosa, and Juana Marin, "Forestry in Mexico," *Journal of Forestry* 75 (1977): 473–477.

46. In South America in the immediate prewar years Brazil and Argentina made similar beginnings. But just as in Mexico, these efforts were frozen by the war and were not revived until about 1950.

47. Caribbean Commission, *Forest Research Within the Caribbean Area* (Washington, D.C.: Caribbean Commission, 1947), 5–18.

48. Gareth Porter, with Delfin J. Ganapin, Jr., *Resources, Population, and the Philippines' Future* (Washington, D.C.: World Resources Institute, 1988); Eric L. Hyman, "Forestry Administration and Policies in the Philippines," *Environmental Management* 7:6 (1983): 511–524.

49. P. Saenger, E. J. Hegerl, and J. D. S. Davie, eds., *Global Status of Mangrove Ecosystems,* Commission on Ecology Papers, No. 3 (Gland: International Union for the Conservation of Nature and Natural Resources, 1983); Lawrence Hamilton and Samuel C. Snedaker, eds., *Handbook for Mangrove Area Management* (Honolulu: East-West Center, 1984).

50. T. C. Whitmore, *Tropical Rain Forests of the Far East,* 2d ed. (Oxford: Clarendon Press, 1984), chaps. 1–4.

51. Savage, *Western Impressions of Nature and Landscape in Southeast Asia.*

52. Karl L. Hutterer, ed., *Economic Exchange and Social Interaction in Southeast Asia: Perspectives from Prehistory, History, and Ethnography* (Ann Arbor: Center for South and Southeast Asian Studies, University of Michigan, 1977).

53. Of the many publications in ethnobotanical archeology and related fields, see for example James L. Cobban, "The Traditional Use of the Forests in Mainland Southeast Asia," Center for International Studies, Ohio University, 1968, typescript.

54. Boomgaard, "Forest Management and Exploitation in Colonial Java, 1677–1897," 4–14.

55. See H. N. Whitford, *The Forests of the Philippines*, Bulletin No. 10 (Manila: Bureau of Forestry, 1911): 1:12–32, for a contemporary's overview of the islands' forest cover. See Whitmore, chap. 17, for a present-day botanical analysis.

56. Larkin, *Sugar and the Origins of Modern Philippine Society*, chaps. 1–3.

57. Richard P. Tucker and J. F. Richards, eds., "Introduction," in *Global Deforestation and the Nineteenth-Century World Economy* (Durham, N.C.: Duke University Press, 1983).

58. Dennis Roth, "Philippine Forests and Forestry: 1565–1920," in *Global Deforestation and the Nineteenth-Century World Economy*, ed. Richard P. Tucker and J. F. Richards (Durham, N.C.: Duke University Press, 1983), 41.

59. Edgar Wickberg, *The Chinese in Philippine Life, 1850–1898* (New Haven: Yale University Press, 1965).

60. Barrington Moore, "Forest Problems in the Philippines," *American Forestry* 16:2 (1910): 75; E. E. Schneider, *Commercial Woods of the Philippines: Their Preparation and Uses* (Manila: Bureau of Forestry, 1916), 13.

61. David W. John, "The Timber Industry and Forest Administration in Sabah under Chartered Company Rule," *Journal of Southeast Asian Studies* 5 (1974): 55–81.

62. See Bernhard E. Fernow, *A Brief History of Forestry, in Europe, the United States and Other Countries* (Toronto: University of Toronto Press, 1911); Gifford Pinchot, *Breaking New Ground* (New York: Harcourt, Brace and Company, 1947). For commentaries see Samuel Hays, *Conservation and the Gospel of Efficiency* (Cambridge, Mass.: Harvard University Press, 1959); Harold K. Steen, *The U.S. Forest Service: A History* (Seattle: University of Washington Press, 1976), chaps. 2–3.

63. Data on Ahern come primarily from Lawrence Rakestraw, "George Patrick Ahern and the Philippine Bureau of Forestry, 1900–1914," *Pacific Northwest Quarterly* 53 (1967): 142–150; see also Roth.

64. Rakestraw, 142–150; Roth, 40–42.

65. Pinchot, 223.

66. Pinchot, 224.

67. Pinchot, 224.

68. Pinchot, 226.

69. Pinchot, 226.

70. Pinchot, 231.

71. Quoted in Roth, 45.

72. Thomas Cox, *Mills and Markets: A History of the Pacific Coast Lumber Industry to 1900* (Seattle: University of Washington Press, 1974), chaps. 5, 7.

73. Dean Worcester, "Philippine Forest Wealth," *American Forestry* 21:1 (1915): 8; Commonwealth of the Philippines, *Forest Resources of the Philippines* (Manila: Government Printing Press, 1939), 4–5; Whitford, 64–65.

74. Moore, "Forest Problems in the Philippines," 150–151.

75. Schneider, 16.

76. Moore, 150.

77. Schneider, 12.

78. Moore, 150–151; Rakestraw, 147, 148.

79. Schneider, 15–16.

80. Frederick L. Wernstedt and J. E. Spencer, *The Philippine Island World, a Physical, Cultural and Regional Geography* (Berkeley: University of California Press, 1967), 428–435, describe Mindoro in some detail.

81. Conklin, *Hanunoo Agriculture,* describes these highlands. Melvin L. Merritt and H. N. Whitford, *A Preliminary Working Plan for the Public Forest Tract of the Mindoro Lumber and Logging Company, Bongabon, Mindoro, P. I,* Bulletin No. 6 (Manila: Bureau of Forestry, 1906), describe the island's forests as of 1906.

82. Rolland Gardner, *Philippine Sawmills, Lumber Market, and Prices,* Bulletin No. 4 (Manila: Bureau of Forestry, 1906), 69; Merritt and Whitford.

83. Worcester, 16.

84. Worcester, 11.

85. Moore, 80.

86. The pioneering research into the tropical botany of the Philippines was Samuel Record's classification work at Yale over the years.

87. Schneider, 13; Raphael Zon, ed., *Conservation of Renewable Natural Resources* (Philadelphia: University of Pennsylvania Press, 1941), chap. 5.

88. Schneider, 13; Raphael Zon and William N. Sparhawk, *Forest Resources of the World* (New York: McGraw Hill, 1923), 1:475.

89. See Zon and Sparhawk, 1:474–475, for partial statistics from 1901 through 1918.

90. Moore, 80.

91. Roth, 47.

92. Worcester, 12.

93. Wernstedt and Spencer, 78–79.

94. Japanese investors also appeared in Central America in the late 1920s. As Japan's post-World War I industrial boom advanced, she began surveying the entire Pacific Basin for sources of raw materials including timber. In 1929 Tom Gill reported that Japanese surveyors were carrying out timber surveys in the Caribbean Basin and were decidedly secretive about their findings. See Gill, *Tropical Forests of the Caribbean,* chap. 12.

95. M. C. Kellman, *Secondary Plant Succession in Tropical Montane Mindanao* (Canberra: Research School of Pacific Studies, Australian National University, 1970), esp. 23–27.

96. Moore, 78, 149.

97. This transformation of land from usufruct to ownership systems began in the Philippines with the first introduction of Spanish colonial law, derived from Spain's own late medieval traditions. See John Liddy Phelan, *The Hispanization of the Philippines: Spanish Aims and Filipino Responses, 1565–1700* (Madison: University of Wisconsin Press, 1959), chap. 8. The issue is of fundamental importance to the imposition of modern forestry management in most of the non-European world.

98. In the Philippines, as elsewhere, this should not be equated with the tension between market economy and subsistence in any simple polarity, especially for modern times. Even relatively remote tribal swiddeners developed complex connections with the market, primarily as providers of a range of forest products for settled lowland populations. For examples from Mindoro, Luzon, and Mindanao see Conklin; Robert Lawless, "Deforestation and Indigenous Attitudes in Northern Luzon," *Anthropology* 2:1 (1978): 1–13; and Stuart A. Schlegel, *Tiruray Subsistence: From Shifting Cultivation to Plow Agriculture* (Quezon City: Ateneo de Manila University Press, 1979).

99. Moore, "Forest Problems in the Philippines," 78.

100. Worcester, though not charitable in his views of most Filipinos' concern for preservation of the forests, did praise the Igorots of the pine forests of northern Luzon for their traditional system of communally limiting the lopping of branches for firewood and controlling grass fires in the pine forests. This, however, was not *kaingin*. Worcester, 2–4. See also Norman E. Kowal, "Shifting Cultivation, Fire, and Pine Forest in the Cordillera Central, Luzon, Philippines," *Ecological Monographs* 36:4 (1966): 389–419; and Lawless, 7–10.

101. Worcester, 11.

102. Phelan, 115–116.

103. Moore, 78; Worcester, 4.

104. Commonwealth of the Philippines, 9–12.

105. Commonwealth of the Philippines, 11.

106. Florencio Tamesis, "Philippine Forests and Forestry," *Unasylva* 2:6 (1948): 324–325.

107. Tamesis, 325.

108. G. Poblacion, "The Lumber Industry in 1946," *Philippine Journal of Forestry* 5:1 (1947): 72. He reports there that at the end of 1946, of the capital invested in the sawmill industry, "24.5% belonged to Filipinos, 41.2% to foreigners, and 34.3% to Filipinos associated with foreigners: American, British, Chinese, Spanish, Swiss and Puerto Rican."

109. Poblacion, 74. Some islands felt the lack of locally available timber and transport facilities more acutely than ever. On Cebu, where the forests had long been depleted and local needs were filled by imports from other islands, peasants expanded the cutting of the few remaining mountain forests. By 1957 Cebu had returned to its former pattern, importing 33 million board feet, mostly from the northern regions of Mindanao. Hardy L. Shirley, "Some Observations on Philippine Forestry, with Special Emphasis on Forestry Education" (unpublished paper, 1960), 8; Wernstedt and Spencer, 44.

110. For statistics see Anonymous, "Commodity Report: Hardwoods," *Unasylva* 12:4 (1958): 183–191; tables are on 186, 189. By the mid-1950s Japan

reappeared on the regional market, preparing to become its primary player. In 1956 Japan imported three times more logs than any other country, mostly lauan, four-fifths of them from the Philippines and one-fifth from North Borneo, for its plywood and lumber industries. Japan's imports of logs rose from an insignificant 12,000 cubic meters in 1948 to 2,331,000 cubic meters in 1956, and that was just the beginning of the great boom that rapidly depleted large areas of hardwood forests throughout the region. From its consumption of 4 percent of the world's hardwood trade in 1950, it rose to importing 50 percent of the global trade in the 1980s. Yet the United States was deeply involved in that pattern of rising consumption too: much of that wood was ultimately re-exported to the United States as milled lumber and high-grade plywood. See James K. Boyce, *The Philippines: The Political Economy of Growth and Impoverishment in the Marcos Era* (Honolulu: University of Hawaii Press, 1993), 227.

111. Boyce, 227.

112. Shirley, 2.

113. Interview with David Smith, Professor at Yale University Forestry School, 20 February 1987.

114. Shirley, 10.

115. Shirley, 8.

116. Hyman, 511–524.

117. David Kummer, *Deforestation in the Postwar Philippines* (Chicago: University of Chicago Press, 1992), 67.

118. In the short period between 1979 and 1982, economist Robert Repetto calculates, timber companies' profits totaled approximately $1.5 billion, but taxes brought only $141 million of that into the public treasury. See Robert Repetto, *The Forest for the Trees? Government Policies and the Misuse of Forest Resources* (Washington, D.C.: World Resources Institute, 1988), chap. 3.

119. See the table in Boyce, 229.

120. Boyce, chap. 8.

121. Kummer, 56.

122. Porter and Ganapin, chap. 3.

123. Nicolas P. Lansigan, "Our Dwindling Forests," *Forestry Leaves* 11 (1959): 19.

124. Lansigan, 20.

125. Winslow L. Gooch, *Forest Industries of the Philippines* (Manila: Bureau of Forestry and U.S. Mutual Security Agency, 1953), 129–137.

126. Tom Gill, "The Menace of Forest Destruction" (unpublished paper, 1959), 5–6.

127. Gill, "The Menace of Forest Destruction," 12–13.

128. Tom Gill, *Forestry Proposals for the Philippines* (Manila: International Cooperation Administration and National Economic Council, 1959), especially 35–36.

129. Four years later another senior U.S. tropical forester, Bruce Lamb, toured the islands. Lamb had had many years' experience in Central America and the Caribbean; his study of mahogany is still the standard work on that species. Lamb's observations in the Philippines reinforced Gill's assessment of

loggers and the rural poor. "The forest resources of the Islands are being destroyed at an alarming rate by small farmers working under a system of shifting cultivation called *kaingin* in the Philippines. Both virgin and selectively cut forest areas are being invaded and converted to worthless *cogon* grassland as cultivation is abandoned." He expressed the same blanket condemnation of tribal subsistence systems in the upland forests, except that in this case the brief visitor's highly simplified perceptions lacked a sense of the political basis of squatter movements or the distinction between tribals and dispossessed lowland peasants. F. Bruce Lamb, "Brief Notes on Forestry in Southeast Asia," *Caribbean Forester* 24:1 (1963): 19.

130. William J. Pomeroy, *An American Made Tragedy* (New York: International Publishers, 1974), 45.

131. Hugh Fraser, "Testing Time for Asia's Forest Products Pioneer," *World Wood* 21:13 (1980): 13.

132. James S. Bethel et al., *The Role of U.S. Multinational Corporations in Commercial Forestry Operations in the Tropics* (Seattle: College of Forest Resources, University of Washington, 1982).

133. Boyce, 223. In the 1970s and 1980s transnational corporations in the Philippines included Georgia-Pacific, Boise-Cascade, International Paper, and Weyerhaeuser, and their largest Japanese competitor, Mitsubishi.

134. Bevan, 52.

135. Callahan, 74–79.

136. Holdridge, Lamb, and Mason, 60–61.

137. Anonymous, "Commodity Report: Hardwoods," 183–191.

138. Anonymous, "Commodity Report: Hardwoods," 186, 188.

139. John A. Zivnuska, *U.S. Timber Resources in a World Economy* (Baltimore: Johns Hopkins University Press, 1967), 61.

140. McNeill, "Deforestation in the Araucaria Zone of Southern Brazil, 1900–1983," 15–32.

141. Anonymous, "Commodity Report: Pulp and Paper," *Unasylva* 12:3 (1959): 139.

142. Holdridge, Lamb, and Mason, 136.

143. F. Bruce Lamb, letter to Richard Tucker, 18 June 1987.

144. Lamb to Tucker.

145. Virgil T. Heath, *Forest Management and Salvage of Beetle Infested Timber in Honduras* (Washington, D.C.: Department of the Interior, Bureau of Land Management, 1964). A similar picture was clear in Guatemala; see Holdridge, Lamb, and Mason, 126–142. FAO reports document similar circumstances throughout Latin America.

146. Tom Gill, "America and World Forestry," 292.

147. United Nations, Food and Agriculture Organization, *Progress Report on Forestry and Forest Products,* February 1946, typescript, pp. 21–30, 37–42.

148. Anonymous, "Commodity Report: Pulp and Paper," 134–141; quotation is on 135. This article summarizes the full statistical survey in United Nations, Food and Agriculture Organization, *World Forest Products Statistics: A Ten-Year Summary, 1946–1955* (Rome: UNFAO, 1958).

149. United Nations, Food and Agriculture Organization, *World Forest Products Statistics*, 135, 138.

150. Bethel et al., 141.

151. Gustavo Gomez, "Case History of a South American Paper Mill," *Unasylva* 42: 1 (1988): 7–13.

152. David H. Blake and Robert E. Driscoll, *The Social and Economic Impacts of Transnational Corporations: Case Studies of the U.S. Paper Industry in Brazil* (New York: Fund for Multinational Management Education, 1976), 6–7.

153. Blake and Driscoll, 5–6. Patricia Marchak reports that Olinkraft more recently has switched to a primary emphasis on eucalyptus plantings. See *For Whom the Tree Falls* (Montreal: Queens McGill University Press, 1996), 441.

154. Robert K. Winters, "How Forestry Became a Part of FAO," *Journal of Forestry* 69 (1971): 574–577.

155. Egon Glesinger, *The Coming Age of Wood* (New York: Simon and Schuster, 1949), 9.

156. United Nations, Food and Agriculture Organization, *Report of the Latin-American Conference on Forestry and Forest Products* (Rio de Janeiro: UNFAO, 1948), 17–18.

157. United Nations, Food and Agriculture Organization, *Report of the Latin-American Conference on Forestry and Forest Products*, 8.

158. United Nations, Food and Agriculture Organization, *Report of the Latin-American Conference on Forestry and Forest Products*, 13.

159. Hardy L. Shirley, 564.

160. Shirley, 566.

161. Shirley, 567.

162. Similar perspectives were exported by Martin A. Huberman, another senior American forester who was active in FAO consultancies in the late 1940s. See his "Our Good Neighbors' Forestry," *Journal of Forestry* 46 (1948): 81–98.

163. Gill, "America and World Forestry," 291.

164. For details see Irvine T. Haig et al., *Forest Resources of Chile as a Basis for Industrial Expansion* (Washington, D.C.: U.S. Forest Service, 1946).

165. For further background on that process, see Thomas T. Veblen, "Degradation of Native Forest Resources in Southern Chile," in *History of Sustained-Yield Forestry: A Symposium*, ed. Harold K. Steen (Durham, N.C.: Forest History Society, 1984), 344–352.

166. Tom Gill, "Paraná Pine—A Source of Wood for Reconstruction in Europe," *Unasylva* 1:2 (1947): 30–32.

167. For a broad assessment of the state of the art in the aftermath of the war, see Caribbean Commission, *Forest Research Within the Caribbean Area* (Washington, D.C.: Caribbean Commission, 1947).

168. Lamb, *Mahogany of Tropical America*, 158–159.

169. F. Bruce Lamb, C. B. Briscoe, and G. H. Englerth, "Recent Observations on Forestry in Tropical America," *Caribbean Forester* 21:1–2 (1960): 47.

170. Hugh M. Raup, "Notes on Reforestation in Tropical America, I" (typescript, 1949).

171. Hugh M. Raup, "Notes on Reforestation in Tropical America, II" (typescript, 1950), 7–12, 44–63.

172. Raup, "Notes on Reforestation in Latin America, II," 2–6.

173. Raup, "Notes on Reforestation in Latin America, II," 5.

174. Lamb, Briscoe, and Englerth, 46–59; quotation is on 47.

175. In the Miskito pine forests of Nicaragua, in the watershed above Puerto Cabezas, the American-owned Nicaragua Longleaf Pine Lumber Company played a major role in the expansion of Nicaraguan pine exports after 1945. Denevan, 297–98.

176. Gustavo Gomez, "Case Study of a South American Paper Mill," Unasylva 42:1 (1988): 8–9.

177. Parsons, "The Miskito Pine Savanna of Nicaragua and Honduras," 57.

178. Heath, 29.

179. Heath, 26.

180. Heath, 31.

181. Ultimately, in 1974 the Honduran government confronted the situation by creating COHDEFOR, a national forestry corporation that henceforth was to oversee all timber exploitation, the first of its kind in the region. This transformed the structure of logging in Honduras, and made it more feasible for foreign forestry aid programs such as FAO, Canadian CIDA and USAID to work in contact with the small local firms which were doing most of the actual logging work. But that development was characteristic of a later era, beyond the scope of this book.

182. Interview with Leslie Holdridge, July 1987.

183. Gerardo Budowski, "The Opening of New Areas and Landscape Planning in Tropical Countries" (paper delivered at XII Congress of the International Federation of Landscape Architects, Lisbon, September 1970), 2.

184. Leslie R. Holdridge, "The Possibility of Close Cooperation for Mutual Benefit between Agriculture and Forestry in the American Tropics," Caribbean Forester 1:3 (1940): 28.

185. Bevan, 50. For further indication that the Puerto Rican forestry station was ahead of its time in understanding the social implications of forestry priorities, see similar arguments in Frank H. Wadsworth, "An Approach to Silviculture in Tropical America and Its Application in Puerto Rico," 245–256.

186. See Gerardo Budowski, "Middle America: The Human Factor," in Future Environments of North America, ed. F. Fraser Darling and John P. Milton (Garden City, N.Y.: Natural History Press, 1966), 150. Budowski points particularly to A. Aguirre, "Estudio Silvicultural y Economico del Sistema Taungya en las Condiciones de Turrialba," Turrialba 13:3 (1963): 168–171; and John Cater, "The Formation of Teak Plantations in Trinidad with the Assistance of Peasant Contractors," Caribbean Forester 2:4 (1941): 144–153.

187. For details of the Americans' links in the 1940s with the British in Trinidad, British Guinea, and British Honduras, the Dutch in Surinam, and the French in Mexico and Central America, see W. A. Gordon, "Forest Management in the Caribbean," Caribbean Forester 22:1–2 (1961): 21–26.

188. Wadsworth, "An Approach to Silvilculture in Tropical America and Its Application in Puerto Rico," 246.

189. Wadsworth, "An Approach to Sivilculture in Tropical America and Its Application in Puerto Rico," 255.

190. Wadsworth, "An Approach to Sivilculture in Tropical America and Its Application in Puerto Rico," 249.

191. William Vogt, "Latin-American Timber, Ltd.," *Unasylva* 1: 1 (1947): 19.

192. See also Vogt's important book, *Road to Survival* (New York: W. Sloane, 1948).

193. Vogt, *The Population of Costa Rica and Its Natural Resources,* 21.

194. United Nations, Food and Agriculture Organization, *Report of the Ninth Session of the Latin American Forestry Commission* (New York: UNFAO, 1964), 3–4.

195. See Budowski, "The Opening of New Areas and Landscape Planning in Tropical Countries," 13.

196. United Nations, Food and Agriculture Organization, *Report of the Ninth Session of the Latin American Forestry Commission,* especially 3–4.

197. See Bethel et al. for details.

198. Boyce, 233.

199. See François Nectoux and Yoichi Kuroda, *Timber from the South Seas* (Tokyo: Tsukiji Shokan, 1989).

200. Eugene F. Horn, "The Lumber Industry of the Lower Amazon Valley," *Caribbean Forester* 18:3–4 (1957): 56.

201. Louise P. Fortmann and Sally K. Fairfax, "American Forestry Professionalism in the Third World," *Economic and Political Weekly,* 12 August 1989, p. 1839.

202. Fortmann and Fairfax, 1840.

203. In striking contrast, only fourteen African addresses appeared on the list, and not one of those names was African. Independence had not yet quite arrived for most of the European colonies there.

204. Gill, "America and World Forestry," 282. His momentary spark of optimism was not yet justified. Moreover, the ISTF itself faded into quiescence in the late 1960s. But it was revived by Frank Wadsworth and others around 1970, and became a major force within the profession.

205. Norman K. Carlson and L. W. Bryan, "Report of the Standing Committee on Forestry—Tenth Pacific Science Congress, Hawaii," *Malayan Forester* 24: 4 (1961): 252–260.

206. And third: development infrastructure such as high dams and mines—which are not covered in this book.

CONCLUSION

1. The following figures are taken from David McCullough, *The Path Between the Seas: The Creation of the Panama Canal, 1870–1914* (New York: Simon and Schuster, 1977), 590–613.

Bibliography

UNPUBLISHED SOURCES

MANUSCRIPTS

Anonymous. "The Role of Forestry in the Development of the Commonwealth Caribbean." Draft manuscript, 1985.

Cobban, James L. "The Traditional Use of the Forests in Mainland Southeast Asia." Center for International Studies, Ohio University. Typescript, 1968.

Fukunaga, Larry K. "A History of the Hawaiian Sugar Planters' Association." Typescript, n. d.

Gill, Tom. "The Menace of Forest Destruction." Unpublished paper, 1959.

Raup, Hugh M. "Notes on Reforestation in Tropical America, Part I." Unpublished paper, 1949.

——. "Notes on Reforestation in Tropical America, Part II." Unpublished paper, 1950.

Shirley, Hardy L. "Some Observations on Philippine Forestry with Special Emphasis on Forestry Education." Unpublished paper, 1960.

United Nations, Food and Agriculture Organization. *Progress Report on Forestry and Forest Products*. Typescript, 1946.

THESES AND DISSERTATIONS

Duncan, K. "Some Aspects of the Economic Geography of the Forests of British Honduras." M.A. thesis, University of Edinburgh, 1966.

Ellis, Frank. "The Banana Export Activity in Central America 1947–1976." Ph.D. diss., University of Sussex, 1978.

Fenner, Bruce L. "Colonial Cebu: An Economic-Social History, 1521–1896." Ph.D. diss., Cornell University, 1976.

Horn, Sally Peterson. "Fire and Paramo Vegetation in the Cordillera de Tala-
    manca, Costa Rica." Ph.D. dissertation, University of California, Berkeley,
    1986.
Legarda, Benito F., Jr. "Foreign Trade, Economic Change and Entrepreneurship
    in the Nineteenth Century Philippines." Ph.D. diss., Harvard University,
    1955.
McLennan, Marshall. "Peasant and Hacendero in Nueva Ecija: The Socio-
    Economic Origins of a Philippine Commercial Rice-Growing Region." Ph.D.
    diss., University of California, 1973.
Murray, Gerald. "The Evolution of Haitian Peasant Land Tenure: A Case Study
    in Agrarian Adaptation to Population Growth." Ph.D. diss., Columbia Uni-
    versity, 1977.
Russell, Edmund P. "War on Insects: Warfare, Insecticides, and Environmental
    Change in the United States, 1870–1945." Ph.D. diss., University of Mich-
    igan, 1993.
Scheffey, Andrew J. W. "Natural Resources and Government Policy in Coa-
    huila, Mexico." Ph.D. diss., University of Michigan, 1958.
Soluri, John. "Landscape and Livelihood: An Agroecological History of Export
    Banana Growing in Honduras, 1870–1975." Ph.D. diss., University of Mich-
    igan, 1998.
Thee, Kian Wee. "Plantation Agriculture and Export Growth: An Economic
    History of East Sumatra, 1863–1942." Ph.D. diss., University of Wisconsin,
    1969.
Wadsworth, Frank H. "The Development of the Forest Land Resources of the
    Luquillo Mountains, Puerto Rico." Ph.D. diss., University of Michigan,
    1949.

PAPERS

Budowski, Gerardo. "The Opening of New Areas and Landscape Planning in
    Tropical Countries." Paper presented at XII Congress of the International
    Federation of Landscape Architects, Lisbon, September 1970.
Butzer, Carl W. "Cattle from Old to New Spain: Historical Antecedents." Paper
    presented at the Latin American Geographers' Conference, Merida, Mexico,
    January 1987.
Doolittle, William E., and Terry G. Jordan. "Marismas to Panuco: The Transfer
    of Lowland/Wetland Cattle Herding from Iberia to Mexico." Paper pre-
    sented at Latin American Geographers' Conference, Merida, Mexico, Jan-
    uary 1987.
Escobar, Francisco. "Gone with the Beef: The Social History of a Case of Nat-
    ural Resource Use in Costa Rica." Paper presented for workshop, "Lands at
    Risk in the Third World: Local Level Perspectives," Institute of Development
    Anthropology, Binghamton, N.Y., October 1985.
Gibbs, Christopher, and Jeff Romm. "Institutional Aspects of Forestry Devel-
    opment in Asia." Paper presented at conference on Forestry and Develop-
    ment in Asia, Bangalore, India, 1982.

Gill, Tom. "The Menace of Forest Destruction." Paper presented to Philippine Lumber Producers' Association, Manila, 1959.

Tucker, Richard P. "U.S. Corporations and Timber Exploitation in Central America, 1890–1950." Paper presented at conference of American Society for Environmental History and Forest History Society, Duke University, April 1987.

PUBLISHED MATERIALS

GOVERNMENT DOCUMENTS

Anonymous. *The International Coffee Agreement.* Washington, D.C.: U.S. Government Printing Office, 1963.

Anonymous. *Philippine Forestry and Wood Industry Development.* Manila: Presidential Committee on Wood Industries Development, 1971.

Anonymous. *Raw Material Resources Survey Bulletin, Series I: General Tables.* Manila: National Economic Council, 1959.

Caribbean Commission. *Forest Research Within the Caribbean Area.* Washington, D.C.: Caribbean Commission, 1947.

Commonwealth of the Philippines. *Forest Resources of the Philippines.* Manila: 1939.

Great Britain, Imperial Economic Committee. *Cattle and Beef Survey: A Summary of Production and Trade in British Empire and Foreign Countries.* London: His Majesty's Stationery Office, 1934.

Holsoe, Torkel. *Third Report on Forestry Progress in Liberia, 1951–1959.* Washington, D.C.: International Cooperation Administration, 1961.

Pan American Coffee Bureau. *Annual Coffee Statistics: 1958.* Washington, D.C.: Pan American Coffee Bureau, 1958.

Philippine Bureau of Forestry. *Annual Reports,* from 1901.

Philippine Bureau of Forestry. *Forestry Golden Book.* Manila: 1950.

United Nations. *Plenary Meetings.* Vol. 1 of *Proceedings of the United Nations Scientific Conference on the Conservation and Utilization of Resources.* New York: United Nations, 1950.

United Nations, Development Programme and Food and Agriculture Organization. *The Philippines: Range Management.* FO:SF/PHI 16, Technical Report 7. Rome: UNFAO, 1971.

———. *The Philippines: Watershed Management.* FO:SF/PHI 16, Technical Report 6. Rome: UNFAO, 1971.

United Nations, Food and Agriculture Organization. *Coffee in Latin America: Productivity Problems and Future Prospects.* 2 vols. New York: UNFAO, 1958.

———. *Proceedings of the Conference on Pulp and Paper Development in Asia and the Far East, Held in Tokyo, 17–31 October 1960.* Bangkok: UNFAO, 1962.

———. *Report of the Latin-American Conference on Forestry and Forest Products.* Rio de Janeiro: UNFAO, 1948.

———. *Report of the Ninth Session of the Latin American Forestry Commission.* New York: UNFAO, 1964.

————. *Survey of Agricultural and Forest Resources: Nicaragua, Final Report.* Vol. I: General. Rome: UNFAO, 1969.

————. *Tropical Forest Resources Assessment Project: Forest Resources of Tropical Asia.* Rome: UNFAO, 1981.

————. *The World Banana Economy, 1970–1984: Structure, Performance and Prospects.* Rome: UNFAO, 1986.

————. *World Coffee Trade.* New York: UNFAO, 1963.

————. *World Forest Products Statistics: A Ten-Year Summary, 1946–1955.* Rome: UNFAO, 1958.

U.S. Department of Agriculture, Foreign Agricultural Service. *World Livestock and Poultry Situation.* Washington, D.C.: 1985.

U.S. Department of Commerce, Bureau of Foreign Commerce. *American Lumber in Foreign Markets: Special Consular Reports XI.* Washington, D.C.: U.S. Government Printing Office, 1896.

U.S. Department of State. *Draft Environmental Report on the Philippines.* Washington, D.C.: U.S. Department of State and U.S. Man and the Biosphere Secretariat, 1980.

————. *Draft Environmental Profile of Honduras.* Washington, D.C.: U.S. Department of State, 1981.

BOOKS

Abbott, George C. *Sugar.* London: Routledge, 1990.

Adamic, Louis. *The House in Antigua.* New York: Harper and Brothers, 1937.

Adams, Frederick Upham. *Conquest of the Tropics: The Story of the Creative Enterprises Conducted by the United Fruit Company.* Garden City, N.Y.: Doubleday Page, 1914.

Adler, Jacob. *Claus Spreckels: The Sugar King in Hawaii.* Honolulu: University of Hawaii Press, 1966.

Agnew, D. B. *The Outlook for Hamburger Livestock and Meat Situation.* Washington, D.C.: U.S. Department of Agriculture, 1979.

Ahern, George P. *Special Report of the Forestry Bureau, Philippine Islands.* Washington, D.C.: War Department, 1901.

Albion, Robert G. *Forests and Sea Power.* Cambridge, Mass.: Harvard University Press, 1926.

Allen, George C., and Audrey G. Donnithorne. *Western Enterprise in Indonesia and Malaya: a Study in Economic Development.* New York: Macmillan, 1957.

Allen, Merritt P. *William Walker, Filibuster.* New York: Harper Brothers, 1932.

Alonzo, Anna Maria. *Thread of Blood: Colonialism, Revolution and Gender on Mexico's Northern Frontier.* Tucson: University of Arizona Press, 1995.

Arévalo, Juan José. *The Shark and the Sardines.* New York: Lyle Stuart, 1961.

Arnson, Cynthia. *El Salvador: A Revolution Confronts the United States.* Washington, D.C.: Institute for Policy Studies, 1982.

Ashcraft, Norman. *Colonialism and Underdevelopment: Processes of Political*

Economic Change in British Honduras. New York: Columbia University Teachers College Press, 1973.

Atkins, Edwin F. *Sixty Years in Cuba.* New York: Arno Press, 1980.

Auslander, Leora. *Taste and Power: The Life-Cycle of Parisian Furniture, 1750–1940.* Berkeley: University of California Press, 1996.

Aykroyd, W. R. *Sweet Malefactor: Sugar, Slavery and Human Society.* London: Heinemann, 1967.

Babcock, Glenn D. *History of the United States Rubber Company: A Case Study in Corporation Management.* Bloomington: Bureau of Business Research, Indiana University, 1966.

Bailey, John P. *Central America: Describing Each of the States of Guatemala, Honduras, Salvador, Nicaragua, and Costa Rica.* London: Saunders, 1850.

Bailyn, Bernard. *The New England Merchants in the Seventeenth Century.* New York: Harper and Row, 1955.

Bakewell, P. J. *Silver Mining and Society in Colonial Mexico: Zacatecas, 1546–1700.* Cambridge: Cambridge University Press, 1971.

Barbour, Thomas. *A Naturalist in Cuba.* Boston: Little, Brown, 1945.

Barham, Bradford L., and Oliver T. Coomes. *Prosperity's Promise: The Amazon Rubber Boom and Distorted Economic Development.* Oxford: Oxford University Press, 1996.

Barlow, Colin. *The Natural Rubber Industry: Its Development, Technology and Economy in Malaysia.* Kuala Lumpur: Oxford University Press, 1978.

Barry, Tom, Beth Wood, and Deb Preusch. *Dollars and Dictators.* New York: Grove Press, 1983.

Bartlett, P. S. *Agricultural Choice and Change: Decision-Making in a Costa Rican Community.* New Brunswick, N.J.: Rutgers University Press, 1982.

Bartolome Francisco, Luzviminda, and Jonathan Shepard Fast. *Conspiracy for Empire: Big Business, Corruption and the Politics of Imperialism in America, 1876–1907.* Quezon City: Foundation for Nationalist Studies, 1985.

Beaglehole, J. *Exploration of the Pacific.* 3d ed. Stanford: Stanford University Press, 1966.

Beard, J. S. *The Natural Vegetation of the Windward and Leeward Islands.* Oxford Forestry Memoirs. Oxford: Clarendon Press, 1949.

Beckford, George L. *Persistent Poverty: Underdevelopment in Plantation Economies of the Third World.* Oxford: Oxford University Press, 1972.

Beechert, Edward D. *The American Frontier in Hawaii: The Pioneers, 1789–1843.* Stanford: Stanford University Press, 1942.

———. *Working in Hawaii: A Labor History.* Honolulu: University of Hawaii Press, 1985.

Bell, John Patrick. *Crisis in Costa Rica: The 1948 Revolution.* Austin: University of Texas Press, 1971.

Benjamin, Medea, Joseph Collins, and Michael Scott. *No Free Lunch: Food and Revolution in Cuba Today.* San Francisco: Institute for Food and Development Policy, 1984.

Bennett, Hugh H. *The Soils of Cuba.* Washington, D.C.: Tropical Plant Research Foundation, 1928.

Bernstein, Marvin, ed. *Foreign Investment in Latin America*. New York: Knopf, 1966.

Bethel, James S., ed. *World Trade in Forest Products*. Seattle: University of Washington Press, 1983.

Bethel, James S., et al. *The Role of U.S. Multinational Corporations in Commercial Forestry Operations in the Tropics*. Seattle: College of Forest Resources, University of Washington, 1982.

Bethell, Leslie, ed. *Cambridge History of Latin America*. 3 vols. Cambridge: Cambridge University Press, 1984.

Blake, David H., and Robert E. Driscoll. *The Social and Economic Impacts of Transnational Corporations: Case Studies of the U.S. Paper Industry in Brazil*. New York: Fund for Multinational Management Education, 1976.

Boeke, J. H. *Economics and Economic Policy of Dual Societies, as Exemplified by Indonesia*. New York: Institute of Pacific Relations, 1953.

———. *The Evolution of the Netherlands Indies Economy*. New York: Institute of Pacific Relations, 1946.

Boorstein, Edward. *The Economic Transformation of Cuba*. New York: Monthly Review Press, 1968.

Bourgois, Philippe. *Ethnicity at Work: Divided Labor on a Central American Banana Plantation*. Baltimore: Johns Hopkins University Press, 1989.

Boxer, Charles R. *The Dutch Seaborne Empire: 1600–1800*. New York: Knopf, 1970.

Boyce, James K. *The Philippines: The Political Economy of Growth and Impoverishment in the Marcos Era*. Honolulu: University of Hawaii Press, 1993.

Bradley, H., and Michael Blaker, eds. *Development Assistance to Southeast Asia: The United States and Japanese Approaches*. New York: Columbia University Press, 1984.

Brandes, Joseph. *Herbert Hoover and Economic Diplomacy: Department of Commerce Policy, 1921–1928*. Pittsburgh: University of Pittsburgh Press, 1962.

Braudel, Fernand. *The Structures of Everyday Life: The Limits of the Possible*. Vol. 1 of *Civilization and Capitalism, 15th–18th Century*. New York: Harper and Row, 1979.

Brennan, Joseph. *The Parker Ranch*. New York: Harper & Row, 1974.

Bresnan, John, ed. *Crisis in the Philippines: The Marcos Era and Beyond*. Princeton: Princeton University Press, 1986.

Brewer, J., and R. Porter, eds. *Consumption and the World of Goods*. London: Routledge, 1993.

Brookfield, Harold, Lesley Potter, and Yvonne Byron. *In Place of the Forest: Environmental and Socioeconomic Transformation in Borneo and the Eastern Malay Peninsula*. Tokyo: United Nations University Press, 1995.

Brown, William H. *Vegetation of Philippine Mountains*. Manila: Bureau of Printing, 1919.

Brown, William H., and Arthur F. Fischer. *Philippine Mangrove Swamps*. Bulletin No. 17. Manila: Bureau of Forestry, 1918.

Browning, David. *El Salvador: Landscape and Society.* Oxford: Clarendon Press, 1971.

Burbach, Roger, and Patricia Flynn. *Agribusiness in the Americas.* New York: Monthly Review Press, 1980.

Burgess, Eugene W. *Casa Grace in Peru.* Washington, D.C.: National Planning Association, 1954.

Burley, T. M. *The Philippines: An Economic and Social Geography.* London: G. Bell, 1973.

Burner, David. *Herbert Hoover: A Public Life.* New York: Knopf, 1978.

Burns, E. Bradford. *The Poverty of Progress: Latin America in the Nineteenth Century.* Berkeley: University of California Press, 1980.

Bushnell, David. *The Making of Modern Colombia: A Nation in Spite of Itself.* Berkeley: University of California Press, 1993.

Bustas-Sanvictores, Josefina, ed. *Philippine Forestry and Wood Industry.* Quezon City: Philippine Association for Permanent Forests, 1971.

Caiger, Stephen L. *British Honduras, Past and Present.* London: George Allen and Unwin, 1951.

Caldwell, Malcolm. *The Wealth of Some Nations.* London: Zed, 1977.

Callahan, John C. *The Fine Hardwood Veneer Industry in the United States: 1838–1990.* Lake Ann, Mich.: National Woodlands Publishing Company, 1990.

Callis, Helmut G. *Foreign Capital in Southeast Asia.* New York: Institute of Pacific Relations, 1942.

Campbell, Charles S. *Special Business Interests and the Open Door Policy.* New Haven: Yale University Press, 1951.

———. *The Transformation of American Foreign Relations, 1865–1900.* New York: Harper and Row, 1976.

Cardoso, Ciro F. S., and Hector Perez Brignoli. *Centro America y la Economia Occidental (1520–1930).* San Jose: Editorial Universidad de Costa Rica, 1977.

Cardoso, F. H., and E. Faletto. *Dependency and Development in Latin America.* Berkeley: University of California Press, 1978.

Carlquist, Sherwin. *Hawaii, a Natural History: Geology, Climate, Native Flora and Fauna above the Shoreline.* 2d ed. Honolulu: SB Printers, 1980.

———. *Island Biology.* New York: Columbia University Press, 1974.

Carlson, Oliver. *Hearst, Lord of San Simeon.* New York: Viking, 1936.

Carstensen, Vernon, ed. *The Public Lands: Studies in the History of the Public Domain.* Madison: University of Wisconsin Press, 1962.

Casey Gaspar, Jeffrey J. *Limon 1880–1940: Un Estudio de la Industria Bananera en Costa Rica.* San Jose: Editorial de Costa Rica, 1979.

Chaloner, Edward. *The Mahogany Tree in the West Indies and Central America.* Liverpool, n.p., 1850.

Chambers, J. D., and G. E. Mingay. *The Agricultural Revolution, 1750–1880.* New York: Schocken Books, 1966.

Champion, Harry G., and S. K. Sethi. *General Silviculture for India.* 3d ed. Delhi: Government of India, 1968.

Chaney, Lindsay, and Michael Cieply. *The Hearsts: Family and Empire—The Later Years*. New York: Simon and Schuster, 1981.

Chaudhuri, K. N. *Asia Before Europe*. Cambridge: Cambridge University Press, 1990.

Chevalier, Francois. *Land and Society in Colonial Mexico: The Great Hacienda*. Trans. Alvin Eustis. Berkeley: University of California Press, 1963.

Chomsky, Aviva. *West Indian Workers and the United Fruit Company in Costa Rica, 1870–1940*. Baton Rouge: Louisiana State University Press, 1996.

Clepper, Henry. *Professional Forestry in the United States*. Baltimore: Johns Hopkins University Press, 1971.

Clower, Robert, et al. *Growth Without Development: An Economic Survey of Liberia*. Evanston, Ill.: Northwestern University Press, 1966.

Colby, Gerard. *Thy Will Be Done: The Conquest of the Amazon: Nelson Rockefeller and Evangelism in the Age of Oil*. New York: Harper Collins, 1995.

Collins, Joseph. *Nicaragua: What Difference Could a Revolution Make? Food and Farming in the New Nicaragua*. Rev. ed. San Francisco: Institute for Food and Development, 1985.

Coni, Emilio. *Historia de las vaquerias de Rio de la Plata, 1555–1750*. Buenos Aires: Editorial Devenir, 1956.

Conklin, Harold. *Hanunoo Agriculture*. Rome: Food and Agriculture Organization, 1955.

Conway, Gordon, and Jeff Romm. *Ecology and Resource Development in Southeast Asia*. New York: Ford Foundation, 1973.

Cooper, George, and Gavan Daws. *Land and Power in Hawaii*. Honolulu: University of Hawaii Press, 1985.

Coquery-Vidrovitch, Catherine. *Le Congo au temps des grandes compagnies concessionnaires, 1898–1930*. Paris: Mouton, 1972.

Cortes Conde, Roberto, and Stanley J. Stein, eds. *Latin America: A Guide to Economic History, 1830–1930*. Berkeley: University of California Press, 1977.

Cowan-Smith, Virginia, and Bonnie Domrose Stone. *Aloha Cowboy*. Honolulu: University of Hawaii Press, 1988.

Cowdrey, Albert E. *This Land, This South: An Environmental History*. Lexington: University of Kentucky Press, 1983.

Cox, Thomas R. *Mills and Markets: A History of the Pacific Coast Lumber Industry to 1900*. Seattle: University of Washington Press, 1974.

Cox, Thomas R., et al. *This Well Wooded Land: Americans and Their Forests from Colonial Times to the Present*. Lincoln: University of Nebraska Press, 1985.

Cronon, William. *Changes in the Land: Indians, Colonists and the Ecology of New England*. New York: Hill and Wang, 1983.

———. *Nature's Metropolis: Chicago and the Great West*. New York: Norton, 1991.

Crosby, Alfred W., Jr. *The Columbian Exchange: Biological and Cultural Consequences of 1492*. Westport, CT: Greenwood Press, 1972.

———. *Ecological Imperialism*. Cambridge: Cambridge University Press, 1986.

Crowther, Samuel. *The Romance and Rise of the American Tropics.* Garden City, N.Y.: Doubleday Doran, 1929.

Cuddihy, Linda W., and Charles P. Stone. *Alternation of Native Hawaiian Vegetation: Effects of Humans, Their Activities and Introductions.* Honolulu: University of Hawaii Press, 1990.

Cunningham, Clark E. *The Postwar Migration of the Toba-Bataks to East Sumatra.* Southeast Asia Studies Cultural Report Series. New Haven: Yale University Press, 1958.

Curtin, Philip. *Two Jamaicas: The Role of Ideas in a Tropical Colony, 1830–1865.* Cambridge, Mass.: Harvard University Press, 1955.

Dargavel, John, et al., eds. *Changing Tropical Forests: Historical Perspectives on Today's Challenges in Asia, Australasia and Oceania.* Durham, N.C.: Forest History Society, 1988.

Dasmann, Raymond. *The Destruction of California.* New York: MacMillan, 1965.

———. *Environmental Conservation.* New York: Wiley, 1984.

Davies, Peter N. *Fyffes and the Banana: A Centenary History, 1888–1988.* London: Athlone Press, 1990.

Daws, Gavan. *Shoal of Time: A History of the Hawaiian Islands.* Honolulu: University of Hawaii Press, 1968.

Dean, Warren. *Brazil and the Struggle for Rubber.* Cambridge: Cambridge University Press, 1987.

———. *The Industrialization of São Paulo, 1880–1945.* Austin: University of Texas Press, 1969.

———. *Rio Claro: A Brazilian Plantation System, 1820–1920.* Stanford: Stanford University Press, 1976.

———. *With Broadax and Firebrand: The Destruction of the Brazilian Atlantic Forest.* Berkeley: University of California Press, 1995.

Deerr, Noel. *The History of Sugar.* 2 vols. London: Chapman and Hall, 1949–1950.

Denevan, William M., ed. *The Native Population of the Americas in 1492.* Madison: University of Wisconsin Press, 1976.

Dennett, Tyler. *Americans in Eastern Asia.* New York: Macmillan, 1922.

Denny, Harold M. *Dollars for Bullets: The Story of American Rule in Nicaragua.* Westport, Conn.: Greenwood Press, 1980. Reprint of 1st ed., 1929.

Development of Upland Areas in the Far East. New York: Institute of Pacific Relations, 1951.

Diskin, Martin. *Agrarian Reform in El Salvador: An Evaluation.* San Francisco: Institute for Food and Development Policy, 1985.

Dobson, Narda. *A History of Belize.* Trinidad and Jamaica: Longman Caribbean, 1973.

Dodge, Ernest S. *Island and Empires: Western Impact on the Pacific and East Asia.* Minneapolis: University of Minnesota Press, 1976.

Donner, Wolf. *Land Use and Environment in Indonesia.* Honolulu: University of Hawaii Press, 1987.

Dorner, Peter, ed. *Land Reform in Latin America: Issues and Cases.* Madison: University of Wisconsin Press, 1971.

Dosal, Paul J. *Doing Business with Dictators: A Political History of United Fruit in Guatemala, 1899–1944.* Wilmington, Del.: Scholarly Resources Books, 1993.

Dourojeanni, Marc J. *Renewable Natural Resources of Latin America and the Caribbean: Situation and Trends.* Washington, D.C.: World Wildlife Fund—U.S., 1980.

Dozier, Craig L. *Nicaragua's Mosquito Shore: The Years of British and American Presence.* Tuscaloosa: University of Alabama Press, 1985.

Dulles, Foster R. *America in the Pacific: a Century of Expansion.* Boston: Houghton Mifflin, 1932.

Dunn, Robert W. *American Foreign Investments.* New York: B. W. Huebsch and Viking Press, 1926.

Durham, William H. *The Soccer War: Scarcity and Survival in Central America.* Stanford: Stanford University Press, 1979.

Echauz, Robustiano. *Apuntes de la Isla de Negros.* Manila: Tipo-lit, 1894.

Eckes, Alfred E., Jr. *The United States and the Global Struggle for Minerals.* Austin: University of Texas Press, 1979.

Edelstein, Michael. *Overseas Investment in the Age of High Imperialism: The United Kingdom, 1850–1914.* New York: Columbia University Press, 1982.

Edminster, Lynn R. *The Cattle Industry and the Tariff.* New York: MacMillan, 1926.

Eichner, Alfred S. *The Emergence of Oligopoly: Sugar Refining as a Case Study.* Baltimore: Johns Hopkins University Press, 1969.

Eisenberg, Peter L. *The Sugar Industry in Pernambuco, 1840–1910: Modernization without Change.* Berkeley: University of California Press, 1974.

Elchibegoff, Ivan M. *United States International Timber Trade in the Pacific Area.* Stanford: Stanford University Press, 1949.

Elson, Robert E. *Javanese Peasants and the Colonial Sugar Industry: Impact and Change in an East Java Residency, 1830–1940.* Singapore: Oxford University Press, 1984.

Faber, Daniel. *Environment under Fire: Imperialism and the Ecological Crisis in Latin America.* New York: Monthly Review Press, 1993.

Fader, Ernest. *The Rape of the Peasantry: Latin America's Landholding System.* Garden City, N.Y.: Anchor Books, 1971.

Faulk, Odie B. *The Last Years of Spanish Texas, 1778–1821.* London: Mouton, 1964.

Feis, Herbert. *The Diplomacy of the Dollar, 1919–1932.* New York: Norton, 1950.

———. *Europe: The World's Banker, 1870–1914.* New Haven: Yale University Press, 1930.

Fernow, Bernhard E. *A Brief History of Forestry, in Europe, the United States and Other Countries.* Toronto: University of Toronto Press, 1911.

Fickle, James E. *The New South and the "New Competition": Trade Association Development in the Southern Pine Industry.* Urbana: University of Illinois Press for the Forest History Society, 1980.

Fifield, Russell. *Americans in Southeast Asia.* New York: Crowell, 1973.

Firestone, Harvey S. *Men and Rubber: The Story of Business*. Garden City, N.Y.: Doubleday, Page, 1926.

Fisher, Charles A. *South-east Asia: A Social, Economic and Political Geography*. London: Methuen, 1964.

Fisher, Raymond H. *The Russian Fur Trade, 1500–1700*. University of California Publications in History, vol. 31. Berkeley: University of California Press: 1943.

Fite, Gilbert C. *Cotton Fields No More: Southern Agriculture, 1865–1980*. Lexington: University of Kentucky Press, 1984.

Flader, Susan L., ed. *The Great Lakes Forest: An Environmental and Social History*. Minneapolis: University of Minnesota Press, 1983.

Flink, James J. *The Automobile Age*. Cambridge, Mass.: MIT Press, 1988.

———. *The Car Culture*. Cambridge, Mass.: Harvard University Press, 1975.

Fosberg, F. R., ed. *Man's Place in the Island Ecosystem*. Honolulu: Bishop Museum Press, 1963.

Fox, Richard Wightman, and T. J. Jackson Lears, eds. *The Culture of Consumption: Critical Essays in American History, 1880–1980*. New York: Pantheon Books, 1983.

Franck, Harry A. *Roaming Through the West Indies*. London: T. Fisher Unwin, 1921.

Frank, Andre Gunder. *ReORIENT: Global Economy in the Asian Age*. Berkeley: University of California Press, 1998.

Friend, Theodore. *Between Two Empires: The Ordeal of the Philippines, 1929–1946*. New Haven: Yale University Press, 1965.

Fuchs, Lawrence. *Hawaii Pono: "Hawaii the Excellent": An Ethnic and Political History*. Honolulu: Bess Press, 1961.

Furnivall, J. S. *Netherlands India: a Study of Plural Economy*. Cambridge: Cambridge University Press, 1944.

Furtado, J. I., ed. *Tropical Ecology and Development*. Kuala Lumpur: International Society of Tropical Ecology, 1980.

Galbraith, J. K. *The Affluent Society*. New York: New American Library, 1958.

Galbraith, John S. *The Hudson's Bay Company as an Imperial Factor, 1821–1869*. Toronto: University of Toronto Press, 1957.

Galeano, Eduardo H. *Open Veins in Latin America: Five Centuries of the Pillage of a Continent*. New York: Modern Review, 1973.

Galloway, J. H. *The Sugar Cane Industry: An Historical Geography from Its Origins to 1914*. Cambridge: Cambridge University Press, 1989.

Garcia Marquez, Gabriel. *One Hundred Years of Solitude*. New York: Avon Books, 1970.

Gardner, Rolland. *Philippine Sawmills, Lumber Market, and Prices*. Bulletin No. 4. Manila: Bureau of Forestry, 1906.

Gates, Paul. *The Farmer's Age: Agriculture, 1815–1860*. New York: Holt, Rinehart, Winston, 1960.

Gellman, Irwin F. *Good Neighbor Diplomacy, 1933–1945*. Baltimore: Johns Hopkins University Press, 1979.

Genovese, Eugene. *The World the Slaveholders Made*. New York: Pantheon, 1969.

Gershoni, Yekutiel. *Black Colonialism: The Americo-Liberian Scramble for the Hinterland.* Boulder, Colo.: Westview, 1985.

Gettleman, Marvin, et al., eds. *El Salvador: Central America in the New Cold War.* New York: Evergreen, 1981.

Gibson, Charles. *Aztecs under Spanish Rule.* Stanford: Stanford University Press, 1964.

Gibson, James R. *Otter Skins, Boston Ships and China Goods.* Seattle: University of Washington Press, 1992.

Giedion, Siegfried. *Mechanization Takes Command.* New York: Oxford University Press, 1948.

Gill, Tom. *Forestry Proposals for the Philippines.* Manila: International Co-operation Administration and National Economic Council, 1959.

———. *Tropical Forests of the Caribbean.* Washington, D.C.: Charles Lathrup Pack Foundation, 1931.

Gillis, R. Peter, and Thomas Roach. *Canada's Forest Industries, Forest Policy and Forest Conservation.* Durham, N.C.: Forest History Society and Greenwood Press, 1986.

Glesinger, Egon. *The Coming Age of Wood.* New York: Simon and Schuster, 1949.

Goetzmann, William H. *When the Eagle Screamed: The Romantic Horizon in American Diplomacy, 1800–1860.* New York: John Wiley, 1966.

Golay, Frank, ed. *The United States and the Philippines.* Englewood Cliffs, N.J.: Prentice Hall, 1966.

Gooch, Winslow L. *Forest Industries of the Philippines.* Manila: Bureau of Forestry and U.S. Mutual Security Agency, 1953.

Goodrum, Charles, and Helen Dalrymple. *Advertising in America: The First 200 Years.* New York: Abrams, 1990.

Goodwin, Neva R., Frank Ackerman, and David Kiron, eds. *The Consumer Society.* Washington, D.C.: Island Press, 1997.

———. *Costa Rica before Coffee: Society and Economy on the Eve of the Export Boom.* Baton Rouge: Louisiana State University Press, 1986.

Gordon, Burton LeRoy. *Anthropogeography and Rainforest Ecology in Bocas del Toro Province, Panama.* Berkeley: University of California Press, 1969.

Gould, James W. *Americans in Sumatra.* The Hague: Martinus Nijhoff, 1961.

Grattan, C. Hartley. *The Southwest Pacific to 1900: A Modern History.* Ann Arbor: University of Michigan Press, 1963.

———. *The Southwest Pacific Since 1900.* Ann Arbor: University of Michigan Press, 1963.

———. *The United States and the Southwest Pacific.* Cambridge, Mass.: Harvard University Press, 1961.

Gregersen, Hans M., and Arnaldo Contreras. *U.S. Investment in the Forest-Based Sector in Latin America: Problems and Potentials.* Baltimore: Johns Hopkins University Press, 1975.

Gregg, A. R. *British Honduras.* London: Her Majesty's Stationery Office, 1968.

Grieb, Kenneth J. *Guatemalan Caudillo.* Athens: Ohio University Press, 1979.

Griffin, Keith. *Underdevelopment in Spanish America.* Cambridge, Mass.: MIT Press, 1969.

Grigg, D. B. *The Agricultural Systems of the World.* Cambridge: Cambridge University Press, 1974.

Grilli, Enzo R., Barbara Bennett Agostini, and Maria J. 't Hooft-Welvaars. *The World Rubber Economy: Structure, Changes, and Prospects.* Baltimore: Johns Hopkins University Press, 1980.

Grindle, Merilee S. *State and Countryside: Development Policy and Agrarian Politics in Latin America.* Baltimore: Johns Hopkins University Press, 1986.

Grinnell, Joseph, et al. *Fur-bearing Mammals of California.* 2 vols. Berkeley: University of California Press, 1937.

Griswold, A. Whitney. *The Far Eastern Policy of the United States.* New York: Harcourt, Brace, 1938.

Grove, Richard. *Green Imperialism: Colonial Expansion, Tropical Island Edens and the Origins of Environmentalism, 1600–1860.* Oxford: Oxford University Press, 1995.

Grunwald, Joseph, ed. *Latin America and the World Economy.* Los Angeles: Sage, 1978.

Grunwald, Joseph, and Philip Musgrove. *Natural Resources in Latin American Development.* Baltimore: Johns Hopkins University Press, 1970.

Gudmundson, Lowell. *Central America, 1821–1871: Liberalism before Liberal Reform.* Tuscaloosa: University of Alabama Press, 1995.

Guerra y Sanchez, Ramiro. *Sugar and Society in the Caribbean: an Economic History of Cuban Agriculture.* New Haven: Yale University Press, 1964.

Guggenheim, Harry F. *The United States and Cuba: A Study in International Relations.* New York: Macmillan, 1934.

Gullick, John. *Malaysia: Economic Expansion and National Unity.* London: Benn, and Boulder, Colo.: Westview, 1981.

Haig, Irvine T., et al. *Forest Resources of Chile as a Basis for Industrial Expansion.* Washington, D.C.: U.S. Forest Service, 1946.

Halberstam, David. *The Fifties.* New York: Villard Books, 1993.

Hall, Carolyn O. *Costa Rica: A Geographical Interpretation in Historical Perspective.* Boulder, Colo.: Westview, 1985.

Halperin-Donghi, Tulio. *Economy and Society in Argentina in the Revolutionary Period.* Cambridge: Cambridge University Press, 1975.

Hamilton, Lawrence, and Samuel C. Snedaker, eds. *Handbook for Mangrove Area Management.* Honolulu: East-West Center, 1984.

Handy, E. S. Craighill, and Elizabeth Green Handy. *Native Planters in Old Hawaii: Their Life, Lore and Environment.* Honolulu: Bishop Museum Press, 1972.

Hanks, Lucien. *Rice and Man: Agricultural Ecology in Southeast Asia.* Chicago: Aldine, 1972.

Hanson, Simon G. *Argentine Meat and the British Market.* Stanford: Stanford University Press, 1956.

Hao Yen-ping. *The Commercial Revolution in Nineteenth Century China: The Rise of Sino-Western Mercantile Capitalism.* Berkeley: University of California Press, 1968.

Harms, Robert. *River of Wealth, River of Sorrow.* New Haven: Yale University Press, 1981.

Hartendorp, A. V. H. *History of Industry and Trade of the Philippines.* Manila: American Chamber of Commerce, 1958.

Hawaiian Sugar Planters' Association. *Sugar in Hawaii.* Honolulu: Hawaiian Sugar Planters' Association, 1949.

Hawes, Gary. *The Philippine State and the Marcos Regime: The Politics of Export.* Ithaca: Cornell University Press, 1987.

Hays, Samuel P. *Conservation and the Gospel of Efficiency.* Cambridge, Mass.: Harvard University Press, 1959.

Heath, Virgil T. *Forest Management and Salvage of Beetle Infested Timber in Honduras.* Washington, D.C.: Department of the Interior, Bureau of Land Management, 1964.

Hecht, Susanna, and Alexander Cockburn. *The Fate of the Forest: Developers, Destroyers and Defenders of the Amazon.* New York: Harper Perennial Books, 1989.

Heckadon, Stanley H., and Alberto McKay, eds. *Colonizacion y Destruccion de Bosques en Panama.* Panama City: Asociacion Panamena de Antropologia, 1982.

Helms, Mary W. *Middle America: A Cultural History of Heartland and Frontier.* Englewood Cliffs, N.J.: Prentice-Hall, 1975.

Henderson, H. D. *Colonies and Raw Materials.* New York: Farrar and Rinehart, 1939.

Hennessy, Alistair. *The Frontier in Latin American History.* London: Edward Arnold, 1978.

Henry, O. [William S. Porter]. *Cabbages and Kings.* New York: Doubleday, Page, 1912.

Higman, B. W. *Slave Population and Economy in Jamaica, 1807–1834.* Cambridge: Cambridge University Press, 1976.

Hitch, Thomas K. *Islands in Transition: The Past, Present and Future of Hawaii's Economy.* Honolulu: First Hawaiian Bank, 1992.

Holdridge, Leslie, F. Bruce Lamb, and Harold Mason. *Forests of Guatemala.* Privately printed, 1950.

Honig, Pieter, and F. Verdoorn, eds. *Science and Scientists in the Netherlands Indies.* New York: Board for The Netherlands Indies, Surinam and Curaçao, 1945.

Horn, Stanley F. *This Fascinating Lumber Business.* Indianapolis and New York: Bobbs Merrill, 1951.

Horowitz, Daniel. *The Morality of Spending: Attitudes toward the Consumer Society in America, 1875–1940.* Baltimore: Johns Hopkins University Press, 1985.

Huke, Robert E. *Shadows on the Land: An Economic Geography of the Philippines.* Manila: Bookmark, 1963.

Humphrey, Don D. *American Imports.* New York: Twentieth Century Fund, 1955.

Hutterer, Karl L., ed. *Economic Exchange and Social Interaction in Southeast Asia: Perspectives from Prehistory, History, and Ethnography.* Ann Arbor: Center for South and Southeast Asian Studies, University of Michigan, 1977.

———. *Interaction Between Tropical Ecosystems and Human Foragers: Some General Considerations*. Honolulu: East-West Center Working Paper, 1982.

Hutterer, Karl L., A. Terry Rambo, and George Lovelace, eds. *Cultural Values and Human Ecology in Southeast Asia*. Ann Arbor: Center for South and Southeast Asian Studies, University of Michigan, 1985.

Instituto Cubano de Estabilización del Café. *Segunda Conferencia Panamericana del Café*. Havana: Instituto Cubano de Estabilización del Café, 1937.

International Union of Forest Research Organizations. *Congress Proceedings*. Vienna: IUFRO.

Jackson, James C. *Planters and Speculators: Chinese and European Agricultural Enterprise in Malaya, 1786–1921*. Kuala Lumpur: University of Malaya Press, 1968.

Jackson, Kenneth T. *Crabgrass Frontier: The Suburbanization of the United States*. Oxford: Oxford University Press, 1985.

Janvry, Alain de. *The Agrarian Question and Reformism in Latin America*. Baltimore: Johns Hopkins University Press, 1981.

Janzen, Daniel, ed. *Costa Rica: A Natural History*. Chicago: University of Chicago Press, 1983.

Jarvis, Lovell S. *Livestock Development in Latin America*. Washington, D.C.: World Bank, 1986.

Jenkins, Shirley. *American Economic Policy Toward the Philippines*. Stanford: Stanford University Press, 1954.

Jenks, Leland H. *Our Cuban Colony: A Study in Sugar*. New York: Vanguard Press, 1928.

Johannessen, Carl L. *Savannas of Interior Honduras*. Berkeley: University of California Press, 1963.

Johnson, Arthur M., and Barry E. Supple. *Boston Capitalists and Western Railroads: A Study in the Nineteenth-Century Railroad Investment Process*. Cambridge, Mass.: Harvard University Press: 1967.

Jones, Eric L. *The European Miracle: Environments, Economies and Geopolitics in the History of Europe and Asia*. Cambridge: Cambridge University Press, 1981.

Jordan, Terry G. *North American Cattle-Ranching Frontiers: Origins, Diffusion, and Differentiation*. Albuquerque: University of New Mexico Press, 1993.

Josephson, Matthew. *The Robber Barons: The Great American Capitalists, 1861–1901*. New York: Harcourt, Brace and World, 1962.

Judd, Richard W. *Maine, the Pine Tree State, from Prehistory to the Present*. Orono: University of Maine Press, 1995.

Kahn, Joel. *Minangkabau Social Formations: Indonesian Peasants and the World Economy*. Cambridge: Cambridge University Press, 1980.

Karasch, Mary. *Slave Life in Rio de Janeiro, 1808–1850*. Princeton: Princeton University Press, 1987.

Karnes, Thomas L. *Tropical Enterprise: The Standard Fruit and Steamship Company in Latin America*. Baton Rouge: Louisiana State University Press, 1978.

Katz, Friedrich. *Life and Times of Pancho Villa.* Stanford University Press, 1998.

Kellman, M. C. *Secondary Plant Succession in Tropical Montane Mindanao.* Canberra: Research School of Pacific Studies, Australian National University, 1970.

Kepner, Charles D., Jr. *Social Aspects of the Banana Industry.* New York: Columbia University Press, 1936; reprint, New York: AMS Press, 1967.

Kerkvleit, Benjamin J., ed. *Political Change in the Philippines: Studies of Local Politics Preceding Martial Law.* Honolulu: University of Hawaii Press, 1974.

Kimber, Clarissa Therese. *Martinique Revisited: The Changing Plant Geographies of a West Indian Island.* College Station: Texas A&M University Press, 1988.

Klein, Julius. *The Mesta: A Study in Spanish Economic History, 1273–1836.* Cambridge, Mass.: Harvard University Press, 1920.

Knight, Franklin W., and Peggy K. Liss, eds. *Atlantic Port Cities: Economy, Culture, and Society in the Atlantic World, 1650–1850.* Knoxville: University of Tennessee Press, 1991.

Knight, Melvin M. *The Americans in Santo Domingo.* New York: Vanguard Press, 1928.

Krasner, Stephen D. *Defending the National Interest: Raw Materials Investments and U.S. Foreign Policy.* Princeton: Princeton University Press, 1978.

Kummer, David. *Deforestation in the Postwar Philippines.* Chicago: University of Chicago Press, 1992.

Kuykendall, Ralph S., and A. Grove Day. *Hawaii: A History, from Polynesian Kingdom to American State.* Rev. ed. Englewood Cliffs, N.J.: Prentice-Hall, 1961.

LaFeber, Walter. *Inevitable Revolutions: The United States and Central America.* New York: Norton, 1983.

———. *The New Empire: An Interpretation of American Expansion, 1860–1898.* Ithaca: Cornell University Press, 1963.

Lamb, F. Bruce. *Mahogany of Tropical America: Its Ecology and Management.* Ann Arbor: University of Michigan Press, 1966.

Landsberg, Hans H., Leonard L. Fishman, and Joseph L. Fisher. *Resources in America's Future: Patterns of Requirements and Availabilities, 1960–2000.* Baltimore: Johns Hopkins University Press, 1963.

Langley, Lester D. *The Cuban Policy of the United States: A Brief History.* New York: Wiley, 1968.

Langley, Lester D., and Thomas Schoonover. *The Banana Men: American Mercenaries and Entrepreneurs in Central America, 1880–1930.* Lexington: University of Kentucky Press, 1995.

Lanly, Jean Paul. *Tropical Forest Resources.* United Nations, Food and Agriculture Organization, Forestry Paper No. 30. Rome: UNFAO, 1983.

Larkin, John A. *Sugar and the Origins of Modern Philippine Society.* Berkeley: University of California Press, 1993.

Lasch, Christopher. *The Culture of Narcissism.* New York: Norton, 1978.

Lawrence, James C. *The World's Struggle with Rubber, 1905–1931.* New York: Harper, 1931.

Lea, Tom. *The King Ranch*. 2 vols. Boston: Little Brown, 1957.

Leach, William. *Land of Desire: Merchants, Power, and the Rise of a New American Culture*. New York: Pantheon Books, 1993.

Lears, Jackson. *Fables of Abundance: A Cultural History of Advertising in America*. New York: Basic Books, 1994.

Lebergott, Stanley. *Pursuing Happiness: American Consumers in the Twentieth Century*. Princeton: Princeton University Press, 1993.

LeGrand, Catherine. *Frontier Expansion and Peasant Protest in Colombia, 1850–1936*. Albuquerque: University of New Mexico Press, 1986.

Leonard, H. Jeffrey. *Natural Resources and Economic Development in Central America*. New Brunswick, N.J.: Transaction Press, 1987.

Leopold, Aldo. *The River of God and Other Essays*, ed. Susan L. Flader and J. Baird Callicott. Madison: University of Wisconsin Press, 1991.

Leuchtenburg, William E. *A Troubled Feast: American Society since 1945*. Boston: Little, Brown, 1973.

Levenstein, Harvey A. *Paradox of Plenty: A Social History of Eating in Modern America*. Oxford: Oxford University Press, 1993.

———. *Revolution at the Table: The Transformation of the American Diet*. Oxford: Oxford University Press, 1988.

Levin, Jonathan. *The Export Economies: Their Pattern of Development in Historical Perspective*. Cambridge, Mass.: Harvard University Press, 1960.

Lewis, Cleona. *America's Stake in International Investments*. Washington, D.C.: Brookings Institution, 1938.

Liebenow, J. Gus. *Liberia: The Evolution of Privilege*. Ithaca: Cornell University Press, 1969

Lief, Alfred. *The Firestone Story*. New York: McGraw Hill, 1951.

Limerick, Patricia Nelson. *The Legacy of Conquest*. New York: Norton, 1987.

Lister, Florence C., and Robert H. Lister. *Chihuahua: Storehouse of Storms*. Albuquerque: University of New Mexico Press, 1966.

Lloyd, John W. *Pan American Trade, with Special Reference to Fruits and Vegetables*. Washington, D.C.: U.S. Department of Agriculture, 1942.

Lockhart, James, and Stuart B. Schwartz. *Early Latin America: A History of Colonial Spanish America and Brazil*. Cambridge: Cambridge University Press, 1983.

Logan, R. W. *Haiti and the Dominican Republic*. London: Oxford University Press, 1968.

Long, W. Rodney. *Railways of Central America and the West Indies*. Trade Promotion Series, No. 5. Washington, D.C.: Department of Commerce, 1925.

Lopez-Gonzaga, Violeta. *Voluntary Land-Sharing and Transfer Scheme in Negros*. Bacolod: Social Research Center, La Salle College, 1986.

Love, Joseph. *Sao Paulo in the Brazilian Federation, 1889–1937*. Stanford: Stanford University Press, 1980.

Lower, Arthur R. M. *The North American Assault on the Canadian Forest*. Toronto: University of Toronto Press, 1938.

Lynch, Frank. *A Bittersweet Taste of Sugar: A Preliminary Report on the Sugar*

Industry in Negros Oriental. Quezon City: Ateneo de Manila University Press, 1970.

MacArthur, R. H., and E. O. Wilson. *The Theory of Island Biogeography.* Princeton: Princeton University Press, 1967.

Machado, Manuel A., Jr. *The North Mexican Cattle Industry, 1910–1975: Ideology, Conflict, and Change.* College Station: Texas A & M University Press, 1981.

MacLeod, Murdo J. *Spanish Central America: A Socioeconomic History, 1520–1720.* Berkeley: University of California Press, 1973.

Macquoid, P. *History of English Furniture.* New York: Putnam and Sons, 1904.

Maguire, Andrew, and Janet Welsh Brown, eds. *Bordering on Trouble: Resources and Politics in Latin America.* Bethesda, Md.: Adler and Adler, 1986.

Marchak, Patricia. *For Whom the Tree Falls.* Montreal: Queens McGill University Press, 1996.

Marshall, Herbert, Frank A. Southard, Jr., and Kenneth W. Taylor. *Canadian-American Industry.* New Haven: Yale University Press, 1936.

Marshall, Jonathan. *To Have and Have Not: Southeast Asian Raw Materials and the Origins of the Pacific.* Berkeley: University of California Press, 1995.

Martin, Lynn J., ed. *Na Paniolo o Hawai'i.* Honolulu: Honolulu Academy of Arts, 1987.

Marx, Leo. *The Machine in the Garden: Technology and the Pastoral Ideal in America.* Oxford: Oxford University Press, 1964.

Masefield, G. B. *A History of the Colonial Agricultural Service.* Oxford: Clarendon Press, 1972.

Matthews, D. M. *Ipil-Ipil: A Firewood and Reforestation Crop.* Bulletin No. 13. Manila: Bureau of Forestry, 1914.

May, Ernest R. *American Imperialism: A Speculative Essay.* New York: Atheneum, 1968.

May, Ernest R., and John K. Fairbank. *America's China Trade in Historical Perspective.* Cambridge, Mass.: Harvard University Press, 1986.

May, Glenn Anthony. *Social Engineering in the Philippines: The Aims, Execution, and Impact of American Colonial Policy, 1900–1913.* Westport, Conn.: Greenwood Press, 1980.

May, Jacques Mayer. *The Ecology of Malnutrition in the Caribbean.* New York: Hafner, 1973.

May, Stacy. *Costa Rica.* New York: Twentieth Century Fund, 1952.

McCann, Thomas P. *An American Company: The Tragedy of United Fruit.* New York: Crown, 1976.

McCoy, Alfred W. *Priests on Trial.* New York: Penguin, 1984.

McCoy, Alfred W., and Ed. C. de Jesus, eds. *Philippine Social History: Global Trade and Local Transformations.* Quezon City: Ateneo de Manila University Press, 1982.

McCullough, David. *The Path Between the Seas: The Creation of the Panama Canal, 1870–1914.* New York: Simon and Schuster, 1977.

McKendrick, Neil, John Brewer, and J. H. Plumb. *The Birth of a Consumer Society: The Commercialization of Eighteenth Century England.* London: Europa Publications, and Bloomington: Indiana University Press, 1982.

McNeill, John R. *Atlantic Empires of France and Spain: Louisbourg and Havana, 1700–1763*. Chapel Hill: University of North Carolina Press, 1985.

Meijer, Willem. *Indonesian Forests and Land Use Planning*. Washington, D.C: National Science Foundation and Agency for International Development, 1975.

Melville, Elinor. *A Plague of Sheep*. Cambridge: Cambridge University Press, 1994.

Merritt, Melvin L., and H. N. Whitford. *A Preliminary Working Plan for the Public Forest Tract of the Mindoro Lumber and Logging Company, Bongabon, Mindoro, P. I.* Bulletin No. 6. Manila: Bureau of Forestry, 1906.

Miller, Daniel, ed. *Acknowledging Consumption: A Review of New Studies*. London: Routledge, 1995.

Mintz, Sidney. *Caribbean Transformations*. Chicago: Aldine, 1974.

———. *Sweetness and Power: The Place of Sugar in Modern History*. New York: Viking, 1985.

Monbeig, Pierre. *Pionniers et Planteurs de São Paulo*. Paris: A. Colin, 1952.

Montejo, Esteban. *The Autobiography of a Runaway Slave*. Harmondsworth: Penguin, 1970.

Montgomery, Tommie Sue. *Revolution in El Salvador*. Boulder, Colo.: Westview, 1982.

Moore, John Hebron. *Andrew Brown and Cypress Lumbering in the Old Southwest*. Baton Rouge: Louisiana State University Press, 1967.

Moreno, S. H. *Cuando Se Acaban Los Montes*. Panama City: Smithsonian Tropical Research Institute, 1983.

Morgan, Q. Martin. *The Beef Cattle Industries of Central America and Panama*. Washington, D.C.: U.S. Department of Agriculture, 1973.

Morison, Samuel Eliot. *The Maritime History of Massachusetts, 1783–1860*. Boston: Houghton Mifflin, 1941.

Moriyama, Alan T. *Imingaisha: Japanese Emigration Companies and Hawaii, 1894–1908*. Honolulu: University of Hawaii Press, 1986.

Morley, James W., ed. *The Pacific Basin: New Challenges for the United States*. New York: Columbia University Press, 1986.

Mowat, Farley. *Sea of Slaughter*. Boston: Atlantic Monthly Press, 1984.

Munro, Dana G. *The United States and the Caribbean Republics, 1921–1933*. Princeton: Princeton University Press, 1974.

Murphy, Martin. *Dominican Sugar Plantations*. New York: Praeger, 1991.

Myers, Norman. *The Primary Source: Tropical Forests and Our Future*. New York: Norton, 1984.

———. *A Wealth of Wild Species: Storehouse for Human Welfare*. Boulder, Colo.: Westview Press, 1983.

Nations, James D. *Tropical Moist Forest Destruction in Middle America: Current Patterns and Alternatives*. Austin, Tex.: Center for Human Ecology, 1980.

Nectoux, François. *Timber! An Investigation of the U.K. Tropical Timber Industry*. London: Friends of the Earth, 1985.

Nectoux, François, and Yoichi Kuroda. *Timber from the South Seas*. Tokyo: Tsukiji Shokan, 1989.

Nelson, Samuel H. *Colonialism in the Congo Basin, 1880–1940.* Athens: Ohio University, 1994.

Nevins, Allan, and Frank E. Hill. *Ford: Expansion and Challenge, 1915–1933.* New York: Scribners, 1954.

Nichols, Roy F. *Advance Agents of American Destiny.* Philadelphia: University of Pennsylvania Press, 1956.

Nietschmann, Bernard. *Between Land and Water: The Subsistence Ecology of the Miskito Indians, Eastern Nicaragua.* New York and London: Seminar Press, 1973.

Nishihara, Masashi. *The Japanese and Sukarno's Indonesia: Tokyo-Jakarta Relations, 1951–1966.* Honolulu: East-West Center Books, 1976.

Norris, James D. *Advertising and the Transformation of American Society, 1865–1920.* New York: Greenwood Press, 1990.

North, Douglass C. *Economic Growth of the United States, 1790–1860.* New York: Norton, 1966.

Ogden, Adele. *The California Sea Otter Trade, 1784–1848.* Berkeley: University of California Press, 1941.

Oliver, Douglas L. *The Pacific Islands.* Rev. ed. Honolulu: University of Hawaii Press, 1975.

Olivier, Sydney Haldane. *Jamaica, the Blessed Land.* London: Faber and Faber, n.d.[1935?].

O'Reilly, Maurice. *The Goodyear Story.* Elmsford, N.Y.: Benjamin Press, 1983.

Ortiz, Fernando. *Cuban Counterpoint: Tobacco and Sugar.* New York: Knopf, 1947.

Orwin, Christabel S., and Edith H. Whetham. *History of British Agriculture 1846–1914.* London: Longmans, 1964.

Osborn, Fairfield. *Our Plundered Planet.* New York: Pyramid Books, 1948.

Owen, Norman G. *Prosperity Without Progress: Manila Hemp and Material Life in the Colonial Philippines.* Berkeley: University of California Press, 1984.

Owen, Norman G., ed. *Compadre Colonialism: Studies on the Philippines under American Rule.* Papers on South and Southeast Asia, No. 3. Ann Arbor: University of Michigan, 1971.

———. *The Philippine Economy and the United States: Studies in Past and Present Interactions.* Papers on South and Southeast Asia, No. 22. Ann Arbor: University of Michigan, 1983.

Packenham, Robert. *Liberal America and the Third World.* Princeton: Princeton University Press, 1973.

Paige, Jeffery M. *Coffee and Power: Revolution and the Rise of Democracy in Central America.* Cambridge, Mass.: Harvard University Press, 1997.

Palacios, Marco. *Coffee in Colombia, 1850–1970: An Economic, Social and Political History.* Cambridge: Cambridge University Press, 1980.

Pares, Richard. *Yankees and Creoles: The Trade between North America and the West Indies before the American Revolution.* Cambridge, Mass.: Harvard University Press, 1956.

Parry, J. H. *The Age of Reconnaissance: Discovery, Exploration and Settlement, 1450 to 1650.* London: Weidenfeld and Nicholson, 1963.

Parry, J. H., and Philip Sherlock. *A Short History of the West Indies.* 3d ed. London: MacMillan, 1971.

Parsons, James J. *Antioqueño Colonization in Western Colombia.* Rev. ed. Berkeley: University of California Press, 1968.

Payson, William F. *Mahogany: Antique and Modern.* New York: E. P. Dutton, 1926.

Pelzer, Karl. *Pioneer Settlement in the Asiatic Tropics: Studies in Land Utilization and Agricultural Colonization in Southeastern Asia.* New York: American Geographical Society, 1945.

———. *Planter and Peasant: Colonial Policy and the Agrarian Struggle in East Sumatra, 1863–1947.* The Hague: Nijhoff, 1978.

Pendergrast, Mark. *Uncommon Grounds: The History of Coffee and How It Transformed Our World.* New York: Basic Books, 1999.

Petulla, Joseph. *American Environmental History.* San Francisco: Boyd and Fraser, 1977.

Phelan, John Liddy. *The Hispanization of the Philippines: Spanish Aims and Filipino Responses, 1565–1700.* Madison: University of Wisconsin Press, 1959.

Phillips, John F. V. *The Development of Agriculture and Forestry in the Tropics.* Rev. ed. New York: Praeger, 1967.

Pinchot, Gifford. *Breaking New Ground.* New York: Harcourt-Brace, 1947.

Platt, D. C. M. *Foreign Finance in Continental Europe and the United States, 1815–1870.* London: Allen and Unwin, 1984.

Pluvier, Jan. *South-East Asia from Colonialism to Independence.* Kuala Lumpur: Oxford University Press, 1974.

Pollen, J. H. *Ancient and Modern Furniture and Woodwork.* London: Chapman and Hall, 1874.

Pomeroy, William J. *An American Made Tragedy.* New York: International Publishers, 1974.

Ponting, Clive. *A Green History of the World: The Environment and the Collapse of Great Civilizations.* New York: Penguin, 1993.

Pope, Daniel. *The Making of Modern Advertising.* New York: Basic Books, 1983.

Popenoe, Wilson. *Manual of Tropical and Subtropical Fruits.* New York: Hafner Press, 1920.

Porter, Gareth, with Delfin J. Ganapin, Jr. *Resources, Population, and the Philippines' Future.* Washington, D.C.: World Resources Institute, 1988.

Potter, Neal, and Francis T. Christy, Jr. *Trends in Natural Resources Commodities, Statistics of Prices, Outputs, Consumption, Foreign Trade and Employment in the United States, 1870–1957.* Baltimore: Johns Hopkins University Press, 1962.

Pratt, Julius W. *Expansionists of 1898: The Acquisition of Hawaii and the Spanish Islands.* Baltimore: Johns Hopkins University Press, 1936.

Pringle, Robert. *Indonesia and the Philippines: American Interests in Island Southeast Asia.* New York: Columbia University Press, 1980.

Pulp and Paper Industry in the Philippines. Manila: National Economic Council, Survey and Research Department, 1957.

Pyne, Stephen. *Fire in America: A Cultural History of Wildland and Rural Fire.* Princeton: Princeton University Press, 1982.

Quirino, Carlos. *History of the Philippine Sugar Industry.* Manila: Kalayaan Publishing Co., 1974.

Ragatz, Lowell. *The Fall of the Planter Class in the British Caribbean, 1763–1863.* New York: Century, 1928.

Rappaport, Roy A. *Pigs for the Ancestors.* New Haven: Yale University Press, 1968.

Ratner, Sidney. *The Tariff in American History.* New York: Van Nostrand, 1972.

Rauch, Basil. *The American Interest in Cuba, 1848–1855.* New York: Columbia University Press, 1948.

Record, Samuel J., and Clayton D. Mell. *Timbers of Tropical America.* New Haven: Yale University Press, 1924.

Reid, Anthony. *The Lands Below the Winds.* Vol. 1 of *Southeast Asia in the Age of Commerce, 1450–1680.* New Haven: Yale University Press, 1988.

Repetto, Robert. *The Forest for the Trees? Government Policies and the Misuse of Forest Resources.* Washington, D.C.: World Resources Institute, 1988.

Repetto, Robert, ed. *The Global Possible: Resources, Development, and the New Century.* New Haven: Yale University Press, 1985.

Repetto, Robert, and Malcolm Gillis, eds. *Public Policies and the Misuse of Forest Resources.* Cambridge: Cambridge University Press, 1988.

Rifkin, Jeremy. *Beyond Beef: The Rise and Fall of the Cattle Culture.* New York: Dutton, 1992.

Ripperton, J. C., and E. Y. Hosaka. *Vegetation Zones of Hawaii.* Bulletin No. 89. Honolulu: Hawaii Agricultural Experiment Station, 1942.

Rippy, J. Fred. *The Capitalists and Colombia.* New York: Vanguard Press, 1931.

———. *Globe and Hemisphere: Latin America's Place in the Postwar Foreign Relations of the United States.* Chicago: Regnery, 1958.

———. *Latin America in the Industrial Age.* New York: Putnam, 1944.

———. *Rivalry of the United States and Great Britain over Latin America, 1808–30.* Baltimore: Johns Hopkins University Press, 1929.

Robbins, Roy M. *Our Landed Heritage: the Public Domain, 1776–1970.* 2d ed. Lincoln: University of Nebraska Press, 1976.

Robequain, Charles. *Malaya, Indonesia, Borneo, and the Philippines.* London: Longmans, Green, 1958.

Robison, Richard. *Indonesia: The Rise of Capital.* Sydney: Allen and Unwin, 1986.

Rohrbough, Malcolm J. *The Land Office Business: the Settlement and Administration of American Public Lands, 1789–1837.* Oxford: Oxford University Press, 1968.

Romney, D. H., ed. *Land in British Honduras.* Colonial Research Publication No. 24. London: Her Majesty's Stationery Office, 1959.

Rosenberg, Emily S. *Spreading the American Dream: American Economic and Cultural Expansion, 1890–1945.* New York: Hill and Wang, 1982.

Roth, Dennis. *The Friar Estates of the Philippines.* Albuquerque: University of New Mexico Press, 1977.

Rouse, John E. *The Criollo: Spanish Cattle in the Americas.* Norman: University of Oklahoma Press, 1977.

———. *World Cattle.* 2 vols. Norman: University of Oklahoma Press, 1970.

Rowe, J. W. F. *Primary Commodities in International Trade.* Cambridge: Cambridge University Press, 1965.

———. *The World's Coffee.* London: Her Majesty's Stationery Office, 1963.

Saenger, P., E. J. Hegerl, and J. D. S. Davie, eds. *Global Status of Mangrove Ecosystems.* Commission on Ecology Papers, No. 3. Gland: International Union for the Conservation of Nature and Natural Resources, 1983.

Sauer, Carl. *The Early Spanish Main.* Berkeley: University of California Press, 1966.

Savage, Victor. *Western Impressions of Nature and Landscape in Southeast Asia.* Singapore: Singapore University Press, 1984.

Schama, Simon. *The Embarrassment of Riches: Amsterdam in the Golden Age.* New York: Knopf, 1987.

Schlebacker, John T. *Cattle Raising on the Plains, 1900–1961.* Lincoln: University of Nebraska Press, 1963.

Schlegel, Stuart A. *Tiruray Subsistence: From Shifting Cultivation to Plow Agriculture.* Quezon City: Ateneo de Manila University Press, 1979.

Schmitt, Robert C. *Demographic Statistics of Hawaii: 1778–1965.* Honolulu: University of Hawaii Press, 1968.

———. *Historical Statistics of Hawaii.* Honolulu: University of Hawaii Press, 1977.

Schneider, E. E. *Commercial Woods of the Philippines: Their Preparation and Uses.* Manila: Bureau of Forestry, 1916.

Schuler, Monica. *"Alas, Alas, Kongo," A Social History of Indentured African Immigration into Jamaica, 1841–1865.* Baltimore: Johns Hopkins University Press, 1980.

Schwartz, Norman B. *Forest Society: A Social History of Peten, Guatemala.* Philadelphia: University of Pennsylvania Press, 1990.

Schwartz, Stuart B. *Sugar Plantations in the Formation of Brazilian Society: Bahia, 1550–1835.* Cambridge: Cambridge University Press, 1985.

Scobie, James R. *Argentina: A City and a Nation.* London: Oxford University Press, 1971.

———. *Revolution on the Pampas: A Social History of Argentine Wheat, 1860–1910.* Austin: University of Texas Press, 1964.

Scott, James. *The Moral Economy of the Peasant.* New Haven: Yale University Press, 1977.

———. *Weapons of the Weak.* New Haven: Yale University Press, 1985.

Scott, Rebecca J. *Slave Emancipation in Cuba: The Transition to Free Labor, 1860–1899.* Princeton: Princeton University Press, 1985.

Scott-Kemmis, Don. *Transnational Corporations and Tropical Industrial Forestry.* Sussex: Science Policy Research Unit, Sussex University, 1983.

Sedjo, Roger A., and Samuel J. Radcliffe. *Postwar Trends in U.S. Forest Prod-*

ucts Trade: A Global, National, and Regional View. Washington, D.C.: Resources for the Future, 1980.

Shalom, Stephen Rosskamm. *The United States and the Philippines: A Study of Neocolonialism.* Philadelphia: Institute for the Study of Human Issues, 1981.

Shane, Douglas R. *Hoofprints on the Forest: An Inquiry into the Beef Cattle Industry in the Tropical Forest Areas of Latin America.* Philadelphia: Institute for the Study of Human Issues, 1986.

Sheridan, Thomas E. *Where the Dove Calls.* Tucson: University of Arizona Press, 1988.

Shineberg, Dorothy. *They Came for Sandalwood: A Study of the Sandalwood Trade in the South-West Pacific.* Melbourne: University of Melbourne Press, 1967.

Shurz, William L. *The Manila Galleon.* New York: Dutton, 1959.

Sicat, Gerardo P., ed. *The Philippine Economy in the 1960s.* Quezon City: Institute of Economic Development and Research, University of the Philippines, 1964.

Silliman, James, and Peter Hazelwood, compilers. *Draft Environmental Profile of Honduras.* Tucson: University of Arizona Arid Lands Information Center, 1981.

Simmons, Roger E. *Lumber Markets of the West and North Coasts of South America.* Special Agents Series, No. 117. Washington, D.C.: Department of Commerce, Bureau of Foreign and Domestic Commerce, 1916.

Simon, Laurence, and James Stephens, Jr. *El Salvador Land Reform, 1980–81.* Boston: Oxfam America, 1982.

Simonian, Lane. *Land of the Jaguar: A History of Conservation in Mexico.* Austin: University of Texas Press, 1995.

Simpson, James R., and Donald E. Farris. *The World's Beef Business.* Ames: Iowa State University Press, 1982.

Sitterson, J. Carlyle. *Sugar Country: The Cane Sugar Industry in the South, 1753–1950.* Lexington: University of Kentucky Press, 1953.

Skutch, Alexander. *A Naturalist in Costa Rica.* Gainesville: University of Florida Press, 1971.

Slatta, Richard W. *Comparing Cowboys and Frontiers.* Norman: University of Oklahoma Press, 1997.

———. *Cowboys of the Americas.* New Haven: Yale University Press, 1990.

Smith, Earl E. *The Forests of Cuba.* Maria Moors Cabot Foundation Publication No. 2. Petersham, Mass.: Harvard Forest; and Cienfuegos, Cuba: Atkins Garden and Research Laboratory, 1954.

Smith, Henry Nash. *Virgin Land: The American West as Symbol and Myth.* Cambridge, Mass.: Harvard University Press, 1950.

Smith, Peter. *Politics and Beef in Argentina: Patterns of Conflict and Change.* New York: Columbia University Press, 1969.

Smith, T. Lynn. *Colombia: Social Structure and the Process of Development.* Gainesville: University of Florida Press, 1967.

Spencer, J. E. *Land and People in the Philippines: Geographic Problems in Rural Economy.* Berkeley: University of California Press, 1952.

———. *Shifting Cultivation in Southeast Asia.* Berkeley: University of California Press, 1966.

Stakman, E. C., Richard Bradfield, and Paul C. Mangelsdorf. *Campaigns against Hunger.* Cambridge, Mass.: Harvard University Press, 1967.

Staley, Eugene. *Raw Materials in Peace and War.* New York: Council on Foreign Relations, 1937.

Standley, Paul C., and Samuel J. Record. *The Forests and Flora of British Honduras.* Botanical Series, vol. 12. Chicago: Field Museum of Natural History, 1936.

Stanley, Peter W., ed. *Reappraising an Empire: New Perspectives on Philippine-American History.* Cambridge, Mass.: Harvard University Press, 1984.

Stannard, David E. *Before the Horror: The Population of Hawaii on the Eve of Western Contact.* Honolulu: Social Science Research Institute, University of Hawaii, 1989.

Starbuck, Alexander. *History of the American Whale Fishery.* Waltham, Mass.: the author, 1878.

Starrs, Paul. *Let the Cowboy Ride: Cattle Ranching in the American West.* Baltimore: Johns Hopkins University Press, 1998.

Stebbing, E. P. *The Forests of India.* 3 vols. London: John Lane, 1922–1926.

Steen, Harold K. *The U.S. Forest Service: A History.* Seattle: University of Washington Press, 1976.

Steen, Harold K., ed. *History of Sustained-Yield Forestry: A Symposium.* Durham, N.C.: Forest History Society, 1984.

———. *Plantation Forestry in the Amazon: The Jari Experience.* Durham, N.C.: Forest History Society, 1997.

Stein, Stanley J. *Vassouras: A Brazilian Coffee County, 1850–1900.* Cambridge, Mass.: Harvard University Press, 1957.

Steinberg, David Joel, et al. *In Search of Southeast Asia: A Modern History.* Honolulu: University of Hawaii Press, 1985.

Stern, H. J. *Rubber, Natural and Synthetic.* New York: Palmerton, 1967.

Stern, Paul C., et al., eds. *Environmentally Significant Consumption.* Washington, D.C.: National Academy Press, 1997.

Stevenson, G. C. *Genetics and Breeding of Sugar Cane.* London: Longmans Green, 1965.

Stewart, Watt. *Henry Meiggs: Yankee Pizarro.* Durham, N.C.: Duke University Press, 1946.

———. *Keith and Costa Rica.* Albuquerque: University of New Mexico Press, 1964.

Stolcke, Verena. *Coffee Planters, Workers and Wives.* Oxford: Macmillan, 1988.

Stoler, Ann Laura. *Capitalism and Confrontation in Sumatra's Plantation Belt, 1870–1979.* New Haven: Yale University Press, 1985.

Stone, Charles P., and M. J. Scott, eds. *Hawaii's Terrestrial Ecosystems: Preservation and Management.* Honolulu: University of Hawaii Press, 1985.

Strasser, Susan. *Satisfaction Guaranteed: The Making of the Mass Market.* New York: Pantheon Books, 1989.

Strauss, W. Patrick. *Americans in Polynesia, 1783–1842*. East Lansing: Michigan State University Press, 1963.

Suret-Canale, Jean. *Afrique Noire de la colonisation aux independances, 1945–1960*. Paris: Editions Sociales, 1977.

———. *Afrique Noire, L'ere coloniale, 1900–1945*. Paris: Editions Sociales, 1962.

Swanberg, W. A. *Citizen Hearst*. New York: Scribner's, 1961.

Sweigart, Joseph E. *Coffee Factorage and the Emergence of a Brazilian Capital Market, 1850–1888*. New York and London: Garland Publishing, 1987.

Szekely, Ladislao. *Tropic Fever: The Adventures of a Planter in Sumatra*. Kuala Lumpur: Oxford University Press, 1979.

Takaki, Ronald. *Pau Hana: Plantation Life and Labor in Hawaii, 1835–1920*. Honolulu: University of Hawaii Press, 1983.

Tannenbaum, Frank. *The Mexican Agrarian Revolution*. Washington, D.C.: Brookings Institution, 1930.

Tedlow, Richard S. *New and Improved: The Story of Mass Marketing in America*. New York: Basic Books, 1990.

Thirsk, Joan. *Economic Policy and Projects: The Development of a Consumer Society in Early Modern England*. Oxford: Oxford University Press, 1978.

Thomas, William L., Jr. *Man's Role in Changing the Face of the Earth*. 2 vols. Chicago: University of Chicago Press, 1956.

Tinker Salas, Miguel. *In the Shadow of the Eagles: Sonora and the Transformation of the Border during the Porfiriato*. Berkeley: University of California Press, 1997.

Totman, Conrad. *The Green Archipelago: Forestry in Preindustrial Japan*. Berkeley: University of California Press, 1989.

Tower, Walter S. *A History of the American Whale Fishery*. Philadelphia: University of Pennsylvania Press, 1907.

Tucker, Richard P., and J. F. Richards, eds. *Global Deforestation and the Nineteenth-Century World Economy*. Durham, N.C.: Duke University Press, 1983.

Tulchin, Joseph S. *The Aftermath of War: World War I and U.S. Policy Toward Latin America*. New York: New York University Press, 1971.

Turner, B. L. II, et al., eds. *The Earth as Transformed by Human Action*. Cambridge: Cambridge University Press, 1990.

Ukers, William H. *All About Coffee*. New York: Tea and Coffee Trade Journal Company, 1922.

Van Alstyne, Richard W. *The Rising American Empire*. New York: Norton, 1974.

Vandercook, John W. *King Cane: The Story of Sugar in Hawaii*. New York and London: Harper and Brothers, 1939.

Vandermeer, John, and Ivette Perfecto. *Breakfast of Biodiversity*. Oakland, Calif.: Institute for Food and Development Policy, 1995.

Vassberg, David E. *Land and Society in Golden Age Castile*. Cambridge: Cambridge University Press, 1984.

Vernon, Raymond. *Two Hungry Giants: the United States and Japan in the Quest for Oil and Ores*. Cambridge, Mass.: Harvard University Press, 1983.

Vernon, Raymond, and Debora L. Spar. *Beyond Globalism: Remaking American Foreign Economic Policy.* New York: Free Press, 1989.

Vlekke, Bernard H. M. *Nusantara: A History of Indonesia.* The Hague: van Hoeve, 1965.

Vogeler, Ingolf. *The Myth of the Family Farm: Agribusiness Dominance of U.S. Agriculture.* Boulder, Colo.: Westview, 1981.

Vogt, Paul. *The Sugar Refining Industry in the United States: Its Development and Present Condition.* Philadelphia: University of Pennsylvania Press, 1908.

Vogt, William. *The Population of Costa Rica and Its Natural Resources.* Washington, D.C.: Pan American Union, 1946.

———. *The Population of El Salvador and Its Natural Resources.* Washington, D.C.: Pan American Union, 1946.

———. *The Population of Venezuela and Its Natural Resources.* Washington, D.C.: Pan American Union, 1946.

———. *Road to Survival.* New York: W. Sloane, 1948.

Volker, Tys. *From Primeval Forest to Cultivation.* Medan: Deli Planters Association, 1924.

Wachtel, Paul. *The Poverty of Affluence: A Psychological Portrait of the American Way of Life.* New York: Free Press, 1983.

Walker, Herbert S. *The Sugar Industry in the Island of Negros.* Manila: Bureau of Science, 1910.

Wallerstein, Immanuel. *The Modern World-System: Capitalist Agriculture and the Origins of the European World-Economy in the Sixteenth Century.* New York: Academic Press, 1976.

———. *The Modern World-System II: Mercantilism and the Consolidation of the European World-Economy, 1600–1750.* New York: Academic Press, 1980.

Ward, Barbara, and Rene Dubos. *Only One Earth: The Care and Maintenance of a Small Planet.* New York: Norton, 1972.

Wasserstrom, Robert. *Class and Society in Central Chiapas.* Berkeley: University of California Press, 1983.

Watson, Andrew. *Agricultural Innovation in the Early Islamic World.* Cambridge: Cambridge University Press, 1983.

Watters, R. F. *Shifting Cultivation in Latin America.* Rome: Food and Agriculture Organization of the United Nations, 1971.

Watts, David. *The West Indies: An Environmental History.* Cambridge: Cambridge University Press, 1987.

Webb, Walter P. *The Great Frontier.* Boston: Houghton Mifflin, 1952.

Weber, David J. *Myth and the History of the Hispanic Southwest.* Albuquerque: University of New Mexico Press, 1988.

———. *The Spanish Frontier in North America.* New Haven: Yale University Press, 1992.

Webster, J. B., and A. A. Boahen. *The Growth of African Civilisation: The Revolutionary Years, West Africa since 1800.* London: Longman, 1968.

Weinberg, Albert K. *Manifest Destiny: A Study of Nationalist Expansionism in American History.* Chicago: Quadrangle Books, 1963.

Weinstein, Barbara. *The Amazon Rubber Boom, 1850–1920.* Stanford: Stanford University Press, 1983.

Weintraub, D., M. Shapiro, and B. Aquino. *Agrarian Development and Modernization in the Philippines.* Jerusalem: Jerusalem Academic Press, 1973.

Wernstedt, Frederick L., and J. E. Spencer. *The Philippine Island World, a Physical, Cultural and Regional Geography.* Berkeley: University of California Press, 1967.

———. *The Role and Importance of Philippine Interisland Shipping and Trade.* Data Paper No. 26. Ithaca: Southeast Asia Program, Cornell University, 1957.

West, Robert C. *Sonora: Its Geographical Personality.* Austin: University of Texas Press, 1993.

West, Robert C., and John P. Augelli. *Middle America: Its Lands and Peoples.* 2d. ed. Englewood Cliffs, N.J.: Prentice-Hall, 1976.

West, Robert C., N. P. Psuty, and B. G. Thom. *The Tabasco Lowlands of Southeastern Mexico.* Baton Rouge: Louisiana State University Press, 1969.

White, Alastair. *El Salvador.* New York: Praeger, 1973.

White, Richard. *The Roots of Dependency.* Lincoln: University of Nebraska Press, 1983.

Whitford, H. N. *The Forests of the Philippines.* Bulletin No. 10. 2 vols. Manila: Bureau of Forestry, 1911.

Whitmore, T. C. *Tropical Rain Forests of the Far East.* 2d ed. Oxford: Clarendon Press, 1984.

Whitten, Anthony J., et al. *The Ecology of Sumatra.* Yogyakarta: UGM Press, 1984.

Whyte, Robert Orr. *Tropical Grazing Lands: Communities and Constituent Species.* The Hague: Junk, 1974.

Wickberg, Edgar. *The Chinese in Philippine Life, 1850–1898.* New Haven: Yale University Press, 1965.

Wickizer, V. D. *Coffee, Tea and Cocoa.* Baltimore: Johns Hopkins University Press, 1977.

Wilkins, Mira. *The Emergence of Multinational Enterprise: American Business Abroad from the Colonial Era to 1914.* Cambridge, Mass.: Harvard University Press, 1970.

———. *The Making of Multinational Enterprise: American Business Abroad from 1914 to 1970.* Cambridge, Mass.: Harvard University Press, 1974.

Wilkins, Mira, and Frank Ernest Hill. *American Business Abroad: Ford on Six Continents.* Detroit: Wayne State University Press, 1964.

Williams, Eric. *From Columbus to Castro: The History of the Caribbean, 1492–1969.* New York: Harper & Row, 1970.

Williams, Michael. *Americans and Their Forests: A Historical Geography.* Cambridge: Cambridge University Press, 1989.

Williams, Robert G. *Export Agriculture and the Crisis in Central America.* Chapel Hill: University of North Carolina Press, 1986.

———. *States and Social Evolution: Coffee and the Rise of National Governments in Central America.* Chapel Hill: University of North Carolina Press, 1994.

Wilson, Charles M. *Liberia: Black Africa in Microcosm.* New York: Harper and Row, 1971.

Winkler, Max. *Investments of United States Capital in Latin America.* Boston: World Peace Foundation, 1929.

Wisdom, Harold W., James E. Granskog, and Keith A. Blatner. *Caribbean Markets for U.S. Wood Products.* Research Paper SO-225. New Orleans: U.S. Department of Agriculture, 1986.

Wolf, Eric. *Europe and the People Without History.* Berkeley: University of California Press, 1982.

Wolfskill, George, and Stanley Palmer, eds. *Essays on Frontiers in World History.* Arlington: University of Texas Press, 1983.

Womack, John. *Zapata and the Mexican Revolution.* New York: Knopf, 1969.

Wood, Bryce. *The Making of the Good Neighbor Policy.* New York: Columbia University Press, 1961.

Wood, Harold A. *Northern Haiti: Land, Land Use, and Settlement.* Toronto: University of Toronto Press, 1963.

Woodrum, Don. *This Is Hawaii.* Honolulu: Book Publishers Hawaii, n. d.

Worcester, Dean. *The Philippines, Past and Present.* 2 vols. New York: Mac-Millan, 1914.

World Resources 1986. New York: Basic Books, 1986.

Worsley, Peter. *The Three Worlds: Culture and World Development.* London: Weidenfeld and Nicholson, 1984.

Worster, Donald. *Dust Bowl: The Southern Plains in the 1930s.* New York and Oxford: Oxford University Press, 1979.

———. *Nature's Economy.* San Francisco: Sierra Club Books, 1977.

———. *Rivers of Empire: Water, Aridity and the Growth of the American West.* New York: Pantheon, 1985.

Wrigley, Gordon. *Tropical Agriculture: The Development of Production.* New York: Praeger, 1969.

Wynn, Graeme. *Timber Colony.* Toronto: University of Toronto Press, 1981.

Yergin, Daniel. *The Prize.* New York: Simon and Schuster, 1991.

Yoshihara, Kunio. *Japanese Investment in Southeast Asia.* Honolulu: University of Hawaii Press, 1978.

Zivnuska, John A. *U.S. Timber Resources in a World Economy.* Baltimore: Johns Hopkins University Press, 1967.

Zon, Raphael, ed. *Conservation of Renewable Natural Resources.* Philadelphia: University of Pennsylvania Press, 1941.

Zon, Raphael, and William N. Sparhawk. 2 vols. *Forest Resources of the World.* New York: McGraw Hill, 1923.

ARTICLES

Aguirre, A. "Estudio Silvicultural y Economico del Sistema Taungya en las Condiciones de Turrialba." *Turrialba* 13:3 (1963): 168–171.

Aiken, S. Robert, and Michael R. Moss. "Man's Impact on the Tropical Rainforest of Peninsular Malaysia: A Review." *Biological Conservation* 8 (1975): 213–229.

Anonymous. "Commodity Report: Hardwoods." *Unasylva* 12:4 (1958): 183–191.

Anonymous. "Commodity Report: Pulp and Paper." *Unasylva* 12:3 (1958): 134–141.

Atkinson, I. A. E. "A Reassessment of Factors, Particularly *Rattus rattus L.*, That Influenced the Decline of Endemic Forest Birds in the Hawaiian Islands." *Pacific Science* 31 (1977): 109–133.

Aubey, Robert T. "Entrepreneurial Formation in El Salvador." *Explorations in Entrepreneurial History* 6 (1969): 59–75.

Baker, Will. "Divided They Fall." *Whole Earth Review* 45 (1985): 51–63.

Baldwin, Mark. "Soil Erosion Survey of Latin America." *Journal of Soil and Water Conservation* 9:4 (1954): 158–168; 9:5 (1954): 214–229, 237; 9:6 (1954): 275–280.

Benya, Edward. "Forestry in Belize, Part I: Beginnings of Modern Forestry and Agriculture, 1921 to 1954." *Belizean Studies* 7:1 (1979): 16–28.

———. "Forestry in Belize, Part II: Modern Times and Transition." *Belizean Studies* 7:2 (1979): 13–28.

Bevan, Arthur. "A Forest Policy for the American Tropics." *Caribbean Forester* 4:2 (1943): 49–53.

Bishko, C. J. "The Peninsular Background of Latin American Cattle Ranching." *Hispanic American Historical Review* 32 (1952): 491–515.

Boomgaard, Peter. "Forest Management and Exploitation in Colonial Java, 1677–1897." *Forest and Conservation History* 36 (1992): 4–14.

Bryan, Patrick. "The Transition of Plantation Agriculture in the Dominican Republic, 1870–84." *Journal of Caribbean History* 10–11 (1978): 82–105.

Budowski, Gerardo. "La conservación de los recursos forestales de Cuba." *Agrotecnica* (Havana) (May–June 1954): 71–79.

———. "La influencia humana en la vegetación natural de montañas tropicales americanas." *Colloquium Geographica* 9 (1968): 157–162.

Caballero, Miguel, Victor Sosa, and Juana Marin. "Forestry in Mexico." *Journal of Forestry* 75 (1977): 473–477.

Callahan, John C. "The Mahogany Empire of Ichabod T. Williams & Sons, 1838–1973." *Journal of Forest History* 29:3 (1985): 120–130.

Carlson, Norman K., and L. W. Bryan. "Report of the Standing Committee on Forestry—Tenth Pacific Science Congress, Hawaii." *Malayan Forester* 24:4 (1961): 252–260.

Cater, John. "The Formation of Teak Plantations in Trinidad with the Assistance of Peasant Contractors." *Caribbean Forester* 2:4 (1941): 144–153.

Caufield, Catherine. "Mindanao Plantation Sparks Controversy." *Multinational Monitor* (1983): 8–9.

Crane, Julian. "Coffee is Gold for El Salvador." *Agriculture in the Americas* 7:4–5 (1947): 69–72.

Crist, Raymond E. "Cattle Ranching in the Tropical Rainforest." *The Scientific Monthly* 56 (1943): 521–527.

Currie, A. W. "British Attitudes toward Investment in North American Railroads." *Business History Review* 34 (1960): 194–215.

Davis, Harlan. "Aid to the Small Farmer: The El Salvador Experience." *Inter-American Economic Affairs,* 29 (1975): 37–51.

Dean, Warren. "Forest Conservation in Southeastern Brazil, 1900–1955." *Environmental Review* 9:1 (1985): 55–69.

Denevan, William M. "The Upland Pine Forests of Nicaragua: A Study in Cultural Plant Geography." *University of California Publications in Geography* 12:4 (1961): 251–320.

Dorner, Peter, and Rodolfo Quiros. "Institutional Dualism in Central America's Agricultural Development." *Journal of Latin American Studies* 5:2 (1973): 217–232.

Dove, Michael R. "Theories of Swidden Agriculture and the Political Economy of Ignorance." *Agroforestry Systems* 1 (1983): 85–100.

Dyer, Donald R. "Sugar Regions of Cuba." *Economic Geography* 32 (1956): 177–184.

Edwards, Clinton R. "The Human Impact on the Forest in Quintana Roo, Mexico." *Journal of Forest History* 30:3 (1986): 120–127.

Fortmann, Louise P., and Sally K. Fairfax. "American Forestry Professionalism in the Third World." *Economic and Political Weekly,* 12 August 1989, pp. 1838–1841.

Fox, J. E. E. "Selective Logging in the Philippines Dipterocarp Forest." *Malayan Forester* 30 (1967): 182–190.

Fraser, Hugh. "Testing Time for Asia's Forest Products Pioneer." *World Wood* 21:13 (1980): 13–17.

Friend, Theodore. "American Interests and Philippine Independence, 1929–1933." *Philippine Studies* 11 (1963): 505–523.

———. "Paraná Pine—A Source of Wood for Reconstruction in Europe." *Unasylva* 1:2 (1947): 30–32.

———. "The Philippine Sugar Industry and the Politics of Independence, 1929–1935." *Journal of Asian Studies* (1963): 179–192.

———. "Tom Gill Looks at Tropical Forestry: 1928–1971." *Forest History* 15: 1 (1971): 16–21.

Glori, Antonio V. "Some Problems and Needs of Reforestation Research in the Philippines." *Conservation Circular* 9:8 (1973): 1–4.

Gomez, Gustavo. "Case History of a South American Paper Mill." *Unasylva* 42:1 (1988): 7–13.

Gomez-Pompa, Arturo, C. Vasquez-Yaniz, and S. Guevara. "The Tropical Rain Forest: a Non-Renewable Resource." *Science* 177 (1972): 762–765.

Gordon, W. A. "Forest Management in the Caribbean." *Caribbean Forester* 22: 1–2 (1961): 21–26.

———. "Obstacles to Tropical Forestry: Land Tenure." *Unasylva* 15:1 (1961): 6–9.

Grammer, A. R. "A History of the Experiment Station of the Hawaiian Sugar Planters' Association, 1895–1945." *The Hawaiian Planters' Record* 51:3–4 (1947): 177–228.

Guess, George. "Pasture Expansion, Forestry and Development Contradictions: The Case of Costa Rica." *Studies in Comparative International Development* 14 (1979): 42–55.

Hall, Carolyn O. "The Tuis Archives: Cattle Ranching on the Frontiers of Colonization in Costa Rica: 1873–1876." *Revista Geografica* 86–87 (1977–1978): 101–117.

Hart, Ansell. "The Banana in Jamaica: Export Trade." *Social and Economic Studies* (Kingston) 3:2 (1954): 212–229.

Hidy, Ralph W., and Muriel E. Hidy. "Anglo-American Merchant Bankers and the Railroads of the Old Northwest, 1848–1860." *Business History Review* 34 (1960): 150–169.

Holdridge, Leslie R. "The Pine Forests of Haiti." *Caribbean Forester* 4:1 (1942): 16–21.

———. "The Possibility of Close Cooperation for Mutual Benefit between Agriculture and Forestry in the American Tropics." *Caribbean Forester* 1:3 (1940): 25–29.

Horn, Eugene F. "The Lumber Industry of the Lower Amazon Valley." *Caribbean Forester* 18:3–4 (1957): 56–67.

Hosmer, Ralph Sheldon. "The Beginning Five Decades of Forestry in Hawaii." *Journal of Forestry* 57 (1959): 83–89.

Hotchkiss, H. Stuart. "Operations of an American Rubber Company in Sumatra and the Malay Peninsula." *Annals of the American Academy* 112 (1924): 154–162.

Huberman, Martin A. "Our Good Neighbors' Forestry." *Journal of Forestry* 46 (1948): 81–98.

Hyman, Eric L. "Forestry Administration and Policies in the Philippines." *Environmental Management* 7:6 (1983): 511–524.

James, Preston E. "Trends in Brazilian Agricultural Development." *Geographical Review* 43:3 (1953): 302–327.

John, David W. "The Timber Industry and Forest Administration in Sabah Under Chartered Company Rule." *Journal of Southeast Asian Studies* 5 (1974): 55–81.

Johnson, Dennis V., ed. "The Northern Andes: Environmental and Cultural Change." *Mountain Research and Development* 2:3 (1982): 327–332.

Juvik, James O., Sonia P. Juvik, and Lawrence S. Hamilton. "Altitudinal Resource Zonation versus Vertical Control: Land Use Conflict on Two Hawaiian Mountains." *Mountain Research and Development* 12:3 (1992): 211–226.

Karush, Gerald E. "Plantations, Population and Poverty in El Salvador." *Studies in Comparative International Development* 13 (1978): 59–75.

Kirch, P. V. "The Impact of Prehistoric Polynesians on the Hawaiian Ecosystem." *Pacific Science* 36:1 (1982): 1–14.

Kolb, Albert. "Die japanische Ackerbaukolonie in Davao, Philippinen." *Koloniale Rundschau* 29 (1939): 209–218.

Kowal, Norman E. "Shifting Cultivation, Fire, and Pine Forest in the Cordillera Central, Luzon, Philippines." *Ecological Monographs* 36:4 (1966): 389–419.

Kudela, Michael. "Los problemas actuales de la silvicultura cubana." *Silvaecultura Tropica et Subtropica* (Prague) 4 (1976): 59–76.

Kudela, Michael, Richard Hochmut, and Roman Leontovyc. "Proteccion for-

estal en Cuba." *Silvaecultura Tropica et Subtropica* (Prague) 4 (1976): 97–112.

Lamb, F. Bruce. "Brief Notes on Forestry in Southeast Asia." *Caribbean Forester* 24:1 (1963): 18–21.

———. "Status of Forestry in Tropical America." *Journal of Forestry* 46 (1948): 721–726.

Lamb, F. Bruce, C. B. Briscoe, and G. H. Englerth. "Recent Observations on Forestry in Tropical America." *Caribbean Forester* 21: 1–2 (1960): 46–59.

Lansigan, Nicolas P. "Our Dwindling Forests." *Forestry Leaves* 11 (1959): 17–21.

Lawless, Robert. "Deforestation and Indigenous Attitudes in Northern Luzon." *Anthropology* 2:1 (1978): 1–13.

Leopold, A. Starker. "Adios, Gavilan." *Pacific Discovery* 2:1 (1949): 4–13.

———. "Vegetation Zones of Mexico." *Ecology* 31 (1950): 507–518.

Lewis, Laurence A., and William J. Coffey. "The Continuing Deforestation of Haiti." *AMBIO* 14:3 (1985): 158–160.

Lind, Ian. "Blemishes on the Top Banana: A Critical Look at Castle and Cooke." *Multinational Monitor* 2 (1981): 10–18.

Lombardi, John V., and James A. Hanson. "The First Venezuelan Coffee Cycle, 1830–1855." *Agricultural History* 44:4 (1970): 355–368.

Lopez Lara, A. "The Mexico of Our Children: Brief History of Deforestation." *Mexican Forester* 50:2 (1976): 14–15.

Lytle, Mark H. "An Environmental Approach to American Diplomatic History." *Diplomatic History* 20:2 (1996): 279–300.

McCreery, David J. "Coffee and Class: The Structure of Development in Liberal Guatemala" *Hispanic American Historical Review* 56:3 (1976): 438–460.

McNeill, John. "Of Rats and Men: A Synoptic Environmental History of the Island Pacific." *Journal of World History* 5:2 (1994): 299–349.

Miller, Elbert E. "The Raising and Marketing of Beef in Central America and Panama." *Journal of Tropical Geography* 41 (1975): 59–69.

Momsen, Janet D. "Crisis in the Caribbean Sugar Industry." *Geography* 56: 253 (1971): 338–340.

Moore, Barrington. "Forest Problems in the Philippines." *American Forestry* 16:2 (1910): 75–81; 16:3 (1910): 149–154.

Morrissey, Richard J. "The Northward Expansion of Cattle Ranching in New Spain, 1550–1600." *Agricultural History* 25 (1951): 115–121.

Morton, F. W. O. "The Royal Timber in Late Colonial Bahia." *Hispanic American Historical Review* 58:1 (1978): 41–61.

Murphy, Charles J. V. "The Fabulous House of Kleberg." *Fortune* (June 1969): 112–119, 218–219, 224–225.

———. "The King Ranch South of the Border." *Fortune* (July 1969): 132–136, 140, 142, 144.

———. "Treasures in Oil and Cattle." *Fortune* (August 1969): 165–167.

Myers, Norman. "The Hamburger Connection." *Ambio* 10:1 (1981): 3–8.

Myers, R. M. "The Utilization of Philippine Mahogany in the United States." *Economic Botany* 17 (1963): 233–237.

St. John, H. "History, Present Distribution and Abundance of Sandalwood on Oahu, Hawaiian Islands." *Pacific Science* (1947): 5–20.

Stouse, Pierre. "The Instability of Tropical Agriculture: The Atlantic Lowlands of Costa Rica." *Economic Geography* 46 (1970): 78–97.

Tamesis, Florencio. "Philippine Forests and Forestry." *Unasylva* 2:6 (1948): 316–325.

Tanner, J. C. "U.S. Cattlemen Buy Spreads in Central America to Exploit Good Grazing, Growing Demand for Beef." *Wall Street Journal*, 27 July 1972, p. 30.

Tanouye, Elyse. "Goodbye Big Five." *Fortune* 103 (1983): 36–39.

Teng, Shu-Chun. "The Early History of Forestry in China." *Journal of Forestry* 25 (1927): 564–570.

Thompson, John. "Production, Marketing and Consumption of Cattle in El Salvador." *The Professional Geographer* 8:5 (1961): 18–21.

Thrupp, Lori Ann. "Pesticides and Policies: Approaches to Pest-Control Dilemmas in Nicaragua and Costa Rica." *Latin American Perspectives* 15:4 (1988): 37–70.

———. "Sterilization of Workers from Pesticide Exposure: The Causes and Consequences of DBCP-Induced Damage in Costa Rica and Beyond." *International Journal of Health Services* 21:4 (1991): 731–757.

Van Niel, Robert. "The Effect of Export Cultivations in Nineteenth-Century Java." *Modern Asian Studies* 15:1 (1981): 25–58.

Veblen, Thomas T. "The Urgent Need for Forest Conservation in Highland Guatemala." *Biological Conservation* 9 (1977): 141–154.

Vogt, William. "Latin-American Timber, Ltd." *Unasylva* 1:1 (1947): 19–26.

Wadsworth, Frank H. "An Approach to Silviculture in Tropical America and Its Application in Puerto Rico." *Caribbean Forester* 8:4 (1947): 245–256.

———. "Import Substitution: Forestry." *Industrial Puerto Rico* (September–October 1971).

———. "Notes on the Climax Forests of Puerto Rico and Their Destruction and Conservation Prior to 1900." *The Caribbean Forester* 11:1 (1950): 38–46.

Wagner, Philip L. "Parras: A Case History in the Depletion of Natural Resources." *Landscape* (Summer 1955): 19–28.

Wernstedt, Frederick L., and Paul D. Simkins. "Migration and the Settlement of Mindanao." *Journal of Asian Studies* 25:1 (1965): 83–103.

White, Benjamin. " 'Agricultural Involution' and Its Critics: Twenty Years After." *Bulletin of the Committee of Concerned Asian Scholars* 15:2 (1983): 18–31.

Wickberg, Edgar. "The Chinese Mestizo in Philippine History." *Journal of Southeast Asian History* 5 (1964): 62–100.

Wilcox, Walter D. "Among the Mahogany Forests of Cuba." *National Geographic* 19 (1908): 485–498.

Winters, Robert K. "How Forestry Became a Part of FAO." *Journal of Forestry* 69 (1971): 574–577.

Womack, John, Jr. "El Salvador and the Central American War." *Socialist Review* 12 (1982): 9–30.

Worcester, Dean C. "Philippine Forest Wealth." *American Forestry* 21:1 (1915): 1–18.

CHAPTERS

Barraclough, Solon L. "Agricultural Policy and Strategies of Land Reform." In *Masses in Latin America,* ed. Irving Louis Horowitz, 95–171. New York: Oxford University Press, 1970.

Beltran, Enrique. "Forestry and Related Research in Mexico." In *Forestry and Related Research in North America,* ed. Frank H. Kaufert and William H. Cummings, 254–271. Washington, D.C.: Society of American Foresters, 1955.

Brazier, S. A. "The Rubber Industry in the 1939–1945 War." In *History of the Rubber Industry,* ed. P. Schidrowitz and T. R. Dawson. Cambridge: Heffer, 1952.

Brennan, Peter, and Mark Merlin. "Biogeography and Traditional Use of *Santalum* in the Pacific Region." In *Sandalwood in the Pacific Region,* ed. F. H. McKinnell, 30–38. Honolulu: Pacific Science Association, 1992.

Budowski, Gerardo. "Middle America: The Human Factor." In *Future Environments of North America,* ed. F. Fraser Darling and John P. Milton, 144–155. Garden City, N.Y.: Natural History Press, 1966.

Burbach, Roger, and Patricia Flynn. "Modern Plantation Systems: Del Monte in the Pacific." In *Agribusiness in the Americas,* 192–205. New York: Monthly Review Press, 1980.

Caldwell, J. A. M. "Indonesian Export and Production from the Decline of the Culture System to the First World War." In *The Economic Development of Southeast Asia: Studies in Economic History and Political Economy,* ed. C. D. Cowan, 72–101. New York: Praeger, 1964.

Cardoso, Ciro F. S. "The Formation of the Coffee Estate in Nineteenth-Century Costa Rica." In *Land and Labour in Latin America,* ed. Kenneth Duncan and Ian Rutledge, 165–201. Cambridge: Cambridge University Press, 1977.

Crosby, Alfred. "Ecological Imperialism: The Overseas Migration of Western Europeans as a Biological Phenomenon." In *The Ends of the Earth,* ed. Donald Worster, 103–117. Cambridge: Cambridge University Press, 1988.

Cullinane, Michael. "The Changing Nature of the Cebu Urban Elite in the 19th Century." In *Philippine Social History: Global Trade and Local Transformations,* ed. Alfred W. McCoy and Ed. C. de Jesus, 251–296. Quezon City: Ateneo de Manila University Press, 1982.

Darby, H. C. "The Medieval Clearances." In *Man's Role in Changing the Face of the Earth,* ed. William L. Thomas, 183–216. Chicago: University of Chicago Press, 1956.

D'Arcy, W. C. "Endangered Landscapes in Panama and Central America: The Threat to Plant Species." In *Extinction Is Forever,* ed. G. T. Prance and T. S. Elias. New York: New York Botanical Gardens, 1977.

Denevan, William M. "Latin America." In *World Systems of Traditional Resources Management,* ed. Gary L. Klee. New York: Halsted Press, 1977.

DeWalt, Billie R. "The Agrarian Bases of Conflict in Central America." In *The Central American Crisis: Sources of Conflict and the Failure of U.S. Policy,* ed. Kenneth Coleman and George Herring, 43–54. Wilmington, Del.: Scholarly Resources, Inc., 1985.

Duncan Baretta, Silvio R., and John Markoff. "Civilization and Barbarism: Cattle Frontiers in Latin America." In *The Frontier in History: North America and Southern Africa Compared*, 587–620. New Haven: Yale University Press, 1981.

Edgerton, Ronald K. "Americans, Cowboys, and Cattlemen on the Mindanao Frontier." In *Reappraising an Empire: New Perspectives on Philippine-American History*, ed. Peter W. Stanley, 170–197. Cambridge, Mass.: Harvard University Press, 1984.

———. "Frontier Society on the Bukidnon Plateau, 1870–1941." In *Philippine Social History: Global Trade and Local Transformations*, ed. Alfred W. McCoy and Ed. C. de Jesus, 361–390. Quezon City: Ateneo de Manila University Press, 1982.

Gill, Tom. "America and World Forestry." In *American Forestry: Six Decades of Growth*, ed. Henry Clepper and Arthur B. Meyer, 282–294. Washington, D.C.: Society of American Foresters, 1960.

Gladwin, Thomas H. "Environment, Development, and Multinational Enterprise: An Overview." In *Business Matters: Multinational Corporations, the Environment, and Development*, ed. Charles Pearson, 3–31. Durham, N.C.: Duke University Press, 1986.

Golay, Frank H. "Economic Collaboration: The Role of American Investment." In *The United States and the Philippines*, ed. Frank H. Golay, 95–124. Englewood Cliffs, N.J.: Prentice Hall, 1966.

———. "Manila Americans and Philippine Policy: The Voice of American Business." In *The Philippine Economy and the United States: Studies in Past and Present Interactions*, ed. Norman G. Owen, 1–36. Ann Arbor: University of Michigan, Center for South and Southeast Asian Studies, 1983.

———. "Taming the Multinationals." In *The Philippine Economy and the United States: Studies in Past and Present Interactions*, ed. Norman G. Owen, 131–176. Ann Arbor: University of Michigan, Center for South and Southeast Asian Studies, 1983.

Goodman, Grant K. "America's Permissive Colonialism: Japanese Business in the Philippines, 1899–1941." In *The Philippine Economy and the United States: Studies in Past and Present Interactions*, ed. Norman G. Owen, 37–62. Ann Arbor: University of Michigan, Center for South and Southeast Asian Studies, 1983.

Heinrichs, Jay. "Forests and Rangelands." In *World Resources 1987*, 57–76. New York: Basic Books, 1987.

Jimenez, Michael F. " 'From Plantation to Cup': Coffee and Capitalism in the United States, 1830–1930." In *Coffee, Society, and Power in Latin America*, ed. William Roseberry, Lowell Gudmundson, and Mario Samper Kutschbach, 38–64. Baltimore: Johns Hopkins University Press, 1995.

Jimenez Codinach, Guadalupe. "An Atlantic Silver Entrepot: Vera Cruz and the House of Gordon and Murphy." In *Atlantic Port Cities: Economy, Culture, and Society in the Atlantic World, 1650–1850*, ed. Franklin W. Knight and Peggy K. Liss, 149–167. Knoxville: University of Tennessee Press, 1991.

Juvik, Sonia P., and James O. Juvik. "Valuations and Images of Hawaiian Forests: An Historical Perspective." In *Changing Tropical Forests: Historical*

Perspectives on Today's Challenges in Asia, Australasia and Oceania, ed. John Dargavel et al., 377–392. Canberra: Australian National University, 1988.

Konrad, Herman W. "Tropical Forest Policy and Practice During the Mexican Porfiriato." In *Changing Tropical Forests: Historical Perspectives on Today's Challenges in Central and South America,* ed. Harold K. Steen and Richard P. Tucker, 123–133. Durham, N.C.: Forest History Society, 1992.

Kuethe, Allan J. "Havana in the Eighteenth Century." In *Atlantic Port Cities: Economy, Culture, and Society in the Atlantic World, 1650–1850,* ed. Franklin W. Knight and Peggy K. Liss, 13–33. Knoxville: University of Tennessee Press, 1991.

Laarman, Jan G. "Export of Tropical Hardwoods in the Twentieth Century." In *World Deforestation in the Twentieth Century,* ed. John F. Richards and Richard P. Tucker, 147–163. Durham, N.C.: Duke University Press, 1988.

LaFeber, Walter. "The Alliances in Retrospect." In *Bordering on Trouble: Resources and Politics in Latin America,* ed. Andrew Maguire and Janet Welsh Brown, 337–388. Bethesda, Md.: Adler and Adler, 1986.

Legarda, Benito, Jr., and Roberto Y. Garcia. "Economic Collaboration: The Trading Relationship." In *The United States and the Philippines,* ed. Frank Golay, 125–148. Englewood Cliffs, N.J.: Prentice Hall, 1966.

McCoy, Alfred W. " 'In Extreme Unction': The Philippine Sugar Industry." In *Political Economy of Philippine Commodities,* 135–179. Quezon City: Third World Studies Center, University of the Philippines, 1983.

———. "A Queen Dies Slowly: The Rise and Decline of Iloilo City." In *Philippine Social History: Global Trade and Local Transformations,* ed. Alfred W. McCoy and Ed. C. de Jesus, 297–358. Quezon City: Ateneo de Manila University Press, 1982.

McLennan, Marshall S. "Changing Human Ecology on the Central Luzon Plain: Nueva Ecija, 1705–1939." In *Philippine Social History: Global Trade and Local Transformations,* ed. Alfred W. McCoy and Ed. C. de Jesus, 57–90. Quezon City: Ateneo de Manila University Press, 1982.

McNeill, John. "Deforestation in the Araucaria Zone of Southern Brazil, 1900–1983." In *World Deforestation in the Twentieth Century,* ed. J. F. Richards and Richard P. Tucker, 15–32. Durham, N.C.: Duke University Press, 1988.

Merlin, Mark, and D. Van Ravenswaay. "The History of Human Impact on the Genus *Santalum* in Hawaii." In *Proceedings of the Symposium on Sandalwood in the Pacific,* ed. Lawrence Hamilton and C. Eugene Conrad, 46–60. Honolulu: USDA Forest Service, 1990.

Mosher, Lawrence. "At Sea in the Caribbean?" In *Bordering on Trouble: Resources and Politics in Latin America,* ed. Andrew Maguire and Janet Welsh Brown, 235–269. Bethesda, Md.: Adler and Adler, 1986.

Naunton, W. J. S. "Synthetic Rubber." In *History of the Rubber Industry,* ed. P. Schidrowitz and T. R. Dawson, 100–109. Cambridge: Heffer, 1952.

Owen, Norman G. "Philippine-American Economic Interactions: A Matter of Magnitude." In *The Philippine Economy and the United States: Studies in Past and Present Interactions,* ed. Norman G. Owen, 177–208. Ann Arbor: University of Michigan, Center for South and Southeast Asian Studies, 1983.

Potter, Lesley. "Indigenes and Colonisers: Dutch Forest Policy in South and East Borneo (Kalimantan), 1900 to 1950." In *Changing Tropical Forests: Historical Perspectives on Today's Challenges in Asia, Australasia and Oceania*, ed. John Dargavel et al., 127–154. Durham, N.C.: Forest History Society, 1988.

Rai, Shobha N. "Status and Cultivation of Sandalwood in India." In *Proceedings of the Symposium on Sandalwood in the Pacific*, ed. Lawrence Hamilton and C. Eugene Conrad, 66–71. Honolulu: USDA Forest Service, 1990.

Roth, Dennis. "Philippine Forests and Forestry: 1565–1920." In *Global Deforestation and the Nineteenth-Century World Economy*, ed. Richard P. Tucker and J. F. Richards, 30–49. Durham, N.C.: Duke University Press, 1983.

Salvucci, Linda K. "Supply, Demand, and the Making of a Market: Philadelphia and Havana at the Beginning of the Nineteenth Century." In *Atlantic Port Cities: Economy, Culture, and Society in the Atlantic World, 1650–1850*, ed. Franklin W. Knight and Peggy K. Liss, 40–57. Knoxville: University of Tennessee Press, 1991.

Shirley, Hardy L. "Obstacles to Sustained-Yield Forestry." In *Proceedings of the Inter-American Conference on Conservation of Renewable Natural Resources*, 564–571. Washington, D.C.: U.S. Department of State, 1948.

Smith, T. Lynn. "Land Tenure and Soil Erosion in Colombia." In *Proceedings of the Inter-American Conference on Conservation of Renewable Natural Resources*, 155–160. Washington, D.C.: U.S. Department of State, 1948.

Tengwall, T. A. "History of Rubber Cultivation and Research in the Netherlands Indies." In *Science and Scientists in the Netherlands Indies*, ed. P. Honig and F. Verdoorn, 344–351. New York: Board for the Netherlands Indies, Surinam and Curacao, 1945.

Tuggle, H. D. "Hawaii." In *The Prehistory of Polynesia*, ed. J. D. Jennings, Cambridge, Mass.: Harvard University Press, 1979.

Veblen, Thomas T. "Degradation of Native Forest Resources in Southern Chile." In *History of Sustained-Yield Forestry: A Symposium*, ed. Harold K. Steen, 344–352. Durham, N.C.: Forest History Society, 1984.

Wagner, Philip L. "Natural Vegetation of Middle America." In *Natural Environment and Early Cultures*, ed. Robert C. West, 216–264. Austin: University of Texas Press, 1964.

Weber, David J. " 'From Hell Itself': The Americanization of Mexico's Northern Frontier." In *Myth and the History of the Hispanic Southwest*, 105–115. Albuquerque: University of New Mexico Press, 1988.

Weiskel, Timothy. "Toward an Archeology of Colonialism: Elements in the Ecological Transformation of the Ivory Coast." In *The Ends of the Earth: Perspectives on Modern Environmental History*, ed. Donald Worster, 162–169. Cambridge: Cambridge University Press, 1988.

West, Robert C. "The Natural Regions of Middle America." In *Natural Environment and Early Cultures*, ed. Robert C. West, 363–383. Austin: University of Texas Press, 1964.

Wharton, Clifton R., Jr. "Rubber Supply Conditions: Some Policy Implications." In *The Political Economy of Independent Malaya: A Case-study in*

Development, ed. T. H. Silcock and E. K. Fisk. Berkeley: University of California Press, 1963.

Wilkins, Mira. "The Impacts of American Multinational Enterprise on American-Chinese Economic Relations, 1786–1949." In *America's China Trade in Historical Perspective,* ed. Ernest R. May and John K. Fairbank, 259–294. Cambridge, Mass.: Harvard University Press, 1986.

Wilson, Arthur M. "The Logwood Trade in the Seventeenth and Eighteenth Centuries." In *Essays in the History of Modern Europe,* ed. Donald C. McKay. New York: Harper Brothers, 1936.

Wolf, Edward C. "Managing Rangelands." In *State of the World 1986,* ed. Lester R. Brown. New York: Norton, 1986.

Worster, Donald. "The Vulnerable Earth: Toward a Planetary History." In *The Ends of the Earth,* ed. Donald Worster, 3–20. Cambridge: Cambridge University Press, 1988.

Index

Paper Industries Corporation of the Philippines (PICOP), 387–88, 412
Paper industry: demand for products in, 393; effect on rainforests, 390; Latin America, 401; markets for, 409
Pará grass, 303–4, 323, 327
Paraíba valley, Brazil: *fazendas* of, 183–184; watershed of, 185
Paraná pine: Brazilian, 196, 402; European market for, 390
Paraná state (Brazil), 196, 198
Pará rubber, 231
Pará state (Amazonia), 258; investment in, 232; population of, 233
Parker, John Palmer, 312, 313, 314
Parker, Sam, 314
Parker Ranch (Hawaii), 314–15
Parsons, James, 304, 405
Pasturelands. *See entries for grasslands*
Pasumil plantation (Philippines), 110
Payne-Aldrich Tariff (1909), 106
Peace Corps, forestry program of, 423
Pearl Harbor, bombing of, 93, 95
Peasantry, Central American, 212; coffee crops of, 224; of Costa Rica, 132, 217, 218; effect of coffee industry on, 212; labor protests by, 154; marginalization of, 132, 178, 220, 455n118
Peasantry, Colombian: coffee crops of, 204, 205; conflict with landlords, 208; effect of coffee industry on, 200; multicropping of, 420
Peasantry, Cuban: living standard of, 49; in sugar industry, 42
Peasantry, Filipino: effect of timber industry on, 377–78, 380; landlessness of, 113, 386; on Negros, 101, 113
Peasantry, Indonesian: unions of, 270; subsistence farming, 240
Peasantry, Javanese, 242; under Dutch cultivation system, 236
Peasantry, Latin American: of Amazonia, 258; landlessness of, 410; of Mexico, 307–8
Peasantry, Salvadoran: coffee groves of, 221; marginalization of, 220
Peasantry, under American imperium, 418
Pedro I (emperor of Brazil), 182–83
Peele, Hubbell and Company, 102
Pelzer, Karl, 271
Pepper trade, 238
Pereira Brazil, Raymundo, 258
Pernambuco coast (Brazil), 58
Perón, Juan, 337
Peru: development of, 454n82; timber imports of, 475n35

Pesticides, 454n89; in banana industry, 162, 168, 178; in cattle industry, 315; in Hawaiian sugar industry, 90, 94–95, 97; petroleum-based, 422; in Philippine sugar industry, 116; in pineapple industry, 175; in rubber industry, 281; in sugar industry, 119. *See also* Agrochemicals
Philadelphia, trade with Cuba, 31
Philippine Bureau of Forestry, 367–80, 381; budget of, 386; establishment of, 366; in postwar era, 384; reforestation by, 385
Philippine Lumber and Development Company, 369
Philippine Lumber Manufacturers Association, 375
Philippine Lumber Producers Association, 386
Philippine National Bank, 106–7
Philippine Packing Corporation, 320
Philippines, 429; American annexation of, 99, 103, 104–5; botanical research in, 478n86; Catholic Church in, 100, 104, 105; debt peonage in, 379; deforestation of, 10, 101, 102, 112–13, 114, 117, 383–85, 388, 412; environmental degradation in, 98–99; forest cover of, 477n55; forest ownership in, 366; forestry operations in, 92; forestry school of, 372, 383; landlord class of, 104–5, 106, 107, 109, 110, 114–17; land tenure systems of, 479n97; Republic (1896), 103–4; rice crop of, 101, 103, 108, 320, 373; rubber of, 249–50; sandalwood of, 76; softwood imports of, 375; Spanish American war in, 99, 104; Spanish control of, 98, 100–103, 366; squatters of, 383–84, 386–87, 481n129; sugar plantations in, 98–99; tenancy system of, 100; timber imports of, 270, 367; tobacco cultivation in, 462n26; War of Independence, 103–4; weaving industry of, 101, 113; during World War II, 114, 319. *See also* Cattle industry, Philippine; Negros; Sugar industry, Philippine; Timber industry, Philippine
Philippines (Commonwealth), 114–17; cattle industry of, 319–20; corruption in, 114–15; food riots in, 117. *See also* Marcos, Ferdinand
Philippines (U.S. colony): constitution of 1902, 105; forestry law in, 370, 378; social organization of, 107–8; sugar board of, 106; sugar corporations in, 8; timber industry of, 367–80

Text:	10/13 Sabon
Display:	Sabon
Composition:	Binghamton Valley Composition, LLC
Printing and binding:	Sheridan Books, Inc.
Maps:	Bill Nelson
Index:	Roberta Engleman